American Literary Scholarship 1994

American Literary Scholarship
An Annual 1994

Edited by David J. Nordloh

Essays by David M. Robinson, Leland S. Person, Benjamin F. Fisher, John Wenke, Martha Nell Smith, Tom Quirk, Greg W. Zacharias, Michael Coyle, Laura Cowan, Philip Cohen, Albert J. DeFazio III, William J. Scheick, Robert E. Burkholder, Laura E. Skandera-Trombley, Jo Ann Middleton, Catherine Calloway, Jerome Klinkowitz, Timothy Materer, Lorenzo Thomas, James J. Martine, Gary Lee Stonum, Daniel Royot, Christoph Irmscher, Algerina Neri, Hiroko Sato, Jan Nordby Gretlund, Elisabeth Herion-Sarafidis, and Hans Skei

Duke University Press   *Durham and London*   *1996*

Contents

Foreword

In his foreword to *ALS 1985* the late J. Albert Robbins reported on plans for two new histories of American literature, *The Columbia History of American Literature* and *The Cambridge History of American Literature*. The former has since appeared in a single large volume (1988), and the latter, longer in the preparation, issues the first two of eight planned volumes this year. Al Robbins suggested that the newer projects might make their predecessor, *The Literary History of the United States* (1948), obsolete. Critical opinion will have to settle whether they manage to do that or only stand beside it as alternative versions of the national narrative.

Meantime, these attempts to overthrow an older critical tradition by writing books to replace other books seem almost archaic by contrast to the explosion of CD-ROM databases and research archives, and World Wide Web sites featuring images of manuscripts, printed materials, photographs of persons and places, even voice-recordings. Increasingly the contributors of essays to *ALS* include electronic publications among the items they review. Since reviewing presumes that the same material in the same form is widely available for others to use, however, we have made it working policy to review only those electronic materials "published" in the sense of being reproduced in multiple identical copies. We do not review electronic on-line archives, because these exist in only one form and can be altered at any time; the version a reviewer comments on here may no longer exist when a reader of *ALS* attempts to use it. This policy coincides with a natural prejudice of the discipline: our concern is American literature, and American literature begins as words on the page.

The explosion of electronic publication certainly has not dented print scholarship, to judge by the amount of material covered in this year's chapters. Thanks to the success of my co-editor, Gary Scharnhorst, in identifying new contributors last year, every chapter in our proposed table of contents, newly expanded by the division of the chapter on "19th-Century Literature" into two more manageable parts, is represented by an essay here. Martha Nell Smith, who because of health problems could not complete the "Whitman and Dickinson" chapter last year, more than compensates by supplying coverage of publications for both 1993 and 1994. Christoph Irmscher prepares the section on German scholarship, absent for several years from the "Foreign Contributions" chapter. The only changes in the table of contents planned for next year also involve "Foreign Contributions": to more correctly identify its coverage, the title of the chapter will become "Scholarship in Languages Other Than English"; and a section in that chapter devoted to both American literature in Spanish and Spanish-language scholarship will be provided by Antonio Marquez of the University of New Mexico.

Other chapters will change hands. Kent P. Ljungquist, Worcester Polytechnic Institute, former contributor of the "Poe" chapter, returns to that post for a year while Benjamin F. Fisher takes a library-remodeling-induced leave of absence. John Samson, Texas Tech University, takes over the "Melville" chapter from John Wenke. Kenneth M. Price, College of William and Mary, assumes "Whitman and Dickinson" from Martha Nell Smith. Alan Gribben, Auburn University at Montgomery, will contribute "Mark Twain," replacing Tom Quirk. Lawrence J. Oliver, Texas A & M University, assumes "Late-19th-Century Literature" from Laura Skandera-Trombley. And in a now almost ritual exchange, Keiko Beppu takes the turn at "Japanese Contributions" from Hiroko Sato. Sincerest thanks to departing contributors for their fine work.

Electronic bibliography may be fast and easy, but it has yet to prove itself thorough and accurate. Authors and publishers can assist us in assuring the comprehensiveness of *ALS* by forwarding offprints and review copies to David J. Nordloh, Department of English, Indiana University, Bloomington, IN 47405.

I am grateful to the many contributors to this volume of *American Literary Scholarship* for their timely and professional effort as well as their tolerance of my editorial incursions into their prose. I am indebted to Ann Bristow and her staff in the Reference Department, Indiana University, Bloomington, for their assistance in bibliographical searches and verification; to the staff of the MLA Center for Bibliographic Services, under the direction of Terence Ford, for once again making a preprint of the *International Bibliography* available for our use; to the secretarial staff in the English Department at Indiana University for continuing help and constant forbearance; and especially to Pam Morrison and Bob Mirandon of Duke University Press, who make impossible deadlines seem possible and demonstrate that professionals are people who work hard and well every day.

David J. Nordloh
Indiana University

Key to Abbreviations

Festschriften, Essay Collections, and Books Discussed in More Than One Chapter

Affirmation and Negation / Gerhard Hoffmann and Alfred Hornung, eds., *Affirmation and Negation in Contemporary Culture* (Winter)

American Literary Naturalism / Paul Civello, *American Literary Naturalism and Its Twentieth-Century Transformations: Frank Norris, Ernest Hemingway, Don DeLillo* (Georgia)

American Realism and the Canon / Tom Quirk and Gary Scharnhorst, eds., *American Realism and the Canon* (Delaware)

The Black Columbiad / Werner Sollors and Maria Diedrich, *The Black Columbiad: Defining Moments in African American Literature and Culture* (Harvard)

Cambridge History of American Literature I / Sacvan Bercovitch, ed., *The Cambridge History of American Literature—vol. 1: 1590–1820* (Cambridge)

Cambridge History of American Literature II / Sacvan Bercovitch, ed., *The Cambridge History of American Literature—vol. 2: 1820–1865* (Cambridge)

Conceived by Liberty / Stephanie A. Smith, *Conceived by Liberty: Maternal Figures and Nineteenth-Century American Literature* (Cornell)

Critical Reconstructions / Robert M. Polhemus and Roger B. Henkle, eds., *Critical Reconstructions: The Relationship of Fiction and Life* (Stanford)

A Cultural History of the American Novel / David Minter, *A Cultural History of the American Novel: Henry James to William Faulkner* (Cambridge)

Cultures of United States Imperialism / Amy Kaplan and Donald Pease, eds., *Cultures of United States Imperialism* (Duke, 1993)

Deferring a Dream / Ernst Rudin and Gert Buelens, eds., *Deferring a Dream: Literary Sub-versions of the American Columbiad* (Birkhäuser)

The Discourse of Slavery / Carl Plasa and Betty J. Ring, eds., *The Discourse of Slavery: Aphra Behn to Toni Morrison* (Routledge)

Engendering Romance / Emily Miller Budick, *Engendering Romance: Women Writers and the Hawthorne Tradition, 1850–1990* (Yale)

The Ethos of Romance / William J. Scheick, *The Ethos of Romance at the Turn of the Century* (Texas)

Excursions in Fiction / Andrew Kennedy and Orm Øverland, eds., *Excursions in Fiction: Essays in Honour of Professor Lars Hartveit on his 70th Birthday* (Novus)

The Fable of the Southern Writer / Lewis P. Simpson, *The Fable of the Southern Writer* (LSU)

Fathers and Mothers in Literature / Henk Hillenaar and Walter Schönau, eds., *Fathers and Mothers in Literature* (Rodopi)

Faulkner and Psychology / Donald M. Kartiganer and Ann J. Abadie, eds., *Faulkner and Psychology / Faulkner and Yoknapatawpha, 1991* (Miss.)

Feminist Nightmares / Susan Ostrov Weisser and Jennifer Fleischner, *Feminist Nightmares: Women at Odds: Feminism and the Problem of Sisterhood* (NYU)

Fictions of Masculinity / Peter F. Murphy, ed., *Fictions of Masculinity: Crossing Cultures, Crossing Sexualities* (NYU)

Framing the Margins / Phillip Brian Harper, *Framing the Margins: The Social Logic of Postmodern Culture* (Oxford)

Get the Guests / Walter A. Davis, *Get the Guests: Psychoanalysis, Modern American Drama, and the Audience* (Wisconsin)

Going Abroad / William W. Stowe,

Going Abroad: European Travel in Nineteenth-Century American Culture (Princeton)

Healing the Republic / Joan Burbick, *Healing the Republic: The Language of Health and the Culture of Nationalism in Nineteenth Century America* (Cambridge)

History and Memory in African-American Culture / Geneviève Fabre and Robert O'Meally, *History and Memory in African-American Culture* (Oxford)

Images of Persephone / Elizabeth T. Hayes, ed., *Images of Persephone: Feminist Readings in Western Literature* (Florida)

Intertextuality in Literature and Film / Elaine D. Cancalon and Antoine Spacagna, eds., *Intertextuality in Literature and Film: Selected Papers from the Thirteenth Annual Florida State University Conference on Literature and Film* (Florida)

Listening to Silences / Elaine Hedges and Shelley Fisher Fishkin, eds., *Listening to Silences: New Essays in Feminist Criticism* (Oxford)

Mastery and Escape / Jewel Spears Brooker, *Mastery and Escape: T. S. Eliot and the Dialectic of Modernism* (Mass.)

Memory, Narrative, and Identity / Amritjit Singh et al., eds., *Memory, Narrative, and Identity: New Essays in Ethnic American Literature* (Northeastern)

Modernist Quartet / Frank Lentricchia, *Modernist Quartet* (Cambridge)

"Modernist" Women Writers / Kathleen

Wheeler, *"Modernist" Women Writers and Narrative Art* (NYU)

Muscular Christianity / Donald E. Hall, ed., *Muscular Christianity: Embodying the Victorian Age* (Cambridge)

The Origins of Modernism / Stan Smith, *The Origins of Modernism: Eliot, Pound, Yeats and the Rhetorics of Renewal* (Harvester Wheatsheaf)

The Other American Drama / Marc Robinson, *The Other American Drama* (Cambridge)

Poetics of the Feminine / Linda A. Kinnahan, *Poetics of the Feminine: Authority and Literary Tradition in William Carlos Williams, Mina Loy, Denise Levertov, and Kathleen Fraser* (Cambridge)

The Prairie in Nineteenth-Century American Poetry / Steven Olson, *The Prairie in Nineteenth-Century American Poetry* (Okla.)

Recovering American Literature / Peter Shaw, *Recovering American Literature* (Dee)

Regionalism Reconsidered / David Jordan, ed., *Regionalism Reconsidered: New Approaches to the Field* (Garland)

Religion in a Revolutionary Age / Ronald Hoffman and Peter J. Albert, eds., *Religion in a Revolutionary Age* (Virginia)

Rereading Modernism / Lisa Rado, ed., *Rereading Modernism: New Directions in Feminist Criticism* (Garland)

Roads to Rome / Jenny Franchot, *Roads to Rome: The Antebellum Protestant Encounter with Catholicism* (Calif.)

Semeia / Loretto Innocenti et al., *Semeia: Itinerari per Marcello Pagnini* (Bologna: Il Mulino)

The Sermon and the African American Literary Imagination / Dolan Hubbard, *The Sermon and the African American Literary Imagination* (Missouri)

Storied Cities / Michael L. Ross, *Storied Cities: Literary Imaginings of Florence, Venice, and Rome* (Greenwood)

The Style's the Man / Louis Auchincloss, *The Style's the Man: Reflections on Proust, Fitzgerald, Wharton, Vidal, and Others* (Scribner's)

The Text and the Voice / Alessandro Portelli, *The Text and the Voice: Writing, Speaking, and Democracy in American Literature* (Columbia)

Tricksterism in Turn-of-the-Century American Literature / Elizabeth Ammons and Annette White-Parks, eds., *Tricksterism in Turn-of-the-Century American Literature* (New England)

The Trouble with Genius / Bob Perelman, *The Trouble with Genius: Reading Pound, Joyce, Stein, and Zukofsky* (Calif.)

T. S. Eliot at the Turn of the Century / Marianne Thormählen, ed., *T. S. Eliot at the Turn of the Century* (Lund)

Understanding Narrative / James Phelan and Peter J. Rabinowitz, eds., *Understanding Narrative* (Ohio State)

Voices of Persuasion / Michael E. Staub, *Voices of Persuasion: Politics of Representation in 1930s America* (Cambridge)

*Walt Whitman: The Centennial
Essays* / Ed Folsom, ed., *Walt Whit-
man: The Centennial Essays* (Iowa)
Walt Whitman of Mickle Street /
Geoffrey M. Sill, ed., *Walt Whit-
man of Mickle Street: A Centennial
Collection* (Tennessee)
Warriors, Conjurers and Priests / Joyce
A. Joyce, *Warriors, Conjurers and
Priests: Defining African-Centered
Literary Criticism* (Third World)
The White Logic / John W. Crowley,
*The White Logic: Alcoholism and
Gender in American Modernist Fic-
tion* (Mass.)
Writing After War / John Limon,
*Writing After War: American War
Fiction from Realism to Postmodern-
ism* (Oxford)

Periodicals, Annuals, and Series

AAR / *African American Review*
ABSt / *A/B: Auto/Biography Studies*
Acoma
AEB / *Analytical & Enumerative Bibli-
ography*
Aethlon
AI / *American Imago*
AIQ / *American Indian Quarterly*
AL / *American Literature*
ALR / *American Literary Realism,
1870–1910*
AmBR / *American Book Review*
AmDram / *American Drama*
Americana (Univ. de Paris IV)
*American Journal of Theology and Phi-
losophy*
American Music
American Review (Tokyo)
AmerS / *American Studies*

AmerSS / *American Studies in Scan-
dinavia*
AmLH / *American Literary History*
AmPer / *American Periodicals*
Amst / *Amerikastudien*
*Anglia: Zeitschrift für Englische Phi-
lologie*
*ANQ: A Quarterly Journal of Short Ar-
ticles, Notes, and Reviews*
AQ / *American Quarterly*
AR / *Antioch Review*
ArAA / *Arbeiten aus Anglistik und
Amerikanistik*
ArielE / *Ariel: A Review of Interna-
tional English Literature*
ArkQ / *The Arkansas Quarterly: A
Journal of Criticism*
ARLR / *American Renaissance Literary
Report*
ArQ / *Arizona Quarterly*
ASch / *American Scholar*
Athanor (Ravenna, Italy)
ATQ / *American Transcendental Quar-
terly*
Biblion
Biography / *Biography: An Interdisci-
plinary Quarterly*
Boulevard
BoundaryII / *Boundary 2: An Interna-
tional Journal of Literature and Cul-
ture*
BSJ / *The Baker Street Journal: An Ir-
regular Quarterly of Sherlockiana*
Caliban (Toulouse Le Mirail)
The Californians
*Callaloo: A Black South Journal of Arts
and Letters*
C&L / *Christianity and Literature*
CanL / *Canadian Literature*
CE / *College English*
CEA / *CEA Critic*
ChH / *Church History*

ChiR / Chicago Review
CimR / Cimarron Review
CL / Comparative Literature
CLAJ / College Language Association
 Journal
CLAQ / Children's Literature Associa-
 tion Quarterly
ClioI / CLIO: A Journal of Literature,
 History, and the Philosophy of His-
 tory
CLQ / Colby Library Quarterly
Clues: A Journal of Detection
CML / Classical and Modern Litera-
 ture
CollL / College Literature
Commentary
Comparatist: A Journal of the Southern
 Comparative Literature Assn.
Il Confronto Letterario
ConL / Contemporary Literature
Connecticut Review
Connotations
Constructions
ContempR / Contemporary Review
 (London, England)
Cresset (Valparaiso, Indiana)
CRevAS / Canadian Review of Ameri-
 can Studies
Crit / Critique: Studies in Modern Fic-
 tion
The Critic
Criticism: A Quarterly for Literature
 and the Arts
CrSurv / Critical Survey
CS / Concord Saunterer
Diacritics: A Review of Contemporary
 Criticism
Dionysos
DLB / Dictionary of Literary Biogra-
 phy
DNR / Dime Novel Roundup
DQ / Denver Quarterly

DUJ / Durham University Journal
Dyade
EA / Etudes Anglaises
EAL / Early American Literature
EAS / Essays in Arts and Sciences
EDJ / The Emily Dickinson Journal
EGN / Ellen Glasgow Newsletter
EigoS / Eigo Seinen (Tokyo)
Éire / Éire-Ireland: A Journal of Irish
 Studies
ELH [formerly *Journal of English Lit-*
 erary History]
ELN / English Language Notes
ELS / English Literary Studies Mono-
 graph Series
ELT / English Literature in Transition
 (1880–1920)
ELWIU / Essays in Literature (Western
 Ill. Univ.)
EONR / Eugene O'Neill Review
Ergo
ERR / European Romantic Review
ES / English Studies
ESP / Emerson Society Papers
ESQ: A Journal of the American Re-
 naissance
EuWN / Eudora Welty Newsletter
Expl / Explicator
Extrapolation: A Journal of Science Fic-
 tion and Fantasy
FaulkSt / Faulkner Studies (Kyoto,
 Japan)
Fitzgerald Newsletter
FJ / Faulkner Journal
GaR / Georgia Review
GettR / Gettysburg Review
GLQ: A Journal of Gay and Lesbian
 Studies
GPQ / Great Plains Quarterly
Gramma: Journal of Theory and Crit-
 icism
HC / Hollins Critic

Heath Anthology of American Literature Newsletter

History of Philosophy Quarterly

HJR / *Henry James Review*

HLB / *Harvard Library Bulletin*

HN / *Hemingway Review*

HPLR / *High Plains Literary Review*

HudR / *Hudson Review*

IEB / *Illinois English Bulletin*

IFR / *International Fiction Review*

Il Lettore di Provincia

Il Piccolo Hans

Il Ponte

Indice

L'Indice

ISLE: Interdisciplinary Studies in Literature and Environment

ItC / *Italian Culture*

JAAR / *Journal of the American Academy of Religion*

JACult / *Journal of American Culture*

JAmS / *Journal of American Studies*

JASAT / *Journal of the American Studies Assn. of Texas*

JEP / *Journal of Evolutionary Psychology*

JER / *Journal of the Early Republic*

JHI / *Journal of the History of Ideas*

JHS / *Journal of the History of Sexuality*

JML / *Journal of Modern Literature*

JMS / *Journal of Men's Studies*

JNT / *Journal of Narrative Technique*

Journal of Black Psychology

Journal of Black Studies

Journal of the Fantastic in the Arts

Journal of Feminist Studies in Religion

Journal of Literature and Theology

JPC / *Journal of Popular Culture*

Kerouac Connection

KR / *Kenyon Review*

Kritik (Copenhagen)

LaLit / *Louisiana Literature*

LALR / *Latin American Literary Review*

LAmer / *Letteratura d'America: Rivista Trimestale*

L&P / *Literature and Psychology*

L&T / *Literature and Theology: An Interdisciplinary Journal of Theory and Criticism*

L&U / *The Lion and the Unicorn: A Critical Journal of Children's Literature*

Lang&Lit / *Language and Literature*

Lang&S / *Language and Style: An International Journal*

Legacy: A Journal of Nineteenth-Century American Women Writers

Leggere

LetP / *Letras Peninsulares*

LFQ / *Literature/Film Quarterly*

LHRev / *Langston Hughes Review*

Linea d'Ombra

LIT / *Literature Interpretation Theory*

LRB / *London Review of Books*

The Marjorie Kinnan Rawlings Journal of Florida Literature

Markers: The Annual Journal of the Association for Gravestone Studies

Mark Twain Circular

MD / *Modern Drama*

MELUS: The Journal of the Society for the Study of Multi-Ethnic Literature of the United States

Menckeniana: A Quarterly Review

MFS / *Modern Fiction Studies*

Midamerica: The Yearbook of the Society for the Study of Midwestern Literature

Mississippi Review

Missouri Historical Review

MissQ / *Mississippi Quarterly*

MLR / *Modern Language Review*

MLS / *Modern Language Studies*
MMisc / *Midwestern Miscellany*
ModA / *Modern Age: A Quarterly Review*
Modernism/Modernity
Mosaic: A Journal for the Interdisciplinary Study of Literature
MP / *Modern Philology*
MQ / *Midwest Quarterly: A Journal of Contemporary Thought* (Pittsburg, Kans.)
MQR / *Michigan Quarterly Review*
MR / *Massachusetts Review*
MSEx / *Melville Society Extracts*
MTJ / *Mark Twain Journal*
N&Q / *Notes and Queries*
Narrative
NCF / *Nineteenth-Century Literature*
NConL / *Notes on Contemporary Literature*
NDQ / *North Dakota Quarterly*
NEQ / *New England Quarterly*
NERMS / *New England Review*
NewC / *The New Criterion*
NewL / *New Letters*
New Republic
Newsboy
NHR / *Nathaniel Hawthorne Review*
NLH / *New Literary History: A Journal of Theory and Interpretation*
Novel: A Forum on Fiction
NTQ / *New Theatre Quarterly*
NWSA Journal: A Publication of the National Women's Studies Assn.
NY / *New Yorker*
NYRB / *New York Review of Books*
OASIS
Obsidian / *Obsidian II: Black Literature in Review*
OhR / *The Ohio Review*
OL / *Orbis Litterarum: International Review of Literary Studies*

Paideuma: A Journal Devoted to Ezra Pound Scholarship
Panta
Paragone
PArtsJ / *Performing Arts Journal*
PBSA / *Papers of the Bibliographical Society of America*
PennH / *Pennsylvania History*
P.E.O. (Odense)
Pittsburgh History
PLL / *Papers on Language and Literature*
Plys
PM / *Pembroke Magazine*
PMLA: Publications of the Modern Language Assn.
PoeS / *Poe Studies*
Poesia
POMPA / *Publications of the Mississippi Philological Assn.*
Prospects: An Annual Journal of American Cultural Studies
PULC / *Princeton University Library Chronicle*
PUUHS / *Proceedings of the Unitarian Universalist Historical Society*
PVR / *Platte Valley Review*
QDLLSM / *Quaderni del Dipartimento di Lingue e Letterature Straniere Moderne* (Univ. di Genova)
QJS / *Quarterly Journal of Speech*
RALS / *Resources for American Literary Study*
R&L / *Religion and Literature*
Raritan, A Quarterly Review
RCF / *Review of Contemporary Fiction*
REAL / *RE Arts & Letters: A Liberal Arts Forum*
Representations
RFEA / *Revue Française d'Etudes Américaines*
RFR / *Robert Frost Review*

RMR / *Rocky Mountain Review of Language and Literature*
RSAJ / *RSA Journal: Rivista de Studi Nord-Americani*
Ruth Suckow Newsletter
SAD / *Studies in American Drama, 1945-Present*
SAF / *Studies in American Fiction*
Sagetrieb: A Journal Devoted to Poets in the Pound–H.D.–Williams Tradition
SAIL / *Studies in American Indian Literature*
SAJL / *Studies in American Jewish Literature*
SALit / *Chu-Shikoku Studies in American Literature*
SAQ / *South Atlantic Quarterly*
SAR / *Studies in the American Renaissance*
SB / *Studies in Bibliography*
SCR / *South Carolina Review*
SCS / *Stephen Crane Studies*
SDR / *South Dakota Review*
SELit / *Studies in English Literature* (Tokyo)
SFolk / *Southern Folklore*
SFS / *Science-Fiction Studies*
SGym / *Siculorum Gymnasium*
Short Story
SHR / *Southern Humanities Review*
The Sinclair Lewis Society Newsletter
Si Scrive
SlavR / *Slavic Review: American Quarterly of Soviet and East European Studies*
SLitI / *Studies in the Literary Imagination*
SLJ / *Southern Literary Journal*
SNNTS / *Studies in the Novel* (North Texas State Univ.)
SoAR / *South Atlantic Review*
Sociological Quarterly

SoQ / *Southern Quarterly*
SoR / *Southern Review*
Southwestern American Literature
Southwest Historical Quarterly
SPAS / *Studies in Puritan American Spirituality*
SR / *Sewanee Review*
SSF / *Studies in Short Fiction*
StAH / *Studies in American Humor*
StHum / *Studies in the Humanities* (Indiana, Pa.)
StWF / *Studies in Weird Fiction*
SVEC / *Studies on Voltaire and the Eighteenth Century*
SWR / *Southwest Review*
T&P / *Text & Presentation: The Journal of the Comparative Drama Conference*
TCL / *Twentieth-Century Literature*
TDR / *The Drama Review*
Testo a Fronte
Text: Transactions of the Society for Textual Scholarship
TFSB / *Tennessee Folklore Society Bulletin*
Thalia: Studies in Literary Humor
Theater
THJ / *The Thomas Hardy Journal*
ThS / *Theatre Studies*
TJ / *Theatre Journal*
TSB / *Thoreau Society Bulletin*
TSLL / *Texas Studies in Language and Literature*
TSWL / *Tulsa Studies in Women's Literature*
TUSAS / *Twayne's United States Authors Series*
TWN / *Thomas Wolfe Review*
USA Today
Veltro / *Il Veltro: Rivista della Civiltà Italiana*
Verri / *Il Verri: Rivista di Letteratura*

Village Voice
VMHB / *Virginia Magazine of History
and Biography*
WAL / *Western American Literature*
W&I / *Word and Image: A Journal of
Verbal/Visual Enquiry* (London,
England)
WCPMN / *Willa Cather Pioneer Me-
morial Newsletter*
WCWR / *William Carlos Williams Re-
view*
Western Forum
Wild West
WL&A / *War, Literature, and the Arts*
WMQ / *William and Mary Quarterly*
Women's Review of Books
Women's Writing
WS / *Women's Studies*
WVUPP / *West Virginia University
Philological Papers*
WWR / *Walt Whitman Quarterly Re-
view*
YER / *Yeats Eliot Review*
YES / *Yearbook of English Studies*
YJC / *The Yale Journal of Criticism:
Interpretation in the Humanities*
YR / *Yale Review*
ZAA / *Zeitschrift für Anglistik und
Americanistik*

Publishers

Åbo Akademi (Turku, Finland)
Abrams / New York: Harry N.
Abrams
Addison-Wesley / Redding, Mass.:
Addison-Wesley Publishing Co.
Alabama / Tuscaloosa: Univ. of Ala-
bama Press
Algonquin / Chapel Hill, No. Car.:
Algonquin Books of Chapel Hill
(div. of Workman Publishing)

Almqvist and Wiksell / Stockholm:
Almqvist and Wiksell
Anchor / New York: Anchor Books
Applause / New York: Applause The-
atre Books
Arizona / Tucson: Univ. of Arizona
Press
Beacon / Boston: Beacon Press
Benjamins / Philadelphia: John Ben-
jamins North America
Birkhäuser / Basel, Boston: Birk-
häuser Verlag
Black Rose Books (Montreal, New
York)
Blackwell / Oxford: Basil Blackwell,
Ltd.
Bodley Head / London: Bodley Head
Borgen / Copenhagen: Borgen
Borgo / San Bernardino, Calif.: Borgo
Press
Bowker / New York: R. R. Bowker
Bowling Green / Bowling Green,
Ohio: Bowling Green State Univ.
Popular Press
Broadview / Peterborough, Ontario:
Broadview Press
Bucknell / Lewisburg, Pa.: Bucknell
Univ. Press (dist. by Associated
Univ. Presses)
Bulzoni / Rome: Bulzoni Editore
Calgary / Calgary: Univ. of Calgary
Press
Calif. / Berkeley: Univ. of California
Press
Cambridge / New York: Cambridge
Univ. Press
Camden House / Columbia, S.C.:
Camden House
Campus / Frankfurt: Campus Verlag
Carroll / New York: Carroll & Graf
(dist. by Publisher Group West)

Center for Mark Twain Studies /
Elmira College for Mark Twain
Studies at Quarry Farm
Chelsea / New York: Chelsea House
Publishers (div. of Main Line Book
Co.)
Chicago / Chicago: Univ. of Chicago
Press
Chicago Historical Bookworks (Ev-
anston, Ill.)
Columbia / New York: Columbia
Univ. Press
Continuum / New York: Continuum
Publishing Co. (dist. by Harper &
Row Pubs.)
Cornell / Ithaca, N.Y.: Cornell Univ.
Press
Dalkey Archive / Elmwood Park, Ill.:
Dalkey Archive Press
Dee / Chicago: Ivan R. Dee
Delaware / Newark: Univ. of Dela-
ware Press (dist. by Associated
Univ. Presses)
Doubleday Canada / Toronto: Dou-
bleday Canada
Dover / New York: Dover Publica-
tions
Dramatic / Woodstock, Ill.: Dramatic
Publishing Co.
Duckworth / London: Gerald Duck-
worth & Co.
Duke / Durham, N.C.: Duke Univ.
Press
East European Monographs (dist. by
Columbia Univ. Press)
Fairleigh Dickinson / Teaneck, N.J.:
Fairleigh Dickinson Univ. Press
(dist. by Associated Univ. Presses)
Farrar / New York: Farrar, Straus &
Giroux
Fiction Collective Two (Normal,
Col.)

Florida / Gainesville: Univ. Press of
Florida
Fordham / New York: Fordham Univ.
Press
Garland / New York: Garland Pub-
lishing
Georgia / Athens: Univ. of Georgia
Press
Gordian / New York: Gordian Press
Greenwood / Westport, Conn.:
Greenwood Press
Gunter Narr / Tübingen: Gunter
Narr Verlag
Hall / Boston: G. K. Hall & Co. (div.
of Macmillan Publishing Co.)
HarperCollins / New York: Harper
Collins Publishers
Harvard / Cambridge: Harvard Univ.
Press
Harvester Wheatsheaf (New York)
Hopkins / Baltimore: Johns Hopkins
Univ. Press
Human Technology / Fayetteville,
N.C.: Human Technology Inter-
face, Ink
Huntington Library (San Marino,
Calif.)
Illinois / Champaign: Univ. of Illinois
Press
Indiana / Bloomington: Indiana
Univ. Press
Iowa / Iowa City: Univ. of Iowa Press
Julian Messner / New York: Julian
Messner
Kent State / Kent, Ohio: Kent State
Univ. Press
Kingsbridge Historical Society (New
York)
Kluwer / Boston: Kluwer Academic
Publishers
Knopf / New York: Alfred A. Knopf
(subs. of Random House)

Lehigh / Bethlehem, Pa.: Lehigh Univ. Press (dist. by Associated Univ. Presses)

Library of America / New York: Library of America (dist. by Viking Penguin)

Lindisfarne / Hudson, N.Y.: Lindisfarne Press

Locust Hill / West Cornwall, Conn.: Locust Hill Press

LSU / Baton Rouge: Louisiana State Univ. Press

Lund / Lund, Sweden: Lund Univ. Press

Macmillan / London: Macmillan Publishers

McFarland / Jefferson, No. Car.: McFarland & Co.

Madison House / Madison, Wis.: Madison House

Manchester / Manchester: Manchester Univ. Press (dist. by St. Martin's Press, subs. of Macmillan Publishing Co.)

Mass. / Amherst: Univ. of Massachusetts Press

Mass. Historical Soc. / Boston: Massachusetts Historical Society (dist. by Northeastern Univ. Press)

Mayfield / Mountain View, Calif.: Mayfield Publishing Co.

Meany / Toronto: P. D. Meany

Mellen / Lewiston, N.Y.: Edwin Mellen Press

Mentor / New York: Mentor Books (imprint of New American Library, subs. of Pearson)

Meridian / Utica, N.Y.: Meridian Publications

Michigan / Ann Arbor: Univ. of Michigan Press

Mich. State / East Lansing: Michigan State Univ. Press

Minnesota / Minneapolis: Univ. of Minnesota Press

Miss. / Jackson: Univ. Press of Mississippi

Missouri / Columbia: Univ. of Missouri Press

Mouton de Gruyter / Berlin and New York: Mouton de Gruyter

National Poetry Foundation / Orono: University of Maine

NCTE / Urbana, Ill.: National Council of Teachers of English

Nebraska / Lincoln: Univ. of Nebraska Press

Neimeyer (Tübingen)

New Directions / New York: New Directions Publishing Corp. (dist. by W. W. Norton & Co.)

New England / Hanover, N.H.: Univ. Press of New England

New Mexico / Albuquerque: Univ. of New Mexico Press

No. Car. / Chapel Hill: Univ. of North Carolina Press

No. Ill. / DeKalb: Northern Illinois Univ. Press

Northeastern / Boston: Northeastern Univ. Press

Northern Lights / Orono, Me.: Northern Lights

Northouse & Northouse (Dallas)

Northwestern / Evanston, Ill.: Northwestern Univ. Press

Norton / New York: W. W. Norton & Co.

Novus / Oslo, Norway: Novus Press

NYPL / New York Public Library

NYU / New York: New York Univ. Press

Odense / Odense Univ. Press

Ohio / Athens: Ohio Univ. Press
Ohio State / Columbus: Ohio State Univ. Press
Oxford / New York: Oxford Univ. Press
Pace / New York: Pace University
Parnassus / Orleans, Mass.: Parnassus Imprints
Penguin / New York: Penguin Books
Penn. / Philadelphia: Univ. of Pennsylvania Press
Penn. State / University Park: Pennsylvania State Univ. Press
Peter Lang / New York: Peter Lang Publishing (subs. of Verlag Peter Lang AG [Switzerland])
Pittsburgh / Pittsburgh: Univ. of Pittsburgh Press
Praeger / New York: Praeger Publishers
Pratt / Baltimore, Md.: Enoch Pratt Free Library
Prentice Hall / Englewood Cliffs, N.J.: Prentice Hall
Princeton / Princeton, N.J.: Princeton Univ. Press
PUF / Paris: Presses Universitaires de France
PUP / Presses Universitaires de Perpignan
Random House / New York: Random House
Rodopi / Amsterdam: Editions Rodopi BV
Routledge / New York: Routledge, Chapman & Hall
Sage / Thousand Oaks, Calif.: Sage Publications
St. James / Chicago: St. James Press
St. Martin's / New York: St. Martin's Press (subs. of Macmillan Publishing Co.)

Saur / London: K. G. Saur
Scandinavian / Oslo: Scandinavian Univ. Press
Scarecrow / Metuchen, N.J.: Scarecrow Press (subs. of Grolier Educational Corp.)
Scolar / Aldershot, Hants, England: Scolar Press
Scribner's / New York: Charles Scribner's Sons
Signet / New York: Signet Books
Simon & Schuster / New York: Simon & Schuster (div. of Paramount Communications)
Skinner / Boston: Skinner House Books
Smith and Kraus (Lyme, N.H.)
Smithsonian / Washington, D.C.: Smithsonian Institution Press
So. Ill. / Carbondale: Southern Illinois Univ. Press
Southeastern Louisiana State University (dist. by University Press of America)
Stanford / Stanford, Calif.: Stanford Univ. Press
Steerforth Press (South Royalton, Vt.)
SUNY / Albany: State Univ. of New York Press
Susquehanna / Selinsgrove, Pa.: Susquehanna Univ. Press (dist. by Associated Univ. Presses)
Swedenborg Foundation (New York)
Syracuse / Syracuse, N.Y.: Syracuse Univ. Press
Talisman House (Hoboken, N.J.)
Tennessee / Knoxville: Univ. of Tennessee Press
Texas / Austin: Univ. of Texas Press
Texas A & M / College Station: Texas A & M Univ. Press

Texas Tech / Lubbock: Texas Tech
Univ. Press
Third Side / Chicago: Third Side
Press
Third World / Chicago: Third World
Press
Toronto / Toronto: Univ. of Toronto
Press
Twayne / New York: Twayne Pub-
lishers (imprint of G. K. Hall &
Co., div. of Macmillan Publishing
Co.)
Univ. Press / Lanham, Md.: Univer-
sity Press of America
Utah / Salt Lake City: Univ. of Utah
Press
Viking / New York: Viking Penguin
Virginia / Charlottesville: Univ. Press
of Virginia

Washington Square / New York:
Washington Square Press (imprint
of Pocket Books, div. of Simon &
Schuster)
Wayne State / Detroit: Wayne State
Univ. Press
Wesleyan / Middletown, Conn.:
Wesleyan Univ. Press
Winter / Heidelberg: Carl Winter
Wisconsin / Madison: Univ. of
Wisconsin Press
Yale / New Haven, Conn.: Yale Univ.
Press
Yoknapatawpha / Oxford, Miss.: Yok-
napatawpha Press
York / Fredericton, N.B., Can.: York
Press

Part I

1 Emerson, Thoreau, Fuller, and Transcendentalism

David M. Robinson

The publication of a comprehensive modern history of the Transcendentalist movement must be singled out as the year's major event in this field. But much more accompanied it, notably an outpouring of work on Margaret Fuller, confirming that we are indeed experiencing a significant Fuller revival. And, with no pause or abatement, the explosion of Emerson studies continues, fueled both by important textual work and contemporary political concerns.

i History of Transcendentalism

It is curious that in a field long distinguished for its historical scholarship, no satisfactory comprehensive history of the Transcendentalist movement has appeared since 1876. Barbara Packer's "The Transcendentalists" (*Cambridge History of American Literature II*, pp. 329–604) answers that need effectively in an engagingly written study grounded in fresh readings of primary sources and a synthetic command of the best recent scholarship. The past three decades have yielded several important insights that are reflected persuasively in Packer's study. To begin with, Packer presents Transcendentalism as an evolution from its religious context rather than a break from it, noting how the Unitarian emergence in the early 19th century made a new generation receptive to the influence of European Romanticism. She presents fresh readings of such theological texts as Convers Francis's *Christianity a Purely Internal Principle* (1836), George Ripley's "Schleiermacher as Theologian" (1836), and Theodore Parker's "A Discourse of the Transient and Permanent in Christianity" (1841), reminding us again of their importance in any full comprehension of the movement.

Packer's presentation of the evolutionary nature of Transcendentalism is complemented by an emphasis on its social and communal qualities; it is the mutual work of several important thinkers rather than the careers of Emerson, Thoreau, and a few Concord hangers-on. This is most evident in Packer's extensive and perceptive treatment of Fuller, whose accomplishment was vital to the movement, even though her most innovative and important work came after her closest connections to it had passed. Packer notes the significance of Fuller's work with New York's imprisoned women on *Woman in the Nineteenth Century*, "a book of hope" whose millennial qualities suggest that Fuller was preparing herself unknowingly for the political and personal crisis she would undergo in Italy. Her witness to the unfolding of powerful historical forces there made her dispatches to the *Tribune* among "the most absorbing, brilliant, and far-ranging of all texts written by the Transcendentalists." Packer's attention to Fuller's achievement by no means diminishes the achievement of Emerson, who is disclosed here in part as a leader despite himself, but perhaps more importantly as part of a group that he worked hard to cultivate, thriving in its mutual relations despite his isolationist rhetoric. For Packer, he is less centrally a visionary than an uncompromisingly honest religious and ethical thinker whose evolution toward intuitive religion was conditioned in large part by his profound struggle with the philosophical skepticism of Hume. Packer also accentuates the work of Parker, Bronson Alcott, Frederic Henry Hedge, and Orestes Brownson, reminding us in every case of their stature and complexity as historical figures and of the consequent necessity of framing an inclusive definition of the movement based on relationship and mutual influence.

Fuller's importance to the Transcendentalist movement and Emerson's sustained growth through his relations within it evince a third important emphasis of Packer's study, the recognition of the social and political nature of the movement. Packer is aware of the subtleties that make this issue an easy one for scholars to mishandle, either in the facile assumption that we are dealing with uncomplicated progressives, or the presentist dismissal of the movement as unengaged in issues of cultural moment. While Packer is frank on the movement's political shortcomings, noting that its "quietism" and "self-absorption" tended to favor "existing institutions, even the ones the Transcendentalists criticized," she also demonstrates that political engagement, and the larger question of effective action in the world, permeated the thought and career of everyone who could be considered part of the movement. The work of

Alcott, Parker, and Brownson, as well as Emerson and Fuller, is therefore of crucial importance to a full picture of the movement; her reading of Thoreau's career as a struggle for a sense of ethically worthy engagement with society is enormously persuasive. "Resistance to Civil Government," in Packer's reading, is an answer to Emerson's conventionalism as well as the transcript of the "secular conversion experience" that provided Thoreau with a glimpse of America's ruthless society from its margins. In many ways the representative Transcendental individualist, Thoreau is also shown as a thinker molded by his interaction with his friends.

Conrad Wright's *The Unitarian Controversy: Essays on American Unitarian History* (Skinner), which brings together nine of Wright's essays published between 1967 and 1992 on early 19th-century Unitarianism, includes some of Wright's most characteristic and significant work. Essays of particular importance are his account of Henry Ware's election as Hollis Professor of Divinity at Harvard, the event that initiated the Unitarian Controversy (pp. 1–16); his vivid portrait of Jedediah Morse, the Calvinist archenemy of the early liberals (pp. 59–82); his groundbreaking analysis of the Dedham case, the court decision that enabled Unitarian control of many of the churches in eastern Massachusetts (pp. 111–35); and his well-documented analysis of the connections between church affiliation and economic and social standing in early 19th-century Boston (pp. 37–58). Wright's detailed scholarly command of this period and his trenchant thinking about early American religious developments are abundantly evident. This excellent collection will help scholars of Transcendentalism know his work better and, I hope, use it more consistently. For analysis of Wright's work in Unitarian history and the present state of that field, see the special issue of *PUUHS* (22, pt. 2 [1992–94]), which includes my "Unitarian History and the Unitarian-Universalist Identity: The Work of Conrad Wright," an overview of Wright's work with comments on its impact on Transcendentalist studies (pp. 1–11); David D. Hall's "The Renewal of Unitarian-Universalist Studies," a discussion of new directions in Unitarian historiography (pp. 12–20); Cynthia Grant Tucker's "Unjustified Margins and Other Irregularities: When Our History Goes Out of Bounds," a call for a "broader format" of Unitarian historiography that would deepen our sense of the roles of women in the movement (pp. 21–32); Alan Seaburg's " 'Wake Up and Smell the Coffee': Writing Histories of Local Unitarian-Universalist Churches," a discussion of the role of parish histories in

Unitarian historiography (pp. 33–40); and William R. Hutchison's "Conrad Wright in His Rising and at High Noon," a personal tribute to Wright (pp. 41–44). My essay "John White Chadwick and Theological Change," pp. 67–74 in Warren R. Ross, ed., *Regaining Historical Consciousness: Proceedings of the Earl Morse Wilbur History Colloquium* (Starr King School), describes Chadwick's construction of Unitarian history in his *Old and New Unitarian Belief* (1894), noting his treatment of the Unitarian Controversy, the Transcendentalist movement, and the Free Religion movement.

Several solid studies of less prominent Transcendentalists further our understanding of the movement. Larry A. Carlson's edition of "Bronson Alcott's 'Journal for 1838' (Part Two)" (*SAR*, pp. 123–93) covers the months June through December 1838 (see also *ALS 1993*, p. 5), with extensive annotations and a solid introductory overview of this period of Alcott's life, one of an "anguished weighing of options" as Alcott closed his Temple School, finally abandoned his book *Psyche* as unpublishable, and attempted to reestablish his career as a teacher and public advocate of educational reform. The journal includes, in addition to Alcott's self-analysis, extensive references to the active schedule of lectures, meetings, and personal conversations and encounters among the Transcendentalists at a time of high excitement for their movement. In "Bronson Alcott's Developing Personalism and the Argument with Emerson" (*ATQ* 8:311–27) Bernard Schmidt describes the lifelong debate between Alcott and Emerson, emphasizing Alcott's belief in "the personality of the deity." Schmidt notes "the social tendency" integral to Alcott's views, and he connects it with that of Whitman and the American philosopher Borden Parker Bowne. In " 'A Fearful Price I Have Paid for Loving Him': Ellery Channing's Troubled Friendship with Ralph Waldo Emerson" (*SAR*, pp. 251–69) Kathryn B. McKee describes the gradual deterioration of this friendship, noting Emerson's mixture of generous support and consistent criticism of Channing's verse, and Channing's expression of "periodic resentment for Emerson" in the middle 1840s as the friendship began to deteriorate. Dean Grodzins and Joel Myerson have edited "The Preaching Record of Theodore Parker" (*SAR*, pp. 55–122), a week-by-week account of the dates, places, and topics of Parker's preaching career; they provide a reference that will be helpful in understanding more fully the theological grounding of Transcendentalism. Kent P. Ljungquist's "Martha Le Baron Goddard: Forgotten Worcester Writer and Thoreau Critic" (*CS* n.s. 2: 149–56) introduces a member of a mid-

19th-century literary circle in Worcester, Massachusetts, influenced by Transcendentalism.

ii Emerson

a. Scholarly Editions and Reference Materials   A new edition of *English Traits,* vol. 5 of *The Collected Works of Ralph Waldo Emerson,* ed. Philip Nicoloff et al. (Harvard), will help to bring into clearer focus the importance of Emerson's increasing concern with ethics and social institutions in the late 1840s, a transition that was advanced by his lecture tour in England and his attempt in the following decade to assess what he had seen there. Nicoloff's thorough "Historical Introduction" recounts the essential details of both of Emerson's journeys to England, noting his "new rush of admiration for the practical bent of the English" in the second tour of 1847–48. Nicoloff provides a solid overview of the evolution of *English Traits* through Emerson's journals and lectures after his return to the United States, and his narrative is supplemented by some 200 pages of detailed informational and explanatory notes prepared by Robert E. Burkholder. The text of *English Traits* is established by Douglas Emory Wilson, using the first edition of 1856 as the copy-text.

Glen M. Johnson's edition of vol. 3 of *The Topical Notebooks of Ralph Waldo Emerson* (Missouri) presents four notebooks from the later period of Emerson's career which show that his work in collecting, indexing, and arranging his journal and other manuscript material had become, by the middle 1840s, a formidable chore. As these notebooks suggest, he worked in part by placing ideas in conjunction, thus creating new and more comprehensive intellectual categories. Of particular interest is his gathering of material on poetic theory in Notebook "Z O" in preparation of "Poetry and Imagination." The volume also includes Notebook "OP Gulistan," with material on his biographical projects; Notebook "M L," containing his reflections on the "Moral Law"; and Notebook "S Salvage," a general compilation of earlier journal material.

The ninth volume of *The Letters of Ralph Waldo Emerson* (Columbia), ed. Eleanor M. Tilton, containing letters from 1860 through 1869 not included in Ralph L. Rusk's earlier edition, indicate Emerson's growing stature as a public figure and his extensive network of friendships and relationships. The Library of America volume of Emerson's *Collected Poems and Translations,* ed. Harold Bloom and Paul Kane, is a comprehensive gathering of Emerson's poetry, including the texts of the first editions of *Poems* (1847), *May-Day and Other Pieces* (1867), 85 other poems and translations published during his lifetime, and 450 "poems, fragments of poems, and translations of poems" from texts unpublished. The editors offer clear-text versions of poems and fragments published in *The Poetry Notebooks of Ralph Waldo Emerson* (see *ALS 1986,* pp. 3–4) and other more recent scholarly editions of his manuscript material. This volume will prove useful to students of Emerson's poetry.

Albert J. von Frank's *An Emerson Chronology* (Hall) is a year-by-year calendar of the major events of Emerson's life after 1826, including records of significant reading, key letters from him and to him with brief synopses, important acts or events in the lives of those close to him, and a "complete record of Emerson's public performances in the delivery of sermons, lectures, and readings." Von Frank also includes clear indications of the sources for all events listed, 68 biographical sketches of the men and women who appear most frequently in the entries, and a brief overview, at the beginning of each year, of important events in Emerson's life. Produced with scholarly thoroughness and a comprehensive knowledge of his milieu, career, and reputation, this volume will be a resource of continuing value for Emerson studies.

With *Ralph Waldo Emerson: An Annotated Bibliography of Criticism, 1980–1991* (Greenwood) Robert E. Burkholder and Joel Myerson extend their earlier *Emerson: An Annotated Secondary Bibliography* (see *ALS 1985,* pp. 3–4). The entries, arranged chronologically, continuing the numerical sequence of the earlier volume, include complete bibliographical information and descriptive and informative annotations. It is remarkable to see how much has been written on Emerson in the past decade— 1,055 entries; Burkholder and Myerson's thorough and well-arranged bibliography will make it easier for us to retrieve that information. In "Emerson and the Examiner Club: An Unpublished Conversation" (*NEQ* 67: 476–86) Alfred G. Litton describes Emerson's participation in the Examiner Club, which was connected with the *Christian Examiner,* relating that connection to his general interest in clubs and social organizations in his later career. Litton publishes the record of a conversation on education from one of the club meetings in 1870, including comments by Emerson, Frederic Henry Hedge, Edward Everett Hale, and James Freeman Clarke. Kent P. Ljungquist's " 'Warrington' Reviews Emerson: Some Uncollected Reviews and Notices" (*ESP* 5, ii: 1–3) gathers several of William S. Robinson's notices of Emerson's work from the 1840s and 1850s, and J. Frank Schulman discusses "An English Review of *Nature*" (*ESP* 5, i: 3) in an 1842 issue of *The Inquirer*.

b. Sources, Contexts, and Intellectual Development   Two notable essays demonstrate the continuing importance of source studies to our comprehension of Emerson's early development, a phenomenon that, despite years of scholarly analysis, still seems to have something of the miraculous about it. In "'A Seraph's Eloquence': Emerson's Inspired Language and Milton's Apocalyptic Prose" (*MP* 92: 36–63) Robin Sandra Grey persuasively connects Emerson's sense of "the grandiose possibility of omnipotent speech" and his desire for "the singular status of a prophet" with his understanding of the apocalyptic urgency of Milton's prose. Grey argues that Milton's models of "inspired, efficacious language" helped Emerson construct the image of "an all-powerful, prophetic orator" which guided his ministerial ambitions. Grey is especially perceptive in describing how this oratorical model "recoil[ed] upon him during the period leading to his ministerial ordination," resulting in his growing dissatisfaction with "the clergy's substitution of formulaic speech for inspired verbal gifts." In "Emerson, Paris, and the Opening of the Scientific Eye" (*Prospects* 19: 315–47) Lee Rust Brown argues with convincing detail that Emerson's 1833 visit to the Jardin des Plantes in Paris provided him with "a stunning paradigm for his own project of systematic composition" through its exemplification of his belief that "techniques of research and display might recover the stable universal sense hidden behind the hieroglyphic scramble of visible nature." Emerson, himself struggling toward a new form of expression, observed there a "strategy of representation" consonant with both the French Realist novelists and his own work in the journals and essays. Of particular importance was the Jardin's demonstration of the very modern suggestion that "the idea or meaning of nature was identical with techniques of production and delivery," an insight that laid great stress on the role of the perceiving subject in the construction and comprehension of nature.

Other studies of Emerson's intellectual context include Susan L. Roberson's reading of his sermons as part of the Victorian advocacy of "muscular Christianity" (" 'Degenerate Effeminacy' and the Making of a Masculine Spirituality in the Sermons of Ralph Waldo Emerson," pp. 150–72 in *Muscular Christianity*). Roberson argues that Emerson's affirmative preaching of the process of self-culture was accompanied by a "persistent call to repudiate and control the appetites and impulses of the body," resulting in a dialectic in which "self-denial and abstinence" became "empowering, masculinizing strategies." Elisabeth Hurth's "William and Ralph Waldo Emerson and the Problem of the Lord's Supper: The Influence of German 'Historical Speculators' " (*ChH* 62 [1993]: 190–206) explains how the German Higher Criticism altered the developing religious belief and the intended career pattern of two of the Emerson brothers. By 1830 William had rejected the permanent ordinance of the Lord's Supper as a Christian rite, following the analysis of J. J. Griesbach. His encounter with the Higher Criticism influenced Ralph Waldo in his first years of ministry at the Second Church, as shown in the Vestry Lectures of March 1831 on biblical history and interpretation, and eventually in his resignation sermon of 1832 on the Lord's Supper. In *The Code of Concord: Emerson's Search for Universal Laws* (Almqvist and Wiksell) Anders Hallengren explains how the categories of "Ethics and Aesthetics, Poetics and Politics" merge as Emerson's philosophy develops and matures. Hallengren's book is best described as an influence study; he revisits many sources familiar to Emerson scholars, adding his own shades of emphasis in which Swedenborg is prominent. Emerson scholars should also be aware of the new volume of works by Sampson Reed (*Sampson Reed: Primary Source Material for Emerson Studies*, comp. George F. Dole [Swedenborg Foundation, 1992]), one of the key sources of Emerson's Swedenborgian ideas. The volume contains the texts of four of Reed's works, including the hitherto unpublished *A Dissertation: On the Evidence from the Light of Nature of a Future Retribution* (1820), discovered in 1985 by Sylvia Shaw, along with Shaw's preface on Reed's influence on Emerson.

Ronald Bosco offers an insightful account of Emerson's use of Plutarch biographical practice and his departure from it in " 'What Poems Are Many Private Lives': Emerson Writing the American Plutarch" (*SLitI* 27, i: 103–29). Bosco describes Emerson's adherence to the Plutarchan model of the exemplary life in the "Biography" lectures (1834), but his detailed consideration of the structure of *Representative Men* shows Emerson's development beyond that model. Bosco also demonstrates how Emerson's later biographical essays on Thoreau and Samuel Hoar and his unfinished biography of Bronson Alcott represent the application of the principles of *Representative Men* to his contemporaries; these later works illustrate Emerson's conviction that "intellect and virtue had not been exhausted by the great men of earlier ages." William W. Stowe's chapter on Emerson in his *Going Abroad* (pp. 74–101) emphasizes Emerson's contradictory attitudes toward travel that arose from his troubled sense of "the conflicting demands of self and other, experience and authority." Stowe shows that despite Emerson's resistance to travel, he both enjoyed and profited from it, and he discusses in some detail Emerson's first European journey and *English Traits.* Stowe also includes (pp. 102–24) a new version of his published discussion of Fuller's experience as a traveler (see *ALS 1991,* p. 17). With *Anglo-American Antiphony: The Late Romanticism of Tennyson and Emerson* (Florida) Richard E. Brantley continues his study of the empirical and evangelical roots of English and American Romanticism. Brantley's *Coordinates of Anglo-American Romanticism* (see *ALS 1993,* p. 7) demonstrated the ways that Lockean empirical epistemology and Wesleyan experiential religion were reflected in Emerson's *Nature.* His new study extends his reading into the major texts of the late 1830s and 1840s, where he sees Emerson continuing to preach "experiential faith" (Divinity School Address) and a broadly Lockean epistemology that stresses a "blend of subject and object" and reflects a preference for "common experience" ("Self-Reliance"). As Brantley notes, this is a far different Emerson from Bloom's "quasi-gnostic" poet; Brantley offers instead "a broadly experiential basis for redefining Emersonian self-reliance, which is too often defined nowadays in terms of narrow inner experience alone." In " 'Too Pathetic, Too Pitiable': Emerson's Lessons in Love's Philosophy" (*ESQ* 40: 139–82) Eric Murphy Selinger offers welcome attention to both "Love" and "Friendship" as important, problematic texts. Selinger argues that Emerson's philosophy of love reflects the Puritan concern about the idolatry of the loved one, resulting in the necessity for a certain self-restraining strictness in our expectations of love. Emerson both articulates this restraint and struggles against it, advocating in "Friendship" the act of self-bestowal that is "unavoidably complicated by [Emerson's] continuing assumption that love must be deserved." In *The Esoteric Emerson: The Spiritual Teachings of Ralph Waldo Emerson* (Lindisfarne, 1993) Richard Geldard presents Emerson as a "purveyor of a radically new yet ancient esoteric knowledge" centered principally in the Platonic and neo-Platonic traditions.

c. Political Reputation and Cultural Influence   Although book reviews are generally beyond the scope of this essay, I want to call readers' attention to Harold Bloom's "Grandfather Emerson" (*LRB* 7 April: 12–

13), a review of Richard Poirier's *Poetry and Pragmatism.* These two critics, with Stanley Cavell, have been central to what we have come to think of as the Emerson revival of the 1970s and 1980s, and the different Emersons propounded by each of them help to account for the vitality of contemporary Emerson studies and the pervasiveness of Emerson in American cultural historiography. Bloom delineates the difference between his Emerson, "who essentially was a religious writer, akin to other gnostics ancient and modern," and Poirier's more skeptical, pragmatic, and modern figure.

Much of the current critical discussion of Emerson concerns his political stature, and political theorist George Kateb's explication of Emersonian individualism in *The Inner Ocean: Individualism and Democratic Culture* (Cornell, 1992) is becoming a focal point for the discussion (see also *ALS 1990,* p. 6). Kateb undertakes a persuasive "renovation of liberalism" based on the concept of "democratic individuality" of which Emerson, Thoreau, and Whitman are the "principal theorists." He distinguishes "*democratic* individuality" from a narrow and self-serving "individualism pure and simple," because it cultivates "the disposition to disobey bad conventions and unjust laws," encourages an "autonomy" in which "one's self must become a project," and makes possible an "impersonal individuality" that frees one of a "sickly self-interest and blinding anxiety for success." Kateb poses democratic individuality against the "radical anti-individualist" positions of "such otherwise diverse writers as Althusser, Barthes, Foucault, and Derrida," finding in the work of Emerson and his followers an articulation of "everybody's inexhaustible internal turbulent richness and unused powers." Partly in response to Kateb, Cyrus R. K. Patell ("Emersonian Strategies: Negative Liberty, Self-Reliance, and Democratic Individuality," *NCF* 48: 440–79) argues that Emerson struggles, not always successfully, "against the limitations of his cultural moment," at times "unable to realize the full egalitarian potential of his doctrine of individualism." Patell resists Kateb's belief that "the development of individuality leads not to egoism but to a sense of connectedness." "The language of community," he argues, "has been incorporated and subordinated within the idealizing logic of individualism." In "What Is the Emersonian Event? A Comment of Kateb's Emerson" (*NLH* 25: 951–58), a response to what apparently was a draft of a portion of Kateb's *Emerson and Self-Reliance* (Sage, 1995), which will be reviewed here next year, Stanley Cavell describes his fundamental agreement with Kateb that Emerson "is a figure of democratic inspiration and aspiration" and that this "democratic inspiration is of essential importance to Emerson's work." Cavell takes exception, however, to what he sees as Kateb's distinction "between thinking and acting," arguing that Emerson's "imagining" of democratic perfection "enables us to act, that is, to exist in freedom from a despair of democracy." Cary Wolfe cogently examines Cavell's attempt to reclaim "the power and promise of Emersonian selfhood" in "Alone with America: Cavell, Emerson, and the Politics of Individualism" (*NLH* 25: 137–57), a project based on Cavell's recognition of "the very transience of the self, the provisionality of any proof of selfhood." For Wolfe, however, this theory of the self and its necessary autonomy is "radically *antisocial*"—"it is difficult to see how such a self could ever engage in social and political praxis."

Kenneth Dauber's "On Not Being Able to Read Emerson, or 'Representative Man'" (*BoundaryII* 21, ii: 220–42) is a cogent defense of Emerson's political values. Dauber finds Emerson's quality of "representivity" a key to his continuing influence as a political progressive, arguing that his centrality as an American spokesman is not hegemonic because of his capacity to voice "nationality" as "the mutuality of contending voices." "The One was, for him, many from the start." Dauber finds Emerson's persistent orientation to the particular occasion, to sustaining "openness to experience," of particular importance in his achievement, locating this texture of presence even in his most mystical passages, such as the transparent eyeball experience in *Nature*. In "Emerson and the Climates of Political History" (*BoundaryII* 21, ii: 179–219) Eduardo Cadava focuses on Daniel Webster's comment, "You cannot keep out of politics more than you can keep out of frost," to trace Emerson's various comments on the connection between "the political" and "the natural." Noting his "call to responsibility" as the Civil War approached, Cadava finds that "Emerson's analysis of the place of nature within the arena of the historical or the political . . . suggests the strength of his social criticism."

Barbara Ryan's "Emerson's 'Domestic and Social Experiments': Service, Slavery, and the Unhired Man" (*AL* 66: 485–508) is an interesting examination of Emerson's attempts to establish "'family-style' domestic service" at his home. Ryan links Emerson's attempts to reformulate domestic service to his thinking about slavery, noting that he became forceful in his opposition to slavery only after he had failed to integrate servants into the family and had therefore reconciled himself to the necessity of waged servants. She connects Thoreau's early boarding with the Emersons with these experiments, an arrangement reached by "mutual decision, pleasing both to the servant-conscious Emerson and the service-conscious Thoreau." In "Negotiating Claims of Race and Rights: Du Bois, Emerson, and the Critique of Liberal Nationalism" (*MR* 35: 169–201) Anita Haya Goldman argues that Emerson "shared many of the racist perceptions of his time, even when such perceptions contradicted his belief in democratic first principles." His affirmation of Anglo-Saxon racialism as the basis for the American identity ironically provided Du Bois with a precedent for affirming "racial unity" as an alternative to "the insufficiencies of the liberal discourse of rights."

Lively critical discussion continues of Emerson's link with modern writers, even including those ordinarily considered anti-Emersonian. William Bedford Clark offers a well-crafted reconsideration of Robert Penn Warren's connection with Emerson in "In the Shadow of His Smile: Warren's Quarrel with Emerson" (*SR* 102: 550–69), arguing that the differences between the two writers are "more superficial than fundamental." Clark observes that Warren and Emerson shared the view "that humankind's fallen state is inextricably linked to the question of self-awareness and inadequate self-definition," and he finds that "each longed for an atonement in which the denatured self might reclaim nature through a new holism." Similarly impressive is Steven Helmling's "Emersonian Eliot" (*SR* 102: 46–69), a lucid reconsideration of the overlooked similarities in sensibility and outlook between Emerson and T. S. Eliot. Helmling stresses "Eliot's unquestioned commitment to *the* definitively Emersonian project, the project of self-making," noting that for both men, "the self is made, or makes itself, in relation to culture, but antithetically: *against* culture." Henry Hart's "Robert Lowell, Emerson, and the American Sublime" (*ESQ* 39 [1993]: 279–307) examines Lowell's "Oedipal combativeness" with Emerson, noting both Lowell's attraction to Emerson's idealism and his distrust of it, born of both "New Critical biases" and Lowell's "manic-depressive illness and his tragic sense of history." Hart argues that Lowell's early contempt for Emerson softened as he came "to realize that Emerson's ambivalence [toward religious enthusiasm and sublime idealism] reflected his own." Martin Bickman's "From Emerson to Dewey: The Fate of Freedom in American Education" (*AmLH* 6: 385–408) is a plea to recover the vitality of an innovative educational tradition which includes Emerson and John Dewey as its preeminent spokesmen. Bickman focuses on "The American Scholar" as the key to Emerson's theory of education, one that "stresses active intelligence over passive absorption." Dewey worked explicitly within this framework, advocating "a truly dialectical and energizing relationship" between thought and action. But despite the promise of Alcott's work at Temple School, which Bickman discusses in some detail, these ideas "never entered the mainstream of American education." Len Gougeon ("Holmes's Emerson and the Conservative Critique of Realism," *SoAR* 59, i: 107–25) investigates Oliver Wendell Holmes's attempts to construct Emerson's legacy in accordance with "conservative and genteel values" in his influential 1884 biography. Working with both the text of the biography and Holmes's manuscript notes for it, Gougeon cogently explains how Holmes attempted to separate Emerson from what he felt were the "degenerate eccentricities" of Thoreau and Whitman as part of a larger resistance to the trend toward realism represented by the fiction of Zola. Holmes was answered during the 1880s by William Dean Howells, who often resorted to Emerson's advocacy of aesthetic innovation to support his conversion to realism. In " 'Demonology': Emerson on Dreams" (*ATQ* 8: 5–16) Richard R. O'Keefe analyzes the little-studied "Demonology," noting that Emerson's analysis of dreams directly anticipates Freud. Emerson characterized dreams as "traces of memories" that reveal "a wish," both central tenets in Freud; most importantly, O'Keefe notes, both men believed that "dreams hold *significance*" in our comprehension of the inner life. Daniel J. Nadenicek discusses Emerson's influence on the design of Sleepy Hollow Cemetery in "Sleepy Hollow Cemetery: Philosophy Made Substance" (*ESP* 5, i: 1–2, 8).

iii Thoreau

Henry S. Salt's *The Life of Henry David Thoreau* (Illinois, 1993) has been newly edited by George Hendrick et al., with a detailed introduction to the development and significance of Salt's influential early biography. While earlier editions had been published in 1890 and 1896, the editors present the revised 1908 version, for which Salt never found a publisher; the biography was preserved in the papers of the pioneering Thoreau scholar Raymond Adams. Jane Bennett's *Thoreau's Nature: Ethics, Politics, and the Wild* (Sage) is a study of Thoreau's political significance, presenting his superficially apolitical attitude as in fact profoundly important to contemporary politics. Bennett argues that Thoreau understood that conventional politics "cultivates skills and habits of mind inimical to a deliberate life," so he turned away to his own work of self-fashioning. But this inward turn had political importance. "Unlike Foucault," Bennett observes, "Thoreau views the deliberating, inward-dwelling individual" as an effectual counter to "forces of normalization." His project of self-fashioning included his recognition of nature's "Wild indeterminacy and excessiveness" and his concomitant desire to be part of a rich "heterogeneity"—a "heteroverse" as opposed to a "universe"—that links his political significance to his commitment to nature.

William Rossi makes a substantial addition to the growing discourse on Thoreau and science in his "Poetry and Progress: Thoreau, Lyell, and the Geological Principles of *A Week*" (*AL* 66: 275–300), a nuanced explanation of how Charles Lyell's version of the progress of scientific advance through lapse and recovery is reflected in the discontinuities of *A Week*'s narrative structure. While on one level Thoreau "defers to scientific authority," his alignment of "poetry with science serves to displace scientific authority" in the construction of his narrative perspective. The resulting "representation of the process of knowing as discontinuously progressive and perpetually incomplete" mirrors Lyell's depiction of the discontinuously progressive advance of scientific knowledge. Ning Yu's "Thoreau and the New Geography: The Hydrological Cycle in 'Ktaadn' " (*ESQ* 40: 113–38) is an instructive essay on the appeal of the " 'new geography' " of Alexander von Humboldt and Carl Ritter, which situated humans as "only part of the complex network of nature" rather than as "masters of the earth." Yu thus reads "Ktaadn" as "a metaphoric journey in reverse order of the hydrological cycle," which culminates in Thoreau's discovery of "a 'Titanic' nature that has ontological priority over the self-centeredness of human beings." In an essay that gives us a glimpse of Thoreau's knowledge and activities as a naturalist, Francis B. Dedmond ("Thoreau and the Glowworms," *CS* n.s. 2: 131–36) recounts Thoreau's efforts to identify specimens of glowworms sent him by Marston Watson in 1857.

Walden continues to be a focal point for Thoreau studies, as readings of the text are connected in new ways to aspects of 19th-century culture. David C. Miller's "The Iconology of Wrecked or Stranded Boats in Mid to Late Nineteenth-Century American Culture" (pp. 186–208, 327–31 in David C. Miller, ed., *American Iconology: New Approaches to Nineteenth-Century Art and Literature* [Yale, 1993]) links Thoreau's meditation in *Walden* on a rotting boat he observed at Flint's Pond to a shift in the iconological significance of the wrecked boat in American luminist painting. Miller argues that in both Thoreau's text and the paintings of the luminists, "an emerging conception of natural history," with its cyclical pattern of development, "undermined or complicated the notion of human progress" and thus deflated "the theatrical, human-centered mood permeating the traditional iconology of shipwreck." I found Miller's essay an engaging example of interdisciplinary cultural analysis and a perceptive reconsideration of luminist painting. In "Performing Experiments: Materiality and Rhetoric in Thoreau's *Walden*" (*ESQ* 39 [1993]: 253–77) Timothy Melley presents a discerning account of the tension between material and rhetorical performance in *Walden,* grounding his reading in J. L. Austin's contention that speech acts tend inevitably to undermine themselves. Melley believes that Thoreau wants his text to dissolve itself into the material experiment that it describes, but Thoreau also fears this loss of intellectual perspective. *Walden* thus demonstrates "the way that self-representation continually threatens to separate one's self from the material acts which underwrite that self." I was impressed with Suzanne D. Rose's investigation of Native American myth on *Walden* ("Following the Trail of Footsteps: From the Indian Notebooks to *Walden,*" *NEQ* 67: 77–91). Rose argues that Thoreau's 11 manuscript notebooks of Native American material are "a neglected resource" for Thoreau scholars. To demonstrate their significance, she shows how Thoreau's adaptation of the myth of the Earth Diver helped him transform his account of the loon "from fact into myth." John Bird's "Gauging the Value of Nature: Thoreau and His Woodchucks" (*CS* n.s. 2: 139–47) treats Thoreau's numerous and varied references to woodchucks in *Walden* as indicative of his "ambivalence about wildness." Etsuko Taketani ("Thoreau's Domestic Economy: Double Accounts in *Walden,*" *CS* n.s. 2: 65–76) argues that "Economy" can be read as Thoreau's "literary appropriation of the tenets of domestic economy" in 19th-century American culture; Taketani stresses the importance of Thoreau's narratives of domestic stories that involve Irish immigrants. Helen Lojek's "Thoreau's Bog People" (*NEQ* 67: 279–97) surveys Thoreau's comments on the Irish, finding that he "shared, apparently without thought, most of society's prevailing anti-Irish sentiments." Lojek places these prejudices in the context of the negative reaction to Irish immigration in New England at mid-century, noting that Thoreau's attitude is free from "the prevailing harshness or cant that would signal deep-seated fear or dislike."

Lively discussion also continues of Thoreau's place in the tradition of

American nature writing, most recently *ISLE*'s publication of three papers and a response from a 1993 session at the Modern Language Association. In "Academic Campfire Stories: Thoreau, Ecocriticism and the Fetishism of Nature" (*ISLE* 2: 53–64) Paul L. Tidwell uses Thoreau as a reference point for a critique of contemporary ecocriticism, arguing for a criticism that fully takes into account both the construction of nature by the human observer and "the linked environmental and social consequences of adopting one or another construction of nature's economy." Ralph W. Black ("From Concord Out: Henry Thoreau and the Natural Sublime," pp. 65–75) uses the "Contact" passage in "Ktaadn" as the focal point of his study of the tension between "*locus*" (presence) and "*logos*" (interpretation) in Thoreau's accounts of the sublime. At the summit of Katahdin, Thoreau "can relinquish his claim as scribe," integrating himself more completely in the natural elements. In "Forest Life and Forest Trees: Thoreau and John S. Springer in the Maine Woods" (pp. 77–84) Stan Tag discusses the impact on *The Maine Woods* of Springer's *Forest Life and Forest Trees* (1851), one of some 30 narratives on Maine's woods written in the 19th century. Springer provided "the lumberman's perspective" against which Thoreau was able to formulate "his ability to perceive the natural world on its own terms." William Howarth's "Thoreau and the Cultural Construction of Nature" (pp. 85–89) is a response to the panel, calling for an expansive practice of ecocriticism that engages cultural theory and natural science. Also of relevance for ecocriticism is Victor Carl Friesen's "Thoreau's Sauntering: The 'Adventure of the Day' " (*CS* n.s. 2: 21–31), a description of Thoreau's practice of "sauntering" and its close connection to his intellectual life and literary work.

Analyses of Thoreau's cultural reputation included David A. Wells's "Thoreau's Reputation in the Major Magazines, 1862–1900: A Summary and Index" (*AmPer* 4: 12–23), a useful survey of Thoreau's 19th-century reputation, emphasizing James Russell Lowell's "vitriolic analysis of Thoreau's mind and character" in the *North American Review* of 1865. Lowell's influential attack was gradually overcome by defenders such as Thomas Wentworth Higginson and Henry S. Salt. Wells includes a listing of "every mention of Henry David Thoreau and his works" in 10 major American magazines from 1862–1900. Donald W. Linebaugh (" 'The Road to Ruins and Restoration': Roland W. Robbins, Henry D. Thoreau, and the *Discovery at Walden*," *CS* n.s. 2: 33–62) recounts Robbins's archaeological recovery of Thoreau's cabin site at Walden, noting Robbins's personal engagement with Thoreau as an intellectual and professional model. In "Young Men and Women of Fairest Promise: Transcendentalism in Concord" (*CS* n.s. 2: 5–18) Robert A. Gross describes the distinctive outlook and experience of the generation born in Concord from 1815 through 1825, who "witnessed a remarkable transformation of New England life." Gross offers sketches of Thoreau's contemporaries George Moore, John Shepard Keyes, and Martha L. Prescott. Ethel Seybold identifies "The Source of Thoreau's 'Cato-Decius Dialogue'" (*SAR,* pp. 245–50) as "Addison's *Cato,* II, ii," printing Addison's original and notes on Thoreau's translation. Students of Thoreau should be aware of expansive new initiatives taken by the Thoreau Society, including the establishment of a Thoreau Educational Center, as outlined in Joel Myerson's 1994 presidential address ("The State of the Thoreau Society, 1994 and Beyond," *TSB* 208: 1–3).

iv Fuller

One of the chief sources of the current revival of interest in Fuller has been Robert N. Hudspeth's edition of *The Letters of Margaret Fuller* (Cornell), the sixth and concluding volume of which was published this year. This final volume includes letters describing Fuller's life in Florence in the winter of 1850, and her difficult decision to return with her family to the United States to find a publisher for her history of the Italian Revolution. Also here are Fuller's accounts not only of political events in Italy, but of her daily life with Ossoli and their son, Angelo, and her relations with the expatriate English and American community in Florence. The volume includes a section of undated letters and fragments of letters, and newly discovered letters, dominated by 84 letters to James Freeman Clarke, which add significant detail to our sense of Fuller's important friendship with him and of her intellectual development in the early 1830s. Some of these letters, Hudspeth observes, "repair some of the damage done by the *Memoirs*" by providing complete and uncorrupted texts of fragments published there and by establishing a more complete context for many of Fuller's statements. This edition will remain central to Fuller studies and, I believe, to all future work on the origins and development of New England Transcendentalism. A new letter from the winter of 1841–42, commenting on Julia Ward Howe's poetry, is published in Judith Mattson Bean's "Margaret Fuller on the Early Poetry of Julia Ward Howe" (*ANQ* 7: 76–80).

With *Minerva and the Muse: A Life of Margaret Fuller* (Mass.) Joan von Mehren has provided a biography that both reinforces our sense of Fuller's accomplishment and underlines the tragedy of her lost potential. Von Mehren's reading of Fuller's early years emphasizes "the mixture of Unitarian self-culture and Goethe's quest philosophy of continual 'generous seeking'" that fueled both her philosophical striving and her desire for fulfilling relationships with others. Von Mehren treats Fuller's friendship with Emerson with balanced judgment, understanding both his importance to her development and the sense in which he left her unfulfilled. "'Sweet Child.—Great Sage—Undeveloped Man!'" she wrote of him in 1844. Von Mehren also observes the change in their relationship in 1842–43, when, "no longer in thrall to Emerson," Fuller "no longer unsettled him," thus deepening in some ways their mutual respect and support.

Von Mehren's account of Fuller's achievement of "a solid place among the New York literati" is one of the most satisfying portions of the book, a discussion that includes portraits of Fuller's crucial and complicated relationships with James Nathan and Horace and Mary Greeley and her increasing closeness with William Henry Channing. The simultaneous development in New York of her literary prowess, her social concern, and her desire for close relationships helped to dictate the nature of her experience in Italy. Fuller's sense of the need to shield her relationship with Giovanni Angelo Ossoli from her friends and family results in some lacunae in the surviving biographical record, but von Mehren succeeds nevertheless in presenting Fuller's achievement of a full maturity and profound sense of both justice and tragedy in the last years of her life. We come to see that Fuller understood the essential drama of her life, even as she lived it. Von Mehren writes of Fuller with profound sympathy and respect, and with the necessary critical judgment for a balanced and persuasive assessment.

Marie Mitchell Olesen Urbanski has edited *Margaret Fuller: Visionary of the New Age* (Northern Lights), a collection of essays structured to highlight major phases of Fuller's development and achievement. Joan von Mehren's "Margaret Fuller: Woman of Letters" (pp. 18–51) is a useful overview of Fuller's life and literary career. Renate Delphendahl's "Margaret Fuller: Interpreter and Translator of German Literature" (pp. 54–100) surveys Fuller's work in German literature, noting her "linguistic versatility and competence" and arguing that "translation became the cornerstone for her intellectual development in a patriarchal society."

Urbanski's "The Ambivalence of Ralph Waldo Emerson Towards Margaret Fuller" (pp. 105–21) is a revision of a 1978 essay in which Urbanski posits a mutual romantic attraction between Emerson and Fuller, as revealed in part in Emerson's "tantalizingly ambiguous remarks that could be interpreted romantically by a reader eager to do so." Urbanski writes that "the tone of their correspondence cooled" after a crisis point in 1840, but that Emerson "tried to revive their 'romance' in Europe" during his lecture tour of 1847–48 without success. In "Letters: A Lady's Cameo Art" (pp. 122–41) Urbanski surveys Fuller's correspondence, placing it in the context of 19th-century women's writing and noting its autobiographical value. She pays particular attention to Fuller's correspondence with James Nathan. In "The Seeress of Prevorst: The Central Jewel in *Summer on the Lakes*" (pp. 142–59) Urbanski disagrees with previous views of this section of the book as a digression, arguing that "the Seeress episode is both the literal and thematic center of this book." Fuller found in the episode a "validation of spiritual power" that helped to clarify "the meaning of her trip west." Margaret A. Lukens's "Columnist of Conscience: Margaret Fuller's New York Years" (pp. 183–96) surveys Fuller's "often-neglected social criticism" of 1844–46 for the *Tribune*. Lukens discusses the impact of Fuller's western travel and her contact with imprisoned women in broadening Fuller's social perspective, and she perceptively treats the probable impact of her relationship with James Nathan on her writing of this period. Judith Strong Albert's "Currents of Influence: 'The electrical, the magnetic element in woman . . . ' " (pp. 199–239) analyzes Fuller's impact on later developments in American culture, arguing that she "set the intellectual foundations for major future breakthroughs for her sex." Albert focuses on Fuller's early influence on Elizabeth Palmer Peabody, Lydia Maria Child, and Caroline Healey Dall, and she traces the cultural work of this "first circle" of her audience. The volume also reprints Urbanski's 1980 essay "*Woman in the Nineteenth Century*: Genesis, Form, Tone, and Rhetorical Devices" (pp. 160–80), includes brief personal essays from each of the contributors discussing her relationship to Fuller's work, and adds an appendix of Fuller's translations from Goethe (pp. 245–372).

The importance of Fuller's "Conversations" for women to American cultural development has long been acknowledged, but scholars have been frustrated by the lack of detailed accounts of them. In "Margaret Fuller's Boston Conversations: The 1839–1840 Series" (*SAR*, pp. 195–226) Nancy Craig Simmons has edited Elizabeth Palmer Peabody's record of one series of the conversations from a manuscript in the American Antiquarian Society. This is indeed a significant addition to our information on Fuller. The manuscript records in some detail the conversations from early November 1839 through late March 1840, providing important information on Fuller's procedures in the conversations and the nature of the dialogue that she was able to create with her participants.

Two studies of Fuller in the context of rhetorical history were published. In "Margaret Fuller: A Rhetoric of Citizenship in Nineteenth-Century America," pp. 110–36 in Gregory Clark and S. Michael Halloran, eds., *Oratorical Culture in Nineteenth-Century America: Transformations in the Theory and Practice of Rhetoric* (So. Ill., 1993), P. Joy Rouse situates Fuller "in the context of the history of rhetoric" by describing how her "practice of self-culture, when applied to women, called for a revision of gender relations in society" and "required social reform." Using the ideals of "Republican Motherhood and True Womanhood . . . subversively," Fuller helped transform self-culture into a vehicle that made women aware of themselves "as a social and historical group." Annette Kolodny ("Inventing a Feminist Discourse: Rhetoric and Resistance in Margaret Fuller's *Woman in the Nineteenth Century*," *NLH* 25: 355–82) argues that *Woman in the Nineteenth Century* should be read as Fuller's experiment in "a pluralistic discourse that was both collaborative and noncoercive." Kolodny notes Fuller's use of Richard Whateley's *Elements of Rhetoric* in framing her text, but she argues that Fuller rejected "persuasion as a tactic for feminist discourse," resulting in a treatise that was not ordered "in the conventional manner." Kolodny finds that Fuller's "conversational strategies proved revolutionary and enduring," empowering the early feminist movement in its earliest organizational phases. Related to these studies is Stephanie A. Smith's discussion of Fuller's use of maternal metaphors in her aesthetic theory (*Conceived by Liberty*, pp. 69–86). Smith argues that "Fuller's work questioned the metaphysical grounds on which the twentieth-century parallelism between masculinity and the American writer would grow" and that she developed an "image of dynamic maternity as a primary source of creative power."

In "Texts from Conversation: Margaret Fuller's Influence on Emerson" (*SAR*, pp. 227–44) Judith Mattson Bean argues convincingly that Fuller was "a partner [with Emerson] in a stimulating dialogue that enlivened many of Emerson's literary texts." Her influence can be discerned not only in Emerson's "Friendship," long recognized as deriving from Emerson's relationship with Fuller, but in "Love," "Heroism," and "Art." Bean describes Emerson's increasing respect for Fuller as a critic of his own work, especially in the *Dial* years, but Bean finds that he resisted some of Fuller's "feminist arguments" after 1843. He attempted to minimize the record of her influence through the *Memoirs*, which "limited later estimations of Fuller's pervasive cultural influence." Shirley Smith's "Anglo-Saxon Women's View of Mazzini: The Case of Margaret Fuller" (*ItC* 10 [1992]: 85–96) discusses Fuller's encounters with Mazzini and her involvement in the Italian cause.

In conclusion, I would observe that the growing interest in Fuller is not only important for our understanding of her accomplishment, but may lead us to emphasize the "movement" aspect of Transcendentalism rather than its individual participants. The study of the relations among the Transcendentalists and the reliance on such texts as letters or the records of public "Conversations" provide a historical grounding that promises much important work in the future.

Oregon State University

2 Hawthorne

Leland S. Person

Despite the appearance of only one critical book, this year features an important new volume in the Centenary Edition and a valuable collection of 19th-century reviews. Debates prompted by New Historicism continue to dominate, but the year's contributions also include an interesting variety and breadth of coverage, with solid essays on all four major novels and several provocative essays on the tales. Especially heartening: after virtually no attention last year, *The House of the Seven Gables* merited three excellent essays.

i Editions and Bibliography

Hawthorne's *Miscellaneous Prose and Verse* (Ohio State), ed. Thomas Woodson, Claude M. Simpson, and L. Neal Smith, will prove a gold mine for Hawthorne scholars—a vital source of hard-to-find items with the potential to reshape our views of the man and the writer. Although appearing in print before volumes 21 and 22, this volume (23) concludes the Centenary Edition, a remarkable publishing venture greatly indebted in recent years to Thomas Woodson. To have readily available in one place Hawthorne's biographical sketches ("Mrs. Hutchinson," "Sir William Phips," et al.), his "lost" American notebook (with new and revised explanatory notes), the notorious campaign biography of Franklin Pierce (supplemented by Pierce's Mexican diary), and the increasingly important essay, "Chiefly about War-matters," along with a more recently discovered companion piece, "Northern Volunteers," as well as juvenilia, poetry and reviews (including one of Melville's *Typee,* praising Melville's "tolerance" for "codes of morals that may be little in accord with our own"), prefaces to edited volumes (such as *Peter Parley's Universal History*), and several newly discovered letters—this treasure trove should spark renewed scholarly interest. A meticulous "Historical and Textual Commentary," which runs to 150 pages, offers a wealth of background information and scholarly reference. The extended commentaries on the Pierce biography and on "Chiefly about War-matters" are especially valuable.

Another major addition to Hawthorne studies, *Nathaniel Hawthorne: The Contemporary Reviews* (Cambridge), ed. John Idol and Buford Jones, will prove invaluable. In addition to healthy selections of reviews (20–40 pages on most of the major book publications) this 500-page, double-columned volume includes at the end of each section checklists of other known reviews. Space limitations prevent my sharing the best ones, but anyone interested in Hawthorne's contemporaneous reputation will find this work indispensable.

ii Critical Books

The only book exclusively on Hawthorne this year, Thomas R. Moore's *A Thick and Darksome Veil: The Rhetoric of Hawthorne's Sketches, Prefaces, and Essays* (Northeastern) complements G. R. Thompson's *The Art of Authorial Presence* (see *ALS 1993*, pp. 23–24) in arguing that Hawthorne's nonfictional prose most fully reveals his "preoccupation with the slippery, untrustworthy nature of language and rhetoric." Like Thompson's, Moore's Hawthorne negotiates with his readers, creating shifting authorial personae and writing doubly for different audiences. For sentimentally inclined readers, Hawthorne employed a "rhetoric of escape" that reinforced "normative cultural taste"; for more "astute" readers (his preferred audience, in Moore's view), Hawthorne relied on a "rhetoric of subversion" to suggest a darker, more ambiguous, antisentimental world. Not a new idea, but Moore's application of it to rarely treated sketches and especially his astute analysis of Hawthorne's opaque, hypotactic prose style (e.g., in "The Old Apple Dealer" and "Monsieur du Miroir") and uncomfortable, evasive relation to his audiences (especially in his prefaces) represent a useful contribution.

Mediating between an older generation of romance critics (descending from Richard Chase) and the current generation of New Americanists (e.g., Sacvan Bercovitch), Emily Miller Budick in *Engendering Romance: Women Writers and the Hawthorne Tradition* (Yale) provocatively places Hawthorne at the head of a female and even matriarchal tradition of romance writing that includes Carson McCullers, Flannery O'Connor, Toni Morrison, and Grace Paley. Deriving a line of strong maternal protagonists from Hester Prynne, Budick redefines the romance tradition as philosophically and sexually skeptical by grounding skepticism in fathers' inability to verify their own paternity. Emphasizing consent rather than consensus (with help from Stanley Cavell), this tradition, which Budick sees inaugurated in *The Scarlet Letter,* "has intimately to do with questions of choice and responsibility" and with "choosing a place within history and tradition and with assuming responsibility both for oneself and for one's progeny." While Budick devotes most of her attention to other writers, she highlights a protofeminist, antipatriarchal Hawthorne and offers a compelling analysis of *The Scarlet Letter* as double family romance (with Hawthorne, Hester, and Surveyor Pue/ Edgar Allan Poe forming the less obvious "family").

iii General Essays

In the role of new literary history revisionist, Jonathan Arac (*Cambridge History of American Literature 1,* pp. 641–51, 708–24) reinscribes the early Hawthorne as a "Massachusetts local writer," whose writing was motivated by a desire for fame and financial success and whose career was nationalized, in "an extraordinary process of construction," by his politically connected friends in the publishing and reviewing industry. Figuring Hawthorne as a waffling political conservative (Democrat) whose methods are "intensely individualizing" and "alienating" and whose writing "reenacts the contradiction of Jacksonianism," Arac argues that Hawthorne's romances reflect his embattled condition as a writer, his split between public and private lives, his sense of disconnection and disunion, his preference for inaction and providential solutions to problems like slavery.

Robert E. Abrams, "Critiquing Colonial American Geography: Hawthorne's Landscape of Bewilderment" (*TSLL* 36: 357–79), insightfully contrasts the "free-floating sense of the unsettled" in Hawthorne's New England tales with the positivistic model of knowledge inscribed in colonial American maps. The "hermeneutic black hole" that Abrams discovers in Hawthorne's presentation of cultural space produces a more radical Hawthorne (a cartographic as well as cultural deconstructionist) than the consensualist of Sacvan Bercovitch and others. Hawthorne blurs what Abrams calls the "jealously sustained opposition" between the "civil and the wild" that was so fundamental to 17th-century New England cartography and sense of space. Hawthorne's "countertendency," Abrams contends, suggests a "less definitively bordered" sense of space in which the "residually alien character of reality" cannot be "quarantined to the far side of a mapped cultural edge." With treatments of "Young Goodman Brown," "My Kinsman, Major Molineux," and *The Scarlet Letter,* Abrams's is the best essay I know on Hawthorne's spatial imagination.

With some theoretical help from Stephen Greenblatt (e.g., on "resonance," "wonder," "wounded artifacts"), Christopher D. Felker in *Reinventing Cotton Mather in the American Renaissance* (Northeastern, 1993) argues perceptively that Hawthorne discovered a metaphor (the wonder-cabinet) for historical fiction in Cotton Mather's *Magnalia Christi Americana.* Comparing Hawthorne's antiquarianism to Mather's and, most originally, to Charles Willson Peale's exhibition techniques at his Philadelphia museum, Felker examines "The Virtuoso's Collection," "The Old Manse," "The Custom-House," and especially *Grandfather's Chair,* which offers the "ideal antiquarian laboratory for testing the combinatorial possibilities of fragments" and for achieving a resonant, contextual history.

Samuel Coale, "The Romance of Mesmerism: Hawthorne's Medium of Romance" (*SAR,* pp. 271–88), claims that "mesmerism as a cultural influence" deeply affected Hawthorne's vision and the form rather than just the themes of his fiction. Hawthorne's long, "clause-ridden" sentences draw readers into a dark, neutral territory to discover "universal and often mysterious human sympathies." Coale goes further than previous critics in discovering parallels between mesmeric process and Hawthorne's fictional theories.

Alessandro Portelli (*The Text and the Voice,* pp. 72–77 and passim) puts Hawthorne into conversation with numerous others on the subversive potential of orality (to undermine national institutions "by feeding memories, rituals, aggregations, and passions, which escape the controls and certainties of written reason and law"), and he finds examples in the scarlet letter, which "scatters 'literal' truth and documentary authority, historical certainty and narrative credibility," and in the inner voice unfettered by Dimmesdale's forest walk with Hester.

Edgar Bowers, "Hawthorne and the Extremes of Character" (*SR* 102: 570–87), compares Hawthorne with Emily Dickinson and Wallace Stevens in their use of character extremes marked by "torpor" and "exuberance." To exemplify "torpor caused by a guilty conscience suddenly released into exuberance," he cites Dimmesdale's return from the forest,

Clifford's manic rail excursion with Hepzibah, the rapture of Miriam and Donatello after the monk's murder, and, most significantly, Hilda's postconfession feelings of love ("*eros* in the form of *agape*"). Taking his cue from Trollope's and Hawthorne's mutual admiration for each other's very different writing, William H. Pritchard, "Reading Hawthorne" (*HudR* 46: 757–64), wonders whether anyone still reads Hawthorne for simple pleasure. The answer that Pritchard gives seems to be "No," as he cites studies by G. R. Thompson, Sacvan Bercovitch, and Richard Millington—all learned and sophisticated in their ways, but "severed," in Pritchard's view, from the "pleasures of [reading] the text." Furthermore, the pleasures Pritchard has in mind derive from the "minor" notes in Hawthorne's writing—his "quaintness," for example. "A lot of the time, while reading Hawthorne," Pritchard admits (apparently on behalf of other unnamed, "amateurish" readers), "we're not just sure how significant is the experience we're having."

iv Essays on the Novels

a. *The Scarlet Letter*   Given the recent outpouring of *Scarlet Letter* criticism, especially by New Historicists, a backlash seemed inevitable. Michael J. Colacurcio, "Puritans in Spite" (*R&L* 26, ii: 27–54), reminds us that in spite of the recent emphasis on 19th-century politics and history, Hawthorne's Puritan connection deserves to be an ongoing question. In a provocative review-essay, "The Irresistibleness of Great Literature: Reconstructing Hawthorne's Politics" (*AmLH* 6: 539–58), Eric Cheyfitz indicts F. O. Matthiessen's *American Renaissance,* Lauren Berlant's *The Anatomy of National Fantasy,* and Sacvan Bercovitch's *The Office of* The Scarlet Letter (on this last, see *ALS 1991,* pp. 22–23) for contributing to "the problem of patriarchal homogenization under the name of pluralism." Valorizing Hawthorne's complexity and the multi-valent representativeness of *The Scarlet Letter,* in Cheyfitz's view, excuses Hawthorne's "reprehensible" politics and promotes his canonization. *The Scarlet Letter,* which Cheyfitz has not taught in some time, cannot and should not be a "central text," because in the "multicultural Americas" there "are no central texts because no single text can figure these Americas." Anticanonically considered, *The Scarlet Letter* becomes the most important novel *not* to teach.

At the opposite end of the "po-literary" spectrum Peter Shaw (*Recovering American Literature,* pp. 23–47) usefully reviews two broad trends in

Scarlet Letter criticism, even as he tries to rescue the novel from the "radical revisionism" of political correctness. Shaw prefers 1950s' and 1960s' critics (e.g., Hyatt Waggoner, Darrel Abel, Richard Harter Fogle) for their sterner antiromantic view of Hester, while he verbally spanks "childlike" later critics for projecting their own radicalism on Hester while attacking Hawthorne's political conservatism, "ideologically interrogating" rather than interpreting the novel and ignoring "literary values" that are, not unexpectedly, conservative. Shaw oversimplifies much criticism in this reactionary exercise, but every critical generation needs *some* disciplining, if not the heavy-handed punishment Shaw doles out.

Citing *The Scarlet Letter*'s "simultaneous involvement in the discourses of pro- and anti-Catholicism," Jenny Franchot (*Roads to Rome*, pp. 260–69) ingeniously argues that the novel reflects the "disturbing depths of the mid-century liberal Protestant engagement with 'popery.'" Linking the detective plot to the "domain of Catholic sensuality and secrecy," Franchot glosses the narrative as "overheard confession," noting that Hawthorne's narrative reserve announces "resistance to the Roman confessional's excessively intimate communications" at the same time that the narrator legitimates his own "probings." Hawthorne, she claims, images "ideological struggles between the white light of Protestantism and the stained-glass corruptions of a mediated Catholicism" in light and color imagery, and Pearl, as "animate stained glass," recalls the Puritans' "abandoned Anglo-Catholic culture."

In "A 'H—ll-Fired Story': Hawthorne's Rhetoric of Rumor" (*CE* 56: 30–45) Scott Harshbarger finds a new angle (rumor theory) on Hawthorne's familiar ambiguity. Arguing that Hawthorne gleaned a "rhetoric of rumor" from New England witchcraft literature, Harshbarger shows him demonstrating and "harnessing" the "double-edged" power of gossip, emphasizing how the "social imagination" makes meaning and thereby reveals its innermost anxieties. Hawthorne presents each major character through rumor, Harshbarger notes in reminding us of his acute perceptions of social dynamics and the social constructedness of "truth."

Juxtaposing *The Scarlet Letter* and *Uncle Tom's Cabin*, Joan Burbick (*Healing the Republic*, pp. 210–22) provides a new twist on head vs. heart approaches to the novel. Historicizing and politicizing the "language of the heart," which values the "speaking subject" and carries the potential to "heal the nation," Burbick sees Hawthorne placing more limits than Stowe on "heart language" and implying that nationhood must be based on "patriarchal, religious law" rather than on the "utterances of the heart."

Critics often compare *The Scarlet Letter* to other works. In a convincing study Hedda Ben-Bassat, "Marginal Existence and Communal Consensus in *The Scarlet Letter* and *A Fringe of Leaves*" (*Comparatist* 18: 52–70), focuses primarily on the adulterous heroines (Hester Prynne and Ellen Roxburgh in Patrick White's 1976 novel) to show how a "similar model of cultural deviance" (based on Victor Turner's *The Ritual Process*) involving separation-marginality-reintegration functions in both works. Louis Auchincloss (*The Style's the Man*, pp. 167–77) groups *The Scarlet Letter* with *Wuthering Heights* and *The Great Gatsby* as a "perfect" novel—a "dazzling artifact, compact, cohesive, a fine hard jewel that can be turned round and round, and admired from every angle." Auchincloss stresses the continuing appeal of Hester's "existential" condition. Rod Phillips, "Purloined Letters: *The Scarlet Letter* in Kathy Acker's *Blood and Guts in High School*" (*Crit* 35: 173–80), argues that Acker plagiarizes from Hawthorne in her 1978 "punk" novel, which he considers a "radical feminist reworking," a "kind of 'taking back' of a woman's story from a male author," as her 10-year-old heroine (Janey) "melts" into Hester Prynne.

In two short pieces in the *Nathaniel Hawthorne Review* Arnold G. Tew, "Hawthorne's P.P.: Behind the Comic Mask" (20, i: 18–22), finds Alexander Pope and John Gay's "Memoirs of P.P., Clerk of this Parish" (1727) lurking behind Hawthorne's "P.P." in "The Custom-House"; while Carmen Valero-Garcés, "Translations of *The Scarlet Letter* into Spanish" (20, ii: 21–30), lists some 20 translations between 1894 and 1985.

Finally, two new paperback editions of *The Scarlet Letter* deserve some mention because of the supplemental materials each contains. Editor John Stephen Martin (Broadview) reprints the first edition rather than the Centenary text and provides 12 appendices, ranging from historical background and notebook passages to contemporary reviews and letters. Monika Elbert (Washington Square Press) also provides excerpts from notebook entries as well as from selected criticism to augment her excellent introduction.

b. *The House of the Seven Gables* Unlike 1993, this year features several significant studies of Hawthorne's second novel, all of them dealing with historical or cultural connections. Susan S. Williams, " 'The Aspiring Purpose of an Ambitious Dialogue': Portraiture and *The House of the*

Seven Gables" (NCF 49: 221–44), examines intersections of word and image to explore both narrative and cultural issues. Hawthorne "inverts" artistic properties, she argues, so that portraits come to "narrative" life, while narratives threaten to become static textual "bodies." This inversion reveals Hawthorne's fear that when fiction enters the marketplace it becomes just another "mass-produced image." A model of cultural criticism.

Peter J. Bellis, "Mauling Governor Pyncheon" (SNNTS 26: 199–217), tries to answer claims by Bercovitch and others that Hawthornian romance evades political and social conflict. On the contrary, romance becomes the "site of radical, even violent, conflict and a powerful cultural critique" in Seven Gables, he claims, and he proves his point by examining two "moonlight scenes" in the novel: Holgrave's hypnotic reading to Phoebe and Jaffrey Pyncheon's death. Most provocatively, Bellis argues that in the famous scene of Jaffrey Pyncheon's death, Hawthorne aligns his romance with the "oral or folk culture of the dispossessed Maules" and, in claiming an "openly adversarial role for the genre," he represents himself as a "Maule who can kill off the Pyncheon line without parricidal guilt," a writer aligned against "Salem's merchant classes" and the "dominant Whig establishment."

From a different but also countercultural point of view, Joan Burbick (Healing the Republic, pp. 235–39, 295–99) notes Hawthorne's emphasis on healthy and debilitated bodies in arguing that he represents "hegemonic demise" through "nervous debility" and renewed health through interclass marriage. To support her class-leveling view of the novel, Burbick, like Bellis, also discusses the democratic, documentary power of daguerreotypy.

In a fascinating study of "literary associationalism," "When Life Imitates Art: Charles Francis Adams, Jr.'s Curious Reader-Response to Hawthorne's The House of the Seven Gables" (ATQ 8: 77–95), Gregory M. Pfitzer shows how the financial and personal disasters striking the Adams family in the 1890s uncannily resembled the Pyncheon family's demise in Hawthorne's novel and, more importantly, how Henry's brother Charles used Seven Gables to help him cope with catastrophic change. Pfitzer goes further, however, by forging connections between Adams's and Hawthorne's interest in Thomas Morton; both were "haunted by a sense of complicity in the events leading to Morton's fall"—Adams, because his family's estate occupied the very land on which Morton had built the house the Puritans burned down. Pfitzer suggests that Hawthorne may well have had the Adams family in mind as he created the Pyncheons. Charles Adams thought so.

c. *The Blithedale Romance*   Harvey L. Gable, Jr., "Inappeasable Longings: Hawthorne, Romance, and the Disintegration of Coverdale's Self in *The Blithedale Romance*" (*NEQ* 67: 257–78), continues his work on Hawthorne and the "pathology of the Self" (see *ALS 1992*, p. 29). Astutely piecing together Hawthorne's fluid-exchange model of the Self from writings of the 1837–50 period, Gable reads *Blithedale* as the "moral journey of Miles Coverdale as his Self is seduced, debilitated, enslaved, and finally destroyed" by the "attractive but pernicious" idea that the Self can live in a "realm of pure theory." Gable's approach to *Blithedale* (and his references) will seem old-fashioned to new-fashioned readers, but his close reading of imagistic patterns offers a new, more sympathetic view of Coverdale and also discloses a Hawthorne more engaged with contemporary philosophy than most other critics have allowed. Nicholas O. Pagan, "The Governing Rhetoric of Theatricality in Hawthorne's *Blithedale Romance*" (*MQ* 35: 324–37), cites Coverdale's frequent use of theater references to make the conventional point that he traps himself in a "distant, aloof" spectator's role.

d. *The Marble Faun*   A cohort of critics examines Hawthorne's efforts to assimilate complex Roman experience in his last novel. Answering previous criticism, epitomized by Milton R. Stern's "savage attack on Hilda" (see *ALS 1991*, p. 24), Emily Schiller, "The Choice of Innocence: Hilda in *The Marble Faun*" (*SNNTS* 26: 372–91), wrestles with the difficult issue of Hilda's moral position in the novel. Schiller raises many good questions about narrative voice, authorial responsibility, and reader responses in arguing finally that Hilda represents a "deconstruction of the idea of adult, feminine innocence." Hilda is a "presumptive" daughter of the Puritans, an ironic re-creation of popular fictional heroines, because she renounces the human condition and the felt depravity that accompanies it. In contrast, Donatello engages in the kind of (Catholic) introspection that produces real moral growth.

Neill Matheson, "Heavy Spirits: Depression and Materiality in *The Marble Faun*" (*JNT* 24: 237–55), deftly conjoins materiality and narrativity (in the idea of material history) in exploring the relationship among history, narrative, and individual subjectivity (especially melancholy). Kenyon's transformation of the Venus de Medici fragments represents the ideal, but more often romance fails to convert an overwhelming materiality into intellect. The result: melancholy becomes the "locus for a disfiguring perception of the materiality of various forms of representation." A solid essay with especially valuable insights into the "characterological transformations" (and failed transformations) at the novel's thematic core.

Jenny Franchot (*Roads to Rome*, pp. 350–58) also focuses on materiality in judging *The Marble Faun* the "era's most significant Protestant fiction of Rome," albeit a "painstaking, ultimately failed, Protestant effort to comprehend Catholicism." Hawthorne's problem, in her view, involves adapting his romance strategies to a city of "excessive representations" and materiality that clogs his efforts to "distill" them and thereby establishes a "religiously fearful relation" between the novel and "itself as narrative."

Udo Natterman, "Dread and Desire: 'Europe' in Hawthorne's *The Marble Faun*" (*ELWIU* 21: 54–67), explores the "extremely troubled relationship between travelers and the host environment" behind Hawthorne's "threefold critique" of American tourism. Natterman cites the dialectic of repulsion and attraction, dread and desire, in arguing that *The Marble Faun* is a "particularly self-conscious international novel" that dramatizes the "Disneyfication" of Europe and the failure of Americans and Europeans to bridge the cultural gap between them. Citing no previous criticism, Michael L. Ross (*Storied Cities*, pp. 231–45) works over well-known ideas—e.g., Rome's role as the "supreme site of creative human suffering and recognition," Hilda's serene ahistoricality versus Miriam's immersion in history.

e. The Children's Books Laura Laffrado, "The Persephone Myth in Hawthorne's *Tanglewood Tales*" (*Images of Persephone*, pp. 75–83), reworks a section of her book on the children's tales (see *ALS 1992*, p. 24) in examining "The Pomegranate-Seeds" as a story of loss, prompted by events in Hawthorne's life (the deaths of his sister Louisa and Sophia's mother and his estrangement from Melville). Laffrado concludes, however, that refashioning the myth helped Hawthorne deal with loss and "move on" with his life (as Liverpool consul, for example). In "The Picturesque Scenery: A Nineteenth-Century Epideictic" (*Oratorical Cul-*

ture in Nineteenth-Century America [So. Ill., 1993], pp. 226–46) S. Michael Halloran places the legend of Philemon and Baucis (*A Wonder
Book*) and "The Old Manse" within the picturesque tradition as examples of "epideictic" discourse that helps define a national identity.

f. The Unfinished Novels Klaus P. Stich, "The Saturday Club as Intertext in Hawthorne's *The Elixir of Life Manuscripts*" (*NHR* 20, ii: 11–20),
addresses the impact (e.g., on characters' names) of Hawthorne's election
to the Boston Saturday Club, his enjoyment of its "vinicultural fringe
benefits," and his friendship with such old "salts" as Cornelius Conway
Felton, Charles Eliot Norton, and Oliver (aka "Dolliver") Wendell
Holmes on his unfinished *Elixir* manuscripts.

v Essays on the Tales and Sketches

Expanding on ideas in his recent book, G. R. Thompson, "Literary
Politics and the 'Legitimate Sphere': Poe, Hawthorne, and the 'Tale
Proper'" (*NCF* 49: 167–95), uses Poe's reviews of *Twice-Told Tales* (in
1842) and *Mosses from an Old Manse* (in 1847) to analyze "large defini-
tional problems" in the two writers' understanding of generic taxonomy.
Misreading Hawthorne's short fiction in the (self-) interest of imposing a
"sensational" paradigm on tale-writing, Poe illustrates the "two major divergent lines of formal development of short fiction"—the "tale proper"
and the "sketch," or essay. Thompson cogently enhances our understanding of Hawthorne's varied methods and achievements in short
fiction, showing that, because he wrote "romantic tale-sketches" featuring an "intrusive narrative persona" rather than the dramatized, presen-
tational fiction that Poe and later writers (e.g., James) prized, his achievement was undervalued.

In a long, exhaustively researched essay, Jonathan A. Cook, "New
Heavens, Poor Old Earth: Satirical Apocalypse in Hawthorne's *Mosses
from an Old Manse*" (*ESQ* 39 [1993]: 209–51), persuasively examines
Hawthorne's seven allegorical fantasies in *Mosses* as "quasi-apocalyptic
dream visions of a 'distracted' world" that both embody and critique a
contemporary "millenialist ideology." In "old" historicist fashion Cook
finds Hawthorne deeply engaged with his biblical sources, contemporary
moral reform movements, and ideologies (e.g., pre- and postmillenial-
ism). One of the best studies we have of these neglected sketches ("The

Celestial Rail-Road," "Earth's Holocaust," "The New Adam and Eve," "The Hall of Fantasy," "The Procession of Life," "The Intelligence Office," and "A Select Party").

Monika Elbert, "Nathaniel Hawthorne, *The Concord Freeman,* and the Irish 'Other' " (*Éire* 29, iii: 60–73), brilliantly employs "Mr. Higginbotham's Catastrophe" in her argument that Charles Creighton Hazewell, who reprinted the 1834 tale in the *Concord Freeman* in 1844, "appropriated" Hawthorne in a "conspiracy against the immigrant Irish." Her analysis of the "underlying insidious elements of hatred and bigotry" in the story and her claim that "rampant xenophobia" lies at the "heart of the story," as well as the ambivalent comments about the Irish she discovers in Hawthorne's notebooks and travel sketches, open a challenging new topic for Hawthorne studies.

Kathryn B. McKee, " 'A Small Heap of Glittering Fragments': Hawthorne's Discontent with the Short Story Form" (*ATQ* 8: 137–47), claims that "The Artist of the Beautiful," "Drowne's Wooden Image," and "The Snow-Image" (all written between 1844 and 1849 and all featuring "deteriorating" art objects) reflect Hawthorne's growing doubts about the tale as a "suitable vehicle for his creativity." In arguing that Hawthorne turned to the novel for financial and aesthetic reasons, McKee usefully explores the intersection of circumstance and creativity in these three tales.

In a provocative example of feminist revisionism Angela M. Kelsey, "Mrs. Wakefield's Gaze: Femininity and Dominance in Nathaniel Hawthorne's 'Wakefield' " (*ATQ* 8: 17–31), positions herself with Mrs. Wakefield, a "separate subject" who refuses to "play object" for her husband; Kelsey then analyzes the struggle of Hawthorne's male narrator to "regulate access" to Mrs. Wakefield's alternative point of view. Readers inclined to roll their eyes at claims of castration anxiety will miss Kelsey's deft demonstration of how a shift in readerly focus can produce valuable new insights, especially into narrative gender dynamics and power struggles among characters, the narrator, and (female) readers.

Benjamin Franklin V, "Goodman Brown and the Puritan Catechism" (*ESQ* 40: 67–88), extends Robert Grayson's insight (see *ALS 1990,* p. 38) that John Cotton's *Milk for Babes* is the specific catechism Brown failed to learn from Goody Cloyse. In explaining how his "decidedly non-Puritan faith in the goodness of humanity" ill prepares Brown to cope with the sudden awareness of human corruption, Franklin fills in important gaps in the religio-historical background of this fascinating tale.

Several short essays add modestly to our understanding of selected tales. Mark Harris, "A New Reading of 'Ethan Brand': The Failed Quest" (*SSF* 31: 69–77), considers Brand's "quest" for the Unpardonable Sin a failure and Brown himself just an ordinary, "deluded" man, motivated by a desire for acceptance. A. James Wohlpart, "Allegories of Art, Allegories of Heart: Hawthorne's 'Egotism' and 'The Christmas Banquet' " (*SSF* 31: 449–60), labels both tales critiques of a "Transcendentalist aesthetic" whose idealism promotes separation from humanity. J. Lasley Dameron, "Faust, the Wandering Jew, and the Swallowed Serpent: Hawthorne's Familiar Literary Analogues" (*NHR* 20, i: 10–17), cites the prevalence of the three figures in his title in popular journals and then points out the appearance of those analogues in tales such as "Young Goodman Brown," "Ethan Brand," and "A Bosom Serpent."

William J. Scheick, *The Ethos of Romance*, pp. 31–41, updates his 1978 *ESQ* article on "Roger Malvin's Burial." Hawthorne represents an ethical (rather than eventuary or aesthetic) romance tradition that influenced James, Robert Louis Stevenson, Rudyard Kipling, and others, while the tale exemplifies "knotted" ethical ambiguities and writers' direct elicitations of reader responses to "ethical conundrums."

vi Miscellaneous

In a compelling essay, "Delia Bacon: Hawthorne's Last Heroine" (*NHR* 20, ii: 1–10), Nina Baym explains Hawthorne's fascination with Bacon by showing how he assimilated her to type, part "individual whose obsession determines the shape of the inner and outer life," part "antinomian heroine who defies social conventions." Hawthorne represents Bacon, Baym concludes, as one more "principled" woman who resists the "law of the dead father."

Targeting a popular more than a scholarly audience, David Laskin, *A Common Life: Four Generations of American Literary Friendship and Influence* (Simon and Schuster), rehearses the Hawthorne-Melville "comradeship in letters" in familiar and enthusiastic terms, borrowing from the standard biographies while hinting about the "reams of commentary" that the puzzling relationship has "spawned." An engaging refresher course in the well-known Lenox-Pittsfield events of 1850–51 and the literary fallout in *The Blithedale Romance* and *Pierre*. Carefully researching various letters, Margaret B. Moore, "Elizabeth Manning Hawthorne, Nathaniel's Enigmatic Sister" (*NHR* 20, i: 1–9), usefully fleshes out the portrait of Ebe, Hawthorne's "prickly older sister."

Hawthorne's influence spreads far and wide, as demonstrated by Cecelia Tichi's *High Lonesome: The American Culture of Country Music* (No. Car.), where Hawthorne's "wild rose heroine" in *The Scarlet Letter* lurks behind the "hillbilly rose" tradition of country music and, for example, the "flower power" of Dolly Parton's "Wildflowers," the heroine of Calder Willingham's novel *Rambling Rose* (1972), adapted for the screen in 1991, and Emily Lou Harris's "Timberline" and "Red, Red Rose." At the other end of the musical scale, Thomas M. Brodhead, "Ives's *Celestial Railroad* and His Fourth Symphony" (*American Music* 12: 389–424), analyzes parallels between Charles Ives's unpublished piano "Phantasy" and Hawthorne's tale.

Southern Illinois University at Carbondale

3 Poe

Benjamin F. Fisher

i Bibliographical, Textual, and Biographical Work

The "International Poe Bibliography: 1992–1993" (*PoeS* 27: 5–27), compiled by Scott Peeples and others, cites a far-reaching range of works, many of them useful. Noticing an incorrect title for Burton Pollin's article on the Philadelphia *Saturday Museum*, however, makes one wary of more such lapses. John E. Reilly's revised edition of *John Henry Ingram's Poe Collection at the University of Virginia* (Virginia) corrects some of the work by the original compiler, John Carl Miller, and makes for greater accessibility to this important material. Poe's name, naturally, appears repeatedly in another bibliographical work, Don L. F. Nilsen's *Humor in American Literature* (Greenwood, 1992), although Nilsen's citations by no means exhaust the available materials that assess Poe and humor. Burton R. Pollin's "Poe's Word Coinages: Supplement III" (*PoeS* 27: 28–39) expands his earlier publications on this subject. Pollin's "A New Englander's Obituary Eulogy of Poe" (*AmPer* 4: 1–11) reprints in handy form Benjamin Lindsey's favorable commentary (which challenged Griswold's slanders) in his newspapers, the New Bedford (Mass.) *Daily Mercury*, 20 October 1849, and the *Weekly Mercury*, 26 October. (Both issues also reprinted "The Bells" from Sartain's *Union Magazine*.) The obituary sketch of Lindsey, dating from 1889, with additional remarks concerning Catharine Maria Sedgwick are extraneous, to my view, and the inconsistent spelling of Sidney Moss's name in the notes may confuse the uninitiated. Challenging John A. Hodgson's proposal against a Poe attribution, Terence Whalen persuasively suggests that the solution to a cryptograph found in the letter to *Graham's* from "W. B. Tyler" is probably by Poe himself and thus constitutes a new Poe text: "The Code for Gold: Edgar Allan Poe and Cryptography" (*Representa-*

tions 46: 35–58). More on the theoretical content of Whalen's essay appears in the Tales section, below.

ii Books, Parts of Books

Furnishing a different slant on an old topic, Dennis W. Eddings, in *Poe's Tell-Tale Clocks* (Pratt and The Edgar Allan Poe Society), focuses principally on five tales: "The Devil in the Belfry," "How to Write a Blackwood Article—A Predicament," "The Angel of the Odd," "The Masque of the Red Death," and "A Descent into the Maelström." For Eddings, Poe's narrators, rather than Poe himself, become slaves to the clock instead of giving free rein to the imaginative element in their selves; consequently, they turn into "maniacs of time." This monograph builds on and extends the readings of Poe and time presented by Richard Wilbur, Jean-Paul Weber, and Gerhard Hoffmann. Eddings's discerning analysis highlights Poe's language, notably his wordplay, and invites further exploration.

Poe figures repeatedly in Joseph Andriano's *Our Ladies of Darkness: Feminine Daemonology in Male Gothic Fiction* (Penn. State, 1993). Of greatest interest to Poe scholars, probably, are the critiques of "Usher" (pp. 6, 84, 86, 148) and "Ligeia" (pp. 84–90), which illuminate how the male narrator's inability to comprehend female nature results in catastrophe. Andriano challenges Martin Bickman's interpretation of Ligeia as an anima figure, arguing that the narrator cannot distinguish "mother archetype from anima," and that he also perceives woman as a "blank page on which he writes his text, 'Ligeia'." Poe and curricular matters recurringly occupy David R. Shumway in *Creating American Civilization: A Genealogy of American Literature as an Academic Discipline* (Minnesota); we glean useful information regarding Poe's shifting status among critics, anthologizers, and editorial evaluators for academic journals. Jack G. Voller's observations in chapter 8 of *The Supernatural Sublime: The Metaphysics of Terror in Anglo-American Romanticism* (No. Ill.) on Poe as "the progenitor of the Western fantastic tradition, which consistently has been a literature of isolation and alienation," range over many tales, "Sonnet—To Science," and *Eureka*, offering illuminations about Poe's achievements and interesting face-offs of his fiction with Hawthorne's. Voller should be read along with G. R. Thompson, cited below. Connections of Gothic and fantastic literature are important in Voller's discussion.

iii Poe, Gender, Race

A double issue of *Poe Studies* (26 [1993]), guest-edited by Michael J. S. Williams, includes three studies under this rubric. They might well be read alongside of Andriano, cited above. Joan Dayan's "Poe's Women: A Feminist Poe?" (pp. 1–12) ranges over the canon, from early verse through *Eureka,* to argue ultimately that Poe was no feminist. If femininity is destroyed in Poe's writings, "women's sexed bodies remain." That reading the first "To Helen" necessitates the recalling of "another hideous ground for her 'hyacinth hair,' 'classic face,' and 'Naiad airs' " is a dubious line of approach, to my way of thinking—not that such a rereading is impossible, but that, in the terms set forth here, it seems more tenuous than essential. One also wonders why, given the statement that recent attempts to come to terms with Poe's feminist perspective concentrate most on the detective fiction," especially on "The Mystery of Marie Rogêt" (p. 11), Dayan's evidence in support of such a proposal chiefly concerns "The Purloined Letter" rather than the cigar girl's story.

Jacqueline Doyle's "(Dis)figuring Woman: Edgar Allan Poe's 'Berenice' " (pp. 13–21) treats that tale as a text being created by Egaeus, the margins of which Berenice continues to haunt. Otherwise, we find little new here; the link with Egeus in *A Midsummer Night's Dream* has long been established as crucial to the inability of Poe's narrator to love and the ensuing catastrophe. Monika Elbert's "Poe's Gothic Mother and the Incubation of Language" (pp. 22–33) incorporates much Kristevan substance to support a Freudian approach to many of Poe works. The deaths of Elizabeth Poe, Frances Allan, and Virginia Clemm Poe remained preeminent in Poe's mind and offered preeminent metaphors for the dying women in his works. Elbert's handling of the "preverbal (semiotic, feminine) and symbolic (analytical, masculine)," especially in "Eleonora"—that oft-neglected tale (along with "The Assignation," which is also tellingly drawn in here) in discussions of Poe's women-centered writings—and her sketching of the mania-depression elements in "Usher" are showpieces. Michael Williams, the guest editor, concludes the collection with "Poe on Women: Recent Perspectives" (pp. 34–40), a judicious evaluation of Leland S. Person's *Aesthetic Headaches* (1988) and Cynthia S. Jordan's *Second Stories* (1989) that takes into account other pertinent studies of contemporaneous feminism in light of Poe's. Indicating Jordan's fairly procrustean tack, Williams also notes that her view of Poe as hostile to patriarchal culture may be questioned. This issue of *Poe*

Studies will call forth supplements and rejoinders; for that reason, among others, it should have been better proofread.

Worthwhile companion reading for the *PoeS* assemblage and for Andriano may be found in David Punter's "Death, Femininity and Identification: A Recourse to Ligeia" (*Women's Writing* 1: 215–28). Punter challenges Elisabeth Bronfen's hypothesis in *Over Her Dead Body* (1992) that the narrator eventually gains possession of Ligeia's knowledge, and he brings in Freudianism via Mikkel Borch-Jacobsen to support a reading of Poe's heroine as no mother figure but rather a locus of dynamic, if forbidden, (hetero-)sexual desire. Punter thus furnishes ideas that concur with and diverge from some of those found in the other essays on gender; his study will doubtless provoke lively responses. Joan Dayan's "Amorous Bondage: Poe, Ladies, and Slaves" (*AL* 66: 239–73) may logically be considered at this point. Although we find many stimulating ideas concerning individual works by Poe, as well as about his more general cultural outlook, this essay duplicates too much that appears in Dayan's *PoeS* piece, already noticed. A major problem for many readers will doubtless be her unhesitating ascription to Poe of the much-discussed "Paulding-Drayton review," which Joseph V. Ridgely has shown (I thought once for all) to be Beverley Tucker's. The linking of the women in Poe's works with African American slaves may be timely, but the statement that his "awfully corporeal ghosts are always women" overlooks the "ghosts" in "Metzengerstein," "Loss of Breath," *Pym,* and "Thou Art the Man." True, Ligeia might emanate from Poe's (American) racism, but what about Scott's Rebecca and Rowena and the German issue underlying the tale? Furthermore, do curling hair and large eyes inevitably call up racial issues? The "less than thou" passage from "For Annie" may hint in larger terms than Dayan implies if not truncated from the passage in which it appears (and are we reading "For Annie" or "To Annie"?). Additional cloudiness occurs in regard to "Silence—A Fable"; the composition date remains uncertain, and publication occurred in 1837, not 1835. Similarities between apes and African Americans have long been recognized and have been held up as such by Richard Kopley in greater detail than we find documented here (see *ALS 1991,* p. 51), but ape-human ramifications are by no means exclusively racial. Dayan's citations of Buffon and Long are but two of how many additional sources in these contexts? More and better information (stronger ammunition?) on this topic would strengthen Dayan's argument and be a valuable contribution to the subject in larger terms. As is the case elsewhere in studies of Poe's writings that feature women, "The Assignation," his first published prose tale on the theme, goes begging in this essay. In sum, this speculative essay should be read cautiously alongside several predecessors, and not taken as groundbreaking or authoritative.

iv Tales

G. R. Thompson's commentary in *The Art of Authorial Presence* (Duke, 1993) is by no means to be missed. His comparisons of Poe's and Hawthorne's art in the short-story form, as well as their ideas—explicit and implicit—concerning that genre, are informative and provocative. Relevant, too, is his "Literary Politics and the 'Legitimate Sphere': Poe, Hawthorne, and the 'Tale Proper'" (*NCF:* 49: 167–95). In general, in both works Thompson accords greater latitude in creativity within the short story form to Hawthorne. John Barth's "It's a Short Story" (*Mississippi Review* 21, i–ii [1993]: 25–40) credits Poe with "codifying" and Maupassant and Chekhov with "purifying" the short story, and he asserts that short story writers from Poe to Paley attempt to try "how much they can leave out." Barth's own experiences in the Johns Hopkins Writing Workshops were guided by "Bob," a man completing a dissertation on Poe, because presumably such a person could oversee the workshop.

Poe's early tales are often overlooked in favor, say, of "Usher," "Wilson," "Murders," "Masque," and "Cask." Barbara Cantalupo's "The Lynx in Poe's 'Silence'" (*PoeS* 27: 1–4) is therefore particularly welcome, providing, as it does, a synopsis of antecedent interpretations and going on to argue sensibly that the lynx in "Silence—A Fable" may be a more positive force than others have thought, although Poe's depiction of lynx elements in "Marginalia" and "Thou Art the Man" reinforces the ambiguity inherent in that animal's symbolic proportions. Cantalupo's examination of the different versions of "Silence—A Fable" reinforces her analysis.

Poe's originating of detective fiction is questioned by Christopher A. Lee in "E. T. A. Hoffmann's 'Mademoiselle de Scudery' as a Forerunner of the Detective Story" (*Clues* 15, ii: 63–74), a zealous plea that the German's tale (1818) "bears many traits of the detective story well in advance of [its] actual invention by Poe." Since the candidacies of other works—among them Godwin's *Caleb Williams* (1798), Austin's "Peter Rugg" (1824), and Hawthorne's "Mr. Higginbotham's Catastrophe" (1834)—as forerunners of detective fiction have been submitted, Lee's hypothesis is obviously worth consideration. (For Poe's influence on recent detective fiction, see also the items by Jan Whitt and Penelope K. Majeske, below.) Terence Whalen's ideas about Poe's aims and methods in "The Gold-Bug" ("The Code for Gold: Edgar Allan Poe and Cryptography," *Representations* 46: 35–58) take issue with and expand Shawn Rosenheim's opinions (1989) to demonstrate in a thoroughly factual, but unflaggingly readable, account just how the tale embodies Poe's thoughts on the conflict between mass and elite audiences and between fiction written for money (to satisfy the mass audience) and that for art's sake (to appeal to the elite). Biographical information is also used to advantage. So, no mere chronicle of mystery and adventure in this tale, even though it took a prize in a newspaper competition. To me, Whalen's is the most significant piece of analytic work on Poe this year. A short leap takes us to another crime tale, which Arthur A. Brown in "Death and Telling in Poe's 'Imp of the Perverse' " (*SSF* 31: 197–205) perceives as kindred to "The Purloined Letter." Both tales dramatize a failure to "read": the victim and the coroner in "Imp" remain unaware of the centrality of the poisoned candle. Moreover, perverseness cannot be defined but only acted out. Finally, bringing the artillery of another theoretical perspective to bear, Tracy Ware offers a plausible Barthesean analysis of "The 'Salutary Discomfort' in the Case of M. Valdemar" (*SSF* 31: 471–80). We come away with a sense that "Valdemar" has far deeper implications than have often been credited to this "hoax."

v Sources, Influences, Miscellaneous

Source studies continue to play an important role in works on Poe. Michele Valerie Ronnick's "Seneca's *Medea* and Ultima Thule in Poe's 'Dream-Land' " (*PoeS* 27: 41–42) reasonably demonstrates that Poe's inspiration may have come from Irving's *History of . . . Columbus* (1828), in which the "ultima Thule" passage from Seneca appears on the title page. Kent P. Ljungquist likewise meticulously advances three items from M. M. Noah's *New-York Enquirer* of 11 March 1829 and the *Courier and Enquirer* for 5 February and 12 March 1830 as sources for Poe's "Diddling": " 'Raising the Wind': Earlier Precedents" (*PoeS* 27: 42). Ljungquist's findings supplement those of John E. Reilly and Burton R. Pollin, which cite source materials with later dates, and they also necessitate our rethinking of ideas proposed by Claude Richard and Alexander Hammond.

A thoughtful comparison of Poe's methods with those of a contemporary is Gary Hoppenstand's "Robots of the Past: Fitz-James O'Brien's 'The Wondersmith'" (*JPC* 27, iv: 13–30). O'Brien carried along the "imaginative macabre story" after Poe, although the former's contemporary urban settings distinguish his tales from Poe's, in which we find "historically remote European settings" (a point for debate, I and many other Poe scholars would say). Poe's popularity at the end of the 19th century is undeniable, despite what long-standard accounts, such as Matthiessen's, might imply of a lesser repute. Another late 19th-century Poe connection receives extended treatment by Burton R. Pollin and J. A. Greenwood—"Stevenson on Poe: Unpublished Annotations of Numerous Poe Texts and a Stevenson Letter" (*ELT* 37: 317–49). Using Robert Louis Stevenson's annotated set of Poe's writings, ed. J. H. Ingram, along with Stevenson's letter to Ingram concerning several biographical and textual aspects of Poe studies (all the Stevensoniana now in the Berg Collection of the New York Public Library), Pollin and Greenwood amplify our knowledge of Stevenson's conception of Poe as person and writer. Poe's impact on Stevenson's own fiction is examined, especially the affinity of each of them for exploiting "the disturbed personality of the evil doer and the anti-social 'loner.'"

My "Poe in the 1890s: Bibliographical Gleanings" (*American Renaissance Literary Report* 8: 142–68) cites editions of his works, his influences (e.g., on Arthur Conan Doyle, Arthur Machen, M. P. Shiel, H. G. Wells, many overlooked writers of detective-mystery-science fiction, and those who are remembered for their grimly realistic fiction), his popularity among illustrators—and much more—to support an image of him as a great creative writer and critic as well as a much-misunderstood person. The latest in the continuing Poe-Conan Doyle linkages are Walter P. Armstrong, Jr., on "The Literary Holmes" (*BSJ* 44: 135–40), where we learn that Holmes's readings in American literature included Poe—Holmes would employ Dupin's methods in "The Resident Patient" and "The Cardboard Box"—and Robert E. Robinson on "The So-Called Porlock Enigma" (*BSJ* 44: 223–34), an argument that Professor Moriarity intentionally teased Holmes by means of ciphering à la "Fred Porlock," who leaked information concerning the professor's activities, such that Poe's name was encoded as a means of reminding Holmes of his antipathies toward Dupin. Numbered among 20th-century descendants of Poe's detective fiction is Jessica B. Fletcher on network television's *Murder, She Wrote*, who—according to Jan Whitt in "The 'Very Simplicity of the Thing': Edgar Allan Poe and the Murders He Wrote" (*Clues* 15: 25–40)—derives her methods and much of her personality from Dupin. Penelope K. Majeske calls our attention to another descendant: Adam Dalgliesh is "P. D. James's Auguste Dupin . . . the completive rational modern man" ("P. D. James's Dark Interiors," *Clues* 15: 119–32). Majeske strongly bolsters her claim in outlining the similarities of the sleuths.

Poe and literary modernism coalesce in Denis Donoghue's *The Old Moderns* (Knopf). Donoghue's opinion that the text of "The Man of the Crowd" gives no evidence of the old man's connection with crime—a link imagined by the narrator—will startle some fans of that tale. Donoghue also argues that Poe's urban vision in this piece anticipates the outlooks of Dickens, Conrad, Dreiser, Fitzgerald, and Pynchon, and influences T. S. Eliot's "Burnt Norton." Poe's impact on Hart Crane is involved in John T. Irwin's "The Triple Archetype: The Presence of *Faust* in *The Bridge*" (*ArQ* 50, i: 51–73), specifically that of the agate lamp from the first "To Helen" on Crane's phrase, "eyes like agate lanterns." Irwin suggests that Crane also shows affinities with Poe in terms of an American poet's fated quest after beauty.

In our own day Poe's name might not be foremost among those bracketed with that of Eudora Welty, but Ruth D. Weston's repeated comparisons of the two in *Gothic Traditions and Narrative Techniques in the Fiction of Eudora Welty* (LSU)—for example, Poe adumbrates Welty's modernism in turning landscape into mindscape, both use houses and other closed spaces to symbolize psychological states, Poe's narrative techniques anticipate Welty's, though they differ in handling supernaturalism (Welty is more like Hawthorne in arousing a sense of the mysterious than she is like Poe or Mrs. Radcliffe, who explain it away)— assuringly illuminate such affinities, despite Welty's disclaimers about being a "Gothic" writer as she understands the term. Another book that might not initially seem to have a place in the Poe world, Craig Hansen Werner's *Playing the Changes: From Afro-Modernism to the Jazz Impulse* (Illinois), nevertheless demonstrates the Poesque in writings by Charles Chesnutt, Melvin B. Tolson, Richard Wright, and August Wilson.

A more readily divined kinship informs Burton R. Pollin's "Stephen King's Fiction and the Legacy of Poe" (*Journal of the Fantastic in the Arts* 5, iv [1993]: 2–25). Proceeding chronologically through King's canon and drawing on the work of earlier commentators, Pollin demonstrates the pervasiveness of Poe's writings in King's fiction and critical pronouncements. Pollin's observations on the importance of "Usher" and "The

Raven" in several King pieces may be the article's showpieces. Other than giving Kenneth Gibbs's name as Stephen Gibbs, this is a first-rate study. Pollin's "Music and Edgar Allan Poe: A Third Annotated Check List" (*PoeS* 27: 41–58), dealing mostly with work published from 1980 until 1993, extends knowledge of Poe's impact on musicians.

University of Mississippi

4 Melville

John Wenke

The year 1994 was not one for book-length studies, though *American Literature* did devote an entire issue to a "New Melville." Prominent among the year's essays and chapters are discussions of the ideologies of icon-making and icon-breaking, the complexities of cultural and cross-cultural resonances, and the problems of gender representation.

i Canonical Issues

Paul Lauter in "Melville Climbs the Canon" (*AL* 66: 1–24) explores the critical and cultural dynamics involved as Melville's status changed from "an obscure teller of South Sea Island tales into the preeminent American novelist." In concentrating on the Americanness of the Melville revival Lauter claims that " 'Melville' was constructed in the 1920s as part of an ideological conflict which linked advocates of modernism and of traditional high cultural values." Sufficiently allusive and recondite for modernist tastes, this Melville was set "against a social and cultural 'other,' generally, if ambiguously, portrayed as feminine, genteel, exotic, dark, foreign, and numerous." Lauter discusses Melville's association with primitivism and his image as heroic masculine artist defeated by a philistine society. Similarly, Myra Jehlen in her introduction to *Herman Melville: A Collection of Critical Essays* (Prentice Hall, pp. 1–14) considers the meaning of Melville's "literary 'greatness' as it has surprisingly survived its fall from transcendence." Jehlen remarks on Melville's penetration into the complex worlds he represents, and she contends that critical discourse has moved away from a consideration of "eternal verities" toward "a variety of local verities," replacing the author's "authority" with "autonomy."

In a discussion that reflects how Melville's canonical status makes possible a profound cross-cultural influence Arnold Rampersad's "Melville and Race" (*Herman Melville: A Collection of Critical Essays,* pp. 160–73) examines Melville's "impact . . . on black American writers and intellectuals." Melville merges a sense of "bohemianism with disturbing ideas about race. These ideas intimidated the black writer almost as much as they have challenged the white world." Rampersad links Babo and Richard Wright's Bigger Thomas and finds that Melville impinged on Ralph Ellison's "decisive modification of naturalism by impressionism and surrealism." Among other figures, Rampersad discusses Melville and C. L. R. James, W. E. B. Du Bois, John Edgar Wideman, Charles Johnson, and Toni Morrison. Melville is "one of the principal interpreters of the American obsession with race and commitment to racism." In "Newton Arvin Reviews Mumford" (*MSEx* 97: 7–9) George Monteiro contributes to our historical understanding of Melville's canonization by reprinting Arvin's 1929 review of Mumford's biography of Melville.

ii General

David Suchoff in "Melville: Ironic Democracy" (*Critical Theory and the Novel: Mass Society and Cultural Criticism in Dickens, Melville, and Kafka* [Wisconsin], pp. 89–135) examines Melville's troubled relation to his literary marketplace and its expression through a doublespeak that could "assure the audience that he complied with their taste even as he violated it." In *Typee, Redburn, White-Jacket,* and *Pierre* Melville views "the novel as a commodity, ironically shaping its constraints into cultural criticism which speaks through the limits of the mass-cultural work." In *White-Jacket* Melville satirizes "mass-cultural populism" as well as racial stereotypes and other forms of theatrical representation. In *Moby-Dick* Melville's deflating juxtaposition of high and low culture encourages his audience to question accepted premises. In taking a more topical approach to Melville's representation of cultural complexes Caleb Crain in "Lovers of Human Flesh: Homosexuality and Cannibalism in Melville's Novels" (*AL* 66: 25–53) explores how the discussion of cannibalism provides rhetorical forms that evoke the unspeakability of homosexuality: "Among [Melville's] innovations was to associate . . . cannibalism and voluptuousness with each other." Crain speculates on related "assumptions about homosexuality and cannibalism" and how they are manifest in symbols of love and power. In also considering the contemporary milieu Richard Hardack's "Stocks and Bonds: Pantheism and the Chain of Being in the American Renaissance" (*SAR*, pp. 21–42) concentrates on intellectual and spiritual fusion. Hardack discusses Melville's pantheism, especially insofar as it displaces the hierarchical Puritan chain of being with a means of reconciling disparate theological, naturalistic, and social traditions. In this prescient argument Hardack examines the pantheistic complex in *Mardi, Redburn*, Melville's letters to Hawthorne, *Moby-Dick*, and *Pierre*. In *Moby-Dick* "democracy's broken chains can only be reforged through the tyrannical pantheistic fusions of Ahab, or the mystical pantheistic fusions of Ishmael." Throughout the essay Hardack convincingly links the thought of Melville and Emerson.

In "Melville, Twain, and Quixote: Variations on the Comic Debate" (*StAH* n.s. 3, i: 1–27) John Bryant considers Cervantes's influence on the conflict between integrative and subversive forms of 19th-century humor. Bryant reads Melville's markings in his copy of *Don Quixote* as they illuminate the narrative voice and interpolated tales in *The Confidence-Man*. Hennig Cohen in "Melville and the Art Collection of Richard Lathers" (*MSEx* 99: 1–25) provides materials that will facilitate the discovery of new biographical and aesthetic influences. Cohen catalogs and discusses the art collection of Richard Lathers, Allan Melville's brother-in-law and Melville's friend: "Taken as a whole, the Lathers collection represents the taste of cultivated cosmopolitan privileged gentility." Cohen, analyzing some of the paintings, speculates on Melville's divided sense of Lathers and his art; ultimately, "Lathers embodied an ambivalent vision of civilized America that had a counterpart in the ambivalences Melville had discovered early on in the primitive world of the Marquesas." Eric Collum and Hershel Parker in "The Lost Lathers Collections: Suggestions for Further Research" (*MSEx* 99: 26–28) summarize the relatively scant work done on the Melville/Lathers connection and sketch the lives of the Latherses' children and their wills. Robert K. Wallace in "Melville and Other Arts" (*MSEx* 96: 5) considers recent research on Melville's relation to multiple art forms. Ernest Suarez in "Dickey on Melville" (*SCR* 26, ii: 114–26) discusses James Dickey's 1940 Vanderbilt master's thesis on Melville's shorter poems and illuminates Melville's influence on Dickey's work, especially the recurring figures of "whiteness."

iii Gender Matters

In "Disquieting Encounters: Male Intrusions/Female Realms in Melville" (*ESQ* 40: 91–111) Judith Hiltner explores a recurrent and "psychically charged" scenic matrix: "a male curiously observes or intrudes upon a female realm." During these many encounters the female body often seems a "tireless, unstoppable machine." Hiltner deftly links Tommo's observation of female tappa-makers in *Typee* with its "bleaker" counterpart, the female millworkers in "The Tartarus of Maids." Such scenes also appear in *Moby-Dick, Pierre,* and *Benito Cereno.* Melville dramatizes "the full range of gender anxieties rooted in his own experience in mid-nineteenth-century American culture, and especially in female-dominated households." In "Melville, Monstrosity, and Euthanasia: Pierre's Mother and Baby Budd" (*Conceived by Liberty,* pp. 163–88) Stephanie A. Smith takes a more typal approach, exploring Melville's depictions of "Woman" as "emblem . . . of Mother Nature . . . she is . . . the mute vessel/vassal/slave." This "hybridized monster" lacks individual identity "because Melville's feminine is that which can no longer speak for itself." Smith incisively examines Melville's "confrontation with femininity and maternal reproduction" in *Pierre.* Later, her discussion of Pip as outcast and silenced child grounds her consideration of *Billy Budd*'s "murderous logic" of male authority and Billy's metaphorical configuration as "the child/slave/woman/worker."

Three brief accounts suggest the open and complex issues associated with Melville's biographical relations to and literary representations of women. Joyce Adler Sparer in "Melville and Misogyny?" (*MSEx* 98: 11–12) counters the notion of Melville's putative misogyny by summarizing a host of characters and imagery: "The real Melville is to be found in his work, not in interpretations about his marriage, the length of its difficult period in the course of many years, [and] the difficulties of living with many relatives." Wyn Kelley in "The Mood for Composition: The Melville Family Letters" (*MSEx* 98: 12) concentrates on letters written by Melville's wife and mother and reflects on how Melville's works might have been influenced by "the chatty, expansive style of the family correspondence." In "Melville and Feminist Biography; Or, A Look at Some Fine, Upstanding Biographical Phallacies" (*MSEx* 98: 12–13) Laurie Robertson-Lorant outlines her biography in progress and disputes the notion that some single secret exists "that will open the floodgates of [Melville's] psychosexual pathology." Arguing that Melville's writings reflect America's "most naked cry of wounded masculinity," she proposes "to place Melville in the matrix of family, history, and culture—to honor the multiplicity of selves, the personal conflicts resolved and unresolved."

In "Herman Melville, Wife Beating, and the Written Page" (*AL* 66: 123–50) Elizabeth Renker dispenses with such subtlety and wields a Cromwellian ax. Translating innuendo into supposition and supposition into foundational evidence, Renker focuses on Melville's marital troubles of the mid-1860s as documented in two well-known, supposedly "silenced," ignored, or misconstrued letters discovered by Walter D. Kring and Jonathan S. Carey that were not only published by the Massachusetts Historical Society but reprinted by the Melville Society (with commentary by many scholars) and mailed free of charge to 800 persons and institutions worldwide. Melville's alleged "wife beating" has its source in something Charles Olson reportedly said, but here the absence of reliable documentation verifies the putative incident's suppressed truth. This factoid is not to be approached as one possible event in a crowded life with a multitude of far more reliable evidence qualifying and complicating its import; here, "wife abuse" resounds as "one crucial element in a network that also includes his tortured relation to writing and his simultaneous dependence on and resentment of the Melville women whose labor he needed to produce his texts." With invidious determinations all fixed, Melville's craft of intense revision does not reflect writing's one true pleasure but an "agonized relation"; "he disfigured the surface of his writing paper, filling out every available white space with writing, as well as with cross-outs, revision, carets, circles, and other manipulations." Manipulated syntax is cognate to misogyny: "These frustrations in his writing illuminate a series of textual effects that associate women with blank pages and textual production." From this view "Fragments from a Writing Desk" and "The Tartarus of Maids" seem to be Melville's most defining and self-reflexive texts.

iv Typee

This year's pieces mostly contend with the ethnographic implications of Melville's cross-cultural narrative. Malini Johar Schueller's "Colonialism and Melville's South Sea Journeys" (*SAF* 22: 3–18) describes how Melville critiques even as he repeats "colonial *topoi*." Though Melville "makes a conscious effort in *Typee* to undermine any ethnocentric assumptions his readers might have," he also "retains a conflicted subtext of colonial imperatives." Schueller sees Tommo as a voyeur making an "imperialistic survey" of Typee life. Turning himself into a hero possessing the "symbols of European power," Tommo upholds the western sense of racial superiority as well as the power philosophy inherent in "binary thinking." In "Oedipus in the South Seas: The Case of Herman Melville's *Typee*" (*ELWIU* 21: 218–34) Dan Latimer complements Schueller's reading. In *Typee,* Latimer contends, Melville delineates "two irreconcilable points of view," not as diametrical opposition but as dialectical process: "Melville's righteous indignation against colonialism seems qualified by a selective valorization of other colonial enterprises." Tommo's lameness evokes the figure of Oedipus.

Samuel Otter in "Of Tattooing" (*MSEx* 96: 7–8) links tattooing and ethnography, Melville's *Typee* and the " 'American School' of ethnology, which sought to divide the human body into significant features and to trace lines of difference on its surface." Tommo is disturbed "about the vulnerability and the transformational possibilities of his own 'white skin.' " Sylvie Andre in "The Inner Adventurer in the *Mariage de Loti* and *Typee*" (*Literature and Travel,* ed. Michael Hanne [Rodopi, 1991], pp. 39–52) discusses the psychological dynamics of cross-cultural travel, especially Tommo's "quest for the Other." This journey leads to an abridged attempt to escape law as well as an incomplete regression to "a state of infantile dependency."

Carol Colatrella in "Bercovitch's Paradox: Critical Dissent, Marginality, and the Example of Melville" (*Cohesion and Dissent in America,* ed. Colatrella and Joseph Alkana [SUNY], pp. 229–50), argues that Sacvan Bercovitch's "own critical position resembles Melville's self-determined position as a writer whose alienation from the world of his father led him to disdain systems and systems making." Thus, *Typee* demonstrates "how in the interest of continuity a community demands the absorption of dissent and resists true social change." Against the background of 19th-century prison reform, Colatrella explores Tommo as narrator, captive, and divided ethnographer, offering an illuminating presentation of his attachment to and dissociation from Typee society. Finally, Kevin J. Hayes in "Toby's *Typee* Lecture" (*MSEx* 96: 1–4) reprints newspaper passages chronicling Richard Tobias Greene's 1855 lecture tour. Hayes reveals "that the American reading public not only remembered *Typee* nine years after its publication, they also remained curious about its truthfulness."

v Moby-Dick

Kevin J. Hayes's *The Critical Response to Herman Melville's* Moby-Dick (Greenwood) reprints material under the rubrics "Contemporary Reviews," "The Melville Revival," and "Academic Attention." His "Introduction: *Moby-Dick* and the Aesthetics of Response" (pp. xv–xxvii) provides a balanced and useful survey of the narrative's popular and critical reception. Hayes also identifies a hitherto unnoticed comment from E. M. Forster. In "*Moby-Dick*: Cutting a Classic Down to Ideological Size" (*Recovering American Literature*, pp. 48–74) Peter Shaw delivers a spirited jeremiad. In the 1980s *Moby-Dick* became "reduced to precisely the settled answers of allegory that Melville had warned against." With the "imposition . . . of contemporary political issues deemed important to academics on the left," the text became a happy hunting ground where one could assert Melville's empathy with victims past, present, and to come. The overtly ideological bent of recent critical practice, Shaw contends, is little more than a narcissistic projection. Traditional historicists, cowed by charges of theoretical naïveté, have taken the beating quietly: "the free discussion of American literature is being stifled by a new, radical orthodoxy." Shaw recommends a turn from ideology toward aesthetics, claiming that the "primary allegiance of criticism must be the integrity of the literary object, not to politics." Shaw will either comfort the already converted or be dismissed by antagonists who view aesthetics as inherently ideological.

The matter of "size" and ideology also pertains to Julian Markels's "The *Moby-Dick* White Elephant" (*AL* 66: 105–22). He finds the "Historical Note" to the Northwestern-Newberry edition of *Moby-Dick* not simply too long but infected with the editors' "deeply compromised ideology of scholarship." While applauding the textual scholar who identifies variants as the fluid perimeters for interpretative possibilities, he attacks the companion scholar who allegedly works "to obscure the dynamic process of *Moby-Dick* scholarship." Despite a massive and diverse list of works cited, Markels claims the editors seal "the book off from scholars and critics through its manner of ignoring objections and alternatives while codifying the judgments of a self-chosen remnant." Markels seems incensed by the association in a "Historical Note" of textual with genetic materials, an odd complaint since Melville composed and amended this text during production. Markels raises a number of valid concerns about what needs to be included within such a note. However, in advancing his Righteous Cause, Markels infuses his contumacious discussion with insults. Of two eminent scholars, Markels berates one for evincing "quasi-positivist assumptions" and the other for "vulgar misogyny."

P. Marc Bousquet in "Mathew's Mosses? Fair Papers and Foul: A Note on the Northwestern-Newberry Edition of 'Hawthorne and His Mosses'" (*NEQ* 67: 622–49) also takes exception to a Northwestern-Newberry text. Bousquet explores the genesis of this essay, especially the "antichauvinist revisions" of Melville's fervid rhetoric of literary nationalism. Bousquet argues that Melville's revisions were arrested because of Evert Duyckinck's departure from Pittsfield. Thus, an editor might justly "*extend* the revision trajectory by canceling the remaining chauvinisms of the fair copy."

A number of essays engage *Moby-Dick*'s relation to cultural and literary contexts. Etsuko Taketani's "*Moby-Dick*: Gnostic Re-writing of History" (*ATQ* 8: 119–35) makes a valuable contribution to our understanding of Melville and heretical theology. Taketani associates Gnostic thought in 19th-century America with "a growing skepticism about the historical veracity of Christianity." Along with examining Andrews Norton's critique of Gnosticism, Taketani discusses Melville's dramatization of such topoi as the dual divinity and matter's intrinsic evil. Ahab's Gnostic strain impels his attempt to redefine history. In "Melville as Lexicographer: Linguistics and Symbolism in *Moby-Dick*" (*MSEx* 98: 1–6) Neal Schleifer finds that "Etymology" is a key to the narrative, especially as it suggests a symbolic opposition between "grace and retribution." Schleifer examines Melville's incorrect translations of the Hebrew and Greek words for whale and plausibly concludes that they are clever cryptograms. Mark Niemeyer in "*Moby-Dick* and the Spirit of Revolution" (*The Critical Response to Herman Melville's* Moby-Dick, pp. 221–39) examines Melville's conflicted political sensibility as expressed in both conservative and iconoclastic attitudes. Ishmael projects the "optimistic vision of the democratic ideal," while Ahab embodies the "extreme form of revolutionary zeal." Niemeyer considers the "usurpation of power" as dramatized in the *Pequod*'s encounters with such ships as *The Town-Ho* and *The Jeroboam*. Michael C. Berthold's "*Moby-Dick* and American Slave Narrative" (*MR* 35: 135–48) explores Melville's "dialogical engagement with the strategies and tropes of the American slave narratives." Berthold reads "The *Town-Ho*'s Story," with its energies of repression and rebellion, as a captivity narrative. The "Epilogue," especially Queequeg's coffin, becomes Melville's version of the "talking book," a fundamental element of the slave narrative tradition. In "A Window on the Prey: The Hunter Sees a Human Face in Hemingway's 'After the Storm' and Melville's 'The Grand Armada' " (*HN* 14, i: 25–35) Nathaniel Philbrick delineates how the shadow of Melville falls on Hemingway's first sea story. Philbrick pursues the numerous connections between these two writers, arguing that both of them "undercut the traditional hunter-prey relationship."

Two essays examine gender. Leland S. Person, Jr., in "Melville's Cassock: Putting on Masculinity in *Moby-Dick*" (*ESQ* 40: 1–26) argues that Melville "explores and challenges a traditional, essentially phallocentric masculinity (individualistic, instrumental, projective, competitive)." Within the narrative Melville unsettles, constructs of male identity, crossing and confusing "gender lines that bracket acceptable male behavior." Ishmael offers a radical alternative to Ahab's male ethos not simply through his cooperative sensibility but by encouraging "the freedom to choose among a range of possibilities." Person sees "A Squeeze of the Hand," "The Cassock," and "The Try-Works" as a "triptych on the economic and political status of masculinity." Emily Miller Budick in "Worlds Without Women: Herman Melville and Edgar Allan Poe" (*Engendering Romance: Women Writers and the Hawthorne Tradition, 1850–1990* [Yale], pp. 59–74) sees Melville's works as "antipatriarchal" and makes a case for their influence on "the 20th-century women's tradition, especially southern women's fiction with its decidedly gothic strain." The world without woman, she argues, is depicted as inherently sterile. Ahab, whose "tragedy" is that he "will not go home," has his counterpoint in Ishmael's "desire for unbirth and self-contracting rebirth." The novel projects Melville's "self-conscious rendering of one man's all-consuming, self-deluding fantasy of self-contained male potency and self-generation."

In "The National Narrative of Monomania" (*Healing the Republic*, pp. 156–75) Joan Burbick explores how the "language of health and the disorders of the brain weave themselves in dense layers." Ahab's monomania and "moral insanity" lead to isolation. As expressions of American possibility, Ahab's hegemonic impulses are destructive to self, ship, and state. Elizabeth Schultz's "Rockwell Kent's Illustrations of *Moby-Dick*: Ordering Infinitude" (*MSEx* 96: 6) contends that Kent's illustrations provide an ongoing critical account in visual figures—mimetic, impressionistic, and symbolic. Mark Dunphy in "*Moby-Dick* and Woody

Allen" (*MSEx* 96: 12) cites recurring references to the novel in the film *Zelig* (1983), where the book is more owned than read, and thus a source of neurosis.

vi   From *Pierre* to *The Confidence-Man*

Samuel Otter's "The Eden of Saddle Meadows: Landscape and Ideology in *Pierre*" (*AL* 66: 55–81) shows how the "excess and distortion" of the language in the Saddle Meadows portion anticipate "the antebellum nightmare that follows. . . . Melville's excess does not simply subvert the Romantic conventions: the excess breathes new life into it." Specifically, Melville debunks the tendency of the picturesque to "idealize American 'difference.' " Otter compares Melville's "contorted representations" with works of Thomas Cole, Nathaniel Parker Willis, and William Cullen Bryant. Besides delineating a tenuous Eden, Pierre's ancestral home evokes those who have been dispossessed of Eden. Tomoyuki Zettsu's "*Pierre* and Pierre Bayle on Androgyny" (*MSEx* 97: 1–4) identifies Bayle's *An Historical and Critical Dictionary* as a source for Melville's dramatization of "gender ambiguity." Zettsu discusses Pierre's affinities not only with Lucy and his mother but also with typal Adam, the "original androgyne." Nancy Fredericks in "The Valorization of Music in *Pierre*'s Allegory of the Arts" (*MSEx* 96: 6–7) sees the relationship among Pierre, Lucy, and Isabel as an allegory of "literary, visual and musical arts." In "Federated Fancies: Balzac's *Lost Illusions* and Melville's *Pierre*" (*Intertextuality in Literature and Film,* pp. 37–47) Benjamin Sherwood Lawson examines these novels' many similarities—their aristocratic families, their uses of representative portraits, their protagonists' status as writers, their scenic shift from country to city, and their dramatizations of suicide.

Douglas Robillard in "The Dead Letter Office" (*MSEx* 96: 8–9) suggests that Francis Copcutt's chapter "A Day in the Dead Letter Office," though published in 1860 as part of *Leaves from a Bachelor's Book of Life,* could have come to Melville's attention when a shorter version was anonymously published in *The United States Magazine and Democratic Review* in December 1846. With collateral evidence Copcott's arresting phrase "burned by cartloads" lends plausibility to the case. In "Bartleby: Representation, Reproduction, and the Law" (*JACult* 17, ii: 65–73) Susan Weiner explores "Bartleby" as a metanarrative that "questioned the efficacy of writing as the predominant mode of discourse both

for interpreting experience and for organizing society." Weiner places
Melville in opposition to Oliver Wendell Holmes on the new photographic technology.

Wyn Kelley in "'I'm Housewife Here': Herman Melville and Domestic Economy" (*MSEx* 98: 7–10) takes a cookbook called *The Modern
Housewife's Recipe Book,* which Melville gave to his wife in July 1854, and
applies it to considerations of gender and domesticity in "The Paradise
of Bachelors and the Tartarus of Maids" and "Poor Man's Pudding and
Rich Man's Crumbs." While pointing out that the stories were written
before Melville's purchase, Kelley argues that the cookbook provides a
social measure by which the stories can be understood. Karen A. Weyler's
"Melville's 'The Paradise of Bachelors and the Tartarus of Maids': A
Dialogue about Experience, Understanding, and Truth" (*SSF* 31: 461–
69) considers the blending of sketch and tale as analogous to the
narrator's transformation from passivity to activity. The diptych dramatizes an unfolding dialogue about universals, ultimately attesting to
Melville's "anxiety about the limitations of language." From the cyber-
space of previously unidentified pieces comes Joel Pfister's "Melville's
Birthmarks: The Feminization Industry" (*The Production of Personal
Life: Class, Gender, and the Psychological in Hawthorne's Fiction* [Stanford,
1991], pp. 104–21). Pfister deftly reads "The Bell-Tower" and "The
Tartarus of Maids" as conscious redactions of Hawthorne's "The Birth-
mark"; Melville reimagines "his friend's criticism of gender construction
and American culture." Melville takes Hawthorne's use of alchemy and
transfigures it in industrial terms. For Melville "the construct of femininity was connected to and complicit with structural social contradictions
at the base of the domestic tensions represented by Hawthorne." Melville
dramatizes intersections between the "ideology of industrial 'progress'
and the cultural production of feminized women." Pfister sees the stories
as "letters" to Hawthorne on "the management of labor, labor-slaving
devices, and the conquest of female nature."

Kris Lackey's "The Two Handles of *Israel Potter*" (*CollL* 21, i: 32–45)
explores Melville's "management of irony" as it reflects his dualistic
imperatives: upholding the Revolutionary War mythos (and thus selling
books) and debunking this mythos (and thus ensuring his book's un-
popularity). Applying economic and historical paradigms from Terry
Eagleton's *Criticism and Ideology,* Lackey discusses Melville's "contradictory politics" as dramatized in conventional and subversive depictions,
through such epochal figures as Benjamin Franklin, Ethan Allen, and

John Paul Jones, and especially through the relation of the United States
to Great Britain and young Israel Potter.

Benito Cereno continues to attract fresh assessments. Bernard B.
Bloch's "Babo and Babeuf: Melville's 'Benito Cereno' " (*MSEx* 96: 9–12)
examines "name changes and wordplay" as indications of Melville's
rejection of Amasa Delano's racism. Block speculates that Babo may have
resonated in Melville's mind with Francis Noel Babeuf and his doctrine
known as "Babouvism," a utopic vision of equality. If so, it would be an
ironic reference, especially in light of Babo's separationist intentions.
Carol Colatrella's "The Significant Silence of Race: *La Cousine Bette* and
Benito Cereno" (*CL* 46: 240–65) argues that both narratives "exploit
the interactive relationship of reader and text," and they demand that
readers "criticize views expressed by characters and narrators." In distinguishing between "narrative audience" and "authorial audience" Colatrella offers a rich examination of how racial ideology is continually
dependent on and transfigured by a "reader's reception of narrative
ambiguity." Robert S. Levine in "Teaching in the Multiracial Classroom:
Reconsidering Melville's 'Benito Cereno' " (*MELUS* 19, i: 111–20) details
his changing relation to the reading and teaching of this racially explosive narrative. He recounts a progress from allegorical/metaphysical to
more historical approaches. Melville's historical and transhistorical narrative turns on an understanding of narrative point[s] of view. Levine
critiques his own attempt to make the narrative too "representative"—of
Melville and "the black experience under slavery." One solution he
identifies is to surround Melville's narrative with texts that reflect multiple experiences of slavery.

Three source studies enlarge our understanding of Melville's adaptations. David Ketterer's " 'Tray Comes Back': 'The Piazza' and Thomas
Campbell's 'The Harper' " (*MSEx* 97: 10–12) convincingly proposes the
Scottish poet Thomas Campbell's "The Harper" (1799) as a primary
source for "The Piazza." Jonathan Cook's "Rabelais' Solar Lamp: A
Source for *The Confidence-Man*" (*MSEx* 97: 1, 4–7) examines scenic
parallels in order to locate one source of Melville's "solar lamp" in "a
related episode at the conclusion of Rabelais's *Fifth Book [of Gargantua
and Pantagruel]*." Both works parody "romance convention depicting
the fulfillment or non-fulfillment of the hero's quest." Rabelais offers "a
joyous affirmation of life," while *The Confidence-Man* "terminates in
an absurdist drama of isolation, deception, and (potentially) death."
Mark C. Taylor in "Discrediting God" (*JAAR* 68: 603–23) explores the

"theological and economic" complexes that make *The Confidence-Man* a "contemporary" text. Taylor contends that Poe's "The Gold-Bug" antici-pates Melville's exploration of signified value—a concern that includes questions about the authenticity of any text.

vii **Late Works**

Three articles respectively consider psychological, terrestrial, and cos-mological concerns of *Clarel.* Zephyra Porat's provocative and rich "To-wards the Promethean Ledge: Varieties of Sceptic Experience in Mel-ville's *Clarel*" (*L&T* 8: 30–46) sees the poem as an extended dialogue on 19th-century cultural history. In depicting an "inverted pilgrimage" Melville projects a dialectic between Promethean rebellion and Christian acceptance. Porat finds that Melville conflates "Gnostic heresy with Jewish apostasy"; Judaism becomes the form within which Melville celebrates rebellion, and Rolfe articulates an "open-ended and unde-cided" redaction of "Gnostic allegory." In "From 'Revery' to Nightmare: The Limits of the Optimistic Metaphor in the Private Voices of Dickin-son and Melville" (*The Prairie in Nineteenth-Century American Poetry*, pp. 106–29) Steven Olson finds that "the prairie is nightmarish. . . . In *Clarel* (1876) and *John Marr and Other Sailors* (1888), Melville echoes the conventional, nationalistic theme associated with the prairies, but he subverts their significance and uses them to emphasize the isolation of the artist in a democracy." The prairie images a haunted region of past failure—both personal and collective. In Brett Zimmerman's "Stars and Spiritual Navigation in Melville's *Clarel*" (*EAS* 23: 21–38) celestial imag-ery illustrates the theme of religious questing. The association of theol-ogy and astronomy reflects natural piety and a range of theological traditions. In the poem, stars serve as guides for the pilgrims.

In "Melville's Handsome Sailor: The Anxiety of Innocence" (*AL* 66: 83–103) Nancy Ruttenberg offers Whitman's belief that an "aesthetics of innocence" is a prerequisite for the prospective American bard, "as if only the poet's inarticulateness and illiteracy guaranteed the purity of the national essence he was invented to contain." Billy Budd manifests such qualities: "Melville's final novel . . . textually enacts the paradox of inarticulate innocence as that which both legitimated and promised to redress the nation's enduring silence about itself." In positioning Budd in relation to artists in Emerson's "The Poet" and Whitman's "Democratic Vistas" Ruttenberg presents Melville's image of the "vocal curent electric" as the novel's "dynamic principle." Lawrence Douglas in "Discursive Limits: Narrative and Judgment in *Billy Budd*" (*Mosaic* 27, iv: 141–60) examines the intersections of law and literature and contends that "the act of judging should be seen as a species of nuanced reading." Douglas explores the connection between "narrative voice and juridical temper," showing how the novel "presents the arguments for and against literature's relevance to the law." The narrator and Captain Vere continually confront "the limits of discourse—historical, literary, juridical." Clyde Taylor's "The Ironies of Palace-Subaltern Discourse" (*Black American Cinema,* ed. Manthia Diawara [Routledge, 1993], pp. 177–99) generates a methodology that reflects the "practice of representational politics." His metaphor of "Palace-Subaltern" delineates the inequity between dominant and repressed classes and points to the forms of discourse most reflective of these classes. Taylor views such "cultural politics as a dialectic of ironies, the ironies of domination." Taylor contends that the movie version of Charles Fuller's *A Soldier's Story* offers a "paraphrase" of *Billy Budd.* Taylor incisively aligns parallel elements of character, action, and theme. And in another note for moviegoers Colette Michael in "*Billy Budd*: An Allegory on the Rights of Man" (*Allegory Old and New in Literature, the Fine Arts, Music and Theatre and Its Continuity in Culture,* ed. Marlies Kronegger and Anna-Teresa Tymieniecka [Kluwer], pp. 251–58) begins with the inaccurate notion that Melville finished *Billy Budd* "[s]hortly before his death"; she then juxtaposes *Billy Budd* and the 1962 film of that name, directed and cowritten by Peter Ustinov. The movie does it better: "In the book . . . Melville *tells us about good and evil*; in the movie . . . Ustinov *shows us about good and evil*" (emphasis in original).

Salisbury State University

5 Whitman and Dickinson

Martha Nell Smith

The early 1990s have seen Dickinson and Whitman scholars attempt to ground each poet much more firmly in the material world. Critical conversations about the life and work of the writer who sang the body electric and claimed to be poet of the body have long attended to matters corporeal, and in a climate of burgeoning lesbian, gay, and/or queer studies and sustained developments in feminist and African American scholarship such interests have expanded and intensified. Purporting to restore a sense of the bardic through Whitman's literal utterance, the recently rediscovered recording by Thomas Edison of Whitman speaking four lines from "America" is perhaps the most poignant symbol of efforts to situate his spiritual and intellectual philosophies in the physical world. Dickinson critics no longer take her lyric "I am afraid to own a body" as a mandate for biographical interpretation, and ownership of her textual body, for a century virtually unquestioned as a goal, has been effectively placed out of reach by contemporary analysis of the complexities of her holographs and transcriptions. The struggle now involves what counts as a Dickinson poem and even what among her writings counts as poetry.

Compensating for the absence of this chapter in *ALS 1993*, I review here Whitman and Dickinson scholarship for both 1993 and 1994, examining in the first section Whitman studies, in the second, Dickinson studies, and in the third, articles and book chapters devoted to both poets. Following *ALS* format, I include the year in citation if an item was published before 1994.

i Walt Whitman

Four books devoted completely to Whitman appeared in 1993–94. For readers concerned with the materialities and distribution of Whitman's writings, Joel Myerson's thorough, analytical *Walt Whitman: A Descrip-*

tive Bibliography (Pittsburgh, 1993) is essential. An important complement to this catalog of primary texts is M. Jimmie Killingsworth, *The
Growth of* Leaves of Grass: *The Organic Tradition in Whitman Studies*
(Camden House, 1993), a metanarrative of the critical tradition which
argues that the primary models of this tradition lie in the organic
metaphors initiated by the poet himself—those of vegetative growth,
technical innovation, architectural feat. In *Walt Whitman's Native Representations* (Cambridge) Ed Folsom examines dictionaries, baseball, Native Americans, and photography to analyze Whitman's work in the
context of some of its "particularly intimate relationship[s] with its
cultural surroundings" and Whitman as a spokesperson for the first
generation of those considering themselves "native" Americans. By examining the Whitmanian Self as urban citizen, especially of Manhattan,
and tracing affinities with Jacob Riis, John Sloan, T. S. Eliot, William
Carlos Williams, Alfred Stieglitz, Charles Sheeler, and Berenice Abbott,
James Dougherty critiques the project of the "poet who introduced the
city to American literature" in *Walt Whitman and the Citizen's Eye* (LSU,
1993).

Two collections of centennial essays feature the paths of critical travel
most often taken in Whitman studies during this year and last. A series
of conferences subsequent to the establishment of a Whitman Studies
Program at Rutgers University–Camden in 1985 has resulted in *Walt
Whitman of Mickle Street,* a collection of 27 essays originally published in
issues of *Mickle Street.* Dedicated to Gay Wilson Allen, the "Dean of
Whitman Scholars," *Walt Whitman: The Centennial Essays* divides its 19
essays (generated by "Walt Whitman: The Centennial Conference,"
held in Iowa City in March 1992) into four sections—"The Life: The
Biographical Whitman," "The Texts: Origins and Style," "The Culture:
Politics and Sexuality," and "The Influence: Whitman Among Others."
The topics encompass three major preoccupations of the scholarship—
the literal body, the textual body, and the body politic.

a. Biography and the Body   Martin G. Murray's " 'Pete the Great': A
Biography of Peter Doyle" (*WWR* 12: 1–51) offers the first sustained
portrait of the streetcar conductor, described by his niece as a homosexual, who had such profound influence on Whitman's emotional life. The
narrative recounts Doyle's immigration as a boy from Ireland, his brief
conscription into the Confederate army, his meeting Whitman, his
eyewitness account of Lincoln's assassination, his and Walt's frequenting

of a bar in Georgetown's Union Hotel, their correspondence, his discovery of baseball, their visit with Whitman's mother, their falling-out and reconciliation (which "did not include a fulfillment of Whitman's wish to share a home with Pete"), Whitman's removing Doyle from his will, their reconnection before Whitman's death, and Doyle's ultimate faith in their tie: "Walt realized I never swerved from him—he knows it now— that is enough." In the process of telling Doyle's story, Murray also fleshes out and makes more real images of Whitman, humanizing the poet through this record of a crucial male relationship.

Thomas Eakins's photographs of Whitman—or his "body-double . . . still giving us," as poet Philip Dacey imagined it, "The Good Gray Poet down to his last disguise"—offer images of the literal body, "mystical, nude." They complement the Edison recording of the physical voice and are discussed by Ed Folsom in "Whitman Naked?" (*WWR* 11: 200–202). The photographs were among those of the "naked series" locked away until the late 1970s in the safety deposit box of the chairman of the committee on instruction of the Pennsylvania Academy, which had dismissed Eakins in 1886. That Whitman should pose naked for Eakins, who painted him and took several photographic portraits of him in the late 1880s, should come as no surprise. "What is unmistakable is that Whitman's sexual emotions were so strong that he made them a part of his poetic program and would protest all his life against prudish suppression of sex in literature," remarks Gay Wilson Allen in "Whitman Biography in 1992" (*Walt Whitman: The Centennial Essays,* pp. 3–9), an essay that evolves into a reverie on Whitman's influence.

By focusing on the work that "brought together on the fiftieth anniversary of the first publication of *Leaves of Grass* most of the known facts about the poet's life in a lively, readable narrative that links Whitman's life and work with the emerging international stature of the United States," Jerome Loving in "The Binns Biography" discusses the influence of various historical moments on critical emphases, noting how Henry Bryan Binns argued that "Whitman experienced a literary awakening as the result of 'an intimate relationship with some woman of higher social rank' " at a time when homosexuality was being pathologized (*Walt Whitman: The Centennial Essays,* pp. 10–18). Yet, as Loving asserts in "Whitman's Idea of Women" (*Walt Whitman of Mickle Street,* pp. 151–67), no sexually intimate relationship with a woman led to his literary awakening, for his "open and 'fraternal' treatment of women" and their "feminine vitality" is "just as poetical and just as impractical as Poe's idea of Helen, or Hawthorne's vision of Hester." When woman is Muse for Whitman, she is Mother.

As Vivian R. Pollak compellingly argues in "Whitman Unperturbed: The Civil War and After" (*Walt Whitman: The Centennial Essays,* pp. 30–50), "death as a 'Dark Mother'" and democracy as mother are creative inspirations evident in "When Lilacs Last in the Dooryard Bloom'd." Especially important too is Pollak's observing how "he imagines that death alone has the power to interrupt a relentless socioerotic narrative in which he, 'Whitman,' is eternally marginalized," for he "discovers in the fact and in the idea of death a community of mourners when no other social relationships are imagined as capable of sustaining him." Pollak's "Death as Repression, Repression as Death: A Reading of Whitman's 'Calamus' Poems" (*Walt Whitman of Mickle Street,* pp. 179–93) interprets his "Calamus" sequence in the context of "Out of the Cradle Endlessly Rocking" to show how he "uses death tropes both to deny the fulfillment of his eroticism and to affirm its vitality in the face of social and psychological oppression." Pollak elaborates more fully on the "homosocial, homoerotic, and homosexual elements that inform Whitman's conception of his gender identity," and she offers a "fuller understanding of the tonal and psychological range of the 'Calamus' lover" and his social context.

Noting in "The Biographer's Problem" (*Walt Whitman of Mickle Street,* pp. 18–27) that a century of Whitman biography "is to a large extent the history of a pussyfooting accommodation to the issue of sexuality, and, more specifically homosexuality," and that biography has been repeatedly "skewed in the interest of literary public relations," Justin Kaplan concludes that "what *does* matter is the way Whitman defines himself as homosexual in his poetry, in his letters and journals, in his daily conduct, in his frequently tormented relations with younger men and his evasive relations with women, in the way he uses democratic political models as a way of emancipating sexuality, in the way he invokes androgyny as a liberating imaginative mode." Indeed, in "Whitman: Bibliography as Biography" (*Walt Whitman: The Centennial Essays,* pp. 19–29) Joel Myerson interprets the facts of the corporealizations of Whitman's thought, his books, to deduce facts about the man. Myerson amply demonstrates the underappreciated reach of analytical primary bibliographies as he examines such details as engravings and photographs of the poet's likeness and when and where they appear in particular editions to trace the evolution of Whitman's career and poetic agenda.

b. The Textual Body: Style and Form The iambic tetrameter regularity
of "A Sketch" and its conventional theme "that the next life awaits to
relieve us from the burdens of this one," discussed by Jerome Loving in
"A Newly Discovered Whitman Poem" (*WWR* 11: 117–22), show how
profoundly Whitman's poetics evolved even as they reveal early faint
articulations of his lifelong preoccupation with manly love. Several
insightful studies explore Whitman's manipulations of rhetoric. In
"'Tallying, Vocalizing All': Discourse Markers" (*Walt Whitman: The
Centennial Essays*, pp. 61–67) C. Carroll Hollis, concerned with the
probability that Whitman wrote with the intention that his poems be
read aloud, examines his use of four "discourse markers" or routine
"particular expressions used to organize conversational interaction" to
demonstrate that there is an "oral basis" for *Leaves of Grass*. Hollis's
explication of Whitman's repeated strategic (often anaphoric) use of
"*Now, and, so, but*" underscores how Whitman's reader was intimately
cast as "listener-on-the-page." Applying Whitman's own deepened sense
of the word "reconstruction" in "Reconstructing Language in *Democratic
Vistas*" (*Walt Whitman: The Centennial Essays*, pp. 79–87), James Perrin
Warren interrogates this "basic textual strategy" of "making anew" in the
"figural crossings" of the "combined acts of saying and seeing" the
"compound word" that enacts the "Hegelian dialectic" and the "oracular
voice" of "syntactic parallelism" and "cataloging." Warren argues that
"by defining democratic culture in terms of audience, Whitman effectively dissolves the boundaries between high and low or elite and popular
culture." In "Only the Dead Know Brooklyn Ferry: The Inscription of
the Reader in Whitman" (*ArQ* 49, ii [1993]: 23–51) Tom Cohen alerts
readers "to the violent implications of rhetorical technique," the "*negative* power wielded by naming and addressing the other (reader) in a
hortatory manner," power that "substantially complicate[s] and revise[s]
any pretended immediacy, transparency or [authorial] presence, and for
that matter, the very integrity of the [authorial] voice itself." Similarly,
Terry Mulcaire observes in "Publishing Intimacy in *Leaves of Grass*"
(*ELH* 60 [1993]: 471–501) that the "total alienation of death becomes the
limit and perfection of Whitman's imagination of intimacy, and, consequently, of his standard of poetic value," and that such "relation between
author and public . . . at once deeply alienated and erotically intimate" is
"impossible to imagine . . . outside of an era of the mass production of
books under the conditions of capitalism."
  More telling, however, is Arthur Golden's thorough investigation of

the simple facts of Whitman's writing life: that he "spent a lifetime writing poetry, establishing various public personalities, and covering his tracks." "The Obfuscations of Rhetoric: Whitman and the Visionary Experience" (*Walt Whitman: The Centennial Essays*, pp. 88–104) also scrutinizes the disappointing and more complicated fact that "when the prose Whitman speaks outside of *Leaves of Grass* of an 'American' he is typically talking about a white native American." Whatever our late 20th-century desires, real inclusiveness was not at the heart of Whitman's vision, for he supported an Oregon law prohibiting the residence of "Colored Persons" because of their competition with white labor, and the grounds of his opposition to slavery was that it "totally degraded" white labor. Sadly, he also wrote, "It is also to be remembered that no race ever can remain slaves if they have it in them to become free. Why do slave-ships go to Africa only?"

How "Whitman's special manipulation of the physical medium of his poems" connects "literate and political life in a way that transforms both aspects of the reader's experience" is M. Jimmie Killingsworth's interest in "Whitman's Physical Eloquence" (*Walt Whitman: The Centennial Essays*, pp. 68–78). Elegantly elaborating how Whitman invites the reader, "offering signs of companionship and desire in a continued search for an accepting, indeed a loving, relationship," Killingsworth makes much of a concept he designates as "physical eloquence." This entails a wide range of confirmations, contradictions, removals, and beckonings—such as the fact of the "distance implicit in the literate medium" being "undermined by the figures and conventions of orality and physical presence." The essay is richly imbued with historical contexts, drawing particularly on Charles Sumner's use of "the trope of sexual violence to oppose the extension of slave power into Kansas"—"It is the rape of a virgin Territory, compelling it to the hateful embrace of Slavery"—as the most powerful demonstration of the fact that "in Whitman's day, the body of the reader was rendered prominent for cultural and political reasons." Christopher Beach's "Walt Whitman, Literary Culture, and the Discourse of Distinction" (*WWR* 12: 73–85) argues that "Whitman incarnates in the nineteenth century Bourdieu's 'counter-artist,'" launching a "radical 'carnivalization' of past literary modes and genres" to enable the "fragmentation and subversion of literary formulas." In "*Leaves of Grass* as a 'Woman's Book'" (*WWR* 10 [1993]: 195–208) Maire Mullins contends that the "qualities of receptivity, expansiveness, and connection" imbuing Whitman's writing "can be understood as stemming from the kind of writing which Hélène Cixous and other French feminists describe," particularly in its "plurality of being and sexual desire, thus creating body/textual consciousness."

Constructing Whitman as seducer, Joseph Coulson's "The Poem Is the Body: Pronominal Relation in 'Song of Myself'" (*Walt Whitman of Mickle Street*, pp. 123–28) argues, at least implicitly, for approaching the poems as one approaches a new lover, as a body of infinite discovery to be luxuriated in, and as a rewarding enticement repeatedly offering "opportunity for an intuitive, mutual understanding." Focusing on Whitman's attribution of preternatural active powers "both to his poems and to the figure of the poet who stands at their center" in "Whitman's Addresses to His Audience" (*Walt Whitman of Mickle Street*, pp. 129–41), Tenney Nathanson analyzes how Whitman relies on readerly collaboration and how "remarkedly sophisticated" are his apparently simple "flirtatious gestures"—"I might not tell everybody, but I will tell you." Two of the things he will tell or argue, of course, are a "eugenic premise" for the "physiological upgrading and transformation of the American citizenry" and the "development of full-fledged personalities and their integration into a new body politic" by means of an "inspirational democratic literature," remarks Harold Aspiz in "The Body Politic in *Democratic Vistas*" (*Walt Whitman: The Centennial Essays*, pp. 105–19). In "Whitman as Jeremiah" (*Walt Whitman of Mickle Street*, pp. 70–79) Peter Balakian scrutinizes the darker side of Whitman's vision of and for America in *Democratic Vistas*, finding that his "waning antebellum idealism and his growing cynicism about his wayward Zion [are] dramatized in the alternating currents of his rhetoric."

c. The Body Politic: Foreign and Domestic Relations and Literary Affinities "Alternating currents" is an apt phrase for the sexual expressions at the core of this poet's vision, and numerous articles interrogate Whitman's homotextualities. Implicitly extending arguments made by Thomas Yingling in "Critical Indifference; or, Tradition and the Homosexual Talent in American Poetry," the opening chapter of *Hart Crane and the Homosexual Text* (1990), Christopher Newfield interrogates the political homosexuality of Whitman in "Democracy and Male Homoeroticism" (*YJC* 6, ii [1993]: 29–62), noting that homosexuality is particularly threatening to the military because it challenges "not just straight homosociality in general, but a male homosociality that consists of submissions to superiors." Though Betsy Erkkila engages in unnecessary hairsplitting between her own contentions about public and private and those of other scholars working in this area like Robert K. Martin, M. Jimmie Killingsworth, and Michael Moon, she makes some important observations in "Whitman and the Homosexual Republic" (*Walt Whitman: The Centennial Essays*, pp. 153–71). Versions of the interpretation have been rendered before, but Erkkila's elaborations substantially extend the insights that "argue the fluidity of Whitman's articulation of same-sex love among men as the language of democracy intersects with other languages, including the languages of temperance, sexual reform, artisan republicanism, labor radicalism, phrenology, heterosexual love, familial and specifically father-son relationships, and spirituality." Her "Whitman and the American Empire" (*Walt Whitman of Mickle Street*, pp. 54–69) studies some of the same paradoxes and contradictions brought to light by Golden; Erkkila focuses on the fact that "Whitman's celebration of an ideal artisan republic of strong, healthy, and virtuous farmers and laborers becomes simultaneously bound up with a national imperial policy of expansion, conquest, and violation." By contrast, in "Whitman and the Erotics of Lyric" (*AL* 65 [1993]: 703–30) Onno Oerlemans contests the conclusions of "politicizing" critics like Erkkila "that Whitman's politics amount to a 'position,'" because "what is important and original in Whitman's poetry is its representation not of the process of forming ideology but of resisting such formations" as he struggles to depict "relations of what he calls the 'Me' to the 'Not-me.'" A thorough assessment of contests such as these over Whitman's politics and the meanings of his sexuality is "Whitman and His Doubles: Division and Union in *Leaves of Grass* and Its Critics" (*AmLH* 6: 119–39), Mark Maslan's review essay of books by Erkkila, Kerry C. Larson, Moon, and a collection by Martin.

In "Whitman and the Politics of Identity" (*Walt Whitman: The Centennial Essays*, pp. 172–81) Robert K. Martin plumbs some of the paradoxes pertaining to sexual identities, and in the process he gives a very complicated interpretation of fluid intersections and confusions between the public and private as he explains, among other things, Whitman's distancing of himself from John Addington Symonds and his homosexual "exuberance in the early editions of *Leaves of Grass* and his duplicitousness in 1890": "Poem 19 is a crucial moment in 'Calamus' because it attempts to mediate between two models of gay male sexuality, one based on ideal friendship and one based on repeated anonymous encounters, because it locates a public act of affection between men as a political act in America, as such an act remains even today." Reminding us that in the 19th century "deviant sexual behavior was regarded as a vice so abhorrent that it was scarcely ever mentioned," Louis Simpson adroitly analyzes "Strategies of Sex in Whitman's Poetry" (*Walt Whitman of Mickle Street,* pp. 28–37), matter-of-factly explaining how Whitman's generalizing the "love of one man for another" into the love "of men for one another" is a tactic desirous of acceptance and played into a general ignorance of homosexuality on which the poet could rely. What Whitman wanted, for himself and for America, as David S. Reynolds points out in "Whitman and Nineteenth-Century Views of Gender and Sexuality" (*Walt Whitman of Mickle Street,* pp. 38–45), was sexuality untainted by the sensationalistic debaucheries so prominent in popular culture writers like George Thompson. "Throughout his poetry, his exploration of sexual organs and functions is guided by his impulse to remove sex from the lurid indirections of the popular love plot." By moving us "from the shameful body-parts of our first parents to the body of the text, especially the shameful part of the text, and its coverings," Linda Munk considers biblical influences and Whitman's hallowing of sex in "Giving Umbrage: The Song of Songs Which is Whitman's" (*Journal of Literature and Theology* 7 [1993]: 50–65). By contrast, in "Walt Whitman Camping" (pp. 113–20), posthumously published in *Camp Grounds: Style and Homosexuality,* ed. David Bergman (Mass., 1993), Karl Keller asserts "that the persona that the 'Chanter of Personality' slips into is often a camp one," and concludes with a characteristically flamboyant but nonetheless insightful query, "Does it go too far to suggest that Walt Whitman is the Mae West of American literature?"

Explorations of the politics of identity do not all focus on the sexual, and Whitman scholars also probed his perceptions, "snapshots," portraits of labor. In "The Politics of Labor and the Poet's Work: A Reading of 'A Song for Occupation'" (*Walt Whitman: The Centennial Essays,* pp. 120–32) Alan Trachtenberg asks how labor figures in Whitman's work, noting (as does Golden) that Whitman "hated the system of bondage [slavery] not mainly because it oppressed black people . . . but because it threatened white laborers." Musing on the intertwinings of Whitman's conceptions of work and his poetry, Trachtenberg concludes that "from the contradiction between use and exchange he extracted a heroic celebration of labor as life, work as art," asking "what does it mean to be occupied, to possess an occupation, to repossess oneself within an occupation?" In "Whitman's Visionary Politics" (*Walt Whitman of Mickle Street*, pp. 94–108) Trachtenberg extends questions that necessarily arise when examining Whitman's celebration of white laborers, questions about what he "*means* by politics, by democracy," and about "how" those meanings figure in what makes Whitman so continually alive for us: the power of his poetry "to beguile, to magnetize, to transform." Celebrating a quarrel he hopes will never be resolved between those who would historicize Whitman and those for whom his poetic presence is *supra*historical, M. Wynn Thomas in "Whitman and the Dreams of Labor" (*Walt Whitman: The Centennial Essays*, pp. 133–52) notes that the poet himself, "one of the best self-levitation acts in the whole poetic business," is in fact responsible for such disputes. Looking to the romanticizing portraits of French painter Jean-François Millet, and adhering to the blind faith of "romantic capitalism" that the rich industrialists became successful simply through their hard work, Whitman likely found "relief from the real intractable labor problems" of his day as well as "grounds for a continuing belief in a 'single society' theory of American life" in the "sentimentalization of labor."

Especially after the Civil War, Whitman found romanticization of the individual and of the ideal of equal opportunity for all necessary to maintain his faith in democracy and its possibilities. In " 'Hankering, Gross, Mystical, Nude': Whitman's 'Self' and the American Tradition" (*Walt Whitman of Mickle Street*, pp. 1–17) Daniel Hoffman traces Whitman's articulation of democratic theory. Commentary on *Leaves of Grass* in "A Backward Glance" clarifies that "equality is known, is apprehended, is felt, by the 'simple, separate person' " and therefore "completely to know, to believe in, to feel that all persons are equal changes the way one apprehends reality." While for many Whitman's love of being photographed is simply part of his relentless self-promotion, Ed Folsom urges readers to think beyond the obvious in "Whitman and the Visual Democracy of Photography" (*Walt Whitman of Mickle Street*, pp. 80–93) and makes a strong case for Whitman's having embraced this new technology as a medium of great democratic possibilities: "Painting's hierarchy of selectivity and distillation gave way to photography's brash informality and speed," and "what may not have seemed worth a painter's time was, for the photographer, always worth a few seconds and a few cents."

Though several essays review literary influences on Whitman in ways that critical stories about American literary history have long made familiar to us, two studies situate him anew, as it were, in relation to Native American traditions. In "Heartbeat: Within the Visionary Tradition" (*Walt Whitman of Mickle Street,* pp. 224–35) Norma Wilson draws distinctions between the mystic, who submits to earthly life, and the visionary, who acts "to bring about the ideal earthly existence," as she connects Whitman's poetic objectives to those of the Aztecs, Navajos, and Lakota, and then analyzes his influence on contemporary writers, particularly Laguna Indian Leslie Marmon Silko. Similarly, James Nolan maintains that the "influences of Whitman and of American Indian poetry seem to blend indetectably into each other, as if they sprang from almost identical poets" in his noteworthy comparative study *Poet-Chief: The Native American Poetics of Walt Whitman and Pablo Neruda* (New Mexico). Another "largely unexplored topic" is Whitman's "legacy to the African-American literary tradition," and in "The Whitman Legacy and the Harlem Renaissance" (*Walt Whitman: The Centennial Essays,* pp. 201–16) George B. Hutchinson probes his profound inspiration of Alain Locke, James Weldon Johnson, and Jean Toomer. Xilao Li opens his "Whitman and Ethnicity" (*Walt Whitman of Mickle Street,* pp. 109–22) assessing Whitman's influence on Native American Joseph Bruchac, black woman poet June Jordan, Jewish writer Michael Gold, Chicano writer Tomas Rivera, and Chinese-American writer Maxine Hong Kingston as he probes writings such as Whitman's "The Spanish Element in Our Nationality," "Real American Red Men," "Ethiopia Saluting the Colors," and his comments on immigration to conclude that "while we can say that Whitman is the voice of ethnic American people, the harbinger of multiculturalism, we do not mean that he is a saint without human weaknesses and failings." An even more thorough investigation of one avenue of Whitman's influence is Li's "Walt Whitman and Asian American Writers" (*WWR* 10 [1993]: 179–94).

Among the most interesting investigations of Whitman's influence on American writers are Denise D. Knight's " 'With the First Grass-Blade': Whitman's Influence on the Poetry of Charlotte Perkins Gilman" (*WWR* 11 [1993]: 18–29) and J. W. Walkington's "Mystical Experience in H.D. and Walt Whitman: An Intertextual Reading of *Tribute to Angels* and 'Song of Myself' " (*WWR* 11: 123–36). Though more conventional in their delineation of the "American" tradition, other useful studies of influence are Daniel Aaron, "Whitman and the Founding Fathers" (*Walt*

Whitman of Mickle Street, pp. 46–53), which situates this brother of "George Washington Whitman, Thomas Jefferson Whitman, and Andrew Jackson Whitman" in relation to those and other pioneers of the American democratic experiment; William H. Shurr's investigation of Whitman's reading of an American history in "The Salvation of America: Walt Whitman's Apocalypticism and Washington Irving's *Columbus*" (*Walt Whitman of Mickle Street,* pp. 142–50); James E. Miller, Jr.'s wide-ranging and "perhaps eccentric" survey of Whitman's influence on Thoreau, Swinburne, Lanier, William James, D. H. Lawrence, Henry Adams, Kate Chopin, and Muriel Rukeyser in "Whitman's Multitudinous Poetic Progeny: Particular and Puzzling Instances" (*Walt Whitman: The Centennial Essays,* pp. 185–200); and Kenneth M. Price's case study of his impact on American novelists in "Whitman's Influence on Hamlin Garland's *Rose of Dutcher's Coolly*" (*Walt Whitman of Mickle Street,* pp. 194–204). Though Amy Lowell wrote that "it would be utter folly to consider that the vignettes in modern work derive from Whitman when Emily Dickinson did the same thing better," Lorelei Cederstrom convincingly analyzes his influence on Lowell and Richard Aldington, as well as Pound and others, in "Walt Whitman and the Imagists" (*Walt Whitman of Mickle Street,* pp. 205–23). And Kenneth M. Price locates the "key narrative strand in [John Dos Passos's] work" and a link to Whitman in the character of "deplorable opinions," "Jay Pignatelli," in "Whitman, Dos Passos, and 'Our Storybook Democracy'" (*Walt Whitman: The Centennial Essays,* pp. 217–26).

Whitman's cosmopolitan milieu is the subject of two richly informative essays: M. Wynn Thomas, "Whitman's Tale of Two Cities" (*AmLH* 6: 633–57); and Christine Stansell, "Whitman at Pfaff's: Commerical Culture, Literary Life, and New York Bohemia at Mid-Century" (*WWR* 10 [1993]: 107–26). Reminding readers that Whitman was a New Yorker, not a New Englander, Roger Asselineau surveys the profound influences on this cosmopolitan poet of Shakespeare, Goethe, Kant, Fichte, Schelling, Hegel, Voltaire, Victor Hugo, and "Dantesque" George Sand in "The European Roots of *Leaves of Grass*" (*Walt Whitman: The Centennial Essays,* pp. 51–60). Asselineau also remarks Whitman's wanting particularly to absorb "'the element of courageous and lofty manhood'" from these sources while eschewing any "antidemocratic doctrines." In "When Walt Whitman Was a Parisian" (*Walt Whitman of Mickle Street,* pp. 270–75) Asselineau offers a more extensive analysis of the influence of Hugo, Rousseau, and Sand as he examines the hold that elements of

exotic France had on the imagination of he who in "Salut au Monde"
wrote "I am a real Parisian."

The two centennial volumes offer several essays spinning off of and
updating Gay Wilson Allen's generation-old *Walt Whitman Abroad*
(1955), one by the good gray scholar himself, "Kornei Chukovsky, Whitman's Russian Translator" (*Walt Whitman of Mickle Street*, pp. 276–82).
In the same collection, Yassen Zassoursky reviews "Whitman's Reception
and Influence in the Soviet Union" (*Walt Whitman of Mickle Street*,
pp. 283–90), while William Heyen examines his influence in Poland in
"Piety and Home in Whitman and Milosz" (*Walt Whitman of Mickle
Street*, pp. 291–96). Others studying Whitman's foreign relations are
Walter Grunzweig, in two essays—"'Teach Me Your Rhythm': The
Poetics of German Lyrical Responses to Whitman" (*Walt Whitman: The
Centennial Essays*, pp. 226–39) and "'Inundated by This Mississippi of
Poetry': Walt Whitman and German Expressionism" (*Walt Whitman of
Mickle Street*, pp. 244–56); S. J. Simkin, "'Extremes Meet': Hopkins and
Walt Whitman" (*MLS* 30: 1–17); V. K. Chari, "Whitman Criticism in
the Light of Indian Poetics" (*Walt Whitman: The Centennial Essays*,
pp. 240–50); Sigurdur A. Magnusson, "Whitman in Iceland" (*Walt
Whitman of Mickle Street*, pp. 236–43); Brooks Toliver, "*Leaves of Grass* in
Claude Debussy's Prose" (*WWR* 11 [1993]: 67–81); Maria Clara Bonetti
Paro, "Walt Whitman in Brazil" (*WWR* 11 [1993]: 57–66); and Alexander
Coleman, "The Ghost of Whitman in Neruda and Borges" (*Walt Whit-
man of Mickle Street*, pp. 257–69).

ii Emily Dickinson

a. Editing and Textual Reproduction   One of the most important
observations made about Dickinson studies occurs in a book with a
section, not a chapter, devoted to her and focusing specifically on her
currency in feminist inquiries. In "The Politics of the Oral and the
Written," the third chapter of *Theory in Its Feminist Travels* (Indiana),
Katie King remarks that various "agents and interests contest for Emily
Dickinson and for what counts as a poem" and that what is at stake are
"contests for the literary canon and assumptions of literary value that the
construction of 'Emily Dickinson' both challenges and embodies." She
thus aptly characterizes Dickinson scholarship in general, not just the
work of those whose especial interests are feminist. Dickinson's writing
technology for the formal presentation of her texts to contemporary

audiences was almost always her own holograph. Print, the preferred technology of transmission for scholars and general readers alike for centuries, was not Dickinson's preferred medium.

Through her correspondences, she "published" at least one-third of her poems, and she sewed 40 manuscripts books of poetry which she tacitly bequeathed to posterity. After the photographic presentation of these handmade books in R. W. Franklin's edition *The Manuscript Books of Emily Dickinson* (1981), interest in what the manuscripts reveal as material artifacts of her poetic process and progress has increased exponentially. Specifically, critical energies have focused on Dickinson's attention to the stationery page and ways in which it features her pen and pencil marks, her conception of the lyric poem, and her notions about its relationship to and function as a letter. A detail of scholarly enterprise serves as a poignant symbol of this surge of scholarly interest in the poet's actual documents rather than in the print translations which for a century have served as the primary site of critical inquiry: however unintentionally, the logo of *The Emily Dickinson Journal*—an artist's reconstruction which imitates Emily Dickinson's holograph, as if she had actually written out precisely this phrase—signals the new view of her holographic designs as constitutive parts of her poetics.

Some of the most exciting interrogations of Dickinson's manuscript productions are those of Jeanne Holland, Jerome McGann, Ellen Louise Hart, and Marta Werner, who each examine the material artifacts and their meaning-making physicalities, and whose work generatively intersects with Susan Howe's focus on "visual intentionality," featured again in "These Flames and Generosities of the Heart: Emily Dickinson and the Illogic of Sumptuary Values," a chapter in her *The Birth-mark: Unsettling the Wilderness in American Literary History* (Wesleyan, 1993). In *HOW(ever)* (1986) and *Sulfur* (1991), Howe has made these arguments, or their prototypes, before. Yet situated amid her reveries on Anne Hutchinson, Mary Rowlandson, and on the "ordained" history of New England by Winthrop and Mather, Howe's interpretations more persuasively than ever contend that "the issue of editorial control is directly connected to the attempted erasure of antinomianism in our culture" as it appropriates and domesticates wayward writings like Emily Dickinson's.

Essays by both Holland and McGann appear in *Cultural Artifacts and the Production of Meaning: The Page, the Image, and the Body*, ed. Margaret J. M. Ezell and Katherine O'Brien O'Keeffe (Michigan).

Holland's "Scraps, Stamps, and Cutouts: Emily Dickinson's Domestic Technologies of Publication" (pp. 139–81) astutely chronicles the poet's progressive refinements of "her own domestic technologies of publication": she chose to "sew together her own fascicles (rather than purchasing ready-made blank notebooks)," then to include "more and more variant readings in the fascicles"; sharing her work with her contemporaries, she circumscribed "her readership to family, friends, and chosen outsiders," refused to print, and ultimately wrote "on household detritus." Holland's emphasis on the shift "away from making The Book in fascicles toward materially locating her poems in the private home" discloses new ways in which Dickinson's "late work interrogates the relation of sexuality and textuality," her "joyful play with writing's construction of the body." Holland scrutinizes Dickinson's appending "Alone and in a Circumstance" (P 1472) with both a three-cent locomotive stamp commemorating the completion of the transcontinental railroad and cutouts from a *Harper's Magazine* review of George Sand—the words "GEORGE SAND" and "Mauprat" scissored to make "legs" for the stamp. By this view, the textual body, the cutout, is prone on the page (and the stamp is pasted sideways, its top to the left). Of course, the locomotive stamp is not just a random bit of Dickinson's culture, for Edward Dickinson worked to bring the railroad to Amherst and died while making a speech about a railroad tunnel. Noting these particular connotations, Holland's analytical explication deftly exploits this image's connotations that from the "father's perspective," symbolized by an engine of industrialist triumph, "the daughter's texts . . . are thrown out of kilter, and vice versa." And she elaborates her critique by noting George Sand's similarities to Susan Dickinson and Susan's incisive, privileged understanding of "Dickinson's resistance to printing." Profoundly commonsensical, Holland's argument is that in Dickinson we see two competing ideological positions—that of the male creator and that of the female tending to the domestic sphere—physically embodied in literary productions which increasingly incorporate remnants of the "private" into "publications" of her writings.

In "Composition as Explanation (of Modern and Postmodern Poetries)" (pp. 101–38) McGann likewise reflects on the "very different kind of 'household' editions that Dickinson was producing" concurrently with those formally published by Houghton Mifflin of Longfellow, Whittier, and other Fireside poets. As do Hart, Howe, Holland, Werner, and I, McGann believes in the significance in the dramatic shifts that begin to evolve so clearly in Fascicle 9 and are evident throughout the 30 following, shifts in the relation between scriptural style and metrical units and in Dickinson's "performance" script. When "Dickinson decided to use her text page as a scene for dramatic interplays between a poetics of the eye and a poetics of the ear," "modernism's subsequent experiments with its many 'visible languages' are forecast." In the first eight fascicles Dickinson's holographic copying imitated the conventions of print and the way in which she saw her lyric was bound by the "horizon of publication"; in Fascicle 9 and following, her horizon is the manuscript page, "in the textuality of personal correspondence," and she began to see her poems in that epistolary medium. McGann admonishes editors—"editing Dickinson, these [visual] scripts [of lineation, punctuation] must be faithfully followed, whether the visible language of the texts appears to us as prose or as poetry"—and explicates Johnson's genre-determined overriding of Dickinson's scriptural conflations via her third letter to Higginson featuring the poem "As if I asked a / Common Alms." As Ellen Louise Hart also points out in "Poetic License" (*Women's Review of Books* II, iv: 24), Thomas H. Johnson indents and regularizes the lineation of writings he deems to be poetry and does not follow Dickinson's scriptural, epistolary form. Thus in Johnson and Theodora Ward's edition *The Letters of Emily Dickinson* (Harvard, 1958), poetry is markedly set off from prose according to the conventions of typesetting, whether Dickinson arranged her lines that way or not. Since after the earliest stages of her writing she usually did not arrange her writings according to print-determined indentations and predictable lineations, Johnson and Ward's print translation obscures the extent to which her writing practices blended the genres. McGann's essay is a revised version of one by the same title in *Black Riders: The Visible Language of Modernism* (Princeton, 1993), and portions also appear—together with some of his commentary on Dickinson that concludes "Modernism and the Renaissance of Printing," the first chapter of *Black Riders*—in "Emily Dickinson's Visible Language" (*EDJ* 2, ii [1993]: 40–57).

Studies like these of the actual manuscripts are the most valuable contributions to editing Dickinson's works during these two years, although the University of North Carolina Press announced its publication of *New Poems of Emily Dickinson*, ed. William H. Shurr with Anna Dunlap and Emily Grey Shurr (1993) with much fanfare. The title suggests a new cache of previously undiscovered manuscripts, and Shurr fully exploits this language of retrieval and discovery. These "new poems" are not, however, taken from manuscripts newly found in someone's attic but from the texts of the *Letters* edited by Johnson and Ward. The "facts" presented in this volume are often questionable: "poems" are often not "new" but had been previously identified by other scholars in dissertations or recent articles or books; and Shurr persistently distorts their epistolary contexts to bolster his belief in a "Master" lover for whom Dickinson pined (e.g., he edits poetic lines from a letter and excises names to suggest that a condolence note to sister-in-law Susan on the passing of her eight-year-old son, Gilbert, is in fact an elegy for Reverend Charles Wadsworth). However sloppy the scholarship, Shurr takes full advantage of a decade of renewed interest in the manuscripts, especially in Dickinson's blending poetry and prose so effectively that, as Johnson remarked in his introduction to the letters, the reader often doubts "where the letter leaves off and the poem begins." Since Shurr edits Johnson's print translations, not Emily Dickinson's manuscripts, this volume would more appropriately be titled "Shurr-Johnson Poems, based on the letters of Emily Dickinson."

Lewis Turco is much more clear about his reformulation of Dickinson's epistolary lines into poems when he offers the title "Poems and Centos from Lines in Emily Dickinson's Letters" to describe one section of *Emily Dickinson: Woman of Letters* (SUNY, 1993). The poems are Turco's, and he represents them as such as he uses Dickinson's words and adds a few of his own to produce 60 lyrics whose subjects are sunsets, sunrises, snowfalls, seasonal changes, housekeeping, birds, holidays, calendars, and clocks. Readers may find this use of Dickinson's words off-putting, but finally Turco's practice demonstrates, from yet another perspective, how the epistolary and poetic imbue all her writing. Some of his ventures, like "The Pearl Jail," about winter, are especially entertaining.

Another Turco section title, "Essays on the Subject by Various Hands," refers to essays by Ellen Louise Hart, Jeanne Holland, David W. Hill, and Marta Werner. In "The Encoding of Homoerotic Desire" (pp. 99–128; reprinted from *TSWL* 9 [1990]: 251–72) Hart begins by identifying a late letter to Susan Dickinson, "Morning / might come / by Accident – / Sister –" (L 912), as a letter-poem, and she situates it among a score or more other letter-poems from this creative wellspring of correspondence. She then persuasively demonstrates how central, how thoroughly intertwined this emotional, erotic, spiritual, intellectual en-

tanglement was to Dickinson's poetic productions. In " 'Knock with /
tremor': When Daughters Revise 'Dear Father' " (pp. 84–97) Holland
analyzes the larger cultural significances of a letter-poem written upon
her father's death as she explains its challenges to "patrilinearity and
power" and her pirouette between "paternal law" and the semiotic of the
"erased mother." Hill's "Words Doing: Dickinson's Language as Autonomous Action" (pp. 129–46) probes Dickinson's epistolary poetics to argue
that these linguistic framings served as windows and doors which
"pierced beyond the world of contexts." Werner's "The Shot Bird's
Progress: Emily Dickinson's 'Master Letters' " (pp. 147–52) interprets
these pored-over documents for their literary significance instead of for
unreliable biographical suggestions, and in an eight-section operatic suite
she reveals how Dickinson's transgressions of generic boundaries redefine
boundaries of the self by exposing the fictions of endings and other
borders. In these essays and poetic appropriations the generic instability
of Dickinson's texts is underscored, and the notion of "definitive" identification neatly distinguishing poems from letters debunked.

Interpreting Dickinson's fascicles, using her "books" and not her lyrics
as the primary units of study, is a burgeoning area of Dickinson studies,
and in *Emily Dickinson's Fascicles: Method and Meaning* (Penn. State)
Dorothy Oberhaus argues that Fascicle 40, the last bound book in
Franklin's *Manuscript Books,* is both a culmination of Dickinson's poetic
endeavors and profound religious statement. From this view, the fascicles
are a long single work recounting Dickinson's spiritual and poetic pilgrimage, and Fascicle 40 a "long dramatic monologue" of "epic dimensions" comparable to *The Waste Land.* Whether one agrees with
Oberhaus's religious interpretations, her elucidations of the interdepen-
dencies of poems within the last fascicle, as well as of the interconnections of the 40 fascicles with one another, persuasively elaborate the
rapidly growing consensus (sharply dissenting from the long-entrenched
view that her poetics were static) that Dickinson's poetic practices and
sensibilities profoundly evolved over decades of writing. By focusing on
one fascicle, Oberhaus critiques the creative methods and production
designs of the entire corpus of manuscript books.

All of these books and articles feature photographic reproductions of
the manuscripts, depictions invaluable in their presentation of Dickinson's various holographs, layouts, and stationery choices. Taken together,
these implicitly argue for wider availability of such facsimile representations of all of the Dickinson documents, not just her manuscript books.

b. Reception   Another important intervention troubling critical commonplaces about Dickinson is Willis Buckingham's "Poetry Readers and Reading in the 1890s: Emily Dickinson's First Reception," pp. 164–79 in *Readers in History: Nineteenth-Century American Literature and the Contexts of Response,* ed. James L. Machor (Johns Hopkins, 1993). This essay both condenses and extends the evidentiary argument of Buckingham's *Emily Dickinson's Reception in the 1890s: A Documentary History* (1989) as it refutes the mistaken, but nevertheless widely held, critical notion that Dickinson was poorly received and misunderstood on initial publication of print volumes of work at the turn of the last century. In fact, she was widely praised for her "masculine" genius, occasionally compared to Thoreau, more frequently to Whitman, but most of all to Emerson. At the same time that she was admired for her forceful thought, she was loved for her womanly feeling and ability to draw readers into communion with her. Her unconventional forms, which were usually the subject of any review's faults, were to many a "refreshingly aboriginal presence in a literary world" already crowded with adept formalists. In "Editorial Policy in *The Poems of Emily Dickinson, Third Series*" (*EDJ* 3, ii: 56–77) Caroline Maun examines Mabel Loomis Todd's changes in editorial policy for the third volume of Dickinson's poetry published in the 1890s, including the deletion of entire stanzas from 21 poems in order to mute unladylike tones and to mask irreverence toward social conventions and traditions. Though useful, the article suffers because Maun writes as if no other recent work than hers has evaluated Todd's practices, when in fact several substantial articles have been published over the past decade; had she taken these into account, her argument might have been even more advanced. Besides this essay, several other noteworthy pieces in the *Emily Dickinson Journal,* a fine forum for scholarly exchange, are unnecessarily limited because they do not join critical conversations in progress.

Challenging the critical commonplace that Dickinson did not confront the public concerns of her day and was withdrawn into a rather dour reclusion is *Comic Power in Emily Dickinson* (Texas, 1993), which Suzanne Juhasz, Cristanne Miller, and I coauthored. "Comedy and Audience in Emily Dickinson's Poetry" (pp. 1–25) and "Comic Power" (pp. 137–40), the first and last chapters, introduce and draw collective conclusions from our individual examinations of Dickinson's probative feminist critiques of patriarchal power, of its attendant suffocating social conventions, and of its coercive political, sexual, religious, and literary institutions. Stressing the necessity of audience involvement to enact comedy and humor, we study Dickinson's gleeful, sly, ironic, bawdy performances, which employ "formal comic structures, humor, wit, teasing, parody, visual and verbal cartooning, the grotesque, satire," and more.

In "The Big Tease" (pp. 26–62) Juhasz investigates Dickinson's trope of teasing that is not simply a trope, arguing that "with tease rather than with direct attack, Dickinson questions and negotiates [patriarchal] power relationships as they are traditionally structured in terms of hierarchies and dominance" and noting that "teasing is defense as well as invitation." As her readers are well aware, Dickinson's teasers assume many poses with which audiences are invited to play—"like a rural Eliza Doolittle," or ballerina, or hick, or bad girl—so that "both reader and poet might be ransomed from complete acculturation, coming together to make her (our) new meanings." Presenting a "mistress of excess and of the grotesque" in "The Humor of Excess" (pp. 103–36), Miller observes that "through the very exuberance or weirdness of her expression . . . Dickinson creates moments of linguistic and narrative incongruity, disruption, chaos; yet because these same poems ultimately exult in the individual's powers of endurance and the poet's power of expression . . . they are humorous rather than merely frightening." Concurring with Karl Keller's assertion that the 20th-century term "camp" most accurately describes Dickinson's exaggerated style, figures, images, and sexual posing, Miller concludes that the humor of excess "demands excess from the reader: only if he or she is also willing to let go of prescribed boundaries separating the serious, the zany, the grotesque, the sentimental will the reader gain entrance to this marginal edge of wildness that constitutes humor in a number of Dickinson's poems." Like the manuscript studies discussed above and my previous work, my chapter "The Poet as Cartoonist" (pp. 63–102) examines artifacts of Dickinson's creative processes, four of which she sent to Susan Dickinson and one of which she sent to her brother, Austin. "Though to call her sketches and layouts 'cartoons' makes liberal use of the term, such liberties have been taken since the advent of Dickinson study: to print and distribute the Amherst poet's private 'publications' is to make liberal use of the term 'literature,' which we conventionally associate with the productions of writers who, like Dickinson's contemporaries Hawthorne, Whitman, and Stowe, work specifically to see their writings mechanically reproduced to as wide an audience as possible." The cartooning layouts and sketches I explicate specifically "challenge the literary, political, and family institutions that have helped reproduce the cartoon-like image of a woman poet commodified," and the analyses are situated in relation to humorous illustrations that Dickinson would have seen in *Harper's New Monthly Magazine* and *Frank Leslie's Illustrated Newspaper;* analyses of her "cartooning" comedic linguistic sketches are situated in relation to storytelling series of paintings like Thomas Cole's *The Course of Empire* or *The Voyage of Life* with which the Dickinson households would have been familiar.

In "Emily Dickinson's Volcanic Punctuation" (*EDJ* 2, i [1993]: 22–46) Kamilla Denman explores Dickinson's meaning-making punctuation, maintaining (and thereby implicitly nodding to feminist critics such as Adrienne Rich and Sandra Gilbert and Susan Gubar) that the volcano is metaphor for "woman writing from within the male organ(ization) itself," and that it describes the poet's dynamic and extensive (from nearly excessive to restrained) use of the "dash." Denman's generative study, plumbing musical and linguistic connotations, ignores the holographic signs appropriative of rhetorical notation and thus does not really contextualize Dickinson's use within 19th-century practices; she only gestures toward two later handbooks (1876 and 1916), neither of which could have informed Dickinson's writing practices of the '50s and '60s. Also, though she claims to be current on the scholarship concerning Dickinson's punctuation, Denman is apparently unaware of extensive interrogations by Susan Howe and others working with the manuscripts. Though engaging because of its comparative analyses, Jay Ladin's "Breaking the Line: Emily Dickinson and William Carlos Williams" (*EDJ* 3, i: 41–58) suffers from a similar lack of critical contextualization by overlooking Howe's, Hart's, and McGann's fruitful examinations of Dickinson's strategic line breaks.

By contrast, in " 'This World is not Conclusion': Dickinson, Amherst, and 'the local conditions of the soul' " (*EDJ* 3, ii: 38–51) Benjamin Lease situates Dickinson's religious attitudes within a complex assessment of those of her contemporaries and argues that "a greater awareness of the daring unorthodoxies of Amherst's spiritual leaders enlarges our understanding of Emily Dickinson's distinctive voice—her music of sacred play, her language experiments, her haunted and haunting visions of nature (outer and inner)." Lease's fleshing out of her religious milieu complements Rowena Revis Jones's earlier argument in "A Taste for

'Poison': Dickinson's Departure from Orthodoxy" (*EDJ* 2, i [1993]: 47–
64). Jones contextualizes Dickinson's religious attitudes by recovering
the influence of the radical Unitarian Theodore Parker's humanizing of
the divine figure Jesus Christ, holding him up not as divine but as
exemplary, and stressing that humans must work out their own salvation.
Demonstrating the abolitionist Parker's undeniable influence on Bowles
and Higginson, as well as Dickinson's congenial familiarity with his
opinions, Jones's essay implicitly argues for a more thorough investigation of her convictions concerning the slavery issue that she supposedly
ignored, a literary "fact" increasingly suspect (especially since we now
know that three of her contemporaneous publications were in the *Drum
Beat,* a Northern fund-raising paper; see Karen Dandurand, "New Dickinson Civil War Publications," *AL* 56 [1984]: 17–27).

Interrogating "Emily Dickinson and the Limit of War" (*EDJ* 3, ii: 1–
18), Tyler B. Hoffman projects a nuanced sense of Dickinson's relationship as alien civilian to a war in which she could not participate, his most
compelling insights phonetically linking the last word in the line "The
name – of it – is 'Autumn' " (P 506) with "Antietam." Ironically, proposing to correct Shira Wolosky's overarching assessment of Dickinson's
"total identification" with the war, and to consider especially Dickinson's
status as woman, Hoffman overlooks the fact that the country for which
she could not fight was one that did not even grant her voting rights. Yet
his supple moves between analyzing stunned responses to Matthew
Brady's photographs and Dickinson's awareness of the war's gory horrors
perpetuate an important critical intervention and a new cycle of reception, acknowledging her "interest in events of public history."

Offering her own illuminating spin on the kind of argument more
powerfully made by Jane Donahue Eberwein and Joanne Dobson,
Shirley Sharon-Zisser argues in "To 'See – Comparatively': Emily Dickinson's Use of Simile" (*EDJ* 3, i: 59–84) that "Dickinson's similes may be
grouped into two broad thematic categories: 'centripetal' and 'centrifugal,' " signs of a "dialectical process by means of which limitation is
transformed to an advantage." In "Emily Dickinson's Poetics of Translation" (*EDJ* 3, i: 85–104) Kim Hosman extends Juhasz's previous observations about Dickinson's subversive doublings to remark that a "dynamic
tension exists between Dickinson's refusal to submit to the vocabulary of
Calvinism . . . and her creation of a poetics that also acknowledges value
and beauty in that vocabulary . . . to make permeable, at least, the
socially imposed boundaries language places on subjectivity."

c. Contexts The topic of the 1992 Emily Dickinson International Society conference was "Translating Emily Dickinson." Some proceedings were published as a number of *The Emily Dickinson Journal* (2, ii [1993]); all probe contextualizations of the poet and her work, and essays by Sandra Gilbert and Cheryl Walker serve as contrasting bookends for the volume. An exhilarating reverie on eight definitions of the word "translate," Gilbert's " 'If a lion could talk . . .': Dickinson Translated" (pp. 1–13) introduces the range, depth, and diversity of critical endeavors featured at the conference and in this special conference issue— "to express in another language, systematically retaining the original sense"; "to put in simpler terms, explain"; "to convey from one form to another, convert"; "to transfer (a bishop) to another see"; "to forward or retransmit (a telegraphic message)"; "to convey to heaven without natural death"; "motion of a body in which every point of the body moves parallel to, and the same distance as, every other point of the body"; "to transport, enrapture." In "Teaching Dickinson as a Gen(i)us: Emily Among the Women" (pp. 172–80) Cheryl Walker contextualizes Dickinson's poetry with that of the women poets of her day and argues against seeing the long-celebrated poet as "exceptional" and thus the "only kangaroo" worthy of study, while she argues for more broad-based interrogations of the long-dismissed women poets who were Dickinson's contemporaries.

The other studies published in this issue of *EDJ* constitute a broad intellectual base indeed. Jerome McGann's is discussed above. Gracefully illustrating Dickinson's literary affinities in "Emily Dickinson's Poetic Covenant" (pp. 14–37), Roland Hagenbüchle remarks that "the European reader is amazed to discover that Dickinson's work functions like a sounding board of much that is central to his own culture: medieval texts (such as Langland and Dante), Shakespeare, English Metaphysical and pre-Romantic poetry as well as the Romantic and Victorian writers," and that this "deeply provincial writer" is also "transatlantic, even cosmopolitan."

The rest of the papers attest to Hagenbuchle's assertion. "Emily Dickinson's Books" (pp. 58–65) by Dorothy Huff Oberhaus argues that Dickinson's readings in world literature—and particularly of the Bible— are often crucial to comprehending her poems. Judith Farr's "Disclosing Pictures: Emily Dickinson's Quotations from the Paintings of Thomas Cole, Frederick Church, and Holman Hunt" (pp. 66–77) shows not only that Dickinson knew about but also that she may well have "profited thematically and imagistically from some visual texts of her own day." In "Emily Dickinson and *The Indicator:* A Transcendental Frolic" (pp. 78–96) Barton St. Armand yokes elements of Dickinson's sublime wit, her integration of romantic and Transcendentalist thought into her poetic project, and her "consummate appreciation of the ridiculous" to the elegant Amherst College monthly magazine which first published her nonsense prose-poetic Valentine "Awake ye muses nine, sing me a strain divine" (P 1). To plumb Dickinson's strategies of defamiliarization, Alice Fulton defines the "foreign" as "connotations of wrongness or insubordination that surround the strange" and as violations of "cultural and aesthetic assumptions concerning propriety, cohesiveness, and proportion" in "Outlandish Powers: Dickinson's Capsizals of Genre and Tone" (pp. 97–103). Three essays show how familiar indeed Dickinson's poetry can seem to natives on foreign shores: Yoko Shimazaki, "A Perspective on Reading Dickinson in Japan" (pp. 104–8); Masako Takeda, " 'After great pain, a formal feeling comes –': The Problems of Translating Dickinson's 'Poetry' into Contemporary Japanese 'Verse' " (pp. 153–59); and Dorothy Z. Baker, "A Russian Translation/Imitation of Emily Dickinson: 'After great pain, a formal feeling comes –' " (pp. 147–52). In "Challenges of Portraying Emily Dickinson in William Luce's Play *The Belle of Amherst*" (pp. 124–29) Maravene Loeschke, author of a biographical novel about Martha Dickinson Bianchi, outlines seven challenges to the actress who translates Dickinson's life to the stage. And in "Translation and the Emily Dickinson Lexicon" (pp. 130–46) Cynthia L. Hallen and Laura M. Harvey note that "because Dickinson uses multiple lexical connections to tie the words of a poem together into an unusually dense network," and because "sometimes words relate cross-textually from one poem to another," an unabridged Webster's 1841 *American Dictionary of the English Language* is imperative for the translator; thus they argue for the necessity of *The Emily Dickinson Lexicon,* which "will have entries for all of the words in Dickinson's poems" and which Hallen is in the process of assembling.

Two of the liveliest contributions to this special conference issue are by a well-known literary biographer and an eminent poet-critic. In "[Im]pertinent Constructions of Body and Self: Dickinson's Use of the Romantic Grotesque" (pp. 109–23) Cynthia Griffin Wolff "wonders whether we have not gone too far" in the critical sophistication that separates the life from the work, "whether . . . we are missing something when we do not respond to the *apparently* 'biographical' element in the

poetry." Exploring Dickinson's riddling and use of the Romantic grotesque to plumb psychic extremes, Wolff astutely speculates that the
need to see her as "mildly mad or marginally hysterical" may likely be a
displacement of the "pain of insight" and of "deep fears about the issues
that her poetry explores." Alicia Ostriker's most stimulating intertextual
analysis of Dickinson's play with her culture's most sacred text, "Re-
playing the Bible: My Emily Dickinson" (pp. 160–71), extends Ostriker's
already wide-ranging studies of women rewriting culture. Connecting
Emily Dickinson's work as poet "re-imagining the Bible" to her own "as a
poet and critic in the field of feminist religion, or the higher sacreligious-
ness," Ostriker is especially interested in poems that impudently challenge God and that even, like "It always felt to me – a wrong" (P 597), go
so far as to describe Him as pouty and petulant, as well as others that
feminize "him." Before offering two poems of her own, which retell
biblical stories from erased perspectives—"The Songs of Miriam" and
"The Story of Joshua"—Ostriker challenges anyone who would presume
to speak Dickinson's religious beliefs: "To read Dickinson on God
(etcetera), then, is to divest oneself of the desire for a single 'correct'
interpretation of scripture, to accept willy-nilly a plurality of interpretations, and to begin to realize that the Bible *asks* to be read like this, to be
plurally and not singly interpreted." Complementing this feminist analysis is Lee Upton's "Coming to God: Notes on Dickinson, Bogan,
Cixous" (*Denver Quarterly* 27, iv [1993]: 83–94).

Several other articles contextualizing or contesting contextualizations
of Dickinson appear in other numbers of the *Emily Dickinson Journal*. In
"Emily Dickinson's Circumference: Figuring a Blind Spot in the Romantic Tradition" Laura Gribben interprets Dickinson's insistence on "Circumference" as a challenge to Romanticism's tenet that "humankind can
transcend material reality" to become part of God (*EDJ* 2, i [1993]: 1–21).
A consciously female vision, Dickinson's focus is on the absence of the
sublime in the here and now. Likewise persuaded of Dickinson's persistent critique of patriarchal valuations, Joanna Yin in " 'Arguments of
Pearl': Dickinson's Response to Puritan Semiology" (*EDJ* 2, i [1993]: 65–
83) contends that the poet "unmasks the illusory power and compassion
of the Calvinist God by denaturalizing Calvinist semiology, a way of
knowing" that hierarchizes divine over human and male over female. By
" 'Regard[ing] a Mouse' in Dickinson's Poems and Letters" (*EDJ* 2, i
[1993]: 84), Susan M. Anderson examines the poet's complex manipulations of gendered hierarchies by means of her repeated exploitations of

the figure of the deceptively negligible domestic pest. Investigating how Dickinson designates the "problematic notion of context as an aspect of the feminine predicament" in "No Frame of Reference: The Absence of Context in Emily Dickinson's Poetry" (*EDJ* 3, ii: 19–37), Lynn Shakinovsky probes the "tension between the constant searching and not finding, the presence and absence, the telling and not telling, all of which result in the peculiar mixture of secretiveness and exhibitionism so characteristic of the poems."

Refreshing for its storytelling, its overlapping autobiographical and biographical narratives, is " 'My George Eliot' and My Emily Dickinson" (*EDJ* 3, i: 24–40), in which Karen Richardson Gee compares her frustrated and fascinated appropriations of biographical elements attached to the author Dickinson to those of Eliot that the Amherst poet made function for her own poetic and personal ambitions. In "From Aaron 'Drest' to Dickinson's 'Queen': Protestant Typology in Herbert and Dickinson" (*EDJ* 3, i: 1–23) Diane Gabrielson Scholl revisits analytical comparisons and unwitting conflations (by Millicent Todd Bingham) of George Herbert and Dickinson to examine how "her poems gain significant tension from the implicit struggle between biblical text" and her own "countertext." That "countertext" is perhaps most dramatically embodied in Dickinson's hand-sewn books, and John Gerlach joins the chorus of arguments to regard the fascicles as "designed groupings" in "Reading Dickinson: Bolts, Hounds, the Variorum, and Fascicle 39" (*EDJ* 3, ii: 78–99). Arguing for complexity of interpretation that, in Whitmanian fashion, invites contradiction as it does not insist on bending poems to particular thematic or theoretical interpretations, Gerlach concludes that the "strongest argument for taking the fascicles seriously is that unlike other forms of organizing her poems, these groupings do not reduce or distort the individual poems but rather allow them to be at once themselves, firmly paradoxical and ironic, while interacting with other poems, gaining energy from contrast or similarity." Happily, "generative" and "admitting of more, not less, possibility" aptly characterize Gerlach's argument, as well as these most productive years of Dickinson scholarship.

iii General Studies: Whitman and Dickinson

The standard comparative critical strategy of examining the 19th century's two most celebrated poets in tandem yielded several studies, some of which probed well-worn geographies, a couple of which explored new terrain, and all of which generated some refreshing insights.

In "Walt Whitman's Six Children" in his *Fictions of Form in American Poetry* (Princeton, 1993), Stephen Cushman plumbs the contradictions inherent in Whitman's emphatic assertions that "aesthetic formalism leads directly to disconnection from America." Railing against the artifice that tethers American poetry to the rhymes and meters of Europe even as he invokes cultivated nature (gardens, groves, orchards) as metaphor for his ideal poetic form, Whitman launches spirited, iambic defenses of poetry that ignores rules of meter and form, indeed of artifice itself. Cushman adroitly connects such protesting-too-much to Whitman's 1876 caveat in the preface for the centennial *Leaves of Grass* that the "special meaning" of *Calamus* "mainly resides in its political significance," which he appends 14 years later with his outrageous claim to John Addington Symonds of having fathered six children. During the centennial year Whitman uses America to shield his poetic project from dismissiveness regarding the homosexual, just as he invokes nationalism elsewhere to defend against overwrought aestheticism. By his example in both instances Whitman shows how to fictionalize form and sexuality and thus effectively resist any reductive shortchanging that would render either without spirit.

In "The Broken Mathematics of Emily Dickinson" in the same volume Cushman argues that Dickinson's poetic form reflects the physical world, which is not a "mathematically harmonious framework" but broken, disrupted, and disrupting, and which threatens "congruence, likeness, integrity." Trying to salvage these with her "poetics of mending," Dickinson's rigorous unique formalism reveals the seams among constituencies rather than fusing incongruities into some mythical seamless whole. Her fiction of America, which emphasizes that it is isolated from others by seas, aligns with her own appropriations of conventions of form which simultaneously embody the very gulfs her poetry attempts to bridge. Cushman's appreciations of the powerful fictiveness of both poets attend to their poetics in ways that refuse easy conclusions about their objectives and that open up their writings, reminding readers that even nationalism, Cushman's (and our) purported arc of inquiry, is itself a fiction of our critical endeavors.

In "Personalism and Fragmentation in Whitman's *Leaves of Grass* (1855–1860)" in his *Splintered Worlds: Fragmentation and the Ideal of Diversity in the Work of Emerson, Melville, Whitman, and Dickinson*

(Northeastern, 1993) Robert M. Greenberg examines Whitman's efforts
to "answer alienation by connecting the individual with the deep forces
of existence" by studying four variants of "Personalism" that imbue the
poems with "emotional power and sustained perspective": mystic/
mythic, homosexual, tragic, fragmentary. Greenberg thus investigates
Whitman's mining of the self's interiorities while simultaneously seeking
to encompass and engage as much multiplicity as possible. Most valuable
in interrogating Whitman's acceptance of diverse male white personalities, this study perhaps unintentionally acknowledges its own glossing
over of "harsh social divisions and unpleasant individualism," for race
and gender do not inform this argument. Greenberg is most acute when
speculating about the diversities of the poet's homosexualities. Dickinson, however, addresses alienation via "particularism," and in another
chapter, "Disconnection and Reconnection in the Poetry of Emily Dickinson," Greenberg covers familiar territory in probing her strategies of
contraction, her building worlds within poems that "contain a fullness
fashioned from the triumph of language over the abyss." Yet the contrasts
he draws between her "particularism" and his "personalism" offer telling
but not overly neat analytical vocabularies.

In *The Regenerate Lyric: Theology and Innovation in American Poetry*
(Cambridge, 1993) Elisa New examines Whitman's "Great Construction
of the New Bible," territory familiar to studies exploring the Puritan
origins of American selves. Yet she is most insightful analyzing the real
nature of the quarrel between Emerson and Whitman when the former
urged the poet of the body to dispense with his sexual frankness. If "Song
of Myself" is "Whitman's Genesis," then " 'The Sleepers' is his Leviticus
and Deuteronomy" and "Children of Adam" "troubled more than Emerson's sense of propriety: it must have offended his faith as well." On
Dickinson, New quibbles that positing gender as the factor determining
both Dickinson's limitations and the nature of her responses to those
social constrictions is too deterministic and/or Romantic. Seeking to
return the poet to an American tradition of individual power acquired
through resistance shaped by Emerson and rejuvenated by Harold
Bloom, she reminds readers that feminist work like that of Gilbert and
Gubar is in fact predicated on the anxiety-of-influence paradigm. New's
energies are better spent interrogating Dickinson's poetry, and she is
much more illuminating interpreting individual poems such as "It always felt to me – a wrong" (P 597).

Though her political emphases are on abolition and feminism rather than on sexual reconstitutions of the individual body and thus of the body politic, Karen Sanchez-Eppler in *Touching Liberty: Abolition, Feminism, and the Politics of the Body* (Calif., 1993) reinterprets the body to redefine the political, and she implicitly extends compelling arguments like those of Michael Moon. By contrasting the poet's incarnation of social divisions as the source for authorial power that absorbs and is absorbed by his nation with Harriet Jacobs's experience of identifications between "the flesh, world, and word" as oppression, Sanchez-Eppler astutely situates Whitman's privilege amid American political struggles grounded in facts of race and gender. Similarly, she contextualizes Dickinson's claim that her "Country is Truth" within the "divided nation in which she lived." Asserting Dickinson's interests in identity to be precisely in "its unresolvable doubleness," and its corporeality "not in terms of the differences that rend society but rather as a split within the self," Sanchez-Eppler notes that in this scheme of things, then, "liberty, domesticity, sexuality, and identity" are all unstable and social programs are impossible. While turnings of phrase such as "actively antipolitical" and "detachedly depoliticized" may be a bit too neat, they do descry, at least in the insights they inspire, important facts of life by making other categories not nearly so clear and fixed—reminding us, for example, that national issues and public division may well be "nonsocial," "lodged within the interiority of the self"—and thereby provocatively examine how the personal indeed inheres in the political.

James Olney's poetics-centered *The Language(s) of Poetry: Walt Whitman, Emily Dickinson, and Gerard Manley Hopkins* (Georgia, 1993) results from a lecture series and argues that in the sprung rhythms, (un)common meters, barbaric yawps, and tropes of presence and absence that differently imbue their work, these three poets "make it new" and profoundly determine the shape and nature of modern English poetry. Hopkins as buffer and catalyst for the comparison of Whitman and Dickinson enables, as provocative triangles often do, insights that seem obvious and simple once noted but that usually go unremarked; for example, that for all three "every individual who really is individual is almost like a separate species." In his study of *The Prairie in Nineteenth-Century American Poetry* Steven Olson compares the "private voices" in Dickinson and Melville and concludes that "writing for a common, democratic audience would constrain" Dickinson's "poetic imagination and, ironically, her artistic freedom," and that Melville is even more extreme, accusing "America of denigrating and isolating its poets" and of attempting to maintain a "too conventional and too simplistic" view of itself that can only contribute to its own "spiritual and artistic" demise.

Two essays by prominent feminist poet/critics revisit issues each has previously addressed to elaborate new but related avenues of critical inquiry. In " 'Now in a Moment I know What I am for': Rituals of Initiation in Whitman and Dickinson" (*Walt Whitman of Mickle Street*, pp. 168–78) Sandra M. Gilbert begins by asking whether "poetic myths of origin" are gendered and then scrutinizes their "rituals of initiation" to expand her argument about these two who were producing "not poetry." "Out of the Cradle Endlessly Rocking" and "My Life had Stood – a Loaded Gun" focus Gilbert's examination of how this father and mother of American poetry "condensed into language a significant account of the moment when 'I know What I am for,' and in doing so . . . each has discovered 'the law of my own poems.' " Though she recycles some misinformation as literary "fact," in "Beginners" (*KR* 15, iii [1993]: 12–19) Adrienne Rich ruminates on the receptions of this "strange, uncoupled couple," who "at the end of the twentieth century . . . are still hardly known beyond the masks they created for themselves and those clapped on them by the times and customs," this "wild woman" and "wild man" "writing their wild carnal and ecstatic thoughts, self-censoring and censored," this wild couple who are "Americana now." But Rich does not conclude with the obvious critical sigh that they will each always elude our taxonomies, paradigms, metanarratives. Instead, she uses their unique strategies and positions to examine the underappreciated work of Muriel Rukeyser, who sought to recover "lost connections between science and poetry" by continuously addressing the "largest questions of her time—questions of power, technology, gender."

Those "largest questions" are the same for us, and for the continued study of these two major poets of America's 19th century. The years 1993 and 1994 also witnessed the beginnings of implementations of technological advances in the storage, retrieval, and manipulation of both poets' texts. In other words, having seen their work through so many permutations, readers may now look to electronic publishing to access Whitman's *Leaves of Grass* (http://www.cc.columbia.edu/acis/bartleby/whitman/) and a Dickinson listserv (emweb@lal.cs.byu.edu). Plans for a hypermedia archive of Dickinson's writings began development this year. "Dwell[ing] in Possibility," these poets and the work they inspire continue to lead us "In Paths Untrodden."

University of Maryland at College Park

6 Mark Twain

Tom Quirk

This year saw an abundance of highly capable and interesting biographical work. Long-standing errors were corrected, many possible influences (both personal and literary) were advanced, new materials relating to Twain were located, several literary sources were identified, and, perhaps most importantly, Twain's social and intellectual contexts were brought into a clearer and more secure focus. In a word, our understanding of Samuel Clemens, and of his creation Mark Twain, was modified and enriched. This is not to say that interpretive work was not plentiful or that it was not still principally concerned with the same basic set of problems or with the most familiar texts, though the critical approaches vary enormously and are sometimes without precedent.

i Editions, Biography, and Reference

The Library of America published Twain's *Historical Romances*: The Prince and the Pauper, A Connecticut Yankee in King Arthur's Court, Personal Recollections of Joan of Arc this year. The texts of the first two are those of the Iowa/California editions, that of *Joan of Arc* is the first American edition. Susan K. Harris prepared the volume's notes. My own edition and introduction of Twain's *Tales, Speeches, Essays, and Sketches* (Penguin) also appeared.

Kevin Hayes in "Mark Twain's Earliest London Lecture: Three Unknown Reports" (*StAH* n.s. 3, i: 116–19) supplies three newspaper reports on Twain's 13 October 1873 lecture, "Our Fellow Savages of the Sandwich Islands." Louis Tanner and Gary Scharnhorst in "Mark Twain Speaking: Three New Documents" (*MTJ* 30, ii [1992]: 23–25) reprint three documents relating to Twain as a lecturer: a letter from Joseph Goodman concerning the offer a rope dancer made to Twain to join forces and divide the profits; an article in the *Boston Globe* recounting a *Roughing It* lecture for which Paul Fatout had been unable to ascertain date or topic; and, most interesting, a transcription in the *San Francisco Examiner* of a story Twain told in private and of which no other text survives. Louis J. Budd in "A Recovered Mark Twain Speech: New Laws and Old Yarns" (*EAS* 23: 59–66) reprints a speech not included in Fatout's *Mark Twain Speaking*. Twain spoke on behalf of an international copyright bill then being debated in Congress at a reception given by the Ladies' Literary Association on 2 February 1889. The centerpiece of the speech, published in the *Washington Post*, is the anecdote of Clemens as a young boy returning home late at night and deciding to sleep in his father's office. In the moonlight he discerns a naked corpse on the floor and escapes through the window, taking the sash with him. The anecdote, Budd points out, was one of Twain's favorites (he used it as early as 1866 and as late as the mid-1890s in his world lecture tour), but this is the fullest and most elaborate of the recorded versions.

A CD-ROM, "Twain's World," is now available and will serve as a concordance for some 80,000 pages of Twain's works. I have not inspected this item, but a full review of its virtues and limitations is published in the *Mark Twain Circular* (8, iii: 3–5). In an instructive and highly readable review-essay, "Twain and Edison: The Intellectual Heritage as Monument" (*EAS* 23: 89–98), David E. E. Sloane discusses the first two volumes of *The Papers of Thomas A. Edison* and the University of California Press editions of the third volume of Twain's *Letters* and the revised edition of *Roughing It.*

Edgar M. Branch's "Bixby vs. Carroll: New Light on Sam Clemens's Early River Career" (*MTJ* 30, ii [1992]: 2–22) corrects long-standing errors about the beginnings of Clemens's riverboating career. The new evidence uncovered by Branch derives from the legal records of a suit that Horace Bixby brought against Captain John W. Carroll in 1857. Apart from the nature of the dispute (interesting in itself), the new evidence indicates that Clemens began his riverboat apprenticeship in early March 1857, two months earlier than has been supposed. Also, the boat for this initial ascent up the Mississippi was not the *Paul Jones,* as Twain recalled, but the *Colonel Crossman.*

In what is likely to be the fullest history we are apt to have of the origin of Clemens's appropriation of the "Mark Twain" label, Horst H. Kruse clears up several misapprehensions, introduces new evidence, and places familiar evidence in a more productive context. "Mark Twain's *Nom de*

Plume: Some Mysteries Resolved" (*MTJ* 30, i [1992]: 1–32) is a thorough and thoroughly intricate account of Clemens's supposed theft of the pseudonym used by Isiah Sellers soon after Sellers's death. Among the several mysteries resolved in this essay: Clemens's "standard" version of how he adopted the name in 1863, though it is not historically accurate, was one that he believed to be true at least until 1882; no evidence is extant that Sellers ever used "Mark Twain" as his own nom de plume; an apparently mistranscribed or misunderstood telegraph message announcing the death of one Isiah Russell probably led Clemens to believe that Sellers was dead and therefore that his pen name was up for grabs; and in 1882, when Clemens did recognize a discrepancy between his standard story and certain facts, he sustained his own version by quiet omission.

If Kruse's essay establishes the origins of Clemens's persona, Greg Zacharias's "Henry Rogers, Public Relations, and the Recovery of Mark Twain's 'Character' " (*MTJ* 31, i [1993]: 2–17) adds to our understanding of Henry Huttleston Rogers's part in rehabilitating the author's borrowed good name. Zacharias, largely on the basis of circumstantial but convincing evidence, suggests that Rogers did more than to put his business savvy at Clemens's disposal after the financial failure of the Webster Company. Instead, his efforts to rebuild Twain's reputation consisted of (1) using "Standard Oil assets such as corporate lawyers, inside stock information, and at least one overseas agent on Clemens's behalf"; (2) using Standard Oil publicity agents to record, publish, and to a degree manufacture Twain's reinvigorated character; and (3) insuring a certain consistency in newspaper reports between 1893 and 1900 that revealed Twain to be a man of stainless character. Zacharias also speculates in a commonsensical way on Rogers's motivation in interceding on Twain's behalf and on the nature of their friendship.

In "Mark Twain's First Joke on the German Language" (*MTJ* 31, i [1993]: 18–21) Holger Kersten notes that it was possible, even likely, that young Sam Clemens did some typesetting work for the St. Louis German language newspaper, *Anzeiger des Westens,* in 1853. His duties would not have required him to know German but merely to reposition for the weekly edition articles that had appeared earlier in the week in the dailies. In fact, the only German words he would have had to set up were "*Eingegangene Subscription-Gelder,*" along with the names of those whose subscriptions were paid in full. The fact that during the period when Clemens most likely worked for the paper this phrase was distorted or mangled every week points an accusing finger at Clemens himself and identifies his first joke on the German language. Lynn Denney in "Next Stop Detroit: A City's Views of Mark Twain's Evolution as a Literary Hero, 1868–1895" (*MTJ* 31, i [1993]: 22–28) views Twain through the lens of Detroit newspaper reviews and interviews spanning almost 40 years. On a different note, Gary Scharnhorst modifies our understanding of the Twain-Harte falling out. In "The Bret Harte-Mark Twain Feud: An Inside Narrative" (*MTJ* 31, i [1993]: 29–32) Scharnhorst demonstrates that, contrary to popular belief, Harte did not bear Twain's angry insults with silence and fortitude. Instead, he took a more "nuanced" path of retribution. In the stories "The Illiad of Sandy Bar," "Amity Claim," "The Heiress of Red Dog," and most particularly in "An Ingenue of the Sierras" Harte told his side of the story; in the last of these he represented a fictionalized version of Twain as a highwayman who is so diminished that he can no longer sell his stolen goods.

In the fourth in the series of Quarry Farm Papers Mary Boewe provides two essays on vastly different subjects—Twain's first lecture at Elmira, New York, and an examination of magic and miracle in *A Connecticut Yankee* (discussed below). In "The American Vandal Goes A-Courting; or Mark Twain's First Elmira Lecture and Its Romantic Aftermath" (Center for Mark Twain Studies, pp. 1–25) Boewe places the occasion of this lecture in the middle of a year crowded with incident and ardent courting. She notes that Twain's lecture "The American Vandal Abroad," though it was delivered in Cleveland and Pittsburgh first, was surely prepared with Olivia Langdon in mind. Its dominant subject matter (much of it having to do with the behavior of young women in Venice), its cautious exclusion of anything that might be deemed irreverent, and a number of parallels and details that only his intended might catch were meant to sway Olivia in his favor.

In *Mark Twain in the Company of Women* (Penn.) Laura Skandera-Trombley reexamines Clemens's life in the context of his lifelong association with, and often indebtedness to, women. These women were a rich and interesting assortment of individuals, and part of Skandera-Trombley's achieved ambition is to show that they were not a monochromatic, even pesky or hostile, presence in Twain's life or a debilitating obstacle to his creative growth. Instead, they were typically intelligent, vital, articulate, and distinct personalities whose varying commitments and perspectives Twain appreciated and responded to. Predictably, one finds extensive reference to Olivia Langdon Clemens, "Mother" Mary Fairbanks, the Clemens daughters, and of course Twain's "Angelfish," but one also encounters instructive discussions of Grace King, Anna Elizabeth Dickinson, Susan Crane, Isabella Beecher Hooker, Julia Beecher, Isabel Lyon, and others. Moreover, Skandera-Trombley describes in some detail the intellectual and political climate of Elmira, New York, before Clemens's arrival on the scene in 1868. Along the way, we learn a great deal about the Elmira "Water Cure" and the Swedish Movement Cure; we also learn of the involvement of Olivia and others in local reading groups, female and freedmen's education, the underground railroad and abolitionist movement, women's suffrage, and the WCTU.

Skandera-Trombley makes good use of the Mark Twain Papers and other archival materials and adds substantially to our store of knowledge about Twain and his social and domestic environment. She corrects many long-standing misapprehensions, particularly about Olivia's health and her intellectual and personal substance; she also recapitulates the debunking argument about Olivia's skating accident, ill health, and miracle cure, which is presented more fully in her "Mark Twain's Fictionalizing of Dr. Newton's Miraculous Cure" (*ALR* 26, ii: 82–92). Skandera-Trombley provides an ampler context in which to locate Twain's moral, political, and imaginative development. Finally, she ably and conclusively dispenses with the notion that Twain was "anti-female," even misogynistic. However, the evidence she adduces does not always lead so ineluctably to the conclusions she draws, and her ambition to establish that Clemens was a fully "integrated personality" jars with his evident reliance on the company he kept. In fact, she comes closer to the point of view of Van Wyck Brooks (whose thesis she particularly sets out to repudiate) than one might suppose when she announces that her intention is to reveal "an author so dependent upon female interaction and influence that without it the sublimity of his novels would have been lost." It is true that Brooks and most of the biographers who followed him viewed the female influence on Twain as detrimental, but the notion of influence as a sufficient explanatory principle is the same. For it was Brooks who maintained that Twain was one of the most "tractable" writers of genius this country has produced, one who set great—perhaps much too great—store in the opinions of others. A case in point is Skandera-Trombley's assertion that as Clemens's "charmed circle" dissolved—gradually as his daughters matured, most poignantly with the death of his daughter Susy in 1896, and permanently with the death of his wife in 1904—Twain's powers likewise dissolved into ill-conceived and uncompleted attempts at creation. Depending on how utterly "bad" one considers Twain's late writing to be, I suppose the question of causes has some urgency. Twain *was* old and tired, and the depredations of circumstance, including the losses of Susy and Olivia, were a sad accompaniment to his condition. Whether or not those losses were the cause of it is more problematic. Nevertheless, this biography is rewarding—rich in detail and, at points, thoroughly engrossing.

In "Negro Wench and Platonic Sweetheart: Images of Splitting and Integration in Samuel Clemens' Dreams" (*EAS* 23: 67–88) Suzi Naiburg provides the sort of image of Clemens and his relation to women that Skandera-Trombley means to combat. Through a modified Freudian reading of Clemens's recorded dream of an attractive "Negro wench" and a series of dreams about his "Platonic sweetheart" (mixed with a dash of Jung and a brief excursion into Celtic mythology), Naiburg rather nimbly argues, contrary to Skandera-Trombley, for a portrait of someone who is fragmented because he rejects communion with the female Other. In his disgust with the seductive "wench" and his repeated loss of the idealized, platonic sweetheart, Clemens projected parts of himself into dreams that held the promise of going beyond cultural stereotypes of gender but ultimately remained suppressed.

Following Skandera-Trombley's lead, Lawrence Berkove's *Ethical Records of Twain and His Circle of Sagebrush Journalists* (Center for Mark Twain Studies) might have been titled "Mark Twain in the Company of Men." This, too, is an influence study that measures Twain's moral, artistic, and political development against the prepossessions of the company he kept. Specifically, Berkove addresses the question, How ethical a journalist was Twain when he worked for the *Territorial Enterprise* in Virginia City? Berkove sees this apprenticeship period as crucial to Twain's growth, a time when "Twain changed from a seemingly frail reed to the writer whose integrity the world has come to respect."

Twain's circle in Nevada was something less than "charmed," or charming, of course, but in his depiction of the figures Joseph Thompson Goodman, Rollin Mallory Daggett, Dan De Quille, James Townsend, and Charles Carroll Goodwin, Berkove paints an interesting and idiosyncratic spectrum of moral influences, both positive and negative, that variously affected the young journalist. In Joseph Goodman, owner and publisher of the *Enterprise,* Twain found a man of fierce integrity, ever ready to expose a hoax with hard fact and, sometimes, to back his words with an actual, physical confrontation. Rollin Daggett was as pugnacious and feisty as Goodman, but he often took a premature and fiery stand before gathering all the facts. Dan de Quille was one of the more talented and trustworthy journalists on the *Enterprise* staff, but he was constitutionally timid and his virtue, such as it was, was often compromised; by dancing lightly over controversial issues, or by not telling everything he knew of the pervasive underhanded and shady deals in and around Virginia City, De Quille more than once committed what Twain many years later would call the "lie of silent assertion." James Townsend (the model for Bret Harte's "Truthful James") was an inveterate liar and so fond of the hoax that he often deliberately involved himself in fraudulent and illegal schemes. And Carroll Goodwin, though talented, was too easily impressed by power and wealth. Though by no means an angel himself, Twain fares well in the company of these men, and he sought to emulate the best of them, Joseph Goodman.

Taken together, Skandera-Trombley's and Berkove's biographical studies tell us something about Twain's supposed "tractability" and his moral nature. Clearly, so-called influences, moral or other, work only on those sensibilities ready to receive them. Twain chose, consciously or unconsciously, the individuals and forces that he would allow to shape him, and, by and large, he chose with an eye to his own personal and professional development. Moreover, judging from these two studies, there may well be questions of gender differences bound up in any consideration of Twain's ethical nature. The women whom Twain responded to tended to embody a set of general convictions, and many of them spoke eloquently from a coherent and relatively stable moral and political foundation. By contrast, the Sagebrush Bohemians, or the best of them, seemed to react scattershot and sometimes violently to whatever happened to get their dander up. Twain participated in both sorts of behavior, and Gregg Camfield's treatment of Twain's wanderings in the "maze" of moral philosophy (see below) offers additional insights into the question of his moral character.

ii General Interpretations

If Samuel Clemens had taken as his alias the name "Mark Multiplicity" or "Mark Monad," I wonder whether the character and emphasis of Twain criticism might have been different. In any event, J. D. Stahl in his *Mark Twain, Culture and Gender: Envisioning America Through Europe* (Georgia) gives us yet another variation of the Mark Twain-divided-against-himself theme. In this instance the terms are original if not wholly persuasive. Stahl's thesis runs something like this: Clemens, through the persona of Mark Twain, projected his own anxieties about gender and his obsession with the lost father onto European settings. He conflated his fear and fascination of woman as Other with the Otherness of Europe and thus translated cultural questions into questions of male identity and, in turn, the male's relation to alternately demonic and seductive or innocent and idealized versions of the female as they were represented by European women, both fictional and real. Stahl rides this thesis through a good number of Twain's works, often to good effect.

In *Innocents Abroad,* by eliminating the perspective of American women aboard the *Quaker City,* Twain reserved the feminine quality of the innocent for himself and thereby achieved a certain cultural authority over his material; by pairing readings of "A Memorable Midnight Experience" and the privately circulated *1601,* Stahl is able to identify in vastly different representations of Queen Elizabeth anxieties about female power and to distinguish between the public and private rhetorical means of addressing gender issues. *The Prince and the Pauper* is deftly treated as a complicated and often paradoxical search for the father, and *A Connecticut Yankee* deals with, among other things, sexual rivalry between Hank Morgan and Morgan Le Fay, and the Yankee's desire to offer himself as the surrogate father to a new generation of boys who would be men. In his reading of *Joan of Arc,* Stahl focuses on the narrator as a semiautobiographical representation of Clemens himself, a narrator who contemplates Joan as the innocent and steadfast woman warrior. Finally, the three "Mysterious Stranger" manuscripts reveal in Twain a blurring of gender boundaries and a willingness to see beyond the limiting possibilities imposed by sex.

Stahl might have benefited from and built on Peter Stoneley's *Mark Twain and the Feminine Aesthetic* (1992), but perhaps his book had gone to press before Stoneley's was published. At any rate, he might well have declared far sooner his allegiances to French theorists or that "I have been appropriating Clemens's texts and reading them in my own fashion, in some cases against the grain of what appear to have been Clemens's intentions." Made early on, such disclosures might have helped the reader follow the argument; instead, these points are reserved for the concluding chapter. More curiously, Stahl elects to eliminate *A Tramp Abroad* from his consideration of Twain's European books. However, his mention in a footnote that in *A Tramp Abroad* Twain treated dueling "admiringly" and described Heidelberg fraternity life "without a trace of irony" indicates to me that it is just as well that he left that work alone. Comments such as these (or his remark that the duke is the "most depraved" character in *Huckleberry Finn*) make me realize that Stahl and I dwell in rather different interpretive communities. Nevertheless, his book is written with verve and earnest conviction, peppered with insights that have an interest apart from the thesis they are meant to support.

In *Sentimental Twain: Samuel Clemens in the Maze of Moral Philosophy* (Penn.) Gregg Camfield in his preface is more straightforward and helpful in identifying and locating his intentions; he means to "create thick historical contexts" and "to explore the power of those contexts over our culture's development." And he elegantly expresses his additional ambition to say something meaningful about Twain—for he wants "to see how a mind negotiates the fissures" in a cultural context and "to find the possibility of creativity within social and psychic restraint." This is a widespread and long-standing ambition, of course, and I know from my own attempts at it that intellectual history can be a tricky business. Camfield's task is all the trickier in dealing with a man like Twain, a notorious autodidact and jokester whose rigorously sly confusions are difficult to separate from seemingly haphazard and accidental insights. On balance, Camfield succeeds admirably.

The sentimentalism referred to in Camfield's title is not the conventionally understood "tears and flapdoodle" kind (though it is not wholly exempt from that application) but the sort that Thomas Jefferson identified as "a generous spasm of the heart." That is, it derives from the conviction shared by Shaftesbury, the Scottish Common Sense philosophers, and others (and in reaction to the idealism of Berkeley and the empiricism of Hume and Locke) that moral intuitions, or "benevolent affections," are part of human nature and do not rely on reason or experience for support. This "unofficial metaphysic" of American democracy during the first half of the 19th century did not simply evaporate, as Perry Miller would have it, because by the 1870s it was no longer reflected in the college curriculum; and Camfield is right to insist that its influence lingered, and lingers still in unacknowledged forms, in the liberal political sensibility. Besides, Twain did not go to college and would not have noted curricular revisions of this sort anyway.

The upshot of Camfield's study, then, is to show that the "doubleness" of Twain is not to be found operating both inside and outside the genteel tradition, but wholly within that tradition. The early journalistic writings and *Innocents Abroad* derive much of their comedy from exposing the piously sentimental, but they also dramatize Twain's attachment to conventionally idealized notions of women, children, courage, and the like. *The Gilded Age* reflects not only collaborative authorship with Charles Dudley Warner, but a shared moral point of view; the novel is, at once, a burlesque of sentimental excess and an endorsement of domestic virtues.

As Twain attempted to become a serious literary moralist, prompted in part by his involvement with the literary community of Hartford, he began seriously to explore familiar sentimental notions as they were affected or modified by naturalist or Spencerian assumptions. Thus, "The Recent Carnival of Crime" and *Huckleberry Finn* wrestle unevenly with questions of the efficacy of conscience and suggest that conscience is a hurtful *ignis fatuus,* while *A Connecticut Yankee* ponders, then abandons, the possibility that training may be genetically transmitted over several generations (à la Lamarck) and eventually lead to social and moral progress. When Twain came to view humor as a powerful instrument of political reform, he produced work like *The American Claimant* and *Puddn'head Wilson,* but he then vacillated between idealist and materialist accounts of human motivation. By 1900, if not before, he recognized that the "humor perception" was not the objective perception of incongruities but the result of subjective tensions within the individual consciousness. That recognition led him in a variety of directions—to describe an absolute cultural relativism in *Following the Equator,* to flirt with the idea of solipsism in the "Mysterious Stranger" manuscripts, and, in a return to the earlier faculty psychology of Common Sense realists, to indulge himself in nostalgic associationism as a warrant for his creative method in his *Autobiography.*

Although the eventual result of Camfield's able study is a thoughtful account of Twain's development as a moralist and a humorist, what distinguishes it, to my mind, is its sense of proportion. Camfield is perfectly aware that he often runs the risk of draining Twain's works of their humor and making him a rather ordinary philosopher instead of an extraordinary writer, or that in an overeager pursuit of an explanatory principle for Clemens's development, he may altogether exclude the object of this explanation from view. Appropriately, Camfield inserts disclaimers and qualifications throughout that serve to spare his readers making the painful choice between a commitment to a well-crafted thesis or a fuller understanding of an important dimension of an extremely complicated figure.

In *Mark Twain: A Collection of Critical Essays* (Prentice Hall) Eric J. Sundquist has gathered some 14 previously published essays or portions of books. Sundquist's introduction to this collection is not so much an effort to introduce the selections that follow as to contextualize Twain and his work, and it deserves to be read as a discrete essay. Like Camfield, Sundquist wishes to see Twain as both representative of and distinct from his culture. Thus, Twain is both implicated in a racist, imperialist American culture and, to a degree, extenuated from active complicity in its more damning features. The culmination of Twain's life and work is a world of "fright and blankness." Sundquist concludes, "After producing a body of work whose moral complexities replicated those of the nation, Twain's art reached the point at which genius and despair, vision and betrayal were one, and true freedom the fire that burned away any illusion to the contrary."

A good deal less ponderous, though I think no less insightful, is Fred Setterberg's "Roughing the Truth with Mark Twain" (*HPLR* 8, i [1993]: 35–62). Part appreciation of Twain, part autobiographical reminiscence, part cultural criticism, and part fiction, Setterberg's piece dramatizes Twain's relation to his time and his occupation as journalist and teller of tall tales by discerning any number of correspondences between Twain's Gilded Age and our own. In his friend and fellow journalist Sandy Fitzgerald, Setterberg detects survivals of a compulsion "to mock the credulous nation whose disregard for truth in the pursuit of convenience could not be exaggerated." This essay is well-written and immensely entertaining.

iii Individual Works Through 1884

Wesley Britton's "Mark Twain, 'Cradle Skeptic': High Spirits, Ghosts, and the Holy Spirit" (*SDR* 30, iv: 87–97) is a thoughtful and wide-ranging essay which argues that even in his earliest journalistic pieces Twain had a "lack of reverence for Christianity" and was, from the beginning, inclined to expose human hypocrisy and credulity. The seeds, and to some extent the literary devices, for the irreverent late fables may be found even in a young journalist on the frontier. The real difference between the early and late skepticism is that the late skepticism lacks "playfulness" and vitality.

In "Melville, Twain and Quixote: Variations on the Comic Debate" (*StAH* n.s. 3, i: 1–27) John Bryant examines the narrative strategies of Melville's and Twain's liars and con men and demonstrates a common debt to Cervantes. Specifically, the 19th-century debate over how to read *Don Quixote*—as humor or satire—has its echoes in the narrative thimble-rigging of *The Confidence-Man* and in the narrative frames of the tall tale. The "Jumping Frog" and "Grandfather's Ram" tales are "subversive" narrative structures that simultaneously rely on the comic put-down and foster democratic notions of community. From a different angle, Peter Gibian in "Levity and Gravity in Twain: The Bipolar Dynamic of the Early Tales" (*StAH* n.s. 3, i: 80–94) contemplates the same two tales and explains the tactics and metaphors operating in them. Gibian locates the "dividedness" of Twain in the cultural polarity epitomized by the terms and concepts of "levity" and "gravity" as they apply to physics, theology, and, of course, humor. The first term resists linear and literal statements and straightforward conclusions; the second insists on somber and serious closure.

Richard H. Cracroft's "'Exactly the German Way': Mark Twain's Comic Strategies with 'The Awful German Language'" (*Thalia* 13, i-ii: 11–21) explores Twain's lifelong fascination and frustration with the German language. By enlisting the familiar comic devices of exaggeration, hyperbole, and irony, he "sounds his barbaric yawp" over German grammar, syntax, and diction, and he treats German as he would any other sacred cow that needs an occasional comic comeuppance.

iv   Adventures of Huckleberry Finn

In "Mark Twain and George MacDonald: The Salty and the Sweet" (*MTJ* 30, ii [1993]: 26–32) Kathryn Lindskoog sketches the relation between Twain and George MacDonald and provides as an appendix a chronology of their association. She nominates MacDonald's *Sir Gibbie* (1880) as a possible influence on *Huckleberry Finn* and notes 20 parallels in plot and incident, including the friendship between a poor and barely literate young boy and an adult black man. Lindskoog also remarks on MacDonald's (and, not so coincidentally, C. S. Lewis's) appreciation of Twain. Karen Alkalay-Gut in "If Mark Twain Had a Sister: Gender-Specific Values and Structure in *Daddy-Long-Legs*" (*JACult* 16, iv [1993]:

91–99) discerns in her comparison of *Huckleberry Finn* and *Daddy-Long-Legs* (1912), a novel by Twain's grand niece Jean Webster, the same sort of differences that some critics have found in comparisons between English and American novelists. Alkalay-Gut attributes these differences to a "male/female causality," however, and observes that while male protagonists often find self-fulfillment by avoiding education and through escape from corrupting society, female protagonists such as the narrator of *Daddy-Long-Legs* achieve fulfillment through "involvement and reform of society." She also suggests that this difference may explain why Webster's novel has "escaped" canonization.

Without suggesting actual influence, Michael Kiskis examines the correspondences between *Huckleberry Finn* and *Heart of Darkness* in "Of Huck and Marlow: The Compelled Storyteller in Mark Twain and Joseph Conrad" in *Heart of the Nation: Polish Literature and Culture,* ed. James S. Pula and Mieczyslaw B. Biskupski (East European Monographs, pp. 143–53). Conrad and Twain (and Coleridge in "The Ancient Mariner") have fashioned narrative strategies in which the storyteller is compelled by past experience to tell the story of painful disillusionment and of redemptive human connectedness. Such compulsion invests the narrative voice with an agressive seductiveness: "Each takes immediate hold of his audience by lunging into the act of storytelling. There is no time to run and no place to hide."

In "*Huck Finn's* Ending: The Intimacy and Disappointment of Tourism" (*JNT* 24: 55–68), Richard M. Gardner treats the structure of the novel in a schematized but ingenious way. Applying Jafar Jafari's analysis of tourism as a model of the archetypal journey, Gardner sees *Huckleberry Finn* as an epitome of the traveler's experience, one that passes through several distinct stages. Thus, the disappointment over the novel's conclusion is largely the result of the lost spirit of animation and intimacy that the traveler has experienced but also knows is impermanent; Huck's acquired virtues are "frighteningly contingent on circumstance."

Kelly Anspaugh published two essays on *Huckleberry Finn* this year. In "Illustrating 'Mark Time's Finist Joke'" (*Thalia* 14: 21–29) he sees the novel as a Derridean "autothanatography"—that is, a species of "self-death-writing" in which the narrator is dead or may as well be—and he argues that E. W. Kemble is something of a collaborator in illustrating this subtext. He concludes with remarkable self-assurance: "That Kemble was an excellent reader of Huck's thanatography, and that his illustrations contribute significantly to the getting up of 'post-mortem effects,' must be allowed." Perhaps, but I am more disposed to allow the argument of the second essay, " 'I Been There Before': Biblical Typology and *Adventures of Huckleberry Finn*" (*ANQ* 7: 219–23). There, Anspaugh maintains that Huck may be seen as both a Moses and a Christ figure if one accepts the novel as a sort of "typological realism" in which Moses is the prefiguring of Christ. He suggests that Twain might have been encouraged in this direction by his reading of Hannah More's "Moses in the Bulrushes"; even so, Twain so consistently inverts biblical analogues that he looks forward to modernists like Joyce instead of back to Victorian writers such as Hannah More.

v Individual Works After 1884

Paul Alkon gives over a significant portion (pp. 115–38) of his genre study, *Science Fiction before 1900: Imagination Discovers Technology* (Twayne), to an extended analysis of *A Connecticut Yankee in King Arthur's Court*. His warrant for lingering over Twain's novel is that it represents a milestone in the subgenre of science fiction—time travel. *A Connecticut Yankee* is "the first story of travel to and from the past. This motif does not occur in previous literature or folklore." And within this broad stroke of originality, there are traces of other forms of originality: no one before, and few after, had had a protagonist actually try to alter the past; other time travelers had served merely as passive spectators. Moreover, Hank Morgan does not merely travel in time but in space; unlike, say, *Looking Backward,* which moves from Boston of the present to Boston of the future, Twain's novel moves from Hartford, Connecticut, to Arthur's England and thus conflates temporal and spatial perspectives. For this reason, too, Alkon notes that *A Connecticut Yankee* owes nearly as much to *Robinson Crusoe* as it does to Malory's *Morte d'Arthur* in its examination of progress and primitivism. Twain was also original in moving from the present to Camelot (a legendary place/time) because he was thus able to explore not merely history but myth. Through his dramatized dialogues with the past, Twain brought romance and realism, experience and legend, technology and magic, progress and primitivism, and much more into active and boisterous conversation.

In " 'Iron Dudes and White Savages in Camelot': The Influence of Dime-Novel Sensationalism on Twain's *A Connecticut Yankee in King Arthur's Court*" (*ALR* 27, i: 42–58) Gregory M. Pfitzer argues that the impulses, the reading, and perhaps much of the work that went into the abandoned *Huck Finn and Tom Sawyer among the Indians* were transferred and reshaped when Twain came to write *A Connecticut Yankee*. Aware that the market for westerns had become saturated, Twain's interest in the project evaporated, but he incorporated many of the ideas he had for the earlier work into his story of King Arthur's England. The novel dramatizes many of the conventions of the western dime novels, reinvigorating them through the dramatic difference in setting and occasion. A particular influence, Pfitzer suggests, may have been Edward S. Ellis's *The Huge Hunter; or the Steam Man of the Prairies* (1882); Ellis also contemplated the consequences of importing technology into a land not ready for such progress. In this case, the land is the Western prairies, and the huge hunter is a steam-powered robot that terrifies miners and Indians alike. Pfitzer notes several parallels between the two novels, including the resemblance of a pipe-smoking Hank Morgan dressed in armor to Ellis's steam man. Joe Boyd Fulton in "*A Connecticut Yankee in King Arthur's Court*" (*Expl* 53: 34–36) also addresses Twain's attitude toward technology, noting that in the novel and the sketch "A Telephonic Conversation," the telephone is comically unable to "connect" people. Considered in this light, Hank's dying words, cast in the form of a telephonic conversation that fails to go through, are apt and moving.

In "Morgan vs. Merlin: The Case for Magic and Miracle in *A Connecticut Yankee in King Arthur's Court*" (Center for Mark Twain Studies, pp. 29–39), Mary Boewe examines the function of magic in Twain's novel. She demonstrates that the first two chapters of W. E. H. Lecky's *History of the Rise and Influence of the Spirit of Rationalism in Europe* were an important source for several incidents and, in part, for his conception of the role that Merlin would play. She nominates Lecky as the source for Hank Morgan's ingenious use of the eclipse as evidence of his own magical powers as a means to save his skin and to secure his advantage over his rival Merlin, and she teasingly observes that an entire monograph might be written on the marked passages in Lecky that have direct reference to the Established Church. Boewe also notes the resemblances between Morgan Le Fay and Hank Morgan as well as Twain himself, and she observes that Sandy is the true antithesis of Le Fay, but that Sandy's primary role is to allow us as readers to feel what it is like to be enchanted.

Henry B. Wonham's "Getting to the Bottom of *Pudd'nhead Wilson*; or, a Critical Vision Focused (Too Well?) for Irony" (*ArQ* 50, iii: 111–26) serves a double purpose. On the one hand, the essay is a sensible critique of New Criticism and New Historicism as sharing an unacknowledged kinship, for both look for some stable ground for interpreting the novel and by virtue of what the book fails to say deem it a success or a failure. On the other hand, Wonham argues convincingly that the novel is meant for the reader with a vision "focused for irony," though not the sort of irony that provides safe detachment from the narrative events or the insidious and complacent ethos of Dawson's Landing. Wonham maintains that *Pudd'nhead Wilson* offers a "paradigm for cultural criticism *in* the novel, not to say *of* the novel." The ironies that even the sophisticated reader is drawn into implicate him or her in specious legal logic and ideological assumptions that one might prefer to expose rather than to experience.

Coincidentally, Vidar Petersen in "Of Slaves and Masters: Constructed Identities in Mark Twain's *Pudd'nhead Wilson*" (*Excursions in Fiction*, pp. 174–90) arrives at parallel conclusions, though he begins with different premises. Petersen argues that the novel consciously dramatizes what we now term a "Foucauldian system of power relations," and, like Wonham, he finds it significant that David Wilson is absorbed into the very system he consistently criticized. Like Wonham, too, Petersen finds the ironies pervasive and telling—that Roxy's efforts to spare her son wind up sending him down the river; that fingerprinting as a "race neutral" form of evidence is used to shore up the division between black and white; and that Wilson, in his blindness to the consequences of his efforts, becomes a real "pudd'nhead." For both Wonham and Petersen, the New Historicist impulse to emphasize context over text tends to obscure or eliminate important features in the novel itself.

In "Mark Twain's First Chestnut: Revisions in 'Extracts from Adam's Diary'" (*EAS* 23: 49–58) Joseph McCullough traces the complicated process of revision of "Adam's Diary." Composed in 1892, the piece was rejected by *Cosmopolitan* and the *Century* and was first published in Irving S. Underhill's *The Niagara Book*, a volume intended to attract tourists to Niagara Falls. Twain revised the text accordingly, making Niagara the scene of the Garden of Eden, but he was never happy with the changes. He revised it twice afterward (in 1895 and 1904). The substance of the revisions has to do with assigning the causes of the Fall not to pride and disobedience, but to a compassion for God's creatures— Eve notices that the sharp-toothed tiger and a morose buzzard are not happy with a diet of grass, and she is thus intent on bringing death into the world for their sake. Twain also wanted to strike the right balance between being sufficiently shocking to be interesting but not so heretical that he might alienate his readers; he reserved his bitterest attacks on biblical myths for works to be published after his death.

Laura Skandera-Trombley touches on some of the same issues in her *Mark Twain in the Company of Women,* but in "Mark Twain's Last Work of Realism: The Ashcroft-Lyon Manuscript" (*EAS* 23: 39–48) she gives a fuller discussion of Clemens's association with Isabel Lyon and argues that the 400-page manuscript he wrote about her might best be regarded as a fiction in which Lyon becomes a character of Twain's invention. According to Skandera-Trombley, Lyon was already a fiction in the Clemens household when she was obliged to play the part of the "unofficial replacement" for Olivia, who had died in 1904. Skandera-Trombley also notes that the work bears some similarities to Edith Wharton's *The House of Mirth,* which both Lyon and Twain had read. The manuscript apparently satisfied negative emotional impulses in Twain. He wished to appease his daughter Clara's objections to Lyon and to alleviate the sense of estrangement from their father that the daughters felt, and he wanted to vent his own fury over Lyon's marriage to Ralph Ashcroft.

University of Missouri-Columbia

7 Henry James

Greg W. Zacharias

In his discussion of canonization and the main currents in James criticism (which I notice below) Richard A. Hocks also touches on the reason for the range of critical perspectives and the sheer volume of contemporary James scholarship: "one cannot get around the *fact* of . . . James's corpulent corpus, its mass and diversity. . . . " That "mass and diversity," in addition to affirming the richness and depth of James's body of work, continues to motivate as much published scholarship on James as on any other American writer. Though the tension and sharp differences generated by the diversity of scholarship might seem unresolvable, Wayne C. Booth, David Golumbia, Garry Hagberg, and Mary Ann Caws contributed to finding a resolution. Meanwhile, interest in James biography remains high. That more than 80 previously unpublished Henry James letters were published this year, and that work continues in the location and cataloging of thousands of "missing" letters, indicate the enormous amount of fundamental scholarship yet to be done.

i Reference Works, Biographical Studies, Bibliography, Editions

The excellent third volume of *The Correspondence of William James: William and Henry, 1897–1910,* ed. Ignas K. Skrupskelis and Elizabeth M. Berkeley (Virginia), has arrived; it contains 110 letters by Henry James, of which, by my count, 88 are published for the first time. This volume is the last of three devoted to the brothers' correspondence and, like the first two, adds substantially to our understanding of Henry's relationship with William, at least. The brothers discuss, among many other things, the Dreyfus Affair, the Spanish-American War, the 1904–05 American tour, the major-phase novels and the New York Edition, and Henry's depression. What may be most remarkable about the correspondence here is how the brothers' competition for fame and publicity merges with a deeply felt sense of mutual understanding and compassion, nearly in the realm of the unspoken, like something from one of James's later novels.

The William-Henry letters should be embraced and celebrated by Jamesians. At the same time, it is estimated that thousands of Henry James letters remain unpublished, even uncataloged, and thus are practically lost. But those interested in James studies should know that Steven Jobe of Hanover College is working to locate those letters and thus make them available for scholars. Jobe has completed a *Partial Calendar of the Correspondence of Henry James* (privately published and available through Jobe), which catalogs "8,544 letters and telegrams, only 2,762 of which have been published and 5,782 of which are not known to have been published" as of October 1994. Even more useful will be the full calendar of 10,500–11,000 letters, which Jobe, working with Susan Gunter of Westminster College (Salt Lake City), with support from the NEH, anticipates completing in December 1997.

Biographical essays continue a dialogue with Leon Edel's *Henry James* and with James's autobiography. In "The Traditions of Gender: Constance Fenimore Woolson and Henry James" (*Patrons and Protégées,* pp. 161–83), Cheryl B. Torsney not only replies forcefully and fairly to Edel's account of and rationale for the James/Woolson friendship and explains the cause of Woolson's depression later in life, but she reminds us of Woolson's place in American letters and of the importance of the traditions of women's writing in American literary history. More, Torsney points out parallels between Woolson's *Anne* and James's *The Portrait of a Lady* which suggest James's attention to Woolson's fiction. Susan Goodman also investigates James's relation to an important woman writer in *Edith Wharton's Inner Circle* (Texas). In general, Goodman's analysis of James's place in Wharton's "inner circle," which, in addition to James, included Howard Sturgis, Percy Lubbock, Walter Berry, Robert Norton, John Hugh Smith, Gaillard Lapsley, and Bernard Berenson, puts into clearer focus what has been accepted for some time: that James played a central role in the group, and that its members saw him as the point of orientation for their shared views on art and life.

Pierre A. Walker and Alfred Habegger in "Young Henry James and the Institution Fezandié" (*HJR* 15: 107–20) use Paris city archival material to offer a new explanation for the James sons' attendance at the institution, to discuss the particular financial circumstances surrounding the James family's residence in Paris, and to correct the traditional attribution of Fourierist sympathies at Fezandié. In so doing, Walker and Habegger supplement James's own version of the Paris stay in *A Small Boy and Others,* the source for the accounts of the period given by James biographers Edel and Fred Kaplan.

Engaging for its exploration of Henry James, Sr., Alfred Habegger's *The Father: A Life of Henry James, Sr.* (Farrar) also contributes to our understanding of the life of his second son, Harry. What I found most useful, among many other details and issues Habegger brings to light, were discussions of Henry Sr.'s powerfully coercive style of managing his children and wife, descriptions of everyday life in James's New York neighborhoods during the 1840s and '50s, new information about the residency in France during the later 1850s, the embarrassment and shame Habegger contends Harry James felt from what he perceived as errors in his father's judgment, and the son's adoption of his father's fascination with the melodramatic and sensational, such as the elder's "alert interest in shocking murders."

Reading contextually the sequence of three "memory clusters" in *A Small Boy and Others,* Paul S. Nielsen in "How Henry James Regularized the Autobiographical Memory of His Father; Or, That Day in the Whorehouse" (*HJR* 15: 190–98) shows how James attempts to "explain himself to himself" by reworking and re-presenting the events of his life "to regularize the memorial portrait of the father and to make it consistent with the culturally dominant modes of masculine self-expression and identity." Nielsen reads in the sequence James's explanation "for a lifelong lack of sexual self-expression."

In "Jamesiana: Assessments of James and His Work by Marianne Moore, Beerbohm, Forster, Madox Ford, and George Stonier" (*HJR* 15: 199–218) Arthur Sherbo supplements the "evergrowing bibliography of writings on James." In addition to excerpts on James from previously published poems, literary essays, and reviews, Sherbo gleans material from less easily located sources, such as Moore's occasional essays and the *Marianne Moore Newsletter,* Beerbohm's and Forster's letters, a Forster lecture to Cambridge undergraduates, and five anonymous pieces by Ford in the *English Review.* Sherbo also includes large portions of essays by C. H. Rickword and George Walter Stonier, which have not been noted in relation to James.

John F. Sears introduces the new Penguin edition of *The American*

Scene, which, given the renewed critical interest in the work, and thus, one assumes, its inclusion in university courses, is welcome.

ii Parallels and Influences

Placing James in the context of two American contemporaries in "Rewriting the Necessary Woman: Marriage and Professionalism in James, Jewett, and Phelps" (*HJR* 15: 242–56), Valerie Fulton studies the politics of reputation and literary history. Fulton argues that the "presumed aesthetic superiority" of James's novels has undermined the way that we read contemporary fiction written by women whose work represents cultural forces and tensions that "work against received notions of canonicity, even in scholarship that presumes to challenge the traditional American literary canon."

In "James and Stevenson: The Mixed Current of Realism and Romance" (*Critical Reconstructions,* pp. 127–49) George Dekker puts forward three main points, each of which uses James to elevate Robert Louis Stevenson's reputation: (1) To distinguish James from Stevenson in terms of "background, temperament, theory, and fictional practice"; (2) to locate what for James made Stevenson "so 'great' as a man and author"; and (3) to identify "distinct Stevensonian reverberations" in the discussion of realism and romance in the Preface to *The American.*" Dekker locates Stevenson's importance to James in the "imaginative play" of James's style and in James's admiration for the way Stevenson conducted his life, which James "prized" as a "moral exemplar."

Joseph Wiesenfarth in "Art and Life: Henry James' Great Expectations," pp. 275–87 in *Das Natur/Kultur-Paradigma,* ed. Konrad Gross et al. (Gunter Narr), examines the influence of early Dickens, in particular "'the half-gothic narrative mode'" of *Great Expectations* on James's style, especially "The Aspern Papers," and explains that the later Dickens did not appeal to James, who believed that the English novelist "did not know *man.*"

In "Framing Fears, Reading Designs: The Homosexual Art of Painting in James, Wilde, and Beerbohm" (*ELH* 61: 923–54) Christopher Lane investigates James's sense of "in-betweenness," marginality, in terms of "what narratives [including painting, speech, and writing] can express and what, of the sexual, is ultimately representable." Ranging from the textual to the cultural and political, Lane explores his subject in

James's "The Liar," Wilde's *The Picture of Dorian Gray,* and Beerbohm's *The Happy Hypocrite.*

iii Critical Books

From beginning to end, intertextually as well as chronologically, using a broad and conceptually useful definition of "the ghostly," T. J. Lustig is likely to persuade readers of *Henry James and the Ghostly* (Cambridge) that "the ghostly" does indeed rest at the center of James's imagination, interests, style, and thus fiction. From "The Romance of Certain Old Clothes" (1868) through James's experiments in realism and naturalism, into the late novels and the Prefaces to the New York Edition, up to the deathbed dictation in 1916, Lustig discusses the ghostly as an aspect of James's investigations of consciousness, as a potent central metaphor, "as a form of subjectivity rather than an object for subjectivity," as an expression of the uncanny, and as a locus of "the great principles of James's fiction—the strange and the familiar, the romantic and the real, the explosive principle and economic mastery." More, Lustig finds the ghostly related to temporal, structural, and linguistic "blanks" or absences. Of course, Lustig discusses the phantasmagoric, characters who are haunting, and those who are haunted. Yet another element of the book is Lustig's discussion of Hawthorne's "ghost" in James's own fiction and criticism. At the same time, without underestimating the significance of Hawthorne's presence, Lustig surveys the British ghost tradition, received through Romantic and Enlightenment thought, that also haunts James and that, like Hawthorne and the popularity of the contemporary ghost story, provides Lustig with a context within which he can discuss the ghostly in James.

In *Henry James: History, Narrative, Fiction* (Oxford, 1993) Roslyn Jolly explains that James's various narrative representations of history function, on the one hand, as strategies to counter "long-standing moral charges against fiction's false epistemology" and, on the other, to assert the importance of the novelist in society. Jolly argues that in "antiromances" James emphasizes the "truth" in the narrative by contrasting it "with another narrative which appears false or romantic." Characters in the antiromances abandon romantic "plots" of living for ones grounded in "history." One strength of Jolly's study is her attention to the complexity of James's management of romance and history. While she maps the "anti-romance" strain, she also traces James's articulation of the power of the romantic narrative imagination to define personal histories and to resist the efforts of others who seek to impose definitions. More, in *The Ambassadors, The Golden Bowl,* and essays written within a few years of his death, Jolly elaborates "James's commitment to the authority of the imagination, thus of fiction, in shaping and revising experience," in producing "counter-realities," and "for addressing problems in social and moral life."

Garry L. Hagberg in *Meaning and Interpretation: Wittgenstein, Henry James, and Literary Knowledge* (Cornell) seeks a way to overcome the traditional division in James studies between those who investigate James's treatment of form (aesthetics) and those concerned with James's implicit discussions of life (ethics). Applying his method to "The Tree of Knowledge," "The Author of Beltraffio," "The Figure in the Carpet," and "The Lesson of the Master," Hagberg centers on Wittgenstein's "language-game strategy," which attempts to understand the conventions by which language generates meaning, in particular "miniscule context[s]" to "yield at least provisional insight into problems of artistic coherence, expansion, invention, expressive limits, intelligibility, mastery, exhaustion, depth, stylistic integrity, the cohesion of materials, and the like. . . . " Language games, then, help us to " 'learn the language' of a given artist." For Hagberg, that "language" includes the ethics of James's transgressions of the limits of any particular language-game convention and the effects of those transgressions on meaning.

Paul G. Beidler in *Frames in James*: The Tragic Muse, The Turn of the Screw, What Maisie Knew, *and* The Ambassadors (ELS 59 [1993]) investigates "James's fascination with the marginal and the subordinate" through Derrida's study of the parergon (or supplemental) frame. With each chapter complicating the relation between James's frames and Derrida's commentary on the parergon, Beidler discusses "the literal frame as it operates within the narrative" of *The Tragic Muse,* analyzes James's experimentation in *The Turn of the Screw* with framing in terms of plot elaboration and completion, literary genres, and the notion "that the frame/work relationship can be found in relations between people in the realm of fiction as well as between elements of a work of art." In *What Maisie Knew* Beidler argues that Maisie herself may be read as a parergonal frame within the work. Maisie is therefore "used to compensate for the lack of decency in her parents' adulterous relationships . . . ." James combines the framing technique in both the structure of *The Ambas-*

sadors and "the parergonal nature of the hero," Strether, for whom Paris is both a "story" and an "aesthetic" from which he must free himself in order to reach the framing place in his own life, where he can see the "truth." Throughout his analysis of James's use of parergon, Beidler makes us realize once again James's extraordinary complexity, the range of his formal experiments, and his deep interest in the nature of language and meaning.

"Starting from the principle that, for [C. S.] Peirce, every creation, scientific or artistic, results in an *icon*," Sigrid Renaux in her readable, interesting, and suggestive The Turn of the Screw: *A Semiotic Reading* (Peter Lang, 1993) conducts an analysis of James's great ghost story, not only in terms of its "verbal/symbolic" language, but, and here is the advantage, of its "visual/iconic language." Since for Renaux the "iconic" includes physical and verbal gestures of the narrator and characters, architectural details of Bly, recurrent figures of speech, music references, and other "phonological-visual icons," which she explains as "the heuristic sign *par excellence*" at the level of text and fiction, her study provides an analytic method that may be applicable to much, if not all, of James's fiction.

In *Henry James and Masculinity* (St. Martin's) Kelly Cannon notes that many of James's male characters, including Rowland Mallet, Strether, Hyacinth Robinson, the *Aspern Papers* narrator, John Marcher, the narrator in "The Figure in the Carpet," Ralph Touchett, Pemberton, Morgan Moreen, and Miles of *The Turn of the Screw*, "defy" or fail to meet contemporary stereotypes of masculinity. Such failure or defiance both places characters at the margins of their fictive societies and "unsettles rather than appeases the reader's longing for conventional manhood," which Cannon locates in Chad Newsome. Cannon investigates James's inquiry into the marginalized male, the particular language he uses to locate and describe that experience, and the effects of such language on readers' imaginations. Cannon also reads autobiography in James's marginal male characters. But marginality is not all agony. Recalling Ross Posnock in *The Trial of Curiosity* (Oxford, 1991), Cannon also recognizes the potential freedom to be found in the margin. At the same time, calling for a reexamination of "James's life in order to trace the pattern of marginality that contradicts the notion that James freely chose his 'life of the imagination,'" Cannon's argument links with Michael Davitt Bell's discussion of masculinity and realism in *The Problem of American Realism* (Chicago, 1993).

Although W. R. Martin and Warren U. Ober's *Henry James's Apprenticeship: The Tales, 1864–1882* (Meany) follows in general the traditional dates of James's early period as a fiction writer and critic, it is odd to call the novelist of *The Portrait of a Lady* (1881) or *The American* (1877) an "apprentice." Nevertheless, a book-length discussion of the 38 earlier tales affirms again the mass of the James oeuvre. Since the authors focus their study on parallels with and borrowings from Shakespeare and Chaucer, the book provokes readers to consider the relation of James's fiction to the poetry of those English writers. Each of the tales, which are taken up in order of publication, is treated with the same procedure: plot summary, brief discussion of details pertinent to the apprenticeship (such as the use of Shakespeare, Chaucer, and other canonical texts, and broad judgments about themes, characters, style, and method), and attention to elements that predict later fiction.

While each of the 10 essays in *Henry James: A Collection of Critical Essays*, ed. Ruth Bernard Yeazell (Prentice Hall), has appeared elsewhere over the past 45 years, with six of the 10 having been published in the last 15, the collection should be useful for students and seasoned Jamesians alike, who now have within one volume essays on some of the main critical issues in James studies by some of the most perceptive and creative James scholars since World War II. A great deal could be (and indeed has been) written about each of the essays in the collection. But the most concise way to describe them is simply to list them: "The Melodrama of Consciousness" by Peter Brooks, "Gender and Value in *The American*" by Carolyn Porter, "Aestheticism and *The Portrait of a Lady*" by Jonathan Freedman, "*The Princess Casamassima*" by Lionel Trilling, "Surveillance in *The Princess Casamassima*" by Mark Seltzer, "The First Paragraph of *The Ambassadors*" by Ian Watt, "The Logic of Delegation in *The Ambassadors*" by Julie Rivkin, "The Beast in the Closet" by Eve Kosofsky Sedgwick, "The Imagination of Metaphor" by Ruth Bernard Yeazell, and "The Consuming Vision" by Jean-Christophe Agnew.

Finally, *Critical Essays on Henry James*, ed. Peter Rawlings (Scolar), surveys English and American periodical literature on Henry James's fiction and criticism from 1878 to 1982 and adds a review of Fred Kaplan's *Henry James: The Imagination of Genius*. The aim of the volume and of the series is to "attempt to recover the controversies that have surrounded the great critics of the modern age." This volume contains the expected signed essays by Howells, George Saintsbury, Robert Louis Stevenson, T. S. Eliot, H. G. Wells, Van Wyck Brooks, and R. P. Blackmur. It also includes unsigned essays and pieces written by less well-known reviewers and critics. The essays are photographically reproduced from the originals, which helps to convey the immediacy of the original publications.

iv Criticism: General Essays

Reminding all Jamesians of the inevitable relation of critical fashion to canon formation, Richard A. Hocks in "Recanonizing the Multiple Canons of Henry James" (*American Realism and the Canon*, pp. 154–69) reviews three currents of James scholarship and the effect of each on canonicity. Hocks defines the currents thus: "pre-postmodern" criticism before 1980; 1980 to the present, which "pushed off center stage" *The Portrait of a Lady* and *The Ambassadors*; and a third phase in which a range of critical perspectives will "rebaptize" "venerable" works. Hocks's is an extremely cogent and thoughtful article, which could do a great deal to calm contentious scholars working in traditions of any of the three phases.

Henry James's novels, especially *The Portrait of a Lady*, play an important role in David Minter's *A Cultural History of the American Novel*. Minter shows that James's novels helped "to socialize readers," and he uses them to remind "us that a novel can expose the secret fears and hopes of an age even if it cannot resolve them."

Michael E. Nowlin in "'Reality in America' Revisited: Modernism, the Liberal Imagination and the Revival of Henry James" (*CRevAS* 23, iii [1993]: 1–29) presents an informative essay on Lionel Trilling's radical cold war project in the construction of Henry James's reputation. Nowlin explains how Trilling and others "within the *Partisan Review* orbit" claimed James as a representative for American dissidents by championing him as a modernist.

Two essays discuss James as his own editor/reviser and also the procedures of editing itself. In "Deconstructing *The Art of the Novel* and Liberating James's Prefaces" (*HJR* 14 [1993]: 284–307) Hershel Parker works to free the Prefaces from Blackmur's arrangement in *The Art of the Novel*, which misleads readers in at least two ways: first about the actual sequence in which the Prefaces were written and second about the association of ideas present when James actually composed them. Jerome

McGann's "The Case of *The Ambassadors* and the Textual Condition," pp. 151–66 in *Palimpsest: Editorial Theory in the Humanities,* ed. George Bornstein and Ralph G. Williams (Michigan, 1993), uses the controversy over the proper place of chapter 29 in *The Ambassadors* to warn editors (and those aspiring to such an office) that a particular text must be "grasped theoretically as a complex (and evolving) set of material and sociohistorical events. . . . [A] historical dialectics [is required] to supply [our analyses] with real critical and reflexive power."

Everett Carter in "Realists and Jews" (*SAF* 22: 81–91) surveys James's attitudes toward Jews in his fiction and nonfiction in the context of Jewish characters in Howells, Trollope, and Thackeray. Most significant is the way Carter reads Prince Amerigo's deprecation of and Maggie Verver's sympathy with the Jewish antique dealer in *The Golden Bowl* as James's strategy to direct readers' sympathies away from the Prince and Charlotte Stant and toward Maggie and Adam Verver.

In "Realism, Ideology, and the Novel in America (1886–1896): Changing Perspectives in the Work of Mark Twain, W. D. Howells, and Henry James" (*Revisionary Interventions,* pp. 189–210) Robert Weimann, like Minter (above), argues cogently that the realism of the last 15 or so years of the 19th century was sharply critical of the dominant culture and used that implicit criticism in an effort to "confront and comprehend the changing nature of society."

In a highly readable introduction to James's late style, the beginning of which she marks from *The Awkward Age,* Cynthia Ozick argues in "What Henry James Knew," pp. 276–304 in *The Ordering Mirror: Readers and Contexts* (Fordham, 1993), that James's ability to face the "sacred terror" of his life and career enabled him to reach a level of personal introspection and complication in his fiction that has enabled it to endure. That terror includes James's failure in the theater, the deaths of Constance Fenimore Woolson and his sister, Alice, and his own loneliness.

Discussing *The Aspern Papers,* "The Figure in the Carpet," "The Lesson of the Master," and *The Tragic Muse,* Michael Wilson in "Lessons of the Master: The Artist and Sexual Identity in Henry James" (*HJR* 14 [1993]: 257–63) contrasts James's depiction of the artist's conflicts with mainstream society, where both the artist and the homosexual are "abject, freakish and unnatural," and "desexualized," "to a representation of artistic life" in "*fin-de-siècle* Parisian bohemia."

v Criticism: Individual Novels

In "The Fiction of Art: Roderick Hudson's Pursuit of the Ideal" (*HJR* 15: 231–41) Craig A. Milliman analyzes characterization in *Roderick Hudson* together with James's remarks on art and artists elsewhere to understand James's implicit argument in the fiction on art and artists. Milliman concludes that "James would align himself with Gloriani."

Surveying references in *The American* to the Western United States, Lewis O. Saum argues in "Henry James's Christopher Newman: 'The American' as Westerner" (*HJR* 15: 1–9) that the idea of the West, "the most American part of this new country," informs James's characterization of Newman and indicates the level of James's knowledge of and attention to the Western United States.

While Michael Kearns in "Henry James, Principled Realism, and the Practice of Critical Reading" (*CE* 56: 766–87) takes *Washington Square* as the subject of his rhetorically based analysis, the implications of his article extend beyond James's novel. For at the center of Kearns's argument is a call for readers "to look at the rhetoric of intention embodied in all of the choices that comprise a novel." In addition, Kearns uses *Washington Square* to advance a discussion of how "naive realism" ("which privileges tangible facts and representational language") differs from "principled realism" (which insists both on the lack of a privileged perspective and the necessity of making ethical choices).

Four essays discuss *The Portrait of a Lady*. In "Narrative Instability in *The Portrait of a Lady*: Isabel on the Edge of the Social" (*JNT* 24: 43–54) Sophia Andres locates the conflict that James identified in his society between "art (and its related values of idealism) and the marketplace (and its related values of materialism and individualism)" in "the tension between the novel's structure and content." Andres argues that James used the New York Edition of the novel to attempt to resolve this tension through Isabel Archer's elision "of the distinction between human beings and material possessions." At the same time, Andres judges from evidence in the novel that James managed to resist full capitulation to "the emerging materialist ethic in England." Paul M. Hadella offers two key points in "Rewriting Misogyny: *The Portrait of a Lady* and the Popular Fiction Debate" (*ALR* 26, iii: 1–11): first, that *The Portrait* should be read in the context of contemporary popular fiction, from which it took "stock characters and incidents," leaving behind the "happy resolution of tensions"; second, that the prototype text for *The Portrait* is Frank Lee Benedict's *Mr. Vaughn's Heir* (1875). Eleanor Cook's "The Italian Journey: From James to Eliot to Browning," pp. 41–52 in Bruno Magliocchetti et al., eds., *The Motif of the Journey in Nineteenth-Century Italian Literature* (Florida), examines *The Portrait* as a *bildungsreise*, in which the education depends on Italy for its meaning. In addition, Cook examines *The Portrait* for what it suggests about James's own educational journey in Italy, including an understanding of the "Italianness" of characterization, which James learned from Robert Browning.

Wai Chee Dimock uses *The Bostonians* in "Gender, the Market, and the Non-trivial in James" (*HJR* 15: 24–30) as a point of departure to discuss social dynamics, gender, identity, and sexual politics in a consumer society, "whose ambition is to 'account for' the world in a quite literal way, to make people and things not only calculable but absolutely transparent, absolutely explainable [and thus equivalent] in their calculability."

Wendy Graham adds to the body of scholarship on power studies in *The Princess Casamassima*. In "Henry James's Subterranean Blues: A Rereading of *The Princess Casamassima*" (*MFS* 40: 51–84) Graham examines the novel as James's attempt to define the relation of the socially marginalized homosexual (Hyacinth Robinson) to contemporary "regulatory norms governing class hierarchy and . . . heterosexual hegemony."

Through Miriam Rooth, Steven H. Jobe in "Representation and Performance in *The Tragic Muse*" (*ALR* 26, ii: 32–42) discusses "the characteristically Jamesian question of how best to live." In Miriam, Jobe reads Jamesian reconciliation between "public and private roles, past and present experiences, and independent and related identities." The discipline of the highly trained performer is key for finding meaning and purpose in "a difficult world of conflicting allegiances, fragmented identities, and changing times."

In "James and the Tribal Discipline of English Kinship" (*HJR* 15: 127–40) Nancy Bentley examines *The Spoils of Poynton* through the lens of contemporary ethnographic literature. In so doing, she makes the point that throughout James's fiction the bonds that link kin are indistinguishable from those that link owners to their property. In "Reconsidering Poynton's Innocent Patriarch" (*HJR* 15: 141–51) Carol Faulkner, like Bentley, also places the novel in a contemporary cultural context; for

Faulkner, however, analysis focuses on the dynamics of patriarchy and primogeniture as "the real center of power" in the novel.

Three articles are concerned with *The Wings of the Dove*. Wayne C. Booth's "The Ethics of Forms: Taking Flight with *The Wings of the Dove*" (*Understanding Narrative*, pp. 99–135) provides two services for its readers. First, it develops an ethical analysis of the novel, which is based on strategies Booth employed in *The Company We Keep: An Ethics of Fiction* (Calif., 1988). Second, it supplies a detailed outline of both "The Chronological Story" and "The Story-as-Told (The Narrative, the Discourse)," which could be helpful for first-time readers. Booth's discussion of ethics in *Wings* deals directly with what seem to be two contradictory demands of the text on the reader: (1) to consider the harmful effects of the commodification of aesthetics, and (2) to examine ethical implications of James's late style, which offers itself as a commodity to be "used" by the critical reader. To accomplish this analysis, Booth argues for a way of reading that reconciles "the ethical powers of a work as being actually in the work, regardless of readers' differences" and "a work's actual ethical effects." In " 'A Circle of Petticoats': The Feminization of Merton Densher" (*HJR* 15: 38–54) Julie Olin-Ammentorp reads *The Wings of the Dove* as a chronicle of how social limits enforce gender roles. Olin-Ammentorp regards Merton Densher as an illustration of the way gender roles "constrict" and also "define," both of which are necessary conditions of identity in the world of the novel.

Allen W. Menton notices in "Typical Tales of Paris: the Function of Reading in *The Ambassadors*" (*HJR* 15: 286–300) that aside from the geographical Paris there are the "mythical" ones of fiction and of Strether's past. Shaping Strether's imagination, the mythical versions of Paris affect the way he conducts his life and understands himself. Pierre A. Walker also discusses Strether's imagination in "Reading the Berne Bears in the End of James's *The Ambassadors*" (*MLS* 22, ii [1992]: 4–14). For Walker, attention to James's allusions to Balzac's *Louis Lambert,* to the legend of Origen, and to the mechanical bears on the Berne *Zeitglockenthurm* would lead readers to an understanding of Strether's particular gain in insight concerning "the duality of human nature and society—that everything contains to some extent its opposite."

All five articles on *The Golden Bowl* deal significantly, if not centrally, with seeing, knowing, and possessing; thus all address issues of form, imagination, and living. For me, one of the best essays of the year is

Thomas Galt Peyser's "James, Race, and the Imperial Museum" (*AmLH* 6: 48–70). Peyser reads the Ververs' tendency in the novel and James's in *The American Scene* to understand the world in aesthetic terms as an expression of a particular imperialism that is capable of reconstructing the multicultural world into a kind of national museum. In that museum, the colonizer or possessor is required to understand and empathize with the collected (and must then also fear the collected) in a relationship that is analogous to that of the White Man to his Burden. Mary Ann Caws in "What Can a Woman Do for the Late Henry James?" (*Raritan* 14, i: 1–17) develops an analysis of the novel's rhetorical construction—its "gynocentric epistemics"—and its ethical component, which she finds interrelated. Caws's essay depends on at least two Jamesian premises: that "seeing is the self" and that "thoughts are material things in the Jamesian consciousness." In addition, with an orientation to the novel similar to that contained in Wayne C. Booth's essay on *The Wings of the Dove*, which I noted above, Caws looks for a way to answer a question that concerns both readers and, in a slightly different way, characters: "How can fictions save?" Beth Sharon Ash works a rather elaborate psychoanalytic inquiry, which is also centered on seeing, in "Narcissism and the Gilded Image: A Psychoanalytic Reading of *The Golden Bowl*" (*HJR* 15: 55–90). Arguing from a post-Freudian set of assumptions about the social constitution of the self, Ash responds to readings of Maggie's motivation in the novel by Bersani, Seltzer, and Foucault. Key to her analysis are the complexity and importance of Oedipal and pre-Oedipal fantasies, which implicate all four of the novel's main characters. The bowl metaphor is also central to Ash's argument because it represents Maggie's "infantile belief . . . that . . . [her public] image is so brilliant on the outside that the parent will not think to look into the secret recesses where the deficient and impotent self actually resides." Cultural and psychological attitudes toward photography and knowing, expressed in James's fiction and representative of his own anxieties, ground Julie Grossman's argument in " 'It's the Real Thing': Henry James, Photography, and *The Golden Bowl*" (*HJR* 15: 309–28). Grossman contends that those attitudes and anxieties drove James to "reinvent realism" by replacing "reality" with "images" and analogies that amount to "evocative senses of things." Similarly, Phyllis van Slyck in " 'An innate preference for the represented subject': Portraiture and Knowledge in *The Golden Bowl*" (*HJR* 15: 179–89) discusses the way both characters and readers gain knowledge by evaluating imaginative "portraits" constructed from fictive worlds or from the text. For van Slyck, a narrative portrait in James is a moment of suspended action during which "one character places another within an enclosing frame" and then interprets that portrait by imposing "an illusory coherence and reliability on a complex, fragmented, and only partially knowable subject." Van Slyck argues that such portraiture demonstrates "both the extreme limitations and the creativity inherent in the act of knowing."

vi Criticism: Individual Tales

Adeline R. Tintner, "*Daisy Miller* and Chaucer's 'Daisy' Poem: *The Prologue to the Legend of Good Women*" (*HJR* 15: 10–23), places "Daisy Miller" in the 14th-century French poetical tradition of "the *marguerite* or 'daisy' poems . . . in which the daisy is the object of adoration and worship connected with the God of Love . . . ." The tradition was carried into the 19th century, "without the daisy symbolism," by Tennyson and Robert Browning.

Combining post-Freudian theory involving orality with cultural studies in "Toxic Mothers, Cultural Criticism: 'In the Cage' and Elsewhere" (*HJR* 14 [1993]: 264–72), William Veeder finds that details of the telegraphist's childhood, including family dysfunction, class, and occupation, account for the way she "behave[s] as she does." In addition, analysis of the telegraphist's childhood brings Veeder to the point that "James views experience . . . fundamentally from the child's point of view. His is the voice of the victim, of the young person of promise damaged from the start."

Two articles concentrate on *The Turn of the Screw*. Working to explain James's career-long "struggle" to integrate various fictional modes, especially realism and romance, William J. Scheick in "Aesthetic Romance: James," pp. 57–74 in *The Ethos of Romance,* discusses *The Turn of the Screw* as "aesthetic romance" ("a self-referential artifact" that "relentlessly insists upon enigma"), which James achieved by converting the ghost story, a formula of "eventuary romance" ("in which mystery is dispelled when its plot reinstates simple reason, social order, and the known world of fact"). One important inference Scheick draws from James's manipulation of romantic form is that "an appreciative paralysis" rather than an assertion of a particular ethos constitutes an "ideal response" to our inability, like the governess's, to know " 'the hideous author of our woe.' "
Lisa G. Chinitz in "Fairy Tale Turned Ghost Story: James's *The Turn of*

the Screw" (*HJR* 15: 264–85) also explores James's "genre confusion" along with his experiments in testing the boundaries of textual meaning and the meaning of the world outside it. For Chinitz, such testing, in addition to James's deliberate confusion of the ghost story and fairy tale, forces readers to frame and reframe the main story, producing for readers, like the tale's characters, "a crisis in reality testing that is nothing less than uncanny."

In "Toward an Ethics of Cultural Acts: The Jamesian Dialectic in 'Broken Wings'" (*HJR* 15: 152–69) David Golumbia reads "Broken Wings" as James's attempt to "mediate between aesthetic and ethical concerns." James's effort to interweave the two suggests the need for Jamesian criticism to avoid separating these realms of inquiry; instead, it ought to examine the dialectical tension of form and ethics.

Two essays on "The Beast in the Jungle" deserve notice. Margaret Faurot in "The Tyranny of the Moment: Time and Tense in 'The Beast in the Jungle'" (*Lang&S* 23 [1990]: 335–50) contends that the story merits attention for the way James's management of verb tense and of the subjunctive and conditional, among other strategies, merges his own style with Marcher's. Studies of the body and of physical motion in geographical space in the narrative of the story and in 19th-century culture establish key frames of reference for Ilana Bar'am in "Bodily Movement as Narrative Strategy in 'The Beast in the Jungle'" (*HJR* 15: 170–78). Bar'am's thesis is that "bodily movement on the metaphorical and nonmetaphorical levels suggests a displacement of meaning from the primary to the secondary frames of reference."

Finally, Norman E. Stafford argues cleverly in "Rediscovering Henry James's 'Hugh Morrow'" (*CEA* 56, ii: 61–68) that "Hugh Morrow" has been neglected because its commentators regard it as a fragment. Stafford explains that no compelling evidence supports this claim and that the story, as it is, especially when paired with "The Real Thing," "enlarges our perception of the relationships between artists and their subjects." More, the work's symbolism and "richness of ambiguity" suggest its worth.

Creighton University

8 Pound and Eliot

Michael Coyle and Laura Cowan

This year Pound and Eliot studies proved more than ever to be a heterogeneous *field* of activity rather than a standardized *industry*. Contributions to the study of both figures, or studies in which Pound and Eliot figured importantly in the ongoing revaluation of modernism, came from a variety of distinct and sometimes competing critical discourses. The year's best work resists either the merely contentious dismissal of their political or ideological commitments, or the uncritical veneration of their poetic accomplishments. This development has been some time in the making, and it suggests that modernist criticism becomes increasingly and genuinely critical because it at last becomes historical. Michael Coyle is responsible for the Pound commentary here, Laura Cowan for the Eliot.

i Pound

a. Text, Biography, and Bibliography   Two important collections of correspondence appeared this year: *Ezra Pound and James Laughlin: Selected Letters,* ed. David M. Gordon (Norton), and *Pound, Thayer, Watson, and* The Dial, ed. Walter Sutton (Florida). Although both collections add to our knowledge of the important role that editors played in Pound's career, and both have been prepared by experienced Pound scholars, the Sutton volume is finally the more impressive.

Gordon explains that, "faced with the immense bulk and diversity" of the material Pound and Laughlin exchanged, he determined to "gather the analects of Pound in these letters." This phrase, "the analects of Pound," reproduces Pound's own Confucianist metaphor; but it also suggests that the editor aims more to present a synopsis of Pound's principal thematics than to chart the course of a complicated relationship between two very different men. Laughlin showed great courage, both in defending Pound and in standing up to him on such questions as Pound's anti-Semitism; the selected inclusion of his side of the correspondence greatly enhances the volume's historical value. But Gordon goes further still, including 11 different correspondents, frequently linked together with short, contextualizing narratives; an appendix reprints John Berryman's rejected introduction to *Selected Poems of Ezra Pound* (Pound did not like what many readers since have regarded as fine work). Nevertheless, Gordon's work is marred by the nearly 50 factual errors identified by Richard Taylor in his review of the volume (*Paideuma* 24, i: 129–36), and by the tendency of Gordon's editorial commentary to read like apologetics.

Sutton's book differs chiefly in its more detached tone. It offers reliable scholarly apparatus, including a biographical appendix and an informative introduction. The introduction details the history of Pound's relations with the *Dial* and explains his distance from it between 1923 and 1926. With the discovery of Watson's papers, Sutton is able to revise prevailing views of the comparative importance of Thayer and Watson; Watson heretofore has been regarded as "a rather shadowy figure in the background." In the course of this correspondence it becomes clear that at least for a brief while Pound invested more of his hopes in the *Dial* than in the other periodicals with which he was variously associated.

A Guide to Ezra Pound and Ernest Fenollosa's Classic Noh Theatre of Japan (National Poetry Foundation), ed. Akiko Miyake et al., is all that it promises to be and more. Copublished with the Ezra Pound Society of Japan, the volume brings together the commentaries, glossaries, and annotations to the Fenollosa manuscripts of 15 scholars and translators. This *Guide* differs from Carroll Terrell's *A Companion to the Cantos* (1980) in its close attention to textual history, making available for the first time a record of Pound's adaptation and transformation of Fenollosa's notebooks. Broader rewards are offered here as well, since the introductory and glossary materials reconstruct the historical context within which Pound undertook this work. For example, at the time that Pound first published *Classic Noh Theatre of Japan,* the only published authority in English was Marie Stopes, the then infamous advocate of birth control. She understandably felt slighted by Mary Fenollosa's choice of Pound and refused to help him in any way. However, contextual questions are occasionally muddied by distracting, Joseph Campbell-like assertions of universality; we are told, for instance, that "the Japanese god danced and the chorus sang the same story of nature mythology that the Westerners sang in Greece and Provence," and that the legend presented in "Hagoromo" exists "practically all over the world." Although consonant with Pound's own published opinions, such comparisons are unlikely to help shape precise understandings of his engagements with Noh. If "the same" story can be found almost anywhere, why go to Noh? Nonetheless, the *Guide* will likely make this part of Pound's work available to new readers and scholars.

Less imposing but no less useful in the classroom is A. Walton Litz's new edition of *Diptych: Rome-London* (New Directions), which juxtaposes "Homage to Sextus Propertius" with "Hugh Selwyn Mauberley." Litz's bibelot reprints in inexpensive form the limited edition of 1958. The primary significance of the original *Diptych* has been apparent since 1990, when the Baechler-Litz edition of *Personae* changed the subtitle of "Mauberley" from "Life and Contacts" to "Contacts and Life." In his introduction to *Diptych,* Litz explains that the change reflects Pound's final sense of the relation between the two parts of the poem.

G. Singh has published two different guides to Pound's prose work. The slighter of the two—*The Sayings of Ezra Pound* (Duckworth)—is nevertheless interesting because it demonstrates that Pound remains something more than an academic subject. Collecting "gists and piths" from Pound's sprawling and heterogeneous prose writings, Singh displays a thorough familiarity with his subject. In conformity with the other titles in what is actually a series of little books, Singh divides his quotations into 12 thematic categories such as "Poetry and Literature," "Music," or "Politics and Economics." In *Ezra Pound as Critic* (Macmillan/St. Martin's) Singh again takes his cue from Pound—as well as from Eliot's introduction to *Literary Essays of Ezra Pound* (1954)—and proposes that Pound's literary criticism offers a coherent program. *Pound as Critic* no more offers to criticize the critic than does *The Sayings,* but Singh is an experienced guide who knows the terrain. His appendix of 60 "salient examples of the Poundian dicta on poetry, criticism, culture, art, religion," however, reads like a draft for the *Sayings* volume; in the context of this more serious project it signifies an attempt to preserve Pound from contemporary criticism rather than negotiate with it.

Marking the completion of a long and demanding project, J. J. Wilhelm's *Ezra Pound: The Tragic Years, 1925–1972* (Penn. State) displays something of the same spirit, but it adopts a more responsive strategy. It is not often that the *revisionist* biography of a celebrated poet is the one that comes to his or her defense, but that is just the case here. In fact, as Wilhelm pointedly reminds us, Pound's biographers have been among his most hostile critics. At different points acknowledging and even addressing the conclusions of Charles Norman, Noel Stock, and Humphrey Carpenter, Wilhelm forthrightly sets out to disengage fact from the momentum of narrative. This effort brings forth the strengths and limits of Wilhelm's study. *The Tragic Years* is the last part of a trilogy, begun with *The American Roots of Ezra Pound* (1985) and followed by *Ezra Pound in London and Paris* (1908–1925) (1990). The division into three volumes says much. The first volume describes Pound's boyhood and education, and the second the 17 years he spent in Paris and London. By comparison, the final volume is telescopic, covering the nearly half-century in which Pound published the separate volumes that make up the *Cantos* as we now have them. While it is true that Wilhelm has already written about the cantos composed in St. Elizabeths (*The Later Cantos of Ezra Pound*, 1977), that earlier book was not biographical. In other words, the very structure of this trilogy constitutes an implicit judgment of Pound's career. Since 1925 was the year in which Pound published *A Draft of XVI Cantos,* the first permanent collection of *Cantos,* Wilhelm's division perhaps inadvertently identifies the period in which Pound composed the *Cantos*—which Wilhelm usually calls Pound's "masterwork"—with tragedy. Tragedy does not necessarily mean waste or failure, but this volume begins: "The last part of Ezra Pound's life was not as happy as the first."

All said and done, Wilhelm's three-volume opus differs qualitatively from previous biographies. If it reads less smoothly than Carpenter's biography (though not than Stock's), its slightly annalistic textures are more given to detail than to potted judgment. The work here is careful, more sympathetic to Pound than not, unafraid to acknowledge some of Pound's mistakes but disinclined to transform the perception of error into a brief against a life's work. Wilhelm's sometimes lengthy discussions of individual cantos remain distinct from the biographical commentary, but the quality of his literary perceptions is the best yet offered by any of the biographers.

b. General Studies and Relation to Other Writers   Reminding us of the root meaning of the phrase "masterpiece," a piece of work submitted for the position of master in a guild, Bob Perelman's *The Trouble with Genius* opens by considering genius as a kind of discourse or career strategy;

within this discourse the word "masterpiece" assumes its more mystify-
ing modern aura, often seeming inseparable from the notion of genius.
Perelman's study proceeds from this association; the four writers who
constitute his subject, Pound, Joyce, Stein, and Zukofsky, all attempted a
"life-writing" rather than poems or fictions understood as such. Perelman's notion of "genius-language" is thus an alternative to more ag-
gressively politicized critical notions of "ideology" or "discourse," even if
it is conceived in analogous ways. Perelman is himself a published poet,
wholly at home in contemporary theoretical discourse. Drawing on
Derrida or Lacan when it suits him to do so, he is finally more concerned
with the texture of writing itself than with translating Pound's poetry
into something else that might make more sense. For example, he writes
of Joyce that critical models often want to use modernist "works as
examples of linguistic processes that are widely representative, if not
universal . . . whereas only an extreme need for singularity could have
produced anything like *Ulysses*."

In Pound's case this same sensibility leads Perelman to a striking
departure from previous opinion on the difficulty of the *Cantos*. The
general tendency of criticism has been, Perelman suggests, to regard
Pound's difficulty as the result of an undereducated readership; consequently, book after book endeavors to supply the identifications and
other information necessary to a real understanding of the poem. In
contrast, Perelman considers such difficulty to be a constitutive feature
of Pound's work: "the blankness" that these works "proffer the naive
reader" is "an integral part of their meaning." Consequently, to explain
away the difficulty is to transform the work and to remove from it a
most characteristic feature. Interrogating Hugh Kenner's assertion that
Pound's poetry "is difficult as all poetry is difficult, but the hard shell is in
most places very thin," Perelman asserts that the unriddling of the
majority of the poem's allusions "can ultimately be a barrier to a comprehension of the 'WHY' of Pound's writing." This basic tenet serves
Perelman well as he describes particular features of the *Cantos;* for
example, he describes the Poundian ideogram as "a never-ending gesture
of verbal discontinuity designed to evoke masterful artistic distance."
Similarly, he sees Pound's use of foreign words, ideograms, and picto-
grams as part of an impulse to "purify, isolate, and sacralize his words."
While drawn to formal issues, Perelman's attentions are not restricted to
them. Rather, his sensitivity to formal issues brings him to challenge
those instances of *idéologie critique* which regard readers as powerless

sheep: "[Pound's] work can be morally dismal if its referents are followed out carefully in certain areas, but the trails that lead to Hitler and the Jews need not be taken: there are other trails from most of Pound's words." Perelman speaks, in other words, for the power of readerly choice, and his discussion here borrows from the Derridean insistence that semiosis can never be wholly controlled. *The Trouble with Genius* is an exciting and finely written book that persuasively submits we have yet really to see Pound's work.

In *Changing Voices: The Modern Quoting Poem* (Michigan, 1993) Leonard Diepeveen turns an insistently formal attention to the task of reframing the way that we approach certain modernist texts. Like Perelman, Diepeveen considers four primary figures, in this case all poets: Cummings, Moore, Eliot, and Pound. But Diepeveen makes no arguments about genius. Instead, his choices follow from the perception that each of these poets quotes in a distinctive way. Such distinctions shape the tenor of this book, which begins by differentiating between quotation and allusion. Allusion tends to work by indirection, while quotation "is specific: the *exact* transferring of a text into another, new text." For Diepeveen the precise identification and annotation of quotations is generally beside the point. It is, he repeatedly affirms, "the *texture* of the quotation in which these poets are most interested," the *difference* of the quoted material from the surrounding text. Considered together with Perelman's *The Trouble with Genius*, *Changing Voices* suggests a small resurgence of formalist study, though one informed by 30 years of poststructuralist activity and that reads closely without expectation of final unity.

"Quotation" is also an important issue for Lawrence Rainey, who this year launched with Robert von Hallberg *Modernism/Modernity* (thrice annually), a new interdisciplinary journal aiming "to bring into dialogue humanists analyzing the history of modernism and social scientists assessing the forces of modernity," and to do so in international contexts. The quality of the journal in its first year was impressive. Volume 1, number 3 included Rainey's own "'The Creation of the Avant-Garde: F. T. Marinetti and Ezra Pound" (pp. 195–219), which considers, in Peter Bürger's formulation, "the extent to which the avant-garde can be defined as an attack on the status of art in bourgeois society," as well as "the ways in which that attack overlaps with the avant-garde's use of motifs, materials, and artifacts from mass or popular culture." Reconsidering the effect of futurism on Pound, Rainey pays special attention to Marinetti's

London visit of 1914, at which time he sought to cross the traditional boundaries between "art" and commercial culture. Rainey explains that Marinetti failed because he did not recognize that the music hall in England "was no longer a hybrid creation of popular culture, but a prototype of mass commodity culture"; moreover, Marinetti "failed to see that quotation and bricolage are strictly one-way streets. By this I mean that Marinetti's effort to appropriate, legitimate, and transform a still illegitimate genre such as the music hall had the effect not of delegitimating art, as he supposed, but of reaffirming its legitimacy." The essay closes by considering the lessons Pound learned from Marinetti's spectacle.

The essays published in *The Violent Muse: Violence and the Artistic Imagination in Europe, 1910–1939,* ed. Jana Howlett and Rod Mengham (Manchester), in a sense pick up where Rainey leaves off, following Marinetti's futurism into the horrific mass or machine violence of World War I. Two essays are of particular interest to Pound studies, touching on him while treating insistently pertinent historical and theoretical questions. Mengham's own "From Georges Sorel to *Blast*" (pp. 33–44) and Tim Mathews's "The Machine: Dada, Vorticism and the Future" (pp. 124–40) both consider "whether the rhetoric of violence in the literary and plastic arts reflects other, more palpable forms of aggression, or whether it issues from the internal logic of evolving arts forms and the changing social role of art." The language of this question in itself suggests exacting standards, for it asks that we study not only ideology and history, but also the history of the social institutions of art and of criticism: all of this without losing the sensitivity to particulars that comes from formal attention.

Frank Lentricchia attends less explicitly to Pound's negotiations with mass culture, but in the Pound chapter of his *Modernist Quartet* he returns to a concern broached last year by Cary Wolfe: Pound's "embarrassment as a male lyricist feeling out of place in a lyric territory that he believed his culture had feminized so much the better to trivialize it." Like Perelman and Diepeveen, Lentricchia studies Pound in the context of four principal subjects—Frost, Stevens, Pound, and Eliot—and like them too he aims to establish, not the essence of modernism, but its diversity; "we have forgotten," he writes, explaining what might seem his odd decision to include Frost in his "Quartet," "the heterogeneous character of modernist literature." Lentricchia's study of Pound differs from these others, however, in its overt interest in ethical and ideological questions. Moreover, although able to speak of Pound's later work, Lentricchia implicitly focuses on the early prose of *Patria Mia* and to a lesser extent on Pound's first published book of poetry, *A Lume Spento*.

Lentricchia proposes that *Patria Mia* is Pound's "single most important piece of literary and social criticism," and presents the writer as "the reverse immigrant," noting that Pound went to Italy "seeking cultural life in the very period when millions of Italians from the south were fleeing their homes (such as they were) for America in the hope of improving an economic base that Pound's family had already secured." And yet, Lentricchia goes on to say, "the unstated assumption of Pound's poetics is that his typical reader is not everyman but an American like himself, in need of what he needs." *A Lume Spento* figures in this argument because in it, Lentricchia finds, "Pound stages the predicament of his empty American 'I' gazing into the mirror of desire." The poems of the volume, "so unmodern in diction," nevertheless "escape mere conventionality by the extremity of their representation of the self seeking inspiration and poetic selfhood." Despite stylistic changes, Lentricchia concludes that from this extremity "Pound never really evolved as a poet."

Notions of poetic selfhood play no role in Denis Donoghue's *The Old Moderns: Essays on Literature and Theory* (Knopf), a gathering of essays that reflects on the very notion of modernism and how that notion changes under the pressure of changing literary theories. The culminating essay of the volume is also the essay most concerned with Ezra Pound: "Is There A Perennial Literature?" Opening with a discussion of R. P. Blackmur's 1956 lecture at the Library of Congress, "Irregular Metaphysics," Donoghue gracefully delivers an unfashionable polemic against the poststructuralist insistence on historical discontinuity as the founding principle of literary study. Blackmur's comments on Pound's "Medallion" provide particular occasion for pause, and Donoghue then recalls meeting Blackmur several years later and asking "how he could have assumed that his audience at the Library of Congress would cope, at first hearing, with those four lectures, with themes so difficult, sentences so compact and arcane, citations so opaque." Blackmur's response leads Donoghue to observe the risk that would attend any contemporary attempt to invoke "the human condition." "A distinction between perennial and capricious experience goes against the modern grain," Donoghue remarks, just as we are now encouraged (after Edward Said) to "think of beginnings, because they are historical, but not of origins, because they are mythic." Donoghue attempts, however, not to discredit contemporary critical theory but to comment on some of the excesses of its victories. *The Old Moderns* is a balanced and thoughtful book that makes highly reasonable requests. Donoghue defends no "essentialist" program, but suggests merely "that there are forms of literature that change far more slowly than literary historians are inclined to say, and that this fact should modify their (our) account of modern literature."

Stan Smith's innovative *The Origins of Modernism* might seem to exemplify the tendencies that Donoghue regrets, but Smith himself is alert to the interaction between critical paradigms and literary history. For this reason the title of Smith's book, apparently promising another historical narrative, is misleading. Smith is actually more interested in teasing out what he calls modernism's "double-edged promise": "originality must be matched by a sense of origins." While reconstructing the historical pressures that could make "restoration" the most radical "revolt" of all is part of Smith's project, he also engages the ways in which we, at the end of the 20th century, understand ourselves. To this end, Smith expertly marshals an array of poststructuralist warrants—most interestingly Julia Kristeva and her now ubiquitous notion of "intertextuality." But this book rarely becomes *about* its own premises; instead, Smith's theoretical sophistication tends to show in the kinds of questions that he does and does not ask. Ultimately, this powerfully revisionist study offers to reframe our increasingly noisy discussions of the relations between modernism and postmodernism. Rather than demonstrating that his three subjects were particularly "always already" postmodern, Smith documents that "the term 'postmodernism' in a book title predates by a year what is generally thought to be the first comparable usage 'Modernist,' in the title of Graves's and Riding's *Survey of Modernist Poetry*" (1927). Postmodernism is thus "in a sense coeval with Modernism, its originary twin, the perpetual but repressed other." Smith writes economically, with wit and verve, and with a keen sense for resonant phrases. It is fitting that a book concerned with "the rhetoric of renewal" should itself hold such promise for the revitalization of modernist studies.

Michael North's compelling and groundbreaking *The Dialect of Modernism: Race, Language, and Twentieth-Century Literature* (Oxford) treats the relations among Anglo-American modernists and African American writers. North triangulates attempts from 1880 until 1920 to "standardize" English with minstrelsy and the development of "aesthetic modernism." His chapter "Old Possum and Brer Rabbit: Pound and Eliot's Racial Masquerade" is especially rich in this regard, at once distinguishing between Pound's and Eliot's use of dialect and also establishing that dialect became "the private double of the modernist poetry they were jointly creating and publishing in these years." While African American dialect made its way into both Pound's and Eliot's work early on, it did so in different ways and ultimately to different purposes. Pound came to regard Eliot's language as having been "emasculated" by his popular success, while Pound attempted to draw on the popular literature of his youth to create a more inclusive notion of culture. Alert to the disruptive interplay of other presences in Pound's work that worked against this inclusivity, North's work maps out a plenitude of further directions in the relation of high modernist activity to popular culture.

Ann Ardis's "Reading 'as a Modernist'/Denaturalizing Modernist Reading Protocols: Wyndham Lewis's *Tarr*" (*Rereading Modernism*, pp. 373–90), essays the relations between modernism and mass culture from a distinct vantage. Possibly from her concern with the binary opposition that Pound and Eliot established between realism and modernism, Ardis calls this relation a "dialectic." The central purpose of this carefully argued piece is to call attention to the reading practices whereby Eliot and Pound proposed Lewis's *Tarr* "for canonization as a modernist masterwork by discrediting other ways of reading, other aesthetic practices (e.g., realism) that were flourishing in the early twentieth century." Anyone familiar with Ardis's first book on "the New Woman" novelists of the period will recognize the important purchase of this work: certainly it is not the likes of Arnold Bennett or John Galsworthy for whom she wishes to recover academic respect. Her concerns prompt her to avoid both "the facile indictment of modernism's misogyny . . . and the blanket endorsement of modernist experimentalism as an instance of what French feminists such as Julia Kristeva or Hélène Cixous have called *écriture feminine*." Ardis's work thus serves to remind us of the heterogeneity not only of modernism but of contemporary feminisms.

c. Shorter Poems and Translations   The special double issue of *Paideuma* (23, ii–iii) presents two essays of importance on the topic of Pound's translations. Songpin Jin's "Observation of Natural Scenes: Ta Hsüeh and Pound's Later Cantos" (pp. 7–44) discusses "certain Confucian ideas" that Pound absorbed while translating *The Great Learning*. In "Rediscovering Ezra Pound: A Post-Postcolonial 'Misreading' of a West-

ern Legacy" (pp. 81–105) Xiaomei Chen confronts expectations of politically correct relativism by resubmitting her notion of "Occidentalism":
that is, in this case, the politically liberating force of Pound's work in
contemporary post-Maoist China.

In "Beyond Language: Ezra Pound's Translation of the Sophoclean
Elektra" (*Paideuma* 23, ii–iii: 107–39), Christine Syros considers what
Pound's *Elektra* (1990) can tell us about his sense of tragedy. Syros finds
there the basis for broad distinctions: "for Pound the 'Make It New'
postulate did not entail rewriting the Greek drama in accordance with
modern ideology, as had been done by otherwise competent authors like
O'Neill, Giraudoux, Cocteau, or Hofmannsthal. Rather, it meant that
the translation had to achieve a linguistic and conceptual timeliness by
creating an analogon to the world registered in the original text." Syros's
essay carefully demonstrates how Pound's translation attempts to forge
an "analogon"—a forging, in Stan Smith's phrase, that is also a forgery.

Classicist Niall Rudd in "Pound and Propertius: Two Former Moderns," a chapter in his *The Classical Tradition in Operation* (Toronto),
suggests that much of the controversy surrounding Pound's *Homage to
Sextus Propertius* "had to do with post-war cultural changes, and with the
general decline of Latin in the educational system." Unfortunately, Rudd
does not develop that point. He finally has little sympathy with Pound,
charging that he turns some parts of Propertius's elegy into burlesque
and degrades others into "juvenile spoof." Rudd's outspoken defense of
the much-maligned William Gardner Hale—the Chicago classicist who
advised that if Pound were a card-carrying member of his own profession
"there would be nothing left for him but suicide"—is just. And in Rudd's
grudging counsel that the real problem "centres not so much, perhaps,
on Pound's competence in Latin (though one has recurrent doubts about
that) as on his attitude to it" resides the beginnings of a new understanding. But, unable to move to fresh ground, Rudd only enlarges a target
that eventually includes others of Pound's generation like F. R. Leavis,
J. P. Sullivan, and Donald Davie. Rudd insists on Pound's "hideous
blunders" and objects that, even if Pound's poem *is* to be judged on
political grounds rather than on the ground of accurate translation, it
still "seems a strangely inadequate response to the disasters of 1914–17."
In this respect, Rudd's conclusions are wholly at odds with those of Litz
or Smith. If this disagreement marks Rudd's imaginative failure, it is
nevertheless useful because it reminds us that we yet lack a fully histor-
icized account of Pound's *Homage* and that when we get that account

Hale will be something more than a stock villain as surely as Pound will emerge as something more than the isolated genius. The controversy resonated with contemporaneous readers—and with contemporary readers—because even beyond the possibly unlicensed vigor of Pound's creation it signified major cultural and institutional shifts in American ideas about education.

d. *The Cantos* Peter Crisp in "Pound as Gnostic? Creative Mythology and the Goddess" (*Paideuma* 23, ii–iii: 173–93) returns to the question of Pound's mysticism. Even those uninterested in such questions should appreciate Crisp's establishing of the importance of G. R. S. Mead, a contribution that helps historicize an aspect of Pound's work that not infrequently invites assertions of qualities merely recurrent and universal. Mead's influence on Pound was proposed years ago by Leon Surette, but Crisp pursues its historical trace as much as its mythopoeic implications.

Fan A. Shen's "Yijing and Pound's Cantos (1)" (*Paideuma* 23, ii–iii: 45–64) discusses a handful of well-known accounts of Pound's ideogramic method as a way of setting up an argument about the real coherence of the *Cantos*. Shen borrows from traditional Chinese aesthetics and submits the word "yijing," a principle ("kinetic entity") uniting two aspects of mind: image and feeling. After developing the significance of the term, and of its application to Pound, Shen treats Pound's attitudes toward it and proposes an analogy between it and what Derrida calls "decentering." In "Yijing and Pound's Cantos (2)" (*Paideuma* 23, ii–iii: 65–79) Shen elaborates further aspects of this "kinetic entity," discussing in particular "the crucial role" that Chinese ideograms play in the *Cantos*. Apparently part of a larger project, these essays constitute Shen's effort to establish a new criterion for evaluation.

Reed Way Dasenbrock pursues a revaluation no less profound than Shen's, but he does so by taking up the single most familiar notion in criticism of the *Cantos*—the idea of epic. He opens "Constructing a Larger *Iliad*: Ezra Pound and the Vicissitudes of Epic," pp. 248–66 in *Epic and Epoch: Essays on the Interpretation and History of a Genre,* ed. Steven M. Oberhelman et al. (Texas Tech), by noting how ideas about and attitudes toward epic have changed through the ages in response to the changing relations between culture and war. In particular, he notes the general revulsion in the 20th century against the Vergilian epic, a version of the epic of paramount importance throughout Renaissance Europe. The problem for modern writers, including the young Ezra Pound, was Vergil's association with imperialist expansion. At the same time, however, Pound's "sense of epic" owed much to the Renaissance association of the epic with the fashioning of moral exempla. Like such Renaissance writers as Spenser or Tasso, Pound was "far more concerned with this exemplary dimension than with questions of epic action and modes of narration." For Dasenbrock, this context makes the commitments of the infamous Italian cantos (72–73) all the more ironic. At this point Pound turns, as it were, from the *Odyssey* to the *Iliad,* from Propertius to Vergil, and the *Cantos* decline into "a textbook for fascists." In view of his own demonstration of Pound's changing conceptions of his own work, Dasenbrock's last charge is overstated—as though the cantos of the '40s and after could retrospectively rewrite those of the '20s. But this exciting essay reminds us how much we take for granted with overly familiar critical terms.

ii Eliot

a. Text, Biography, and Bibliography   Last year's publication of Eliot's Clark and Turnbull lectures as *The Varieties of Metaphysical Poetry,* ed. Ronald Schuchard (American ed., 1994; see *ALS* 1993, pp. 107–08) remains the signal textual event. Its footfalls will echo in the memory for years. In the "Restorer of the Real" (*New Republic* 19 December: 34–36), Helen Vendler interprets the lectures biographically and sees Eliot's descriptions of John Donne and Jules Laforgue as descriptions of the young Eliot: "a dissociated sensibility, plunged into a time almost wholly uncongenial." I see these interior struggles latent in his earlier essay, "The Metaphysical Poets" (1921): quotations used to demonstrate stylistic principles describe inner conflicts between the desire for unity and completion and inner compulsions which impede them. But Eliot's inner conflicts play out more stridently in these lectures. These personal conflicts could account for his much more critical view of Donne. While "The Metaphysical Poets" emphasized the possibilities in Donne's unifying sensibility, *The Varieties of Metaphysical Poetry* stresses his "catabolic tendency, the tendency towards dissolution." Vendler's review draws generously on Schuchard's "magisterial" notes in her depiction of the lectures as Eliot's "poetic manifesto." *The Varieties of Metaphysical Poetry* is really two books: along with the lectures themselves, Schuchard's thorough, erudite annotations and introduction make a monumental contribution to Eliot studies. Vendler's review expands our understanding of Eliot and modernism by using some of Schuchard's commentary to compare Eliot to Edith Sitwell and the French surrealists and by exploring the lectures' contemporary relevance.

A panel discussion, "Eliot's Standing and Eliot Studies: Diagnoses and Prospects," pp. 215–32 in *T. S. Eliot at the Turn of the Century*, part of the proceedings of a colloquium at Lund University, underscores another textual issue, copyright permissions. Several participants contend that the difficulty involved in getting permissions and the "tremendous" cost of these permissions are obstructing Eliot scholarship, discouraging new scholars from taking up Eliot, and contributing to the general disaffection with him.

b. General Studies   Probably because of the nature of contemporary criticism, which is often ideological or interdisciplinary and at its best tends to inclusive, outward gestures rather than narrow, specializing ones, many of this year's most valuable works fall in the General Studies category. Almost all of these at least implicitly address the explicit subject of *T. S. Eliot at the Turn of the Century*, evaluating Eliot's current status and the viability of his work for the 21st century. Of the conferees, A. David Moody and Barbara Everett address the conference topic most directly. In a study of both Eliot's criticism and his poetry, Moody's "The Mind of Europe in T. S. Eliot" (pp. 13–32) investigates the contemporary relevance of Eliot's "mind of Europe"—the possibility of any sort of European unity in today's fragmented and divisive world. He traces the concept in Eliot's criticism from its origins in a desire to transcend differences in "Tradition and the Individual Talent" through a Christian wisdom of disillusionment in the late essays. Whereas the idea of "a mind of Europe" settled into idealistic orthodoxy in the criticism, it found a much more dynamic enactment in the poetry which is vested in actuality and the real. Everett meets Eliot's detractors head-on in " 'How unpleasant to meet Mr Eliot' " (pp. 198–214). Her subtle readings of single lines and titles and her sensitive appreciation of broader patterns in his work prove her point that the complexities and nuances of poetic texts resist reductive readings as dogma or propaganda. In a more general study Bernard Bergonzi's discussion of the essentially 19th-century nature of "Eliot's Cities" (pp. 59–76) stimulates questions about the definition of modernism.

A revaluation of Eliot is in essence a revaluation of modernism. It is not surprising that some of the most compelling studies of Eliot occur in general examinations of this issue. All tie Eliot's aesthetics to social or political issues. In *The Origins of Modernism* Stan Smith's definition of modernism as a conflict between "restoration" and "revolt" underlines the "decentered, polyphonic, and self-unraveling plurality" inscribed in the structure and language of texts that explicitly deny their own multiplicity and instability. Calling Eliot and Pound the "Lenin and Trotsky of Modernism," Smith persuasively argues for the political and social origins of modernism from several angles. His evidence includes Eliot's own insistence that poetry has a political context, Eliot's pervasive political metaphors, and historical parallels (like the Bolshevik call for self-sacrifice that Eliot turns into a call for self-surrender in order to effect a literary revolution). Eliot's political consciousness is also manifest in his attention to dates and especially his deliberate misdating of "Tradition and the Individual Talent" to coincide with the Bolshevik revolution.

Marianne Thormählen (*T. S. Eliot at the Turn of the Century*, pp. 120–32) brings an entirely different perspective to "Tradition and the Individual Talent" in her analysis of Eliot's ambivalence toward self-effacement in his poetry and plays. Thormählen is particularly deft at integrating a wide variety of perspectives, including astute comments on Eliot's Buddhist influences.

Frank Lentricchia includes economics and the modernists' plight in the face of a capitalist commodity culture in his political and cultural study. *Modernist Quartet* was begun as the section on modern American poetry for the new *Cambridge History of American Literature,* and it has retained an introductory flavor. Its initial chapters, "Philosophers of Modernism at Harvard, circa 1900" and "Lyric in the Culture of Capital," make it appropriate reading for generalists and specialists alike. It will become essential reading for students of modernism. Lentricchia's analyses, which address the role of Eliot's background, family, marriage, and employment in his work, demonstrate the importance of context in our evaluations of modernism (in spite of the modernists' desire for universality). Ronald Schuchard's introduction to *The Varieties of Metaphysical Poetry,* which also makes the pressures of Eliot's business, financial, and family life patent, lends credence to Lentricchia. Lentricchia's summaries of the essentials of Eliot's career are sometimes concise to the point of reductive simplicity, but they are often both incisive and cognizant of the complexity of Eliot's work. His acknowledgment of the poetry's emotional power and resonance will act as an important corrective to many of the introductions to modernism which stress the intellectual in Eliot's poetry and the substance of his allusions.

Donald Childs's essay "T. S. Eliot's American Dissent/Descent" (pp. 77–94) appears in a collection of essays, *Cohesion and Dissent in America,* ed. Carol Colatrella and Joseph Alkana (SUNY). All of the essays in this provocative volume draw on Sacvan Bercovitch's ideas about cohesion and dissent as they define American culture; their methodology and their substance distinguish them. Childs sets out to prove Eliot's Americanness and to probe what this identity means to our understanding of him by examining the rhetoric and symbology in his essays. Childs unfolds a narrative of a rejection of the present because of a dedication to an ideal of what-ought-to-be that is similar to Bercovitch's description of the American jeremiad.

Jewel Spears Brooker structures her collection of essays, *Mastery and Escape,* by opposing two modernisms and defining a feature of the high modernists, "the tendency to move forward by spiraling back." This attention to the past is found in a great deal of this year's criticism—much of which is indebted to Jeffrey Perl's *Tradition of Return* (1984). The "escape" in Brooker's title entails a transcendence that moves beyond that which is mastered. While thought-provoking, her frame was less useful to me than many of the points of the learned individual essays which stand on their own.

c. Relation to Other Writers   The sometimes outworn subject of Eliot's relationship to 19th-century writers is repeated in several keys. In "Shelley and Eliot: A Study in Affinity" (*ELH* 61: 955–89) George Franklin places Eliot and Shelley in a tradition of radical skepticism that impels both writers to depict liminal characters or spaces which intersect the real world and a shadow world. The article—one of the most provocative this year—gives an intellectual and historical context for some of Eliot's most evocative passages (e.g., the "familiar compound ghost" passage in "Little Gidding"). The most interesting comments in Asad Al-Ghalith's study of Eliot and Wordsworth, "T. S. Eliot's Poetry: Intimations of Wordsworth's Romantic Concerns" (*MQ* 35: 42–51), discuss structural features and the imagination—subjects George Bornstein treated masterfully in *Transformations of Romanticism in Yeats, Eliot, and Stevens* (1976). Kristian Smidt (*T. S. Eliot at the Turn of the Century,* pp. 181–97) closely examines the poems quoted in "The Metaphysical Poets" to argue that

Eliot makes artificial and strained comparisons between the metaphysical poets and the Victorians to disavow a close connection between
himself and the 19th century.

Three articles on anthropology interweave recurrent themes in original ways. David Spurr's "Myths of Anthropology: Eliot, Joyce, Lévy-
Bruhl" (*PMLA* 109: 266–80) has affinities with both George Franklin
and Stan Smith. Spurr defines modernism as a self-origination which requires the recovery of the past. He illustrates the differences between Eliot's and Joyce's "artistic projects" by pointing out their different orienta-
tions toward the French ethnologist Lucien Lévy-Bruhl: "Whereas Eliot
mythologizes history, Joyce . . . historicize[s] mythology." Spurr accounts
for some of the "indeterminate" passages that preoccupy Franklin with
Lévy-Bruhl's theories about a prelogical primitive mentality which "collapses a number of distinctions essential to rational thought: between
sensible reality and the beyond, or the dream; between present and past
or future; between the sign and the cause of an event." This discussion
sets the stage for Eliot's troubling depiction of Jews (which contrasts
with Joyce's). Spurr sees the "figures of the savage and Jew in polar
opposition."

James Buzard analyzes anthropology and ethnology to very different
ends in "Eliot, Pound, and Expatriate Authority" (*Raritan* 13, iii: 106–
22). He sees Pound's and Eliot's self-appointed roles as "exiles" as a way to
legitimize their quest for a unified, cultural vision. Voicing a "sense of
dissatisfaction with this venerable trope" of exile, Buzard dubs Eliot and
Pound "optional expatriates" whom he compares to two other types of
voluntary expatriates—the professional ethnographer and the tourist.
The quest romance's journey toward cultural authority offers a model for
all three expatriates. Buzard interprets "Burbank with a Baedeker: Bleis-
tein with a Cigar" as a "dramatization of failed antitourism." He ends his
article reminding us of the ways in which both Pound's and Eliot's texts
undermine the unity and authority sought by the writers. In "The Case
of the Missing Abstraction: Eliot, Frazer and Modernism" (*Mastery and
Escape,* pp. 110–22), Jewel Spears Brooker dismisses prevailing definitions of the "mythical method" to offer her own based on Frazer's
scientific method.

Gareth Reeves's lucid and stimulating " 'The Present Self-Conscious
Century': Eliot on Valéry" (*YER* 13: 42–47) could be a companion piece
to Thormählen's on "Tradition and the Individual Talent," discussed
above. Eliot's early ideas about impersonality seemed to have been

shaped by reading Valéry, and his evolving attitudes toward impersonality and *poésie pur* can be charted through his essays on the French
poet. Eliot's comments in these essays about philosophical poems and
about the collapse of civilization because of self-consciousness voice
concerns of *The Varieties of Metaphysical Poetry* and suggest other avenues
for exploration.

d. Poems and Plays   The only full-length study of the plays this year,
Randy Malamud's *Where the Words Are Valid: T. S. Eliot's Communities of
Drama* (Greenwood) takes as central to all Eliot's drama a recurring
theme of this year's criticism: the importance of community. Readers of
Malamud will want to turn to Lentricchia for philosophical and political
backgrounds to these ideas. Because he has chosen to conduct a play-by-
play analysis, Malamud sometimes belabors his point and also perhaps
exaggerates drama's pivotal role in Eliot's changing aesthetics, politics,
and style. Equating the young Eliot with Prufrock and the other early
personae, he—like several other of this year's critics—is dismissive of
Eliot's early verse.

Several of the articles on a wide range of works and subjects implicitly
address questions of poetic method and creation and their consequent
interpretative strategies. Jewel Spears Brooker and Lois A. Cuddy read
"Gerontion" and *Four Quartets,* respectively, as unified structures whose
underlying aesthetics allow the poems to achieve a transcendent unity
beyond their apparent disparate or fragmented parts. Brooker's "The
Structure of Eliot's 'Gerontion': An Interpretation Based on Bradley's
Doctrine of the Systematic Nature of Truth" (*Mastery and Escape,* pp. 81–
109) is a philosophical defense of spatial readings (as conceived by Joseph
Frank). It is an informed reminder of the roots of New Criticism. A silent
backdrop to many of these articles, *The Varieties of Metaphysical Poetry*
calls these roots into question. The New Critics grounded their organic
interpretations of poems in part on Eliot's desire for a unified, integrated
text and his description of Donne's (at least partial) achievement of it in
"The Metaphysical Poets." According to Eliot's analysis of Donne and
Crashaw in *The Varieties of Metaphysical Poetry,* these exemplars of New
Critical tenets would fail the New Critical test of unity. Dante's poems
are unified structures—"every part of the system felt and thought in its
place." However, Donne's and Crashaw's poems are *sequences* rather than
systems: "In Donne you get a sequence of thoughts which are felt; in
Crashaw . . . you have a sequence of feelings which are thought. In

neither do you find a perfect balance." While Brooker studies idealism in philosophers such as Hegel and Bradley, Cuddy turns to science, theories of evolution, and John Boodin's cosmic idealism in " 'Making a Space in Time': T. S. Eliot, Evolution, and the *Four Quartets*" (*T. S. Eliot at the Turn of the Century*, pp. 77–90).

Gareth Reeves shares an emphasis on the reader's experience with Brooker. His book, *T. S. Eliot's* The Waste Land (Harvester Wheatsheaf), offers a comprehensive reading of the poem, its historical and cultural context, its critical reception, and its theoretical perspectives. The conviction that its notorious difficulty and mysterious inscrutability are essential to *The Waste Land* gives focus to his wide-ranging study. Reeves, one of today's most promising Eliot scholars, is well-versed in contemporary critical theory and Eliot studies. Murray McArthur's "Deciphering Eliot: 'Rhapsody on a Windy Night' and the Dialectic of the Cipher" (*AL* 66: 509–24) draws on theories of Lacan, Derrida, and Freud to pursue the impulses which generate "Rhapsody on a Windy Night" and offer an opinion congruent with Reeves's—the necessity of "cipher" (a secret code) in the composition and interpretation of the poem. The ambiguity and lack of closure that Reeves promotes would question Brooker's drive for unity.

This year has witnessed some attention to Eliot's religion—a legacy no doubt of Lyndall Gordon's biography. John Timmerman's book, *T. S. Eliot's Ariel Poems: The Poetics of Recovery* (Bucknell), the first full-length study of the Ariel poems (including "Ash-Wednesday") unabashedly takes a religious approach to an analysis of the poems' use of and attitudes toward history. The scholarship sometimes overwhelms the readings and robs the poems of their spirituality and magic, but valuable information about Eliot's sources, the biblical and religious backgrounds of the poems, dates of publication and composition, and close examinations of recurring themes, motifs, and images enlarge and integrate our views of the works.

One of the year's most tantalizing articles is Rudolf Germer's "T. S. Eliot's Religious Development" (*T. S. Eliot at the Turn of the Century*, pp. 91–104). Germer's study differs from many others in the importance he attaches to the different types of religious influences (e.g., Calvinism vs. Puritanism vs. Catholicism) and his relative neglect of Eliot's personal life. The brevity imposed on Germer by the colloquium format clearly constrains him, but what he does present is dense and informative. Artur Blaim and Ludmila Gruszewska's linguistic analysis, "Languages at War:

T. S. Eliot's *Murder in the Cathedral*" (*YER* 13: 17–25), interprets the play according to competing systems of discourse: mythological, secular/political, and religious. The eventual victory of a religious language signals the victory of a unified and transcendent religious worldview.

Spirituality and the occult have gained increasing prominence in recent reconsiderations of modernism (and its super-rational critics). As background to his article "*The Waste Land* in the Light of the 'Cross-Correspondence Scripts' of the Society for Psychical Research" (*YER* 13: 7–16) Thomas Gibbons locates a strain of occultism and psychical research in an array of modernist pronouncements by E. M. Forster, Virginia Woolf, H. G. Wells, and D. H. Lawrence. A bounty of information about psychical research and in particular the "Cross-Correspondence Scripts" shores up his assertion that *The Waste Land* has an underlying unity based on these scripts. Shamans—living people who journey to the underworld—offer a point of departure for Grover Smith's examination of *The Cocktail Party*, "Eliot and the Shamans" (*T. S. Eliot at the Turn of the Century*, pp. 162–80), the most compelling work on Eliot's drama this year. Smith focuses on three manifestations of the shamanistic traditions as they influence the play: the Greek myths in Euripides' *Alcestis*, Charles Williams's development of the occult tradition, and academic and scientific studies of shamanism. Smith's study captures the phantasmagoric nature of Eliot's texts and renders the profundity and spirituality that his works can achieve.

e. Criticism   Analyses of Eliot's critical theory figure in almost all the works discussed here, but few treat the criticism solely. The most frequently discussed essay is "Tradition and the Individual Talent." In its political and historical focus, Gary Day's article "Past and Present: T. S. Eliot's 'Tradition and the Individual Talent' " (*SHR* 28: 17–26) is typical of many. The most intriguing part of Day's analysis is his treatment of Eliot's disruptive use of analogy, conventionally a familiarizing device.

Several of the essays in Brooker's *Mastery and Escape* focus on the criticism. She has read Eliot's prose thoroughly, and her work draws on diverse works from all periods. "Common Ground and Collaboration" (pp. 65–80) refutes the frequent accusation of elitism and argues that Eliot wished to reach people from all classes and cultures throughout his career because of his sense of the collaborative nature of all art. There has been a valuable surge of criticism on Eliot's dissertation over the last several years. This wave has died down, but Brooker continues to elucidate. "F. H. Bradley's Doctrine of Experience in T. S. Eliot's *The Waste Land* and *Four Quartets*" (pp. 191–206) cites the empirical nature of Bradley's idealism to dispute the notion that Bradley and Eliot are solipsists. "T. S. Eliot and the Revolt against Dualism: His Dissertation on F. H. Bradley in Its Intellectual Context" (pp. 172–96) is a useful reminder of Eliot's (and most of the modernists') resolute stance against dualism—particularly valuable because contemporary critics are sometimes too ready to analyze Eliot dualistically from a perspective he would renounce and that he hoped his writings would disprove. This year's criticism suggests such debates are not over and that the multiplicity of Eliot's work will continue to provoke admiration and controversy and offer "perpetual possibility" for scholars.

Colgate University
University of Maine

9 Faulkner

Philip Cohen

One of the most noticeable trends in Faulkner criticism over the past few years has been the shift from masculinist Freudian and poststructuralist Lacanian psychoanalytic readings of the fiction to feminist psychoanalytic approaches that take as their starting point the French feminist, especially Julia Kristeva's, revision of Lacan's revisions of Freud's premises, procedures, and concepts. This work is characterized by a turn away from the patriarchal Freudian emphasis on the Oedipal conflict between fathers and sons and the transition from nature to culture and away from the still patriarchal Lacanian emphasis on the constitution of the self within the Symbolic Order by means of the subject's fall into language during the Oedipal conflict. Instead, feminist psychoanalytic accounts of Faulkner have stressed the primacy of the pre-Oedipal symbiotic relationship between mother and infant, which is characterized by an emphasis on the nonverbal language of physical gesture and rhythm. Usually this methodology privileges the language of the Kristevan semiotic over that of the Symbolic Order. This year, the influence of the French school of "writing the body" on criticism and scholarship on Faulkner can be seen in significant work by Diana York Blaine, Deborah Clarke, Michel Delville, Doreen Fowler, Anne Goodwyn Jones, Carolyn Porter, and Bonnie Woodbery. Essays by Michael Zeitlin and Donald Kartiganer, however, reveal that examining Freud's influence on Faulkner and using Freud to interpret Faulkner can still produce much good work. I also want to single out for particular praise Diane Roberts's cultural and historical-feminist account of Faulkner's negotiations in his fiction with a variety of female stereotypes and Barbara Ladd's New Historicist

I want to thank Nancy Wood, my department chair, for a faculty development leave that gave me the time to prepare this chapter.

discussion of *Absalom, Absalom!* in the context of American nationalist narratives.

The only distressing aspect of preparing a Faulkner chapter for this volume has been witnessing how frequently the work of previous scholars is repeated. In part, this tendency simply reflects the sheer mass of scholarly material currently being published. But it is not going to get any better. Electronic information technology is opening the floodgates to a deluge of information. As courses in research methods continue to disappear from our curricula, I think it important that students, both graduate and undergraduate, be encouraged to use gatekeeping tools like *ALS.*

i Bibliography, Editions, and Manuscripts

Some new Faulkner texts appeared this year from Random House, including *Big Woods* in a Vintage paperback and the Snopes trilogy in a Modern Library trade edition with George Garrett's short introduction. David Minter has produced a second edition of his fine Norton Critical Edition of *The Sound and the Fury.* With a text established by Noel Polk, extracts from relevant letters and interviews, Faulkner's introductions to the novel, the Compson appendix, and a generous selection of representative criticism, the volume is perfect for undergraduate and graduate use. The Library of America has released another handsome Faulkner volume: *Novels 1942–1954: "Go Down, Moses," "Intruder in the Dust," "Requiem for a Nun," "A Fable,"* ed. Joseph Blotner and Noel Polk.

No student of Faulkner can afford to miss Neil R. McMillen and Noel Polk's "Faulkner on Lynching" (*FJ* 8, i [1992]: 3–14), which prints Faulkner's "virtual defense of lynching as an instrument of justice" in a newly discovered 1931 letter he published in the *Memphis Commercial-Appeal.* Their extensive commentary provides biographical and historical contexts for this strikingly racist piece that appeared at the same time as "Dry September," his classic indictment of lynching. The near-simultaneous publication of these two documents should caution us against monolithic accounts of Faulkner's attitudes on race, whether progressive or conservative. James G. Watson's "Two Letters about William Faulkner, 1918," one of which is by Phil Stone announcing Faulkner's arrival in New Haven in April 1918, appears in *FJ* 8, i (1992): 15–19. In "Senator John Sharp Williams, Phil Stone, and a Postmaster's Job for Faulkner" (*FJ* 8, ii [1993]: 95–98) Arthur F. Kinney and David Berman print and discuss a letter Stone wrote in 1922 concerning Faulkner's application for the postmaster's position at Ole Miss.

It is hard to know under what heading to place William Boozer, Dean Faulkner Wells, and Lawrence Wells's *"The Faulkner Newsletter": Collected Issues* (Yoknapatawpha), which brings together with an index more than 13 years of this publication. Faulkner scholars will find this cornucopia of formal and informal essays and notes, interviews, photographs, and book reviews ideal for browsing.

ii Biography

I received Richard Gray's *The Life of William Faulkner* (Blackwell) too late for inclusion, but I will discuss it next year. In the meantime, Thomas C. Moser's important "Faulkner's Muse: Speculations on the Genesis of *The Sound and the Fury*" (*Critical Reconstructions*, pp. 187–211) gives us a fascinating if controversial preview of the psychobiographical study of Faulkner's creativity that Moser is writing. Drawing together and extending the insights in much biographical work on Faulkner, especially Judith Sensibar's, he argues that Faulkner's pursuit, loss, and eventual union with his personal muse, Estelle Oldham, was central to the creation of Caddy as well as many of his other female characters. This groundbreaking but perhaps mistitled essay articulates causal connections "between Faulkner's relationship with Estelle from her 1918 marriage to its 1927 collapse and his literary production during that same period."

iii General Criticism

In *Faulkner and Southern Womanhood* (Georgia) cultural and historical feminist Diane Roberts reads a variety of female stereotypes of the Confederate woman—the mammy, the belle, the tragic mulatta, the spinster, and the mother—"against the South that created them for different social purposes, or reinvented them at crucial moments in history" to recover cultural anxieties and aspirations. More specifically, she examines how Faulkner's work is the product of "a writer making fiction out of a time and a place." In this solid contribution to the ongoing contemporary reinterpretation of Faulkner's work for our time, each chapter summarizes the representation of a particular female stereotype in Southern culture, the context of its reappearance, and the social and biographical settings of Faulkner's examination of that stereotype. By revising and questioning these stereotypes, Roberts argues, Faulkner's fiction destabilizes the binary oppositions that constitute such Southern hierarchies as race, class, and gender. Methodologically, she uses Bakhtin, French feminist theory, and Minrose Gwin's *The Feminine and Faulkner* (Tennessee, 1990) to produce ideological readings that situate Faulkner in social, historical, and cultural discourses of his day, although curiously she ignores religious ones. That she is not all that interested in grounding the texts in biography would be no problem except that she selectively uses biographical evidence to support claims for Faulkner's intentions in writing particular texts. Thus, it is disconcerting to have her argue that Faulkner's overlapping fictional treatments of incest and miscegenation are purely conscious responses to contemporary stereotypes of the tragic mulatta without referring to some combination of conscious and unconscious psychopathology. In keeping with much recent work, Roberts articulates a conflicted but perhaps too progressive view of Faulkner as a reviser of conservative Southern representations and roles of women despite his sometime acceptance of such types and the ideology behind them. She values Faulkner's fiction by how much it questions these stereotypes, and she generally believes that his negotiations with stereotypes are often paradoxical and without resolution. I enjoyed her discussion of how female stories in *Absalom* destabilize the gender, race, and class certainties sought in the male stories and her view of Judith as inhabiting multiple roles rather than accepting the unitary roles assigned by the male narrators. She also has interesting things to say about Faulkner's subversive negotiations of space between the mulatta, the white lady, and the mammy, and between males and females. I remain skeptical, however, of her claim that Quentin Compson desires to be a woman and represents that site of conflict between feminine and masculine discourses.

Drawing on American and French feminist psychoanalytic theory, especially Kristeva's and Madelon Sprengnether's work, Deborah Clarke's *Robbing the Mother: Women in Faulkner* (Miss.) is another concise if ahistorical contribution to scholarship on gender in Faulkner's fiction that complements Roberts's cultural and historical feminism. Without referring to biographical, historical, or social contexts, Clarke argues that Faulkner's novels reveal his need to undo and erase the mother whose female sexuality is the source of artistic creativity and vision. Beneath its patriarchal emphasis on Oedipal conflict, she locates a maternal subtext in Faulkner's fiction: that creativity is based on matricide, unlike the Bloomian emphasis on literary patricide, since it must be wrested from the mother and posited as a substitute for the female body. For Clarke, maternal power in seven of Faulkner's novels is often a source of language and identity and a challenge to the homogenizing impulses of the symbolic language, fixed gender boundaries, and stable self of patriarchy. Her treatment of the masculine fear of female sexuality in *The Sound and the Fury* is illuminating, especially her contention that the book's problematic mothers like Caddy and Mrs. Compson undermine the masculine order and survive. Although I find a fairly symbolic order to Benjy's language and rhetoric, Clarke is interesting on his narrative as a Kristevan semiotic discourse. Her discussion of how the cold and selfish Mrs. Compson achieves a kind of power by undermining the patriarchal structures of motherhood and marriage are useful correctives to other feminist attempts to rehabilitate Mrs. Compson, and her comments on Dilsey serve as a corrective to racial and sexual stereotyping in some of the critical responses to the servant. Clarke's argument that motherhood and female sexuality "pose serious threats to male autonomy and the cultural order" in *Sanctuary* and *The Hamlet* qualifies critical emphasis on masculine oppression in the two novels by focusing on female resistance, as does her discussion of how the presence of and the fantastic nature of women, both white and black, undermine *Absalom*'s masculine thematic and structural premises.

Faulkner and Psychology (Miss.) is the latest volume of papers from the annual Faulkner Conference at Ole Miss. These essays from the 1991 conference on Faulkner and Psychology represent a diverse array of psychoanalytic approaches—classical Freudian, revisionist Lacanian, post-Freudian feminist, and even post-Freudian masculinist. Most of them share a focus on psychoanalysis and the text while eschewing an interest in the biographical data of Faulkner's life. Although this prejudice against the authorial orientation produces much good work, it cuts off a priori a category of evidence that some still find useful in evaluating how Faulkner's fiction grapples with the racism and sexism of his day. General essays here and papers on individual works are discussed below under the appropriate headings.

First up, Anne Goodwyn Jones's "Male Fantasies?: Faulkner's War Stories and the Construction of Gender" (pp. 21–55) is an intriguing feminist Lacanian investigation of such war fictions as *Flags in the Dust*, *The Unvanquished*, "Ad Astra," "Crevasse," and "Turnabout," although

A Fable is regrettably absent. Goodwyn Jones argues that the inability of men in these works to accept the loss of the wholeness of the pre-Oedipal phase and to move on to mature individual identities leads to sexual anxieties and militarism. The male characters thus resort to war as a way of experiencing the engulfment of the ego, the return to the mother, without losing control completely. Faulkner remains committed, she argues, to traditional binary hierarchies of gender, displacing them from patriarchal structures to linguistic and narrative structures: that is, narration and language are masculinized in stories that critique wars and the impulses that lead to wars. The essay also addresses some earlier psychoanalytic readings of Faulkner that emphasize the masculine Oedipal stage at the expense of the feminine pre-Oedipal stage. Goodwyn Jones herself is more interested in the difference between the pre-Oedipal union with the mother and the post-Oedipal sense of loss that results in the construction of a masculinity based on the rejection and degradation of the feminine and the separation from the mother.

Carolyn Porter's lengthy "Symbolic Fathers and Dead Mothers: A Feminist Approach to Faulkner" (pp. 78–122) is a Lacanian meditation on the power of the maternal presence, specifically Addie Bundren in *As I Lay Dying* and Rosa Coldfield in *Absalom,* to disrupt patriarchal language, structures, and systems of exchange, especially the patriarchal concealment of the gap between the signifier and the signified. Although Porter spends as much time explicating Lacan as she does applying Lacan to Faulkner, I found her essay notable for its revisionist portrait of Rosa Coldfield as an agent of revenge against patriarchy as well as a victim of it.

Jay Watson's "Faulkner's Forensic Fiction and the Question of Authorial Neurosis" (pp. 165–88) offers a preview of his Lacanian *Forensic Fictions: The Lawyer Figure in Faulkner* (Georgia) (see *ALS 1993,* pp. 116–17). He too employs Lacan to focus on the individual's passage from the Imaginary register to the Symbolic and on the acquisition of language, which leads to submission to the Symbolic Order and to the experience of alienation. If this submission of the speaking subject does not occur, the self becomes neurotic as it tries to maintain the illusion of a unified self. Watson explores whether or not Faulkner and his fiction accept this alienation as the price of becoming a speaking self, and he argues that Faulkner investigates this dilemma in his lawyer figures, whom he sees as ambivalent authorial figures. In particular, he looks at "An Odor of Verbena" and *The Reivers.* Some may find exaggerated his claims that Faulkner's decision to delineate the lawyer figure of Horace Benbow in

Flags in the Dust made his discovery of Yoknapatawpha and the subject matter of his career possible.

A similar version of John T. Irwin's "Horace Benbow and the Myth of Narcissa" (pp. 242–71) appeared in *AL* 64 (1992): 543–66 (see *ALS 1992*, p. 133). David Wyatt's "Faulkner and the Reading Self" (pp. 272–87) helpfully views Faulkner as an existentialist rather than a postmodernist who was interested in how the self emerges and in how the self in the act of reading becomes the self interpreting itself. He suggestively examines Ike McCaslin in "The Bear" and Bayard Sartoris in "An Odor of Verbena" to chart Faulkner's movement from a receptive apprentice self to a assertive, self-authoring self.

Jay Martin's "Faulkner's 'Male Commedia': The Triumph of Manly Grief" (pp. 123–64) differs from other essays in the collection in its post-Freudian masculinist view, based on contemporary developmental psychology, of male psychosexual development as different from that of women. After stressing the difficulty caused by the male child's closeness to the differently sexed mother, which causes the male child to develop an arsenal of defenses that the female child does not require, Martin discusses Faulkner's life and fiction in terms of the young Faulkner's closeness to his mother and his struggle both to become a boy and to deny his masculinity. With some speculation offered as assertion, Martin presents Faulkner's development in terms of his deep childhood division between his attachments with his mother and father, seeing the fiction as "a grand drama of the varieties of male experience." Though Martin does not deal with the modern social or cultural phenomena that make masculinity so precarious, and his taxonomy of male psychosexual development in Faulkner is perhaps too neat, this is an original, controversial piece.

Gwendolyne Chabrier's *Faulkner's Families: A Southern Saga* (Gordian, 1993) is a traditional biographical and sociological study of the fiction that charts Faulkner's shift from a gloomy to a more rewarding view of family relations. While one of its strengths is the interviews conducted by the author in the late 1970s with Faulkner's friends, lovers, and relatives, one of its flaws is that its secondary bibliography ends for all intents and purpose with the early 1980s, after which only a few biographical items are listed. The family is also the focus of Ineke Bockting's "The Figure of Parental Fusion in the Novels of William Faulkner" (*Fathers and Mothers in Literature*, pp. 123–36). Bockting, however, employs Melanie Klein's object relations theory to analyze the

recurring figures in Faulkner's fiction of intimate, exclusionary parents
and despairing children who feel neglected. Like other psychoanalytic
critics of Faulkner who have begun to concentrate on the pre-Oedipal
period, Bockting argues that pre-Oedipal characters like Quentin and
Darl undergo a traumatic separation from the mother that leads to
psychic disintegration. Reading this essay, though, one would never
guess that many readers find Faulkner's fictional families dysfunctional.

Different chapters of Jeffrey J. Folks's *Southern Writers and the Machine: Faulkner to Percy* (Peter Lang, 1993) discuss Faulkner's ambivalent
attitude toward traditional notions of honor in "Honor" and "Shingles
for the Lord," Temple Drake's self-creation and flight from masculine
authority in both *Sanctuary* and *Requiem for a Nun*, and his response to
the destructiveness and exciting power of mechanization and urbaniza-
tion in *Pylon*.

More insightful than most general introductions to Faulkner, David
Minter's "History and Novels/Novels and History: The Example of
William Faulkner" (*A Cultural History of the American Novel*, pp. 215–
29) reads the novels from *The Sound and the Fury* to *Go Down, Moses* in
terms of how they "bring technical sophistication . . . to bear on [the]
social and moral problems" of the Great Depression. Reflecting our era's
progressive rereading of American authors, Minter's Faulkner generally
critiques but rarely reflects the prejudices of his culture. Arthur F.
Kinney's "Faulkner and Racism" (*Connotations* 3 [1993–94]: 265–78) is a
good general introduction to the irregular progress of Faulkner's career-
long "agonizing recognition of the exacting expenses of racism." Michael
Kreyling's "Fee, Fie, Faux Faulkner: Parody and Postmodernism in
Southern Literature" (*SoR* 29 [1993]: 1–15) argues for a critical stance
toward postmodern Southern literature, a stance that exhibits equal parts
skepticism, irony, and playfulness and recognizes that access to the past,
history, and tradition is thoroughly mediated by representations, especially those authored by earlier writers. His delightful discussion of
parodies of Faulkner by Flannery O'Connor, Eudora Welty, Reynolds
Price, Barry Hannah, and Peter Taylor illustrates his argument.

Drawing primarily on Marjorie Garber's work, Michael Williams's
"Cross-Dressing in Yoknapatawpha County" (*MissQ* 47: 369–90) stakes
out an original slant on Faulkner's fictional realm. Positing gender as a
social construct, Williams usefully examines the clothing, occupation,
and social and sexual behavior of three female characters generally seen
by critics as masculinized: Drusilla Hawk Sartoris from *The Unvan-*

quished, Joanna Burden from *Light in August*, and Linda Snopes Kohl from *The Mansion*. Williams's focus on cross-dressing, sexual and racial ambiguity, and the taking of traditionally masculine work makes visible Faulkner's female-to-male transvestites, who "challenge . . . the supposed rigidity of social categories" like race and gender and show "the boundaries of these categories actually to be quite permeable."

David Lawrence Rogers's "The Irony of Idealism: William Faulkner and the South's Construction of the Mulatto" (*The Discourse of Slavery*, pp. 166–90) argues that Faulkner progressively deconstructs in novels the discourses of slavery and the key figures of the mulatto and the unwed mother "through the central oppositional figures of idealism—the male idealist and his figural counterpart, the virginal woman—from which the antebellum South fashioned its defence against the mulatto." In "Fathers and Virgins: García Márquez's Faulknerian *Chronicle of a Death Foretold*" (*LALR* 21 [1993]: 21–29) John S. Christie discusses parallels between Márquez's and Faulkner's narrative techniques and the use of incest as a metaphor for social and historical corruption. Lewis P. Simpson's "The Tenses of History" (*The Fable of the Southern Writer*, pp. 96–113) originally appeared as "William Faulkner of Yoknapatawpha" (see *ALS 1979*, p. 153).

Finally, two excellent essay-reviews of more recent work on Faulkner, especially feminist studies, also appeared this year: James M. Mellard's "Desire and Interpretation: Reading *The Sound and the Fury*" (*MissQ* 47: 497–519) and Anne Goodwyn Jones's "Female, Feminine, Feminist, Femme, Faulkner?" (*MissQ* 47: 521–45).

iv Individual Works to 1929

In "*The Marble Faun*(s): Hawthorne's Influences on and Parallels with William Faulkner" (*POMPA* [1993]: 73–80) S. Kelly argues on the basis of internal and weak external evidence for Hawthorne's formal and thematic influence on Faulkner's first book. Andrew Scoblionko's "Subjectivity and Homelessness in *Soldiers' Pay*" (*FJ* 8, i [1992]: 61–71) draws on Lacan and Bergson but no previous Faulkner scholarship to contend that the attempts of characters to define themselves spatially in Faulkner's novel "suggest and subvert [their] false consciousness of totality manufactured through spatial identification."

Continuing his excellent work on Faulkner, Freud, and Joyce, Michael Zeitlin in "Faulkner and Psychoanalysis: The *Elmer* Case" (*Faulkner and*

Psychology, pp. 219–41) argues that Faulkner drew on *Three Essays on the Theory of Sexuality* and *Ulysses* in writing his unfinished 1925 novel. Zeitlin concisely examines fetishism in *Elmer*, stressing the fetish as a substitute for Elmer's incestuous desire for the maternal phallus he imagines his sister Jo-Addie has. This fetishism leads to a primal fear of castration in his art and in his relationships. Zeitlin is especially attentive to *Elmer*'s climax as a "nighttown" scene that fuses Freudian dreamwork and Joycean echo structure. Even readers who do not share Zeitlin's high regard for *Elmer* will profit from this essay.

Doreen Fowler's " 'Little Sister Death': *The Sound and the Fury* and the Denied Unconscious" (*Faulkner and Psychology*, pp. 3–20) is well worth reading. In this accessible feminist Lacanian essay Fowler reads the novel as a narrative of failed male passages into adulthood that results in the Compson brothers victimizing Caddy and other women as a means of masking and assuaging the true sources of their failure. While Benjy is not a speaking subject and does not exist in the Lacanian Symbolic Order, Quentin and Jason have not accepted the Lacanian lack that generates their transition to the condition of speaking subjects in that order. Consequently, they repress their desire for and fear of a pre-Oedipal fusion with the mother-figure and of unmediated union with the world. Their projection of their own lack onto their surrogate mother, Caddy, who becomes the return of their repressed, is the most prominent example of their projection of their loss onto women who lack the post-Oedipal phallus. Like Clarke, Fowler is very good on Quentin and Jason's sense of inadequacy and masculine impotence.

Michael Zeitlin's fine "Faulkner, Joyce, and the Problem of Influence in *The Sound and the Fury*" (*Faulkner Studies* 2, i: 1–25) besides discussing how Faulkner "might be said to have gained possession of and gone beyond the discursive possibilities" of *Ulysses*, provides a "partial inventory of the traces of Joyce's presence" in Faulkner's novel. If only this essay were more widely available. In his "Mind Style as an Interdisciplinary Approach to Characterization in Faulkner" (*Lang&Lit* 3: 157–74) Ineke Bockting usefully employs a combination of narrative psychology, psychiatry, and literary stylistics to examine the implications for characterization of the differences in attributive style between the Compson brothers, but without citing any previous stylistic studies of the novel.

Faulknerians might also be interested in James L. W. West III's photographic facsimile reproduction of William Styron's *"Inheritance of Night": Early Drafts of* Lie Down in Darkness (Duke, 1993). This failed attempt at what would eventually become *Lie Down in Darkness*, West notes, reveals the influence of *The Sound and the Fury*—probably in the 1946 Modern Library dual edition of *The Sound and the Fury* and *As I Lay Dying*—looming over the young novelist. The most intriguing echo of Faulkner here is Styron's prospectus for the novel: it resembles Faulkner's lengthy appendix, which appeared first in the 1946 *Portable Faulkner* and then in the Modern Library dual edition. *The Explicator* published three notes on the novel: Gene Fant, Jr.'s "Faulkner's *The Sound and the Fury*" (52: 104–6); Irene Visser's "Faulkner's *The Sound and the Fury*" (52: 171–72); and Donna L. Potts's "Faulkner's *The Sound and the Fury*" (52: 236–37). Fant comments on the significance of Benjy's possible confusion of the words "Candace" and "candles"; Visser traces the repetitions and symbolic scenes and images that reveal Caddy's tragic presence in the fourth section of the novel; and Potts relates Faulkner's description of Dilsey's church to folk art and Christianity.

v Individual Works, 1930–1939

As I Lay Dying received the lion's share of critical attention this year. Nathan P. Tinker's "Geomancy: The Triangular Structures of Landscape and History in *As I Lay Dying*" (*Constructions* [1993]: 37–55) connects the novel's "geometric structure and imagery" to its "critique of history in a world where time itself has been rendered relative," while Darryl Hattenhauer's formalist "The Geometric Design of *As I Lay Dying*" (*CLQ* 30: 146–53) argues that the "geometric spatial abstractions" of circles, horizontals, and verticals inform the novel's setting, plot, and characters, especially Darl. For Hattenhauer, Faulkner ultimately grounds the novel's theme—the metaphysics of antifoundationalism—in the spatiality of its characters. Taking a different tack in "Rewriting Poor White Myth in *As I Lay Dying*" (*Arkansas Quarterly* 2 [1993]: 308–24), Robert Hanson contends that the novel reveals "the relationship between identity and economics" beneath the regional myth of the poor white Southerner as either mentally deficient or bestial. In "Faulknerian Tragedy: The Example of *As I Lay Dying*" (*MissQ* 47: 403–18) Robert Merrill provocatively but intelligently proposes that Faulkner intended the novel to be a modern formal tragedy rather than a dark comedy or a tragicomedy, arguing that Addie and Darl are tragic characters whose fall we anticipate and who, in falling, come to understand "the irreducible facts of suffering and death."

Sharing Clarke's approach, Diana York Blaine's Kristevan "The Abjection of Addie and Other Myths of the Maternal in *As I Lay Dying*" (*MissQ* 47: 419–39) describes the book as a postmodern tragedy of ontological instability and ambivalence about the mother-figure, a tragedy in which "Nothing is what it seems, the traditional narratives of patriarchal power have been usurped, and . . . a problematized figure of the maternal holds brief and uneasy sway." Blaine is especially perceptive on how critical responses to the novel have been inflected by gender. Similarly, Bonnie Woodbery's intelligent "The Abject in Faulkner's *As I Lay Dying*" (*L&P*, 40, i: 26–42) focuses on how linguistic ruptures, interruptions, and silences in Addie's and Darl's monologues create rhythms that suggest Kristeva's notions of the semiotic, the maternal, and the abject. "While Addie's discourse reveals her rejection of the paternal order, Darl's progressively ruptured discourse" reveals him to be a borderline subject, an unstable exile. I found Woodbery particularly illuminating on Darl's visual hallucinations as a form of the abject. Finally, Michel Delville's excellent "Alienating Language and Darl's Narrative Consciousness in Faulkner's *As I Lay Dying* (*SLJ* 27, i: 61–72) is, in part, an exercise in stylistics that analyzes the ultimately unsuccessful verbal strategies that Darl uses in his interior monologues to come to terms with his mother's death and to end his quest "for essences and final, signified certainties." More specifically, Delville argues that Lacan's theory of symbolic language sheds light on Darl's rhetorical practices, which mirror his interest in ontology, abstraction, and authenticity.

In "Translating the Comic: A Case Study of *Sanctuaire*" (*FJ* 8, i [1993]: 67–83) Annick Chapdelaine continues her previous work on French translations of Faulkner's novels by using contemporary translation theory to argue that the French translation of *Sanctuary* emphasized the tragic rather than the comic dimensions of Faulkner's prose and thus helped shape his initial Gallic reception. Andrew J. Wilson's "The Corruption of Looking: William Faulkner's *Sanctuary* as a Detective Novel" (*MissQ* 47: 441–60) discusses how and why the novel is saturated with voyeurism, but without referring to such important work as Noel Polk's essays or Michel Gresset's *Fascination: Faulkner's Fiction, 1919–1936* (Duke, 1989).

Donald M. Kartiganer's elegant, provocative " 'What I Chose to Be': Freud, Faulkner, Joe Christmas, and the Abandonment of Design" (*Faulkner and Psychology*, pp. 288–314) begins with an investigation of the modernist parallels between Freud's abandonment of his seduction theory of neurosis and Joe Christmas's claim in *Light in August* to be partially black. In rejecting his theory, Kartiganer claims, Freud rejected his patients' apparent experience and opened up for them the possibility of choosing origins equal to what they chose to become. Kartiganer then examines the issue of racial ambiguity in the novel, tracing the possibility of choice for Christmas from the beginning and exploding fixed notions of "race" just as Freud reimagined primal scenes of molestation. In "Psychoanalytic Conceptualizations of Characterization, Or Nobody Laughs in *Light in August*" (*Faulkner and Psychology*, pp. 189–218) Lee Jenkins provides a contemporary psychoanalytic reading of the major characters of the novel in terms of obsessive-compulsive, paranoid, borderline, narcissistic personality types. What the different characters share is a resistance to intimacy, which they perceive as a threat to the integrity of the self. Ineke Bockting's "*Light in August* and the Issue of Unreliability" (in *Literature and the New Interdisciplinarity: Poetics, Linguistics, History,* ed. Roger D. Sell and Peter Vedonk [Rodopi], pp. 197–208) draws on social psychology and the distinction between reliability and credibility to explore how both the townspeople and the reader are enticed "to participate in those acts of labelling and prejudice which would make Christmas a murderer." Ralph Watkins's interesting " 'It was like I was the woman and she was the man': Boundaries, Portals, and Pollution in *Light in August*" (*SLJ* 26, ii: 11–24) examines the affinities between the theoretical work of such symbolic anthropologists as van Gennep, Douglas, Leach, and Turner and the novel's treatment of liminality, rites of passage, pollution taboos, and anomaly. In the process Watkins illuminates Faulkner's excavation of "the number of possibilities attached to a person who is simultaneously a part of, yet outside, society."

Hugh Ruppersburg's *Reading Faulkner: "Light in August"* (Miss.) is the first entry in a new series of glossaries and commentaries on Faulkner's fiction under the general editorship of Noel Polk. As with Garland's competing series, each book in this series explains, identifies, and comments on elements of a novel that readers may find unfamiliar or difficult. I especially appreciated Ruppersburg's inclusion of a chronology for the novel. The series itself is a fitting memorial to the late Jim Hinkle, the Faulkner scholar who conceived and nursed the series until his untimely death in 1990.

Richard Godden's densely argued and fascinating "*Absalom, Absalom!,* Haiti and Labor History: Reading Unreadable Revolutions" (*ELH* 61: 685–720) contends that Sutpen's "violent enactment of white supremacy," his repeated fights with his slaves on Sutpen's Hundred, is counter-revolutionary in that it vainly seeks to repress his sense that "mastery is made by [and thus dependent on] bound labor." There is much of value here about class in the novel and on the debate over Sutpen's status as a precapitalist Southern plantation owner or an entrepreneurial liberal capitalist. Godden has more to say on the subject in "*Absalom, Absalom!* and Faulkner's Erroneous Dating of the Haitian Revolution" (*MissQ* 47: 489–94). He returns to economic and political issues in "*Absalom, Absalom!* and Rosa Coldfield: Or, What *Is* in the Dark House?" (*FJ* 8, i [1993]: 31–66), where he contends that Rosa's difficult monologue displays her conservatively stabilizing and establishing a "sexual claim to [Sutpen's] goods" and taking possession of them rather than subverting patriarchy, as recent feminist criticism would have it. Her monologue is thus "a [thwarted] marriage narrative . . . about taking possession of a plantation house" that is the product of black slave labor rather than of white mastery.

Barbara Ladd's sophisticated New Historicist essay " 'The Direction of the Howling' ": Nationalism and the Color Line in *Absalom, Absalom!*" (*AL* 66: 525–51) proposes that the narrative construction of Charles Bon as a white Creole and then reconstruction as a black Creole "points to questions and anxieties that white southerner[s] had . . . in a nationalistic and increasingly imperialistic United States." In Ladd's account, Bon's personal history becomes "a psychologized recapitulation of the nationalist narrative," and his tragic fate "is the destiny that always attends the past in any dream of U.S. redemptive nationalism." Even those unsympathetic to the New Historicism may still admire how Ladd joins together what has often been kept asunder in criticism of *Absalom*: the thematic implications of Sutpen's story and of its attempted reconstruction by different narrators. She argues that the purity which Henry Sutpen tries to protect "is constructed in terms that are nationalistic, familial, or racial [depending] upon who the speaker is, or rather *when* he is."

Nancy E. Batty's fascinating "The Riddle of *Absalom, Absalom!*: Looking at the Wrong Blackbird?" (*MissQ* 47: 461–88) easily wins the prize for this year's most provocative piece. Believing that the novel's valorization of indeterminacy implies "that *even* the facts of the murder, including those pertaining to the identities of perpetrator and victim are speculative, heavily invested and highly motivated narrative constructions," Batty painstakingly analyzes neglected passages to argue that Charles

Bon killed Henry Sutpen in 1865, that Judith and Clytie covered up the facts of the murder, and that Quentin Compson met the dying Bon rather than Henry at the Old Sutpen place.

Originally appearing in 1991, Lewis P. Simpson's "On William Faulkner's *Absalom, Absalom!*" has now reappeared as "War and Memory: Quentin Compson's Civil War" (*The Fable of the Southern Writer*, pp. 73–95). This fine if somewhat general account of the novel places *Absalom* in the context of Civil War memories shaping the identity of many a Southern writer and his or her fictional writer-figures. Simpson's traditional reading ultimately focuses on the autobiographical Quentin Compson's interpretation of Sutpen's story as one embodying the tormented history of the South. Richard Schwartz's poorly researched "Modernist American Classical Tragedy: *Absalom, Absalom!*" (*JEP* 15: 212–21) treats the novel as a paradoxical modernist classical tragedy.

In "On Faulkner and Verbena" (*SLJ* 27, i: 73–84) Robert W. Witt contends that our appreciation of the last story of *The Unvanquished* hinges on our understanding of (1) the complex and shifting symbolism of an odor which the flowering plant traditionally lacks and (2) the fact that Drusilla does not try to seduce Bayard. Finally, Gabriele Gutting's "The Mysteries of the Mapmaker: Faulkner, *If I Forget Thee, Jerusalem*, and the Secret of a Map" (*FJ* 8, i [1993]: 85–93) convincingly shows that two draft maps of the Mississippi delta, found in the manuscript papers of *If I Forget Thee*, do not sketch out part of the novel's geography but rather the grounds of the hunts Faulkner participated in from 1940 to 1957.

vi Individual Works, 1940–1949

Nancy Dew Taylor's *Annotations to William Faulkner's* "Go Down, Moses" (Garland), the latest entry in Garland's Faulkner Annotation Series, glosses the novel's literary and historical biblical allusions, references to small town and rural Mississippi language, customs, flora and fauna, family relationships, chronology, and narrative voice.

vii Individual Works, 1950–1962

In "'Play' within a Play: Gaming with Language in *Requiem for a Nun*" (*FJ* 8, i [1992]: 43–59) Janet Wondra performs a Bakhtinian stylistic analysis of how Faulkner's centrifugal linguistic strategies—his "multiple voices and multiple interpretations at play in dramatic form," "repetition and strategic silences," and that "skilled fragmenter of unitary language and logic: metaphor"—enable marginalized and silenced black women and white women to speak in a language constructed by reworking dominant discursive practices. Hee Kang's French feminist and Derridean close reading in "A New Configuration of Faulkner's Feminine: Linda Snopes Kohl in *The Mansion*" (*FJ* 8, i [1992]: 21–41) argues for an appreciation of "just how different, how unprecedented, and how revolutionary [Linda Kohl] is—within (Southern) cultural and contemporary theoretical contexts" and celebrates Faulkner's construction "of a radically creative and . . . modern feminine" in the novel.

viii The Stories

Chris LaLonde's " 'New Orleans' and an Aesthetics of Indeterminacy" (*FJ* 8, ii [1993]: 13–29) intelligently discusses Faulkner's first nationally published fiction as a metafiction "primarily concerned not with representing the city but with desire and the production of meaning." In "Irony and Isolation: Narrative Distance in Faulkner's 'A Rose for Emily' " (*FJ* 8, ii [1993]: 3–12) Isaac Rodman challenges the conventional view that the story's narrator is representative of the community's point of view, arguing instead that he "is more dedicated to ironic distance than identification with the people of the town." In her more provocative "Gender and Authorial Limitation in Faulkner's 'A Rose for Emily' " (*MissQ* 47: 391–402) Renée R. Curry draws on work by Minrose Gwin and Gaston Bachelard to argue that the story examines the community's different gendered responses to Emily. Curry claims that "gender often controls the eye of a story," but that it does not control Emily's behavior when she is sequestered inside her house. Faulkner's story also "reveals and revels in an authorial lack of knowledge when presented with writing a 'lady' into a patriarchal Southern text." Andrew Hook notes allusions in "Victory" to Sassoon's poems "The General" and "Blighters" in "Faulkner and Sassoon" (*N&Q* 41: 377–78).

R. Rio-Jelliffe's subtle "The Language of Time in Fiction: A Model in Faulkner's 'Barn Burning' " (*JNT* 24: 98–113) is a formalist reading from a well-informed Bergsonian perspective of the story's narrative technique, structure, and style. In analyzing how Faulkner manipulates antithesis, condensation, and juxtaposition—especially in the different viewpoints of the young, bewildered Sarty and the man he later becomes—for "the paradoxical end of creating an illusion of mobility," Rio-Jelliffe provocatively describes Faulkner's metaphysics of time as one of "perpetual resurrections" rather than Sartre's often-echoed conception of Faulknerian time as past-oriented. Still, I wish Rio-Jelliffe had better connected her argument to other studies of the story and of Bergson's influence on Faulkner.

The University of Texas at Arlington

10 Fitzgerald and Hemingway

Albert J. DeFazio III

Perhaps a zephyr from the international conference in Paris this summer whisked us suddenly to the '20s when Fitzgerald and Hemingway, unimaginably international, momentarily matched stride. A biography on each and another on the pair. Studies of identities in *Tender is the Night* and the chronology of *Gatsby* mirrored by one on invention in *For Whom the Bell Tolls* and another on Hemingway's writers. The *Fitzgerald Newsletter*, ed. Ruth Prigozy et al., grows steadily in its fourth year; Charles Oliver's *Hemingway Newsletter* strides through its fourteenth. Editor Susan F. Beegel managed to publish a dozen articles and as many notes and timely reviews while also initiating (and surviving) the upgrade of the *Hemingway Review* from desktop to professional design and typesetting. While Hemingway attracted the preponderance of essays, published 25 "lost" news articles, and saw his *Old Man* dock on the bestseller list again, Fitzgerald had the last word, in the Bruccoli-Baughman *Life in Letters*.

i Text, Letters, the Archives, and Bibliography

Scott Heller's "Novelist's Champion Vows to Keep the Flame Burning" and "How a Dispute Over Editing Led to a Scholar's Resignation" (*Chronicle of Higher Education* 2 Nov.: A10–11, A13ff.) note the "sale and donation" of Matthew J. Bruccoli's extraordinary Fitzgerald collection to the University of South Carolina and announce his withdrawal as editor of Cambridge's projected 12-volume set of Fitzgerald's writings. Bruccoli favors correcting factual errors "since there [is] no reasonable explanation for their inclusion"; the other two trustees do not and overruled him. He allowed some errors to stand, but he "became increasingly ashamed of his capitulation and resigned." James L. W. West III has been appointed general editor. Bruccoli's rationale for emendation appears in *Getting It Right: The Publishing Process and the Correction of Factual Errors—with Reference to* The Great Gatsby (Columbia, S.C.: no pub.), an earlier version of which appeared in *Essays in Honor of William B. Todd* (see *ALS 1992*, p. 143).

Having stepped aside but not away, Bruccoli, with the assistance of Judith S. Baughman, edited the year's best work in primary material, *F. Scott Fitzgerald: A Life in Letters* (Scribner's). Arranged chronologically and selected for their autobiographical content, these letters—211 of which are not in Andrew Turnbull's *Letters* (1963)—allow Fitzgerald to tell his own tale. The sensible editorial policy calls for diplomatic transcription and footnotes identifying literary references and influential friends. The volume commences with a brief life and is divided into five parts, each prefaced with a helpful chronology. Fitzgerald's account of things is a refreshing blend of vulnerability and tenacity, sadness and humor, fear and pride. Indispensable.

New Hemingway materials include three letters, a play, a recording of the author reading "On the American Dead in Spain," and 25 previously unrecognized *Toronto Star* articles (printed in William Burrill's biography and discussed later). Ellen Andrews Knodt publishes a Hemingway letter to her father (8 November 1946 to Jack D. Andrews) and characterizes the author's politics as "Jeffersonian libertarian" in "Always 'Shoveing Off': A Letter as Metaphor" (*NDQ* 62, ii: 87–94). Hemingway's 13 June 1953 letter to Edwin Rolfe as well as rare fliers distributed in response to *For Whom the Bell Tolls* and Hemingway's essay "On the American Dead in Spain" are included in Cary Nelson's pamphlet, *Remembering Spain: Hemingway's Civil War Eulogy and the Veterans of the Abraham Lincoln Brigade* (Illinois), which accompanies a cassette recording of Hemingway reading his tribute; also published here are Nelson's analysis of the political ramifications of the eulogy, "Honor and Trauma: Hemingway and the Lincoln Vets" (pp. 19–39), and Milton Wolff's "Hemingway's 'On the American Dead in Spain'" (pp. 7–17), which explains Wolff's turbulent relationship with Hemingway and documents how the sound recording came to be. (Nelson transcribes another letter to Edwin Rolfe in his article on Hemingway's politics, discussed later.) Bryan Harnetiaux, whose one-act play, *The Killers,* appeared in 1990, now gives us a superb full-length adaptation, *The Snows of Kilimanjaro* (Dramatic).

"News from the Hemingway Collection" (*HN* 13, ii: 120; 14, i: 99–100), by Megan Floyd Desnoyers and Stephen Plotkin, announces grants, acquisitions, and new openings. With support from colleagues near and far, I continue to provide bibliographies for the *Hemingway Review* (13, ii: 114–19; 14, i: 91–98) and the *Fitzgerald Newsletter* (4: 18–21).

ii Biography

In the better of the book-length biographies, Bruccoli improves on his *Scott and Ernest* (see *ALS 1978,* pp. 158–59) with an "enlarged and rewritten study," *Fitzgerald and Hemingway: A Dangerous Friendship* (Carroll). Replacing paraphrase with quotation, providing thorough documentation, and updating factual details, Bruccoli gives us our best accounting of the "friendship and estrangement," using letters, memoirs, and interviews and including numerous illustrations, facsimiles, and photographs. In *Scott Fitzgerald: A Biography* (HarperCollins) Jeffrey Meyers exhibits his considerable skills as a comparatist, yet his volume is suffused with disdain and devoid of mercy. Returning to Fitzgerald as a mature reader, Joseph Epstein in "F. Scott Fitzgerald's Third Act" (*Commentary* 98, v: 52–57) contends that the author accomplishes a second act, albeit posthumously.

While Hemingway enjoyed a "four-year association with the city of Toronto and the *Toronto Star* newspaper," he endured but four months at the home office, under the watchful eye of Harry Hindmarsh. Focusing on early 1920 and late 1923, William Burrill's critical biography, *Hemingway: The Toronto Years* (Doubleday Canada), purposefully revisits ground trod by Charles Fenton's *The Apprenticeship of Ernest Hemingway: The Early Years* (1954), reminding readers that Fenton's excellent analysis has long been out of print and that new materials have surfaced since mid-century. Most notably, Burrill adds 30 stories to those in William White's *Dateline, Toronto: The Complete* Toronto Star *Dispatches, 1920–1924* (See *ALS 1985,* p. 170). Twenty-five of these previously unrecognized stories are published (without a statement of editorial policy) as appendices, many of them delightful to read and excellent sources for scholars (a sampling has also appeared in the *Toronto Star*; see *ALS 1992,* p. 144). A few of them, Burrill reveals, were doubly and trebly dealt to the *Star*'s rivals, the *Globe* and the *Mail and Empire,* as the young author's patience waned; others bore the pen name "Peter Jackson."

Among the 40 photographs are the Connable mansion, the infamous Hindmarsh, downtown Toronto, the Hemingways' apartments and hotels, as well as friends from the *Star* who were gathered for an interview with Carlos Baker in 1965.

A pair of biographical-critical articles recall subjects from the '20s: H. R. Stoneback's "On Bobsledding, Lugeing, Skiing, Tobogganing, Skis Leaning Against Alpine Inn Walls, Frozen Carcasses, Death, Glory, and Transcendence: Winter Sport in Hemingway's Journalism and Fiction" (*Aethlon* 11, ii: 117–29) and Erik Nakjavani's "On Autobiography and Multiple Personality: The Case of Morley Callaghan Remembering Ernest Hemingway" (*NDQ* 62, ii: 55–82). Heeding Stoneback's call for closer attention to Hemingway and winter sport, Andrew Slough's "An Immoveable Feast" (*Ski* 59, iii: 180–87) draws on the letters, life, and work as it details Hemingway's downhill adventures as "the Black Christ" of Schruns. Reexamining Morley Callaghan's *That Summer in Paris* (1963) and challenging its binary oppositions and presentation of "selfhood as an unsegmented whole," Nakjavani mistrusts conventional autobiography and biography, proposing a move to the kind of "fictional autobiography" that we find in *A Moveable Feast* or *Green Hills.*

The '30s and Hemingway's involvement with the Spanish Civil War attract work by William Braasch Watson, "Investigating Hemingway IV. The Scene" (*NDQ* 62, ii: 11–40), and Cary Nelson, "Hemingway, The American Left, and the Soviet Union: Some Forgotten Episodes" (*HN* 14, i: 36–45). Watson's last in a series of articles on Hemingway's actions during the war is rife with detail; he accepts as "quite probably true" Antek Chrost's assertion that Hemingway twice visited Chrost's guerrilla outfit. Nelson pleads for balance from the biographers: "For too long evaluations of Hemingway's politics have been dominated by the cold war ideologies"; readers "have sometimes been subjected to judgments filtered through a cold war anti-Communism that had no place in Hemingway's world."

Addressing the author in the '40s is Donald P. Beistle's "Ernest Hemingway's ETO Chronology" (*HN* 14, i: 1–17), which accounts for Hemingway's movements through Europe from May 1944 until March 1945. And commemorating the 25th anniversary of Carlos Baker's biography, Charles Scribner III offers his father's address to the Princeton Club (1985), "Hemingway: A Publisher's Perspective" (*PULC* 56, i: 15–23).

iii   Sources, Influences, Parallels

Among the modest but noteworthy contributions is D. G. Kehl and
Allene Cooper's "Sangria in the Sangreal: *The Great Gatsby* as Grail
Quest" (*RMR* 47 [1993]: 203–17), which uses Auden's "six essential
elements of the typical quest story" to illustrate Fitzgerald's familiarity
with the grail quest as illustrated in *Gatsby* and " 'O Russet Witch.' "
Charles Nicol's "Finding the 'Assistant Producer'," pp. 155–65 in Charles
Nicol and Gennady Barabtarlo, eds., *A Small Alpine Form: Studies in
Nabokov's Short Fiction* (Garland, 1993), examines the Wilson/Nabokov
correspondence and argues that *The Last Tycoon* inspired "The Assistant
Producer." Without insisting that Gatsby was aware of Platonism,
William T. Liston's "Not Just Personal: Platonism in *The Great Gatsby*"
(*MQ* 35: 378–91) argues that the novel offers "us in the eponymous 'hero'
of the book a parody of Platonism," for certainly Gatsby was aware of his
idealism and organized his emotional life accordingly. Roger Forseth's
"Alcohol, Disease, and the Limitations of Artistic Representation" (*Dionysos* 5, iii: 16–27) claims that alcoholism compromised the conclusion
of *Tender is the Night*: "it simply peters out" because Fitzgerald "was not
able to resolve the book's moral theme or its structure since his own alcoholism remained unresolved." José Maria Rodriguez-García's "Gatsby
Goes to Barcelona: On the Configuration of the Post-Modern Spanish
Novel" (*LetP* 5 [1992–93]: 407–24) notes the "parallel use of constructive
principles" in *Gatsby* and Eduardo Mendoza's *La verdad sobre el caso
Savolta* (1975).

Hemingway's influence on another Nobel laureate is the subject of
Harley D. Oberhelman's *The Presence of Hemingway in the Short Fiction of Gabriel García Márquez* (York). Focusing on García Márquez's
appraisal of Hemingway's work, Hemingway's associations with the
Spanish-speaking world, and his mark on García Márquez's short stories
and novels, this study cites Hemingway's style and his iceberg principle
as major influences; it includes a selected Hemingway bibliography and
list of Spanish translations of his primary works. Elsewhere, Oberhelman
observes in "Hemingway and García Márquez: Two Shipwreck Narratives" (*IFR* 21, i–ii: 1–6) that *The Old Man and the Sea* provides García
Márquez "with short, exemplary sentences as a model for his prose, a
gripping story line, images and similes in accord with the barren waters
that encircle both protagonists, and an exploration of the twilight zone

between reality and fantasy." Overcoming the anxiety of influence is the
focus of James Plath's " 'After the Denim' and 'After the Storm': Raymond Carver Comes to Terms with the Hemingway Influence" (*HN* 13,
ii: 37–51). Tracing 19th-century influences, Jack Jobst and W. J. Williamson in "Hemingway and Maupassant: More Light on 'The Light of the
World' " (*HN* 13, ii: 52–61) chart the "strong affinities of characterization, technique, and theme" with emphasis on irony and allusion; and
Nathaniel Philbrick's insightful "A Window on the Prey: The Hunter
Sees a Human Face in Hemingway's 'After the Storm' and Melville's 'The
Grand Armada' " (*HN* 14, i: 25–35) compares "the chase, the storm, the
underwater view of the prey in its most human-like and potentially
disturbing poses." Damning our propensity to settle for convenient
causality, Paul Smith asks us to reconsider our assumptions about Gertrude Stein's influence on "Big Two-Hearted River" in "Stein's Remarks,
Hemingway's Literature" (*NDQ* 62, ii: 95–102). Without claiming that
the two men ever met, Beatriz Penas Ibáñez in "A Hemingway-Vallejo
Analogue" (*HN* 13, ii: 87–96) contrasts their modified versions of Christian prayers (in "A Clean, Well-Lighted Place" and César Vallejo's "Re-
doble fúnebre a los escombros de Durango" [Funereal Tolling in the
Rubble of Durango]) and suggests that Vallejo's inclusion of "forgiveness" may be the crucial difference. Hemingway's growing influence
concerns Lu Yutai's "Hemingway: A Star in China" (*HN* 13, ii: 97–100),
which discloses Hemingway's favorable status there. With reference to
his *The Study of Ernest Hemingway in China* (Heilongjiang Education,
1990), Ping Rang Qiu's "Letter" (*HN* 14, i: 101–02) corrects a few errors
in Yutai's piece. And George Anastaplo, in "Can Beauty 'Hallow Even
the Bloodiest Tomahawk'?" [*The Critic* 48, ii [1993]: 2–18), links "The
Killers," Flannery O'Connor's "A Good Man Is Hard to Find," and
director Jonathan Demme's film *The Silence of the Lambs* (1991) by way of
explaining our acceptance of violence and pathologically foolish people.

iv Criticism

a. Full-length Studies: Fitzgerald   We are fortunate to have Milton R.
Stern's eminently readable *Tender is the Night: The Broken Universe*
(Twayne), which follows the pattern of the Masterworks Studies, opening with a literary and historical overview, concluding with a dozen
chapters of close reading that not only explicate the story but advance

cogent arguments about the various kinds of *identity* (sexual, national, American) that readers encounter. Polished treatises from Stern's past—his *The Golden Moment* (see *ALS 1970*, p. 145) and his "*Tender is the Night*: The Text Itself" (see *ALS 1986*, p. 169)—are revisited, which is a good thing. Ronald Berman gives followers of the green light required reading in The Great Gatsby *and Modern Times* (Illinois). Observing that the characters "absorb ideas and feelings from what is communicated to them," that "their closest relationships are not with each other . . . but with published, advertised, and perceived images in print," he re-creates the popular culture of Fitzgerald's era, including cinematic techniques, mass print, visual literacy, and best-sellers. This absorbing and accessible text shows us Fitzgerald formulating his sensibilities; observing the "new economy" of things manufactured, marketed, advertised, consumed, and describing the "mental landscape" that they create; assessing how things are perceived, especially time and place, the past and present; and pursuing the links between "identity" and the serials, noting that characters see ideal forms of themselves in magazines. Gatsby, writes Berman, did not so much reinvent himself as he reassembled himself from "found" elements in the culture. Deborah Davis Schlacks's often slow and sometimes forced *American Dream Visions: Chaucer's Surprising Influence on F. Scott Fitzgerald* (Peter Lang) argues that the author uses "Chaucerian structure and themes" to "convey ideas about the artist and creativity" and claims that his knowledge of the medieval period is generally greater than has been acknowledged. Only time will tell if Thomas Pendleton's *I'm Sorry about the Clock: Chronology, Composition, and Narrative Technique in* The Great Gatsby (Susquehanna) offers a lasting contribution. His tripartite ambition includes demonstrating the novel's propensity for temporal incoherence—this Pendleton undeniably does, though often with tiresome repetition; explaining how and why these slips occur—which is chiefly attributable to Fitzgerald's revision process (included is a useful chart depicting the arrangement of chapters during three stages of composition); and finally indicating the significance of these incoherences to the achievement of the novel—which is its chief shortcoming. The implications of Pendleton's discoveries should cause us all to reconsider our assessment of *Gatsby,* but despite giving over one-sixth of his book to "Conclusions," he simply fails to demonstrate the impact of his discoveries on our reading.

b. Full-length Studies: Hemingway   Robert Fleming's *The Face in the Mirror: Hemingway's Writers* (Alabama) asks "how does the writer coexist with the man?" and answers by analyzing many "writers" in the fiction. "Mr. and Mrs. Elliot" and "Banal Story" reflect "early attempts to articulate a writer's relationship to his art and to his fellow human beings," while *Torrents* captures "a growing uneasiness about the integrity of the literary progression" and *The Sun Also Rises* addresses the faults of one writer, Cohn, who lives vicariously and fails to balance his personal and professional life. Short and long works of the '30s (though not *Green Hills of Africa*) broach different questions about the author's relationship to friends, society, and fame. The freshest insights emerge from Fleming's reading of the play, *The Fifth Column,* and the Spanish Civil War stories. He closes with chapters on *Islands in the Stream,* where Hemingway "worked to clarify how he felt in his own mind about the divided loyalties of the artist," and *The Garden of Eden,* whose "provisional ending" contemplates what has hitherto been unthinkable for Hemingway's writers: sacrificing the artistic in favor of the personal. Fleming's study, well-grounded in the archive, provides a sound beginning for what will surely be a lively discussion about Hemingway's writers.

Treating Hemingway's novel of the Spanish Civil War for Twayne's Masterwork Studies is Allen Josephs's For Whom the Bell Tolls: *Ernest Hemingway's Undiscovered Country.* The book opens with six succinct chapters addressing the novel's "literary and historical context"—focusing on Hemingway's personal and professional role in the war and countering the notion that the author was politically naive. With an engaging style and brisk pace, Josephs provides a good overview of the novel's critical reception, of Hemingway's motivation to write the manuscript, and of his desire to relegate political commentary to wartime writing and save his apolitical *Bell* for peacetime. Josephs follows with seven chapters that constitute "A Reading," wherein Josephs emphasizes "that Hemingway *intentionally* wrote an 'invented' novel rather than a personal rendition of the war's reality." He stresses as well the circularity of setting and the "real," "disguised," and "invented" nature of the characters. The plot is treated in four chapters, reflecting particularly on the novel's "continuous presence" and the love affair (after all, Josephs contends, this is "first and foremost a love story"). His reading benefits from the insights of other specialists, and his appendix, "On Language," engages the continuing discussion about *Bell*'s use of Spanish.

Revisiting last year's subject of choice, Nancy R. Comley and Robert

Scholes have collaborated on *Hemingway's Genders: Rereading the Hemingway Text* (Yale), adding one new essay to three previously published. Witty and provocative, these inquiries elevate the issue of gender because it seems to be "a conscious preoccupation for Hemingway" and because "questions of gender keep presenting themselves as the most fruitful questions to pose." Their field of play is the "Hemingway Text," a biobibliographical matrix that is "not as concerned with the borders between individual works or with the differences between published and unpublished writing as some other critics have been." Comley and Scholes treat "the notion of paternity in the myth of Papa," the repertory of female character types, transgressive sexuality, and male homosocial desire. Their ending signals a new beginning: "The Hemingway you were taught in high school is dead. *Viva el nuevo Hemingway*."

c. Collections   Kenneth Rosen's titular allusion in the collection *Hemingway Repossessed* (Praeger) is to Mark Spilka's "Repossessing Papa: A Narcissistic Meditation" (pp. 37–49), which Rosen believes characterizes the anthology as "the latest attempt by these individual scholars . . . to make Hemingway their own . . . in terms of *their* particular needs, *their* specific critical approaches," and so raises once again the vexing question that Josephs urges us to consider: is criticism "sometimes as much of an invention as fiction"? It all depends, these critics seem to say. "Part I. Hemingway and Art" provides four comparatist responses and helps us appreciate the novelist's understanding of the visual arts. Elizabeth Dewberry Vaughn's "*In Our Time* and Picasso" (pp. 3–8) pursues the painter's influence—monoplanic style, resistance to closure, block-shaped interchapters, repetition of words, phrases, and images—and claims that the cubists offered a model for "representation of truth rather than truth itself." Another influential cubist painting, Juan Gris's *The Bullfighter*, is the subject of James Plath's "*Le Torero* and 'The Undefeated': Hemingway's Foray into Analytical Cubism" (pp. 9–16); Plath explains how Hemingway's "The Undefeated" is an "attempt to apply the technique of analytical cubism to fiction—using *Le Torero* as a model." Robert E. Gajdusek visits the Prado to describe a 17th-century influence in "Artists in Their Art: Hemingway and Velásquez—Their Shared Worlds of *For Whom the Bell Tolls* and *Las Meninas*" (pp. 17–27); both artists place themselves within their art, achieving eternity and immortality, transcending—while remaining amid—their subjects. And Thomas Hermann's "Formal Analogies in the Texts and Paintings of Ernest Heming-

way and Paul Cézanne" (pp. 29–33) reveals that as the visual artist purges
his craft of its clichés, so too does the writer eschew "interior decoration";
Cézanne subjected all elements to the motif or narrative just as Hemingway insisted that "the alteration of one word can throw an entire story
out of key."

The trio of essays under the heading of "Part II. Our Old Man" begins
with Spilka's narcissistic meditation: "as we attempt to interpret authorial
intentions . . . [we] begin our own takeover of authorial achievements."
His premise is reasonable. But when he blends life and art (in this case
with "Soldier's Home" and *Bell*) and concludes that "Hemingway liked
to kill people," I do not follow. Donald Junkins is unimpressed not only
with Spilka's claim but with biographical criticism in general ("Mythmaking, Androgyny, and the Creative Process, Answering Mark Spilka,"
pp. 57–67). He urges a study of Hemingway's "darker unconscious self
where the alchemy of creation takes place" because the true gold of
Hemingway's life is his art. Larry Merchant's tribute, "Hemingway's
Influence on Sportswriting" (pp. 51–56), stands like a patient referee
between opposing critical teams, reminding readers that more than one
Hemingway exists out there.

"Part III. On Spanish Earth" might well have been called "inventing
from fact." Susan Beegel's " 'The Undefeated' and *Sangre y Arena*: Hemingway's *Mano a Mano* with Blasco Ibáñez" (pp. 71–85) compares the
short story, the novel, and *La Corrida,* an abridged bilingual edition of
the novel, owned and annotated by Hemingway. "At the very least,"
Beegel concludes, "it is time to add Vincent Blasco Ibáñez to the ever-
lengthening roll of Hemingway's literary mentors." Allen Josephs in
"Reality and Invention in *For Whom the Bell Tolls,* or Reflections on the
Nature of the Historical Novel" (pp. 87–95) demonstrates that Hemingway is equally adept at inventing from life and urges readers to focus on
how this inventive process works. While Erik Nakjavani shrouds his
insights in "Nostalgia, Its Stylistics and Poetics in Hemingway's *For
Whom the Bell Tolls*" (pp. 97–113), H. R. Stoneback's " 'You Sure This
Thing Has Trout in It?': Fishing and Fabrication, Omission and 'Ver-
mification' in *The Sun Also Rises*" (pp. 115–28) proves that learning and
laughter are not mutually exclusive. It is the Fabrica, Stoneback demonstrates with map and text and experience, and not the Irati that Bill and
Jake fish. And Stoneback's explanation of Jake's worm fishing—it has a
history of dignity, he explains—wins him a place with Izaak Walton,
Charles Cotton, and Sylvia Plath.

The last handful of essays is loosely gathered beneath "Part IV. Getting It Right," which echoes Hemingway's reply to George Plimpton, who asked "What was it that had stumped you?" when Hemingway offered that he rewrote the end of *A Farewell to Arms* thirty-nine times. Miriam B. Mandel's "Reading the Names Right" (pp. 131–41) reveals that "proper names that appear in the novels and stories guide us to the facts, rumors, and feelings that attach to the names but that the text does not provide," thus allowing us "to retrieve the erudition that does not show." Point of view is the subject of Paul Smith's "Who Wrote Hemingway's *In Our Time?*" (pp. 143–50), which examines—and finds lacking— evidence for the hypothesis that "*a* Nick Adams is the implied author of the stories in that book." Frank Scafella's "Beginning with 'Nothing'" (pp. 151–57) considers "nothing" as a symbol, the winning (or grasping) of which allows the character "to lose himself to a new possibility for thought and action," rejuvenating imaginative possibilities in him. The dark possibilities of Hemingway's hospital story intrigue Ann L. Putnam, whose "Opiates, Laughter, and the Radio's Sweet Lies: Community and Isolation in Hemingway's 'The Gambler, the Nun, and the Radio'" (pp. 159–68) shows kinship between "The Gambler" and Hemingway's "A Clean, Well-Lighted Place" and reveals Frazer's discovery that "life itself is the ultimate illusion"; having shrunk from community, he ends a solitary figure turned toward his radio. Wolfgang E. H. Rudat's "Hemingway on Sexual Otherness: What's Really Funny in *The Sun Also Rises*" (pp. 169–79) discusses Jake's encounter with Prentiss and the Satirist Satirized and calls for reevaluation of "authorially marginalized characters."

d. General Essays The most significant of this year's useful crop of essays is Rose Marie Burwell's. She uses the recently opened Scribner Archives at Princeton University to begin solving some of "The Posthumous Hemingway Puzzle" (*PULC* 56, i: 24–45) that Gerry Brenner (see *ALS 1982*, p. 181) and Jacqueline Tavernier-Courbin (*ALS 1991*, pp. 150– 51) have been posing. Burwell's single most intriguing find? "The Hotel Ritz Papers"—inspirations for *A Moveable Feast*—exist: "I found stuff here," writes Hemingway to Lee Samuels on 15 January 1957, "that has been in storage for 30 years. Good stuff . . . Mss. of *The Undefeated, Fifty Grand* and most of *In Our Time* and *Men Without Women* all holograph and *Big Two[-]Hearted River* in copybooks. . . ." Susan Beegel's "'A Room on the Garden Side': Hemingway's Unpublished Liberation of Paris"

(*SSF* 31: 627–37) scrutinizes one of five World War II stories that remained unpublished in the author's lifetime. In the seductive Babylon of Paris, dead writers such as Proust, Hugo, Dumas, Baudelaire arise to accuse the narrator of not appreciating his gift of life and choosing to follow the war rather than his craft. By not publishing this story of literary despair—or the other four—Hemingway may have been trying "to leave the Paris of the Ritz" in favor of his own personal Paris. Using *A Moveable Feast* and several other works, David Minter's "War as Metaphor: The Example of Ernest Hemingway" (*A Cultural History of the American Novel*, pp. 113–45) describes the author's faith "in the power of writing to provide models of effective resistance for writers like himself" who are "truly vulnerable" but make their way against great odds.

Grounding her detailed and intelligent study in the scholarship of Charles A. Fenton, Robert O. Stephens, and Michael S. Reynolds, Phyllis Frus's perceptive *The Politics and Poetics of Journalistic Narrative: The Timely and the Timeless* (Cambridge) reconsiders traditional definitions of "journalism" and "literature." Her chapter " 'News That Stays': Hemingway, Journalism, and Objectivity in Fiction" (pp. 53–89) concludes that Hemingway's minimalist style is more plausibly the result of his "desire to critique the discourse of propaganda and patriotism . . . than the influence of writing for a newspaper or magazine or cablese."

Robert E. Gajdusek's "Sacrifice and Redemption: The Meaning of the Boy/Son and Man/Father Dialectic in the Work of Ernest Hemingway" (*NDQ* 62, ii: 166–80) charts these relationships across the canon, observes the death of the boy/son figures, and "suggests the execution of the son as a necessity underwriting the reinstitution of the abstract power of the Father." Nick's dubious prospects prompt Paul Strong's " 'You know me, don't you?': Role Reversal in the Nick Adams Stories" (*NDQ* 62, ii: 132–39), which pursues "something very much like" Michael Reynolds's "echo scene" (see *ALS 1976*, pp. 141–42) in a quartet of short stories. Critics should exhibit care, argues Nadine Devost, who examines the manuscripts in "Hemingway's Girls: Unnaming and Renaming Hemingway's Female Characters" (*HN* 14, i: 46–59), lest they "diminish the purposeful interplay of the common nouns Hemingway used so often to refer to these women."

Overlooked in earlier coverage were Michael M. Boardman's "Innovation as Pugilism: Hemingway and the Reader after *A Farewell to Arms*," pp. 146–88 in his *Narrative Innovation and Incoherence: Ideology in Defoe, Goldsmith, Austen, Eliot, and Hemingway* (Duke, 1992), and Paul W.

Miller's "Hemingway's Posthumous Fiction, 1961–87: A Rorschach Test for Critics" (*Midamerica* 20 [1993]: 98–106). Treating *Death in the Afternoon,* "The Short Happy Life of Francis Macomber," and *To Have and Have Not,* Boardman explains Hemingway's unsuccessful response to the changing demands of his readers in the '30s: mixing "artistic integrity" with "satiric rage," he fails to combine "his universalistic tragedy with social action" and mistakes satire for social commentary. Miller observes a "pattern of critical response" that aligns biographical and style critics, "who regard an author's style as an extension of his person rather than a unifying principle of the entire work under consideration," and aesthetic critics, "who focus their attention on the coherence and excellence of the work as a whole rather than on the work as an extension of the author's psyche." The biographical critics, aided by commercial interests, have carried the day, despite declining enthusiasm for the posthumous work. Miller concludes by mouthing the now-familiar mantra: the trade publications "have established the need for scholarly editions of the major posthumous work to replace the defective versions already supplied."

e. Essays on Specific Works: Fitzgerald   David Minter's *A Cultural History of the American Novel* also treats of *The Great Gatsby* and several short stories in "Class, Power, and Violence in a New Age" (pp. 110–17), reading Gatsby not only as a victim of Tom but of the social pragmatist, Ben Franklin, and the romantic idealist, Hopalong Cassidy, who conspire to make Jay "vulnerable to the machinations of the rich." Lauraleigh O'Meara's "Medium of Exchange: The Blue Coupé Dialogue in *The Great Gatsby*" (*PLL* 30: 73–87) views the car's roles—for Tom, a means of access to Myrtle and the price of silence from George; for George, his ticket west as a successful purveyor of automobiles. Ami M. Krumrey's Jungian reading, "Nick Carraway's Process of Individuation" (*JEP* 15: 249–58), suggests that Nick begins to "find himself" relative to both the "one-sided" characters (Daisy, Tom, Jordan), who are rooted in either "thinking" or "feeling," and the multidimensional, but unsuccessful, Gatsby. Dalton and Mary-Jean Gross contribute a useful note, "F. Scott Fitzgerald's American Swastika: The Prohibition Underworld and *The Great Gatsby*" (*N&Q* 41: 377), which suggests that Wolfsheim's Swastika Holding Company may allude to underworld figures Texas Guinan and Larry Fay, bootleggers whose fleet of taxicabs and whose nightclubs were decorated with the emblem.

Todd H. Stebbins's "*Tender is the Night*: The Last Love Battle" (*Fitzgerald Newsletter* 4: 4–10) discusses the "catalytic agents" that influenced the novel's composition and were brought about by World War I, including "changes in social, political, financial, intellectual, and artistic arenas." John Haegert's "Repression and Counter-Memory in *Tender Is the Night* (*ELWIU* 21: 97–115) considers the 1934 and 1951 editions in terms of "counter-memory," which "impedes and disrupts the narrative of inexorable decline and fall favored by most readers," suggesting that Dick's "dive" may also be seen as a return "to the land of his fathers, driven by the memory of a moral homeland from which he has temporarily 'digressed.' " Robert Silhol's dense psychoanalytic reading, "*Tender is the Night* or the Rape of the Child" (*L&P* 40, iv: 40–63), identifies a "seesaw" structure wherein "apparent happiness" and "sadness and tragic separation" balance on a fulcrum of "flashback" (i.e., the middle portion of the novel as it was originally published). Silhol concludes that "unconscious desire" in the form of the character's quest "to sacrifice himself for the glory of the phallic parent . . . presided over the architecture of Fitzgerald's novel." John W. Crowley's "The Drunkard's Holiday: *Tender Is the Night*" (*The White Logic*, pp. 65–89) attributes the curious depiction of alcoholism in the novel to Fitzgerald's own ambivalence about the disease.

f. Essays on Specific Works: Hemingway   Eight novels or collections received attention. Stephen P. Clifford's "Hemingway's Fragmentary Novel: Readers Writing the Hero in *In Our Time*" (*HN* 13, ii: 12–23) draws on the theories of Teresa de Lauretis to dismantle the notion that *In Our Time* has a single hero, while it joins Joseph M. Flora (see *ALS 1993*, p. 138) in challenging Debra A. Moddlemog's contention that the collection is, in Lawrentian terms, "a short book" or fragmentary novel.

Studies illuminating Hemingway's *Sun* include John W. Crowley's "Bulls, Balls, and Booze: *The Sun Also Rises*" (*The White Logic*, pp. 43–64), Marc D. Baldwin's " 'To Make It into a Novel . . . Don't Talk About It': Hemingway's Political Unconsciousness" (*JNT* 23 [1993]: 170–87), and Doris A. Helbig's "Confession, Charity, and Community in *The Sun Also Rises*" (*SoAR* 58, ii [1993]: 85–110). Crowley claims that despite Hemingway's eventually succumbing to alcoholism, his novel "subtly affirms sobriety as a means to the sheer drunkenness of the writer's art"; Baldwin finds that the novel's silences bespeak both pragmatism and irony, reminding us that society concomitantly unifies and divides; Helbig argues that Jake's confessional narrative allows both him and Bret to unburden themselves of selfishness and win a place in the community.

Paul Civello's *American Literary Naturalism* (pp. 67–111) devotes three of 10 chapters to *Farewell* and *Sun,* considering them examples of "'modern' naturalism" because they exhibit "the collapse of the old order that had imbued the material world with meaning, the subsequent rift between the self and that material world, and the struggle to reconcile the two." The Hemingway hero "puts forth consciousness" as an ordering principle, imbuing his existence with "a personal, rather than divine, meaning" that is based on his experience and not on some abstraction. Because Frederic and Catherine's relationship "apotheosized love to an absolute" in a world cleansed of absolutes, they fail; conversely, Jake Barnes learns "to create an order that gives meaning to existence *within* a world of indifferent material force." Jake succeeds because he creates his own personal order that is not belied by experience.

Miriam Mandel's "Furguson and Lesbian Love: Unspoken Subplots in *A Farewell to Arms*" (*HN* 14, i: 18–24) helps to frame the novel's sexual politics by addressing the "strong sexual component" that complicates the relationship between Furguson and Barkley. Robert Emmett Finnegan in "Adieu Identity: Mirrors and Newspapers in Hemingway's *A Farewell to Arms*" (*DUJ* 86: 259–70) suggests that Frederic's "fundamental difficulty is a lack of self knowledge" and, borrowing Erik Erikson's definition of identity, "the process by which an individual finds his idea of himself affirmed by the community"; Finnegan traces images of mirrors and newspapers en route to determining that Frederic fails in his "search for (re)definition." Margot Norris in "The Novel as War: Lies and Truth in Hemingway's *A Farewell to Arms*" (*MFS* 40: 689–710) explains that the novel "ends as a love story masking and protecting a war story from the truth of its own violence, and its own lies." With reference to Frederic, Rinaldi, and the priest, Ira Elliott's "*A Farewell to Arms* and Hemingway's Crisis of Masculine Values" (*LIT* 4 [1993]: 291–304) examines "the ways in which gender fluidity and sexual indeterminacy function." And William Thomas Hill's "The Roads of the Abruzzi and the Roads of Earthly Paradise in Hemingway's *A Farewell to Arms*" (*Studies in the Humanities* [Kanda, Tokyo] 55: 25–43) explains Frederic's decision to establish an earthly paradise with Catherine rather than visit the priest's sacred home.

Three works were the subject of single essays. Donald Junkins reveals how Hemingway uses tone in *Death in the Afternoon* to overcome his audience's objection to bullfighting in "Hemingway's Old Lady and the Aesthetics of *Pundonor*" (*NDQ* 62, ii: 195–204). Lloyd Halliburton contributes to the ongoing discussion of the author's Spanish in "Hemingway's Use of *Máquina* in *For Whom the Bell Tolls*: A Reconsideration" (*NDQ* 62, ii: 183–92). And explicating a pair of essential allusions in a still-neglected novel is James H. Meredith's "The Rapido River and Hürtgen Forest in *Across the River and Into the Trees*" (*HN* 14, i: 60–66).

In "Lies, Damned Lies, and Autobiography: Hemingway's Treatment of Fitzgerald in *A Moveable Feast*" (*ABSt* 9, i: 64–82) Susanna Egan studies manuscript variants and reveals how Hemingway constructs himself and others. Wolfgang E. H. Rudat's "Hemingway's Revenge on Gertrude Stein: Intertextuality between *A Moveable Feast* and *The Sun Also Rises*" (*JEP* 15, 1–2: 39–50) takes exception to Linda Wagner-Martin's claim (see *ALS 1991*, p. 154) that Jake's disdain for the homosexuals at the *bal musette* should be "widened to include lesbians," arguing that "we should read *Feast* against the background of the *Sun* instead of retroactively viewing the *Sun* in light of the *Feast*." Michael Funch's "The Intentional Phallacy: The Art and Life of Ernest Hemingway—A Biographical Angle?" (*AmerSS* 26, ii: 65–78) uses *Feast* and *Eden* to question the machismo often attributed to Hemingway and finds "that behind the public image is a private one, transgressing maleness into the field of femaleness"; the resulting reading embraces "the range of meanings and significances to be derived from the texts."

H. R. Stoneback ushers in the year's half-dozen treatments of the stories with "Fiction into Film: 'Is Dying Hard, Daddy?' Hemingway's 'Indian Camp'" (pp. 93–108 in Richard L. Chapple, ed., *Social and Political Change in Literature and Film: Selected Papers from the Sixteenth Annual Florida State University Conference on Literature and Film* [Florida]), where he addresses the creation and reception of Brian Edgar's artful adaptation. Lisa Tyler's "Ernest Hemingway's Date Rape Story: Sexual Trauma in 'Up in Michigan'" (*HN* 13, ii: 1–11) clarifies terminology and centers her discussion in earlier scholarship, arguing that Jim raped (not seduced) Liz, and that, just as Nick's trauma in *In Our Time* is war, Liz's trauma is rape. James Plath explains in "Fishing for Tension: The Dynamics of Hemingway's 'Big Two-Hearted River'" (*NDQ* 62, ii: 159–65) that the author accomplishes his visual-to-verbal transformations by employing alternating planes of opposition. Edwin J. Barton's

"The Story as It Should Be: Epistemological Uncertainty in Hemingway's 'Cat in the Rain'" (*HN* 14, i: 72–78) highlights the story's *writerly* nature. "Poor Ernest's Almanac: The Petty Economies of 'Fifty Grand' 's Jack Brennan" (*HN* 13, ii: 24–36) by David Thoreen considers the narrative in terms of earning, saving, and multiplying money, and as being about the capitalist system and its effect on people. John Leonard's " 'A Man of the World' and 'A Clean Well-Lighted Place': Hemingway's Unified View of Old Age" (*HN* 13, ii: 62–73) finds that these stories confront the onset of advanced age and converge on a dozen themes.

g. Miscellaneous Assessing Hemingway's market value is Nina M. Ray's "The Endorsement Potential Also Rises: The Merchandising of Ernest Hemingway" (*HN* 13, ii: 74–86), which explains why Hemingway may serve as an attractive endorser for "socially visible, higher preference products." For Louis Auchincloss in "Three 'Perfect Novels' [*The Scarlet Letter, Wuthering Heights,* and *The Great Gatsby*] and What They Have in Common" (pp. 167–77 in his *The Style's the Man* [Scribner's]), "there is much in common between Fitzgerald's prose and the painting of Edward Hopper. Hopper selects dull houses, drab streets, plain people, and invests them with a glow that is actually romantic."

Part II

11 Literature to 1800

William J. Scheick

This year saw the publication of *The Cambridge History of American Literature, Volume I: 1590–1820,* ed. Sacvan Bercovitch (Cambridge), which is little concerned with literature or history as such, but which by editorial design reflects several of the incompatible approaches to early American culture that are characteristic of our time. Consisting of Myra Jehlen's "The Literature of Colonization" (pp. 11–168), Emory Elliott's "New England Puritan Literature" (pp. 169–306), David Shields's "British-American Belles-Lettres" (pp. 307–44), Robert A. Ferguson's "The American Enlightenment, 1750–1820" (pp. 345–537), and Michael T. Gilmore's "The Literature of the Revolutionary and Early National Periods" (pp. 539–693), this very uneven tome of more than 800 pages is unfortunately a questionable resource for students uninformed about undeclared critical and political agendas. A number of the limitations and strengths of this work are reported in William C. Spengemann's perspicacious "E Pluribus Minimum" (*EAL* 29: 276–94) and Philip F. Gura's "Essaying Early American Literature" (*NEQ* 68 [1995]: 118–38).

i Native Americans and the Colonial Imagination

Into the Wilderness Dream: Exploration Narratives of the American West, 1500–1805, ed. Donald A. Barclay et al. (Utah), is a fine anthology of 33 excerpts, in English, primarily drawn from narratives by Spanish, French, and British individuals who consciously or unconsciously described encounters between their traditional European expectations concerning the New World and their actual experiences in the North American West. Reverse colonization, specifically the influence of early colonial experiences on debates in Spain concerning race and gender, is the subject of James D. Fernández's "The Bonds of Patrimony: Cervantes and the New World" (*PMLA* 109: 969–81). Of related interest is E. Thomson Shields, Jr.'s useful bibliography, "Selected Primary Spanish-Language Sources from Spain's Seventeenth-Century Northern Frontiers Available in English-Language Translation" (*Heath Anthology of American Literature Newsletter* 12: 4–11).

John Smith, John Milton, Benjamin Franklin, William Blake, and Jane Austen are featured in *A New World of Words: Redefining Early American Literature* (Yale), William C. Spengemann's assault on what he perceives as our invention of nationality in early American writings. Spengemann prefers such registers as the vocabulary, grammar, and semiotics of the English language (particularly the features of selection and arrangement) as the means for defining the historical and literary Americaness of narratives concerning early encounters with the New World. He includes all works in English from diverse countries and times that treat the idea of America. Three other discussions relevant to the topic dealt with by Spengemann include *The Imaginary Puritan: Literature, Intellectual Labor, and the Origins of Personal Life* (Calif., 1992), in which Nancy Armstrong and Leonard Tennenhouse consider the influence of Mary Rowlandson's captivity narrative on Samuel Richardson's *Pamela* (see also *ALS 1992*, pp. 166–67); *Culture and Imperialism* (Knopf, 1993), in which Edward W. Said assesses the influence of West Indian plantation slavery on Jane Austen's *Mansfield Park*; and *Spectacles of Strangeness: Imperialism, Alienation, and Marlowe* (Penn., 1993), in which Emily C. Bartels observes the influence of empire construction on Christopher Marlowe's *The Jew of Malta,* among other plays.

What Bernard Rosenthal did last year with the Salem witch trials, Robert S. Tilton does this year with the Pocahontas legend. Tilton's *Pocahontas: The Evolution of an American Narrative* (Cambridge) examines the various, often contradictory, cultural uses of a legend that has influenced such large issues as race relations and national expansion. Roger Williams's *A Key into the Language of America,* Eric Wertheimer similarly argues in " 'To Spell Out Each Other': Roger Williams, Perry Miller, and the Indian" (*ArQ* 50, ii: 1–18), provides bicultural possibilities; it places Native Americans within a metaphorical framework (including typology) that critiques the limitations of Puritan culture and elevates Amer-Indian cultures through the process of translation.

William M. Clements's cautionary "The Jesuit Foundations of Native North American Literary Studies" (*AIQ* 18: 43–59) raises important questions about the reliability of early reports of Native American oral performance; in assessing these reports Clements considers the influence of figurism (natural revelation), traditional *relations,* ethical concepts, theories of the primitive, notions of myth, and the Jesuit preference for oration over song. Other ways whereby Puritans projected religious and cultural beliefs on Native Americans are reviewed in David S. Lovejoy's "Satanizing the American Indian" (*NEQ* 67: 603–21). And the devastating effect of two specific representations of Native Americans intrigues Colin Ramsey, whose "Cannibalism and Infant Killing: A System of 'Demonizing' Motifs in Indian Captivity Narratives" (*ClioI* 24: 55–68) also notes the classical and early Christian appropriation of these images.

ii Rowlandson and Early Colonial Prose

Kathryn Zabelle Derounian-Stodola's "The Indian Captivity Narratives of Mary Rowlandson and Olive Oatman: Case Studies in the Continuity, Evolution, and Exploitation of a Literary Discourse" (*SLitI* 27, i: 33–46) focuses on two best-sellers which mingle fact and propaganda; their exploited genre steadily devolved into a device for furthering the extermination of Native Americans. One application of this captivity narrative paradigm—specifically, the victim's suffering and liberation as the result of divine providence—is documented in John Saillant's " 'Remarkably Emancipated from Bondage, Slavery, and Death': An African American Retelling of the Puritan Captivity Narrative, 1820" (*EAL* 29: 122–40). And an allied appropriation is identified in Dennis Barone's " 'When the Woman Looks, She Changes': The Ambivalent Female Conversion Narrative in American Film" (*StHum* 21: 1–12).

Such cultural cross-fertilization surfaces in both Albert J. von Frank's "John Saffin: Slavery and Racism in Colonial Massachusetts" (*EAL* 29: 254–72) and Michael Elliott's " 'This Indian Bait': Samson Occom and the Voice of Liminality" (*EAL* 29: 233–53). In his debate with Samuel Sewall, von Frank observes, Saffin represented the mercantile class whose claims for slavery increasingly prevailed as Puritanism declined. In his correspondence with Eleazar Wheelock, Elliott explains, Occom occupied a transitional position between two races that empowered him to extract multiple meanings, designed for a dual audience, from the discourses available to him.

In "Narratives of Class in a Culture of Consumption: The Significance of Stories in Sarah Kemble Knight's *Journal*" (*CollL* 21, ii: 33–46)

Scott Michaelson impugns Knight's bourgeois passion for proper behavior as a feature of her class consciousness and her relish for stories; by
"linking hatreds [*sic*] and narrative wit," she "makes class racisms [*sic*]
fun." More than racism was involved in the New York slave trials of 1712
and 1742, which Wilson J. Moses compares to the witch trials of 1692;
the text of paranoia and intolerance typical of these episodes concealed
the role of ritualistic spectacle in supporting the power of the governing
class: "Sex, Salem, and Slave Trials: Ritual Drama and Ceremony of
Innocence" (*The Black Columbiad*, pp. 64–76).

A fear of personal devaluation is William Byrd's theme, and a desire
for continual accumulation is his motive, Jeffrey J. Folks explains in
"Crowd Types in William Byrd's Histories" (*SLJ* 26, ii: 3–10). According
to Susan Manning's "Industry and Idleness in Colonial Virginia: A New
Approach to William Byrd II" (*JAmS* 28: 169–90), Byrd's Southernness
is defined less by his local material than by his meticulous, witty style;
different from its Addisonian model, this style expresses at once a
nostalgia for an imagined lost innocent leisure and a humorous critique
of this nostalgia.

Not nostalgia as such, but the personal and emotional costs of emigration interest Sargent Bush, Jr., in both "After Coming Over: John
Cotton, Peter Bulkeley, and Learned Discourse in the Wilderness" (*SLitI*
27, i: 7–21) and "Epistolary Counseling in the Puritan Movement: The
Example of John Cotton" (*Puritanism: Transatlantic Perspectives on a
Seventeenth-Century Anglo-American Faith,* ed. Francis J. Bremer [Mass.
Historical Soc., 1993], pp. 127–46). Whereas the first of these essays
examines the correspondence of two divines to assess how their sense of
loss was somewhat redressed by fervid ministerial engagement in intellectual exchange pertaining to religious matters, the second reviews the
important contribution of one minister's personal and informal letters to
the emergent inner coherence of Puritan beliefs. Support for Bush's
claims emerges in Francis J. Bremer's thoroughly researched and densely
detailed *Congregational Communion: Clerical Friendship in the Anglo-
American Puritan Community, 1610–1692* (Northeastern), which discloses how the intricate network of interaction among Puritan confreres
provided the hub of an emerging self-definition for an elect subculture
within a dominant, often hostile society.

Previewing his observations about John Cotton and others in *Theocracy in Massachusetts: Reformation and Separation in Early Puritan New
England* (Mellen), Avihu Zakai's "Theocracy in Massachusetts: The Pu-

ritan Universe of Sacred Imagination" (*SLitI* 27, i: 23–31) highlights the subversiveness of a Puritan millennial radicalism that did not support a national church. Several of Zakai's conclusions are implicitly challenged by Janice Knight's findings in *Orthodoxies in Massachusetts: Rereading American Puritanism* (Harvard). Knight contends that the emphases of such "Spiritual Brethren" as John Cotton (accentuating divine benevolence, a nonconditional covenant between God and humanity, a mystical sense of the salvation process, and a genuinely millennialist devotion to the international church) contrasts with the emphases of such "Intellectual Fathers" as Thomas Shepard (accentuating divine power, a conditional covenant between God and humanity, a preparationist attitude toward the salvation process, and a tribal mentality concerning the fulfillment of biblical millennial prophecies). The non-Ramean sermons of the Brethren, whose views were eventually suppressed, fostered a mystical sense of the ineffable wonder of Christic communication and union; they did not imply a position of privilege and tended to be lyrically associative, allusive, incantatory, repetitive, and exegetical rather than logical, plotted, definite, linear in development, and hortatory. Although to be completely convincing, this reading of the technique of the Brethren requires a more sustained analysis, Knight makes a reasonable case for a strain of Puritanism that has been overlooked as such and that may possibly explain some of the odd features of Puritan culture as arising from differences rather than from inconsistencies.

Michael Ditmore's keen exercise in detection, "Preparation and Confession: Reconsidering Edmund S. Morgan's *Visible Saints*" (*NEQ* 67: 298–319), potentially augments Knight's thesis by reducing John Cotton's alleged role and advancing Thomas Shepard's likely role in the establishment of the spiritual relation. The intersection of method and spontaneity in an autobiography of multiple unfoldings, also pertinent to Knight's thesis, interests Constance Post, whose "Making the Random Routine and the Routine Random: Ritual and Anti-Ritual in Cotton Mather's *Paterna*" (*SPAS* 4 [1993]: 125–54) explores these competing dispositions of Puritan piety. Contradiction is likewise highlighted in Christopher D. Felker's insightful *Reinventing Cotton Mather in the American Renaissance*: Magnalia Christi Americana *in Hawthorne, Stowe, and Stoddard* (Northeastern, 1993), which focuses on Mather's self-consciousness as a historian and his experience of cultural instability and transformation; with "novelistic realism" Mather's account presents and displaces both the desires and anxieties of his time, features that made his book highly marketable later to such diverse readerships as children, women, and citizens of a democracy. That other chronicles besides Mather's—such as Sir Walter Raleigh's *History of the World* and Nathaniel Bacon's *Relation of the Fearful Estate of Francis Spira*—were popular among colonial readers is documented in Gillian Avery's *Behold the Child: American Children and Their Books, 1621–1922* (Bodley Head, pp. 13–62). Avery also observes the steady displacement of moral texts by recreational literature as acceptable reading matter for 18th-century youth.

The reception, sources, and place of the first colonial attempt at a comprehensive integration of science and religion are detailed in the extensive introduction to Winton U. Solberg's edition of Cotton Mather's *The Christian Philosopher* (Illinois). In "Prodigies, Puritanism, and the Perils of Natural Philosophy: The Example of Cotton Mather" (*WMQ* 51: 92–105) Michael P. Winship reads Mather's anxiety about science as an indication of his recognition of the constraints on reporting extraordinary phenomena imposed from abroad by mainstream scientists. And William R. Newman's *Gehennical Fire: The Lives of George Starkey, an American Alchemist in the Scientific Revolution* (Harvard) documents that the alchemical interests of New Englanders such as Mather derived from contemporary progressive English and Continental "scientific" thought, which likewise credited dreams, revelations, and intuitions.

The successful combination of two careers by Cotton Mather's father is noted by Joanne M. Gaudio in " 'So many parts of myselfe': Increase Mather, Minister or Politician?" (*CEA* 57, i: 68–76). Increase Mather's disapproval of men and women dancing together is mentioned in Bruce C. Daniels's assessment of the rise of self-gratification and the decline of self-denial in Puritan culture, "Sober Mirth and Pleasant Poisons: Puritan Ambivalence toward Leisure and Recreation in Colonial New England" (*AmerS* 34, i [1993]: 121–37). And Increase Mather also appears in John D. Burton's "Crimson Missionaries: The Robert Boyle Legacy and Harvard College" (*NEQ* 67: 132–40), which documents various ministerial efforts to dilute the aim of the trust fund.

Both Mathers figure in *Authorizing the Past: The Rhetoric of History in Seventeenth-Century New England* (No. Ill.), a well-written book less satisfying or original as a whole than in several of its perceptive parts. Stephen Carl Arch demonstrates that from the 1630s to 1690s a professionalism steadily developed in the practice of Puritan historiography. In

Arch's discussion, Winthrop's journal fails to present an adequate over-view of the various conflicts evident in early Puritan society and so never reconciles its author's conservative notion of social order and his more modern vision of individual attainment. Edward Johnson's *Wonder-Working Providence,* in contrast, recasts confusing cultural events into a cohesive account by subordinating alternative theocratic perspectives to the establishmentarian view of the divine purpose behind New England. Increase Mather's various parochial histories incidentally reveal a social fragmentation for which the historian has no comprehensive explana-tion, even while they promote the acceptance of the historian's percep-tion of and recommendations concerning various crises as responses only to specific cultural episodes. Cotton Mather's *Magnalia Christi Amer-icana,* written in the voice of the historian divinely endowed as *sacer vates,* vacillates between embalming and reviving his readers' lost vision. (See also *ALS 1992,* p. 165, and *ALS 1993,* p. 151, on material drawn from this book.) Another Puritan's effort to remove history from its traditional and mythic configuration on behalf of cultural reform interests Den-nis R. Perry, whose " 'Novelties and Stile Which All Out-Do': William Hubbard's Historiography Reconsidered" (*EAL* 29: 166–82) explores seeming inconsistencies in perspectives that actually represent an at-tempt to reconcile opposing secular and congregational viewpoints.

iii Bradstreet and Early Colonial Poetry

Anne Bradstreet's viewpoint inspired four essays in *SPAS.* Robert Daly's "Powers of Humility and the Presence of Readers in Anne Bradstreet and Phillis Wheatley" (4 [1993]: 1–23) detects the deliberate self-effacing management of several voices fashioned to appeal to different audiences. Kimberly Cole Winebrenner's "Bradstreet's Emblematic Marriage" (4 [1993]: 45–70) reminds us that the poet speaks at once in terms of a wife's physical love of her husband and in terms of a Canticle bride's spiritual love of Christ. Birgit Meany's "The Contemplative Art of Anne Brad-street's 'Contemplations' " (4 [1993]: 71–103) differentiates between a regimented meditative search for truth and a spontaneous contemplative regard for found salvation. And, the best of the group, Peter Shuffelton's "Anne Bradstreet's 'Contemplations,' Gardens, and the Art of Memory" (4 [1993]: 25–43) applies two Renaissance perceptions of the garden: as a rhetorical place where chaotic thought is ordered and can be directed toward poetic invention; and as a place where Edenic splendor and divine presence are remembered. Bradstreet specifically identifies the imagined site of "Contemplations" as "the woods," the opposite of a garden; but if this setting is seen as the deity's garden, and not only as divine art, then Shuffelton's reading is intriguing.

In " 'Contemplations': Anne Bradstreet's Homage to Calvin and Reformed Theology" (*C&L* 42 [1992]: 41–68) Timothy Whelen identifies two perspectives in the poem: in the first part of the verse human knowledge proves inadequate to the poet's needs; in the second part divine knowledge, based on Scripture, satisfies the poet. My "Logonomic Conflict in Bradstreet's 'Letter to Her Husband' " (*ELWIU* 21: 166–84) describes a narrative performance characterized by (1) the sudden intrusion of openly declared biblical allusions that attempt to displace the poet's voice and identity; (2) the unstable relationship of this intrusion between the apparent centrality of intense secular experience and the possible marginality of divine signification in the verse letter; (3) the allied potential narrative inversion of typological discourse, with the antitype serving as a means rather than an end in the authorization of physical love; and (4) the fragmenting of the verse letter into two unequal parts, not only quantitatively but qualitatively, with each segment evidencing a distinct emotional register.

Bradstreet also appears in "Early New England Women Poets: Writing as Vocation" (*EAL* 29: 103–21), Pattie Cowell's review of the negative and positive effects of print culture on female literary creativity. And the writings of three colonial women are reconsidered in biographical-bibliographical essays in *Legacy*: "Bathsheba Bowers (c. 1672–1718)" by Suzanna M. Zweizig (11: 65–73), "Judith Sargent Murray (1751–1820)" by Sharon Harris (11: 152–59), and "Anne Bradstreet (c. 1612–1672)" by Jane Donahue Eberwein (11: 161–69).

Christy Friend's " 'My Case Is Bad, Lord, Be My Advocate': The Use of Classical Rhetoric in Edward Taylor's Meditation 1.39" (*SPAS* 4 [1993]: 105–24) offers an innovative examination of the influence of judicial speech as one paradigm for Taylor's poetic technique. J. Daniel Patterson prints an earlier version of " 'Meditation 2.162': The Last Unpublished *Preparatory Meditation* from Edward Taylor's 'Poetical Works' Manuscript" (*EAL* 29: 273–75). And the management of a classical image of fish in trees to defend the Puritan way is detected by Michele Valerie Ronnick in "A Horatian Influence on the Verse of Samuel Danforth (1626–1674)" (*ELN* 32, ii: 37–39).

iv Edwards, the Great Awakening, and the New Divinity

In *Ecclesiastical Writings,* the 12th volume of *The Works of Jonathan Edwards* (Yale), David D. Hall provides editions of four documents on the sacraments, including a careful reconstruction (based on manuscripts) of Edwards's retrospective narrative on the Lord's Supper controversy. In *The "Miscellanies," a-500,* the 13th volume of *The Works* (Yale) Thomas A. Schafer provides much more than an edition (based on manuscripts) of Edwards's theological notebooks from 1722 to 1731; he also offers a valuable chronology of Edwards's sermons during these years, an index of biblical allusions, an illustrated guide to Edwards's changing handwriting, and a catalog of the ink textures and the watermarks in Edwards's manuscripts.

Focusing on *A Faithful Narrative* in "Jonathan Edwards and the Reconstruction of 'Feminine' Speech" (*AmLH* 6: 185–212), Sandra Gustafson highlights the theologian's early social emphasis on emotional relationships; this emphasis opened a "representational space" that was later occupied by the antebellum female voice, especially in spiritual biographies and sentimental fiction. That Edwards unwittingly participated in the colonial displacement of Native Americans, even while trying to protect them, is noted by Lion G. Miles in "The Red Man Dispossessed: The Williams Family and the Alienation of Indian Land in Stockbridge, Massachusetts, 1736–1818" (*NEQ* 67: 46–76). A survey of approaches to Edwards during the past 15 years is provided by M. X. Lesser in *Jonathan Edwards: An Annotated Bibliography, 1974–1993* (Greenwood). And an Edwardsean whose effort to promote the veneration of the Pilgrims inadvertently resulted in strengthening his adversaries appears in Mark L. Sargent's "The New Divinity in the Old Colony: Chandler Robbins and the Legend of the Pilgrims" (*SPAS* 4 [1993]: 155–84).

v Franklin, Jefferson, and the Revolution

Eric Wertheimer's "Commencement Ceremonies: History and Identity in 'The Rising Glory of America,' 1771 and 1786" (*EAL* 29: 35–58) concludes that the later version of a poem by Philip Freneau and Hugh Henry Brackenridge refines the idiom of innocence; Americans hence emerge as a national force displacing the inchoate and dialetical features of New World identity evident in the earlier version. Michele Valerie Ronnick reinstates two missing lines and revises a classical attribution in "A Note on the Text of Philip Freneau's 'Columbus to Ferdinand': From Plato to Seneca" (*EAL* 29: 81–82). And E. Thomson Shields, Jr., contextualizes and edits an anonymous satire that suggests some of the complexities behind the movement of the Southern colonies toward independence: " 'A Modern Poem,' by the Mecklenburg Censor: Politics and Satire in Revolutionary North Carolina" (*EAL* 29: 205–32).

How the idea of an independent Ojibwa territory emerged from a critique of American pastoral tradition is treated in "Pastoral Landscape with Indians: George Copway and the Political Unconscious of the American Pastoral" (*Prospects* 18 [1993]: 1–27), Timothy Sweet's consideration of one person's belief in combining Anglo-American and Native American cultural matter in an agrarian economy. Sweet's "American Pastoralism and the Marketplace: Eighteenth-Century Ideologies of Farming" (*EAL* 29: 59–80) usefully contrasts the antimarket ideology of the backwoods farming paradigm defended in Benjamin Rush's *Essays Literary, Moral, and Philosophical* with the capitalist ideology of the agrarian social and political theory advanced in J. Hector St. John de Crèvecoeur's *Letters from an American Farmer* and Thomas Jefferson's *Notes on the State of Virginia.*

Early national epistolary exchange is the subject of both "Jefferson and the Familiar Letter" (*JER* 14: 195–220) and " 'Posterity Must Judge': Private and Public Discourse in the Adams-Jefferson Letters" (*ArQ* 50, iv: 1–30). In the former essay Andrew Burstein explores Jefferson's appreciation of language—akin to a spiritual experience for him—as an agent of individual conscience; it fosters people's awareness of their behavior and their assessment of the past and the present. In the latter essay David Haven Blake, Jr., explores Jefferson's and Adams's regard for the difference between personal communication and public discourse; opposing the examples of newspapers, histories, and polemics, these men defended private correspondence as an asylum that provided unity and enlightenment in an otherwise factional cultural milieu.

Without even a nod toward Richard Beale Davis in "Jefferson and Sterne" (*EAL* 29: 19–34), Andrew Burstein and Catherine Mowbray describe the mutual views of these two men concerning thought and feeling, the use of wit in response to mortality, and the reliance on style to resist classical models. Paul K. Conklin's "Priestley and Jefferson: Unitarianism as a Religion for a New Revolutionary Age" (*Religion in a*

Revolutionary Age, pp. 290–307) assesses the impact of *An History of the Corruptions of Christianity* on Jefferson's skepticism. Debunking what he sees as the fabrication of historians, Paul Finkelman contends that Jefferson was unable to join the resistance against slavery and, instead, prevented change in American race relations: "Thomas Jefferson and Antislavery: The Myth Goes On" (*VMHB* 102: 193–228).

A slave whose talents were dismissed by Jefferson appears in "The Other Song in Phillis Wheatley's 'On Imagination' " (*SLitI* 27, i: 71–84) by Michele McKay and me; beneath her ostensible regard for passionless neoclassical verse Wheatley is subtly faithful to her own voice, especially concerning love as the natural bond that reverses inhumane bondage. An edition of the earliest plea for freedom by a slave mulatto appears in Thomas N. Ingersoll's " 'Releese us out of this Cruell Bondegg': An Appeal from Virginia in 1723" (*WMQ* 51: 777–82). The African American custom of using Scripture as *materia medica,* a therapeutic means of revising and transforming a deleterious social reality, is explored in Theophus H. Smith's *Conjuring Culture: Biblical Formations of Black America* (Oxford), which particularly contrasts this alternative polyvalent practice to the monolithic Puritan American tradition of typology.

How, in response to improved literacy, women increasingly developed a historical sense of themselves is the primary topic of " 'Vindicating the Equality of Female Intellect': Women and Authority in the Early Republic" (*Prospects* 17 [1992]: 1–27) by Mary Kelley. The intersection of intellectual convictions and personal conflicts as a medium for establishing a precarious and paradoxical voice of independence is investigated in *Paine, Scripture, and Authority: The Age of Reason as Religious and Political Idea* (Lehigh) by Edward H. Davidson and me; the theatrical performance of Paine's voice negotiates a paratactic identity whose linguistic strategy of opposition unwittingly reenacts the authoritative rhetorical maneuvers of deposed patriarchal figures.

A father who instructed his children not in terms of class hierarchy and patronage, but in terms of the emerging social and economic challenges of republicanism, interests Philip Hamilton in "Education in the St. George Tucker Household: Change and Continuity in Jeffersonian Virginia" (*VMHB* 102: 167–92). A cleric who responded to Franklin's *A Narrative of the Late Massacres* is identified in "The Rev. Thomas Barton's Authorship of *The Conduct of the Paxton Men, Impartially Represented* (1764)" (*PennH* 61: 155–84) by James P. Myers, Jr. The Quaker whose "wisdom and goodness" Franklin praised in *Poor Richard's*

Almanack is commemorated in a special issue of *PennH* (61: 389–490), which includes commentary not only on William Penn's gentry commonwealth and his response to Roman Catholics but on the historical mythologizing of his two wives. And the importance to Franklin of an intellectual as well as a political revolution is assessed in Ralph Lerner's *Revolutions Revisited: Two Faces of the Politics of Enlightenment* (No. Car.), which reprints his analysis of the function of rhetoric in the Silence Dogood papers in fostering individual and social advancement (pp. 3–18; see also *ALS 1993,* p. 154).

vi The Early National Period

In "Anglo-American Clubs: Their Wit, Their Heterodoxy, Their Sedition" (*WMQ* 51: 293–304) David S. Shields explains that social clubs, featuring the play of wit and the pursuit of pleasure, provided occasions for an experimental expression of viewpoints different from the *sensus communis* and the controlling discourse of church and state. The dissenting views of a skeptical South Carolinian Federalist interest Karen O'Brien, whose "David Ramsey and the Delayed Americanization of American History" (*EAL* 29: 1–18) focuses on resistance in 1789 to the belief that the destiny of the new republic would be different from European national patterns. Political belief, not skepticism, figures in Elaine Forman Crane's interpretation of both a needlework by Faith Robinson Trumbull and an account of the battle of Rhode Island by Mary Gould Almy: "Religion and Rebellion: Women of Faith in the American War for Independence" (*Religion in a Revolutionary Age,* pp. 52–86). With the rise of such national faith, Methodism rapidly spread after the Revolutionary War, a trend documented in John H. Wigger's "Taking Heaven by Storm: Enthusiasm and Early American Methodism, 1770–1820" (*JER* 14: 167–94).

Offering a corrective to biographical readings, Joseph Fichtelberg's "Utopic Distresses: Crèvecoeur's *Letters* and Revolution" (*SLitI* 27, i: 85–101) urges a sensitivity to the ideological contradictions in *Letters;* these contradictions point to the limits of the authority of this work, a self-reflexive critique at once boldly resistant to and naively representative of republican culture. Whatever their local differences, Charles E. Clark concludes in *The Newspaper in Anglo-American Culture, 1665–1740* (Oxford), newspapers collectively offered their readers a unified and coherent view of the world; ranging from such figures as John Campbell to

Benjamin Franklin, Clark maps the progression, particularly in Boston, from various publishers' reliance on English models to their gradual discovery of an American place for the genre by the middle of the 18th century.

vii Brown, Rowson, and Contemporaries

Progression informs Daniel E. Williams's introduction to *Pillars of Salt: An Anthology of Early American Criminal Narratives* (Madison House, 1993), which traces the increasing secularization, sensationalization, and anti-authoritarianism of a genre initially designed to reinforce theocratic power. Williams has previously explored this thesis in such essays as "From Damnation to Dollars: The Motivations of Malefactors in Two Eighteenth-Century American Criminal Narratives" (*SVEC* 303 [1992]: 388–91).

Reviewing 550 post-1777 addresses in "Reinventing Native Americans in Fourth of July Orations" (*SLitI* 27, i: 47–69), Klaus Lubbers reports that since the indigenous people of the New World were perceived as resisting acculturation, they were represented either as doomed to extinction or as deleterious to national expansion. This essay is drawn from Lubbers's *Born for the Shade: Stereotypes of the Native American in United States Literature and the Visual Arts, 1776–1894* (Rodopi), which examines examples of fiction, poetry, drama, Fourth of July orations, occasional essays, school texts, peace medals, documentary art, paintings, and sculpture with attention to changes in Anglo-American representations of Native peoples. Over the years, for example, the white party imaged on ceremonial medals presented to tribal chiefs moved to the center whereas the red party moved to the margins—an asymmetry (subverting the theme of mutual benefit) that prevails in other contemporary American cultural expressions and coincides with the transformation from temporal to spatial concerns in national meliorist predictions.

Asymmetry similarly concerns John Paul Tassoni, whose "'I can step out of myself a little': Feminine Virtue and Female Friendship in Hannah Foster's *The Coquette*" (*Communication and Women's Friendships: Parallels and Intersections in Literature and Life* [Bowling Green, 1993], pp. 97–111) focuses on how the detrimental effect of rhetoric about virtue—in effect a socially constructed notion of women—hindered female friendship in spite of a cultural milieu that fostered personal freedom. Pertinently, in "The Dialogic Margins of Conduct Fiction:

Hannah Webster Foster's *The Boarding School*" (*JASAT* 25: 59–72)
Gwendolyn Audrey Foster finds that *The Boarding School* sometimes
appears to support male social standards while it subverts the dominant
ideology, especially when its female voices express a desire for education,
economic self-sufficiency, celibacy, and same-sex unions. That the predominantly female-authored letters in another early Republican novel
imply the value of balanced dialogism as a corrective to a cultural
background of repressive monologic male speech is the point of Leonard
Cassuto's "The Seduction of American Religious Discourse in Foster's
The Coquette" (*Reform and Counterreform: Dialectics of the Word in
Western Christianity since Luther* [Mouton de Gruyter], pp. 105–18).

An early Republican portrait of John Smith that entangles an older
view of the virtue of individual labor with an emergent newer ideology
stressing national prosperity attracts Philip Gould's attention in "Representative Men: Jeremy Belknap's *American Biography* and the Political
Culture of the Early Republic" (*ABSt* 10: 83–97). A metaparadigm rather
than a mythologized figure is applied in Lucy Rinehart's "A Nation's
'Noble Spectacle': Royall Tyler's *The Contrast* as Metatheatrical Commentary" (*AmDram* 3, ii: 29–52).

The lack of such a transhistorical motif beset the subject of Steven
Watts's *The Romance of Real Life: Charles Brockden Brown and the Origins
of American Culture* (Hopkins), which contends that the anxious post-
Revolutionary transformation from republicanism to individualism, including the capitalist fragmentation of the self, determined the pattern of
Brown's life and work. Later, Brown began to preach "a bourgeois creed
of genteel self-control" in an effort to accept the competitive market
conditions that had previously frustrated him; he did so in the expectation that the turmoil typical of capitalist society and its restive citizens
would be remedied by a civilized culture. In "'All Was Lonely, Darksome, and Waste': *Wieland* and the Construction of the New Republic"
(*SAF* 22: 37–46), Nicholas Rombes, Jr., argues that Brown challenged
Federalist authority, which depended on a dichotomy between rational
order and irrational anarchy; specifically, Brown resisted the reader's
expectation of a conventional moral and implied through Clara's pluralistic voice a revisionist paradigm of assimilation. In contrast, Jared
Gardner's "Alien Nation: Edgar Huntly's Savage Awakening" (*AL* 66:
429–61) indicts Brown for a proto-Manifest Destiny viewpoint in his
representation of Native Americans as a frontier alien presence that must
be eliminated in the interest of achieving a cleansed and unique national

identity. But such bias against Native Americans is only apparent, Sydney J. Krause claims in "Penn's Elm and *Edgar Huntly*: Dark 'Instruction to the Heart'" (*AL* 66: 463–84); a symbolic subtext in Brown's romance is designed to foster both an awareness of white racial injustice and compassion toward its victims. And "Adventures of the Young Man: Brockden Brown's *Arthur Mervyn*," Warner Berthoff's 1957 discussion of the moral compromises of urban existence, is reprinted in his *American Trajectories: Authors and Readings, 1790–1970* (Penn. State, pp. 53–68).

Here, I conclude with the slightly adapted words of John Josselyn concerning a report on one of his two Restoration voyages to New England: "This homely piece, I protest ingenuously, is prepared for such only who well know how to make use of their charitable constructions towards works of this nature, to whom I submit myself in all my faculties, and [have] proceed[ed] in my [seventeenth] voyage."

University of Texas at Austin

12 Early-19th-Century Literature

Robert E. Burkholder

The general impression given by the work published this year is that of expansiveness, an apt adjective if one assumes that scholarship should somehow capture the tenor of the time that it takes for its subject. Perhaps as a direct result of the evolving focus on cultural studies in the discipline, the criticism of antebellum literature might now more accurately be described as the study of antebellum literature *and* culture. At least such an inference seems fair when looking over the variety of writers, reformers, politicians, and orators represented in the scholarship to be discussed here. In most ways the expansiveness and the openness that produce it is healthy, resulting in fine work on too-long-neglected writers and texts.

There was a noticeably narrow range of work on some writers, however, and in a few cases the messages delivered seemed almost desperately repetitive, as if, for example, Cooper's putative racism needs to be proven using the heavy machinery of theoretical methodologies. If recent concern with the issues of race, gender, and class seems not to have produced much insight in some areas, in others—the intensity of debate over Frances E. W. Harper accompanying the ongoing recovery of her work, or the pioneering biographical scholarship on Lydia Maria Child, Sojourner Truth, and Harriet Beecher Stowe, for instance—it has produced exciting work of high quality.

i General Studies

As if to underscore the importance of cultural studies to scholarship this year, the first three substantial works to be considered feature a cultural studies methodology. What may be most interesting about Stephanie A. Smith's *Conceived by Liberty* is Smith's apparent goal of rehabilitating sentimentalism, a mode that seems to receive increasing scrutiny and intensifying censure from all quarters. But as Smith would have it, such criticism is really conditioned by the attitudes of the patriarchal culture, which appropriated the images of conception, birth, and motherhood, the images that Smith associates most closely with the sentimental mode, and used them politically, socially, and culturally to justify abuses of democratic principles and to privilege aesthetically "conceptual creativity" over actual reproduction. Just as Smith focuses on the image of the maternal in the formation of American identity, William W. Stowe in *Going Abroad* examines the role of American accounts of European travel in shaping Americans' individual and group identities and the national identity in general. In his discussion of travel chronicles, an attempt to demonstrate both what was conventional and unconventional in 19th-century American writing about Europe, Stowe discusses Irving's *Sketch-book* and narratives by Lydia H. Sigourney and Benjamin Silliman, as well as travel accounts by two mid-century African American travelers: William Wells Brown, who used his *The American Fugitive in Europe* to advance the antislavery cause, and David F. Dorr, who employed *A Colored Man Round the World* principally to put forward his own cause. Finally, in *Healing the Republic* Joan Burbick foregrounds medical theory and practice in her study of writings associated with the health of the body that "extend beyond the authority of professional medicine and its institutions" and claim cultural authority to represent the body. Burbick differentiates between the "common-sense" lay medicine of Samuel Thomson, whose theories about health assumed that everyone possessed the power to be healthy, and the professionalized understanding of physiological law that justified specialized forms of authority over the health of men and women. Burbick examines four major body parts—the brain, heart, senses, and eyes—each of which functioned as a key to health in the 19th century. Her assertion is that privileging one body part in health narratives exposes not only national values and the locus of cultural authority, but the conflict over those values. For example, narratives that privilege the brain invariably look to hierarchy and management as the principal means to social order. Obviously, Burbick's ideas are intriguing, as are her analyses of pseudosciences, such as phrenology, and her interpretations of texts by Catharine Beecher, William Alcott, and Oliver Wendell Holmes, among many others.

The real value of Layne Neeper's fine essay on our first literary historians, "Inventing Tradition: America's First Literary Historians"

(*SAR*, pp. 1–19), is that he ably demonstrates that recent concerns with the canon are nothing new. He examines the mechanisms of canon formation in literary histories by Samuel Kettell, Samuel Knapp, Rufus Griswold, George and Evert Duyckinck, and George Cleveland, and he discovers in all of these works what he calls a "rhetoric of plenitude" that is used to justify inclusion of a wide range of writings—from treatises on mathematics and medicine to poetry—and to argue not only for the existence of an American literature, but for its variety and richness. Perhaps the more things change, the more they really do remain the same.

One of the most curious statements to appear in recent years and yet one that serves well as a snapshot of the discipline's progress in the last ten is Judith Fetterley's "Commentary: Nineteenth-Century American Women Writers and the Politics of Recovery" (*AmLH* 6: 599–611). In assessing the progress made in the recovery of the work of women writers since the publication of her landmark anthology *Provisions* (1985), Fetterley finds precious little that is encouraging. The problem, of course, is that while a good bit of neglected work by women has seen print and much of it has found its way into classrooms, little has been done to demarginalize this writing or to discover those "interpretive strategies," to borrow Susan K. Harris's phrase, that will give it a permanent place in the American literature canon. As much in sympathy with Fetterley's assessment as one might be, it is difficult not to see its irony: the initial attempts to expand the traditional canon by pioneers like Fetterley were certainly buttressed by the explosion of interest in critical theory, which Fetterley implies has been a bust in regard to these marginalized texts. Her proposed solution of returning to close reading and thematic criticism of the work of marginalized writers, while the work of white male, canonical writers continues to receive the demystifying scrutiny of theory seems impractical, at the least. Stephen Arch's "Romancing the Puritans: American Historical Fiction in the 1820's" (*ESQ* 39 [1993]: 107–32) is, like Fetterley's commentary, an expression of dissatisfaction, though his is an unhappiness prompted by what he believes is an attempt by feminist scholars to revive interest in Child's *Hobomok* and Sedgwick's *Hope Leslie* at the expense of Cooper's *The Wept of Wish-ton-Wish*. Arch's reading of the three novels points up his belief that none of them is more socially enlightened by our standards than the others and that Cooper's novel also happens to be a more complex and accomplished work of fiction. A reading of Harriet V. F. Cheney's *Peep at the Pilgrims in Sixteen*

Hundred Thirty-Six, which Arch argues is a more accomplished and less noticed work than *Hobomok* or *Hope Leslie,* supports his final assertion that recovery of texts on solely political grounds and a failure to defend writers like Cooper from charges of "historical misdeeds" is a failure of vision on two counts: "in the first, a failure to recognize that we have left the realm of 'art' when the argument depends primarily on political judgments; in the second, a failure to understand that the work of artists like Cooper has been so powerful precisely *because* it is able to describe and explain more than our worst attributes."

ii Cooper, Bryant, and Contemporaries

After a banner year for Cooper criticism in 1993, the perspective on his work narrowed considerably this year. The dominant concern of those who took Cooper for their subject was race, even when depictions of race were only indirectly related to Cooper's writing. I am referring specifically to Gary Edgerton's "'A Breed Apart': Racial Stereotyping and the Promise of Revisionism in *The Last of the Mohicans* (*JACult* 17, ii: 1–20), a comparison of 1920, 1936, and 1992 film adaptations of Cooper's novel which claims that the latest movie version not only rejects multiculturalism but is even more insidiously racist than any of its ten movie predecessors. In "Savagism and Its Discontents: James Fenimore Cooper and His Native Contemporaries" (*ATQ* 8: 211–27) Gary Ashwill creates a range for understanding written images of Native Americans in Cooper's time from *The Life of Ma-Ka-Tai-Me-She-Kia-Kiak or Blackhawk,* which Ashwill reads as expressing an Indian/white separateness comparable to that found in Cooper's novels, to the writings of William Apes and Elias Boudinot, both of whom demonstrate "their ability to manipulate and control white ideas and discursive practices to attain a kind of independence unavailable to Black Hawk." Other studies address Cooper's putative benightedness on matters of race and ethnicity a bit more directly. Randall C. Davis's "Fire-Water in the Frontier Romance: James Fenimore Cooper and 'Indian Nature'" (*SAF,* 22: 215–31) discusses Cooper's use of the stereotypical character of the "drunken Indian" in four novels in order to argue that Cooper's reliance on such a stereotype could be construed as underscoring the impassable gulf between savagism and civilization, thus expressing Cooper's tacit support for the inhuman Indian Removal policies of the 1820s and 1830s. The difficulty with such an argument is the inherent complexity of the depiction of characters like Old John Mohegan in *The Pioneers,* a "drunken Indian" who shows himself to be utterly noble and admirable in his final assertion of his "savagism." In "Anticipated Torments and Indian Tortures in *The Last of the Mohicans*" (*ANQ* 7: 215–19) E. W. Pitcher speculates that Cooper may have relied on the *Affecting History of the Dreadful Distresses of Frederick Mannheim's Family* (1793) as a source for descriptions of the torture of "pitching." Despite an absence of evidence that Cooper had any formal association with nativism or the Know-Nothing Party, Thomas Gladsky's "James Fenimore Cooper and American Nativism" (*SAR,* pp. 43–53) uses Cooper's friendship with Samuel Morse and anti-Catholic and xenophobic passages from his novels to assert that "by 1850, Cooper had assimilated national prejudices about immigrants to the degree that he could repeat them without second thoughts." To Gladsky, Cooper's assimilation and use of these ideas prove "that he sympathized with the spirit of nativism." The title of Mary A. McClay's "Cooper's Indians, Erdrich's Native Americans," pp. 152–67 in *Global Perspectives on Teaching Literature: Shared Visions and Distinctive Visions,* ed. Sandra Ward Lott et al. (NCTE, 1993), more or less captures her point: Cooper is bad and Erdrich is good. With little acknowledgment of the historical situatedness of either writer, McClay argues that while Cooper creates a monologic myth of Anglo-America, Erdrich recaptures Native American myths that are multicultural and polyvocal.

Bryant fares somewhat better. William Cullen Bryant II collects nearly 200 of the thousands of editorials written by Bryant for the *New York Evening Post* in *Power for Sanity: Selected Editorials of William Cullen Bryant, 1829–1861* (Fordham), the largest sampling of Bryant's editorials ever to be recovered and republished. In "Bryant and the American Poetic Tradition" (*ATQ* 8: 53–76) Timothy Morris surveys the evolution of critical opinion on Bryant and implicitly argues for his reestablishment in the canon because of his importance to his contemporaneous audience and his influence on Whitman and others. C. Deirdre Phelps's "The Edition as Art Form: Social and Authorial Readings of William Cullen Bryant's *Poems*" (*Text* [1992]: 6: 249–85) examines such aspects of the physical presentation of literary work as typography, illustration, and binding in editions of Bryant's *Poems* to suggest how such physical aspects of presentation may have been employed to complement Bryant's stated authorial intent. Since Phelps deals with every important edition of Bryant's poetry from 1832 to 1935 and generously illustrates, hers is also a study of the relationship of presentation history to an author's status in the canon.

Following a new edition of two major novels in 1993 (see *ALS* 1993, p. 175), little new work appeared on William Gilmore Simms this year. However, James E. Kibler's "Some Unrecorded English Reviews of W. G. Simms" (*MissQ* 47: 557–66) prints generous portions of 11 reviews and book notices that appeared from 1834 to 1847, with Kibler's informative commentary on their importance. Another native South Carolinian who made substantial contributions to American culture was Washington Allston, the subject of David C. Miller's fine "Washington Allston and the Sister Arts Tradition in America" (*ERR* 5: 49–72). Miller uses W. J. T. Mitchell's concept of "Iconology" to read two paintings by Allston— *Elijah in the Desert* (1818) and *Moonlit Landscape* (1819)—and in turn to show how the development of Allston's approach demonstrates "the richness of visual imagery's instrumental role in historical change." More specifically, Miller finds the noticeable interiority and expression of individuality of each painting consistent with the changing needs of Allston's audience—an increasingly self-conscious Boston elite that was mired in materialism and economic aggression, and one that required landscapes like Allston's to identify with nature and the spiritual values they felt it embodied.

Other than work noticed elsewhere in this essay, the only new work on Irving was "Professional Travelers and A Professional Travel Narrator: Fact and Fancy in Early Nineteenth-Century Narratives," pp. 107–24 in Sharon Rogers Brown's *American Travel Narratives as a Literary Genre from 1542 to 1832: The Art of A Perpetual Journey* (Mellen), which compares Irving's *A Tour on the Prairies* to narratives of the same trip by Henry Leavitt Ellsworth and Charles Joseph Latrobe in order to demonstrate Irving's "accomplishment as a professional writer and American mythmaker." A member of Irving's circle is the focus of Ralph M. Aderman's "Paulding's Anonymous Writings: New Attributions and Speculations" (*SB* 46 [1993]: 370–81), an argument for a reexamination of Paulding's activities in the 1850s based on Aderman's positive and possible attributions to Paulding of a number of political essays published in the *United States Review* and the *Washington Union* after Paulding was thought to have retired.

iii Women Writers and Others at Mid-Century

The writer who seems to have garnered the most attention this year is Harriet Beecher Stowe. Foremost among works dealing with her is

Joan D. Hedrick's *Harriet Beecher Stowe: A Life* (Oxford). Since Hedrick's
is the first full-scale biography of Stowe to be published since Forrest
Wilson's *Crusader in Crinoline* (1941), it is sure to become the standard
biographical reference. What especially recommends it, though, is the
thoroughness of Hedrick's scholarship and the balance she is able to
achieve in describing the life of her subject. Hedrick is exceptional in
showing how the concerns expressed in *Uncle Tom's Cabin* are founded
on Stowe's religion; her education, particularly under her sister Catharine's tutelage; her parlor culture; and the events of her own life.

Besides Hedrick's landmark biography, two critically different books
on the rhetorical issues of *Uncle Tom's Cabin* appeared this year. In the
first chapter of her *Message, Messenger, and Response: Puritan Forms and
Cultural Reformation in Harriet Beecher Stowe's* Uncle Tom's Cabin (Univ.
Press) Gladys Sherman Lewis expresses her dissatisfaction with contemporary criticism that by the extremely narrow focus of its various theoretical concerns minimizes the dramatic cultural impact Stowe's novel had
in its own time. Simply put, Lewis's goal is to account for the novel's
popularity with its contemporaneous audience, and her wide-ranging,
rhetorically oriented study of the novel goes far toward meeting that
goal. In three substantial chapters Lewis examines the novel's message as
Stowe's peculiar adaptation of Puritan rhetorical forms, Stowe's negotiation of the novel's dual narrative voices—those of the preacher or moral
didact and of the storyteller or sentimental novelist—and, finally, the
character of the novel's various audiences—the religious, sentimental,
and sociopolitical. *The Stowe Debate: Rhetorical Strategies in* Uncle Tom's
Cabin, ed. Mason I. Lowance, Jr., et al. (Mass.), a collection of essays
growing out of a 1992 NEH Summer Seminar at the Newberry Library,
has a coherence uncommon in published collections. To a greater or
lesser degree, all of the essays concern themselves with three debates:
that over the institution of slavery itself, which ostensibly prompted
the writing of *Uncle Tom's Cabin;* the professional critical debate that
emerged with the novel's publication; and the discourse of contemporary
theory. Essays by Catherine E. O'Connell, Melanie J. Kirstadt, and Jan
Pilditch explore Stowe's discourse strategies. Pilditch's "Rhetoric and
Satire" (pp. 57–70) is notable for its exploration of Stowe's use of satiric
forms in tandem with the didactic. S. Bradley Shaw, Isabelle White, and
Susan Roberson contribute essays that focus on the rhetoric of domesticity and sentimentality. Helen Petter Westra and Mason I. Lowance, Jr.,
each foreground Stowe's Calvinism in their considerations of her use of

religious rhetoric and biblical types. James Bense, Sarah Smith Duckworth, Michael J. Meyer, and Susan Marie Nuernberg each considers the
rhetoric of race and slavery. Both Bense's "Myth and Rhetoric of the
Slavery Debate and Stowe's Comic Vision of Slavery" (pp. 187–204),
which argues that the comic is a prominent element in the textual power
of *Uncle Tom's Cabin,* and Nuernberg's "The Rhetoric of Race" (pp. 255–
70), which examines popular contemporaneous concepts of race, are
particularly useful. Finally, R. C. De Prospo's clever and apocalyptic
afterword (pp. 271–93) draws this collection's various concerns together
and meditates on the meaning of the debates of *Uncle Tom's Cabin* to
American culture now and in the future. *The Stowe Debate* is a valuable
contribution because it suggests both the conventional concerns of the
criticism of *Uncle Tom's Cabin* and opens new areas worthy of more
exploration.

Two new versions of the novel deserve notice. The Macmillan edition
reprints the introduction and notes of George McMichael from the fifth
edition of his *Anthology of American Literature* (1993). The Norton
Critical Edition of *Uncle Tom's Cabin,* ed. Elizabeth Ammons, offers a
variety of possibilities for teaching the novel's contexts as both an artifact
of popular culture and an object of recent critical attention. Except for
James Baldwin's landmark 1955 essay "Everybody's Protest Novel," all of
the modern critical views that Ammons chooses to reprint date from 1985
and after, including essays by Jane Tompkins, Robert S. Levine, Hor-
tense Spillers, and Christina Zwarg.

One aspect of the context of *Uncle Tom's Cabin,* the "anti-Tom" novel,
is Beverly Peterson's subject in *"Aunt Phillis's Cabin:* One Reply to Uncle
Tom" (*SoQ* 33, i: 97–112). Peterson is persuasive in demonstrating how
the single-minded purpose of Mary Henderson Eastman's novel—that is,
to refute Stowe—is disrupted by the conventions of domestic fiction and
Eastman's tendency to identify with the suffering female victims of
slavery. In a remarkably cogent bit of interpretation, Arthur Riss argues
in "Racial Essentialism and Family Values in *Uncle Tom's Cabin*" (*AQ* 46:
513–44) "that Stowe generates the 'progressive' politics of *Uncle Tom's
Cabin* by means of racial essentialism." And while Riss himself admits
that his claim may seem idiosyncratic, he convincingly shows how
Stowe's attitudes grew out of a cultural context that was pervasively
"biological racialist" in its assumptions. In "Her Holiness" (*NYRB*
1 Dec.: 39–40) Alfred Kazin ordains *Uncle Tom's Cabin* as "New En-

gland's last holiness," suggesting that the novel's success was the perfect blending of Stowe's sense of religious mission with the issue of slavery.

Among considerations of Stowe's writings other than *Uncle Tom's Cabin* is Richard Boyd's "Violence and Sacrificial Displacement in Harriet Beecher Stowe's *Dred*" (*ArQ* 50, ii: 51–69), which places Stowe's novel within the context of the "spiraling cycle of vengeance and retaliation" that characterized the rhetoric of Bleeding Kansas and the "slave insurrection panic of 1856." To Boyd, Stowe's decision to sacrifice Dred ritualistically instead of making him the initiator of some sort of healing regeneration is finally a capitulation to the rhetoric of reciprocal violence that pervaded public debate. Dorothy Z. Baker's detailed reading of *The Pearl of Orr's Island* in "Puritan Providences in Stowe's *The Pearl of Orr's Island*: The Legacy of Cotton Mather" (*SAF* 22: 61–79) is intended to show how the plot, characters, dialogue, and structure of Stowe's novel are heavily informed by the tales of divine providence in book six of Cotton Mather's *Magnalia Christi Americana*.

The work of Louisa May Alcott received a lot of attention in 1994, and the release of a movie version of *Little Women* at the close of the year is sure to increase that attention in the next few years. In "From Emerson to Dewey: The Fate of Freedom in American Education" (*AmLH* 6: 385–408) Martin Bickman discusses Alcott's *Little Men* as a fictional realization of Emersonian educational theories; like the theories themselves, the novel seems unable to locate a balance between unorthodox creative learning experiences and conventional educational practice. Jesse Crisler's "Alcott's Reading in *Little Women*" (*RALS* 20: 27–36) identifies literary allusions in the novel in an attempt to show how Alcott's reading and biography may inform her narrative. In "Seeking Home: Secularizing the Quest for the Celestial City in *Little Women* and *The Wonderful Wizard of Oz*," pp. 153–71 in John C. Hawley, ed., *Reform and Counterreform: Dialectics of the Word in Western Christianity since Luther* (Mouton de Gruyter), Karla Walters also focuses on intertextuality in the novel by reading each of the March sisters' pilgrimages as a transformation of the quest motif into a captivity narrative about imprisonment within female roles that could be alleviated only by "the sense of choice and opportunity women experience when they could imagine themselves domesticating the American frontier." Walters believes that Jo March has such a "sense of choice and opportunity" at Plumfield.

Of course, explorations of sentimentality, domesticity, and gender are standard in Alcott criticism. Mary Elliot's "Outperforming Femininity: Public Conduct and Private Enterprise in Louisa May Alcott's *Behind a Mask*" (*ATQ* 8: 298–310) juxtaposes a reading of mid-19th-century concepts of domesticity, facts of Alcott's life, and a reading of the protagonist of *Behind a Mask,* Jean Muir, in order to demonstrate how Muir's behavior as a governess in the Coventry household is intended to essentialize gender roles and subvert them. Similarly, in wondering about the resilience of female literary critics' interest in *Little Women,* Jill May in "Feminism and Children's Literature: Fitting *Little Women* into the American Literary Canon" (*CEA* 56, iii: 19–27) decides that Alcott's various subtexts, aimed at subverting both conventional female roles and the romance literature that supports such roles, account for that abiding interest and, ironically, for the male ignorance or indifference toward the novel that has excluded it from the canon. In "Subjectivity as Feminist Utopia," pp. 93–106 in *Utopian and Science Fiction by Women: Worlds of Difference,* ed. Jane L. Donawerth and Carol A. Holmerton (Syracuse), Jean Pfaelzer reads Rebecca Harding Davis's "The Harmonists" and Alcott's "Transcendental Wild Oats" as deconstructions of male concepts of utopia, which Pfaelzer believes implicitly incorporate patriarchy, romanticism, sentimentality, and socially destructive individualism. Donna M. Campbell's "Sentimental Conventions and Self-Protection: *Little Women* and *The Wide, Wide World*" (*Legacy* 11: 118–29) argues that Alcott uses conventions of the sentimental novel as they are exemplified by Warner's bestseller in order to distance her own work from the genre. Such an argument is difficult to bring off, for obvious reasons, as is Mary Cappello's in "'Looking About Me with All My Eyes': Censored Viewing, Carnival, and Louisa May Alcott's *Hospital Sketches*" (*ArQ* 50, iii: 59–88). Starting from assumptions that seem to be the opposite of those that inform Campbell's essay, Cappello's goal is to problematize the sensible reading of Elaine Showalter, who claims that in *Hospital Sketches* everything, including gender, is rendered irrelevant "in the face of sickness and death." In Cappello's view, Alcott's narrative is consistently gendered, and "Racism . . . is called in to censor feminism in Alcott's book"; but her jargon-laden explanation of that assertion is never convincing.

Among those who deal with Alcott as a writer for children are Angela M. Estes and Kathleen M. Lant, who in "'Unlovely, Unreal Creatures': Resistance and Relationship in Louisa May Alcott's 'Fancy Friend'" (*L&U* 18: 154–70) present a wonderfully convincing reading of the last story in the six-volume *Aunt Jo's Scrapbag,* an allegorical tale of a young girl named Fancy who creates her own mermaid, receives advice from Aunt Fiction and Uncle Fact, and finally acquiesces to Uncle Fact's realistic (and decidedly male) point of view, destroying the relationship between Fancy and her creation. To Estes and Lant, the story's ending suggests that Fancy's acquiescence to reality is tragic because it represents a compromising of her imagination and sense of self. In "Reading for Profit *and* Pleasure: *Little Women* and *The Story of a Bad Boy*" (*L&U* 18: 143–53) Ellen Butler Donovan focuses on narrative strategies used by Thomas Bailey Aldrich and Alcott that tend to restrict the adult point of view in order to invest moral authority in the perspectives of child characters, a move that Donovan argues was revolutionary in expressing a new understanding of children's experience.

Besides Hedrick's fine new biography of Stowe, the other major new biography to deal with a 19th-century woman writer is Carolyn Karcher's magisterial *The First Woman of the Republic: A Cultural Biography of Lydia Maria Child* (Duke). As in her previous work, Karcher here demonstrates that she is a scholar and writer of exceptional ability, and anyone interested in American culture in the decades before the Civil War will profit from Karcher's richly detailed account of Child's various careers as abolitionist, suffragist, and writer of 47 books and tracts and a considerable amount of uncollected journalism. There is also much to be gained from Karcher's extensive quotation from and detailed analysis of Child's writing, something that sets this biography apart from others. But those expecting an apolitical account of Child's life will be disappointed, since Karcher admits that she was initially attracted to Child as a subject "because she boldly tackled the problems of racial, sexual, and economic justice that our society has yet to resolve," and Karcher clearly works from the premise that we still have much to learn from Child's example. Other work on Child includes Karcher's "Reconceiving Nineteenth-Century American Literature: The Challenge of Women Writers" (*AL* 66: 781–93), which uses Child and her work as the focus of a plea for a canon expanded to include more than the white male writers of romance and transcendental escapism; and Jennifer Fleischner's "Mothers and Sisters: The Family Romance of Antislavery Women Writers" (*Feminist Nightmares,* pp. 125–41), a reading of Child's "The Quadroon" against the Eliza subplot of Stowe's *Uncle Tom's Cabin* to show how Child resists structuring the relationship between her white readership and the slave girl in terms of domination, specifically that of mother and child.

Two substantial studies of Catharine Sedgwick's *Hope Leslie* appeared this year. In "Catharine Sedgwick's 'Recital' of the Pequod War" (*AL* 66: 641–62) Philip Gould shows how Sedgwick's use of the Pequod War as the setting for her novel appropriates an event that Puritan historiography of the early republic consistently cast as an example of masculine "virtue." He then argues that Sedgwick subverts that misogynistic male ideal in her narrative by offering in its place a form of domestic virtue "based on benevolence, Christian love, and the sacredness of the home." T. Gregory Garvey in "Risking Reprisal: Catharine Sedgwick's *Hope Leslie* and the Legitimation of Public Action" (*ATQ* 8: 287–98) suggests that through the characters of Hope Leslie and Magawisca, Sedgwick is demonstrating the point at which woman's intervention in the public sphere is necessary. In both cases the interventions are justified as morally and practically necessary to save their respective societies, and yet both are punished by men for trespassing in the public sphere. Therefore, Garvey believes, Sedgwick shows that the only way women can bridge the private and public spheres is by establishing the public world of community in the household, as Hope does in the end, or by complete surrender to the private sphere, as it is figured in the actions of Hope's cousin, Esther Downing.

Among other considerations of women writers is Paola Gemme's "Rewriting the Indian Tale: Science, Politics, and the Evolution of Anna S. Stephens's Indian Romances" (*Prospects* 19: 375–87), which accounts for substantial revision of the 1838 serialized version of *Mary Derwent* for the novel's 1858 book publication by showing how Stephens's attitudes toward her Native American characters may have been changed as the result of government policies and scientific racialism. Gemme believes that *Mary Derwent* and other works by Stephens did their cultural work by legitimizing an Indian policy that rejected assimilation in favor of segregation. The "wild side" alluded to in Veronica Stewart's "The Wild Side of *The Wide, Wide World*" (*Legacy* 11: 1–16) is the unpredictable Nancy Vawse who, according to Stewart, serves as "a relatively flexible dialogizing element that energizes the novel's discourse" and "reveals a subversive side and creative dimension of Warner's personality and work." In " 'Feet so precious charged': Dickinson, Sigourney, and the Child Elegy" (*TSWL* 13: 317–38) Elizabeth A. Petrino uses several child elegies by Lydia H. Sigourney as negative examples to demonstrate how Dickinson rejected the sentimentality of the conventional child elegy but exploited the form to critique "materialism, women's roles, and the power and function of consolatory verse."

Treatments of work by the once-canonical Schoolroom Poets were few this year. Edward L. Tucker's "References in Longfellow's *Journals* (1856–1882) to His Important Literary Works" (*SAR*, pp. 289–323) compiles and carefully and copiously annotates journal references to seven works by Longfellow. Jeanne Moskal in "John Greenleaf Whittier and Ebeneezer Elliott" (*RALS* 20: 37–44) publishes for the first time an 1881 Whittier letter that demonstrates his interest in Elliott long after his 1849 poetic tribute to "the Corn Law Rhymer." In "Holmes's Emerson and the Conservative Critique of Realism" (*SoAR* 59, i: 107–25) Len Gougeon critiques Holmes's "conservative" portrayal of Emerson in his 1885 biography and implies that Emerson would have been more in agreement with Howells's promotion of literary realism than with Holmes's criticism of it. Also of note is E. N. Feltskog's stunning edition of Francis Parkman's *The Oregon Trail* (Nebraska), which features an authoritative text, illustrations by Frederic Remington, and Feltskog's copious explanatory notes.

Several interesting essays appeared on regional writers who have received scant recent attention. Marisha Sinha in "Louisa Susanna McCord: Spokeswoman of the Master Class in Antebellum South Carolina" (*Feminist Nightmares*, pp. 62–87) reviews McCord's career as a polemicist for slavery and *against* women's rights and argues that her work deserves more attention because it calls into question essentialist and transhistorical views of women. Thomas C. Ware's " 'Where Valor Proudly Sleeps': Theodore O'Hara and 'The Bivouac of the Dead' " (*Markers* 11: 82–111) is also an interesting argument for the recovery of its subject, a Kentucky poet who wrote a famous verse tribute to Civil War bravery. Similarly, in "Charles Sealsfield (1793–1864): German and American Novelist of the Nineteenth-Century" (*MissQ* 47: 633–44) Alexander Ritter implicitly argues for the importance of the emigrant Austrian novelist, who settled in New Orleans, wrote prolifically, and became the subject of hot debate in leading American periodicals in 1844. Maria Mondragon in " 'The [Safe] White Side of the Line': History and Disguise in John Rollin Ridge's *The Life and Adventures of Joaquín Murieta: The Celebrated California Bandit*" (*ATQ* 8: 173–87) asserts that "because of his 'mixed-blood' heritage, his success in the 'white world,' and his controversial embracing of assimilationist policies, Ridge is a problematic figure for those who wish to fix the limit of his cultural or political identity," which is what Mondragon attempts to do in her reading of Ridge's novel as a working out of his own racial and ethnic anxieties. Finally, in "Robots of the Past: Fitz-James O'Brien's 'The Wondersmith'" (*JPC* 27, iv: 13–30) Gary Hoppenstand argues that O'Brien's short story bridges the gap between American literature and the German Märchen, adapts Hugo's hunchbacked romantic hero to an American setting, and introduces to Americans the robot motif that O'Brien may have taken from Mary Shelley's *Frankenstein*.

The most interesting new work on Abraham Lincoln includes Thomas F. Mader's "Burkean Rites and the Gettysburg Address," pp. 131–54 in *Rhetorical Movement: Essays in Honor of Leland M. Griffin*, ed. David Zarefsky (Northwestern), which uses Lincoln's speech in explaining an elaborate rhetorical theory based on Kenneth Burke's dramatism, and the more useful "Lincoln and Douglas Respond to the Antislavery Movement" by David Zarefsky and Ann E. Burnette (pp. 112–30 in the same collection), which examines speeches by Lincoln and Stephen A. Douglas in order to show that the rhetorical and political fates of each man can be understood in terms of the theory of "rhetorical trajectory." Neil Schmitz's "Refiguring Lincoln: Speeches and Writing" (*AmLH* 6: 103–18) is a meditation on Lincoln's meaning based on Schmitz's abundant appreciation for the Library of America edition of Lincoln's *Speeches and Writings 1859–1865* (1989) and Edmund Wilson's *Patriotic Gore* (1962) that settles into a comparative reading of Lincoln's 1852 Eulogy on Henry Clay and a 10 February 1865 Message to Congress on an exchange of communications with Jefferson Davis. Schmitz finds the "Jacksonian Lincoln," whose principal appeal was to Reason, in the 1852 speech, but the imperial Lincoln, Lincoln in an "Ahabian mood," in the 1865 message.

iv African American Writers and the Literature of Abolition

Most notable among general studies of African American literature is *The Black Columbiad,* a collection of relatively brief essays by young scholars that seeks to answer the question, "How did the extremely heterogeneous group of African pioneers manufacture themselves into Americans?" Of particular interest are Carl Pedersen's "Sea Change: The Middle Passage and Transatlantic Imagination" (pp. 42–51), which examines a number of Middle-Passage narratives to expand their symbolic significance; Geneviève Fabre's "Festive Moments in Antebellum African American Culture" (pp. 52–63), which explores the meaning of the Jonkonnu celebration; Stefania Piccinato's "The Slave Narrative and the Picaresque Novel" (pp. 88–98), which argues for a strong methodological and structural relationship between the two genres; Christopher Mulvey's examination of the paradoxical use of Columbus in *Clotel* in his "The Fugitive Slave and the New World of the North: William Wells Brown's Discovery of America" (pp. 99–111); and Rosemary F. Crockett's argument for the significance of the 1857 novel *The Garies and Their Friends* in "Frank J. Webb: The Shift to Color Discrimination" (pp. 112–22). Also of note is Jean Fagan Yellin and John C. Van Horne, eds., *The Abolitionist Sisterhood: Women's Political Culture in Antebellum America* (Cornell). This collection of essays, organized around the broad themes of female antislavery societies, the growth of black women's political culture in the North, and the strategies and tactics of antislavery feminists, is a useful attempt to explore women's political culture in 19th-century America. The intriguing title of Michael Newbury's "Eaten Alive: Slavery and Celebrity in Antebellum America" (*ELH* 61: 159–87) belies the inherent difficulties Newbury faces in arguing a relationship among slavery, authorship, and what could only be termed "marketplace cannibalism" through readings of *Uncle Tom's Cabin, The Scarlet Letter,* and *Incidents in the Life of a Slave Girl.* What may finally be most interesting about Nancy Armstrong's provocative "Why Daughters Die: The Racial Logic of American Sentimentalism" (*YJC* 7, ii: 1–24) is not so much her readings of *Uncle Tom's Cabin* or *Incidents in the Life of a Slave Girl* or *Beloved,* but her sincere attempt to transform the way in which we understand the sentimental novel, which Armstrong believes is read too much in terms of its English predecessor and counterpart. Instead, Armstrong proposes that American sentimental fiction be seen as a working out of the conflict between "family" (which assumes a daughter's marrying in the same race and class as her father) and "household" (which assumes leaving the family and assimilating).

Work on Frederick Douglass was marked by the appearance of the Library of America edition of his *Autobiographies,* which prints the *Narrative, My Bondage and My Freedom,* and the expanded 1893 text of *Life and Times of Frederick Douglass* together with a helpful chronology and explanatory notes on all three texts by Henry Louis Gates, Jr. Perhaps the finest of a number of excellent essays on Douglass that appeared this year is John Sekora's " 'Mr. Editor, If You Please': Frederick

Douglass, *My Bondage and My Freedom,* and the End of the Abolitionist Imprint" (*Callaloo* 17: 608–26). Sekora sets his argument against a background of instances of Douglass's suffering from racist treatment at the hands of his first political allies, the New England abolitionists, especially William Lloyd Garrison and Maria Weston Chapman. His point is to show, through a detailed comparative examination of the structures and other features of the *Narrative* and *My Bondage and My Freedom,* that the former "was shaped as much by the American Anti-Slavery Society as by its author," and that the latter reveals that Douglass was exerting typographical and editorial control over his own story at the same time he was redirecting his political energies away from service to Garrison and his organization. In "The Process of Literacy as Communal Involvement in the Narratives of Frederick Douglass" (*AAR* 28: 363–74) Daniel J. Royer rejects the "strong-text" orientation that Houston Baker and others have used in interpreting the role of literacy in slave narratives and demonstrates in readings of the *Narrative* and *My Bondage and My Freedom* that "the real causes and lasting effects of literacy are . . . social and contextualizing, not solitary and isolating." Both Sekora in "The Legacy of Frederick Douglass" (*AAR* 28: 473–79) and James W. Tuttleton in "The Many Lives of Frederick Douglass" (*NewC* 12, vi: 16–26) discuss Douglass as the foremost black figure of the 19th century.

Winifred Morgan deals with the same concerns as Royer but from a different perspective in "Gender-Related Difference in the Slave Narratives of Harriet Jacobs and Frederick Douglass" (*AmerS* 35, ii: 73–94). Her gendered reading of Jacobs and Douglass produces a conclusion at odds with Royer's: that male narrators accentuate the role of literacy as a solitary and isolating factor in their struggles for freedom, while female narrators like Jacobs emphasize community, relationships, interdependence, and the personal connectedness that allowed women to survive slavery. Among other studies that focus more specifically on Jacobs is Jeanne M. Braxton and Sharon Zuber's "Silences in Harriet 'Linda Brent' Jacobs's *Incidents in the Life of a Slave Girl*" (*Listening to Silences,* pp. 146–55), a lucid exploration of the thesis that "Jacobs's achievement is closely linked to her ability to negotiate [the] multiple layers of silence in her text." Sharon Davie's " 'Reader, my story ends with freedom': Harriet Jacobs's *Incidents in the Life of a Slave Girl,*" pp. 86–109 in *Famous Last Words: Changes in Gender and Narrative Closure,* ed. Alison Booth (Virginia), is an often opaque study of the economic and social constructions of race and gender at the root of the sexual victimization of Linda Brent

and the strategies that Jacobs uses in her narrative to fight such restric-
tions. In "Surviving in the Garret: Harriet Jacobs and the Critique of
Sentiment" (*ATQ* 8: 189–210) Krista Walter explores what she calls "the
double bind of a black woman writer," the victim of a system that she can
escape only by confining herself in an attic and can protest only by
staying within the master's discourse. Walter argues that in *Incidents*
Jacobs uses the limited choices available to her to critique both the
institution and the type of discourse—the sentimental—that imprisoned
her. In "Speech, Listening, and Female Sexuality in *Incidents in the Life of
a Slave Girl*" (*ArQ* 50, ii: 19–49) Deborah M. Garfield examines how
Jacobs negotiates a similar double bind that faced female antislavery
orators who were caught between relating lurid tales of sexual abuse and
the need to shield the sensibilities and assumed innocence of a white
female audience. "Harriet Jacobs's Family History" (*AL* 66: 765–67) is
Jean Fagan Yellin's correction of information regarding the identity of
Jacobs's father as it was reported in her 1987 biography of Jacobs.

Some of the most interesting and important work on any marginalized writer is that being done on Frances E. W. Harper, the subject of
several books and articles this year. There is no way to overestimate the
valuable service to the study of the history of African American literature
represented by Frances Smith Foster's heroic archival and editorial work
in recovering and publishing three novels by Harper—*Minnie's Sacrifice,
Sowing and Reaping, and Trial and Triumph* (Beacon)—previously available only in the pages of the difficult-to-locate *Christian Recorder*. Given
the ongoing recovery and rediscovery of Harper's writings, Melba Boyd's
Discarded Legacy: Politics and Poetics in the Life of Frances E. W. Harper
(Wayne State) is both a much-needed biographical and interpretive
study and an eloquent argument for the importance of Harper's life and
work. Two considerations of Harper's use of the "tragic mulatta" story in
Iola Leroy are Kimberly A. C. Wilson's "The Function of the 'Fair'
Mulatto: Complexion, Audience, and Mediation in Frances Harper's
Iola Leroy" (*CimR* 106: 104–13), an angry indictment of Harper for her
"surrender to audience restraints, her ideological contradictions, and her
self-betrayal" in privileging light-skinned characters over those of darker
cast, and Carla L. Peterson's "'Further Liftings of the Veil': Class,
Gender, and Labor in Frances E. W. Harper" (*Listening to Silences,*
pp. 97–112), a defense of Harper's characterization in *Iola Leroy* based on
Peterson's belief that the character of Iola is intended to deny the
"tragic mulatto plot" by refusing to "pass" as her mother did, rejecting

220 Early-19th-Century Literature

Dr. Gresham's proposal, and working to uplift her race. Phillip Brian Harper's "Private Affairs: Race, Sex, Property, and Persons" (*GLQ* 1: 104–13) features a reading of Harper's treatment of miscegenation in *Iola Leroy* that focuses on the way in which Iola's racial heritage tends, finally, to deprive her of her own subjectivity, which otherwise might have been perceived as a threat to the patriarchy's subjectivity.

A wonderfully smart and effective argument regarding abolitionist uses of the sentimental mode is Stephen Browne's " 'Like Gory Spectres': Representing Evil in Theodore Weld's *American Slavery As It Is*" (*QJS* 80: 277–92). Browne believes Weld's exposé of the brutalities of slavery provides examples through which outraged readers could virtually exhaust their moral indignation over slavery without challenging the system that allowed such an inhuman institution to exist. The great abolitionist and suffragist orator Sojourner Truth is the subject of Erlene Stetson and Linda David's *Glorying in the Tribulation: The Lifework of Sojourner Truth* (Mich. State), an interesting and largely successful experiment in writing biography. David and Stetson do an extraordinary job negotiating their subject's illiteracy and the "complexly shifting shadow" of Truth in the various accounts of her life by white female abolitionists and in newspapers that must of necessity be Stetson and David's principal sources. In " 'Yours Very Truly': Ellen Craft—The Fugitive as Text and Artifact" (*AAR* 28: 509–29) Barbara McCaskill examines the cultural and social significance of the public's fascination with Ellen Craft, whose escape from slavery with her husband, William, is chronicled in his *Running a Thousand Miles to Freedom*. Jo Ann Marx in "Myth and Meaning in Martin R. Delaney's *Blake; or the Huts of America*" (*CLAJ* 38: 183–92) reads Delaney's novel as a narrative that embodies "the archetypal pattern of quest that comprises the world of heroes, gods, and other supernatural forces." John Ernest's "Economies of Identity: Harriet E. Wilson's *Our Nig*" (*PMLA* 109: 424–38) is a fascinating interpretation of Wilson's novel as enacting just what its story represents: a countering of the antislavery argument against capitalism with an appeal for salvation through the values of the marketplace.

v Humor

One of the most substantial contributions to the study of American humor in recent memory is John Bryant's superb *Melville and Repose* (Oxford, 1993). It is really as much a lively, well-written cultural history of humor as it is a focused rhetorical study of Melville's struggles to develop an "amiable" voice. Bryant treats such aspects of Melville's cultural context as the "Grand American Humor Skirmish of 1845–46," a war of words between Young America's William A. Jones and William Gilmore Simms over the social and aesthetic functions of humor. In his attempt to locate the sources of Melville's comic style, Bryant also devotes a chapter to an analysis of Irving's genial satire and part of another to the tall-tale tradition as it is figured in Thomas Bangs Thorpe's "The Big Bear of Arkansas." Sharon Ruzycki O'Brien takes a much different tack to the humor of the old Southwest in "Writing with a Forked Pen: Racial Dynamics and Johnson Jones Hooper's Twin Tale of Swindling Indians" (*AmerS* 35, ii: 95–113). O'Brien describes her main concern as being "to examine the manner in which old Southwest writers used humor to legitimate the political and economic interest of the elites and, especially, with the way in which humor was used to justify racial inequalities." While the later part of this essay indeed examines Hooper's *Adventures of Captain Simon Suggs,* O'Brien's approach actually implicates all Southwest humorists (she discusses Joel Chandler Harris, Thorpe, Joseph G. Baldwin, and Davy Crockett) in using a proto-Social Darwinism to support Whig politics, especially a commitment to economic progress at the expense of republican ideals and to represent Native Americans as inherently inferior to whites.

The real and mythic David Crocketts are the subject of several essays. Royce E. Flood in "Rhetoric in Defense of the Dispossessed: David Crockett and the Tennessee Squatters," pp. 34–54 in *Rhetorical Movement: Essays in Honor of Leland M. Griffin,* ed. David Zarefsky (Northwestern), attempts to account for academic historians' general distaste for Crockett by establishing that his principal political constituency was the lowest class of squatter settler—the class that produced Crockett himself. Flood shows how Crockett responded to land policy that disadvantaged his squatter constituents with a rhetoric charged with anti-intellectualism and invective for Andrew Jackson and his political allies. Crockett's rhetoric, according to Flood, made it "virtually impossible for educated individuals—particularly academic practitioners of history—to sympathize with him." James E. Crisp's "The Little Book That Wasn't There: The Myth and Mystery of the de la Peña Diary" (*Southwest Historical Quarterly* 85: 260–96) is an extensive analysis and refutation of Bill Groneman's *Defense of a Legend: Crockett and the de la Peña Diary* (Plano: Republic of Texas Press), which is itself an attempt to prove that the diary of Lt. Col. José Enrique de la Peña and its account of Crockett's death by torture and execution, rather than on the battlements of the Alamo, is a clever forgery. In the same vein Michael A. Lofaro's light-hearted "Davy Crockett, David Crockett, and Me: A Personal Journey Through Legend into History" (*Tennessee Folklore Society Bulletin* 56: 96–106) seeks to separate the heroic qualities of the historical Crockett from the often ugly mythic figure in the *Crockett Almanacs*.

vi Drama

The emergence of cultural studies has inspired a noticeable increase in scholarship on various aspects of popular culture. This trend in some ways may account for several articles this year on antebellum American drama. In "Bowery B'hoys and Matinee Ladies: The Re-Gendering of Nineteenth-Century American Theater Audiences" (*AQ* 46: 374–405) Richard Butsch supplies an abbreviated social history of American the-aters from the 1820s to the 1890s, tracing them from the rowdy men's clubs of the '20s through the advent of museum theaters, matinee performances, and sensational melodramas in the '60s and '70s. This history admirably illustrates Butsch's thesis that the "re-gendering" of theater audiences involved "the three related processes of domestication, demasculinization, and feminization."

Studies of work by individual actors and playwrights included Thomas M. Kitts's "An Argument for Boker's *Francesca da Remini*" (*AmDram* 3, ii: 53–70), a study of two versions of George Henry Boker's 1853 verse drama. Kitts compares the text of the authoritative version of the play published in the 1856 edition of Boker's collected works to acting versions of the play prepared in part by Boker in 1855 (for Edward Loomis Davenport) and in 1882 (for Lawrence Barrett), both of which feature changes that heighten the play's melodrama but damage its literary qualities. In "*Columbus El Filibustero:* John Brougham's Mirror of Discovery" (*Gramma* 2: 149–57) Pat M. Ryan examines both pre- and postwar treatments of the Columbus story by the prolific Brougham— *Columbus El Filibustero!!* (1857) and *Columbus Reconstructed* (1866)—for the playwright's commentary on and allusions to contemporary events in New York City and the nation. Ryan finds both plays to be mirrors of chauvinistic "nascent 'Monroe Doctrine,' evolving Manifest Destiny, and unbridled filibustering."

The Pennsylvania State University

13 Late-19th-Century Literature

Laura E. Skandera-Trombley

Considering the immense amount of scholarship being generated in these high-volume publishing times, the decision to divide 19th-century materials into two sections, pre- and post-Civil War, makes eminent good sense. With division sometimes comes greater detail, and I found in reading through this year's scholarship that some offerings simply did not fit within past parameters. For this reason I have created several new categories: "Western Writers," "Realism," "Naturalism," and "Utopian/Science Fiction." Articles on authors who formerly lay outside the boundaries of the canon continue to increase, and a particularly strong area this year is cultural studies. Also encouraging to see is the scholarly response to Toni Morrison's call for reconceptualizing American literature to include the Africanist influence. Always necessary and valuable archival research has resulted in editions of primary texts, diaries, and journals that will undoubtedly provide the basis for future theorizing. And it appears that this is the year of Owen Wister.

i General Studies

As part of Joseph N. Riddel's expanding ruminations on the problematics of American origination, his *Purloined Letters: Originality and Repetition in American Literature* (LSU) serves to carry the question of modernism, a series of beginnings and repetitions, back to the 19th century. Riddel undertakes readings of Emerson, Poe, Hawthorne, Melville, James, and Henry Adams—to prove his assertion that "American" literature is an oxymoron. Indeed, Riddel argues, American literature belongs to a conceptual order rather than a historical period or geographical locale. Those responsible for publishing some of the literature that is now being so conceptualized can be found in Ellery Sedgwick's *The*

Atlantic Monthly, 1857–1909 (Mass.). A laudatory overview of the careers and choices made by James T. Fields, William Dean Howells, Thomas Bailey Aldrich, Horace Elisha Scudder, Walter Hines Page, and Bliss Perry, those stalwarts of the 19th-century Yankee publishing class, is provided in this history of the magazine's editors.

A rewarding genre study is Marcia Jacobson's *Being a Boy Again: Autobiography and the American Boy Book* (Alabama), which traces the development of the American boy book from the Civil War to World War I. In discussing works by Aldrich, Howells, Twain, Crane, and Tarkington, Jacobson explores how these authors, faced with the problematics of adult, masculine self-definition, returned to a nostalgic boyhood in fiction. American girlhood as remembered in unpublished 19th-century autobiographies and American boyhood as portrayed by Aldrich in *The Story of a Bad Boy* and Twain in *Adventures of Tom Sawyer* are among the collected essays discussing the relationship between children's fiction and their cultural setting in Anne S. MacLeod's *American Childhood: Essays on Children's Literature of the Nineteenth and Twentieth Centuries* (Georgia).

Joan Burbick provides a new lens for envisioning the 19th-century preoccupation with defining nationalism in *Healing the Republic*. Burbick examines the copious health narratives written between 1820 and 1880 and argues that these too-long neglected texts function as a means of fusing the concept of a healthy body with that of an equally robust polis. Ultimately, these texts serve as codes for differentiating the bodies that form the republic into sexual and racial hierarchies. Health and fitness narratives are highlighted in Claudia Nelson's "Care in Feeding: Vegetarianism and Social Reform in Alcott's America" (pp. 216–42) and Sherrie A. Inness's "'It is Pluck, But—Is it Sense?': Athletic Student Culture in Progressive-era Girls' College Fiction" (pp. 11–33) in *The Girl's Own: Cultural Histories of the Anglo-American Girl, 1830–1915* (Georgia). Editors Claudia Nelson and Lynne Vallone have collected essays drawn from an array of genres and fields—biography, journalism, photography, Progressive-era stories, educational pamphlets, and conduct books—that serve to examine Anglo-American constructions of female adolescence in contemporaneous cultural productions.

Certainly worth mention is the latest volume in Wellesley Studies in Critical Theory, Literary History, and Culture, *Regionalism Reconsidered: New Approaches to the Field* (Garland), ed. David Jordan. Chapters of particular relevance here include Michael Kowalewski's discussion of the relation between place and environment in "Bioregional Perspectives in American Literature" (pp. 29–46); Marjorie Pryse's strategies for reading and teaching women regionalists in "Reading Regionalism: The 'Difference' It Makes" (pp. 47–64); and Peter Caccavari's comparison of Tourgée's novels and the possibilities of reconciling nationalism and regionalism in "Reconstructing Reconstruction: Region and Nation in the Work of Albion Tourgée" (pp. 119–38). *Rethinking Class: Literary Studies and Social Formations,* ed. Wai Chee Dimock and Michael T. Gilmore, is part of the Social Foundations of Aesthetic Forms series from Columbia. This eminently readable collection as a whole formulates the construction of class as an "analyzable artifact" rather than viewing it either as a self-evident concept or a category of Marxist analysis. This way of viewing class then invites a variety of theoretical responses from historical, cultural, and literary perspectives. Previously published essays by Richard H. Brodhead and Eric Lott are included, as well as Amy Schrager Lang's new "The Syntax of Class in Elizabeth Stuart Phelps's *The Silent Partner*" (pp. 267–85). Allene Cooper makes an interesting connection between the rise of science and the decline of sentimental poetry following the Civil War in "Science and the Reception of Poetry in Postbellum American Journals" (*AmPer* 4: 24–46). Cooper concludes that the "cynicism of American culture as reflected in [post-Civil War] poetry . . . grew . . . out of the persistent threat on the human heart posed by science." The second edition of *Contexts for Criticism,* ed. Donald Keesey (Mayfield), adds Chopin's *The Awakening* as a text for analysis, with essays by Cynthia Griffin Wolff, Sandra Gilbert, Patricia Yaeger, and Margit Strange, while the "Deconstructive Epilogue" includes a chapter on poststructural criticism. Another added chapter features New Historicism and cultural criticism. This much expanded collection will doubtless prove a valuable classroom text.

Autobiographical accounts from the 17th to the 20th centuries are collected in Robert F. Sayre's *American Lives: An Anthology of Autobiography Writing* (Wisconsin). Among the post-Civil War autobiographical accounts included are those by Warren Lee Goss, Ulysses S. Grant, Frederick Douglass, Lucy Larcom, Andrew Carnegie, John Muir, and Charlotte Perkins Gilman. Though limited in scope, this useful edition ought to be acquired by libraries. A second autobiography anthology from Wisconsin is *Native American Autobiography,* ed. Arnold Krupat. The collection is exciting and highly recommended. With the exception of part one, all chapters follow a generally chronological order, presenting autobiographies ranging from the 18th century to contemporary times; parts two and three present Native "response" to non-native European-American forces. Parts three—"The Resisting Indians, from Indian Removal to Wounded Knee, 1830–90"—and four—"The Closed Frontier, 1890"—are of particular interest. Part seven—"Traditional Lives Today"—refers to part one—"Traditional Lives"—and completes a cyclical structure.

ii Women's Literature (General)

Coverage of women's literature continues to grow, yet a larger critical perspective is added this year in discussing the kind of work that has been done and where the field is headed. Judith Fetterley's insightful "Commentary: Nineteenth-Century American Women Writers and the Politics of Recovery" (*AmLH* 6, 3: 600–611) lauds the gains made in publishing primary works over the past decade while asking whether this activity takes place in the absence of critical work. Fetterley includes a helpful summary of earlier criticism and with the approach of the 21st century, issues a call for the continued centrality of 19th-century women writers to the study of the literature of that century. Kimberly Rae Connor's *Conversions and Visions in the Writings of African-American Women* (Tennessee) traces the ways religion and literature collaborated in history to promote self-affirmation in African American women. While the focus is on 20th-century women writers, among 19th-century writers discussed are Rebecca Jackson, Sojourner Truth, and Harriet Jacobs. Connor's analysis in "Voluntary Converts" (pp. 43–109) shows that these 19th-century writers created paradigmatic forms in the shape of "sacred stories" that future writers would use to comprehend their personal epistemologies.

In Two Friends *and Other Nineteenth-Century Lesbian Stories by American Women Writers* (Meridian), ed. Susan Koppleman includes short fiction by Constance Fenimore Woolson, Alice French, Mary Wilkins Freeman, Kate Chopin, Alice Brown, and Sarah Orne Jewett, and asserts that these collected stories constitute a lesbian tradition. This claim is intriguing, yet it is left unclear whether these writers were intent on creating a self-consciously lesbian fiction or if contemporary readers are reading such a tradition into these works. This anthology will certainly provoke discussion.

iii Kate Chopin, Sarah Orne Jewett, Charlotte Perkins Gilman, and Post–Civil War Women Writers

Among the writers in this category, Chopin, Jewett, and Gilman again generate the most scholarship. Continuing last year's strong critical commentary is Michele A. Birnbaum's " 'Alien Hands': Kate Chopin and the Colonization of Race" (*AL* 66: 301–23). Birnbaum convincingly argues that Edna Pontellier's sexual liberation is indebted to a 19th-century, Southern, colonialized racial/ethnic difference embodied in what Toni Morrison calls the "Africanist persona." A less effective essay arguing against the canonization of *The Awakening* is Hugh J. Dawson's "Kate Chopin's *The Awakening*: A Dissenting Opinion" (*ALR* 26, ii: 1–18). Dawson takes issue with Chopin's supposedly overblown prose style. Harriet Kramer Linkin points out that, indeed, a cigar is sometimes meant for more than just blowing smoke in " 'Call the Roller of Big Cigars': Smoking Out the Patriarchy in *The Awakening*" (*Legacy* 11: 130–42). By tracing the wafting smoke of cigarettes and cigars throughout the novel, Linkin concludes that a framework emerges for interpreting Edna's relationships with men as well as her connection to Creole society. The possible influence of Poe's poems on Chopin is the subject of Rosemary F. Franklin's provocative article "Poe and *The Awakening*" (*MissQ* 47: 47–57). Michael Hollister offers an insightful reading in "Chopin's *The Awakening*" (*Expl* 52: 90–92) regarding the connection between Mlle Reisz's playing of "Solitude" and Chopin's negotiation of literary realism.

Chopin's short prose is the subject of Martha J. Cutter's "Losing the Battle but Winning the War: Resistance to Patriarchal Discourse in Kate Chopin's Short Fiction" (*Legacy* 11: 17–36). Cutter concludes that a strategy emerges in the late works to resist patriarchal suppression—in part through the increasing willingness of Chopin's female characters to verbalize. Karen Day discusses Chopin's feminine jouissance in "The 'Elsewhere' of Female Sexuality and Desire in Kate Chopin's 'A Vocation and a Voice' " (*LaLit* 11: 108–17). Chopin's unsuccessful short story "The Maid of Saint Phillippe" is viewed by Doreen Alvare Saar in "The Failure and Triumph of 'The Maid of Saint Phillippe': Chopin Rewrites American Literature for American Women" (*LaLit* 11: 59–73) as an important rite of passage that in part enabled Chopin to develop her voice and eventually write *The Awakening*. David Steiling's "Multi-Cultural Aesthetic in Kate Chopin's 'A Gentleman of Bayou Teche' " (*MissQ* 47: 197–200) discusses Chopin's deeply felt pluralism. Janet Goodwyn provides a postcolonial interpretation of Chopin's short fiction in " 'Dah You Is, settin' down, lookin' jis' like w'ite folks!': Ethnicity Enacted in Kate Chopin's Short Fiction" (*YES* 24: 1–11). Jack Branscomb examines Chopin's use of different kinds of time, cycles of nature, religious calendars, and human life cycles in "Chopin's 'Ripe Figs' " (*Expl* 52: 165–67). Chopin's obvious floral imagery is probed in Christopher Baker's brief note, "Chopin's 'The Storm' " (*Expl* 52: 225–26). A commonly accepted assertion is that from the 1920s until the 1960s Chopin's fiction was essentially unavailable and ignored. Bernard Koloski contests this assumption in "The Anthologized Chopin: Kate Chopin's Short Stories in Yesterday's and Today's Anthologies" (*LaLit* 11: 18–30), concluding that after 1921 at least part of Chopin's work was "consistently available."

Jewett's place in contemporary scholarship appears entrenched with the latest publication in Cambridge's American Novel series of critical guides, *New Essays on* The Country of the Pointed Firs, ed. June Howard. The slender volume contains essays by such noted critics as Sandra A. Zagarell ("*Country*'s Portrayal of Community and the Exclusion of Difference," pp. 39–60); Michael Davitt Bell ("Gender and American Realism in *The Country of the Pointed Firs*," pp. 61–80); Elizabeth Ammons ("Material Culture, Empire, and Jewett's *Country of the Pointed Firs*," pp. 81–100); and Susan Gillman ("Regionalism and Nationalism in Jewett's *Country of the Pointed Firs*," pp. 101–18). Howard provides an informative introduction to Jewett's life and 19th- and 20th-century critical reception in "Sarah Orne Jewett and the Traffic in Words" (pp. 1–38), as well as a useful selective bibliography. Francesca Sawaya offers a well-grounded reading of *The Country of the Pointed Firs* within its Progressive-era context in "Domesticity, Cultivation, and Vocation in Jane Addams and Sarah Orne Jewett" (*NCL* 48: 507–28).

Certain to increase the recent plethora of Gilman studies is the publication of Denise Knight's two-volume *The Diaries of Charlotte Perkins Gilman* (Virginia). The diaries date from 1879 through 1935, and Knight's fine edition includes appendices of miscellaneous writings, explanatory and textual notes, and a helpful bibliography. Knight also edited a volume of Gilman's short stories, '*The Yellow Wall-Paper' and Selected Stories of Charlotte Perkins Gilman* (Delaware), a collection divided into five categories reflective of Gilman's life and her social and political views. Last from Knight is her brief note, "Charlotte Perkins

Gilman's Forgotten First Publication" (*ANQ* 7: 223–25); for those interested in the date and title, they are May 20, 1880, "To D.G." John S. Bak reinterprets that dismal nursery in "Escaping the Jaundiced Eye: Foucaldian Panopticism in Charlotte Perkins Gilman's 'The Yellow Wallpaper'" (*SSF* 31: 39–46). Bak argues that even though the narrator does wind up on all fours and "clinically insane," internally she has managed to free herself of "her male-imposed shackles, her Panopticism." If this is freedom, it seems to me a limited victory. Gilman's interest in athletics is the subject of Jane Lancaster's "'I Could Easily Have Been an Acrobat': Charlotte Perkins Gilman and the Providence Ladies' Sanitary Gymnasium, 1881–1884" (*ATQ* 8: 33–52). Despite factual and transcription errors, Lancaster's article provides an interesting discussion of Gilman's physical activity in the early 1880s, a precursor of the emerging "new woman" at the turn of the century.

A scattering of articles appeared on post-Civil War women writers who are still negotiating the canonical margin. An article that echoes Fetterley's warning about critical exclusion is Linda Grasso's "'Thwarted Life, Mighty Hunger, Unfinished Work': The Legacy of Nineteenth-Century Women Writing in America" (*ATQ* 8: 97–118). Two short stories, Mary Wilkins Freeman's "The Poetess" and Constance Fenimore Woolson's "Miss Grief," are viewed by Grasso as protests that, no matter her subject and expertise, a woman author is doomed to exclusion from literary histories composed by men. Indeed, an appropriately irked Cheryl B. Torsney proves Woolson's prophecy true in her article describing the woeful state of the Constance Fenimore Woolson Collection held by Rollins College, in "The Strange Case of the Disappearing Woolson Memorabilia" (*Legacy* 11: 143–51). Despite having published an article a decade ago criticizing the state of the collection, Torsney notes that considerable restoration and cataloging remain to be done.

The genealogy and professional career of Kate Field, once one of the best-known writers of the late 19th century, are traced in Carolyn J. Moss's "Kate Field: The Story of a Once-Famous St. Louisan" (*Missouri Historical Review* 88: 157–75). Karen Oakes profiles "Sarah Pratt McLean Green: 1865–1935" (*Legacy* 11: 55–64), and considers her prose comparable to that of women writers who have managed to survive in literary histories—Stowe, Jewett, Cooke, and Freeman—as well as male writers such as Twain. Robin Riley Fast discusses how Harriet Prescott Spofford moves beyond female gender stereotypes in "Killing the Angel in Spofford's 'Desert Sands' and 'The South Breaker'" (*Legacy* 11: 37–54). While

Spofford was successful in portraying female power, Fast recognizes that
this empowerment is problematized by her use of racial stereotypes and
by her "concern over the relation of sexuality to spiritual experience,
morality, and women's roles in family and society." "Freeman's 'A Church
Mouse'" (*Expl* 53: 43–44) is explicated in Janice B. Daniel's brief piece
focusing on Freeman's incorporation of a sunflower quilt as an important
"storytelling device." Andrew J. Scheiber's "An Unknown Infrastructure:
Gender, Production, and Aesthetic Exchange in Rebecca Harding Davis's 'Life in the Iron-Mills'" (*Legacy* 11: 101–17) builds on scholarship by
Jean Fagan Yellin and Sharon Harris and contends that Davis's "Iron-
Mills" is coded by "self-deconstructive impulses that are currently held as
indices of a work's superior literary merit." Scheiber insightfully concludes that the time has arrived to recognize that the apprehensions
expressed in Davis's work regarding the epistemology of artistic origination are also adopted and transformed by such canonical writers as
Hawthorne and James.

iv Humor

Humor, I am happy to report, has been resuscitated in the form of the
new series issue of *Studies in American Humor.* The inaugural volume
includes one article of particular interest here, Gwendolyn B. Gwathmey's "'Who will read the book, Samantha?': Marietta Holley and the
19th Century Reading Public" (3, i: 28–50). Gwathmey contends that by
invoking humor Marietta Holley did not write against sentimentalism,
as some feminist critics have argued. Instead of privileging one reading
over another, humorist versus sentimentalist, the totality of Holley's
work demands that she be reconstructed as a feminist, sentimental
writer; according to Gwathmey, such a construction is no oxymoron. I
hope that with the resumption of publication, *StAH* will encourage
future scholarship in an area from which too little has been heard in
recent years.

Additional entries this year include M. Thomas Inge's *Perspectives on
American Culture: Essays on Humor, Literature, and the Popular Arts*
(Locust Hill), an invaluable collection of Inge's previously published
essays on 19th-century American humor, popular culture, and American
humor from an international perspective. In addition to the essays, a
checklist is included of Inge's voluminous publications on humor. Also,
nearly forgotten humorist John Kendrick Bangs's short story "Thurlow's

Christmas Story" is interpreted by William J. Scheick in his *Ethos of Romance* as a comical, ethical romance fashioned out of the conventions of the ghost story.

v Western Writers

The paucity of scholarship on Ambrose Bierce is hardly alleviated this year with a lone biographical note by David M. Owens regarding Bierce's deliberate manipulation of geography: "Bierce and Biography: The Location of Owl Creek Bridge" (*ALR* 26, iii: 82–89). The latest entry in Boise State's Western Writers Series is James M. Aton's monograph on *John Wesley Powell.* The text contains an interesting biographical essay and helpful bibliographies of Powell's works and critical secondary sources. Lawrence I. Berkove performs some admirable literary sleuthing with William Wright's (Dan De Quille) unpublished story "The Sorceress of Attu," in a volume with that title (Mardigan Library of the University of Michigan-Dearborn). One of the most popular writers of the Comstock, De Quille has only recently been rediscovered by Western literature scholars; the publication of his last story will contribute to his literary resurrection. The Southwest as an imagined, mythical land is the subject of Karl Doerry's "The American West: Conventions and Inventions in Art," pp. 127–53 in *Essays on the Changing Images of the Southwest,* ed. Richard Francaviglia and David Narrett (Texas A&M). Doerry explores how such writers as Owen Wister in *The Virginian* created the independent, righteous Western hero for whom there was no moral ambiguity or self-doubt.

vi Realism

American Realism and the Canon, ed. Tom Quirk and Gary Scharnhorst (Delaware), is an important, eminently readable volume. After the co-editors lead off with a charged, topical introduction, the collection of essays examines Realism and its representative authors from the formerly marginalized now republished and included in the curriculum in Amy Ling's "Reading Her/stories Against His/stories in Early Chinese American Literature" (pp. 69–86) to the formerly canonized now unanthologized and absent from the classroom in Gary Scharnhorst's "Whatever Happened to Bret Harte?" (pp. 201–11). The collection attempts to determine in part what is meant by American Realism, whether such a term can be used in a poststructuralist age, and how 19th-century authors and their texts have negotiated the canon in both the 19th and 20th centuries. A number of essays here are reprinted. New ones are Patricia Okker's "Native American Literatures and the Canon: The Case of Zitkala-Sa" (pp. 87–101); Sanford E. Marovitz's "Romance and Realism: Children of the New Colossus and the Jewish Struggles Within" (pp. 102–26); Susan K. Harris's "Problems of Representation in Turn-of-the-Century Immigrant Fiction" (pp. 127–42); and Alfred Habegger's "From Painful Cult to Painful Realism: Annie Ogle's *A Lost Love* and W. D. Howells's Ben Halleck and Penelope Lapham" (pp. 170–89). John Limon devotes two chapters to discussions of Realism in *Writing After War*. Limon proposes that war helps create a literary history that eventually represents itself as "uncontainable" by literature. In his discussion of fiction by Howells, Crane, James, and Twain in "Swords to Words: Realism and the Civil War" (pp. 32–58) Limon contends that if Realism functioned as a substitute for the "real thing," that is, the Civil War, then "to imagine war, imagine war imagining you." In "Goddesses on the Battlefield" (pp. 59–83) he explores how and why it is generally accepted that Realism must follow romance; in his readings of Cable, Tourgée, De Forest, and Howells he explores the notion that to "recognize reality" one must have "literary unreality."

vii Naturalism

The Theory and Practice of American Literary Naturalism (So. Ill., 1993) is a collection of Donald Pizer's essays, all previously published except for "William Kennedy's *Ironweed* and the American Naturalistic Tradition" (pp. 187–96). Pizer contends that publishing these essays together constitutes a full-scale interpretation of American Naturalism, and it is left to the reader to concur. Crane, Norris, and Wharton receive their own chapters in a volume divided into four sections: "General Essays," "The Late Nineteenth Century," "The Twentieth Century," and "Reviews." The last portion contains Pizer's comments on books on Naturalism by Harold Kaplan, John J. Conder, Walter Benn Michaels, and Lee Clark Mitchell. A selected bibliography is included.

The big event in Crane studies this year is the publication of *The Crane Log: A Documentary Life of Stephen Crane, 1871–1900* by Stanley Wertheim and Paul Sorrentino (Hall). This extensively documented history of Crane's life corrects past subjective biographical interpretations and provides an abundance of primary source information. A helpful biographical guide is included for many people mentioned in the text. This history is essential to those interested in Crane. Crane's undergraduate hazing experience continues to unfold in Thomas Gullason's "Stephen Crane at Layfayette College: New Perspectives" (*SCS* 3, ii: 2–12).

Fictions of Masculinity, ed. Peter F. Murphy (NYU), reprints Alfred Habegger's "Fighting Words: The Talk of Men at War in *The Red Badge of Courage*" (pp. 185–203). Habegger asserts that when the frequency with which Crane's characters receive head wounds measured against their increasing incapacity to speak, cultural norms are reflected directing that as masculinity increases, verbal dexterity decreases. M. Thomas Inge adds an additional book to the brief list of works Crane may have used as background information in "Sam Watkins: Another Source for Crane's *The Red Badge of Courage*" (*SCS* 3, i: 11–16). A comparison of Crane's "The Open Boat" and his newspaper account of the same incident, "Stephen Crane's Own Story," opens Phyllis Frus's fine study concerning the relationship between journalism and fiction, *The Politics and Poetics of Journalistic Narrative: The Timely and the Timeless* (Cambridge). Frus rejects traditional valuation of texts, as in their universal or aesthetic characteristics/constructions, and instead performs self-conscious and historically based readings of narratives in order to observe how texts create their own reality. "The Open Boat" is featured again in Oliver Billingslea's discussion of how reading becomes a centerless process because of Crane's impressionism in "Why Does the Oiler 'Drown'? Perception and Cosmic Chill in 'The Open Boat'" (*ALR* 27, i: 23–41). Penney Scott traverses the mean streets and anthropomorphized towers of New York in "The Veracious Narrative of 'An Experiment in Misery': Crane's Park Row and Bowery" (*SCS* 3, i: 2–10). William J. Scheick contends in *The Ethos of Romance* that metafictional questions concerning the ethics of storytelling are raised in Crane's "The Blue Hotel" and Richard Harding Davis's novella *In the Fog.* Carl Guldager's biographical article, "Stephen Crane: The Wanderer" (*ModA* 37: 18–26), includes mentions of his major works and details about his relationship with Cora Taylor. And Donald Vanouse continues Crane bibliography with "Stephen Crane: An Annotated Bibliography of Articles and Book Chapters through 1993" (*SCS* 3, i: 22–25).

Frank Norris studies also enjoyed a prolific year. Clare Eby's provocative article, "*The Octopus*: Big Business as Art" (*ALR* 26, iii: 33–51),

departs from past critical assessments of Presley's role in *The Octopus*;
instead of viewing the character as a major flaw in the work or as a critique intended by Norris, Eby proposes that the narrative voice "comes
the closest to representing Norris's own views." Presley's velocipede foray
comes under scrutiny in Reuben J. Ellis's " 'A Little Turn through the
Country': Presley's Bicycle Ride in Frank Norris's *The Octopus*" (*JACult*
17, iii: 17–22). Presley's excursion is no simple, freewheeling matter;
rather, Ellis claims, it signals the intrusion of technology into everyday
life at the end of the 19th century and signifies Presley's evolution from
"detached observer" to "engaged participant." A second article by Eby,
"Domesticating Naturalism: The Example of *The Pit*" (*SAF* 22: 149–
68), begins with an editor and publisher's debate over the cover for the
new paperback edition of *The Pit*—to bear or not to bare? In this
commercial-artistic disagreement lies the subject of Eby's article: how to
read *The Pit*. David Marut examines the political and economic elements omitted by Norris in "Sam Lewiston's Bad Timing: A Note on the
Economics Context of 'A Deal in Wheat' " (*ALR* 27, i: 74–80). Marut
concludes that Norris's focus in the piece was speculators' control of
economic events rather than historical context. John C. Waldmeir provides pertinent background information in "A New Source for Frank
Norris's 'Epic of Wheat' " (*ELN* 31, iii: 53–59). Norris's topic and epic
approach, Waldmeir contends, came from an article, "The Movement of
Wheat," by Ray Stannard Baker. In "Frank Norris, Apprentice Novelist"
(*The Californians* 11, v: 40–45), George Rathmell traces Norris's career in
a compact biographical, pictorial sketch.

viii Utopian/Science Fiction

Utopian and Science Fiction by Women: Worlds of Difference (Syracuse)
ed. Jane L. Donawerth and Carol A. Kolmerten, establishes a continuous
literary history of female-authored utopias and science fiction novels.
Three essays are of particular interest here. Jean Pfaelzer posits in her
foundational essay, "Subjectivity as Feminist Utopia" (pp. 93–106), that
19th-century women writers of utopian fiction offer a revisionist history
that presents female-centered social and biological realities. Carol A.
Kolmerten argues in "Texts and Contexts: American Women Envision
Utopia, 1890–1920" (pp. 107–25) that Rebecca Harding Davis in "The
Harmonists" (1866) and Louisa May Alcott in "Transcendental Wild
Oats" (1872) write to expose patriarchal assumptions within male-

defined utopian communities and anticipate feminist utopias that will reject gender domination. Kolmerten records that more than 30 women, few of them recognized authors, wrote utopian novels between 1890 and 1919. For these largely unknown women, writing and publishing utopian fiction was a "subversive act," hampered by their reliance on sentimental fiction structures that contained elements of the very ideology they were trying to refute. Last, Carol Farley Kessler's "Consider Her Ways: The Cultural Work of Charlotte Perkins Gilman's Pragmatopian Stories, 1908–1913" (pp. 126–36) maintains that Gilman's aim in her utopian fiction—four novels and more than a half-dozen short stories—was purposely didactic; she hoped that through her "cultural work," readers would eventually reject being defined by traditional gender roles.

Jonathan Auerbach takes a new approach to Edward Bellamy's best-seller in " 'The Nation Organized': Utopian Impotence in Edward Bellamy's *Looking Backward*" (*AmLH* 6: 24–47). Choosing not to discuss the text as it is usually interpreted either as socialist theory or literary genre, Auerbach performs an alternative reading: envisioning *Looking Backward* as presenting to its 19th-century audience an economic alternative to market relations while noting the changes that have occurred within a market-driven society. It can be hoped that this provocative article will encourage increased Bellamy scholarship. A second assist in generating scholarly activity on Bellamy is Paul G. Haschak's *Utopian/Dystopian Literature: A Bibliography of Literary Criticism* (Scarecrow). Haschak has compiled the first reference text whose focus is American, British, European, and ancient utopian/dystopian literature; 19th-century American authors listed include Twain, Howells, and Gilman.

ix The Howells Generation

The Howells resurgence continues with *Staging Howells: Plays and Correspondence with Lawrence Barrett* (New Mexico), ed. George Arms, Mary Bess Whidden, and Gary Scharnhorst. This volume provides invaluable information about Howells's stage ambitions and stands as a fitting final work by the late George Arms. The editors gather a host of new material, including 55 recently discovered letters from Howells to Barrett and Howells's original transcription of Manuel Tamayo y Baus's "Un drama neuvo," published here for the first time. *Staging Howells* is an exemplar of fine scholarly editing and, with Walter Meserve's *The Complete Plays of William Dean Howells* (1960) and Brenda Murphy's *A Realist in the*

Theatre (1992), forms a triptych of texts on Howells's stage career. Special attention is paid to Howells's awareness in combining the forms of literary memoir with autobiography in Marcia Jacobson's "Howells' *Literary Friends and Acquaintance*" (*ALR* 27, i: 59–73). Of particular interest is Jacobson's discussion of Howells's growing realization that the relatively innocuous memoir he had initially anticipated producing was becoming increasingly autobiographical. John W. Crowley's "From Intemperance to Alcoholism in the Fiction of W. D. Howells" (*The White Logic*, pp. 1–18) joins traditional literary history with cultural studies in treating the thesis that Howells's tales of addiction signaled the onset of literary modernism.

A volume that should spark future scholarship on Joel Chandler Harris is Hugh T. Keenan's collection of Harris's 1890–1908 letters to his children, *Dearest Chums and Partners: Joel Chandler Harris's Letters to His Children, A Domestic Biography* (Georgia). Interestingly, although this span of time marks Harris's greatest period of production, he makes precious little mention of his fiction in his correspondence; instead, these letters constitute a domestic biography that reveals a previously unseen side of him. Included are the transcriptions, a chronology, genealogical chart, appendix, and bibliography.

Despite the resurgence of American populism in the 1980s, the rise of popular culture studies, and the return to discussions of Realist and Naturalist prose, Bill Brown notes with some irony in "The Popular, the Populist, and the Populace—Locating Hamlin Garland in the Politics of Culture" (*ArQ* 50, iii: 89–110) that Garland's accomplishments in these areas remain largely unmentioned. This does not imply that Garland has been excluded from cultural history altogether; rather, Brown contends, he has been made over to fit into feminist and reformist paradigms. Brown persuasively argues that at the turn-of-the-century Garland was intent on creating a new, popular literature that defied past categorizations.

x Adams and the Fin de Siècle

Four cultural studies share a bond in the person of Buffalo Bill. David Minter's first-rate *A Cultural History of the American Novel* draws on an extraordinary list of literary sources, both 19th- and 20th-century, to examine the social meanings of fiction in such writers as Horatio Alger, Owen Wister, Henry Adams, and Frank Norris by positing them in their cultural milieus. Minter turns to the 1893 World's Columbian Exposition in Chicago and the twin appearances by Buffalo Bill and Frederick Jackson Turner to demonstrate how the convergence of the two helped demarcate a national identity reflected in the fiction of the time. Alger and Wister are featured in Marcus Klein's *Easterns, Westerns, and Private Eyes* (Wisconsin). Klein takes the Gilded Age as the point of origination for these three categories of tales—the rags-to-riches story, the Western saga, and detective fiction. Richard White's essay, "Frederick Jackson Turner and Buffalo Bill" (*The Frontier in American Culture* [California], pp. 7–68), discusses the polemics of Turner's 1893 address and Buffalo Bill's representation of the frontier in his Wild West show. Finally, Wister appears once again along with Alger, Turner, and Norris in David Leverenz's discussion of how constructions of masculinity are linked to developments in American capitalism in "The Last Real Man in America" (*Fictions of Masculinity: Crossing Cultures, Crossing Sexualities* [NYU], pp. 21–53).

Continuing in the same vein as last year's scholarship in viewing the protagonist of *The Education of Henry Adams* as a fiction and a deliberate one at that is Joseph Parkhurst's "The Manikin and the Memorial Bronze: The Figure of Defacement in *The Education of Henry Adams*" (*Biography* 17: 144–60). An important and beautifully researched article by J. C. Levenson, "The Etiology of Israel Adams: The Onset, Waning, and Relevance of Henry Adam's Anti-Semitism" (*NLH* 25: 569–600) focuses largely on Adams's increased post-1893 anti-Semitic expressions, both public and private. Levenson stresses that, viewed in ideological terms, Adams's statements are demonstrative of "how nineteenth-century ideals of civilization could . . . collapse into monstrous nightmare. . . . " Eugenia Kaledin's 1981 biography *The Education of Mrs. Henry Adams* (Mass.) has been reissued in paperback with a new preface.

Part of the recent scholarly surge in Chesnutt studies is Ernestine Williams Pickens's *Charles W. Chesnutt and the Progressive Movement* (Pace). Pickens explores Chesnutt's role in the major social reforms in the United States at the turn of the century. *The Conjure Woman* is interpreted as Chesnutt's challenge to the post-Reconstruction South to remember its historical past and to subvert attempts by white Southerners to re-create it as chivalric myth in Sandra Molyneaux's "Expanding the Collective Memory: Charles W. Chesnutt's *The Conjure Woman* Tales" (*Memory, Narrative, and Identity: New Essays in Ethnic American*

Literatures, ed. Amritjit Singh et al. [Northeastern], pp. 164–78). Darryl
Hattenhauer examines the dialogic combination of tragedy, melodrama,
satire, and comedy, as well as narrative techniques, in "Racial and
Textual Miscegenation in Chesnutt's *The House Behind the Cedars*"
(*MissQ* 47: 26–45), to demonstrate that Chesnutt's narrative, textual
miscegenation provides the entrée into his stories of racial miscegenation. Myles Raymond Hurd closely reads "Uncle Wellington's Wives" in
"Booker T., Blacks and Brogues: Chesnutt's Sociohistorical Links to
Realism" (*ALR* 26, ii: 19–31). And in "Listening to 'The Goophered
Grapevine' and Hearing Raisins Sing" (*AmLH* 6: 684–94) Ben Slote
traces racial and cultural parallels between the post-Reconstruction period portrayed in "The Goophered Grapevine" and the Reagan-Bush
era.

Robert Nowatzki explores the unforgivable in "Race, Rape, Lynching,
and Manhood Suffrage: Constructions of White and Black Masculinity
in Turn-of-the-Century White Supremacist Literature" (*JMS* 3: 161–
70). Prose of this type, Nowatzki argues, justified the victimization and
murder of African American males by creating bestial images and, in
turn, portraying European-American males as brave protectors of help-
less, European-American females. Only through exposing the racist
ideologies contained within this literature, Nowatzki contends, can they
be "deauthorized." Kim Emery's superbly researched article "Steers,
Queers, and Manifest Destiny" (*JHSex* 5, i: 26–57) views John Wesley
Carhart's 1895 fin de siècle novel *Norma Trist* as pivotal in American
semiotics; Emery contends that Carhart, in attempting to define lesbian
identity, marks a rejection of determinism for pragmatism. Robert Myers
reads "Antimodern Protest in *The Damnation of Theron Ware*" (*ALR* 26,
iii: 52–64) as Harold Frederic's critique of modernization, and he views
Frederic's privileging of Roman Catholicism as reflective of the turn-of-
the-century transition from "competitive capitalism to a consumer
culture."

xi Miscellaneous

This year produced an abundance of articles on William James, four of
them in a special issue of *American Journal of Theology and Philosophy.*
"The Stream of Thought" transformed into the "River-Riverbed" is the
subject of Everett J. Tarbox's article on James's influence on Wittgenstein
in "Linguistic Pragmatism: William James and Ludwig Wittgenstein"

(15: 43–58). A second offering on James and Wittgenstein is Russell B. Goodman's "What Wittgenstein Learned from William James" (*History of Philosophy Quarterly* 11: 339–54). Goodman asks a series of questions concerning James's historical influence on Wittgenstein and proceeds to answer them by establishing Wittgenstein's reading of James and his discussions of James's writing in his correspondence. Wittgenstein is abandoned for Buddhism in John Powers's "Empiricism and Pragmatism in the Thought of Dharmakirti and William James" (*American Journal of Theology and Philosophy* 15: 59–85). Powers concludes that while James demonstrated an active interest in non-Western traditions, obvious cultural and religious differences separate his views and those of Dharmakirti. James's *The Varieties of Religious Experience* is the subject of William C. Spohn's "William James on Religious Experience: An Elitist Account?" (*American Journal of Theology and Philosophy* 15: 27–41). Spohn examines recent scholarship that accuses James of systematic elitism in treating religious phenomena, concluding that while the jury is still out on Nicholas Lash's elitism charge, a particular brand of exclusivism does exist in James. *Religious Experience* appears again in Randolph Miller's overview of James's impact on American philosophy, both past and present, in "William James and the American Scene" (*American Journal of Theology and Philosophy* 15: 3–14). Miller provides an excellent account of James's current critical standing and comments on the recent flood of publications, from biographical perspectives to philosophical examinations to explorations of his religious thought. Miller also comments at length on the other James essays in the journal. In "The Polytheism of William James" (*Journal of the History of Ideas* 55: 99–111) Amos Funkenstein makes it clear that he is not much concerned with whether James was a polytheist; instead, his focus is on "the problem of motives" raised in *Religious Experience.* Jonathan Levin discusses James's struggles with formulas purporting to define aesthetics in "The Esthetics of Pragmatism" (*AmLH* 6: 658–83). Levin concludes that for James art is the antithesis of the formulaic and abstract.

State University of New York College at Potsdam

14 Fiction: 1900 to the 1930s

Jo Ann Middleton

As we approach the beginning of a new century, the early years of this one seem to become more and more attractive. Scholars look for clues in turn-of-the-century narratives to late-century issues of class, race, and gender by juxtaposing what we are with what we were. Cather and Wharton share the honors as major figures; the redefinition of Jack London continues. It is fascinating—and unpredictable—to see who resurfaces or disappears from year to year. This year we have *no* articles on B. Traven, and *three* on Gene Stratton-Porter!

i Willa Cather

Cather scholarship expanded and deepened this year with many excellent essays and several fine book-length studies. Clearly the most significant contribution is the eagerly awaited second volume in the Nebraska Cather Edition, *My Ántonia* (Nebraska), ed. Charles W. Mignon with Kari Ronning. *My Ántonia* includes the critical text that follows Cather's intent in preparing the first edition, the original Benda illustrations, a textual commentary that reveals Cather cared deeply about the appearance of this book, and a record of all revisions in various editions of the text. Photographs tying the text to Cather's life are also included, and Cather biographer James Woodress provides comprehensive explanatory notes and the engrossing historical essay that locates the novel in its own time and in Cather's career. Like *O Pioneers!* (see *ALS 1992,* p. 211), this beautiful book reveals meticulous attention to detail and the highest standards of scholarship.

My Ántonia inspired three fine essays this year. In "Willa Cather and 'The Storyteller': Hostility to the Novel in *My Ántonia*" (*AL* 66: 689–717) Richard H. Millington draws on Walter Benjamin's 1936 essay to

demonstrate *My Ántonia*'s much-debated form as "an intergeneric combat." Through her simultaneous simulation of oral storytelling and
attack on novelistic values, Cather achieves the kind of "literary and
cultural renovation" Benjamin advocates. Evelyn I. Funda argues that
Ántonia is an artist with the power to shape her own experience in " 'The
Breath Vibrating Behind It': Intimacy in the Storytelling of Ántonia
Shimerda" (*WAL* 29: 195–215). In a typically female pattern of storytelling, Ántonia's stories ostensibly concern "*others* and their struggle to
create human bonds," but they are actually stories of herself, her fears,
and her desires. David Murphy's interesting "Jejich Antonie: Czechs, the
Land, Cather, and the Pavelka Farmstead" (*GPQ* 15: 85–106), complete
with 10 illustrations, refers to *My Ántonia* and "Neighbour Rosicky" to
connect the Pavelka farmstead with the spatial characteristics of Czech
villages.

   In *Willa Cather's Transforming Vision: New France and the American
Northeast* (Susquehanna) Gary Brienzo proposes that *Shadows on the
Rock,* a pivotal novel in Cather's search for meaning, belonging, and
order, posits a familial order much larger than the domestic heart of
My Ántonia. Using primary research in little-known historical sources,
Brienzo clearly and skillfully explicates *Shadows* as Cather's "statement of
faith in the ability of both individuals and larger societal orders to work
together for the creation of an all-encompassing whole," and he traces
the theme of family connectedness in the works following *Shadows.* Sally
Peltier Harvey in her broader study, *Redefining the American Dream: The
Novels of Willa Cather* (Fairleigh Dickinson), traces Cather's attempt to
"refashion an American Dream without the 'ugly crest of materialism'
stamped on it" through all 12 novels and four short stories to show how
Cather's struggle with the "success ethic" of American society gradually resolved into an acceptance of the "fulfilled self grounded in
community."

   In "Willa Cather, France, and Pierre Loti: A Spirit of Affiliation"
(*WCPMN* 38, iv: 15–18) John P. Anders advances the French homoerotic
literary tradition as a source for Cather's dedication to the French and
proposes that novelist Pierre Loti (Julien Viaud) provided her with "a
stylistic and thematic model for writing about men in love." Mary Titus
argues that George Du Maurier's representation of female creative power
and the relations between men greatly influenced the male spectators
(Professor Wunsch, Ray Kennedy, Spanish Johnny, Dr. Archie, and Fred
Ottenberg) who confirm Thea's creative power in "Cather's Creative

Women and Du Maurier's Cozy Men: *The Song of the Lark* and *Trilby*"
(*MLS* 24, ii: 27–37). The men in *Song of the Lark* are also the subject of
Laura Dubek's "Rewriting Male Scripts: Willa Cather and *The Song of
the Lark*" (*WS* 23: 293–306). Cather identifies not with Thea's integration
of feminine and masculine qualities, but with her male characters, who
negotiate between social definitions of masculine identity and "their
secret, second selves."

John H. Flannigan's superb "Thea Kronborg's Vocal Transvestism:
Willa Cather and the 'Voz Contralto'" (*MFS* 40: 737–63) discusses two
"vital *physical* aspects" of Thea's character: her contralto voice and the
music it produces which underlines its transgressive and transvestite
possibilities. Elizabeth Wood also discusses the "coloratura mezzo" voice
in *The Song of the Lark* and work by Gertrude Atherton, Marcia Davenport, Natalie Barney, and Ethel Smyth ("Sapphonics," pp. 25–66 in
Queering the Pitch: The New Gay and Lesbian Musicology [Routledge],
ed. Philip Brett et al.).

Domna Pastourmatzi focuses her important essay "Willa Cather and
the Cult of Masculinity" (*WCPMN* 38, iv: 2–14) on Cather's portrayal of
several ladies' man or lady-killer character types to illustrate her own
exploration and critique of the masculine ideology of her era. Spanning
more than 20 years, Cather's "playboys" help her castigate male sexism,
possessiveness, and domination in reaction to the "predatory male attitude encouraged by American culture and institutionalized by the novel
of seduction."

Issues of gender inform Ian F. A. Bell's "Re-Writing America: Origin
and Gender in Willa Cather's *The Professor's House*" (*YES* 24: 12–43).
The novel's radical understanding of "origin before birth" and Godfrey
St. Peter's complex apprehension of the female reveals a fear of the
biological intensity of parenthood. Although St. Peter desires an ideology
counter to a matriarchal structure and modern messiness, he discovers
that the future "with Augusta" depends on "a recasting of adventure from
conquest to availability, from the solitary to . . . the relational, from the
privatizing of the male to the complex multiplicity of the female." An
equally compelling essay, Matthew Wilson's "Willa Cather's Godfrey St.
Peter: Historian of Repressed Sensibility?" (*CollL* 21, ii: 63–74), argues
that St. Peter's retreat from modernity is caused by the eruption of
history (the death of Tom Outland in World War I) and his suppression
of that powerfully unmanageable event. Trapped by the patriarchal
assumptions undergirding history, the Spanish conquistadors, and the

war, the Professor cannot resolve, confront, or interpret historical contradictions, and his subsequent alienation makes him another victim of the war's patriarchal violence.

One of Ours engaged two scholars. Margaret R. Higonnet examines the "blurring of dichotomies between men and women, war and peace, death and life" in women's writing about war by reading *One of Ours* in conjunction with Edith Wharton's *A Son at the Front* and Mary Borden's "The Forbidden Zone" in "Women in the Forbidden Zone: War, Women, and Death," pp. 192–209 in Sarah Webster Goodwin and Elisabeth Bronfen, eds., *Death and Representation* (Hopkins, 1993). Asserting that Claude Wheeler "is hardly a male according to Nebraska gendering," John Limon contends that Cather's war is "not merely a consummation of femininity but also a fruition of motherliness" (*Writing After War*, pp. 200–205). Only women like Mrs. Wheeler search for maps of Europe; only the imaginative respond to the call of war; only death equals the perfect fusion of motherhood and sonhood.

Evelyn Helmick Hively's impressive, painstakingly researched *Sacred Fire: Willa Cather's Novel Cycle* (Univ. Press) draws on Cather's reading in the work of historians, philosophers, and mythographers to examine nine novels, from *O Pioneers!* to *Shadows on the Rock*. Hively traces the influence of Giambattista Vico and Jules Michelet on Cather's cyclic design of the rise, maturity, and fall of American civilization. She compellingly argues that Cather incorporates elements of preclassical and classical mystery religions to locate the history of the frontier in a context of universal significance; using mystery rituals devoted to the worship of a goddess also allowed her to write them all for Isabelle McClung. In "The Four Seasons of Marian Forrester" (*JEP* 15: 54–59) Dalma H. Brunauer also draws on the Eleusinian mysteries to read *A Lost Lady* as a cyclic work which includes comedy, romance, tragedy, and irony in a sequence encompassing four "long seasons" of 12 years each that correspond to the seasons of the year as well as to Cather's own life. K. P. Stich in "Woman as Enemy: Willa Cather's 'The Marriage of Phaedra'" (*MLS* 24, ii: 38–47) examines Cather's story as an example of her sensitivity to myth. Reverberating with Amazon myth, "The Marriage of Phaedra" directs "the gaze of the world" from "male-centered preunderstanding" toward "renewed recognition of the power of the feminine."

Locating Cather among modernists whose work questions the nature of reading and the role of the reader (*"Modernist" Women Writers*, pp. 19–50), Kathleen Wheeler demonstrates that through her narrative complexities Cather conveys different kinds of experience, ranging from that unnoticed by the unconscious to that refined into the production of art. In "*Lucy Gayheart:* Sounds and Silences" (*WCPMN* 38, iv: 20–23) Joanna Lloyd argues that readers must focus on what Cather leaves out in *Lucy Gayheart,* an experimental novel that explores "resonant silence" to "extend the boundaries of what we hear in a text." In "Teaching Willa Cather in Japan" (*JEP* 15: 224–30) Dalma Brunauer points out cultural differences that inform reader responses to *My Ántonia* and *A Lost Lady,* and in "*Lucy Gayheart:* A Realistic Novel of Youth's Longings" (*IEB* 81: 31–33) Laura L. Koenig recommends *Lucy Gayheart* for high school students who can identify with Lucy's feeling of alienation. Two biographies for young adults appeared this year: Ann T. Keene's *Willa Cather* (Julian Messner) and Sharon O'Brien's *Lives of Notable Gay Men and Lesbians: Willa Cather* (Chelsea). Keene's straightforward, readable introduction to Cather, focused on her literary career, is fine for all ages; O'Brien's discussion of the complicated issues of sexual identity and socially constructed concepts of gendered roles makes her slim volume better suited to mature adolescents.

Tom Quirk examines the influence of that perennial adolescent, Huckleberry Finn, on Cather, Ring Lardner, and Langston Hughes in his lucid "Huckleberry Finn's Heirs" (pp. 106–46 in *Coming to Grips with Huckleberry Finn* [Missouri]). Cather admired Twain for the quality of language and vitality of feeling in *Huckleberry Finn* and because Twain's work proved that the land and people of *her* youth were also worthy of literary treatment. In "A North American Connection: Women in Prairie Novels" (*GPQ* 14: 21–28) Ann Barnard competently traces the classic tradition distinguished by "spatial archetypes involving motion and diversity" in prairie novels by American and Canadian writers Cather, Sinclair Lewis, Sinclair Ross, Margaret Laurence, and Robert Kroetsch, all of whom centered female characters within the physical space of the prairie "open[ing] the door to new perceptions of gender." Mark Schlenz differentiates between a "symbolic regionalism" and "semiotic regionalism" in his discerning comparison of Cather's and Mary Austin's "critically distinct rhetorical strategies" in "Rhetorics of Region in *Starry Adventure* and *Death Comes for the Archbishop*" (*Regionalism Reconsidered,* pp. 65–85). Cather seeks to erase regional difference through assimilation into a transcendent world community; Austin answers this vision with a "bioregional narrative" that endeavors to comprehend the interactions of people with a particular landscape.

Apparently, Cather brought out competitiveness in others. In her perceptive "Katherine Anne Porter's 'Reflections on Willa Cather': A Duplicitous Homage" (*AL* 66: 719–35) Janis P. Stout questions prevailing feminist models of relationships among women writers by reading Porter's "homage" to Cather as an "artfully duplicitous essay on a literary elder sister" that asserts Porter's own stature while purporting to pay tribute to a literary "foremother." Arguing the need to accommodate the intricacies of sisterhood and daughterhood in discussing literary affiliations, Stout demonstrates that Porter's language reveals her rivalry with Cather and also her sensitivity to the "quasi-familial complexity" of the relationship. In his thorough discussion of *The Folks*, "The Cool Clarity and Secrets of Ruth Suckow's *The Folks*" (*Cresset* 58, ii–iii: 5–10), Charles Vandersee reminds us that Margot finds herself in Greenwich Village reflecting on the apartment house "where . . . Willa Cather had lived" and speculates that Suckow includes this scene as a challenge to compare *her* prose with Cather's "cool clarity." The essay also appears in the Spring 1994/1995 *The Ruth Suckow Newsletter* (pp. 1–15), as does Abigail Martin's "*Cora*: A Feminist Novel" (pp. 16–20), which proposes that *Cora* is Suckow's most explicit discussion of "the woman question."

Loretta Wasserman suggests that Cather's own competitiveness surfaced as she was writing *Sapphira and the Slave Girl*. In "*Sapphira and the Slave Girl*: Willa Cather vs. Margaret Mitchell" (*WCPMN* 38, i: 1–15), Wasserman "fancies" that Cather read *Gone With the Wind* and, irritated at its bland picture of slaves and slavery, countered Mitchell's depiction with *Sapphira*. Wasserman enumerates the myths that Cather challenges, locates the book in the tradition of "tragic mulatto," and divines the unspoken possibility of "an ultimate racial harmony." William Holz reminds us that Cather could be helpful to younger artists in "Willa Cather and Floyd Dell" (*WCPMN* 38, ii: 34–36). Citing a 1960 letter in which Dell remembers Cather as editor at *McClure's*, Holz traces connections between the two and contemplates the effect of Cather's addition to an early Dell poem (which she then published in the magazine.) Of interest here is Douglas Clayton's biography, *Floyd Dell: The Life and Times of an American Rebel* (Dee), an informative, readable, and engaging account of Dell's life and the literary milieu in which he moved. Eight pages of photographs of Dell and his friends, including Sherwood Anderson, Theodore Dreiser, and Upton Sinclair, are included as well as obscure and entertaining information (for example, that Dell, like

Cather before him, lived for a while at 61 Washington Square South, the "House of Genius").

Interest in Cather's short stories has blossomed, and of the 10 essays published on the stories this year, only two concern the same story. Eight notable essays appear in two numbers (38: ii, iii) of the *Willa Cather Pioneer Memorial Newsletter*. In " 'The Old Beauty' and Maternal Purity" (ii: 17–18, 20, 22) John N. Swift presents a Freudian interpretation of "The Old Beauty," with Gabrielle Longstreet as "maternal object" to Henry Seabury's "boyish" desire. Drawing on the stylistic features of French impressionism, Kristy Rimmasch reads "Two Friends" as Cather's attempt to find stability and reality in "Flux and Friendship: Impressionism in 'Two Friends' " (ii: 24, 26, 28). Emily Stark Zitter in "Willa Cather's Early Naturalism: 'A Death in the Desert' (ii: 29–31) weighs competing critical views about "A Death in the Desert," then concludes that its essential gloominess results from the strictly deterministic philosophy on which it is based. Lawrence I. Berkove shares his delight at unearthing a possible source for "Paul's Case" in "Rollin Mallory Daggett's 'My French Friend': A Precursor of 'Paul's Case'?" (ii: 31–34) and reprints extensive excerpts from the now largely unknown story.

In "The Magical Art of Willa Cather's 'Old Mrs. Harris' " (iii: 37–50) Blanche H. Gelfant draws an analogy between the storyteller's art and standard acts of magic to explicate Cather's techniques. Kevin A. Synnott pairs stories from the beginning and the end of Cather's career in "Defining Community in 'Jack-a-Boy' and 'The Best Years' " (iii: 41, 43, 45) to explore the tension between art and family that permeates her work. John J. Murphy's brief, thought-provoking essay, "An American Tradition in 'The Enchanted Bluff' and 'Before Breakfast' " (iii: 47, 49), explores the human process of "poetic or imaginative possession." For Cather, as for Emerson and Twain, the source of all meaning is to be found "within humanity, within intelligence, within spirit, or soul."

Susan J. Rosowski produces yet another clear and cogent explication of Cather's work in "Willa Cather's "Cather's Manifesto for Art— 'Coming, Aphrodite!' " (iii: 51–55). Rosowski reads the inset story of the Aztec princess as a statement of artistic intent wherein Cather discloses the principles of her writing and acknowledges the "issues of privacy fundamental to the intimacy of her art." In a brilliant final analogy Rosowski links Cather's story of Eden Bower/Edna Bowers to that of

Marilyn Monroe/Norma Jean Baker, "our version of Aphrodite as the cultural icon in whom we see reflected . . . the pleasure and pain of our own desires." Paraphrasing Cather's letters of the period after she finished *The Song of the Lark,* Marilyn Arnold expertly traces Cather's thwarted impulse to write another book about the Southwest to the story "full of love and hate"—the Rain Princess legend—in "Coming, Aphrodite!" in "Willa Cather's Other Story of the Southwest" (*Southwestern American Literature* 19 [1993]: 27–34). We can expect more work on Cather's stories as scholars make use of Sheryl L. Meyering's handy reference source, *A Reader's Guide to the Short Stories of Willa Cather* (Hall), with chapters on 60 stories, each containing publication history, circumstances of composition, links to Cather's other work, critical reception, and a bibliography. Virgil Albertini furnishes two bibliographical essays (*WCPMN* 38, i: 1–21).

ii Edith Wharton and Ellen Glasgow

Wharton scholars show no signs of fatigue, producing two biographies, three book-length studies, and a great pile of articles. Shari Benstock's *No Gifts from Chance: A Biography of Edith Wharton* (Scribner's), a major addition to Wharton scholarship, is a highly readable study that draws on government records, legal and medical documents, and recently opened collections of Wharton's letters to disprove several dominant myths about her paternity, her relations with her mother and brothers, her marriage to Teddy Wharton, and her affair with Morton Fullerton. Benstock meticulously documents Wharton's adolescent determination to achieve a writing career, her tough-minded business acumen, her international charity work, and her financial problems near the end of her life. Benstock keeps Wharton's writing life at the center of this splendid biography, and she includes extensive notes, 16 pages of photographs, and a list of archives where unpublished material can be found. Although Eleanor Dwight perpetuates some of the very myths Benstock dispels, her "illustrated biography," *Edith Wharton, An Extraordinary Life* (Abrams), makes a fine companion book with its more than 300 illustrations, including photographs (some by Wharton herself), drawings, paintings, garden plans, letters, and postcards, many here published for the first time. This collection reveals Wharton's lifelong passion for travel, gardening, art, and architecture, and it documents her friendships with Henry James, Henry Adams, and Bernard Berenson. Susan Goodman traces Wharton's relationships with James, Adams, and Berenson, as well as other members of her coterie of asexual and homoerotically oriented men, in her thoroughly engrossing biographical and critical study, *Edith Wharton's Inner Circle* (Texas). This makes an intriguing counterpart to Goodman's earlier study, *Edith Wharton's Women* (see *ALS 1990*, p. 247).

William R. Macnaughton proposes that *The Reef* is both Wharton's "act of homage to Henry James" and a veiled criticism of her friend's actions, attitudes, and depiction of male-female relationships in "Edith Wharton, *The Reef,* and Henry James" (*ALR* 26, ii: 43–59). Macnaughton demonstrates Wharton's position that however convincingly James's female characters wield power and influence, for reasons of gender, age, education, economic status, and class, power does *not* reside in the women. Nicole Tonkovich's feminist "audit" of *The Mother's Recompense* ("An Excess of Recompense: The Feminine Economy of *The Mother's Recompense*" [*ALR* 26, iii: 12–32]) reveals economies linking generic norms, literary evaluation, a patriarchal ideology, and the ultimate production of cultural and sexual standards. Kate's reward/recompense is a new relationship with her daughter within a feminine space; her horror at Anne's marriage results from the interruption of that relationship and the precision of the heterosexual role Anne is to play in the patriarchal system. In "Edith Wharton's 'Inscrutable Totem Terrors': Ethnography and *The Age of Innocence*" (*SFolk* 51: 137–52) Kenneth D. Pimple explicates Wharton's many references to anthropology, totemism, tribalism, rites, rituals, and customs to reveal the contemporary ethnographic model she used to address a social stasis in which "gender relationships tend to imply that all the members of Society feel and behave in exactly the same way." Identifying Undine Spragg as a "perverted Horatio Alger heroine" who has no other means to achieve success but "pluck, luck, lack of scruples, and great natural resources (beauty)" in "Undine Is Us: Wharton's Attack on American Greed" (*EA* 47: 22–31), Peter L. Hays expertly shows how Wharton uses marriage in *The Custom of the Country* as a synecdoche for what is wrong with our patriarchal, materialistic, and thoroughly corrupt culture.

Two articles explore aspects of Wharton's relationship with Morton Fullerton. " 'The Life Apart': Text and Context of Edith Wharton's Love Diary" (*AL* 66: 663–88) by Kenneth M. Price and Phyllis McBride reprints the text of the diary Wharton kept from 29 October 1907 through 12 June 1908. Endnotes contextualize the manuscript, clarify references and allusions, and provide translations of foreign phrases. In a second essay, "The Mediating 'Whitman': Edith Wharton, Morton Fullerton, and the Problem of Comradeship" (*TSLL* 36: 380–402), Price traces the metamorphosis of Wharton's "Whitman" from a liberating force to a misogynist during her affair with Fullerton as she realized that "the homosexual Whitman . . . was likely to deprive her of lasting physical communion with any one individual from the one group of men that consistently took her seriously as an individual." Of interest as well is "Another Reading of Wharton's View of Women in *French Ways and Their Meaning*" (*Edith Wharton Review* 11, iii: 13–14, 16), in which Laurel Fryer-Smith rereads "The New Frenchwoman" to demonstrate that Wharton believed "the French were the most civilized of all people" because she also believed in "the complementary role of men and women."

Locating Wharton's repudiation of female local color writers in her fear of entrapment within that tradition, Donna M. Campbell in "Edith Wharton and the 'Authoresses': The Critique of Local Color in Wharton's Early Fiction" (*SAF* 22: 169–83) finds evidence of that rejection in "Mrs. Manstey's View" and *Bunner Sisters,* written long before Wharton challenged the tradition in *Ethan Frome* or in *Summer.* John Limon proposes that Wharton endangers the validity of her own art by killing only sons (to sever the male artistic heritage) in his discussion of *A Son at the Front* (*Writing after War,* pp. 205–10). Dale Bauer's thoughtful study *Edith Wharton's Brave New Politics* (Wisconsin) examines the interrelation of political and historical issues and their effect on intimate experience in Wharton's late work, and he proficiently argues the thesis that, while Wharton's conventional views on race regrettably never altered, her "celebration of gender and class privilege did change, bravely."

In perhaps the strongest essay of the year, " 'Roman Fever': A Mortal Malady" (*CEA* 56, ii: 56–60), Lawrence I. Berkove explicates the moral issues at stake in "Roman Fever." Not only do Mrs. Ansley and Mrs. Slade violate standards of decency, but "in the course of their lifetime of silent combat against each other, they also negate their marriage vows, poison their lives with hatred and deception, and . . . verge upon murder." By making women the protagonists of her story, Wharton repudiates the notion that women are by nature morally superior to men, and she conveys "the seriousness about the moral standards that women as well as men must obey to rise above the natural human tendency to savagery." Kathleen Wheeler examines Wharton's narrative strategies, imagery, and perspective in "Roman Fever" and *In Morocco* (*"Modernist" Women Writers and Narrative Art*, pp. 77–98).

Evelyn E. Fracasso's fine study, *Edith Wharton's Prisoners of Consciousness: A Study of Theme and Technique in the Tales* (Greenwood), explores Wharton's careful and conscious crafting of narrative techniques to fit the theme of imprisonment in most of her 86 short stories, and she explicates representative stories in four categories: men and women trapped by love and marriage, individuals imprisoned by society, artists torn between the demands of art and morality, and persons paralyzed by fear of the supernatural. The spring 1994 *Edith Wharton Review* (11, i) takes as its topic "Wharton and the Gothic" and includes four excellent essays. In " 'Forbidden Things': Gothic Confrontation with the Feminine in 'The Young Gentlemen' and 'Bewitched' " (pp. 3–9) Kathy Fedorko examines Wharton's contrasting ways of dealing with "fearful" feminine qualities. Richard A. Kaye explores the personal reverberations in the ghost tales through which Wharton dealt with the subject of homoerotic carnality in " 'Unearthly Visitants': Wharton's Ghost Tales, Gothic Form and the Literature of Homosexual Panic" (pp. 10–18). Linking Wharton's Gothic mode to T. S. Eliot's modernism, Monika Elbert finds parallels between "Bottle of Perrier" and Eliot's *The Waste Land,* both attempts to ward off a sense of chaos and fragmentation through some supernatural (or feminine) form of reality in "T. S. Eliot and Wharton's Modernist Guide" (pp. 19–25). In "Is This Indeed 'Attractive'? Another Look at the 'Beatrice Palmato' Fragment" (pp. 26–29) Kristin O. Lauer takes issue with those who have interpreted the pornographic fragment as "startling" or "attractive," and she counters with a reading that reveals "the same rescue scenario ubiquitous in male-female relationships in Wharton's fiction." Martha Banta's "The Ghostly Gothic of Wharton's Everyday World" (*ALR* 27, i: 1–10) locates Wharton within the cultural context of the newly popular science of ethnography, links her narrative art to Walter Benjamin's theories of secrets and revelations, and suggests that Wharton repositioned the Gothic within the everyday world in "Afterward" and *Ethan Frome.*

Ethan Frome figures in three additional essays. Mary D. Lagerwey and Gerald E. Markle read it through a framework developed by Talcott Parsons in "Edith Wharton's Sick Role" (*Sociological Quarterly* 35: 121–34), then explore Wharton's sick role as a social construct and examine the power relations within which this story of illness has been constructed. In "Cold Comfort for Ethan Frome" (*N&Q* 40 [1993]: 498–

500) Jackie Vickers identifies *Ethan Frome* as "one of the [works] bob-
bing about whole and recognisable" in *Cold Comfort Farm* (1932) by
Stella Gibbons. Elsa Nettels's "Thwarted Escapes: *Ethan Frome* and Jean
Stafford's 'A Country Love Story' " (pp. 6–8, 15) is one of three essays on
"Wharton's Legacy to Women Writers" in the fall issue of the *Edith
Wharton Review* (11, ii: 1–16). Nettels illuminates Stafford's story of a
disintegrating marriage by reading it beside Wharton's novel, astutely
locating similarities and telling differences that point to Stafford's "need
to reduce her formidable predecessor to a figure she could satirize." Mia
Manzulli suggests that Alice Walker inherits the garden (a space for
female creativity) which Wharton has revised as "a place of work and
words" in "Edith Wharton's Gardens as a Legacy to Alice Walker"
(pp. 9–12, 16). Meredith Goldsmith in "Edith Wharton's Gift to Nella
Larsen: *The House of Mirth* and *Quicksand*" (pp. 3–5, 15) argues that
Quicksand functions as a critical rereading of *The House of Mirth* in
which Larsen manipulates the conventions of Wharton's plot "to inscribe
her work within a feminine literary tradition that problematizes class and
racial categories."

Scholarship on *The House of Mirth* is plentiful and varied. Cynthia
Griffin Wolff's "Lily Bart and the Drama of Femininity" (*AmLH* 6: 71–
87), a fascinating exploration of Wharton's artistic interest in the "busy,
varied world of Edwardian drama," points out the many allusions to
contemporary drama that Wharton's 1905 readers would understand,
demonstrates the novel's structural resemblance to a five-act play, and
elucidates the tensions Wharton creates between "the platitudes of simplistic stage reality and the intractable complexity of real life." With the
help of Jacques Derrida and Jacques Lacan, Marilyn Maness Mehaffy
explores the means and metaphors by which Wharton's text destabilizes
sexual categories to "extend the radically subversive potentiality of a
female-female nexus of desire" in "Manipulating the Metaphors: *The
House of Mirth* and 'the Volcanic Nether-Side' of 'Sexuality' " (*CollL* 21,
ii: 47–63). Louise K. Barnett discusses *The House of Mirth* as a "speech-
act drama" and sees Lily as a nonconformist who follows Huck Finn,
Natty Bumppo, and Ishmael, refusing adulthood on society's terms and
demanding a latitude available only to women who have "submitted/
married" even as she shrinks from her role as object (*Authority and
Speech: Language, Society, and Self in the American Novel* [Georgia, 1993],
pp. 129–39). In " 'A Barrier of Words': The Tension between Narrative
Voice and Vision in the Writings of Edith Wharton" (*ALR* 27, i: 11–22)

D. Quentin Miller advances tableaux vivants as a metaphor for the conscious struggle between vision and speech that informs Wharton's narrative.

Lily's death is always a compelling topic. Rita di Giuseppe, in "Dialectic of Transvaluation in Edith Wharton's *The House of Mirth,*" pp. 111–124 in John D. Simons, ed., *Literature and Film in the Historical Dimension: Selected Papers from the Fifteenth Annual Florida State University Conference on Literature and Film* (Florida), ties the opposition between free will and determinism in *The House of Mirth* to the psychology of William James and suggests that the unresolved philosophical controversy leaves the reader torn between an impression that Lily is fated to die tragically and a suspicion that she is somehow morally responsible for her own death. Richard Kaye's "Literary Naturalism and the Passive Male: Edith Wharton's Revisions of *The House of Mirth*" (*PULC* 56: 47–72) is a thoroughly engaging scholarly essay that draws on two hand-corrected galleys and an undated synopsis of the novel to propose a new critical understanding of Lawrence Selden and his relationship with Lily and to argue that the determinist logic informing *The House of Mirth* proves Lily's death "is less one of failed character than one of fatefully delayed timing." In a chapter on *The House of Mirth* in her *Psychological Politics of the American Dream: The Commodification of Subjectivity in Twentieth-Century American Literature* (Ohio State) Lois Tyson investigates the psychological payoffs for both genders invested in woman as "commodity fetish" and regards Lily's problematical death as the consummation of both her and her male counterpart's "delusional transcendental project." Shari Benstock ties reader ambivalence about Lily's death to the shifting narrative modes Wharton used to modify the ethical referentiality of art within the context of modern aesthetics (" 'The word which made all clear': The Silent Close of *The House of Mirth,*" pp. 250–28 in Alison Booth, ed., *Famous Last Words: Changes in Gender and Narrative Closure* [Virginia, 1993]).

In "The House of Mirrors: Carrie, Lily, and the Reflected Self" (*MLS* 24, iii: 44–54) Caren J. Town compares notions of identity formation in Wharton and Theodore Dreiser. Carrie creates an identity by abandoning herself to her mirror image, making her appearance *pay;* Lily refuses to relinquish a belief that objects must have meaning. And in *Engendering Romance* Emily Miller Budick locates Wharton with Kate Chopin and Ellen Glasgow in the Hawthorne tradition of romance fiction (pp. 122–39).

In her splendid study *Ellen Glasgow and a Woman's Traditions* (Virginia) Pamela R. Matthews challenges other feminist scholars to follow her lead in revaluating Glasgow in terms of the traditions she faced as a woman writer. Using current feminist psychological theory, Matthews shows that the important and nurturing relationships of Glasgow's life were with women, and she offers fresh readings of Glasgow's novels and five Gothic short stories. Matthews also provides the fine, thoughtful introduction to Glasgow's long-out-of-print autobiography, *The Woman Within* (Virginia). In *Sacred Estrangement: The Rhetoric of Conversion in Modern American Autobiography* (Penn. State, 1993) Peter A. Dorsey situates *The Woman Within* and Wharton's *A Backward Glance* within the American tradition of spiritual autobiography; Glasgow's skepticism inverts the tradition and presents the emotional and intellectual effects of disappointment as conversion experiences (pp. 151–63). Lee Winniford investigates Glasgow's omissions, evasions, and discursions in *Barren Ground* as narrative strategies that force the reader to assent to a feminist story that undermines "the thematic and plot expectations of the male-dominated canon" in "Suppressing the Masculine Metanarrative: The Uncaging of Glasgow's *Barren Ground*" (*JNT* 24: 141–52).

This year's *Ellen Glasgow Newsletter* offers Edgar Macdonald's " 'Remembering Ellen Glasgow'—and Elizabeth Branch Bowie" (31: 1–7); E. Stanley's reflections on his 1972 biography of Glasgow ("A Biography and a Biographer" [32: 4–5]); Glasgow's untouched and retouched 1937 photographs (32: 10–11); Catherine G. Peaslee's account of Glasgow's friendship with her neighbor, Princess Amelie Rives Troubetzkoy ("A Poem for a Dear Friend from Castle Hill" [33: 6–7]); and Stephanie Branson's close reading of works by "female myth-makers" Glasgow and Marie de France similar in plot (a love triangle involving two women) and theme (female generosity) (" 'A Plant for Woman's Troubles': Rue in Marie de France's 'Eliduc' and Ellen Glasgow's 'The Past' " [33: 1, 4–5]).

iii Gertrude Stein and H. L. Mencken

This year's work on Stein should go a long way to alter her public image. In *Gertrude Stein Remembered* (Nebraska), editor Linda Simon gathers 21 memoirs, some previously unpublished, from men and women who knew Stein from her undergraduate days at Radcliffe College until her death in 1946. This charming and provocative book includes Simon's graceful introduction and notes on such contributors as Sherwood An-

derson, Carl Van Vechten, Sylvia Beach, and Cecil Beaton. Editor
Renate Stendhal has selected 360 photographs from Stein's personal
collection and matched them with text from her work and from letters
and memoirs of her friends in *Gertrude Stein in Words and Pictures*
(Algonquin). The collection's richness supports Stendhal's speculation
that Stein left these pictures as a visual chronicle of her life to accompany
her literary record.

Linda Watts's carefully conceived and clearly written " 'Can Women
Have Wishes': Gender and Spiritual Narrative in Gertrude Stein's *Lend a
Hand or Four Religions*" (*Journal of Feminist Studies in Religion* 10, ii: 49–
72) argues that Stein's work should be reassessed in terms of spiritual
issues; Watts makes a solid contribution to that effort by addressing
intersections of gender and spirituality which reveal Stein's "acts of
'revision.'" Bonnie Marranca contributes two essays on Stein's spirituality. In "St. Gertrude" (*PArtsJ* 46: 107–12) Marranca explains how
Stein's spiritual journey, though different from Ignatius's, was "nevertheless toward the perfect state of mind, her stanzas in meditation more
joyous and wondrous in celebrating nature and being and creating." In
"Presence of Mind" (*PArtJ* 48: 1–17) Marranca turns to Stein's understanding of sainthood as a form of genius and the joining of her own life
with Saint Theresa of Ávila's, the writer's life with the saintly life, and
modern Paris with baroque Spain in *Four Saints in Three Acts*. Affirming
that Stein belongs in the company of Pound, Joyce, and Zukofsky, Bob
Perelman in *The Trouble with Genius: Reading Pound, Joyce, Stein, and
Zukofsky* (Calif.) differentiates Stein the writer from Stein the genius and
confirms that in both her difficult and her popular works Stein was
concerned with the problem of addressing the public in language "more
real than it could read."

In "The Poetics of Event: Stein, the Avant-Garde, and the Aesthetic
Turn of Philosophy" (*Sagetrieb* 12, iii: 125–48) Krzysztof Ziarek locates
Stein's work in the philosophical debate on modernist aesthetics and
suggests that Stein's idiom is a response to the event-character of experience and its erasure from linguistic practices. Georg Schiller contributes
to the ongoing discussion of "reference" in Stein's texts by combining
John Dewey's aesthetic theory with Wolfgang Iser's reader-response concept to place Stein's work within the framework of recent pragmatist
approaches to literature in "Organizing Energies: Reference and Experience in the Work of Gertrude Stein" (*Amst* 39: 511–24).

Two essays in *Rereading the New: A Backward Glance at Modernism* ed. Kevin J. H. Dettmar (Michigan, 1992) deal with Stein. Ellen E. Berry expertly explores Stein's ideas concerning the relations between an emerging mass culture and avant-garde art in "Modernism/Mass Culture/Postmodernism: The Case of Gertrude Stein" (pp. 167–89). Anticipating many of the forms and logics of postmodernism, Stein's texts also represent one of the first attempts "to articulate the modern *through* the popular rather than in reaction to it." In " 'Entering the Modern Composition': Gertrude Stein and the Patterns of Modernism" (pp. 137–63) Jonathan Levin observes that most readers fixated on stable meanings or concerned with the promotion of distinct cultural values have little patience reading Stein because she "wants less to clarify a point or drive home a specific idea than to keep the movement—of words, of idea, of self-awareness—on the go"; "Melanctha" illustrates Stein's ability to draw out dynamic, nonconceptual qualities of language while integrating them into the central dramatic conflict of the story. The rhythms of the story point "to nothing universal short of constant change." "Hysteria and the Normal Unconscious: Dual Natures in Gertrude Stein's 'Melanctha' " (*JAmS* 28: 77–83) is Mark Neimeyer's first-rate examination of the influence of William James and two articles Stein published in the *Psychological Review* on the genesis of the two central characters in her story. Stein conceived Melanctha as "an hysteric alternately ruled by one of her two warring personalities" and Jeff as "a normal, though logic-dominated, human being trying to experience a deeply emotional life by liberating his unconscious."

Two articles of note appeared on Picasso and Stein. In "Experiment in Time and Process of Discovery: Picasso Paints Gertrude Stein; Gertrude Stein Makes Sentences" (*HLB* 5, ii: 5–30) Jane P. Bowers focuses her clearly written and thoroughly satisfying essay on the year 1905–06, during which Picasso painted *Gertrude Stein* and Stein returned to her abandoned project, *The Making of Americans,* to identify the portrait of Stein as "a declaration of independence and an act of self-definition for both painter and sitter" and review the consequences of that creative breakthrough for each. Karin Cope's "Painting after Gertrude Stein" (*Diacritics* 24: 190–203) explicates how the famous portrait that reassembled the elements of the model Gertrude Stein in an unexpected and disturbing fashion led Picasso to the pursuit of other bodily forms and Stein to a series of inquiries into the nature, possibilities, and impossibilities of identity. In a related piece, "The 'Convincing Lies' of Gertrude Stein: Cubism in *The Autobiography of Alice B. Toklas*" (*PVR* 22, ii:

5–20), Karla Murphy rejects the term "abstractionism" for Stein's style, arguing that *The Autobiography*'s "intellectualized content" and "timeless and simultaneously fragmented style" instead exemplify cubism.

Several unrelated items deserve mention. In her lucid prose Marianne DeKoven investigates the "mutuality of progressive politics and avant-garde art" by drawing parallels between Gertrude Stein and Jane Addams in " 'Excellent Not a Hull House': Gertrude Stein, Jane Addams, and Feminist-Modern Political Culture" (*Rereading Modernism*, pp. 321–50). Michael Kaufmann examines Stein's use of the physical text, pp. 52–67 in his *Textual Bodies: Modernism, Postmodernism, and Print* (Bucknell). By reteaching readers to *see* print, Stein teaches us how to *hear* it, disordering meaning, exposing forgotten links in language, and showing us that blanks between words are actually filled with "music, memory, musical memory." Wolfgang E. H. Rudat contributes this year's essay on the Stein/Hemingway relationship with "Hemingway's Revenge on Gertrude Stein: Intertextuality between *A Moveable Feast* and *The Sun Also Rises*" (*JEP* 15: 39–50). Hemingway avenged himself on Stein for *The Autobiography of Alice B. Toklas,* lampooning his own description of male homosexuality and turning the tables on Stein.

Three major additions to Mencken scholarship appeared this year, and, given the industry of Menckenites, we should reap critical essays in days to come. A milestone in Mencken scholarship is Fred Hobson's long-awaited and definitive *Mencken: A Life* (Random House), meticu-lously researched, judiciously balanced, and gracefully written. Observ-ing that "rarely has a person written so much about himself . . . and still . . . revealed so little," Hobson goes beyond Mencken's strategies of concealment and diversion to examine the many paradoxes in the man, uncovering a private Mencken more serious, more lonely, and more human than his public image. Hobson's is the "first-rate biography" of Mencken that Louis D. Rubin, Jr., asked for in 1991 (see *ALS 1991*, p. 231).

Thanks to Mencken's foresightedness, he continues to publish long after his demise. *Five Years of Newspaper Work* (Hopkins), ed. Fred Hobson et al., draws from one massive manuscript to present important new material on Mencken's coverage of presidential candidates from 1912 through 1940, the 1925 Scopes trial, his brief stint as a war correspondent in 1917, his trip to Germany in 1938, and his candid, gossipy comments on Baltimore politicians and clerics. The editors have cut the original manuscript to a single volume comprising about 45 percent of Mencken's text and have retained just two of 30 appendixes to present "Mencken abridged but not bowdlerized." The sequel to the best-selling *A Mencken Chrestomathy* (Knopf, 1948), *A Second Mencken Chrestomathy* (Knopf), "selected, revised, and annotated by the author" and discovered among the Mencken papers by editor Terry Teachout, contains 219 of approximately 250 typescript passages edited by Mencken, as well as 19 unrevised articles, Mencken's introductions, and, with the exception of one, the original footnotes. At once an anthology and a deliberate act of "literary and intellectual self-definition," this absorbing volume reprints in book form 147 previously uncollected passages and makes available 62 items from books no longer in print. *Chrestomathy,* according to Mencken, means "a collection of choice passages from an author or authors."

Of note in this year's *Menckeniana* are Louis D. Rubin, Jr.'s, assessment of Mencken as a working newspaperman ("the very best in the business") (131: 1–11); Ray Stevens's comments on the implication of the Mencken controversy for his criticism of Joseph Conrad (132: 1–12); Anne Henley's biographical essay on Sara Haardt (129: 1–12); indefatigable Vincent Fitzpatrick's bibliographic checklist (129: 15–16, 130: 13–16, 131: 16); and S. L. Harrison's account of Mencken's personal and professional relationship with editorial cartoonist Edmund Duffy (129: 12–14). Harrison takes a closer look at the role that partnership played in shaping the course and events of the Scopes trial in "The Scopes 'Monkey Trial' Revisited: Mencken and the Editorial Art of Edmund Duffy" (*JACult* 17, iv: 55–63).

iv Sherwood Anderson, Theodore Dreiser, Sinclair Lewis, and Upton Sinclair

Anderson scholars will welcome Judy Jo Small's *A Reader's Guide to the Short Stories of Sherwood Anderson* (Hall), a handy compendium of historical and critical information on the stories Anderson published in *Winesburg, Ohio, The Triumph of the Egg, Horses and Men,* and *Death in the Woods.* A chapter for each story includes information about composition, sources and influences, publication, its relation to Anderson's other work, critical and interpretive commentary, and a bibliography.

In "Another Look at Community in *Winesburg, Ohio*" (*Midamerica* 20 [1993]: 76–88) Clarence Lindsay extends his earlier essay "The Rhetoric of Community in *Winesburg, Ohio*" (*Midamerica* 15 [1988]: 39–47), which calls into question Anderson's romantic ethic privileging the individual in opposition to larger social configurations. In this reading of *Winesburg*, Lindsay find that community is the audience for selfhoods, interpreter of the fictions of selfhood played out for it by individuals, and creator of its own problematic and indeterminate fictions. David D. Anderson believes that "to Anderson the reality of human life is not found in its community with others." In his important essay "The Dramatic Landscape of Sherwood Anderson's Fiction" (*Midamerica* 20 [1993]: 89–97) David Anderson defines two stories in each work. That of the town is structurally and organically the foundation of the work, but the second, which lays bare the inner turmoil of the people, provides the substance of Anderson's fiction and is his "most durable contribution to the literature of our time and place." Emily Miller Budick asserts that "Sherwood Anderson's *Winesburg, Ohio* stands closely behind Faulkner's [*As I Lay Dying*]" and views these texts as "antiphallocentric romances" which open with similar images of a "nonterminating pregnancy" (*Engendering Romance*, pp. 87–104). One last note: Anderson's *Windy McPherson's Sons* (Illinois, 1993) is out in a new edition that includes the alternate 1922 ending.

Dreiser inspired several additional articles, two books, and a new collection, the Dover Thrift Edition of *Short Stories,* which includes five stories as well as Sherwood Anderson's 1918 introduction. In *Sexualizing Power in Naturalism: Theodore Dreiser and Frederick Philip Grove* (Calgary) Irene Gammel argues that the "survival" and transformation of European naturalist conventions in a North American context is deeply rooted in a preoccupation with sexuality and power. She makes her case by examining the fiction of Dreiser and Frederick Philip Grove, thereby covering the first four decades of this century and three cultures— American, Canadian, and German. Also of note, *The Theory and Practice of American Naturalism: Selected Essays and Reviews* (So. Ill., 1993) reprints some of the best of Donald Pizer's excellent work on the genre.

Sister Carrie commands the spotlight again this year. Jerome Loving ends his ambitious *Lost in the Customhouse* (Iowa, 1993) with *Sister Carrie,* the "culminating fiction about the American woman (waking up) at the end of the nineteenth century" (pp. 195–210). The first workingwoman in American fiction to be vividly drawn from a materialistic society, Carrie is also the first to break out of the domestic cycle and survive in a world of men and money. The world of men is also on the mind of Margaret Rozga, who links Dreiser's novel to Jane Smiley's in

"Sisters in a Quest—*Sister Carrie* and *A Thousand Acres:* The Search for Identity in Gendered Territory" (*MMisc* 22: 18–29). *Sister Carrie* questions social structures and conventional morality to invert the Horatio Alger story, and *A Thousand Acres* reimagines *King Lear* to interrogate a patriarchal structure that results in irremediable conflict between daughters and fathers. Although he proposes to investigate Dreiser's own thought and not to define "conscience" in any particular way, Thomas Pitoniak does both superbly in "Present Feelings, Distant Reason: Conscience in *Sister Carrie*" (*ALR* 26, iii: 65–79).

Jeffrey Hart challenges Lionel Trilling's 1960 disparagement of Dreiser to make a case for *Sister Carrie* and *An American Tragedy* as "major and very potent works of art" in "Reality in America: Yet Once More" (*SR* 102: 631–41). Writing about the aesthetic possibilities of the American city in direct and muscular prose, Dreiser did something new "in the teeth of his moralistic superego, which kept telling him the city and riches were evil." In *Dark Mirror: The Sense of Injustice in Modern European and American Literature* (Fordham) Richard Clark Sterne considers *An American Tragedy* with Martin du Gard's *Jean Barois,* Bertolt Brecht's *The Caucasian Chalk Circle,* and Arthur Koestler's *Darkness at Noon* as examples of varying interpretations of Darwinism by modern social writers (pp. 108–67).

Two miscellaneous items merit attention. In his carefully documented "Dreiser's *'Genius'* in the Making: Composition and Revision" (*SB* 47: 230–52) Louis J. Oldani sheds light on the first edition of *The "Genius"* (1915) by tracing Dreiser's process of construction, beginning with the earliest but abortive draft of 1900 and proceeding to the complete holograph of 1910–11 through successive typescripts and revisions to the final key differences between galley proofs and the published novel. William A. Tieck offers an "apparatus" to accompany Dreiser's *An Amateur Laborer* in *The Locale of Theodore Dreiser's Kingsbridge Experience* (Kingsbridge Historical Society), a documentary guide to the book's topographical details and sites. This guide comes with a fascinating map (adapted by computer from real estate maps of the time).

It was a meager year for Sinclair Lewis after the past two, but new editions of *The Job* (Nebraska), ed. Maureen Honey, and *Ann Vickers* (Nebraska), ed. Nan Bauer Maglin, both with fresh and competent introductions, as well as *The Selected Short Stories of Sinclair Lewis* (Dee), with an introduction by James Tuttleton, should spur some activity on the critical front. Essays of note in *The Sinclair Lewis Society Newsletter* are James M. Hutchisson's "Edith Wharton and Grace Lewis" (3, i: 5–6), which details Wharton's admiration for *Grace* Lewis's novel, and Jacqueline Tavernier-Courbin's "Harvey Taylor and Jack London's Purchase of Sinclair Lewis's Plots: A Posthumous Saga" (3, ii: 6–8), which recounts the convoluted tale of the story plots London bought from Lewis. The *Newsletter* also publishes abstracts of papers presented at conferences and symposia.

Published late but certainly welcome is Hutchisson's "'All of Us Americans at 46': The Making of Sinclair Lewis' *Babbitt*" (*JML* 18 [1992]: 95–114), an exhaustive and perceptive analysis of the notes Lewis prepared and the manuscripts he revised at three stages in the creation of *Babbitt*. In addition to his splendid scholarship, Hutchisson also includes six illustrations from the Lewis papers. Sally E. Parry finds a new reason for the persistent coupling of Sinclair Lewis and Upton Sinclair in "Upton-Sinclair-Lewis: The Crossed Paths of Two American Reformer-Novelists" (*Connecticut Review* 16, i: 81–92), her proficient examination of the intersection of their lives and fortunes. Despite personal differences, Lewis and Sinclair shared progressive ideals and distress at the growing power of business and special interest groups which colored their work and their actions. A new edition of Sinclair's 1935 *I, Candidate for Governor, and How I Got Licked* (Calif.) is out.

v Jack London and John Dos Passos

It remains to be seen if *The Portable Jack London* (Viking), ed. Earle Labor, will do for London what Malcolm Cowley's *Portable Faulkner* did for Faulkner, but this splendid collection of stories, nonfiction, letters, and the complete *The Call of the Wild* with Labor's erudite, convincing introduction and notes just might. Labor's valuable annotated bibliography of critical works includes Franklin Walker's "articulate and definitive" *Jack London and the Klondike* (Huntington Library), which is now available in a new edition with Labor's introductory comments. Completing a literary hat trick, Labor is also joint author with Jeanne Campbell Reesman of a revised edition of his original 1974 *Jack London* (TUSAS 230). Incorporating new scholarship, this impressive study rectifies misconceptions about London's literary strengths and the quality of his late work. In a new chapter Labor and Reesman discuss at length four important neglected stories. Their brief final chapter summarizes everything needed to justify London's place in the canon.

A new addition to the Twayne Masterwork Series is Jacqueline Tavernier-Courbin's The Call of the Wild: *A Naturalistic Romance* (Twayne), which thoughtfully reads this "world classic" as a naturalist, archetypal, mythic, and romantic novel. *The Call of the Wild* is credible as a "tale of devolution" because London maintains an amoral and objective stance; we unconsciously identify with Buck specifically *because* he is not human; Buck's journey echoes the Myth of the Hero, the Pastoral Myth and the Myth of Love; and, finally, in true romantic tradition, *The Call of the Wild* "dramatizes a human dream of adventure, freedom and personal freedom."

In his incisive and thoughtful study, *The Ethos of Romance,* William J. Scheick reads "A Thousand Deaths" as an early political allegory in which London uses the ethical mode of the romance genre to "urge a psychological revision in our perception of human existence," pushing the genre to its "gruesome limits" to demonstrate the disintegration of both the proscriptive patriarchal model and the social definition of romance. In "Gender and Genre: Nature, Naturalism, and Authority in *The Sea-Wolf*" (*SAF* 22: 131–48) Christopher Gair examines the "anti-essentialist impulse" in *The Sea-Wolf* that questions the absolute separation of male and female and links this impulse to the role of the aesthetic at the time to explain how London "reinscribes authorial and gender roles within hegemonic American culture." Charging that critics miss London's obsession with sexual difference by focusing on androgyny or masculine conflation, Andrew J. Furer, "Jack London's New Woman: A Little Lady with a Big Stick" (*SAF* 22: 185–214), explains that London constructs models of "New Womanhood" which insist on an essential femininity and heterosexual attractiveness in physically powerful, capable, intelligent, economically independent women. In *The Little Lady of the Big House* London finally came to terms with the tragic implications of women free "in every way but sex and passion" when faced with the entrenched power of inherited social forms.

The Iron Heel inspired two critics this year. Alessandro Portelli identifies the significant "gaps," "intervals," and "blanks" created by the stratification of voices in *The Iron Heel,* points out that all the crucial events take place within these gaps, and proposes that London's "proletarian revolution" completes an American paradigm of missing revolutions found in Irving, Bellamy, and Hawthorne ("Jack London's Missing Revolution: *The Iron Heel,*" pp. 247–53 in *The Text and the Voice*). By tracing the discourse that London uses to describe Ernest Everhard and qualify his message, Francis Shor, "*The Iron Heel*'s Marginal(ized) Utopia" (*Extrapolation* 35: 211–29), reveals connections between marginalization and utopianism and locates in London's marginalia his perspective on utopian possibilities for power and gender codes.

Taking the title of his groundbreaking study, *The White Logic*, from *John Barleycorn*, John W. Crowley explores the historical formation of concepts of habitual drunkenness and their bearing on the social construction of gender roles, while combining traditional literary criticism and literary history to define "the drunk narrative: a mode of fiction that expresses the conjunction of modernism and alcoholism in a pervasive ideology of despair." London is "the first American writer to drink in the modern spirit" and his book "the prototype for the modernist drunk narrative."

A flurry of activity on the Dos Passos front produced seven items, five on aspects of war. In "'Revolt However Brews': An Unpublished Dos Passos Letter" (*ELN* 32, ii: 53–65) Neale Reinitz shares his 1988 discovery of a seven-page unnoticed and hitherto unpublished letter written by Dos Passos to a Harvard classmate, Roland Jackson. Mark A. Graves in "A World Based on Brotherhood: Male Bonding, Male Representation, and the War Novels of John Dos Passos" (*CLAJ* 38: 228–46) shows how Dos Passos's war novels, particularly *Three Soldiers,* question traditional models of personal and national masculine gender identity and examine the disruption of traditional gender barriers and the reordering of male homosociability on the western front as "a logical outgrowth of the teamwork, loyalty, and camaraderie encouraged in nineteenth-century life."

William E. Matsen's *The Great War and the American Novel: Versions of Reality and the Writer's Craft in Selected Fiction of the First World War* (Peter Lang) examines novels by Dos Passos, Thomas Boyd, William March, and Ernest Hemingway to trace a development from the "near-journalistic narratives" of "witness and testimony" of the early '20s to the final, more crafted war literature of the late '20s and '30s (pp. 96–108). The contrast between "documentary (autobiographical) and fictional renderings of the war experience" and the formal devices used to create these rhetorical effects is Evelyn Cobley's focus in *Representing War: Form and Ideology in First World War Narratives* (Toronto, 1993). By choosing an *openly* fictional form, war novelists such as Dos Passos indicate a greater willingness to shape the raw material and thus give more weight to conceptual abstraction and less to immediate experience (pp. 155–63).

In "The Literary Initiation of John Dos Passos" (*PBSA* 88: 87–92) Stephen Enniss argues that publication delays and public fatigue with the subject of war, not its antiwar message, caused the poor sales of *One Man's Initiation—1917.*

In "Whitman, Dos Passos, and 'Our Storybook Democracy,'" pp. 217–25 in Ed Folsom, ed., *Walt Whitman: The Centennial Essays* (Iowa), Kenneth M. Price locates Whitman's influence on Dos Passos in his fusion of formal literary categories and the mixing of poetry and prose in *U.S.A.,* and he examines the work to illustrate how Dos Passos conceived of himself as "an American modernist" committed to the diversity of American culture. Finally, Brian McHale counters the principles of "classical" literary dialectology with a close reading of the complete repertoire of children's language features he finds in passages from *U.S.A.,* for which Dos Passos drew on the baby-talk stereotype ("Child as Ready-Made: Baby-Talk and the Language of Dos Passos's Children in *U.S.A.*," pp. 202–24 in *Infant Tongues: The Voice of the Child in Literature* [Wayne State], ed. Elizabeth Goodenough et al.).

vi Nella Larsen, W. E. B. Du Bois, Jean Toomer, and Others

Larsen comes first this year because Thadious M. Davis's long-awaited *Nella Larsen, Novelist of the Harlem Renaissance: A Woman's Life Unveiled* (LSU) has arrived and lives up to its promise. In this meticulously researched, engrossing narrative Davis presents the details of Larsen's life traced through a "quagmire of written records and oral testimonies"; explores Larsen's development as a female African American artist; discusses the cultural and racial history that affected her work and life; and brilliantly restores Larsen to her rightful place among the luminaries of the Harlem Renaissance. Thanks to Richard Newman, the texts of two rare holograph letters from Larsen to Edward Wasserman are provided in "Two Letters from Nella Larsen" (*Biblion* 2: 124–29).

Angela Hewett locates *Quicksand* among texts that try to find something utopian within commercial works designed for a female audience in "The 'Great Company of *Real* Women': Modernist Women Writers and Mass Commercial Culture" (*Rereading Modernism,* pp. 351–72). In "*Writing Up the New Negro:* Construction of Consumer Desire in the Twenties" (*JAmS* 28: 191–207) Chip Rhodes compares *Quicksand* with DuBose Heyward's "exemplary [and conservative] Negrotarian novel *Porgy*" to illustrate how Larsen's novel opens up "radical possibilities" that *Porgy* endeavors so hard to defuse. Questions of racial indeterminacy and of geographical place in *Quicksand* become one in Jeffrey Gray's analysis of Helga's shuttling movement between Europe and the United States, which mirrors her movement between black and white and corresponds to "the binarism in which the African-American novel of the time found itself trapped" ("Essence and the Mulatto Traveler: Europe as Embodiment in Nella Larsen's *Quicksand*" [*Novel* 27: 257–70]).

In "Blackness, Betrayal, and Childhood: Race and Identity in Nella Larsen's *Passing*" (*CLAJ* 38: 31–45) Merrill Horton suggests that racial, social, and gender issues in *Passing* are all reducible to racial identity and have their genesis in Larsen's childhood and the childhood games of her characters. Mary Condé notes in "Passing in the Fiction of Jessie Red-mon Fauset and Nella Larsen" (*YES* 24: 94–104) that both novelists use Europe as a metaphor for characters' betrayal of their own identities; passing is *not* a moving away, but a "moving in, and a seizing of those rights to which all American women . . . are entitled." Beth A. McCoy's persuasive " 'Is This Really What You Wanted Me To Be?': The Daughter's Disintegration in Jesse Redmon Fauset's *There Is Confusion*" (*MFS* 40: 101–17) reads *There Is Confusion* "against the grain" to reveal competing narratives that destabilize and question conservative ideology and constitute "an intricate negotiation of a black woman's relationship not only to race, gender, class, and sexuality, but also to art in the time of the New Negro."

This has been another banner year for W. E. B. Du Bois. Keith E. Byerman makes a major contribution to Du Bois scholarship with *Seizing the Word: History, Art, and Self in the Work of W. E. B. Du Bois* (Georgia), the first comprehensive reading of the whole of the Du Bois canon and the first to treat Du Bois primarily as a literary figure. Byerman's clearly written study follows the interaction of the personal, the intellectual, and the political throughout Du Bois's career, positions *The Souls of Black Folk* as a master text which establishes his famous tropes—double consciousness and the veil—and, in superbly lucid analyses that draw on Lacan's Law of the Father and Erikson's work on identity, reads successive works as elaborations of this "master narrative." A look at the human side of Du Bois can be found in Mark D. Higbee's "A Letter from W. E. B. Du Bois to His Daughter Yolande, Dated 'Moscow, December 10, 1958' " (*JNegroHist* 78 [1993]: 188–95), which also provides insight into the creative process by which the posthumously published *Autobiography of W. E. B. Du Bois* was written; in splendid notes, Higbee indicates whole sentences from the letter that were incorporated un-altered into the autobiography.

A special Du Bois issue of *The Massachusetts Review* (35, ii) guest-edited by Robert Gooding-Williams, contains seven substantial essays and David W. Blight's thoughtful comments on David Levering Lewis's 1993 biography, *W. E. B. Du Bois: Biography of a Race, 1868–1919* (see *ALS 1993*, p. 220). In "Negotiating Claims of Race and Rights: Du Bois, Emerson, and The Critique of Liberal Nationalism" (pp. 169–201) Anita Haya Goldman argues that the pattern of contradiction in Du Bois's writings represents a critique of liberal (Emersonian) American dis-courses on national identity; Gooding-Williams, "Du Bois's Counter-Sublime" (pp. 202–24), declares "Of Alexander Crummell" a master-piece of indirection that elaborates Du Bois's critique of Crummell's 1885 repudiation of slave culture and of the alienated model of racial leader-ship which Crummell personified; Dale E. Peterson, "Notes from the Underworld: Dostoevsky, Du Bois, and the Discovery of Ethnic Soul" (pp. 225–48), delineates the affinities between *Notes from the House of the Dead* and *The Souls of Black Folk* to "dis-cover" the "devalued and veiled expressive culture of an ethnic majority still in bondage to the sovereign contempt of modern Western civilization"; and Ronald A. T. Judy, "The New Black Aesthetic and W. E. B. Du Bois, or Hephaestus, Limping" (pp. 249–82), concentrates on the significance of *The Souls of Black Folk* for the New Black Aesthetic (NBA). Puzzling over Du Bois's virtual neglect of the Spanish Civil War in *Dusk of Dawn*, Kathryne V. Lindberg in "W. E. B. Du Bois's *Dusk of Dawn* and James Yates's *Mississippi to Madrid* or 'What Goes Around Comes Around' in *Autobiography*" (pp. 283–308) discovers ways in which James Yates appropriates and nuances Du Bois's "radical and accomodationist lives" to reclaim Spain for "the Civil Rights and radical '60's" in *Mississippi to Madrid* (pp. 283–308). And Brook Thomas in "Schlesinger and Du Bois on the Old New World Order: A History of the Canon Wars" (pp. 309–18) traces the consequences for "cultural politics" of differences between Arthur M. Schlesinger, Jr.'s and Du Bois's attitudes toward the former USSR. William E. Cain also inquires into the Soviet Union's attraction for Du Bois, tracing the trajectory of his political thought to ponder the meanings of socialism and communism in the "struggle of oppressed peoples against Western imperialism" in "From Liberalism to Commu-nism: The Political Thought of W. E. B. Du Bois" (*Cultures of United States Imperialism*, pp. 45–73).

David Blight's "W. E. B. Du Bois and the Struggle for American Historical Memory," pp. 45–71 in Geneviève Fabre and Robert O'Meally, eds., *History and Memory in African-American Culture* (Oxford) is a thorough and important analysis of *Black Reconstruction in America,* in which Du Bois challenged and confronted the "tragic flaws" and false assumptions in the "master narrative" of American history. Paul Gilroy devotes a chapter of his *The Black Atlantic: Modernity and Double Consciousness* (Harvard, 1993) to issues of "travel, movement, displacement, and relocation" that emerge from Du Bois's response to the varieties of racism that deny the historical character and the integrity of black cultures (pp. 111–45).

In an impressive reading of *The Souls of Black Folk* as a bildungs-biographie Shamoon Zamir reinterprets the interplay of its various elements as a critical investigation of the optimism and confidence of "The Talented Tenth" (" 'The Sorrow Songs'/'Song of Myself': Du Bois, the Crisis of Leadership, and Prophetic Imagination," pp. 145–66 in *The Black Columbiad*). Racism and violence constantly thwart the uplift program and lead to a rupture of the prophetic model of leadership; in its place emerges a poetic and prophetic imagination, represented by Du Bois himself and distinct from the American transcendentalism of Emerson or Whitman.

Jan Miller's "Annotated Bibliography of the Washington-Du Bois Controversy" (*Journal of Black Studies* 25: 250–72) compiles a useful list of 91 entries, but only one essay is on the perennial topic this year. Stanley O. Gaines, Jr., and Edward S. Reed take Booker T. Washington's "conciliatory stance regarding ethnic relations" as a starting point for exploring the differences and similarities between the theories of Gordon W. Allport and Du Bois in "Two Social Psychologies of Prejudice: Gordon W. Allport, W. E. B. Du Bois, and the Legacy of Booker T. Washington" (*Journal of Black Psychology* 20: 8–28). Charles Lemert asks why Du Bois has not mattered more to sociologists in "A Classic from the Other Side of the Veil: Du Bois's *Souls of Black Folk*" (*Sociological Quarterly* 35: 383–96), then speculates that "had the most basic concept [the veil drawn across cultures] in Du Bois's sociology come to matter, sociology's investment in its own way of seeing things darkly would have been at risk."

Several good essays discuss Jean Toomer. Naming Toomer "one of the fathers of modern African American literature," Friederike Hajek in "The Change of Literary Authority in the Harlem Renaissance: Jean

Toomer's *Cane*" (*Black Columbiad,* pp. 185–90) demonstrates that Toomer preserved the waning oral tradition as a future source of literary tradition and imagination by transcribing it into a written text which fictionalized the historical process of fundamental cultural loss—and did so as he simultaneously encoded the crisis of changing cultural authority in *Cane*'s "blues" structure: statement, variation, and response. Laura Doyle's strong, feminist analysis of *Cane* focuses on the mother figures in its marginal spaces who "resist the role of reproducing racial, sexual, and metaphysical borders" (*Bordering on the Body: The Racial Matrix of Modern Fiction and Culture* [Oxford], pp. 81–109). George B. Hutchinson's essay, "The Whitman Legacy and the Harlem Renaissance" (*Walt Whitman: The Centennial Essays,* ed. Ed Folsom [Iowa], pp. 201–16), traces the responses of Toomer, James Weldon Johnson, and Alain Locke to outline Whitman's legacy to " 'New Negro' poetic theory, literary language, cultural nationalist ideology, sexuality, and spirituality." Johnson joins Charles Waddell Chesnutt and Paul Laurence Dunbar as examples of the vagaries of anthology editors and their effect on the canon in Keneth Kinnamon's "Three Black Writers and the Anthologized Canon" (*American Realism and the Canon,* pp. 143–53).

Two new anthologies will draw both scholarly and general audiences. *Classic Fiction of the Harlem Renaissance,* ed. William L. Andrews (Oxford), collects stories by Zora Neale Hurston, Rudolph Fisher, and Langston Hughes, major selections from *Cane, Home to Harlem,* and *Quicksand,* a chapter from Wallace Thurman's *Infants of the Spring,* and Fisher's "Introduction to Contemporary Harlemese, Expurgated and Abridged" (1928). *Within the Circle: An Anthology of African American Literary Criticism from the Harlem Renaissance to the Present,* ed. Angelyn Mitchell (Duke), is just as inclusive as its title and also has the advantage of Mitchell's fine introduction.

The complexity of Alain Locke's thought is a constant challenge to scholars. Johnny Washington defines a new academic field he calls "destiny studies" in *A Journey into the Philosophy of Alain Locke* (Greenwood), with a comprehensive reading of Locke's philosophical works that reveals just how prophetic Locke was about the destiny of America's multiethnic society. Two writers discover European influences on Locke's aesthetics. In "Nationalism and Pluralism in Alain Locke's Social Philosophy," pp. 103–19 in Lawrence Foster and Patricia Herzog, eds., *Defending Diversity* (Mass.) Tommy Lee Lott reminds us that Locke adapted Johann G. Herder's ideas of cultural nationalism to advocate African

American folk art as a source of inspiration and as a basis for higher art, then questions Locke's belief that such a cultural nationalism would lead to integration and cultural pluralism. In "From Berlin to Harlem: Felix von Luschan, Alain Locke, and the New Negro" (*The Black Columbiad,* pp. 174–84) Malgorzata Irek announces that the liberal race theories underlying the Harlem Renaissance originated in Germany with Felix von Lushan and fellow anthropologist Rudolf Virchow, and that Lushan—not Picasso—first described objects from Benin as "works of art ranking with the best European achievements."

Claude McKay's prose and his poetry have one essay each. In "Finger-Snapping to Train-Dancing and Back Again: The Development of a Jazz Style in African American Prose" (*YES* 24: 105–16) Alan J. Rice begins with *Home to Harlem* to show how African American writers from McKay to Toni Morrison use alliteration, antiphony, nonstandard punctuation, signifying, and repetition ("riffing") to create "jazzy passages of great rhythmic complexities." Focusing on "Look Within," "Tiger," and "Negro's Tragedy," James R. Keller in " 'A chafing savage, down the decent street': The Politics of Compromise in Claude McKay's Protest Sonnets" (*AAR* 28: 447–56) contends that by joining tradition and dissent McKay "was attempting to create a space in which to challenge white America's claim to cultural superiority" at its most vulnerable points—the ideological disparities evident in its racial inequalities and injustices.

Two final items: the influence of *The Messenger* on issues of racial and cultural amalgamation and George Schuyler's influence on *The Messenger* occupy George Hutchinson in "Mediating 'Race' and 'Nation': The Cultural Politics of *The Messenger*" (*AAR* 38: 531–48), and Schuyler's reaction to comparison with H. L. Mencken enlivens Harry McKinley Williams's fanciful "Why George Schuyler Disliked the Sobriquet 'The Negro's Mencken': A Note on 'Racial' Sensitivity" (*Menckeniana* 130: 5–9).

vii Immigrants, Exiles, and Western Writers

I begin this section with Gert Buelens's important essay, "The New Man and the Mediator: (Non-)Remembrance in Jewish-American Immigrant Narrative" (*Memory, Narrative, and Identity,* pp. 89–113), which focuses on representations of the American Jew "as a rightful aspirant to an American identity," tracing "new manhood and mediatorship" through

Ezra Brudno's *The Fugitive,* Edward Steiner's *The Mediator: A Tale of the Old World and the New,* Louis Pope Gratacap's *Benjamin the Jew,* Elias Tobenkin's *Witte Arrives,* Elizabeth Stern's *My Mother and I* and *I Am a Woman—and a Jew,* and Mary Antin's "key text" *The Promised Land.* In "A Geography of Conversion: Dialogical Boundaries of Self in Antin's *Promised Land,"* pp. 167–87 in Kathleen Ashley et al., eds., *Autobiography and Postmodernism* (Mass.), feminist Kirsten Wasson employs Bakhtinian theories to locate the tension in Antin's response to "the American code of transformation." Betty Bergland objects to the omission from later editions of *The Promised Land* of 18 photographs that constitute an integral part of the original 1912 text, and she reproduces 12 of them to demonstrate that they lead to a "radically altered reading of the narrative that implies a critique of the very discourse [Antin] presumably celebrated" ("Rereading Photographs and Narratives in Ethnic Autobiography: Memory and Subjectivity in Mary Antin's *The Promised Land,"* pp. 45–87 in *Memory, Narrative, and Identity*). Although Antin's *The Promised Land* and Agnes Smedley's *Daughter of Earth* seem to provide apparently contradictory versions of the American Dream, Arázazu Usandizaga in "Two Versions of the American Dream: Mary Antin's *The Promised Land* and Agnes Smedley's *Daughter of Earth"* (*Deferring a Dream,* pp. 37–47) explains that they both end up deferring their explicit intentions of dealing with the ways in which personal destinies are affected by specifically American political events and situations because they are shackled by a tradition of women's silence in public and private matters.

Laura Wexler begins "Looking at Yezierska," pp. 153–81 in Judith R. Baskin, ed., *Women of the Word: Jewish Women and Jewish Writing* (Wayne State), with a photograph of the young Anzia Yezierska to "read" the story of her personal and artistic choices as "a struggle with formalities" and explicates *Bread Givers* as a complex work in which her characters' problematic relations with men represent alternative moral relations that immigrant Jewish women might adopt toward Jewish history. Janet Burstein's thoughtful "Mother at the Center: Jewish American Women's Stories of the 1920s" (pp. 183–96 in the same volume) studies the central narrative figure of the Jewish-American mother in texts of the 1920s. Faithful to constraining traditional roles of self-sacrifice and self-abnegation, these Jewish characters bear little resemblance to "new women" in non-Jewish stories.

Abraham Cahan's was the only male version of the immigrant narrative to receive any attention, and that in three essays, two in *American Realism and the Canon.* Sanford E. Marovitz, "Romance and Realism: Children of the New Colossus and the Jewish Struggle Within" (pp. 102–25), identifies anti-Semitic hostility and the ramifications of mass immigration as distinguishing themes in Jewish-American realism and explores these concerns in Cahan's *The Rise of David Levinsky, Yekl: A Tale of the New York Ghetto,* and *The Imported Bridegroom and Other Tales of the New York Ghetto.* Susan K. Harris, "Problems of Representation in Turn-of-the-Century Immigrant Fiction" (pp. 127–41), offers a close reading of "The Imported Bridegroom" to elucidate problems created by formal and political factors for immigrant writers; only with the advent of modernism were these writers able to "break through the structures of American narrative forms and create immigrant characters who spoke for themselves." In "Abraham Cahan, Capitalist; David Levinsky, Socialist," pp. 134–52 in Philip Goldstein, ed., *Styles of Cultural Activism: From Theory and Pedagogy to Women, Indians, and Communism* (Delaware) Richard S. Pressman theorizes that despite his intention to demonstrate the effects of rampant capitalism on Jewish immigrants, Cahan's power, prestige, and wealth countered his long-standing commitment to socialism, causing him to fall back on "a mystical abstraction," tragic suffering.

Annette White-Parks has had a busy year—and we should all be grateful! After nine years of detective work, she resurrects the founder of the Chinese North American literary tradition in *Sui Sin Far/Edith Maude Eaton: A Literary Biography* (Illinois), a first-rate, absorbing biography that sets the standard for interracial scholarship and brilliantly interweaves biography and literary analysis. With Amy Ling, White-Parks has also coedited Sui Sin Far's Mrs. Spring Fragrance *and Other Writings* (Illinois), which makes available two dozen of the original 37 stories in *Mrs. Spring Fragrance* and a representative sampling of Sui Sin Far's uncollected essays, journalistic articles, and short stories. This landmark contribution is further enhanced by Ling's and White-Parks's fine introductory essays. White-Parks also coedited *Tricksterism in Turn-of-the-Century American Literature* (New England), with Elizabeth Ammons, and contributed " 'We Wear the Mask': Sui Sin Far as One Example of Trickster Authorship" (pp. 1–19), in which she lists the trickster strategies Sui Sin Far used to write against the racial and cultural ideologies of her time. In the same collection Yuko Matsukawa's "Cross-Dressing and Cross-Naming: Decoding Onoto Watanna" (pp. 106–25) proposes that there is more to Sui Sin Far's sister than meets the eye and "decodes" the "culturally and literarily constructed facade" of Onoto Watanna/Winnifred Eaton to reveal a subversive writer who crosses cultural lines to challenge the "conventional boundaries" of ethnicity and authenticity. In "Sui Sin Far and Onoto Watanna: Two Early Chinese-Canadian Authors" (*CanL* 140: 50–58) James Doyle stakes a Canadian claim to the Eaton sisters and catalogs affinities linking Maude to Pauline Johnson and Winnifred to Archie Belaney. Amy Ling's "Reading Her/stories Against His/stories in Early Chinese American Literature" (*American Realism and the Canon*, pp. 69–86), a close analysis of four texts (Lee Yan Phou's *When I Was a Boy in China,* Sui Sin Far's "Leaves from the Mental Portfolio of an Eurasian," Yung Wing's *My Life in China and America,* and Winnifred Eaton's *Me, A Book of Remembrance*), finds that the men describe what they have done, while the women express who they are.

Patricia Okker's "Native American Literatures and the Canon: The Case of Zitkala-Ša" (*American Realism and the Canon,* pp. 87–101) advances the work of Zitkala-Ša (Gertrude Simmons Bonnin) as an example of the difficult and problematic process Native American texts have in gaining entrance to literary anthologies. In " 'A Second Tongue': The Trickster's Voice in the Works of Zitkala-Ša" (*Tricksterism in Turn-of-the-Century American Literature,* pp. 46–60) Jeanne Smith describes Zitkala-Ša's strategy in writing from "the gap between tradition and assimilation" which marginalized her in Lakota, pan-Indian, *and* non-Indian circles and empowered her to transplant oral Lakota trickster tales into written English. Alanna Kathleen Brown explores trickster energy as a strategy that Mourning Dove employed "to survive with an Indian identity intact," and she analyzes Mourning Dove's stories to reveal how she uses the oral storytelling tradition of Native Americans to transcribe their ongoing story of survival into English ("Mourning Dove, Trickster Energy, and Assimilation-Period Native Texts," pp. 126–36 in the same volume). In "Looking through the Glass Darkly: The Editorialized Mourning Dove," pp. 274–90 in Arnold Krupat, ed., *New Voices in Native American Literary Criticism* (Smithsonian, 1993), Brown takes a look at the relationships between Mourning Dove and each of her white male collaborators and finds that "we still hobble our way toward letting a Native American storyteller speak her own truth in her own way." Tiffany Ana López introduces a Mexican-American woman writer to this chapter's diverse array in "María Cristina Mena: Turn of the Century La

Malinche, and Other Tales of Cultural (Re)Construction" (*Tricksterism in Turn-of-the-Century American Literature,* pp. 21–45) with an intriguing discussion of Mena's deliberately female trickster figures.

Mary Austin's efforts to awaken a "transformational childlike sense of wonder in her audience" are the focus of William J. Scheick's careful examination of *The Basket Woman* (*The Ethos of Romance,* pp. 125–34). Austin's text disguises philosophical and aesthetic subtleties in "simplicity of narrative manner and mythic implication of narrative matter." In "Claiming Female Space: Mary Austin's Western Landscape," pp. 119–32 in Leonard Engel, ed., *The Big Empty: Essays on Western Landscapes as Narrative* (New Mexico), Cynthia Taylor attributes Austin's artistic vision to her conviction that the creative spirit of the Southwest speaks with a woman's voice; her landscape is neither exploited nor exploitable and subverts male-defined values and power relationships. To compare Austin's landscape with that of a male contemporary, see *Writing the Western Landscape* (Beacon), ed. Ann H. Zwinger, which contains excerpts from *Earth Horizon* and *The Land of Journeys' Ending* and from John Muir's *The Grand Cañon of the Colorado* and *Travels in Alaska.*

Two of this year's essays offer diametrically opposed visions of the possibilities for women in a patriarchal society. In "Through the Golden Gate: Madness and the Persephone Myth in Gertrude Atherton's 'The Foghorn' " (*Images of Persephone: Feminist Readings in Western Literature,* pp. 84–98) Melissa McFarland Pennell recovers a valuable neglected text in which Atherton revises the Persephone myth to explore the effects of oppression; the narrator achieves freedom in the underworld of madness, but the price is the loss of her voice. On the other hand, demonstrating that even in the most constraining gender paradigms a girl can grow up to be a builder, Ann Romines convincingly argues that Laura Ingalls Wilder perpetuates the traditions of both her parents by writing the Little House books with her daughter ("Writing the *Little House:* The Architecture of a Series" [*GPQ* 14: 107–15]); "in a *serial* context established by Pa and the patriarchal vagaries of manifest destiny, Ma Ingalls taught that enduring houses could be built of order and words."

Interest in Zane Grey never entirely withers away. Struck by the singular set of bizarre motifs shared by Arthur Conan Doyle's *A Study in Scarlet* and Grey's *Riders of the Purple Sage,* Lee Mitchell competently examines "what is hidden" behind traditional formal features of narrative that serve an ideological function and discovers that "the enduring popularity of most popular texts lies in their capacity to resolve ideologi-

cal conflicts far removed . . . from the immediate context of their own
production" ("White Slaves and Purple Sage: Plotting Sex in Zane Grey's
West" [*AmLH* 6: 234–64]). Kent Oswald considers factors in Grey's
continuing popularity in "Critics Lambasted Zane Grey's Western Novels, But His Millions of Readers Couldn't Care Less" (*Wild West* 7, iv: 12–
16), and in "Some Comments on 'The Evil of the West' " (*Western Forum*
33: 3–4) Richard A. Bartlett notes Grey's awareness of the "dark under-
side" of the Western movement, but correlates his plots in which good
always prevails with the emphasis on "glorious achievements" recorded
in accounts by contemporary historians. Karl Doerry's more extensive
discussion of the tension between utopian expectations and the reality of
the West, "The American West: Conventions and Inventions in Art and
Literature," pp. 127–53 in Richard Francaviglia and David Narrett, eds.,
Essays on the Changing Images of the Southwest (Texas A & M), investigates the image of the West shaped in art and literature by Easterners
Frederic Remington, Zane Grey, and Owen Wister. Marcus Klein's
intriguing study, *Easterns, Westerns, and Private Eyes: American Matters,
1870–1900* (Wisconsin), includes a chapter on Wister (pp. 109–30) which
proposes that *The Virginian*, "the essential western," actually returns the
now armed and dangerous hero to the East. Three new studies in the
Western Writers Series belong to this chapter: Abe C. Ravitz's *Rex Beach*
(BSWWS 113), Lawrence V. Tagg's *Harold Bell Wright* (BSWWS 115),
and Norris Yates's *Caroline Lockhart* (BSWWS 116).

viii General Works and Additional Authors

David Minter's vision of the United States as "a still unruly, shifting
cultural scene" and the novel as "a still unruly, shifting genre" informs his
splendid, sometimes irreverent, and always thought-provoking study, *A
Cultural History of the American Novel.* Minter brings the authors and
texts covered by this chapter (and many others), cultural events, and
readers into relationships that raise complex questions about history,
culture, art, and literature, and that address issues of class, race, gender,
and ethnicity to capture the excitement of this richly productive period.
Elizabeth Ammons draws on this very richness and diversity to argue
that the establishment of a "white, male, and American-born" canon has
less to do with objective criteria than with "racism and misogyny" in
"Men of Color, Women, and Uppity Art at the Turn of the Century"
(*American Realism and the Canon,* pp. 22–33). Richard Martin's goal of

recovering "a significant corpus of forgotten or ignored texts" is admirably achieved in his *Reading Life, Writing Fiction: An Introduction to Novels by American Women, 1920–1940* (Peter Lang), which concentrates on women who "fictionalized their own private experiences and concerns" and provides an analytical introduction to 100 novels by more than 30 writers.

Henry Regnery's *Creative Chicago: From* The Chap-Book *to the University* (Chicago Historical Bookworks, 1993) tackles the question, "Why has literary culture . . . not taken permanent hold in Chicago?" and reflects on writers from Cather, Dreiser, Harriet Monroe, and Floyd Dell to Frank Baum and Edgar Rice Burroughs in his thoughtful answers. In a related article Guy Szuberla examines the settlement house novel as a Chicago phenomenon that blended radical politics with conservative cultural beliefs and traditional gender values in "Peattie's *Precipice* and the 'Settlement House' Novel" (*Midamerica* 20 [1993]: 59–75).

Popular fiction has become popular among scholars seeking to investigate cultural definitions of gender roles. Edward Stratemeyer and his Syndicate's role in creating male cultural models produced several essays: Francis J. Molson's "The Boy Inventor in American Series Fiction: 1900–1930" (*JPC* 28: 31–48); Rocco J. Musemeche's "The Rover Boys at School . . . Again, Again, and Again" (*Newsboy* 31, iv [1993]: 12–14); and John T. Dizer's "How Tom and Franklin Got from Allison to Street & Smith (with Side Trips)" (*Newsboy* 31, ii [1993]: 15–18). Deidre Johnson has discovered "Another Syndicate Pseudonym?" (*DNR* 63: 117–18), and Anne Scott MacLeod devotes a chapter (pp. 40–48) of *American Childhood: Essays on Children's Literature of the Nineteenth and Twentieth Centuries* (Georgia) to the influence of Stratemeyer's Nancy Drew. In *Magazines for the Millions: Gender and Commerce in* The Ladies' Home Journal *and the* Saturday Evening Post, *1880–1910* (SUNY) Helen Damon-Moore combines primary sources and current theories to show how the great mass-market magazines shaped modern ideals of femininity and masculinity. Martha Banta surveys the influence of Frederick Winslow Taylor's theories of productivity on gender roles and fiction in *Taylored Lives: Narrative Productions in the Age of Taylor, Veblen, and Ford* (Chicago, 1993) and looks at Dreiser, Lewis, Dell, Sinclair, Yezierska, and Ida Tarbell among others. Patricia Raub's *Yesterday's Stories: Popular Women's Novels of the Twenties and Thirties* (Greenwood) examines the basic beliefs affirmed in fiction written by and for women between the wars to uncover values widely held by middle-class women of the era. In

"Mashes, Smashes, Crushes and Raves: Woman-to-Woman Relationships in Popular Women's College Fiction, 1895–1915" (*NWSA Journal* 6: 48–68) Sherrie A. Inness's intelligent discussion focuses on relatively unknown woman-authored "college texts" that serve as a "barometer of changing social attitudes towards women's homoaffectionate relationships at the turn of the century."

In *Being a Boy Again: Autobiography and the American Boy Book* (Alabama) Marcia Jacobson finds "a particular crisis of male adulthood" behind each of the boy books that she examines, including Booth Tarkington's *Penrod* (pp. 133–59). Michael S. Kimmel refers to works by Zane Grey, Upton Sinclair, and Edgar Rice Burroughs to examine turn-of-the-century masculine anxiety and the concomitant rediscovery of the male body as a "gendered testing ground . . . especially in consumerist fantasies of physical prowess" in "Consuming Manhood: The Feminization of American Culture and the Recreation of the Male Body, 1832–1920" (*MQR* 33: 7–35). "Science Fiction, the World's Fair, and the Prosthetics of Empire, 1910–1915" (*Cultures of United States Imperialism*, pp. 129–63), sets forth Bill Brown's argument that the obsession with "a perfected, eugenic American body" in the science fiction of Burroughs and others serves their agenda of validating this body as "a transcendent, metasocial guarantee of wholeness, of totality."

Joanne E. Gates's enlightening *Elizabeth Robins, 1862–1952: Actress, Novelist, Feminist* (Alabama) draws on Robins's vast collection of private papers to establish her as an early feminist and writer whose fiction shares characteristics with James, Wharton, and Cather. Bonnie Haaland focuses on Emma Goldman's prescient ideas about birth control, voluntary motherhood, and marriage, religion, and homosexual rights in *Emma Goldman: Sexuality and the Impurity of the State* (Black Rose Books, 1993) to situate her within current feminist debates. In *Liberating Literature: Feminist Fiction in America* (Routledge) Maria Lauret explores the links between socialist women's writing of the '30s and feminist fiction of the '70s and '80s, reading Agnes Smedley's *Daughter of Earth*, Meridel LeSueur's *The Girl*, Ann Petry's *The Street*, and Josephine Herbst's *Rope of Gold* beside novels by Marilyn French, Rita Mae Brown, Erica Jong, Alice Walker, and Marge Piercy. Robert Shulman explains how LeSueur, Herbst, and Richard Wright "reconstructed and deconstructed" the traditional American dream by foregrounding gender and racial issues in "Subverting and Reconstructing the Dream: The Radical Voices of Le Sueur, Herbst, and Wright" (*Deferring A Dream*, pp. 24–36).

Martha C. Carpenter cogently foregrounds the radical content of Glaspell's fiction in "Susan Glaspell's Fiction: *Fidelity* as American Romance" (*TCL* 40: 92–113).

The Several Worlds of Pearl S. Buck (Greenwood), ed. Elizabeth J. Lipscomb et al., collects 12 essays presented at the 1992 centennial symposium at Randolph-Macon College, Buck's alma mater. Organized around historical, humanitarian, and literary perspectives, this volume seeks to reintroduce Buck and her ideas about cross-cultural representation and communication, debate over gender, and the treatment of minorities to an audience for whom these issues have become urgent. *Dawn Powell at Her Best* (Steerforth Press), ed. Tim Page, prints two novels, eight stories, and a brief memoir from a charming voice.

Like Zane Grey, Gene Stratton-Porter has never entirely vanished. In "How to Cocoon a Butterfly: Mother and Daughter in *A Girl of the Limberlost*" (*CLAQ* 18: 148–53) Elizabeth Ford reexamines the complex relationship between Katherine and Elnora that illustrates a daughter's development into difference arising out of various methods of mothering. Patricia Raub analyzes the moralistic tone and old-fashioned heroines of Stratton-Porter's novels as emblematic of her era in "A New Woman or an Old-Fashioned Girl?: The Portrayal of the Heroine in Popular Women's Novels of the Twenties" (*AmerS* 35, i: 109–30). Eugene H. Pattison finds that Stratton-Porter and Annie Dillard share attitudes toward authority as well as an awareness of the moral and theological dimension of nature in "The Limberlost, Tinker Creek, Science and Society: Gene Stratton-Porter and Annie Dillard" (*Pittsburgh History* 77: 160–71). A noteworthy item is Mark J. Madigan's "A Newly-Discovered Robert Frost Letter to Dorothy Canfield Fisher" (*RFR*, pp. 24–27), containing a letter found tucked inside Frost's *A Lone Striker,* inscribed to Fisher and her husband John for Christmas 1933.

Late-century, fast-paced life must encourage interest in short stories. Although O. Henry rejected the idea that he was the "American de Maupassant," Richard Fusco in his *Maupassant and the American Short Story: The Influence of Form at the Turn of the Century* (Penn. State) penetrates the smoke screen to show that he did, in fact, borrow the "surprise-inversion" (pp. 118–37). B. M. Ëjxenbaum discusses O. Henry's short story techniques in "O. Henry and the Theory of the Short Story," trans. I. R. Titunik, pp. 81–88 in Charles E. May, ed., *The New Short Story Theories* (Ohio). "Ring Lardner's Rhetoric" (*SSF* 31: 207–16) contains Brian T. Cowlishaw's analysis of *Round Up,* demonstrating opera-

tive patterns in first- and third-person stories which elicit reader participation. Jennifer Jordan Baker examines a story from Glenway Wescott's
Goodbye Wisconsin to demonstrate that, though it undermines the pastoral ideal, it represents Wescott's impulse to embrace a fleeting pastoral
moment (" 'In a Thicket': Glenway Wescott's Pastoral Vision" [*SSF* 31:
187–95]). *The Collected Stories of Max Brand* (Nebraska), ed. Robert and
Jane Easton, reprints 18 of Frederick Schiller Faust's nearly 900 stories,
including the one which introduced Dr. Kildaire.

Finally, Gordon E. Ernst, Jr.'s *Robert Benchley: An Annotated Bibliography* (Greenwood) contains chapters on Benchley's books, essays, journalism, criticism, secondary sources, a filmography, and a discography and
could spur some activity.

Drew University

15 Fiction: The 1930s to the 1960s

Catherine Calloway

Southerners continue to be especially popular. Eudora Welty and Zora Neale Hurston receive the greatest interest, with four books and several articles about Welty and a book and seventeen articles or book chapters about Hurston. Each of eleven other writers covered in this chapter receive at least one book-length study. In addition, *SoQ* devotes a special issue to Peter Taylor and *WAL* to Wallace Stegner, and Pearl S. Buck receives long overdue attention in an essay collection. Several frequently overlooked authors, including Glenway Wescott, Patricia Highsmith, Jane Bowles, Alfred Bester, and Robert Heinlein, feature in single essays. As in previous years, scholarship is sparse on Westerners, iconoclasts, and detectives, although science fiction is briefly revived.

i Proletarians

a. John Steinbeck   Steinbeck scholars will be pleased with *John Steinbeck: Dissertation Abstracts and Research Opportunities* (Scarecrow), ed. Tetsumaro Hayashi and Beverly K. Simpson, considerably updated from the 1980 edition. Aside from a brief introduction by John H. Timmerman and a chronological checklist of Steinbeck's major works, the text consists of 102 detailed dissertation abstracts compiled by the editors. Published in chronological order, the abstracts reveal changes in the Steinbeck canon over a period of 50 years, from more general dissertations to more specific ones, from Steinbeck's role as a 20th-century modernist to the relationship of his works to recent critical theory. In "Research Opportunities," the third section of the book, Christopher S. Busch provides a useful overview and evaluation, decade by decade, of dissertations on Steinbeck. Concluding the volume is an "Index to

Dissertation Abstracts," organized first by author, then by chronology, subject, title, and university.

The Grapes of Wrath continues to be the essential subject for Steinbeck enthusiasts. Nicholas Visser in "Audience and Closure in *The Grapes of Wrath*" (*SAF* 22: 19–36) explores Steinbeck's problem with closure and demonstrates how he writes "to influence public opinion" and not to address either the migrants or the owners; instead, he hopes that through public pressure national government will be persuaded to eliminate the exploitation of migrant workers. In "The Rhetoric of American Protest: Thomas Paine and the Education of Tom Joad" (*MQ* 35: 392–404) Kurt Hochenauer takes issue with other critics and argues that the central political character in *The Grapes of Wrath* is Joad rather than Jim Casey. According to Hochenauer, the novel traces Tom Joad's educational processes, which are responsible for his metamorphosis into an active American rebel in the tradition of Thomas Paine. J. R. C. Perkin in "Exodus Imagery in *The Grapes of Wrath*," pp. 79–93 in *Literature and the Bible*, ed. David Bevan (Rodopi, 1993), draws convincing parallels between Steinbeck's novel and the Old Testament Exodus narratives. These parallels, some of which are ironically inverted, raise the novel to an epic level and enhance the "archetypal American myth about the West as a land of opportunity." Michael J. Meyer in "Finding a New Jerusalem: The Edenic Myth in John Steinbeck," also in Bevan (pp. 95–117), examines the Eden myth in *The Grapes of Wrath, East of Eden,* and *Of Mice and Men,* suggesting that Steinbeck believed Edens to be central to the American dream and capable of restoration. In "Talking Dirty: Alice Munro's 'Open Secrets' and John Steinbeck's *Of Mice and Men*" (*SSF* 31: 595–606) Ildikó de Papp Carrington shows the influence of Steinbeck on Munro's story. Because Munro alludes to *Of Mice and Men* in "Open Secrets," not only can the relationship between her protagonists be compared to that of Steinbeck's, but her allusions to Steinbeck's characters can enhance the reader's active participation as a detective in Munro's story. The mutual correspondence between Steinbeck's interior and exterior landscapes is the subject of John Ditsky's "John Steinbeck, the Interior Landscape, and Tragic Depletion" (*SDR* 32, i: 106–15). Because Steinbeck mirrored in his own life the feelings of his typically lonely characters, his role as an artist led him to feel tragically isolated.

b. James Agee and Henry Roth   Agee shares honors with John Dos Passos in chapter 2 (pp. 20–53) of Michael E. Staub's *Voices of Persuasion.*

Dos Passos in *Facing the Chair* and Agee in *Let Us Now Praise Famous Men* examine the problems inherent in viewing the documentary as a form that could accurately portray the real—the objective—problems that lead them to write fiction rather than nonfiction and that ultimately make the two men, especially Agee, forerunners of the postmodernist New Journalism. Through parody, Staub argues, Agee surpasses Dos Passos in demonstrating that writers' versions of events are not necessarily authoritative and as such cannot succeed as well as documentaries. Ironically, it is through this failure that some works "succeed as truth" and reeducate their audiences. In "Henry Roth's Secret" (*Commentary* 97, v: 44–47) Hillel Halkin discusses Roth's return to fiction six decades after *Call It Sleep. A Star Shines Over Mt. Morris Park,* the first of five projected volumes of *Mercy of a Rude Stream,* indicates that his Jewish heritage may once again be a major influence in Roth's life and writing.

c. Richard Wright, Ralph Ellison, and James Baldwin Wright is well represented in journal articles this year. Jeffrey J. Folks in " 'Last Call to the West': Richard Wright's *The Color Curtain*" (*SoAR* 59, iv: 77–88) views *The Color Curtain: A Report on the Bandung Conference* as Wright's attempt "to understand his own identity in relation to non-Western cultures," such as Asia and Africa. In " 'As True and Direct as a Birth or Death Certificate': Richard Wright on Jim Thompson's *Now and on Earth*" (*SAF* 22: 105–10) Mark J. Madigan explores the possible influence of Wright on Thompson, whose ideologies were similar to Wright's and whose writing grew in stature with the aid of Wright's endorsement. A novella by Wright is the focus of Yoshinobu Hakutani's "Richard Wright's *The Man Who Lived Underground,* Nihilism, and Zen" (*MissQ* 47: 201–13). Hakutani examines the issue of race and the philosophies of existentialism, Zen, and nihilism in *The Man Who Lived Underground* and concludes that the novella is distinctive in the Wright canon because the protagonist gains "enlightenment" before his ironic death, which denies him the chance to share that enlightenment with others. Existentialism is also the subject of James A. Jaye's "Richard Wright's Freedom: The Existentialism of *Uncle Tom's Children*" (*MQ* 35: 420–34). Jaye demonstrates how an "existential awakening" takes place in stories such as "Fire and Cloud," "Down by the Riverside," and "Bright and Morning Star" as well as in *Native Son,* perceptively noting that in these three stories can be found the naturalistic tendencies of Dreiser and other writers that Wright would adopt in his later writing. Dale E. Peterson in

"Richard Wright's Long Journey from Gorky to Dostoevsky" (*AAR* 28: 375–87) details the influence of the two Russian writers, noting how Wright parallels yet moves beyond their intentions in his own works and in doing so retains his "exemplary African-American soul." In "'Toward the Living Sun': Richard Wright's Change of Heart From *The Outsider* to *The Long Dream*" (*CLAJ* 38: 211–27) Eberhard Alsen argues that contrary to critical opinion the two novels are ideologically different in plot, character development, imagery, and structure; such differences demonstrate a shift in Wright's ideology from "philosophical materialism" to "an idealist vision of life." *Native Son* is the subject of Seodial Deena's "The Irrationality of Bigger Thomas's World: A Frightening View for the Twenty-First Century Urban Population" (*CLAJ* 38: 20–30). According to Deena, society is responsible for the fate of Wright's protagonist, even before his trial and execution: "the society that molds Bigger Thomas kills him, but before it kills him, it twists him and makes him a killer." Through numerous allusions to earlier American literary works Joyce A. Joyce in "Richard Wright: A Romantic and a Realist" (*Warriors, Conjurers and Priests,* pp. 49–72) outlines Wright's heavy reliance on the literary traditions of romance, naturalism, and realism in *Native Son* and *The Long Dream*. Wright's travels to Spain are the subject of M. Lynn Weiss's "Para Usted: Richard Wright's *Pagan Spain*" (*Black Columbiad,* pp. 212–25). Weiss notes that Wright's written version of Spain holds a unique place in American literature because his account reveals that even though he may have been living abroad his writing was grounded in American literary tradition and ideology, an indication that expatriation strengthened, not weakened, his ties to his American heritage and his role as an American writer.

Ralph Ellison scholars are well served by Jerry Gafio Watts's *Heroism and the Black Intellectual: Ralph Ellison, Politics, and Afro-American Intellectual Life* (No. Car.), which details Ellison's life, including his literary and political careers, and his use of the blues and folk culture. In contrast to other African American writers of his time, such as Richard Wright, Ellison had faith in his own culture and immersed himself in it. What disturbs Watts is Ellison's tendency to turn to "elitist individualism as a mechanism for protecting and nurturing his creativity and viability as a writer," an act that was not especially successful. Brian K. Reed in "The Iron and the Flesh: History as Machine in Ellison's *Invisible Man*" (*CLAJ* 37: 261–73) offers an alternate view for the novel's hospital scene, which takes place after the protagonist is involved in a factory explosion.

Instead of regarding the machine as "a symbol of external forces working to modify [the protagonist's] behavior," as many critics do, Reed argues that the change comes from within the protagonist, who turns to a "new concept of history" that coldly disregards humanity and thus absolves him from moral responsibility. Tang Soo Ping's "Ralph Ellison and K. S. Maniam: Ethnicity in America and Malaysia, Two Kinds of Invisibility" (*MELUS* 18, iv: 81–97) explores the issue of ethnicity in *Invisible Man* and Maniam's *The Return.* Whereas the ethnicity in Ellison's novel "leads to a discovery of national identity and an understanding of contemporary life," that in Maniam's is "symbolic" and as such dooms the characters to a marginal existence and a lack of "self-creation." Ping reminds his audience, though, that this difference does not necessarily make one novel more successful than the other. The reader must keep in mind that Ellison was writing about four centuries of African American experience in the United States and Maniam about only one century of non-Malay experience in Malaysia. In "The Big E(llison)'s Texts and Intertexts: Eliot, Burke, and the Underground Man" (*CLAJ* 37: 377–401) Sandra Adell notes the influence of T. S. Eliot and Kenneth Burke on Ellison, who, as a modernist himself, was concerned with "the possibilities for a new aesthetic," yet was disillusioned with modernism and wished to reject it. She compares *Invisible Man* with two literary antecedents: Dostoevsky's *Notes from Underground* and Wright's "The Man Who Lived Underground." *The Invisible Man* is more successful, Adell argues, because Ellison's Invisible Man "is the first black American 'hero' to come fully clothed in the 'uniform' of the modern age." Kenneth Burke's influence on Ellison is the subject of Robert G. O'Meally's "On Burke and the Vernacular: Ralph Ellison's Boomerang of History" (*History and Memory in African-American Culture,* pp. 244–60). O'Meally reflects particularly on the presence in Ellison's fiction of "the blues and other vernacular forms," which bring Ellison's protagonists to a "community awareness, a sense of history that spells a responsibility to take meaningful action." Phillip Brian Harper in " 'To Become One and Yet Many': Psychic Fragmentation and Aesthetic Synthesis in Ralph Ellison's *Invisible Man*" (*Framing the Margins,* pp. 116–44), relates Ellison's novel to Lacanian psychoanalysis. Dolan Hubbard in "The Sermon without Limits and the Limits of the Sermon: *Invisible Man*" (*The Sermon and the African American Literary Imagination,* pp. 64–93) notes the importance of the sermon to the African American community. Through the rhetorical device of the sermon, particularly the sermons of Homer A.

Barbee, Ellison's narrator experiences an epiphany that enables him to
rejoin the community that he has so fervently tried to escape.

Hubbard also examines the subject of the black sermon in the writing
of James Baldwin. In "The Sermon as Cultural History: *Go Tell It on the
Mountain*" (*The Sermon and the African American Literary Imagination*,
pp. 94–122) he demonstrates how Baldwin grounds his novel in "distinctly African American sensibilities rooted in the black folk church and
its peculiar eschatology" which emphasizes redemption. Charles Duncan's "Learning to Listen to 'Sonny's Blues'" (*Obsidian* 9, ii: 1–10),
though not original, clearly delineates the aural aspects of Baldwin's
story. As other critics have noted, the story's narrator must learn to listen,
not only to foster his own relationship with his brother, but to gain the
understanding that he needs in order to embrace his African American
heritage. Joyce A. Joyce in "James Baldwin and Black Women Writers:
The Connection Between History and Identity" (*Warriors, Conjurers and
Priests*, pp. 155–77) notes the similarities between the political views of
Baldwin and contemporary black women writers, for example, Toni
Morrison, Sonia Sanchez, and Margaret Walker. Each author believes
that history and identity cannot be separated. It is only by knowing one's
heritage that one can know oneself, a prerequisite for gaining the self-
confidence necessary to extend aid to other people.

ii Southerners

a. Robert Penn Warren   In "Southern Modernism and the Battle of
Literary Succession" (*SLJ* 27, i: 6–17) James H. Justus briefly examines
Warren's criticism of T. S. Stribling, another naturalistic writer, and
concludes that Warren's condemnation of Stribling resulted from Warren's own inability to choose between Southern romance and American
naturalism. James A. Perkins in "Notes on an Unpublished Robert Penn
Warren Essay" (*SoR* 30: 650–53) shares his finding of "Episode in the
Dime Store," a previously unpublished Warren manuscript in which
Warren reacts to three news photos of a beating suffered by a young
white demonstrator in Nashville, Tennessee, in March 1960. According
to Perkins, "Episode in the Dime Store" is especially significant because
it indicates that Warren continued to be concerned about American
racial issues throughout his literary career. Warren and Caroline Gordon
are the subjects of Allison Hersh's "Representations of Temporal Liminality in Caroline Gordon's 'The Brilliant Leaves' and Robert Penn

Warren's 'Meet Me in the Green Glen' " (*SoQ* 32, ii: 79–94). Using their works as examples, Hersh explores "the South's collective ambivalence towards time and history." Warren's characters want to "control" time, whereas Gordon's try to "transcend" it, evidence that Southern modernism and American modernism cannot be equated. In "Warren's Wandering Son" (*SoAR* 59, ii: 75–93) Randy J. Hendricks examines the significance of the figure of the wanderer that Warren was so fond of. While Hendricks focuses primarily on Warren's poetry, he alludes first to Warren's fictional wanderers and provides an inventory of the various roles that the wanderer plays throughout Warren's career. Lewis P. Simpson in "The Loneliness Artist: Robert Penn Warren" (*The Fable of the Southern Writer*, pp. 132–54), discusses Warren's exile to the North from the South and the inclusion of autobiographical elements in his fiction. As a "white southern loneliness artist," Warren prefigures later writers such as Eudora Welty, Elizabeth Spencer, John William Corrington, and Bobbie Ann Mason who would experience the same emotions but not to the same extent.

b. Flannery O'Connor and Eudora Welty   Ruthann Knechel Johansen in *The Narrative Secret of Flannery O'Connor: The Trickster as Interpreter* (Alabama) examines the "narrative landscape" in a number of O'Connor's stories and novels. It is through this landscape, full of "figures, gestures, or actions," that O'Connor's audience can become most involved with the "mystery or secrecy" of her work. Significantly, O'Connor unintentionally relies on the archetypal device of the trickster figure. The trickster is necessary, Johansen argues, because "without the trickster to assist interpretation, Flannery O'Connor's narratives, so reliant on religious myths and allusions, may seem confusing and disorderly or even blasphemous."

In "Art and the Female Spirit" (*Engendering Romance*, pp. 162–80) Emily Miller Budick explores the connections between love and freedom in the romance tradition as they pertain to *The Violent Bear It Away*. According to Budick, O'Connor's thesis in this novella is that humankind should "bear responsibility rather than . . . be borne away by violence." By exercising one's freedom to move toward Christ, one moves in the direction of other people. Gender is the issue in Peter A. Smith's "Flannery O'Connor's Empowered Women" (*SLJ* 26, ii: 35–47). Using examples from a number of O'Connor's short stories, Smith argues that the female characters, particularly those who supervise male laborers, cross gender lines and fail at their attempts to act like both men and women. In "Onomastics in Flannery O'Connor's 'Parker's Back'" (*NConL* 24, iii: 6–8) James A. Grimshaw, Jr., considers that story's structure, symbolism, and verbal and situational irony. Grimshaw notes that O'Connor gives Parker a tripartate role: that of "the prophet, the violence that can be associated with grace, and the grotesqueness of man." Nancy Bishop Dessommes in "O'Connor's Mrs. May and Oates's Connie: An Unlikely Pair of Religious Initiates" (*SSF* 31: 433–40) draws interesting parallels between O'Connor's "Greenleaf" and Joyce Carol Oates's "Where Are You Going, Where Have You Been?" Both stories contain selfish, uncaring protagonists, male intruders, and sexual over-tones; in addition, both protagonists experience revelations or "moments of grace" that make them "religious hero[es]". Karl Martin in "Flannery O'Connor's Prophetic Imagination" (*R&L* 26, iii: 33–58) provides a thorough study of O'Connor's role as a prophet in her work. Martin clearly explains the arguments of a number of theologians who influ-enced O'Connor when she reviewed and annotated their books, par-ticularly the views of Walter Brueggemann, an Old Testament scholar. Then he turns to the beliefs about prophecy in O'Connor's own works, including lectures, letters, and essays. Particularly significant are O'Con-nor's views that her modern audience is guilty of ignoring the voice of the prophet and of overlooking past actions of God and the incarnation, and that writers such as herself are responsible for convincing their readers to once again believe in "both the judgment of God and the action of his grace in the world." In "O'Connor and Her World: The Visual Art of *Wise Blood*" (*StHum* 21: 79–95) Juniper Ellis argues that O'Connor's artwork from high school and college—her cartoons and paintings—are an integral part of her later writing. Using several of O'Connor's works as examples, Ellis demonstrates how she employs physical details, doubles, flat characters, the grotesque, surfaces, distortions, and the surreal for characterization, inversion, reversal, or emphasis.

Eudora Welty is the subject of four books and several articles. Espe-cially valuable is Noel Polk's *Eudora Welty: A Bibliography of Her Work* (Miss.). Polk divides the bibliography into Welty's major books, followed by her shorter works such as book reviews, photographic work, works anthologized in collections not devoted exclusively to Welty, and dust-jacket reviews. This 500-page text is unique in its focus on "the editing, printing, and publishing of Eudora Welty's works . . . the physical formats in which they have appeared, and their textual relationships to one another."

The Critical Response to Eudora Welty's Fiction, ed. Laurie Champion (Greenwood), reprints 46 articles published between the 1940s and the current decade. Champion's introduction gives a useful overview of the book's contents, briefly showing trends and patterns in Welty scholarship over 40 years. Beginning with *A Curtain of Green and Other Stories,* Champion includes chronological sections on each of Welty's novels and short story collections as well as on general criticism for each era and a brief bibliography of selected readings.

A particularly insightful study is Ruth D. Weston's *Gothic Traditions and Narrative Techniques in the Fiction of Eudora Welty* (LSU), which argues that even though Welty resists categorization as a Gothic author the "Gothic overtones" in her work are far more significant than she has admitted and previous critics have recognized. Welty is not a Southern Gothic writer like some of her contemporaries; rather, she has been influenced by such early British and American Gothic authors as Ann Radcliffe, Jane Austen, the Brontë sisters, Washington Irving, Charles Brockden Brown, Nathaniel Hawthorne, and James Fenimore Cooper. Significantly, Welty makes earlier Gothic traditions her own by avoiding the sentimental, incorporating the mythic, and not restricting the subject of confinement to one sex. Weston breaks new ground by demonstrating the pervasiveness of the Gothic in Welty's work, a multifaceted Gothic that supports Welty's "pervasive theme of enclosure, exposure, and escape of women, and some men, in search of selfhood."

Gail L. Mortimer's *Daughter of the Swan: Love and Knowledge in Eudora Welty's Fiction* (Georgia) concentrates on Welty's epistemological concerns and the images by which she conveys those concerns. Mortimer takes a thematic approach, delving into "various themes, images, and issues that illustrate basic features of Welty's imagination and her assumptions about knowledge and language." Mortimer explores additional Welty territory in "A Source for a Name and a Question of Naming in Eudora Welty's 'Moon Lake'" (*SoQ* 32, iv: 80–83). According to Mortimer, a likely source for the name of Welty's protagonist in "Moon Lake" is Nina Hirshfeld, the daughter of New York artist Al Hirshfeld. Evidence suggests that Welty would have been aware that Hirshfeld often hid his daughter's name in his drawings and posters. In "The Domestic Thread of Revelation: An Interview with Eudora Welty"

(*SLJ* 27, i: 18–24) Sally Wolff combines two interviews with Welty, from 26 July 1989 and from 15 June 1993. The subjects covered include Welty's use of rural settings in her stories, love, images of sewing or threading, and characters that drown or images of drowning. The *Eudora Welty Newsletter* also contributes several items. In "Textual Variants in 'The Hitch-Hikers' " (18, i: 1–11) Catherine H. Chengges examines Welty's extensive revision of the story for publication in *A Curtain of Green*. The Summer 1994 issue mainly focuses on bibliographical matters. W. U. McDonald, Jr., in "Works By Welty: A Continuing Checklist" (18, ii: 3–6) provides a brief update of 1993–94 materials, including photographs and interviews, and Suzanne Marrs in "The Clipping File" (18, ii: 13–15) lists newspaper and magazine articles from 1991 through 1994 on Welty and her work. More extensive is Pearl Amelia McHaney's "A Checklist of Welty Scholarship 1993–94" (18, ii: 8–13), which includes bibliographies, books, special journal issues, and theses and dissertations.

c. Zora Neale Hurston   Hurston scholars will be pleased with John Lowe's *Jump at the Sun: Zora Neale Hurston's Cosmic Comedy* (Illinois). Lowe takes an interdisciplinary approach, applying theory from African American humor, from the "cosmic," and from Mikhail Bakhtin's " 'carnivalization of language' " to various dimensions of Hurston's humor. Two articles also treat humor. Christine Levecq in " 'Mighty Strange Threads in Her Loom': Laughter and Subversive Heteroglossia in Zora Neale Hurston's *Moses, Man of the Mountain*" (*TSLL* 36: 436–61) examines the parallels between the Old Testament version of the story of Moses and Hurston's novel of African American slaves, noting that Hurston's humor comes from a "socially, politically, and culturally charged heteroglossia." Helena Woodard in "Expressions of 'Black Humor': Laughter as Resistance in Alice Walker's *The Color Purple* and Zora Neale Hurston's *Moses, Man of the Mountain*" (*TSLL* 36: 431–35) explores Carole Ann Taylor's and Christine Levecq's studies of the humor in Walker's and Hurston's novels. Michael E. Staub's "Zora Neale Hurston: Talking Black, Talking Back" (*Voices of Persuasion,* pp. 79–109) details the many ways that Hurston's *Of Mules and Men* surpasses the anthropological studies of the 1930s to anticipate "the experimental ethnographies" of the past 15 years. Significantly, Hurston excels at taking the black oral vernacular and changing it " *into* the written form"; by abandoning the "Mason jar" method of other writers of her time, Hurston demonstrates the power and vitality of African American speech. Ultimately, Staub argues, Hurston serves not only as the author of the book, but as the protagonist and the ethnographer of the open text that she creates by actively encouraging the reader to add meaning to her stories.

Their Eyes Were Watching God attracts the greatest amount of critical attention. William M. Ramsey in "The Compelling Ambivalence of Zora Neale Hurston's *Their Eyes Were Watching God*" (*SLJ* 27, i: 36–50) maintains that even though Hurston wrote and published her novel, which contains "unresolved tensions," in less than two months, it is a complex text of "remarkable creative intelligence." In "Zora Neale Hurston's *Their Eyes Were Watching God*" (*Marjorie Kinnan Rawlings Journal of Florida Literature* 5 [1993]: 87–90) Ronald F. Anderson refutes an earlier claim that Hurston's protagonist will die of a rabies infection she receives from being bitten by the dying Tea Cake.

A number of articles on *Their Eyes Were Watching God* celebrate the oral tradition, particularly Anita M. Vickers's "The Reaffirmation of African-American Dignity Through the Oral Tradition in Zora Neale Hurston's *Their Eyes Were Watching God*" (*CLAJ* 37: 303–15) and Cathy Brigham's "The Talking Frame of Zora Neale Hurston's Talking Book: Storytelling as Dialectic in *Their Eyes Were Watching God*" (*CLAJ* 37: 402–19). Vickers argues that "the shift in voice" does not weaken the novel; instead, it "permits Hurston to bring in events that are outside of Janie's sphere" and to add "another life to Janie's dream." Brigham regards the structure of Hurston's novel as "a multivocal storytelling dialectic . . . that speaks from, to, and about Janie's cultural perspective, as well as to itself" and that helps to create an African American community discourse which will no longer be restricted to black men. Hazel Carby in "The Politics of Fiction, Anthropology, and the Folk: Zora Neale Hurston" (*History and Memory in African-American Culture*, pp. 28–44), explores the tension that Hurston depicts between the folk community and the intellect, offering yet another view of the debate about Janie, the intellectual, as speaking or silent in *Their Eyes Were Watching God*. Hurston uses Phoeby, Janie's friend, to tell Janie's story; therefore, "Phoeby becomes both Hurston's instrument of mediation and her text is an act of fictionalization." Pearlie M. Peters in " 'Ah Got the Law in My Mouth': Black Women and Assertive Voice in Hurston's Fiction and Folklore" (*CLAJ* 37: 293–302) discusses the significance of Hurston's female characters who, because of the African American oral tradition, cannot survive without the authorial voice of their culture.

Maria J. Racine's "Voice and Interiority in Zora Neale Hurston's *Their Eyes Were Watching God*" (*AAR* 28: 283–92) continues the debate over Janie as silent. Racine argues that by the end of the novel Janie does gain a voice and self-importance. Through Hurston's presentation of Janie's internal consciousness, the reader is made aware that even silent characters like her are important and can achieve the special ability to express their own opinions. Dolan Hubbard in "Recontextualizing the Sermon to Tell (Her)story: *Their Eyes Were Watching God*" (*The Sermon and the African American Literary Imagination*, pp. 47–63) also reads the novel affirmatively. By the end of the book, Janie is elevated to the status of a prophet; her personal quest is fulfilled, and she is able to transcend traditional female gender boundaries. Christine Levecq in " 'You Heard Her, You Ain't Blind': Subversive Shifts in Zora Neale Hurston's *Their Eyes Were Watching God*" (*TSWL* 13: 87–111) disagrees with Hubbard and others. According to Levecq, who acknowledges the positions of her opponents, the novel continually deflates the possibility of Janie's achieving a higher awareness or a clear identity because "the narrator, through her constant and subtle use of humor, heteroglossia, and carnivalesque scenes, subversively works against the protagonist in her presentation of Janie's consciousness and environment by implicitly questioning the way she defines herself, and is defined by others, as a black woman."

Five other articles on Hurston's work deserve mention. Gordon E. Thompson in "Projecting Gender: Personification in the Works of Zora Neale Hurston" (*AL* 66: 737–63) examines the techniques by which Hurston achieves her narrative voice: as narrator and storyteller, Hurston can personify herself as a male, cross gender boundaries, and make storytelling "gender neutral." In "Zora Neale Hurston's *Autobiographie Fictive*: Dark Tracks on the Canon of a Female Writer" (*The Black Columbiad*, pp. 191–200) Paola Boi questions the relationship between fiction and autobiography in *Dust Tracks on a Road;* Hurston's book, though called an autobiography, is instead both an "*autobiographie fictive*" and an "*histoire fictive*." Andrew Crosland in "The Text of Zora Neale Hurston: A Caution" (*CLAJ* 37: 420–24) analyzes "textual complications" in "The Eatonville Anthology," *Mule Bone: A Comedy of Negro Life,* and *Dust Tracks on a Road.* Because some of Hurston's works were not published in her lifetime, Crosland warns, editors may need to provide additional exposition and explanatory material to give them a proper context. In "Zora Neale Hurston as English Teacher: A Lost Chapter Found" (*Marjorie Kinnan Rawlings Journal of Florida Literature*

(5 [1993]: 51–59) Gordon Patterson provides insight into Hurston's character and personality by relating the little-known events of the last two years of Hurston's life, among them her brief stint as an English teacher. Geneva Cobb-Moore in "Zora Neale Hurston as Local Colorist" (*SLJ* 26, ii: 25–34) records Hurston's success in capturing the essence of Eatonville and its residents, and in so doing "expand[ing] the meaning of local color."

d. Katherine Anne Porter and Others   Porter material dwindles significantly this year, although two items merit attention. Janis P. Stout in "Katherine Anne Porter's 'Reflections on Willa Cather': A Duplicitous Homage" (*AL* 66: 719–35) argues that Porter adopts "the Bloomian model of male writer's anxiety" in her essay on Cather, whom she never met but obviously admired and identified with. In "Katherine Anne Porter's 'The Old Order' and *Agamemnon*" (*SSF* 31: 491–93) P. Jane Hafen notes the significance of an allusion to Aeschylus' *Agamemnon* in "The Grave." Like Agamemnon, Porter's Miranda and other characters in the stories in *The Old Order* will undergo change as they bear the weight of the past.

New additions this year are critical commentaries on the work of Marjorie Kinnan Rawlings and Andrew Lytle. Susan Schmidt in "Finding a Home: Rawlings's *Cross Creek*" (*SLJ* 27, ii: 48–57) examines the 1942 reminiscence in terms of Rawlings's affection for that locale. Because Rawlings loves Cross Creek so dearly, her writing about it cannot be considered as only regional literature. *The Marjorie Kinnan Rawlings Journal of Florida Literature* devotes three articles to Rawlings. Language is the subject of Sally E. Parry's "'Make the Message Clear': The Failure of Language in Marjorie Kinnan Rawlings's *New Yorker* Stories" (5 [1993]: 39–49). Parry provides an interesting analysis of the function of language in those five stories: the characters' linguistic inadequacies deny them acceptance into their desired communities. In "The St. Johns River in the Work of Marjorie Kinnan Rawlings" (5 [1993]: 61–66) Rebecca Richie notes the significance of the river in Rawlings's 1933 story "Hyacinth Drift." Two events in Rawlings's life influenced her to write about the St. Johns: an actual journey that she took down the river with Dessie Smith Vinson, a friend, and William Bartram's 1773 *Travels,* which details a river journey that Bartram made 160 years earlier. Anne E. Rowe in "Rawlings on Florida" (5 [1993]: 67–71) also notes the influence of William Bartram on Rawlings, who, like Harriet Beecher Stowe and

Sidney Lanier, writes of Florida as a physical and spiritual paradise. Andrew Lytle occasions one article. William Walsh's "The Nature of the World: An Interview with Andrew Lytle" (*PM* 26: 114–23) focuses on biographical materials, life in the South, the Fugitive poets, environmentalism, and Lytle's move to Florida. The interview, conducted in a congenial spirit, provides rare personal insight into the man, his philosophy, and his work.

e. Peter Taylor and Thomas Wolfe   Catherine Clark Graham in *Southern Accents: The Fiction of Peter Taylor* (Peter Lang) strives to give a frequently overlooked Southern author the scholarly attention he deserves. Graham examines a number of short stories that reflect Taylor's major themes and then demonstrates how these themes culminate in his Pulitzer Prize-winning novel *A Summons to Memphis*. Women are the subject of a brief section of *SoQ* devoted to Taylor. Both Walter Shear in "Women and History in Peter Taylor's Short Stories" (33, i: 41–46) and Linda Kandel Kuehl in "Peter Taylor's Women: Old and New" (33, i: 47–53) focus on the difficulties that women confront when past and present cultures begin to merge. Shear uses a number of Taylor's short stories to illustrate the effects that "historical discontinuity" can have in women's literature; for instance, when female characters suddenly shift to unfamiliar environments, they must "display 'the power of a woman in a man's world,'" or they must deal with other personal or societal changes for which they are not prepared. Similarly, Kuehl explores the contrasting attitudes of two Taylor women in transition. The younger woman in "Her Need," who has been subjugated by men throughout her life and who now faces an increasingly impersonal, urban world, seeks "revenge from the grave" for the men who have betrayed her; while the terminally ill but stoic protagonist of "Three Heroines" graciously teaches her son that women can be heroic even when confronted with impending death.

In "The Influence of Modernist Structure in the Short Fiction of Thomas Wolfe" (*SSF* 31: 149–61) Joseph Bentz notes the influence of modernism, particularly modernist structure, on Wolfe's short fiction. Such stories as "No Cure for It" and "The Lost Boy" illustrate Wolfe's use of modernist characteristics and help categorize him as an experimentalist. Bentz also explores T. S. Eliot's *The Waste Land* as a literary antecedent to some of Wolfe's prose. In "Wolfe and the Wastelanders: T. S. Eliot's Influence on *The Hound of Darkness*" (*TWN* 18, ii: 1–5) Bentz draws parallels between Wolfe's collage-like prose work "A Prologue to America," intended originally as a section of *The Hound of Darkness,* a book-length manuscript, and *The Waste Land.* While Wolfe "American-ize[s] the subject matter," he frequently alludes to *The Waste Land,* uses similar structural patterns, and sets his work in cities. The influence of Ovid is explored in "*Look Homeward, Angel* and Ovid's *Metamorphoses*" (*TWN* 18, ii: 6–12) by Cheryl Cunningham. The works are similar in their structure, tone, and use of water and door symbolism; furthermore, Eugene Gant shares affinities with the mythological Bacchus/Jove figure. Mythology is also the subject of Heather O'Neill's " 'Of Wandering Forever and the Earth Again': Mythology in Thomas Wolfe's *Of Time and the River*" (*TWN* 18, ii: 40–49), which inventories mythological elements, including Telemachus's search for his father Odysseus, the Herculean conquest of Antaeus, the story of Orestes' matricide, and the story of Jason and the Golden Fleece. Two other articles have mythologi-cal overtones. Suzanne Stutman in "The Image of the Child in *The Good Child's River*" (*TWN* 18, i: 19–24) focuses on Wolfe's examination of "the *process* of memory" and "the quest for home," and Douglas S. Johnson in "Eliza Gant's Web: Her Role as Earth Mother and Moral Hub in *The Web of Earth*" (*TWN* 18, i: 42–47) views Wolfe's novel as superior to some of his longer works in its sense of "completeness" and its skillful use of Eliza Gant (Julia Wolfe), the earth mother, as the narrator. Each issue of *TWN* includes a brief, annotated "Wolfe Pack: Bibliography" (18, i: 84–86; 18, ii: 99–101) of critical material on Wolfe and his writing.

iii Expatriates and Émigrés

a. Vladimir Nabokov   Nabokov's influence on contemporary Russian writers is the focus of Arnold McMillin's "Bilingualism and Word Play in the Work of Russian Writers of the Third Wave of Emigration: The Heritage of Nabokov" (*MLR* 89: 417–26). McMillin explores word-play in three Russian writers, Vasili Aksenov, Zinovi Zinik, and Joseph Brodsky, the last of whom is regarded as Nabokov's successor. Biographi-cal matters are the subject of Jeffrey Meyers's "The Bulldog and the Butterfly: The Friendship of Edmund Wilson and Vladimir Nabokov" (*ASch* 63: 379–99). In an effort to reveal the personal and intellectual rea-sons behind the broken friendship, Meyers details the infamous quarrel of the two men over Wilson's biting review in the *New York Review of Books* of Nabokov's 1965 translation of Pushkin's *Eugene Onegin.* Meyers argues that critics have overlooked the extent of Wilson's professional jealousy of Nabokov and have concentrated on Nabokov's point of view at Wilson's expense. Susan Elizabeth Sweeney in " 'April in Arizona': Nabokov as an American Writer" (*AmLH* 6: 325–35) makes a good case for Nabokov as a genuine American author. Drawing first on Brian Boyd's *Vladimir Nabokov: The American Years* (1991), Sweeney then offers her own assessment of Nabokov's nationality, calling *Lolita* "the most cunning, poetic, and incisive American novel of this century" and noting throughout Nabokov's works an extensive use of American settings, even though Nabokov lived in the United States for only two decades before returning to Europe. Ironically, Sweeney concludes, the figure of the exile that Nabokov portrays "may be the most archetypal American figure."

Other articles focus on specific Nabokov works. In "Fathers, Sons, and Imposters: Pushkin's Trace in 'The Gift' " (*SlavR* 53, i: 140–58) Monika Greenleaf argues that in "The Gift" Nabokov creates a tripartate exercise in mourning; he mourns the things that exile has denied him, his fatherland, his father, and his native tongue. In "Maramzin's *Two-Toned Blond* and Nabokov's *Lolita*" (*IFR* 21: 85–89) David Lowe demonstrates that Vladimir Maramzin was influenced by Nabokov, and not only by Mikhail Zoshchenko and Andrey Platonov as many critics believe; *Two-Toned Blond* contains numerous parallels with *Lolita*, which Maramzin parodies and inverts. In her excellent "Playing a Game of Worlds in Nabokov's *Pale Fire*" (*MFS* 40: 299–317) Martine Hennard examines *Pale Fire* in terms of its modernist/postmodernist qualities and techniques. She points out the significance of the debate over the novel's genre. Is *Pale Fire* a parody? A "deconstructive critical strategy"? A poem? A novel? A work of "limit-modernism"? A detective story? By surveying these alternatives Hennard demonstrates the complexity of Nabokov's novel, a book that "can be viewed as enacting the transition between modernity and postmodernity by staging a double-voiced text which, half-nostalgically, half-playfully, celebrates the advent of error as the only certainty." M. Keith Booker's intriguing "Fiction and 'Real Life': Vargas Llosa's *The Real Life of Alejandro Mayta* and Nabokov's *The Real Life of Sebastian Knight*" (*Crit* 35: 111–27) also focuses on ontological concerns. Booker's informative comparison of Vargas Llosa's and Nabokov's self-reflexive novels deals with the postmodernist blurring between fact and fiction. Like Hennard, Booker questions the definition of truth: what, if anything, is true in the metafictive *The Real Life of Sebastian Knight?*

b. Djuna Barnes and Anaïs Nin The best article on *Nightwood* is Andrea L. Harris's "The Third Sex: Figures of Inversion in Djuna Barnes' *Nightwood*," pp. 233–59 in *Eroticism and Containment: Notes from the Flood Plain,* ed. Carol Siegel and Ann Kibbey (NYU). Harris provides an in-depth study of the issues of gender, ambiguity, and the invert, then goes on to demonstrate that ultimately "the truth of gender" cannot be decided within the novel. In " 'Looking for That Dead Girl': Incest, Pornography, and the Capitalist Family Romance in *Nightwood, The Years,* and *Tar Baby*" (*AI* 51: 421–45) Margot Gayle Backus suggests that the novels by Barnes, Virginia Woolf, and Toni Morrison depict capitalistic evil as permeating society and poisoning human behavior. Capitalism is also the subject of Phillip Brian Harper's "Anaïs Nin, Djuna Barnes, and the Critical Feminist Unconscious" (*Framing the Margins,* pp. 55–89). Harper shows how capitalism grants men a way "to enact the fragmentation of female subjectivity." The women in Nin's and Barnes's writing seek their completeness from men, although Barnes's novel does not limit the scope of her book "to the single problem of feminine subjectivity," instead applying it to the population at large.

It is appropriate that Henry Miller and his friend and mentor, Anaïs Nin, are honored by the University of Mississippi Press's Literary Conversation Series in the same year. *Conversations with Anaïs Nin* (Miss.), ed. Wendy M. DuBow, collects 24 interviews conducted from 1965 through 1976. Topics include gender issues, surrealism, politics, the women's movement, and Nin's diaries.

c. Kay Boyle and Others Joan Mellen in *Kay Boyle: Author of Herself* (Farrar) successfully undertakes a most ambitious project—a detailed and interestingly written 670-page tribute to Boyle's life, encompassing her health, marriages, and children as well as her role as a political activist, her job as a foreign correspondent for the *New Yorker,* and her literary career. Mellen documents her research into Boyle papers housed at various libraries in copious endnotes. In *Metamorphosizing the Novel: Kay Boyle's Narrative Innovations* (Peter Lang, 1993) Marilyn Elkins seeks to give Boyle, whose novels have at times been ignored, especially by feminists, the critical attention they deserve. Elkins explores Boyle's modernist artistic transformation: the "early poetry and short fiction fit both the content and style expectations of modernism," but "her longer works focus on women characters and offer a turn toward a new 'horizon' of expectations' about gender issues." The single article on Boyle is

Donna Hollenberg's "Abortion, Identity Formation, and the Expatriate Woman Writer: H.D. and Kay Boyle in the Twenties" (*TCL* 40: 499–517), which examines "problematic maternity as a catalyst in the development of authentic, cohesive selfhood, viewed from an expatriated perspective" in the works of the two women.

Paul Bowles scholars will be pleased with Gena Dagel Caponi's *Paul Bowles: Romantic Savage* (So. Ill.), a chronological study of life and works which moves beyond the work of earlier biographers, such as Christopher Sawyer-Laucanno and Michelle Green, to break new ground by "defining Bowles's place in twentieth-century American culture." Caponi chronicles the influences and relationships most essential to a nuanced view of Bowles, basing that account on interviews with Bowles as well as with friends and literary contemporaries. Michael Pinker in " 'Everyone Exists in Order to Be Entertaining': The Fiction of Paul Bowles" (*DQ* 29, ii: 156–93) traces the themes of violation, alienation, and isolation and the role of travel in a number of works spanning Bowles's writing career. Bowles comments on his own work in Abdelhak Elghandor's "Atavism and Civilization: An Interview with Paul Bowles" (*ArielE* 25, ii: 7–30), which explores such topics as the element of violence in Bowles's writing, cultural encounters, anti-intellectualism, and Morocco. Elghander seeks to employ his non-European voice to ask cultural questions of Bowles not addressed by earlier interviewers.

Jane Bowles is treated in Kathy Justice Gentile's " 'The Dreaded Voyage into the World': Jane Bowles and Her Serious Ladies" (*SAF* 22: 47–60), which studies the "concept of dread," figured particularly in female characters who are reluctant to journey out into the world.

d. Pearl S. Buck Buck scholarship is also revived this year with the publication of *The Several Worlds of Pearl S. Buck: Essays Presented at a Centennial Symposium, Randolph-Macon Woman's College, March 26–28, 1992* (Greenwood), ed. Elizabeth J. Lipscomb et al., a collection of 13 items devoted to various aspects of Buck's life and work. The introduction is provided by Peter Conn, and the keynote address by James C. Thompson, Jr. Charles W. Hayford, David D. Buck, John d'Entremont, and Liu Haiping write on "Historical Perspectives," Grace C. K. Sum, Conn, and Deborah Clement Raessler on "Humanitarian Perspectives," and Jane M. Rabb, Conn, Pradyumna S. Chauhan, and James L. Hoban, Jr., on "Literary Perspectives."

iv Easterners

a. Saul Bellow *Conversations with Saul Bellow* (Miss.), ed. Gloria L. Cronin and Ben Siegel, collects 29 interviews dating from 1953 to the present. They offer insight into Bellow's views on contemporary writing, his own work, his response to his critics, his education, his views on being classified as a "Jewish writer," and his family's problems with "'Americanization and assimilation.'" In "Saul Bellow and the Midwestern Myth of the Search" (*MMisc* 22: 46–53) David D. Anderson examines in Bellow's writing the motif of the journey, the search that has dominated American literature since Twain's *Huckleberry Finn*. Regardless of their backgrounds or ages, Bellow's characters, like numerous other American Midwesterners, still find the search viable. What distinguishes them from earlier American literary figures is their ability to see the search more clearly and to recognize "the elements of chance, of circumstance, of reality that threaten it." Ruth Essex in "Bellow's Sammler and Kosinski's Kosky in New York" (*SAJL* 13: 85–92) examines *Mr. Sammler's Planet* and *The Hermit of 69th St.* in regard to the Holocaust. Both novels include protagonist-writers who need to tell about their Holocaust experiences; use a number of literary techniques, such as analogy, anecdote, and vignette; contain dysfunctional families; lack "nurturing" women; and end in death. Noting the difficulties inherent in writing about such a horrific event, Essex demonstrates how Bellow and Kosinski use their protagonists to set forth not only the Holocaust's horrors, but the fact that the ravaged, urban modernist world has the frightening potential to repeat the past. The connection between Bellow, Nabokov, and Martin Amis is the subject of Victoria N. Alexander's "Martin Amis: Between the Influences of Bellow and Nabokov" (*AR* 52: 580–90). Alexander points out how extensively Amis has been influenced by the other two modernists in spite of differences in their writing philosophies.

b. Bernard Malamud *Dubin's Lives* is the subject of Malcolm O. Magaw's "Malamud's Dubious Dubin: The Biographer and His Square Walk in a Circle" (*ClioI* 23: 219–33). Magaw views the novel as multilayered, with Malamud as well as Dubin playing the role of biographer; Malamud chronicles Dubin's many lives, such as those of Bach, Vivaldi, Nixon, Marco Polo, and Chekhov, while the fictive Dubin processes the lives of many others, including D. H. Lawrence. A "circle *inside* a square" is the image that fits Dubin best, for his "immediate 'life'" and his "biographical 'lives'" are disjointed and incapable of merging or synthesizing; this, Magaw points out in his thorough and insightful reading, is "not only the crux of the matter but the explanation of it." Lawrence M. Lasher in "Plenty of News: Bernard Malamud's 'The Letter'" (*SSF* 31: 657–66) argues that in spite of attracting little critical commentary "The Letter" deserves a higher place in the Malamud canon. According to Lasher, Malamud typically advocates in "The Letter" that a character must read and understand the correct text. Newman's failure to gain the message of Ralph and Teddy's blank four-page letter is a clue to the careful reader that Malamud has included a "letter" in the text for his own audience: the warning that America is too quick to condemn victims such as Ralph and Teddy to institutions where they are unable to convey their messages about the horrible realities of war and other disasters to future generations. The influence of Virginia Woolf on Malamud is the focus of Lucio Ruotolo's "Bernard Malamud's Rediscovery of Women: The Impact of Virginia Woolf" (*TCL* 40: 329–41). Ruotolo shows how Malamud's works, particularly "In Kew Gardens" and "Alma Redeemed," reflect Woolf's own philosophies and writing; parallels are evident in structure and plot, the study of women characters, the style of writing, and the presence of dark humor. Malamud's Jewishness is the concern of Edward A. Abramson in "Bernard Malamud and the Jews: An Ambiguous Relationship" (*YES* 24: 146–56). While many scholars have categorized Malamud as a "Jewish" writer, Abramson thinks it unfair to restrict him in such a way; he should instead be viewed as an author who goes beyond Judaism to a concern with all humanity.

c. Shirley Jackson and James Thurber   Jackson's work inspires two noteworthy articles. Jay A. Yarmove's "Jackson's 'The Lottery'" (*Expl* 52: 242–45) points out the significance of the setting, the time frame, the characters' names, and Tessie Hutchinson's hypocritical behavior. Jackson's techniques remind the reader just how easily American democracy could be sacrificed and a holocaust of our own created. S. T. Joshi's "Shirley Jackson: Domestic Horror" (*StWF* 14: 9–28) provides an insightful analysis of a number of Jackson's stories and novels, considering domestic issues, horror, loneliness, misanthropy, houses, and truth, and concluding that readers should be thankful for Jackson's "weird" fiction.

Thurber is represented in one book and two articles. Neil A. Grauer's

Remember Laughter: A Life of James Thurber (Nebraska) provides an examination of Thurber and his work more personal than critical. Through anecdotes, photographs, and cartoons, Grauer chronologically traces Thurber's life and career. Anthony Kaufman in " 'Things Close In': Dissolution and Misanthropy in 'The Secret Life of Walter Mitty' " (*SAF* 22: 93–104) argues that one of Thurber's most popular stories has been misread. While many scholars see Mitty as a dynamic character, who is "in the process of change," Kaufman points out that Mitty's change is a negative one; he is not regaining a sense of reality, but instead is moving in the opposite direction, "to misanthropy, withdrawal, and final dissolution." In "Thurber's *Fables for Our Time:* A Case Study in Satirical Use of Great Chain Metaphor" (*StAH* n.s. 3, i: 51–61) Douglas Sun posits that Thurber's book of fables is successful precisely because it relies on the concept of the Great Chain; through the use of animals and their place in the chain Thurber reveals his satire—"he forces us to confront and make sense of the impossibilities that animal characters embody, and in doing so he presents us with certain views of human behavior."

v Westerners

a. Wallace Stegner *Western American Literature* (29, ii) devotes an issue to Stegner. Jackson J. Benson in "Finding a Voice of His Own: The Story of Wallace Stegner's Fiction" (pp. 99–121) sets forth an interesting account of Stegner's life and traces his literary career from his earlier to later works, noting his lengthy search for a voice of his own. He moves from remote narrators who do not actively engage the reader in the text to fictional narrators who reflect himself. As Benson notes, one of Stegner's eventual accomplishments was his creation of a first-person Jamesian voice that enabled characters to speak for themselves and that helped him to draw readers more deeply into his fiction. In "Wallace Stegner and the Environmental Ethic: Environmentalism as a Rejection of Western Myth" (pp. 124–42). Brett J. Olsen examines Stegner's views of the West and his role as an environmentalist. In his writing and lectures Stegner tried to debunk the Western myth of "the West as the regional embodiment of hope," stressing instead the significance of the communal environment over the individual environment in Western society. Olsen laments the gap left by Stegner's death in both the academic world and environmentalism.

b. Glenway Wescott   Jennifer Jordan Baker in " 'In a Thicket': Glenway
Wescott's Pastoral Vision" (*SSF* 31: 187–95) argues that in "In a Thicket"
Wescott portrays both the innocence and the dangers of the Midwest
pastoral region. The fall of innocence of Lily, the protagonist, parallels
that which is taking place in the real Midwest, a fall that is lamentable yet
necessary for urban progress.

vi Iconoclasts and Detectives

a. Jack Kerouac   In "Jack Kerouac: An American Tragedy?" (*Kerouac
Connection* 26: 17–29) Gerald Nicosia asks whether Kerouac's life should
be viewed positively or negatively. Nicosia provides interesting details
of Kerouac's private life, including bits of letters and snippets of conversations, and concludes that Kerouac's life was tragic because of his
inability to establish an identity independent of his mother and other
relatives.

b. Nathanael West and Henry Miller   Richard P. Lynch in "Saints and
Lovers: *Miss Lonelyhearts* in the Tradition" (*SSF* 31: 225–35) draws comparisons between West's novel and several other literary works. Like
Dostoevsky's Underground Man or Camus's Tarrou, Miss Lonelyhearts
cannot make the sacrifices necessary to acquire human love, and like T. S.
Eliot in *The Waste Land,* West notes that the lack of human love is the
main problem of modern society. However, Miss Lonelyheart's inability
to acquire human love does not mean that human love is insignificant; in
fact, the contrary is true. Instead, West warns us that the real danger to
the modern world is that "we will not do what humans *can* do." Rita
Barnard in " 'When You Wish Upon a Star': Fantasy, Experience, and
Mass Culture in Nathanael West" (*AL* 66: 325–51) explores West's literary use of the wish, explaining how he was influenced by the Frankfurt
School and Theodor Adorno. In spite of Hollywood's facade, West
admits that it offers some redeeming qualities. Phillip Brian Harper in
"Signification, Movement, and Resistance in the Novels of Nathanael
West" (*Framing the Margins,* pp. 30–54), studies West's novels "to point
out their consistent depiction of a social class whose disenfranchisement
is figured as its inaptitude at linguistic expression." In their effort to find
that which is "real," West's protagonists show that language is incapable
of portraying that reality.

The best work on Henry Miller this year can be found in *Conversa-*

tions with Henry Miller (Miss.), ed. Frank L. Kersnowski and Alice Hughes, with 22 interviews from 1956 through 1977 that provide insight into Miller's life and work and the various roles he played in the world: reader, writer, traveler, talker, and bibliophile. The material discussed includes Miller's commitment to all forms of freedom, his love of Paris, exploitation of and by women, and his friendships with Lawrence Durrell, Anaïs Nin, and Alfred Perles. An informative introduction by the editors and a chronology of Miller's life are included.

c. Raymond Chandler and Others   In "Background Action and Ideology: Grey Men and Dope Doctors in Raymond Chandler" (*Narrative* 2: 29–40) David H. Richter examines the different ways that Chandler achieves unity in *The Big Sleep* and *The Long Goodbye,* particularly through use of background action. Specifically, the background of "grey men and dope doctors" in *The Long Goodbye* allows him to avoid the "centrifugal plot" on which he relies in *The Big Sleep* and demonstrates his versatility as a detective writer. Oscar De Los Santos in "Auster vs. Chandler or: Cracking the Case of the Postmodern Mystery" (*Connecticut Review* 16, i: 75–80) argues that Chandler, in spite of his expertise in writing modern detective stories, does not move beyond the modernist category. Paul Auster, on the other hand, moves into the realm of the postmodern by virtue of his more humanistic character development, his authorial intrusion, his metafictive techniques, and his open texts, all qualities designed to draw his audience more fully into his works. Ronald R. Thomas views Chandler in a more postmodern vein. He compares Chandler's *Farewell, My Lovely* with Walker Evans's *American Photographs* in "The Dream of the Empty Camera: Image, Evidence, and Authentic American Style in *American Photographs* and *Farewell, My Lovely*" (*Criticism* 36: 415–57). Both works concentrate on "a world of photographic artiface" in which the truth is distorted and illusory and the definitive truth can never be known. MaryKay Mahoney in "A Train Running on Two Sets of Tracks: Highsmith's and Hitchcock's *Strangers on a Train,*" pp. 103–14 in *It's a Print! Detective Fiction from Page to Screen,* ed. William Reynolds and Elizabeth A. Trembley (Bowling Green), compares Alfred Hitchcock's 1951 cinematic adaptation to Patricia Highsmith's 1950 novel, from which it departs drastically. Mahoney does not find one version superior to the other; rather, she recognizes each as a unique work of art. This year's publications on Dashiell Hammett would best be avoided.

d. Heinlein, Le Guin, and Alfred Bester   Science fiction makes a modest comeback after a brief hibernation. Donna Glee Williams in "The Moons of Le Guin and Heinlein" (*SFS* 21: 164–72) provides a thorough and perceptive comparison of Ursula K. Le Guin's *The Dispossessed* and Robert Heinlein's *The Moon Is a Harsh Mistress,* which paradoxically bear both distinct likenesses and differences, especially in the treatment of anarchy, a principal subject. The connections between the novels are so strong that Williams considers them companion texts that "orbit each other, exerting strong mutual gravitational forces. Neither can be understood alone." Images of imprisonment are the subject of Fiona Kelleghan's "Hell's My Destination: Imprisonment in the Works of Alfred Bester" (*SFS* 21: 351–64), an intriguing article that will attract even neophyte science fiction readers to Bester. Kelleghan traces "themes of imprisonment and release" in Bester's fiction, noting the similarities in settings and rhetorical devices and the emphasis on "the prison as the site of psychological catalysis."

Arkansas State University

16 Fiction: The 1960s to the Present

Jerome Klinkowitz

The decade of the 1960s marks a transition point in fiction, but also in American life. One-third of a century later, definitive studies look to the nature of that transformation in larger terms. Aspects once seen as extraliterary, such as conditions within the publishing industry, are now considered for their impact on the work itself, while other social, cultural, and political dimensions are treated as generative forces. Yet by no means is fiction reduced to material cause. Instead, scholars show great astuteness in discerning how the world itself was becoming more fictive.

i General Studies

Novelist and critic Ronald Sukenick is considered an icon for the transformative 1960s, but recent work shows his role to be more active than reflective. His *In Form: Digressions on the Act of Fiction* (see *ALS 1985*, pp. 277–78) emphasizes this aggressive force, demonstrating how the era's fiction reconnects art with the energy of experience. In "Love Conks Us All," an introduction added to the fifth edition of his novel *98.6* (Fiction Collective Two), he associates his utopianism with that of Hawthorne and Melville, arguing for an "experimentalism" that is American existence itself, from the original 13 colonies to the commune featured in his own work. Collisions between desire and reality, between the innovative and the canonically literary, characterize the search for a primal language behind the word, for the spirit within matter. Only thus will articulation emerge from the nonsense of chaos, which is fiction's job to do. In an important series of essays Sukenick considers such factors in this process as thought in "Excerpts from the Writers' Roundtable" (*SAQ*

My thanks to Julie Huffman for help with the research toward this essay.

93: 460–87), voice in 'How to be Jewish" (*NewL* 60, iv: 65–76), the role
of Europe versus that of America in "Name of the Dog" (*Boulevard* 9:
227–38), and the conditions of dissemination in "Publishing, 2001"
(*AmBR* 16, iv: 3, 6–7).

A similar look at fiction's role in transforming culture is taken by
Marcel Cornis-Pope, whose "Narrative Innovation and Cultural Rewriting: The Pynchon-Morrison-Sukenick Connection" (pp. 216–37) appears in *Narrative and Culture,* ed. Janice Carlisle and Daniel R. Schwarz
(Georgia). Not merely deconstructive, such fiction in fact resists the
totalizing impulses of realistic narration and the bland normalizing of
"midfiction" by "regrounding sociocultural generalizations in a scrupulous analysis of experiential details and refocusing critical attention on the process of realistic articulation." Thomas Pynchon's self-
reflexiveness, Sukenick's tension between innovation and constraint, and
Toni Morrison's disruption of "the hermeneutic, libinal economy of
narration" all undermine the stability of society's "grand narratives." By
focusing on the fiction-making impulse, these authors raise important
questions about the role self-legitimizing narrative orders play in all types
of cultural construction, in the process both examining and undermining claims of authority.

The broad cultural sweep of such process is studied by Philip D.
Beidler in *Scriptures for a Generation: What We Were Reading in the '60s*
(Georgia). The era's own anticanonical impulse has prevented formation
of a defining myth, yet within that anticanonical stance Beidler finds
another myth of sorts: "a belief that acts of imagination, inspired modes
of thinking *and* doing, might truly change the world." The texts themselves are neither literary items nor facets of popular culture but rather
constitute "an *experience* of language across a range of printed texts
whereby a community of the word found it possible to construct itself
politically and historically as a fact of consciousness and to do so in ways
that have now become part and fabric of our lives." Writers studied
include James Simon Kunen, Kurt Vonnegut, and Richard Brautigan;
Beidler's genius is in discerning their texts in the manner of Sukenick's
introduction to *98.6.*

A similar thesis informs William D. Atwill's *Fire and Power: The American Space Program as Postmodern Narrative* (Georgia). Here, key texts by
Saul Bellow, John Updike, Norman Mailer, Tom Wolfe, Thomas Pynchon, and Don DeLillo plot an increasingly "acute awareness of the
troubled status of 'history' even while it is being written into the collec-

tive memory of a culture." Like Sukenick and Beidler, Atwill sees received narrative being called into question, a three-stage process that begins with the portrayal of irrational individuals (*Mr. Sammler's Planet, Rabbit Redux*), problematizes itself in expressing the inexpressible (*Of a Fire on the Moon, The Right Stuff*), and is resolved by freeing the text for multiple meanings (*Gravity's Rainbow, Ratner's Star*).

Such textual activities, of course, emerge from a larger culture, one that is explained by the ethics of deconstruction. But they reenter the popular culture as usable artifacts via motion pictures. And what a remarkable number of such works have appeared on the screen: *Catch-22, Slaughterhouse-Five, One Flew Over the Cuckoo's Nest, Being There, The World According to Garp, Sophie's Choice, The Color Purple, Ironweed,* and various fictions by Norman Mailer and E. L. Doctorow. Editor Barbara Tepa Lupack has various hands study the process in *Take Two: Adapting the Contemporary American Novel to Film* (Bowling Green), and their conclusions fit the general interpretation advanced by Sukenick, Beidler, and Atwill: that at issue are not representations of one form or another of culture but rather a culture's history-making propensity and all of the problems that activity implies.

Not that this thesis rules the day. There are still ways of marginalizing such effort, and these include the alternatives of tokenism and exoticism. Tokenism is the approach taken by editor Peter Parker and consulting editor Sir Frank Kermode in *A Reader's Guide to the Twentieth-Century Novel* (Oxford). On the one hand, Parker and Sir Frank acknowledge the prevalence of innovation by including John Barth, Donald Barthelme, Kurt Vonnegut, William H. Gass, Thomas Pynchon, John Hawkes, Robert Coover, Richard Brautigan, Don DeLillo, and Joseph Heller in their pantheon. But for the most part their achievements in this cavalcade of each year's most important novels are limited to one-offs. Only Barth, Pynchon, and Vonnegut are represented more than once, and then just twice or three times—this in a volume which memorializes five novels by John Updike and 14 by Evelyn Waugh (compared to just three for William Faulkner). Yet a more effective form of marginalization, understandable when advocated by an educationist-oriented creative writing program geared toward morally praiseworthy realism, is that of branding such efforts as quaintly exotic. Such is the critical impulse behind *Transgressions: The Iowa Anthology of Innovative Fiction,* ed. Lee Montgomery et al. (Iowa), where a foreword by William H. Gass reduces the broad sweep of innovation to the narrow technique of metafiction and an afterword by Robert F. Sayre excuses the historical phenomenon as a countercultural wrinkle of the hippy-dippy '60s.

An issue apart from such theoretical and cultural politics is given sound examination by Barbara Ann Schapiro, whose *Literature and the Representational Self* (NYU) associates three novelists not usually studied together. John Updike's work features sex and religion conjoined; that a loving relationship is fundamental to religious impulses fits current revisionist interpretations of religion, particularly with regard to matters of women, dependency, and power. Yet Updike's application yields a "contemptuous authorial distancing" from his characters as expressed by a language of self-display. Toni Morrison probes "the unconscious emotional and psychic consequences of slavery" where the denial of subjecthood has personal consequences exacerbated by the slaves' inability to read their own story. Ann Beattie's "world of boredom, emptiness, and paralyzing passivity" is explicable as part of the culture of narcissism, here a consequence of depending on social institutions where the personal fails and infantilism is reinforced.

Literary politics as real politics is given an intriguing look by Norman Birnbaum in *Searching for the Light* (Oxford, 1993), in which a French government conference for American fiction writers puts them on the spot answering accusations of cultural imperialism, a reminder of issues raised by Sukenick, above.

ii Women

Issues regarding men appear extensively in recent work addressing the concerns of women, most notably so in the third volume, *Letters From the Front,* of Sandra M. Gilbert and Susan Gubar's *No Man's Land: The Place of the Woman Writer in the Twentieth Century* (Yale). The man question is especially pertinent for fiction of the 1960s, a time when sexual liberation promoted men's uncertainty of their own virility. One consequence was "male masquerading" as found in Vonnegut's "Welcome to the Monkey House," Stanley Elkin's "The Making of Ashenden," Pynchon's *V.,* and Donald Barthelme's novels. In the last of these one finds a true no-man's-land where women have all of the intensity as yearned for but never achieved—leading to the question of how women can achieve personhood in such circumstances. Similar matters occupy Nadya Aisenberg, whose *Ordinary Heroines: Transforming the Male Myth* (Continuum) traces a heroic code that is imprinted but remains no longer functional. As opposed to questing out for conquest, the contemporary heroine privileges moral courage over physical bravery within her own normal life. Subgenres show the highest profile for such actions: the new romance eclipses previous themes of women lacking development, crime novels feature new domestic arrangements, and science fiction promotes women as wise leaders far less tied to realism than are men. Strong skepticism is expressed in Martina Sciolino's "Objects of the Postmodern 'Masters': Subject-in-Simulation/Woman-in-Effect," pp. 157–71 in *Men Writing the Feminine: Literature, Theory, and the Question of Genders,* ed. Thaïs E. Morgan (SUNY). Writing the feminine is something men do for their own purposes, fantasizing a bigendered male body as a way of appropriating the feminine. A key example is Barthelme's *The Dead Father,* where authority is only superficially deconstructed, leaving the closed-circuit source of male domination intact.

In the manner of an old-fashioned reputation study, Lisa Maria Hogeland examines a more specifically political issue in " 'Men Can't Be That Bad': Realism and Feminist Fiction in the 1960s" (*AmLH* 6: 287–305), concluding that "the persuasive power of feminist realist fiction, then, is confirming rather than challenging: rather than confronting political and ideological difference, political realism enables its readers to dismiss as unconvincing or unfair depictions with which they disagree." A broader style of literary politics, however, is seen as beneficial to the career of Tillie Olsen, says Shelley Fisher Fishkin in "Reading, Writing, and Arithmetic: The Lessons *Silences* Has Taught Us" (*Listening to Silences,* pp. 23–48). Against the canon of exclusion or ghettoization Olsen's work exploits silencings as both theme and technique, redirecting critical trends and changing the way we read. Similar redirections are plotted in Lindsey Tucker's *Textual Escap(e)ades: Mobility, Maternity, and Textuality in Contemporary Fiction by Women* (Greenwood). It is Sylvia Plath's *The Bell Jar* that takes narrative beyond Freudian development into a yearning for mobility against the bonds of others' discourses; Alice Walker's *Meridian* explores the problematic conjunction of such mobility and the claims of maternity; Toni Morrison's *Sula* and *Beloved* employ the mode of journey to create a centrifugal force, a force which in turn allows superficial issues to vanish into a vortex, including the problematic nature of all boundaries.

How the field has expanded and developed since 1982 is a readerly subtext evident in the supplemental volume 5 to editors Carol Hurd Green and Mary Grinley Mason's *American Women Writers from Colonial*

Times to the Present (Continuum). How interesting it is to have Kathy Acker side by side with Judy Blume, not only as subjects of illuminating entries but as part of an overview the editors construct.

iii Alice Walker and Other African Americans

There are folk elements in Alice Walker's work well beyond conventional nationalistic designs, argues Madhu Dubey in *Black Women Novelists and the Nationalist Aesthetic* (Indiana). Dubey's general approach is posited against the "race-centered aesthetic" of the nationalistic '60s and '70s, but neither does she fully embrace the subsequent African Americanist feminism so often used to interpret Walker and others. Instead, she draws on Bakhtin to describe a novelistic language that becomes a terrain of ideological struggle, a true dialogia that also reveals nonrealistic modes of characterization in the fiction of Toni Morrison and Gayl Jones. A more familiar yet still illuminating metaphor for such work is provided by Margot Anne Kelley's "Sisters' Choice: Quilting Aesthetics in Contemporary African American Women's Fiction," pp. 49–67 in *Quilt Culture: Tracing the Pattern,* ed. Cheryl B. Torsney and Judy Elsley (Missouri). Such assembly offers a way to recapitulate senses of self, community, lineage, and artistic/social connection. How writers undertake a revision of myth interests Elizabeth T. Hayes, whose " 'Like Seeing You Buried': Persephone in *The Bluest Eye, Their Eyes Were Watching God,* and *The Color Purple*" (*Images of Persephone,* pp. 170–94) examines how Morrison, Walker, and Zora Neale Hurston reject the patriarchal notion that women must suffer if life is to continue (thus rendering Persephone's domination "unnatural, highly repugnant, and destructive"). A specific but illuminating study of the character Shug's role is undertaken by Thomas F. Marvin in " 'Preachin' the Blues': Bessie Smith's Secular Religion and Alice Walker's *The Color Purple*" (*AAR* 28: 411–21).

Mind and God are the center of two Morrison studies, Iyunolu Osagie's "Is Morrison Also Among the Prophets?: 'Psychoanalytic' Strategies in *Beloved*" (*AAR* 28: 423–40) and Deborah Guth's " 'Wonder what God had in mind': *Beloved's* Dialogue with Christianity" (*JNT* 24: 83–97). The first essay identifies psychoanalysis as a "conditional operative" narrative strategy to uncover "buried stimuli," while the second locates religion within the contrary imperatives of remembering and forgetting. How narratives are shaped to anticipate our response, much like an

African American sermon with its participatory rhythms, becomes apparent in Dolan Hubbard's *The Sermon and the African American Literary Imagination,* where *Song of Solomon* and *Beloved* are seen as demanding such feedback. Jazz itself offers double voicings and a tappable metalanguage in *Tar Baby,* Craig Hansen Werner establishes in *Playing the Changes: From Afro-Modernism to the Jazz Impulse* (Illinois); reality is thus more readily seen as a texture of competing myths, with the added feature that for African American fiction all such myths must be apprehended with a double consciousness (in which full knowledge is split between two characters, a factor also present in such innovative works as Pynchon's *Gravity's Rainbow* and Gilbert Sorrentino's *Mulligan Stew*). That Morrison is associated with Sorrentino should not be surprising, as both are veterans of commercial publishing and the endless editorial wars that shape much contemporary fiction; the prevalence of her career in publishing is evident from many of the interviews collected by Danille Taylor-Guthrie in *Conversations with Toni Morrison* (Miss.).

Other figures lack the concentrated study given to Walker and Morrison, but helpful readings do continue. "Recovering the Conjure Woman: Texts and Contexts in Gloria Naylor's *Mama Day*" (*AAR* 28: 173–88) by Lindsey Tucker shows how a reliance on African magico-religious views of the world creates a different narrative mode and demands a reader's response different from that of realism. Suppressed sexuality and commodification of the self are challenges Amy S. Gottfried finds central in "Angry Arts: Silence, Speech, and Song in Gayl Jones's 'Corregidora'" (*AAR* 28: 559–70), while the plight of Sherley Anne Williams's character Dessa Rose is explored by Catherine Clinton in "'With a Whip in His Hand': Rape, Memory, and African-American Women" (*History and Memory in African-American Culture,* pp. 205–27).

New essays collected by editor David C. Estes for *Critical Reflections on the Fiction of Ernest J. Gaines* (Georgia) present this figure as an inclusive rather than dismissive author. This initial comparison, with Richard Wright, is made by Frank W. Shelton in "Of Machines and Men: Pastoralism in Gaines's Fiction" (pp. 12–29), where the issue is not just the weakness but the strength of a Southern rural heritage. The dissonances Gaines cultivates are in history, especially a history that is less endlessly repetitive than influenced by the individual act, according to David Lionel Smith in "Bloodlines and Patriarchs: *Of Love and Dust* and Its Revisions of Faulkner" (pp. 46–61). The greater complexities are found in gender relationships, says Marcia Gaudet in "Black Women: Race, Gender, and Culture in Gaines's Fiction" (pp. 139–57), where the issues are influence, violence, and community.

Charlie Reilly and I deal with two innovators active through four decades. Reilly's *Conversations with Amiri Baraka* (Miss.) includes the editor's new "Interview with Amiri Baraka" (pp. 239–59) in which Baraka clarifies biographical points and argues for the artistic importance of his *The Autobiography of LeRoi Jones.* My own "Clarence Major's Innovative Fiction" (*AAR* 28: 57–63) links Major's earliest innovations with his use of historical and folk materials in more recent years.

The growing importance of Caribbean writing in the American canon is evident in the announcement of editor Maurice Lee's new *Journal of Caribbean Literatures* and in Moira Ferguson's *Jamaica Kincaid: Where the Land Meets the Body* (Virginia). Kincaid's fiction plots relations with mothers as mediated by living as colonial subjects; how complex it is when the idea of a colonial motherland contests the duality of mother and land conjoined. A solution is to become a "voice-giver" in the quest for personal identity, part of the movement beyond memory and "unitary thinking." No single perspective or perception can be adequate, demanding a repoliticization beyond unworkable older attitudes.

iv Indian and Asian Americans: Bharati Mukherjee, Amy Tan, and Maxine Hong Kingston

An exotic novelist's appeal to a small-town newspaper columnist yields sound critical insight in Scott Cawelti's "Interview with Bharati Mukherjee" (*Short Story* n.s. 2, i: 101–11). "Straightforward and direct, that's the Iowa way," Cawelti assures this writer lately living and working in his state, a view Mukherjee complements in her explanation of how her convent education had previously "protected us from contemporary literature, 20th century literature which was supposedly all so raucous and obscene, mind damaging." In the process Mukherjee has become savvy in the matter of grants as well, going well past the more common Writers Workshop feeding-trough mentality to regret the creation of "a kind of stable of writers who are going to write optimistic propaganda, cultural propaganda"—she does admit to having a no-strings MacArthur Fellowship as the ideal. A Mukherjee protagonist's bildungsroman-like progress from India to Iowa is traced by Kristin Carter-Sanborn in " 'We Murder Who We Were': *Jasmine* and the Violence of Identity" (*AL* 66:

573–93); the challenge consists in working through literary and sociopolitical transformations as well as personal ones.

Amy Tan's major novel continues to draw scholars. Noteworthy for its technical insight is Stephen Souris's " 'Only Two Kinds of Daughters': Inter-Monologue Dialogicity in *The Joy Luck Club*" (*MELUS* 19, ii: 99–123). Intended as a collection of stories, Tan's work benefits from a backdoor use of multiple monologues in the tradition of Woolf and Faulkner, yet with the enhancement of decentered, multiperspective forms such as encouraged by Bakhtin. There is a dialogy of difference and agreement across these various monologues, and it is in that dialogy that the novel's import is formed. Thematics play a more important role in "Memory and the Ethnic Self: Reading Amy Tan's *The Joy Luck Club*" (*MELUS* 19, i: 3–18); Ben Xu shows how "The need to ethnicize their experience and to establish an identity is more real and more perplexing to the daughters than to the mothers," who are secure in their Chinese identities. Such community exists only in the remembered past, a situation that demands narratives of memory to form "an experiential relation between the past and the present."

A similar theme informs Debra Shostak's "Maxine Hong Kingston's Fake Books" (*Memory, Narrative, and Identity*, pp. 233–60). Not histories but events as remembered are important; therefore, the various possibilities of memory, especially in its imaginative form, enrich a narrative where individuality combines with communal consciousness.

v Cynthia Ozick, Philip Roth, and Other Jewish Americans

Sarah Blacher Cohen's facility with comedy enriches her important study, *Cynthia Ozick's Comic Art: From Levity to Liturgy* (Indiana). Both author and subject share a laughter of remembering, not of forgetting, a comedy that is neither smiling nor infernal. "The most conspicuous comic element in Ozick's fiction," Cohen understands, "is comedy of character which exposes the tainted nature of her protagonists." Some of these have self-mockery, while most of the others are unaware of their flaws and look askance, in a Bergsonian way, at the flaws of others. The key is understanding that for the Holocaust Ozick uses both retaliatory and restorative humor, techniques other critics tend to weight more heavily one way or the other. Uplifting irony is Cohen's subject in "Cynthia Ozick: Prophet for Parochialism," pp. 283–98 in *Women of the Word: Jewish Women and Jewish Writing*, ed. Judith R. Baskin (Wayne

State); here, Jewish sources for creativity are more important than universal ones, a reminder that before assimilation one must have a value of
one's own to offer others, not the voice of the ghetto but of Sinai. All of
this is seen as more problematic by Victor Strandberg, whose *Greek
Mind/Jewish Soul: The Conflicted Art of Cynthia Ozick* (Wisconsin) perceives the author's attempt to maintain Jewish culture as a major struggle
against Christian values, an argument bolstered by biographical research
and interpretation.

Agreeing with Cohen is Andrew Vogel Ettin; his *Speaking Silences:
Stillness and Voice in Modern Thought and Jewish Tradition* (Virginia) also
covers Grace Paley's "silences of tales untold" (among the marginalized
and excluded) and Philip Roth's protagonist in "The Conversion of the
Jews" whose attitudes are Jewish but whose rhetoric is profoundly Christian. The ideological dimensions of comic narrative are examined by
Thomas Pugh in "Why Is Everybody Laughing? Roth, Coover, and
Meta-Comic Narrative" (*Crit* 35: 67–80) to the point that Roth's "On
the Air" and Robert Coover's *Whatever Happened to Gloomy Gus of the
Chicago Bears?* reflect on comic discourse, choosing Adorno's ideology
over Bergson's or Freud's.

Another look at comedy comes from Robert Murray Davis. His "A
Stand-Up Guy Sits Down: Woody Allen's Prose" (*Short Story* n.s. 2, ii:
61–68) draws insightful contrasts with the art of Donald Barthelme, an
equally comic writer but one who works with comic effect in language
rather than relying on the hit-or-miss of situation. Another comic writer
not frequently associated with Ozick and Roth is Raymond Federman.
Treated as an experimental fictionist rather than as a Jewish writer,
Federman is not accorded the depth that Jewish-based comedy often
receives. The author himself corrects this situation in "The Necessity
and Impossibility of Being a Jewish Writer" (*New Letters* 60, iv: 179–87),
reminding readers that "the linguistic and typographical games I have
played in my fiction may be a mere cover-up, a partial cancellation of the
past, but nonetheless they point to the inadequacy of language in the face
of an event as hideous and as unspeakable as the Holocaust."

vi Walker Percy and Other Southerners

Family has always been an important element in Walker Percy's fiction,
and now one scholar has examined the biographical and literary influences. In *The House of Percy: Honor, Melancholy, and Imagination in a*

Southern Family (Oxford), Bertram Wyatt-Brown recounts a son's unpayable obligation to an adoptive father. The wound of Roy Percy's death motivates a search for self-mastery, a maturity that brings with it dedication to religious conviction. The true core of Percy's work, however, is an intellectual expansiveness which acknowledges but also condemns the "Percy legend" of loss and vengeance. Autobiographical elements in the fiction are established by Wyatt-Brown in a second book, *The Literary Percys: Family History, Gender, and the Southern Imagination* (Georgia), especially the ideals of male power and female submissiveness; "most intriguing of all" is the "singular connection" between *Lancelot* and Catherine Ann Warfield's *The Household of Bouverie,* specifically how both heroes are compulsive not only "to prove their own existence but to reassert their power over those near them, particularly women." Such biographical revelations are also noted by Lewis P. Simpson in *The Fable of the Southern Writer,* prompting the question, "What is the consequence of the gnostic moment when one goes out of history into history and assumes the responsibility for time?" The answer is that Percy "extends the southern prophetic imagination of the moral complicity of the individual in history." Such influence extends to younger writers, as Richard Keller Simon suggests in "John Kennedy Toole and Walker Percy: Fiction and Repetition in *A Confederacy of Dunces*" (*TSLL* 36: 99–116). *The Moviegoer* is itself a text of repetitions; by repeating them again, Toole answers Percy's project with a Boethian corrective rather than a Kierkegaardian affirmation.

Cozier notions of family are considered in Terri Witek's "Reeds and Hides: Cormac McCarthy's Domestic Spaces" (*SoR* 30: 136–42). Most of McCarthy's protagonists flee home, reflecting the pattern of flight in traditional American literature. The author's argument, however, is not with home itself but with our metaphors for it, most of which he finds are unrealistic when set against experience. The complexities of relating to society interest Terry Roberts, whose *Self and Community in the Fiction of Elizabeth Spencer* (LSU) finds complex narrative structures in Spencer's later novels as having evolved to deal with more complex relations to society, especially those of community dynamics and the layerings of relationships. Family life appears as a strong influence in editor Dale Salwak's *Anne Tyler as Novelist* (Iowa), particularly in Elizabeth Evans's "Early Years and Influences" (pp. 1–14) and Stella Nesanovich's "The Early Novels: A Reconsideration" (pp. 15–32), where isolation of the individual within the family prompts growth of self-awareness. In terms of Tyler's mature work, the poetic consciousness of time is appreciated by Joseph Voelker in "Marcel Proust, Involuntary Memory, and Tyler's Novels" (pp. 86–98), while the smooth prose for tangled lives is analyzed in "Everybody Speaks" (pp. 138–46) by Donna Gerstenberger.

Southern writers always seem to be the best interview subjects, a resource exploited to excellent effect in two new collections: editor Susan Ketchin's *The Christ-Haunted Landscape: Faith and Doubt in Southern Fiction* (Miss.), which features Larry Brown being tough on characters, loading them down to see how much they can do, and William Parrill's *The Long Haul: Conversations with Southern Writers* (Southeastern Louisiana), where concerns are directed to professional aspects of literary work, particularly in the publishing business.

vii Sandra Cisneros and Other Writers of the West and Southwest

The growth of protagonists signals the writerly growth of the author itself, according to L. M. Lewis's "Ethnic and Gender Identity: Parallel Growth in Sandra Cisneros' *Woman Hollering Creek*" (*Short Story* n.s. 2, ii: 69–78). As opposed to what Cisneros herself described as the "lazy poems" of her first collection, the stories gathered here show women not just confronting external, dominant sets of values but evolving their own identities by dealing with such alien, exclusive languages. Something similar happens to Louise Erdrich's character in *Tracks,* a novel taken by Laura E. Tanner in *Intimate Violence: Reading Rape and Torture in Twentieth-Century Fiction* (Indiana) as a tale not of empowerment but of vulnerability, as understandings of race, gender, and power are keyed not just by the rape but by the way that act of violence remains present through the victim's imagination. "History, Postmodernism, and Louise Erdrich's *Tracks*" (*PMLA* 109: 982–94) by Nancy J. Peterson considers the context of deconstruction, which calls into question the referential value of history, the authority of narrative and the role of dominant histories with regard to more indigenous tales. Erdrich distinguishes herself from her husband's social interests in *Conversations with Louise Erdrich and Michael Dorris,* ed. Allan Chavkin and Nancy Feyl Chavkin (Miss.), a volume that also answers questions about the nature of their collaboration.

A new darkness in nature writing emerges in the work of Edward

Abbey, according to James I. McClintock in *Nature's Kindred Spirits* (Wisconsin). Abbey develops in the tradition of Thoreau but identifies increasingly with the moods of Jack London and B. Traven, "giving fact emotional and spiritual significance in a threatening Darwinian world," an approach that yields an "anarchist perspective." That protagonists must learn to read radically before telling their own stories is a lesson Michael Hobbs explicates in "Living In-Between: Tayo as Radical Reader in Leslie Marmon Silko's *Ceremony*" (*WAL* 29: 301–12), proving Harold Bloom's thesis that "When you read, you confront either yourself, or another, and in either confrontation you seek power." Lying is one way of avoiding confrontation, and a searing indictment of such practice in the modern-day mythmaking of a nonexistent reality distinguishes more than one contribution to editor Judy Nolte Temple's *Open Spaces, City Places: Contemporary Writers on the Changing Southwest* (Arizona).

viii The Mannerists: John Updike and John Cheever

Editor James Plath's *Conversations with John Updike* (Miss.) presents an unusually rich trove of materials generated by this most articulate and literary of authors. One of the few such writers not affiliated with a university or part of the roving-in-residence crowd, Updike remains preeminently a man of letters whose real world is bookish in the best sense (rather than being academically political). His comments here cover a wide range of interests and show him as adept a critic as he is a novelist—discerning, for example, that *The Sirens of Titan* is Kurt Vonnegut's best work and that his *Slapstick* is an underrated, ambitious novel.

John Cheever's world is neither bookish nor academic; even its suburban WASP texture is woven in a unique style, a technique Michael D. Byrne finds instructive in *Dragons and Martinis: The Skewed Realism of John Cheever* (Borgo). Like other critics Byrne segments Cheever's work after *The Wapshot Chronicle* as a "second period" distinguished by the author's "troubled vision"; but rather than just making an assessment of how unstable characters upset the community in thematic terms, Byrne explores how the fantastic and the mysterious yield new strategies of narrative. Cheever's career then resolves itself in a third period where such narrative forms take a metafictive turn, featuring narrators who intrude with protestations of their factionality.

The most perceptive of Cheever's critics is Robert A. Morace, whose "Tales from the Crypt(o-autobiography): A User's Guide to John Cheever's Journals" (pp. 224–45) bolsters editor Francis J. Bosha's *The Critical Response to John Cheever* (Greenwood). It was *Falconer,* Morace believes, that set the stage for the biographically based criticism that has informed recent discussions of this novelist. But reading the journals reveals more complex connections; as opposed to interpretive simplifications, Morace is able to show how Cheever's life is textualized in various sources. How much richer would studies of realistic authors be if more scholars drew on such theoretics as Foucault's modes of existence in discourse and Bakhtin's understanding of voice, resources that Morace employs to show how there is more of Samuel Beckett than of F. Scott Fitzgerald to this deep and demanding writer.

ix Realists Old and New

John Gardner's *On Moral Fiction* (see *ALS 1978,* p. 431) almost single-handedly made realism an explosive critical issue. Shortly before his death in 1982 Gardner retracted many of his more contentious opinions, but that his understanding was both broadening and mellowing is evident from the material now collected in *On Writers and Writing* (Addison-Wesley). Of particular note is Gardner's long, rich essay, "A Writer's View of Contemporary American Fiction" (pp. 163–98), in which he links his own techniques with those of former archenemy Ronald Sukenick. Of particular note is Gardner's redefinition of what is "moral" fiction: no longer Gerald Graff's dogmatic prescription for how to live one's life but rather a sensitive artist's understanding that a reader's imagination must be involved for a fictive work to be complete.

Individual studies, however, lack Gardner's expansive vision, devoted as they are to specifics of craft. "John Gardner's 'The Ravages of Spring' as Re-creation of 'The Fall of the House of Usher'" (*SSF* 31: 481–90) allows Katherine Feeney Fenlon to show how this master can "out-Poe Poe" in effect and extend his plot. Similar close craftsmanship is appreciated by Michael Trussler in "The Narrowed Voice: Minimalism and Raymond Carver" (*SSF* 31: 23–37), a study that measures what can be implied by absence. That another of these minimalists "participates in the general postmodernist decentralization of dominant cultural paradigms" is clear to Yonka Krasteva, who suggests in "The South and the West in Bobbie Ann Mason's *In Country*" (*SLJ* 26, ii: 77–90) that the author is inventing a new style of regional writing. The contemporary American landscape is what Timothy Peters finds well described in "'80s Pastoral: Frederick Barthelme's *Moon Deluxe* Ten Years On" (*SSF* 31: 175–87), while a more familiar conclusion is reached by Michael Walker in "Boyle's 'Greasy Lake' and the Moral Failure of Postmodernism" (*SSF* 31: 247–55). Yet both Walker's reading of T. Coraghessan Boyle and Fenlon's of John Gardner assume a moralistic, instructive stance for fiction that was one of the terms of combat in 1978; that the leader of this battle had revised his notions by 1982 makes them even more suspect today.

How refreshing, then, to enter the world described by Peter A. Scholl in *Garrison Keillor* (Iowa). Here, a literary artist can be admired for his "narrative ubiquity" without the need of slaying critical enemies in the process. Indeed, Keillor's multiple perspectives and comic attitude toward his materials make self-important claims of moralism the last things one would think of. Of special interest is Scholl's documentation of how Keillor draws on the work of others—for example, employing ghostwriter Gordon Mennenga.

In the world of Sylvia Plath's biography, contentions continue. Janet Malcolm concerns herself, as might be expected, with some of the dirty laundry aired after Plath's death, but she justifies it by establishing how Plath's image has been frozen at the moment of her suicide. Therefore, *The Silent Woman: Sylvia Plath and Ted Hughes* (Knopf) works to defrost and reanimate this image, even if that means dwelling on such subjects as how Hughes allowed *The Bell Jar* to be published because he wanted money for a third home and how the literary-journalistic politics of literary estateship have complicated the historical picture.

x Experimental Realists: Grace Paley and Paul Auster

How Grace Paley combines referentiality and self-referentiality is well described by Adam Meyer in "Faith and the 'Black Thing': Political Action and Self-Questioning in Grace Paley's Short Fiction" (*SSF* 31: 79–89). Paley's own politics are rehearsed by characters created as if for the purpose of such statement; but instead of using fiction as an agitprop soapbox, the author turns her protagonists' developing political consciousnesses into an artistic process which draws on the elements of fiction-making itself. Radical idealism is thus seen to be relative in terms of right and wrong, something Paley's distance from her characters allows her to question even as metafiction interrogates itself.

A similar complexity informs the work of Paul Auster as studied in a special issue of *Review of Contemporary Fiction* (14, i), guest-edited by Dennis Barone. What Auster has in mind beyond simple realism is suggested by Chris Tysh in "From One Mirror to Another: The Rhetoric of Disaffiliation in *City of Glass*" (pp. 46–52), a project that deconstructs "the heavenly tower of the father's city and his language" in a way that parallels "postmodernism's crisis of repetition." The artistic complexity of what Auster devises challenges Steven Weisenburger to research sources and theoretics for "Inside *Moon Palace*" (pp. 70–79); by rejecting the naturalizing conventions of narrative, Auster delegitimizes the "state authority" behind a story, preferring an alternative mode of temporality more useful to the fictionist's purposes. "Things happening for a second time" is Auster's delicate description of memory, an orientation Mary Ann Caws explores in "Paul Auster: The Invention of Solitude" (pp. 30–31). A special feature of *RCF* in its ongoing treatment of living authors is attention to the mechanics of their publication. Editor-in-chief John O'Brien's researches have helped establish how crucial such elements are, and for the Auster issue editor Gerald Howard offers his personal testimony in "Publishing Paul Auster" (pp. 92–95), an account that emphasizes Auster's absorption of literary theory as a key to his success.

xi Innovative Fiction from Barth to Vonnegut

Advertised as a basic introduction to Barth's fiction, *A Reader's Guide to John Barth* (Greenwood) provides author Zack Bowen with too much latitude for fulsome praise. The review of criticism reads like hagiography, and while there are good notes on recurrent themes and techniques, far too little thought is put into evaluating literary trends. A more useful view of Barth appears in Richard Kostelanetz's *On Innovative Performance(s)* (McFarland), a treatment of a typical Barth reading from the late '60s as alternative theater. For a new edition of *LETTERS* (Dalkey Archive) Barth himself supplies a foreword that recounts the novel's genesis during a time of national insufficiency.

"Apocalyptic metafiction" is a term Gabriele Schwab finds helpful for comprehending Thomas Pynchon's dalliance with epistemological crises in a context of real threats; her *Subjects Without Selves: Transitional Texts in Modern Fiction* (Harvard) values such fiction for exposing dangers of apocalyptic myths. Traps of representation are thus avoided without embracing "world-disenchantment" as an alternative. The judgment of

J. Kerry Grant's *A Companion to* The Crying of Lot 49 (Georgia) is that
as Oedipa Maas is paralyzed by interpretation, culture itself moves
toward a state of intellectual inertia, a reading that explains both the
accessibility of this novel and its coherence with Pynchon's larger (and
more difficult) canon. The role of social structures in Pynchon's major
work is explained by Timothy Melley in "Bodies Incorporated: Scenes of
Agency Panic in *Gravity's Rainbow*" (*ConL* 35: 709–38); as Slothrop
disintegrates, "his material body is transformed into a geographical
distribution similar to the map he once made of his innermost experiences," a movement from singular locus to statistical distribution. *Vineland* is given attention in *Pynchon Notes* 30–31 in terms of fantasy,
dystopian fiction, political leftism, and entropy (here seen in economic
rather than physical terms). Most original is John Farrell's "The Romance of the '60s: Self, Community, and the Ethical in *The Crying of Lot
49*" (pp. 139–56), a reminder that so much of the author's fictive activity
takes place within the paradigms of the romance.

Donald Barthelme's *Forty Stories* reminds Morton Gurewitch how
hard it is to pin down irony in absurdist fiction; but as opposed to the
ironist reading advanced by Charles Molesworth (see *ALS 1982*, p. 291),
Gurewitch sees Barthelme's irony as suspensive and ambivalent, with
much of his comedy being farcical in the manner of "furious nonsense"
and therefore qualifying less as irony and more as fun, according to
arguments advanced in *The Ironic Temper and the Comic Imagination*
(Wayne State). Ellen J. Esrock's *The Reader's Eye: Visual Imaging as Reader
Response* (Hopkins) finds a more refined pleasure in William H. Gass's
texts. A "network of substitutions" rather than a fixed response to
something in the world motivates such readings, where the reader's
production of visual images yields a total set of relationships, no one of
which is a clear stamp-to-seal thing. The most serious business of all
takes place among Gaddis's complex narratives, says Gregory Comnes in
The Ethics of Indeterminacy in the Novels of William Gaddis (Florida).
Apparent fragmentation is in fact "dialectics at a standstill," whereas only
a mimesis beyond representation is capable of providing an ethics that
can be justified in terms of epistemological concepts.

Jerzy Kosinski's *Being There* establishes the power of television as its
own reality, Wendy Lesser agrees in *Pictures at an Execution: An Inquiry
into the Subject of Murder* (Harvard), just as Norman Mailer's *The
Executioner's Song* must answer formulaic questions of the murder story
but leave the end open to popular fascination (never pinning down just

why the murder took place). Yet as problematic as such fictive visions are, they cannot come close to matching the quasi-historical stew concocted as fraudulent autobiography by Kosinski. The decade's long argument continues in Russ W. Baker's "Painted Words" (*Village Voice*, 15 March, pp. 58–59), but it makes its first movement toward closure in "Kosinski's War" (*New Yorker*, 10 October, pp. 46–53) by James Park Sloan. A former Kosinski protégé, Sloan is motivated not to defame the novelist but to explore the complexities of autobiographic invention that fed his literary art. To this extent he has researched Kosinski's papers among the Houghton-Mifflin archives at Harvard and, for this essay, traveled to Poland where he interviewed villagers who knew Kosinski as a child—a child whose wartime experiences were far different from what has been accepted as fact.

Despite its title, Lawrence R. Broer's *Sanity Plea: Schizophrenia in the Novels of Kurt Vonnegut* (Alabama) pictures a far more stable subject, one whose struggle against the despair of his time constitutes a true spiritual evolution. To the original edition (see *ALS 1990*, p. 306) Broer adds coverage of *Hocus Pocus* and *Fates Worse Than Death*, works that confirm his thesis about Vonnegut's increased autobiographical candor. Pessimism is not thematic fatalism but rather an element in the writer's psychological plot; all of Vonnegut's heroes, including his protagonist Hartke in *Hocus Pocus*, have a divided nature, part of which fights through this pessimism to overcome apathy and evolve from an imprisoned self to a creative one. That a new round of Vonnegut scholarship is under way becomes evident with Marc Leeds's massive *The Vonnegut Encyclopedia* (Greenwood), an index to characters, locales, and themes not just in the fiction but in Vonnegut's essays. Editor Leonard Mustazza's *The Critical Response to Kurt Vonnegut* (Greenwood) provides a first-class reputation study which in its four decades of coverage testifies to this author's continuing importance. A reminder that Vonnegut's comic impulse has social pertinence is provided by M. Keith Booker in *The Dystopian Impulse in Modern Literature* (Greenwood), particularly in Booker's reading of *Player Piano* within the context of works by Skinner and other social scientists.

A quantum advance in the understanding of an important but understudied author is made by W. C. Bamberger in *William Eastlake: High Desert Interlocutor* (Borgo). Eastlake's fiction ranges from Revolutionary War days to Vietnam and the modern Southwest, but Bamberger looks past thematic superficialities to see an underlying interest in the processes of misinformation and self-deception. In this sense Eastlake's work is an important antecedent to a writer getting much more critical attention, Don DeLillo. Social orders old and new inform *End Zone* and *Libra*, according to Paul Civello's *American Literary Naturalism*. In being unable to come to terms with the old order and working toward a new paradigm in the new, DeLillo's characters attack assumptions of critical science by showing how there can be no such thing as a detached witness. In *American Notes* (Northeastern) Daniel Aaron shares this sense of convergences in events, particularly in such participatory witnessing and especially when it comes to connections that historians fail to see when they are unable to sense feelings. Closer studies of special interests are undertaken by John M. Duvall in "The (Super)Marketplace of Images: Television as Unmediated Mediation in DeLillo's *White Noise*" (*ArQ* 50, iii: 127–53) and by Joseph Kronick in "*Libra* and the Assassination of JFK: A Textbook Operation" (*ArQ* 50, i: 109–32). The United States is awash in protofascistic urges, DeLillo would have us believe; yet any such expressive acts are as hard to decode as any text. Similar readerly concerns occupy Mark Conroy in "From Tombstone to Tabloid: Authority Figured in *White Noise*" (*Crit* 35: 96–110) and Christopher M. Mott in "*Libra* and the Subject of History" (*Crit* 35: 131–45), the Mott article showing how discussions take place within a discourse framed by specific ideologies.

As always, fetishistic aspects of Kathy Acker's work draw critics like flies, sometimes to the extent that they make a fetish of Acker herself. Escaping this fault is Arthur F. Redding's "Bruises, Roses: Masochism and the Writing of Kathy Acker" (*ConL* 35: 281–304), thanks to an ability to see her stimulations as textual rather than simply physical devices. A careful textual experiment is outlined by Rod Phillips in "Purloined Letters: *The Scarlet Letter* in Kathy Acker's *Blood and Guts in High School*" (*Crit* 35: 173–80). Acker feels as deeply about forms as meanings, particularly when it is those forms that have empowered male dominance; thus her borrowings are more than topical satires, for she is ultimately subverting form. The master of formalistic subversion, however, remains Richard Kostelanetz, at least according to the cannily perceptive Raymond Gomez in "Toward a Critical Understanding of Richard Kostelanetz's Single-Sentence Stories" (*Crit* 35: 229–36). By tearing down "prevalent conditions of mid-twentieth-century rhetoric, style, and subject matter in literature" Kostelanetz, in the manner of John Cage, allows truly fresh innovations to emerge. The result is an aphoristic style of literature stripped free of preconceptions, again in the manner of Cage.

xii   Subgenres: Science, Horror, War, and the Nonfiction Novel

Organizational structures lie at the heart of dystopian science fiction, David Seed proposes in "The Flight from the Good Life: *Fahrenheit 451* in the Context of Postwar American Dystopias" (*JAmS* 28: 225–40). Ray Bradbury's character only gradually comes to realize his participation in a system, the consequences of which let the author dramatize his feelings about how a consumer culture can develop in a fully apoliticized way.

Jonathan P. Davis provides a good insight when he says that the horror story is "subtextually a realist portrayal of life, only hidden behind masks, capes, and fangs." *Stephen King's America* (Bowling Green) is thus an illuminating study of how the author covers the "broad landscapes of America" with such narration. Original to this study is a specific under-standing of how King's political altruism and savvy allow him to probe "the human condition" in the United States.

A strong political vision informs Donald Ringnalda's *Fighting and Writing the Vietnam War* (Miss.). Yet as so often happens, when politics are shaded to the left aesthetic judgments become slanted to the right. Ringnalda rejects earlier arguments that because the war itself eclipsed military conventions, the fiction in response to it had to follow a similar path of innovation. Instead, because the conflict's motivating politics were absurd, he believes the resultant fiction was absurd, too—absurdist, in fact, in a high modern sense, an interpretation almost everyone working in the field would reject, given that it ignores the literary theory of an entire era. More responsible is John Limon's response in *Writing After War: American War Fiction from Realism to Postmodernism* (Ox-ford), where with more pertinent originality the author proposes a sports theory to explain disruptions of the war fiction tradition (a theory encompassing ideas by Derrida and others emerging parallel with Viet-nam). A special issue of *Critique: Studies in Modern Fiction* (36, i) is devoted to fiction from the war, where in addition to expectable studies of Tim O'Brien and Larry Heinemann (the two most frequently dis-cussed novelists in recent years) one finds Maureen Ryan's "The Other Side of Grief: American Women Writers and Vietnam" (pp. 41–57), a topic whose consideration has been long overdue.

That conventional journalism is no more objective than fiction seems obvious to Phyllis Frus, whose *The Politics and Poetics of Journalistic Narrative: The Timely and the Timeless* (Cambridge) faults Ernest Hemingway for creating the sham that it is. A crucial feature of the work of Norman Mailer, Truman Capote, Tom Wolfe, and Janet Malcolm is that they reject this Hemingwayesque sham, and that they also realize that much of late 20th-century experience is textual in nature.

University of Northern Iowa

Timothy Materer

William Carlos Williams captures the most critical attention this year as
the subject of six books, one of them his correspondence with Marcia
Nardi, the "Cress" of *Paterson*. Wallace Stevens and Robert Frost also
inspire numerous studies, and there are significant books on Hilda
Doolittle, E. E. Cummings, and W. H. Auden. The year's work includes
an edition of Langston Hughes's poetry and a fine general study, Frank
Lentricchia's *Modernist Quartet* (treating Frost, Stevens, Pound, and
Eliot). Cultural and feminist approaches predominate. The best of the
Williams books analyzes his Puerto Rican heritage, and Stevens's political orientation is analyzed in both Lentricchia and Alan Filreis's *Modernism from Right to Left*. Of the three feminist studies, Linda A. Kinnahan's
Poetics of the Feminine (on Williams and three of his poetic "daughters")
stands out for its insight into literary history and poetics as well as
theoretical issues.

i William Carlos Williams

Julio Marzan's *The Spanish American Roots of William Carlos Williams*
(Texas) explores Williams's two identities: Carlos Williams, the child of
Spanish-speaking immigrants, and Bill Williams the American. Marzan
shows how Williams often obscured his ethnic roots (as in his *Autobiography*) before he finally accepted and acknowledged them. Like
any minority child, he grew up with an awareness that his family's
heritage was devalued by the mainstream culture. This consciousness
motivated his strenuous insistence, in contrast to Ezra Pound and T. S.
Eliot, on a native American culture and poetry. As Marzan puts it, "He
was American and a 'pure product of America' *because* his mother was
Puerto Rican." While developing a "cool, anglicized Bill persona," he

continually returned to the dark, passionate Carlos as his "Dionysian *duende.*"

The key figure in this development is Williams's mother. Although several Williams books this year discuss her influence, Marzan has the keenest insight into their relationship. This relationship was ambivalent "because she was the person in whom Williams saw himself, and as a medium of a foreignizing practice she also foreignized him from 'normal' American culture." As the mother of "Carlos," she does not "figure in the life of Bill" until he draws closer by working with her on Spanish translations and writing *Yes, Mrs. Williams* (1959). Marzan links the books about his mother with both *Paterson* and the autobiography as a "single semantic piece" in a "cosmology in which she is the spiritual core." Marzan's knowledge of Spanish literature and appreciation of multicultural issues enrich his analysis. He corrects many misapprehensions by Paul Mariani and other Williams critics about Spanish-American culture and Williams's ethnic background. (For example, Mariani refers to a "Spanish patois," which does not exist.) Marzan gives illuminating readings of such poems as "The Desert Music," which he says is full of "antagonist cultural symbols" but ultimately celebrates the "moment of discovering the stabilizing triumph of poetry over the agony of possessing a divided soul." Readers of this book will also wish to read Miguel Mota's " 'It looked perfect to my purpose . . .': William Carlos Williams's Contact with the Spanish" (*JML* 18: 447–59).

Peter Halter's *The Revolution in the Visual Arts and the Poetry of William Carlos Williams* (Cambridge) is a useful addition to work on Williams and the visual arts. Thanks to its illustrations and review of past criticism, it is an ideal introduction to the topic. Halter assesses the influence of Marcel Duchamp, Paul Cézanne, and Georges Braque. Duchamp's "belief that chance and accident are creative principles that often triumph over outworn artistic conceptions" influenced Williams's early experimental poetry. Williams admired Cézanne's attack on "the Renaissance perspective [which] entailed an unwanted feeling of separation between the spectator and the depicted world," and he emulated Braque's attempt "to replace the vanishing point, the empty space into which all painted objects receded, with a space that was solid and close to the viewer." Halter also explores Williams's links to such American artists as Charles Demuth, Alfred Stieglitz, Marsden Hartley, Charles Sheeler, and John Marin, whose works adhered to "immediate sensory experience."

In *William Carlos Williams and Alterity* (Cambridge) Barry Ahearn seems to echo Marzan when he says that the failure of Williams's critics to see the importance of his mother's influence is "perhaps due to the tendency of some critics to view his parents as representing values Williams was eager to repudiate." Ahearn focuses on Williams's conflicts about himself, his family, and his social role by making the poet's ambivalence, alienation, or "alterity" his theme. The first three chapters on Williams's biography are an absorbing summary of the multiple conflicts in the poet's nature. Ahearn's conclusion is that Williams found his voice as a poet when he discovered how to express his contradictory selves. The last three chapters on the formal tensions in the poetry (such as the conflict between formal and free meters) are less interesting because the listing of poetic techniques and motifs (for example, various categories of metamorphosis) have inherently less interest. Ahearn's conclusion that Williams surpassed many of his contemporaries because "the tensions of opposing elements [in his poetry] are greater" is unsurprising, but also well supported by the many sensitive readings of specific poems.

Donald W. Markos's *Ideas in Things: The Poems of William Carlos Williams* (Fairleigh Dickinson) recalls George Bagby's *Robert Frost and the Book of Nature* (1993) in its attempt to relate a modern poet to Emersonian Transcendentalism. Both books are brave attempts to counter the current critical tendency to emphasize the skeptical and relativistic qualities of modern poets. The contrary danger, however, is to rely on sometimes superficial similarities between a poet's beliefs and Emerson's. For example, Markos argues that Emerson's term "oversoul" resembles Williams's term "ground"; yet he has no convincing argument that "ground" carries a Transcendentalist connotation. The looseness of the argument is seen particularly in his claim that Williams like Emerson and Whitman "was a visionary poet with an intuitive sense of ideal value beyond but also within the world that appears to the senses." The comparison is supported by the assertion that these three poets share a "life-affirming mood." His argument is more rigorous when he analyzes the Aristotelian conception of the universal in Williams's claim "To make a start,/out of particulars/and make them general." An excellent review by Stephen Hahn of this book, with a reply by Markos, appears in the *William Carlos Williams Review* (20: 62–69).

In *Poetics of the Feminine* Linda A. Kinnahan confesses to uncertainty about whether her book is "about Williams, or modernism, or poetic

daughters in a male tradition, or language innovation, or feminist poetics?" As the title suggests, it is first a book about feminist poetics, but
the range of its concerns keeps it from a narrow theoretical cast. She
anchors it in literary history by discussing Williams's personal and
literary relationships with Mina Loy and Denise Levertov and his literary
influence on Kathleen Fraser—a "language poet" who founded the
feminist journal *HOW(ever)*. Williams's modernism developed at the
same time as what Fraser calls "first-wave feminism." The modernism
was expressed in the "collaged expression" of Williams's early poems and
in the sympathy for feminism he showed in supporting Mina Loy's
poetry and Dora Marsden's writing in the *New Freewoman* (soon retitled
the *Egoist*). Like Ahearn, Kinnahan values Williams's discovery that he
could speak out of conflicting selves, which made him receptive to the
feminist challenge to fixed identities. Williams valued feminism because
it too challenged traditional forms. He conceived of woman's poetry as "a
feminine discourse linked to the body." His repeated call for "contact"
involved "alternative notions of authority and is grounded—philosophically, metaphorically, linguistically, and ontologically—in an idea of the
feminine." His awareness of the innately gendered and sexual reality of
the world made him unusually receptive as a male poet to feminist
concerns. Although one could argue that Williams "essentializes" the
concept of "woman," Kinnahan prefers to emphasize his "interaction
between essentialism and constructivism." Unlike other modernists, his
conception of the individual "relies not upon mastery but upon related-
ness or connectedness." In a discussion of Mina Loy's questioning of
male authority, Kinnahan notes that Williams in poems such as "The
Ogre" and "Housewife" demonstrates the "destabilization of poetic
authority . . . , unsettling traditional authority by questioning the
broader implications of the power of dominance."

Williams showed sympathy for Denise Levertov's "sense of marginality" early in her career. Her "maternal model of empathy and connection" intersected with his willingness to invest the maternal with poetic
authority and so encouraged her poetic development. In the present-day
poet Kathleen Fraser, Kinnahan sees the continuing influence of the
Williams tradition in Fraser's "concern with the interaction between
linguistic innovation, feminist politics, and literary tradition." Kinnahan's sympathy for Williams is the more impressive because she is fully
aware of Williams's male arrogance and condescension as he defined his
own sense of the feminine and maternal. In *Paterson* especially, Kin-

nahan finds a strong assertion of "patriarchal authority" in his mythologizing of the feminine. Her criticism is particularly sharp when she
discusses Williams's use of Marcia Nardi's letters to him to represent the
plight of women in that work; this appropriation of a woman's words
reveals the assertion of "male privilege" and "the traditional inscription
and silencing of the feminine within constructs [such as Williams's epic]
of male authority." She agrees with Nardi when she wrote (in a *Paterson*
letter) "that my thoughts were to be taken seriously, because that too
could be turned into literature."

Readers who wish to explore Williams's relationship to Nardi can now
read *The Last Word: Letters between Marcia Nardi and William Carlos
Williams,* ed. Elizabeth Murrie O'Neil (Iowa). Nardi met Williams when
she asked his advice about the hospitalization of her son. Williams was
interested in her as a woman poet, placing several of her poems in
publications like the New Directions anthology, but not as a woman. She
did not object to her letters appearing in *Paterson* but regretted the
confirmation that to Williams she was interesting only as a type or
symbol of the talented but struggling woman poet. She reflected in 1981
when she was 80 that Williams was actually a "very conventional man":
"no matter how much a man admires a woman's work, or her intelligence . . . his interest in her as a friend (and I mean a *close* friend) depends
very much on his feeling about her sexually. If she has no sex appeal for
him, he tends to keep her at a distance socially, regardless of her achievements." Nardi's letters are no less painful to read in this edition than in
Paterson, and the Afterword caps the gloom with the sad story of Nardi's
later life and estrangement from her son. But the advice Williams himself gave has been honored: "Use *all* her letters. *She* has the last word."

Feminist readings of Williams also appear in Susan Ayer's "Women in
the Later Poems of William Carlos Williams" (*JEP* 15: 168–75), a catalog
of female archetypes, and Sergio Rizzo's "The Other Girls of Paterson—
Old and New" (*WCWR* 20: 38–60), which discusses Williams's short
story "The Colored Girls of Passenack," where the prototype for the
"Beautiful thing" of *Paterson* appears. Williams's relationship to a mater-
nal figure, Emily Dickinson, is discussed in Jay Ladin's "Breaking the
Line: Emily Dickinson and William Carlos Williams" (*EDJ* 3: 41–59).
Noteworthy articles in *WCWR* include Andrew Lawson's "Division of
Labor: William Carlos Williams's 'The Wanderer' and the Politics of
Modernism" (20: 1–22) and an analysis of Williams's ambivalent feelings
about literary fame, " 'Geez, Doc, What Does it Mean?': Reading Wil-

liams Reading *Life*" (20: 23–37). The fall issue of *WCWR* on Williams
and History includes Richard Frye's "Answering Back: History and
William Carlos Williams's 'Impromptu: The Suckers'" (20:2–14) and
Burton Hatlen's "Openness and Closure in Williams' *Spring and All*"
(20: 15–29).

ii Robert Frost

In comparison to Kinnahan's book, Katherine Kearns's feminist reading
of Frost in *Robert Frost and a Poetics of Appetite* (Cambridge) is narrow
and unsympathetic. Her thesis, that Frost's "poetry documents a man's
struggle with his own oppositional impulses of appetite and modera-
tion," seems to bring the poetry down to the biological level. Since all
men fight out these impulses, the book emphasizes Frost's common
characteristics as a man rather than his unique qualities as a poet. On the
basis of Kearns's thesis, the conclusions are predictable: one poem after
another reveals the assertion of masculine dominance in opposition to
female formlessness. Kearns attributes to Frost a conception of language
and human nature that seems alien to him. For example, in describing
the way language subverts itself she writes that "by Frost's terms the
power to undermine any speaking voice lies within the venereal force of
language itself." Terms like "venereal force" belong to Kearns, not to
Frost. Similarly, the Foucauldian term "Heautocratic" is used a dozen
times to describe Frost as phallocentric. She attributes Foucauldian views
to Frost himself, finding it significant that he wrote in an era when "every
malady and physical disturbance would perhaps explain the sexual etiology implicit in his seemingly nonironic appropriation of the art/love
analogy to verify an impulse perceived oppositionally in terms of creation and annihilation." When she says that sexuality in Frost "is made
to confess to its own pathological nature" and that one discerns the
"seeds of nihilism" within Frost's use of "'love' as the figure a poem
makes," the implication that sex is pathological is also hers and not his.

She is much more persuasive in her analyses of individual poems than
in her theoretical statements because the explications stay within the
vocabulary of the poetry. Her stimulating readings of individual poems,
including those of poems she returns to again and again ("Home Burial,"
"The Hill Wife," and "The Witch of Coös") does convince one of Frost's
fear of the feminine and his desire to control "feminine" experience
through poetic form. Like Frank Lentricchia, she notes Frost's concern

about poetry being a feminine art, and she also shows that Frost particularly distrusted irony as a feminine technique.

Kearns's discussion of irony is the most original and persuasive aspect of the book, even though her analysis is sometimes confusing. When she speaks of Frost's "seemingly nonironical appropriation of the nature/art analogy," one must wonder if Frost was ever nonironical. Can one imagine a poet like Frost *not* having ironical reservations about the nature=woman, art=man analogy that Kearns attributes to him? Critics such as Jay Parini, Richard Poirier, and Lentricchia value the doubleness, paradoxes, and modernist irony of Frost's poetry. But Kearns's criticism discovers duplicity rather than doubleness, dishonesty rather than ironic detachment. Her concluding pages are eloquent but flawed with an almost personal bitterness: "Frost wanted to write poetry and still be a man, even as he devalued the vocation as feminine. . . . He wanted to be taken as serious while seeming to jeer at the pukes and prudes who wanted to be taken seriously. He wanted to abjure the egotistical sublime while being egotistical and evoking sublimity. . . . He wanted to be popular and to be an artist, to be both parsnips and caviar, to sell enough books to make himself rich while infiltrating his apparent accessibility with inside literariness. . . . He wanted to be a farmer who wasn't a farmer, a teacher who wasn't a teacher. . . . " One cannot dismiss this indictment, supported as it is by the book's analysis; it should keep Frost critics busy for a while. But I have no doubt that, dark as Frost was as a poet, the design of darkness in Kearns's critical perspective accounts for her indictment more than Frost's work itself.

Lawrence Thompson's saturnine portrait of Frost, which clearly influenced Kearns's book, has inspired a memoir from the poet's granddaughter, Lesley Lee Francis's *The Frost Family's Adventure in Poetry* (Missouri). Although she had resolved not to add to the biographies of Frost, Francis feared that Thompson's "crudely psychoanalytical interpretation had silenced the brilliant and humorous voice of the living poet and seriously misrepresented his relations with family and friends." Through her personal knowledge of her grandfather and access to journals that the Frost children wrote while living on New Hampshire and English farms, Francis portrays Frost's "human and humourous presence." She vividly portrays a family environment that recalls the childhoods of the Brontës and Alcotts. Each child kept extensive journals and gathered to hear Elinor Frost read Scottish classics from Sir Walter Scott, George Mac-Donald, and Robert Burns; their parents gave them the "undivided attention necessary to raise [their] children on reading, writing, and the art of direct observation." She also vividly describes the financial and physical hardships of country living and shows the cold reality behind the romantic idea of "living under thatch." Francis acknowledges the irony that the Frost children, who received such close and loving attention, should have had such troubled lives. Her comments on this irony is a wise summing-up of the family's "adventure": "The personalities that emerge from the pages of the notebooks and the little magazine, uncomplicated and devoid of cynicism, yet rich in emotional texture and artistic development, give no hint of the troubles that would beset these children as adults. Unless we are prepared retroactively to interpret their intuitiveness and natural wonder as a lack of preparedness for life's hard knocks—a fair enough interpretation in retrospect—we can only marvel at the display of talent and inventiveness of the Frost children and their friends, and experience with them the spontaneous delight in their surroundings."

Two essays by poets on Robert Frost, the late Joseph Brodsky's "On Grief and Reason" (*NY* 26 Sept.: 70–78) and Daniel Hoffman's "Robert Frost: The Symbols a Poem Makes" (*GettR* 7: 101–12) are of special interest. Brodsky gives us the perspective of a Russian poet lecturing to French students. He explains that Frost is not "tragic" in the European sense but "terrifying" in the American one, as seen in his confrontations with untamed nature and animals. To conclude his brilliant reading of "Home Burial," Brodsky writes of the detachment one senses in the narrator and thus in Frost himself: "the poem is the author's self-portrait. That is why one abhors literary biography—because it is reductive." Hoffman recalls hearing Frost stating his conception of symbolism, defined in terms explicitly opposed to Eliot's, and he discusses the power of Frost's "metaphorless words" in "Neither Out Far Nor in Deep." Helen H. Bacon reminds us of Frost's profound classicism in " 'Getting among the Poems' in Horace's *Fons Bandusiae* and Robert Frost's *Hyla Brook*" (*CML* 14: 259–67), and Walter Jost reads Frost through Heidegger in " 'It Wasn't Yet It Was': Naming Being in Frost's 'West-Running Brook' " (*TSLL* 36: 5–50). Donald G. Sheehy's "Winter 'Not Quite All, My Dear': Gender and Voice in Frost" (*TSLL* 36: 403–30) gives a balanced account of the dialogue of male and female in poems such as "Two Look at Two," concluding that the male voice predominates since "gender difference is inscribed as hierarchy." Donald G. Sheehy edits " 'To Otto as of Old': The Letters of Robert Frost and Otto Manthey-

Zorn" in two issues of *NEQ* (67: 355–402; 567–602), which highlight Frost as teacher and philosopher rather than as poet. In addition to numerous readings of his poems, the *Robert Frost Review* contains a current bibliography, a letter from Frost to Dorothy Canfield Fisher, and essays on Frost's dualism, anthropomorphism, and religious beliefs. Finally, Frost's address at Brown University (1955) on the vocation of poetry, "For Glory and for Use," appears in *Gettysburg Review* (7: 91–99).

iii Hilda Doolittle (H.D.)

In *Out of Line: History, Psychoanalysis, and Montage in H.D.'s Long Poems* (Stanford) Susan Edmunds is far more self-conscious about her feminist perspective than is Katherine Kearns. She quotes Sarah Schuler's opinion that H.D.'s critics may see in her poetry "versions of current feminist concerns, but only through a biological lens that reflects back at the woman critic her own desire and duplicity." She approves of the feminist critics who have rescued H.D. from a misogynist or homophobic sense of modernism and who have explored H.D.'s "specifically female" quest for wholeness and an authentic voice. However, her book challenges the "optimism" of their interpretation by challenging the notion that H.D. actually achieved a liberated sexual identity. She suggests that these critics are unaware that the liberation they find in H.D.'s poetry is the result of importing contemporary ideas into her texts. Although Edmunds demonstrates their blindness to the major and decidedly unliberated theme of maternal guilt in the poetry, I believe that Edmunds herself does not detect the blindness generated by her own insights.

Her criticism of H.D.'s conception of maternal guilt is grounded in the fascinating story of the poet's sessions (1935–37) with the English psychoanalyst Walter Schmideberg, which seem to have been as momentous for H.D. as her analysis with Freud and which deeply influenced her long poem *Helen in Egypt* (1961). Schmideberg married the daughter of Melanie Klein, the controversial English psychoanalyst. Although his wife, also a psychoanalyst, was a bitter critic of her mother's work, Schmideberg accepted the Kleinian theory of the violent psychic development of early infancy. H.D. wrote that she discussed with Schmideberg chiefly the "guilt and suppressed rage" implied in Klein's notion that the child conceives of both a Good Mother and a Bad Mother—one who satisfies all needs and another who withholds her breast and her warmth, triggering the infant's aggressive instinct to devour the bad mother and the mother's equally strong response. Edmunds approves of the way this theory supports a woman's right to be as aggressive as a man. In H.D.'s *Helen in Egypt* the recognition "that our sex need not enforce our position as victims of male violence" is seen in the "seeker's" invocation of "the original great-mother" who drives "harnessed scorpions/before her." On the other hand, the Kleinian conception of the mother does not serve the seeker well since it replaces the Freudian's castrating father with the equally sinister "cannibalistic Kleinian mother." The Kleinian emphasis on maternal aggression and guilt apparently enforced H.D.'s guilt over leaving her own child while she traveled and wrote. Edmunds deplores the way this guilt shapes H.D.'s rewriting of the Helen myth: "Indeed, the poem's plot eventually turns on a surprisingly conservative application of Melanie Klein's theories of reparation and the good and bad mother, one that diverts blame from the oedipally conflicted fathers and sons who occupy the battlefield at Troy to the very mothers and daughters who are most insistently absent from it" (100).

Edmunds's criticism of *Helen in Egypt* is penetrating, and there is similarly acute analysis of *Trilogy* and *Hermetic Definition*. However, she ignores *Helen* for what it is, a poem, when she disapproves of H.D.'s theme because it does not serve the cause of "women eager to increase their power outside the family" or because it defines maternal power in a way "that feminists can only protest." Edmunds lacks the love for poetry (seen in Kinnahan's admiration for Williams) which can override discomfort with a theme that challenges or offends a reader. Although she usefully counters the optimistic critics of H.D., she should also grant H.D. her poetic donnée of expressing guilt through the myth of Helen. Is H.D.'s Kleinian theme of "mourning as reparation" poetically moving or not? Unfortunately, Edmunds asks instead whether the theme furthers the cause of liberation. Edmunds's analysis of *Helen* will nevertheless help the sympathetic reader to a deeper appreciation of H.D.'s long poems.

Donna Hollenberg also treats the topic of H.D. and maternal guilt in "Abortion, Identity Formation, and the Expatriate Woman Writer: H.D. and Kay Boyle in the Twenties" (*TCL* 40: 499–517). The theme of identity is the focus of Susan Smith Nash's "H.D.'s Dark Night of the Soul: Nights and the Rupture of the Self" (*ArkQ* 1: 337–42). In "Mystical Experience in H.D. and Walt Whitman: An Intertextual Reading of 'Tribute to the Angels' and 'Song of Myself'" (*WWR* 11: 123–36) J. W. Walkington argues that H.D.'s critics have neglected the mystical dimension.

iv Wallace Stevens

The careful recovery of cultural and political contexts that one finds in Marzan on Williams and Edmunds on H.D. distinguishes Alan Filreis's *Modernism from Right to Left: Wallace Stevens, the Thirties and Literary Radicalism* (Cambridge). Although its intensive use of archival material makes it a work to study rather than read, it is essential to anyone who wants to understand the original context of many of Stevens's poems, including the historical events that inspired them and their political implications for contemporary readers. In his first book, *Wallace Stevens and the Actual World* (1991), Filreis concentrated on Stevens's poetry from 1940 through 1950. *Modernism from Left to Right* contains fascinating background on Stevens's work as an insurance adjustor during the depression and his generally compassionate social views on controversial measures such as Social Security (though he detested FDR, whom Filreis identifies as the "pagan in a varnished car" of an early passage in *Blue Guitar*). Filreis shows how poems like "Lions in Sweden" spring out of headline news, and how "Mozart, 1935" emerges from discussions in left-wing publications.

Filreis discredits the "myth of wholly separate radical and modernist spheres" invented by the New Critics in the '50s. His highly detailed accounts of the politicizing of aesthetic issues, especially his perhaps too exhaustive discussion of Stanley Burnshaw's review of Stevens in *New Masses* (1935), shows how profoundly sensitive the poet was to the terms of political discussion. In Stevens's hands, the modernist mode was ideally suited to a "rhetorical dialogism" that was desperately needed but usually missing in political discussion. Stevens proved surprisingly adept in "working in a mode in which adversarial relations were to be casually played out with intense thirties-style dialogic." In both theory and practice, Stevens defended the continuing relevance of the lyric poem and warned his readers that "political repression become aesthetic—can happen here." But his great achievement in this mode was in his long poem *The Man with the Blue Guitar*: "the end of the poem makes thematically clear what the interactive structure of the whole implies all along—that modern poetry overtly and incessantly lyric is no different from other forms of political language in inscribing opposing voices." Filreis's conclusion is that this dialogic is "one of the structural blessings—it is no less than that—bestowed upon American forms of modernism by the radical moment."

Discussing how one teaches certain poems and poets is stimulating in a faculty coffee room. But I soon grew tired of the two dozen essays in *Teaching Wallace Stevens: Practical Essays,* ed. John N. Serio and B. J. Leggett (Tennessee). For one thing, I teach survey courses, and these essays all assume that one can break up into discussion groups (a fine idea in itself), send students to the rare books room, and introduce them to philosophical systems. The most interesting essay is the first, by Helen Vendler, who reminds us that a poem is like a painting and must be taken as a whole. To proceed line by line is like looking at the top corner of a painting and then working down, which is boring and violates the work as a whole. Yet most of the essayists not only take this approach in teaching a poem but also in writing their articles, which often give us too much detail about how the teacher proceeds from stanza to stanza or from one concept to another. However, the volume contains some excellent readings of the poems and serves as an interesting survey of which critics seem most useful (Harold Bloom, A. Walton Litz, Joseph N. Riddel), the poets most often compared to Stevens (Marianne Moore, William Carlos Williams, T. S. Eliot), and the poems most often taught (mostly old favorites like "The Snow Man," but also fresh choices like "Tea at the Palaz of Hoon"). Serio is also the compiler of *Wallace Stevens: An Annotated Secondary Bibliography* (Pittsburgh). In this essential volume, the chronological entries from 1916 through 1990 are clearly described and organized, and they document the tremendous growth in Stevens studies in the past 25 years. A chapter in Krzysztof Ziarek's *Inflected Language: Toward a Hermeneutics of Nearness* (SUNY) concerns Stevens's late poetry but adds little to previous discussions of Heidegger and Stevens. *The 1994 Annual of Hermeneutics and Social Concern,* ed. Justus George Lawler (Continuum), contains Lawler's "Soliloquy of the Interior Paraplegic: Stevens on the Poet and the Philosopher" (pp. 81–91), which explores Stevens's "amicable antagonism" to the philosopher. In "Leaving Things Out" (*SWR* 79: 574–92) James Longenbach analyzes the modernist practice of ellipsis in Stevens's poetry. He shows that "Notes Toward a Supreme Fiction" illustrates the role of interpretation in supplying what the author has omitted. He counters Marjorie Perloff's claim that *Notes* (composed 1941–42) ignores the war with the argument, which Filreis would surely approve, that it reveals wartime conditions in its reflection on the "limitation of the poet's historical power." In addition to many explications of his poems, the *Wallace Stevens Journal* contains two articles on Stevens's friendship with the Irish poet Thomas Egan McGreevy, "Thomas McGreevy and Wallace Stevens: A Correspondence" by Mary Joan Egan (18: 123–45) and "Thomas McGreevy and the Pressure of Reality" by Lee Jenkins (18: 146–56). Janet McCann's "A Letter from Father Hanley on Stevens' Conversion to Catholicism" (18: 3–5) discusses the reports of Stevens's deathbed conversion to Catholicism as well as the reaction to them of Holly Stevens and some of the poet's critics.

v Lentricchia on Frost and Stevens

Frank Lentricchia's *Modernist Quartet,* a study of Frost, Stevens, Pound, and Eliot, represents cultural studies and intellectual history at its best. Lentricchia describes the challenges these poets faced in entering a literary scene formed by the genteel heritage of the Fireside Poets and within a society pervaded by imperialism and capitalism. He also analyzes the influence of three Harvard philosophers—George Santayana, William James, and Josiah Royce—whose works are "themselves collaborative modernist texts, the original metapoetic idiom of the youth of Eliot, Frost, and Stevens—both expression and criticisms of the ideologies of modernism before the fact." Santayana's *The Sense of Beauty* (1896) states the modernist doctrine of the image: "perception caught and crystallized in language, the image *is* the sense of beauty." Santayana also gives a "historically surprising criticism of perceptualist aesthetic" by warning against the extreme inwardness and social alienation that cultivating the image can foster; his theory of the image challenges conventional language with the "authoritative language of immediacy." Similarly, Lentricchia shows the social implications of William James's criticism of the abstractness that not only undermines literary language but is the "major symptom of a society's terminal illness." James's Emersonian stress on the individual is countered by Josiah Royce's on community as both a historical and imaginative consciousness, leading to a historic debate carried on by the romantic Stevens and classicist Eliot.

According to Lentricchia, Frost's guarding of his masculinity is not the character flaw that Kinnahan perceives: the "cultural issue of manliness had for him immediate, personal impact" because he was writing a new kind of lyric poem with no ties to the genteel or elitist traditions. He thought the poet should mirror social change and the world of work as truly as the novelist. No less a modernist than Pound or Eliot, he differed from them in not conceding to prose the mass audience created by the genteel tradition. Lentricchia argues that Stevens's reaction to his milieu is less socially constructive than Frost's. A collector of objets d'art and consumer of exotic foods, Stevens cultivated the self to an extreme of Emersonian individualism. He loved the unique and abhorred the mass-produced. Yet the unique was equally contaminated by a culture of capitalism and imperialism, which made the exotic goods (from China or Africa, for example) available to him. Although Lentricchia loves the vivid transparency of Stevens's poetry, he thinks his long poems cohere merely through the "force of desire for moments" and do not advance, despite what his critics say, in "scope, ambition or high seriousness." Like Yvor Winters, Lentricchia sees cultivation of the exquisite image as Stevens's weakness as well as his strength. He concludes that the "missing term in modernist thinking . . . is community: something larger, something more valuable than isolate selfhood, that would include original selves, nourish and sustain them, while also nourishing and sustaining a network of connection."

Considering the critical attention that Williams receives this year, it is almost surprising that he does not appear in Lentricchia's study, for who would be more significant as a poet of community? However, Lentricchia only regrets leaving out Marianne Moore and Hart Crane. His reason, he suspects, is "insufficient love" for their work. Would that more critics declined writing about poetry for the same reason! A criticism of Lentricchia's treatment of Stevens and gender issues appears in Lee Edelman's *Homographesis: Essays in Gay Literary and Cultural Theory* (Routledge): "Redeeming the Phallus: Wallace Stevens, Frank Lentricchia, and the Politics of (Hetero)Sexuality" (pp. 24–41).

vi E. E. Cummings

Although no anthology of modern poetry would exclude E. E. Cummings, and most poetry lovers number a few of his poems among their favorites, only one major study of him was published in his centenary year. In *E. E. Cummings, Revisited* (Twayne) his biographer Richard S. Kennedy frankly acknowledges that the neglect of Cummings is in part the poet's fault, since he published much bad or trivial work and his paranoid character alienated friends and admirers. However, the main problem is simply that critical opinion finds it difficult to characterize him. Kennedy attempts to revisit or reintroduce Cummings by analyzing three aspects of his style: Apollonian (lyric and mythic), Satyric (erotic

and satiric, often coarse), and Hephaestian ("bending, breaking, twist-
ing, mending, and reshaping materials in order to create new forms of
literary expression"). The creation of the Hephaestian style seems most
likely to merit Cummings his place as a modernist. Although Kennedy
does not neglect the impact of Greek and French literature, or Emersonian Transcendentalism (*Self-Reliance* was Cummings's "bible"), he
shows that art movements from the American "ashcan" school to dada-
ism are the key to the poet's development. Cummings was not only
inspired by the visual artists, but was himself an accomplished draftsman
and painter—as the book's 27 illustrations demonstrate. Cubism had the
deepest influence, as one of his key statements reveals: "The symbol of all
art is the Prism. . . . The goal is unrealism. The method is destructive. To
break up the white light of objective realism into the secret glories which
it contains."

Francis O. Mattson's catalog for an exhibition of Cummings's work,
e.e. cummings @ 100 (NYPL), contains an introduction by Norman
Friedman; and there are comments on the poet's work by Robert Creeley,
Theodore Weiss, and others in the journal of the Cummings society,
Spring.

vii Langston Hughes, Claude McKay

Readers of Hughes will welcome the appearance of *The Collected Poems of
Langston Hughes,* ed. Arnold Rampersad and David Roessel (Knopf).
The poems Hughes published in his lifetime appear in chronological
order according to dates of their first publication. The notes give the
poem's publication history (the text used is always the last published
version), a record of textual changes, and explanatory (not interpretive)
notes. An exception to the chronological order is that the poems in
Montage of a Dream Deferred and *Ask Your Moma* are presented intact to
honor Hughes's sense of them as unified works. The brief introduction
observes that some critics think that Hughes failed to create "a modernist
literature attuned to the complexities of modern life." The full text of
Montage, and the balance of the approximately 600 pages of poetry in
this edition, refute that critical opinion. The *Langston Hughes Review*
contains a tribute to the pioneer of Hughes studies, the late Richard
Barksdale, in Harry B. Shaw's "The Historical Pragmatism of Richard K.
Barksdale" (13: 1–20). This review of Barksdale's scholarship touches on
the major critical events in Hughes's career, such as his feud with James

Baldwin. Hughes's 1930 collaboration with Zora Neale Hurston is discussed in Lisa Boyd's "The Folk, the Blues, and the Problems of *Mule Bone*" (13: 33–44). Boyd attributes the poor critical reception of the play Hughes wrote with Hurston to their separate visions of the play—Hurston's grounded in folkloric narrative and Hughes's in tragicomedy. Hughes's friendship with Cuba's national poet is the subject of Robert Chrisman's "Nicolás Gilluén, Langston Hughes, and the Black American/Afro-Cuban Connection" (*MQR* 33: 807–20). Hughes inspired Gilluén (1909–89), a mulatto who exemplified "the quest for the national synthesis of Cuba," to use the Afro-Cuban *son,* the music of the black masses, as Hughes himself used the rhythms of the African American blues.

In "Never Cross the Divide: Reconstructing Langston Hughes's *Not Without Laughter*" (*AAR* 28: 601–13) John P. Shields tells the story of Hughes's relationship with the wealthy white woman he met in 1927 and called "Godmother," Mrs. Charlotte Mason. In urging him not to "cross the divide" into propaganda, especially while writing his novel *Not Without Laughter,* she also inhibited his developing political voice. His experience with her inspired his poem "Poet to Patron," written in 1930 but not published until his break with her in 1939. In "Heroic 'Hussies' and 'Brilliant Queens': Genderracial Resistance in the Works of Langston Hughes" (*AAR* 28: 333–45) Anne Borden explores Hughes's understanding of the connection between gender and race and the way it shapes identity. She particularly admires Hughes's ability to adopt both male and female voices (as in *Montage*).

Claude McKay's poetry is discussed by James R. Keller in " 'A chafing savage, down the decent street': The Politics of Compromise in Claude McKay's Protest Sonnets" (*AAR* 28: 447–56). Although a "protest sonnet" may seem a contradictory term, Keller argues that the poems successfully join form and content and "tradition and dissent." He analyzes the "subversion/containment model" throughout McKay's sonnets, and he shows how functional McKay's echoes of Shakespeare, Blake, and Milton are in context.

viii Marianne Moore, Louise Bogan, May Sarton

There are two outstanding essays on Moore's poetry this year. The first is Melissa Monroe's "Comparison and Synthesis: Marianne Moore's Natural and Unnatural Taxonomies," pp. 56–83 in *The Text Beyond: Essays in*

Literary Linguistics, ed. Cynthia Goldin Bernstein (Alabama). Moore's brilliance as a modernist innovator, a master of juxtaposed images who crosses linguistic boundaries, is seen in this linguistic analysis of her "noun + noun compounds." For example, in "Jerboa," Moore labels the jerboa a "sand-brown jumping-rat," which is taxonomic in form; however, it is also described as a "Sahara field-mouse" and not a rat (with a further confusion about whether its habitat is a desert or a field); moreover, the term "sand-brown" is a poetic rather than a scientific term. However vivid Moore's descriptions, we finally never fully grasp the nature of what she describes, as in the case of the jerboa: "we only have the sum of the ways it is referred to, various attempts, 'scientific' or 'poetic,' to structure the natural world by means of words." Andrew J. Kappel's "The World Is an Orphan's Home: Marianne Moore on God and Family," pp. 173–92 in *Reform and Counterreform: Dialectics of the Word in Western Christianity since Luther,* ed. John C. Halwey (Mouton de Gruyter), criticizes the account in Charles Molesworth's biography of the religious atmosphere of the Moore household. Although she did not share the sentimental piety of her mother and brother, she was not as unappreciative of it as Molesworth suggests. Kappel gives a perceptive account of Moore's religious life as glimpsed in her poems and allusions to theological works, and he speculates on how the absence of her father, who was institutionalized after a mental breakdown before her birth, may have influenced it. He summarizes his argument through a brilliant analysis of "Silence," the final poem of Moore's *Complete Poems.*

Christine Colasurdo's "The Dramatic Ambivalence of Self in the Poetry of Louise Bogan" (*TSWL* 13: 339–61) describes Bogan as an "outsider to the male-dominated tradition [who] must battle with language not her own, and this battle may at times end in silence." Her strategy in this battle is the bold one of exposing her "female ambivalence"; her "poems do not describe a battlefield, they are the battlefield itself." Colasurdo argues that critics have often misunderstood Bogan's poetic persona through underestimating her irony and failing to see that in her work failure is success and silence is music: "What appear to be victim poems are in fact celebration of the self's emergence from family constraints, failed love, and rigid gender roles."

The late May Sarton (1911–95) is memorialized in *A Celebration for May Sarton,* ed. Constance Hunting (Puckerbrush). Among the 22 essays are discussions of Sarton's poetic affinities with H.D., W. B. Yeats, and Elizabeth Bishop, her maternal imagery, transformation of the (feminine) sentimental tradition, and recurrent themes of death, aging, and loneliness. Sandra M. Gilbert's " 'That Great Sanity, That Sun, the Feminine Power': May Sarton and the (New) Female Poetic Tradition" (pp. 267–85) praises Sarton for her "repudiation of the 'slant' or guarded statement, that signals her allegiance to the newly bardic American muse who inspires the singing of our recent 'homegirls.' " The collection's liveliest essay is Carolyn Heilbrun's "The May Sarton I Have Known" (pp. 3–12), a contentious exploration of why the outspoken and independent Sarton has been so little recognized by the literary establishment.

iv W. H. Auden

Critical Survey devotes an issue to Auden which includes Glyn Maxwell's "Notes on Auden's 'Bucolics' " (6: 351–54) and Tony Sharpe's essay on Auden's poetry of the 1930s, "W. H. Auden and Rules of Disengagement" (6: 336–42). Mihaela Irimia's "The Art of Losing: W. H. Auden and Elizabeth Bishop" (6: 361–65) draws on the marks and marginalia in Bishop's own volumes of Auden (now at Harvard) to demonstrate the affinity between them. Auden's affinity with Thomas Hardy is explored in Andrew Robert Deane's "Tiny Observers of the Enormous World: Thomas Hardy and W. H. Auden" (*THJ* 10: 41–52). The second issue of "Auden Studies" appears as *W. H. Auden: "The Language of Learning and the Language of Love,"* ed. Katherine Bucknell and Nicholas Jenkins (Oxford). The volume is in three sections: previously unpublished writings, which include some brilliantly witty songs and a travel diary, "In Search of Dracula"; Edward Mendelson's bibliography of "Interviews, Dialogues, and Conversations"; and critical essays. Among the best of the essays are Stan Smith's "Persuasions to Rejoice: "Auden's Oedipal Dialogues with W. B. Yeats" (pp. 155–63) and David Luke's essay on Auden's notorious Berlin journal, "Gerhart Meyer and the Vision of Eros: A Note on Auden's 1929 Journal" (pp. 103–11).

x Robert Penn Warren, John Crowe Ransom, Allen Tate

Daniel Duane's "Of Herons, Hags and History: Rethinking Robert Penn Warren's 'Audubon: A Vision' " (*SLJ* 27, ii: 25–35) considers the ambivalence of Warren's judgment on Audubon's aggressive but passionate approach to nature. William Bedford Clark's "In the Shadow of His

Smile: Warren's Quarrel with Emerson" (*SoR* 30: 550–69) contends that Warren's philosophy is closer to Emerson's than his critics, with the notable exception of Harold Bloom, have acknowledged. Randy J. Hendricks discusses Warren's anxiety about retaining a historical identity in a technological world in "Warren's Wandering Son" (*SoAR* 59, ii: 75–93). Warren also figures in Ernest Suarez's "Southern Poetry and Critical Practice" (*SoR* 30: 674–89), which deplores the politicization of modern poetry and offers as a welcome alternative the regional and individual themes of Southern poets such as Warren and David Bottoms.

In William Klein's "A Critic Nearly Anomalous" (*SoR* 30: 392–409) John Crowe Ransom's early essay ("A Poet Nearly Anonymous") on Milton's self-consciousness in "Lycidas" is considered a key to Ransom's sense of himself as a modern poet. Ellen Bryant Voigt in "Narrative and Lyric: Structural Corruption" (*SoR* 30: 725–41) uses Ransom to illustrate how Southern poets "corrupt" narrative form to make their works more lyrical. Jeffrey J. Folks's " 'The Archeologist of Memory': Autobiographical Recollection in Tate's 'Maimed Man' Trilogy" (*SLJ* 27, i: 51–60) explores the interconnections among three poems—"Maimed Man," "The Swimmers," and "Buried Lake"—to demonstrate Tate's turn from myth toward autobiography. Wyatt Prunty's "At Home and Abroad: Southern Poets with Passports and Memory" (*SoR* 30: 745–61) analyzes Tate's work in a discussion of the sense of place as a metaphor. Finally, Louis D. Rubin, Jr., in "A Gathering of Fugitives: A Recollection" (*SoR* 30: 658–74) recalls the 1956 reunion of the Nashville Fugitives, including Warren, Ransom, Tate, Cleanth Brooks, and Donald Davidson, and assesses their place in the history of modern poetry.

University of Missouri, Columbia

18 Poetry: The 1940s to the Present

Lorenzo Thomas

Criticism of poetry this year is notable more for the practical application of theory than for theoretical writing; even so, the tone of much current writing reflects the cultural politics of recent years. There are some attempts to explicate poems for the benefit of the ordinary, curious reader, but more often critical discussion is a matter of contestation, issues of gender and variously perceived structures of hegemony looming just offstage. Sweetness and light seem not to be high priorities these days; indeed, the critical search for such qualities in contemporary poetry is rarely even a concern—a sure sign of impending obsolescence.

These comments should not be construed to mean that no important work is being published. Studies of major figures of the New York School and the Confessional poets continue to appear, with more in the pipeline, and much attention is also directed toward poetry influenced by the Objectivists and the L=A=N=G=U=A=G=E group.

i Mentors: Louise Bogan, Theodore Roethke, Winfield Townley Scott, George Oppen, Louis Zukofsky, Robert Hayden

Given the embattled tone of much recent criticism, readers might find it refreshing that several editors—perhaps to ameliorate Harold Bloom's agonistic drama of "influence"—have encouraged more attention to poetic mentorship. Thomas Simmons's *Erotic Reckonings: Mastery and Apprenticeship in the Work of Poets and Lovers* (Illinois) examines mentorship in the careers of three pairs of 20th-century American poets, including Theodore Roethke and Louise Bogan. In this case, Bogan's pedagogic role was initially complicated by "a crucial combination of romance and instruction." Referring to their letters, Simmons shows how Bogan carefully guided and encouraged Roethke for a decade. "Under Bogan's tutelage," he writes, "Roethke becomes a more careful observer and writer, and his poems begin to command their own audience, until his public reputation rivals and finally surpasses his mentor's."

In "Winfield Townley Scott: The Exile as Mentor" (*OhR* 51: 10–24) Hilary Masters recalls how Scott's metered audacity and his "eulogies for spiritual outcasts" captivated college students of 1950 who were not anxious to go quietly into gray flannel suits. In addition to its qualities as personal memoir, documenting Scott's generosity to younger writers, the essay is a fine reevaluation of Scott's long and distinguished career.

Michael Heller in "Encountering Oppen" (*OhR* 51: 75–88) recalls George Oppen as mentor and friend while demonstrating how Oppen's linguistic precision and method of composition differ from the "programmed experimentations of much of the avant-garde." A number of essays on Oppen—generated by a conference at the University of Notre Dame in March 1994—are collected in a special issue of *Sagetrieb* (12, iii [1993, but copyrighted 1995]) subtitled "Intersections of the Lyrical and the Philosophical" and edited by Stephen Fredman and Henry Weinfield; essayists include Jeffrey Peterson, John Shoptaw, Heller, and Weinfield.

Louis Zukofsky is a poet whose influence on younger writers continues to increase. Bob Perelman's *The Trouble with Genius* is concerned with interrogating modernism to assess the social value of literature. Perelman brings wit and erudition to his subject. "Zukofsky's writing is not separable from Zukofsky writing," writes Perelman as he ponders the implications of "laboring in isolation, producing meaning but not quite embodying it." Of course, Perelman argues for the possibility that "reading and writing, now so professionally separated, can be brought closer together." Sandra Kumamoto Stanley's *Louis Zukofsky and the Transformation of a Modern American Poetics* (Calif.) includes a valuable chapter, "A Legacy: Zukofsky and the Language Poets" (pp. 147–71), that underscores Perelman's point. To paraphrase Richard Wright in *Black Boy*, it is not always clear whether younger poets view Zukofsky as an example or a warning. Stanley notes that some who first encountered Zukofsky's work in the 1970s were interested "in both Zukofsky's formalist innovations and his oppositional politics." She sees poets such as Clark Coolidge, Ron Silliman, Robert Grenier, Barrett Watten, and Charles Bernstein as those who appreciate Zukofsky as a link to a tradition of skeptical social comment that yet believes in "the transformative power of language."

In *Callaloo* (17: 975–1016) Xavier Nicholas presents "Robert Hayden and Michael S. Harper: A Literary Friendship." Letters exchanged by the poets from 1972 until Hayden's death in 1980 show that, while Harper considered Hayden his mentor, they shared a supportive relationship. Between publication of his first book, *Heart Shape in the Dust* (1940), and his appointment in 1976 as Poetry Consultant to the Library of Congress, Hayden was very much an outsider. "His allegiance to models such as William Butler Yeats and W. H. Auden alienated proponents of the 'Black Aesthetic,' at the same time that his fascination with black folk culture barred him from the 'mainstream,'" writes Nicholas. The selection of letters is a valuable contribution to an overdue reassessment of Hayden's underappreciated offices. Another poet who persevered despite obscurity is Amy Clampitt who, says Karen A. Weisman, "is neither confessional, autobiographical, nor hermetically sealed within her own poetic spaces." In "Starving Before the Actual: Amy Clampitt's *Voyages: A Homage to John Keats*" (*Criticism* 36: 119–37) Weisman nevertheless places Clampitt in opposition to Charles Bernstein and other poets who find "lyric fluency" suspect. Clampitt's study of Keats, says Weisman, is also a study of the difficulties of "articulation of felt experience."

ii General Studies

"Poetry sweetens the tongue," says Al Young; and because it has always fostered ingenuity, the "telepoetic" developments reported in Lisa Brawley's informative article "The Virtual Slam: Performance Poetry on the Net" (*ChiR* 40, ii–iii: 164–74) might have been expected. The news that one can virtually attend readings at the Nuyorican Poets Cafe by means of computer modems from anywhere on the planet will, undoubtedly, delight some of us more than others. Much more down-to-earth is Louise Chawla, a psychologist interested in understanding environmental memory. Chawla's *In the First Country of Places: Nature, Poetry, and Childhood Memory* (SUNY) explores how poets use early experiences in their work. Close readings of William Bronk, Henry Weinfield, David Ignatow, Audre Lorde, and Marie Ponsot—supplemented by Chawla's tape-recorded interviews with the poets—result in a delightfully readable work that readers unfamiliar with these writers may find useful as an introduction.

Laurence Goldstein's important and thoroughly fascinating *The American Poet at the Movies: A Critical History* (Michigan) is an ambitious attempt to win recognition for "a new genre." Motion pictures became objects of literary attention early in the century, and Vachel Lindsay's *The Art of the Moving Picture* (1915) was, in fact, the first book of serious cinema criticism and film theory published in the United States. Goldstein begins with Lindsay and presents chapters on Hart Crane, Archibald MacLeish, Winfield Townley Scott, Delmore Schwartz, Karl Shapiro, Frank O'Hara, Adrienne Rich, and Jorie Graham. A chapter on African American poets' response to Hollywood images includes discussion of Wanda Coleman and others.

Vince Gotera's *Radical Visions: Poetry by Vietnam Veterans* (Georgia) is an attempt to place this work in a comparative context of earlier war poetry. Gotera suggests that Vietnam poetry can be categorized as antipoetic, aesthetic, or cathartic, and he studies examples of these modes in works by Michael Casey, Leroy V. Quintana, and Lamont Steptoe in the first group; Walter McDonald and D. F. Brown in the second; and W. D. Erhart, Norma J. Griffiths, and others in the third. Bruce Weigl and Yusef Komunyakaa, "two poets who ultimately transcend these categories," are treated in full chapters of their own. Of related interest is Michael Stephens's "A Bad and Green Dream: Bruce Weigl's Many Voices and Landscapes" (*HC* 31, ii: 1–12), which revisits several earlier books and notes that *What Saves Us* (1992) includes poems that "move subtly and thoroughly explore Weigl's already established obsessions: the war in Vietnam, working-class Ohio, male violence (and violation)." While Gotera clearly intends to interrogate the entire issue of warfare and its relationship to national character, Stephens asks, "What purpose does any of this literature serve beyond its documentary value" and confides: "The idea that a combat soldier would write poetry about that experience years later still flabbergasts me; I find the incongruity beautiful and illuminating." Perhaps the difference between Stephens and Gotera speaks to many Vietnam veterans' continuing sense of discomfort, a feeling reflected in poems by Komunyakaa and others.

On the battlefield of critical theory, each call for a variously defined "diversity" or "inclusion" seems to trigger energetic efforts at fortress-building. Such an exercise is found in Ernest Suarez's "Contemporary Southern Poetry and Critical Practice" (*SoR* 30: 674–88). Suarez joins the debate launched by Dana Gioia's *Can Poetry Matter?* (1993) to suggest that "the origin of poetry's decreased readership can be found in the late '50s and the '60s, when many poets and critics began to stress poems as vehicles for social subversion." All of the poets Suarez finds culpable—

Beats, Confessional, and Black Mountain stalwarts—are still in print, and it is open to question whether the impressive numbers of readers who continue to find those poets of interest are merely responding to what Suarez calls "a romanticized portrait of bohemian marginalization." To counter this faction, Suarez posits that contemporary Southern poetry "has clung to tradition," and he discusses a group of poets disparate enough to include David Bottoms, Ellen Bryant Voigt, and Yusef Komunyakaa as if they were all somehow descendants of the Fugitives.

In "Poems of Popular Common Ground: Four Voices of the Midwest" (*MMisc* 22: 9–17) James P. Saucerman calmly examines the work of Nebraska poets William Kloefkorn, Ted Kooser, Greg Kuzma, and Don Welch. Saucerman does not propose a new school of regionalism, but he notes that all four poets employ a vernacular diction and an Emersonian "focal distance" to express human universals while depicting localized experiences.

iii Major Voices: Robert Lowell, John Berryman, Randall Jarrell, Elizabeth Bishop

Peter Davison's "Out of Bounds: Robert Lowell, 1955–1960" (*YR* 82, iii: 76–100) is part personal memoir, part skillful analysis of the midlife crisis of a poet "famous throughout literary America not only for the power of his lines but for the agonies and scandals of his private life." Davison suggests that Lowell's celebrity was a contributing factor to that crisis, even if balanced by a sense of community that he shared with poets William Alfred, Elizabeth Bishop, Philip Booth, W. S. Merwin, and others. Davison explains how Lowell's friendships and anxieties during this period were transmuted into the extraordinarily original poetry of *Life Studies* (1960).

In "Damaged Grandeur: The Life of Robert Lowell" (*SR* 102: 121–31) Richard Tillinghast assesses the decline in critical esteem Lowell seems to have suffered and questions some of the assumptions popularized by Ian Hamilton's *Robert Lowell: A Biography* (1983), a work that Tillinghast deems "often misleading." He offers a sampling of corrective views from Elizabeth Hardwick, Randall Jarrell, and others. "To Lowell," writes Tillinghast, "life and art were one. His loyalties were, finally, to his work." An unembarrassed loyalist himself, Tillinghast's recent contributions to Lowell scholarship include "Robert Lowell's *Day by Day:* 'Until the Wristwatch Is Taken from the Wrist' " (*NERMS* 16, iii: 54–63) and "Robert Lowell: The Vagaries of a Literary Reputation" (*GettR* 6: 441–52). Also of value is Daniel Hoffman's memoir "Afternoons with Robert Lowell" (*GettR* 6: 480–89).

Lowell's mastery of free verse and metrical forms "allows him to have his poetic cake and eat it too, using tradition while mocking it at the same time" in poems such as "Commander Lowell." So argues Antoine Cazé in "Polyphony in Robert Lowell's Poetry" (*JAmS* 28: 385–401). This linguistic polyphony, says Cazé, is matched by a similar manipulation of cultural referents. Alan Williamson's *Eloquence and Mere Life: Essays on the Art of Poetry* (Michigan) collects Williamson's reviews and essays, including some perceptive comment on Lowell (pp. 3–28), Elizabeth Bishop (pp. 29–41), and Eleanor Ross Taylor (pp. 56–65).

John Berryman is a poet whose stock has fluctuated as wildly as Lowell's. In "Berryman at Thirty-Eight: An Aesthetic Biography" (*NERMS* 16, iii: 36–53) Carol Frost argues against the cult of personality, complaining that for Berryman, "audience interest has had much-too-much to do with the circumstances of the poet's life, which the audience thinks it finds evidence for in the poems to the exclusion of all else." At age 38 Berryman was reading W. B. Yeats and Gerard Manley Hopkins, teaching Shakespeare at the University of Cincinnati, and mistrustful of political poetry. Frost examines aspects of this period and Berryman's childhood in order to reconstruct his aesthetic choices in composing *Homage to Mistress Bradstreet* (1956). With a practicing poet's insight, Frost shows how Berryman's art becomes much more than the sum of his models and even the titillating "nasty bits" of autobiography that obsessed him.

Luke Spencer prefers a psychological reading of the "appropriative ambition" he detects in Berryman's long poem. In "Mistress Bradstreet and Mr. Berryman: The Ultimate Seduction" (*AL* 66: 353–66) Spencer argues that Berryman's motives for writing the poem included a desire to "expiate his guilt about his own adulterous relationships with women." Spencer considers Bradstreet a possible precursor of feminist critiques of patriarchy, but he spends more time demonstrating that Berryman's "self-serving patriarchal ventriloquism" merely replicates the historical victimization of women. Christopher Benfey's "The Woman in the Mirror: Randall Jarrell and John Berryman," pp. 123–38 in *Men Writing the Feminine: Literature, Theory, and the Question of Genders,* ed. Thaïs E. Morgan (SUNY), offers yet another view of Randall Jarrell's "The Face"

(1945) and Berryman's *Homage to Mistress Bradstreet* that differs significantly from Luke Spencer's. Benfey diagnoses Berryman's ventriloquism
as "disguised means of expression for aspects of himself that he regarded
as effeminate." These autobiographical poets, argues Benfey, are less
interested in creating female personae for poetic reasons than they are in
"probing repressed and evaded aspects of the poet's own gender identity."
Another anxious aspect of the female is explored by Alan Williamson in
"Jarrell, the Mother, the Märchen" (*TCL* 40: 283–99). The essay compares Jarrell's metaphors for "primal separation" from the Mother to
psychoanalytic readings of similar patterns in fairy tales.

Susan McCabe's *Elizabeth Bishop: Her Poetics of Loss* (Penn. State) is
grounded in the theories of Julia Kristeva and Hélène Cixous and
proposes that "a sense of personal and primal loss infuses and governs all
Bishop's work." McCabe therefore reads *Questions of Travel* (1965) as
evidence of how Bishop establishes the poem as site for a contest between
"reality" and the imagination. Reviewing all of Bishop's work, McCabe
concludes that while the poet "cannot be assigned to any 'movement,'
the postmodern and feminist permeate her work and become, in their
own right, categories to be questioned." Mutlu Konuk Blasing, however,
works hard to establish Bishop's feminist position. In "From Gender to
Genre and Back: Elizabeth Bishop and 'The Moose'" (*AmLH* 6: 265–
86) Blasing argues that choosing to write sonnets and sestinas, thereby
"aligning herself with a patriarchal tradition," Bishop was in a position to
subversively critique that tradition. From this premise, Blasing turns to
the task—now suddenly more difficult than one would have imagined—
of showing how Bishop's art responded to the lessons of her mentor
Marianne Moore.

Margaret Dickie thoughtfully examines Bishop poems based on experiences in racially mixed societies in Key West and Brazil to determine
whether the upper-middle-class Anglo poet is actually "colonizing, slum-
ming, or reporting." Responding to an earlier discussion by Adrienne
Rich, Dickie's "Race and Class in Elizabeth Bishop's Poetry" (*YES* 24:
44–58) argues that Bishop depicts contacts across race and class lines as
both intimate and dependent relationships. While these relationships
indicate the possibility of transcending imposed boundaries, Dickie also
suggests that Bishop "may have identified the trials of her lesbian experience with figures she distances" through race and class. Zhou Xiaojing
identifies similar distancing strategies in the use of animal personae in
"'The Oblique, the Indirect Approach': Elizabeth Bishop's 'Rainy Sea-

son; Sub-Tropics' " (*ChiR* 40, iv: 75–92). For William Logan, however, Bishop presents an attractive "faux naive" oeuvre and her fictive geographies become "a world in themselves" that he is not embarrassed to explore. Logan's "The Unbearable Lightness of Elizabeth Bishop" (*SWR* 79: 120–38) examines what he calls her "seeming perfection of a minor art" in a manner that does Bishop no disservice. Though he claims to detect timidity in her adherence to conventional verse forms, Logan warns readers to be wary of critical preconceptions that might inhibit the pleasure that awaits them in Bishop's carefully tuned songs.

iv James Merrill, May Swenson, James Dickey, and Others

Spirituality becomes a matter of "visionary discourse" in Helen Sword's unusual discussion "James Merrill, Sylvia Plath and the Poetics of Ouija" (*AL* 66: 553–72). While W. B. Yeats and others were curious about the supernatural, Sword points out that Plath and Merrill "more explicitly address the affinities and alliances between poetic creativity and spiritualist experience" than did their predecessors. Merrill's *The Changing Light at Sandover* (1976–82) and Plath's "Dialogue Over a Ouija Board" (1957) involved using the spiritualist's instrument as a compositional tool. Plath was frightened by the experience, says Sword, but Merrill found in it "a metaphor for metaphor." Focusing on a less occult form of poetic ventriloquism, Eric Murphy Selinger's essay "James Merrill's Masks of Eros, Masques of Love" (*ConL* 35: 30–65), does an excellent job of tracing how Merrill's work of the 1960s explores aspects of love ranging from erotic attraction to disappointment and forgiveness, and—ultimately—an understanding of the meaning of friendship. Selinger quite skillfully employs Roland Barthes and Kristeva in demonstrating how Merrill presents love as metaphor for the creative process.

Sue Russell's essay "A Mysterious and Lavish Power: How Things Continue to Take Place in the Work of May Swenson" (*KR* 16, iii: 128–39) begins by noting Elizabeth Bishop's formative influence on Swenson in the early 1950s and usefully explores how the younger poet has dealt with feminist and lesbian themes. Russell's approach seems to rely on "decoding" Swenson's lines—a task made difficult by the poet's unusually precise attention to how her poems should appear as well as her dislike of "labels." Studying Swenson in an attempt to find the "openly sexual and distinctly female" is rather risky, but Russell's readings are intelligent and informative.

James Dickey, writes Monroe K. Spears, "has always been determined to get his readers involved: it has been a cardinal principle of his poetics that the poem is not merely an object to be contemplated but an action or process to be participated in by the reader—a spell or incantation or ritual or prayer." In "James Dickey's Poetry" (*SoR* 30: 751–60) Spears is nevertheless more concerned with analyzing Dickey as a visionary poet than as a popular one. Seeing in Dickey a Dionysian energy tempered by Apollonian control, Spears offers an insightful and witty discussion. A number of *South Carolina Review* (26, ii) devoted to Dickey includes four critical essays on his poetry: "Going for Broke" by Henry Taylor (pp. 27–39); "James Dickey's Motions" by Dave Smith (pp. 41–60), considering Dickey's identification as a Southern poet; "James Dickey's '*Puella* in Flight'" by Patricia Laurence (pp. 61–71); and Laurence Lieberman's "Erotic Pantheism in James Dickey's 'Madness'" (pp. 72–86).

Employing symbols of Greek myth in a fresh manner, Greg Hewett suggests that Robert Duncan borrowed the trope of Penelope in order to acknowledge the "power source [of poetry] in a historically feminine process." Hewett's "Revealing 'The Torso': Robert Duncan and the Process of Signifying Male Homosexuality" (*ConL* 35: 522–46), citing Kristeva, argues that Duncan articulates "a new masculinity and male sexuality." It is a complex argument, but Hewett balances philosophical inquiry, Duncan's wide-ranging allusions, and his own political purpose quite well. Luke Carson's "The Protesting Furor: Robert Duncan's 'Metaphysical Genius'" (*Sagetrieb* 12, i: 55–81) offers a reading of Duncan's *Ground Work: Before the War* (1984) that stresses the influence of such 16th- and 17th-century poets as Robert Southwell and George Herbert.

Jane Frazier's "W. S. Merwin and the Mysteries of Silence" (*SDR* 32, i: 116–25) examines *The Carrier of Ladders* (1970) to explain how, like Robert Lowell, Merwin also abandoned traditional stanzaic forms for free verse. Frazier sees this as not merely a matter of technique but as an indication of Merwin's philosophical commitment.

Susan Porterfield's "Portrait of a Poet as a Young Man: Lucien Stryk" (*MMisc* 22: 36–45) presents a fine overview of the career of a poet whose commitment to Zen Buddhism guided his development from Midwestern regionalism to a terse, powerful style that is both interior and international in its concerns.

A poet whose concern for the world of nature is as intense as is

Merwin's, Wendell Berry has sometimes been controversial. Berry's attacks on "cultural forgetfulness brought on by the consumer values of an industrial economy" have, says Stephen Whited, caused some to criticize him as anachronistic. In his essay "On Devotion to the 'Communal Order': Wendell Berry's Record of Fidelity, Interdependence, and Love" (*SLitI* 27, ii: 9–28) Whited contends with Charles Hudson and Peter Stitt, arguing that Berry—both in poetry and fiction—effectively "illustrates the manner in which significant traditions are exchanged between generations to preserve community." The stance of embattled critic is also evident in "Wisdom and Sadness in the Poetry of Carl Dennis" (*DQ* 28, iv: 114–35), where Mark Halliday worries that Carl Dennis is a poet so much at odds with our time that "the extreme consistency of Dennis's calm, gentle, moderate voice risks alienating readers." Halliday portrays Dennis as a creator of an alternate world where "Main Street will fill with the swagger of the actual/But you won't bow down anymore." Excellent readings of poems in Dennis's *Meetings with Time* (1992) are offered to show that his work is a quest for "spiritual health," depicted here as sanity and empathy, in the midst of a society prone to "the cramping effect of self-concern and self-pity." It is perhaps noteworthy that neither poet nor critic attempts to equate "spiritual health" with religion. That may be an indication that Carl Dennis is indeed contemporary.

Wary of what he calls "the reflex of disbelief endemic to the modern world," Frank J. Lepkowski rejects categories such as "visionary" or "naturalist poet" for A. R. Ammons. In "'How are we to find holiness?': The Religious Vision of A. R. Ammons" (*TCL* 40: 477–98) Lepkowski argues that Ammons's "idea of God, clearly present in the early poetry, undergoes a period of doubt, reconstruction, and denial in the middle of his career, and after a strong negation becomes a renewed theme in his later poetry." Explications of poems chosen from each of these stages of the poet's career support Lepkowski's thesis.

As carefully argued is "The 'Orient-ation' of Eden: Christian/Buddhist Dialogics in the Poetry of Shirley Geok-lin Lim" by Laurel Means (*C&L* 43: 189–203). Employing Bakhtinian narrative theory, Means demonstrates that Lim's poems—in part because of the Asian-American poet's early education in three cultures—"provide a wide range of Christian biblical images which reflect certain Asian spiritual traditions," including Taoism, Confucianism, and Mahayana Buddhism. Means does not seem to suggest that Lim syncretizes these elements, rather that they are all part of her poetic and spiritual vocabulary.

Bruce Bond in "Metaphysics of the Image in Charles Wright and Paul Cézanne" (*SoR* 30: 116–25) looks at two artists who consider their work "sacramental." Bond interprets Charles Wright's idea that "All great art tends toward the condition of the primitive" as another way of saying that "the artist's powers of volition rival God's" and concern our apprehension of death. For such an artist, Bond argues, transcendence is a function of making art.

William V. Davis's *Robert Bly: The Poet and His Critics* (Camden House) is a thorough and detailed analysis of the critical reception of all of Bly's books of poetry from *Silence in the Snowy Fields* (1962) to *Selected Poems* (1986). An appendix offers an overview of the response to Bly's nonfiction bestseller *Iron John: A Book About Men* (1990), and Davis also provides a bibliography. From a decidedly different "gendered" position, *The Dream and the Dialogue: Adrienne Rich's Feminist Poetics* (Tennessee) is Alice Templeton's straightforward attempt to produce a critical theory from a poet's praxis. Poetry itself is seen as "a process of cultural engagement," implying that its social impact outweighs the personal transactions required. Templeton admits that Rich faces a dilemma similar to that facing writers from ethnic minorities: "how to participate in a culture that so often deludes and oppresses to the degree necessary to change it." *The Dream and the Dialogue* covers Rich's writing between 1971–91.

Meaningful Differences: The Poetry and Prose of David Ignatow, ed. Virginia R. Terris (Alabama), offers critical essays by Ralph J. Mills, Jr., David Ray, Linda Wagner-Martin, Diane Wakoski, Jerome Mazzaro, James Wright, Robert Bly, Gary Pacernick, Michael Heller, and Terris. The second part of the book offers a chapter on each of Ignatow's 17 books that includes a selection of critical comment—both friendly and negative. Terris also provides a chronology, a useful bibliography, and an index of Ignatow's poems. This is a well-conceived collection intended to introduce readers to "the richness beneath the deceptive spareness of Ignatow's poems," and it suggests that Ignatow may, indeed, deserve consideration as one of our major postwar poets.

"Robert Penn Warren's *Audubon:* Vision and Revision" by Anthony Szczesiul (*MissQ* 47: 3–14) pays close attention to the textual history of the poem with excellent results. Szczesiul examines Warren's manuscripts and his correspondence with *New Yorker* poetry editor Howard Moss to show the poet at work and to consider how Warren "is able to define more sharply the interwoven themes of the poem" as a result of responding to his editor's comments.

v The New York School: Frank O'Hara, John Ashbery

The appearance in 1993 of Brad Gooch's thorough and readable biography *City Poet: The Life and Times of Frank O'Hara* (Knopf) predictably inspired a number of memoirs from friends and fellow poets who cherished O'Hara's memory. William Weaver's "Remembering Frank O'Hara" (*SWR* 79, i: 139–46) is a charming portrait recalling the brio of New York in the early 1950s when newcomers like O'Hara and his circle were in love with art, music, and conversation. Weaver admired O'Hara's attitude of "brave defiance" and chides Gooch for an overdependence on interpreting events as sexually determined. Gooch's book is, one should add, accurate in its subtitle: O'Hara's poems are merely quoted as part of the biographer's account of the day they were written or published; one learns next to nothing about the poet's professional relationship with his editors and less about the critical reaction to his books. Gooch makes few attempts at explication, and the poems are treated so much like journal entries that the reader of *City Poet* would hardly guess that anyone other than Frank O'Hara's friends had ever read them.

For a discussion that encompasses both lifestyle and poetic technique, one might turn to Jim Elledge's "The Lack of Gender in Frank O'Hara's Love Poems to Vincent Warren," pp. 226–37 in *Fictions of Masculinity: Crossing Cultures, Crossing Sexualities,* ed. Peter F. Murphy (NYU). Homosexuality was not recognized as an alternative lifestyle in the 1950s, Elledge notes, adding that O'Hara was also "disinterested in using homosexuality per se as a topic for his poetry and disinterested in making his career a vehicle for political statement." In the sequence of poems discussed here, "O'Hara consciously preserved, perhaps even sanctified, the universality of love," Elledge asserts, "by writing his love poems to Vincent Warren without regard to gender-identifying words." Consequently, O'Hara "frees the reader to identify 'you' as anyone of any sex, any age, any race . . . a universal 'you.'" Elledge's intelligent and scrupulous reconstruction of O'Hara's poetic concerns—viewed as a triumphant refusal to accept imposed limitations—may annoy those who would prefer to enlist the poet in other campaigns. As interest in the poet continues to grow, Vincent Prestianni's "Frank O'Hara: An Analytic Bibliography of Bibliographies" (*Sagetrieb* 12, i [1993]: 129–30) is of value.

John Shoptaw in *On the Outside Looking Out: John Ashbery's Poetry*

(Harvard) presents a thorough chronological discussion of all of Ashbery's published works. Arguing that Ashbery's "misrepresentative poetics" is rooted in modernism, Shoptaw suggests that his intentionally fragmented and fractured poems "do not rule out meaning, expression and representation; they renovate them." It is interesting that, in searching for a comparative metaphor, Shoptaw refers more to music than (as previous commentators have done) to the visual arts. Shoptaw's access to Ashbery's papers and manuscripts allows him to demonstrate how the poet's meticulous revisions achieve the amazement he desires "by both consciously and unwittingly misrepresenting his previous work, making each book in some way a departure from the previous one and (by a progressive elimination) from all the others." Notable for clarity and historical accuracy, Shoptaw's *On the Outside Looking Out* is a major contribution to the critical materials available on this major poet. Other noteworthy work on Ashbery includes " 'The Lyric Crash': The Theater of Subjectivity in John Ashbery's *Three Poems*" (*Sagetrieb* 12, ii: 137–48) by Susan M. Schultz.

vi The L=A=N=G=U=A=G=E Group and Others

While Charles Bernstein's prolific statements on poetics continue to have a catalytic impact on discussions of critical theory, more attention is beginning to be focused on the poems produced by members of the "Language poets." In "Poetry as History Revised: Susan Howe's 'Scattering As Behavior Toward Risk' " (*AmLH* 6: 716–37) Ming-Quian Ma rereads Howe's *My Emily Dickinson* (1985) and recent poems and places her work in a milieu that includes the modernist long poem, Charles Olson's *Call Me Ishmael* (1947), and Ron Silliman's *Tjanting* (1981). Rae Armantrout—a poet more concerned with the lyric than epic possibilities—is the subject of Michael Leddy's appreciative " 'See Armantrout for an Alternate View': Narrative and Counternarrative in the Poetry of Rae Armantrout" (*ConL* 35: 739–60). Leddy finds that Armantrout uses wit and vernacular to raise questions about the rhetoric of authority and to inscribe a "counterstory." Armantrout's message, in a poem quoted by Leddy, has a clearly political resonance: "When names perform a function, / that's fiction."

In "Write the Power" (*AmLH* 6: 306–24) Bob Perelman cynically remarks that "poets have claimed a direct access to the divine for mil-

lennia," but the critique of power he reads in the works of Charles
Bernstein and Edward Kamau Braithwaite is unblinkingly of this world.
This essay is also useful in explaining the neo-Joycean wordplay and
what Perelman calls "antiorthographies" found in Braithwaite's *X/Self*
(1987) and many of Bernstein's poems. For both poets, he says, "words
are an engine of social change," inferring that such a change begins with
the very act of reading (or deciphering) their pages. Perelman reinforces
his argument in "Building a More Powerful Vocabulary: Bruce Andrews
and the World (Trade Center)" (*ArQ* 50, iv: 117–32). In recent works
Andrews has proposed "linking radical politics with radical poetics," and
Perelman compares that effort, Maya Angelou's "On the Pulse of Morning," and Clark Coolidge and Larry Fagin's irreverent parody of that
Inauguration ode in order to explore how Language poets might create
their own effective "public poetry." As a poet himself Perelman has
created effective social critiques in *Face Value* (1988) and other collections. He is able, therefore, to view the problem from more than
one perspective and understands that parody and polemic may both
be unreliable weapons: "A basic conundrum surfaces: don't such attacks tend to reinforce their target at least as much as they explode
it?" While Perelman finds Bruce Andrews's politics "either literary or
improbable," the essay endorses the poet's effort to craft a discourse that
is not vulnerable to the mass-marketed Orwellian counterfeit now in
circulation.

John Taggart's engaged and often engaging opinions make *Songs of
Degrees: Essays on Contemporary Poetry and Poetics* (Alabama) a book
worth dipping into. In "On Working with Dancers" Taggart writes: "It is
difficult to speak and to move at the same time. It is more difficult to
speak with articulation and to move with purpose at the same time." But
Taggart is used to making the difficult seem easy. There are good essays
and reviews of Susan Howe, Theodore Enslin, William Bronk, Charles
Olson, Robert Duncan, Frank Sampieri, and Bruce Andrews, as well as
meditations on poetics, music, and—as indicated—even modern dance.
Several essays on George Oppen and Louis Zukofsky make *Songs of
Degrees* worthy of note and help to illuminate the links of the Language
poets with their predecessors. Several of the poets Taggart discusses can
also be found in Edward Foster's *Postmodern Poetry: The Talisman Interviews* (Talisman House). Those included are William Bronk, Clark
Coolidge, Anselm Hollo, Susan Howe, Nathaniel Mackey, Alice Notley,

Ron Padgett, Leslie Scalapino, Gustaf Sobin, Rosemarie Waldrop, and John Yau.

vii Gender and Genealogy: Native American Poets and Others

Robert Dale Parker's excellent essay, lumberingly entitled "To Be There, No Authority to Anything: Ontological Desire and Cultural and Poetic Authority in the Poetry of Ray A. Young Bear" (*ArQ* 50, iv: 89–116), explores the complexities of what is trendily referred to as "multicultural literature." With admirable clarity Parker examines a tension in Ray A. Young Bear's poetry that results from projecting "a post-Wordsworthian transcendence of identity" that the poet himself feels is "at odds with the personal humility of Mesquakie culture and ritual." Young Bear's use of the techniques of surrealism and Native American oral narrative conventions complicates his relationship to a reading audience that has no other access to the sources Young Bear himself refines. Other recent work, quite useful, includes Gretchen M. Bataille, "Ray A. Young Bear: Tribal History and Personal Vision" (*SAIL* 5, ii: 17–20), and "Staying Afloat in a Chaotic World: A Conversation with Ray Young Bear" by David Moore and Michael Wilson (*Callaloo* 17: 205–13).

Jenny Goodman's "Politics and the Personal Lyric in the Poetry of Joy Harjo and C. D. Wright" (*MELUS* 19, ii: 35–58) focuses on "two poets who work consciously at the borders of aesthetics and politics, reshaping the cultural language for both." Harjo, drawing on Native American storytelling, and Wright, experimenting with avant-garde forms and Ozark vernacular, both challenge the "poetic expectations" of readers while encouraging deeper levels of analysis among those who share their political concerns. In "Twin Gods Bending Over: Joy Harjo and Poetic Memory" (*MELUS* 18, iii: 41–50) Nancy Lang focuses on Harjo's use of English to reproduce elements of Creek (Muskogee) oral tradition; Lang also raises the question of whether such a new language is needed to address "pan-tribal experiences and the assimilationist, Anglo-dominated world of much contemporary Native American life."

Patricia Wallace's "Divided Loyalties: Literal and Literary in the Poetry of Lorna Dee Cervantes, Cathy Song and Rita Dove" (*MELUS* 18, iii: 3–20) raises similar questions and wonders, also, if the formal education of these poets possibly estranges them from their ethnic cultural communities. Finding that Cervantes, Song, and Dove—Hispanic,

Asian American, African American, and above all contemporary—
"unsettle categories we customarily freeze into opposition," Wallace
offers excellent close readings of works by all three poets along with
useful biographical information.

viii African American Poets: Sterling A. Brown, Jay Wright, Sam Cornish, Ishmael Reed

Sterling A. Brown first claimed attention as a poet at the end of the
Harlem Renaissance with his extraordinary *Southern Road* (1932) but he
did not publish a second collection until 1975. Mark A. Sanders in "The
Ballad, the Hero and the Ride: A Reading of Sterling A. Brown's *The Last
Ride of Wild Bill*" (*CLAJ* 38: 162–82) explains how and why Brown
was rediscovered by the Black Arts Movement and, indeed, belatedly
"lionized for his strident defense of grassroots folk and for his acute
understanding of African-American culture." Sanders points out that
Brown can be seen as "mentor and progenitor" of the Black Arts Movement for—as a professor at Howard University—Brown had students
who included Amiri Baraka, musician Marion Brown, activist Stokely
Carmichael, and others who were leaders during the 1960s. Sanders
presents an excellent study of Brown's poems and his dynamic recon-
figuration of folklore motifs. Readers also will be pleased that Joanne V.
Gabbin's *Sterling A. Brown: Building the Black Aesthetic Tradition,* first
published in 1985, has been reissued (Virginia). Gabbin's outstanding
book offers reliable biography, a useful bibliography, and a thorough
critical appraisal of Brown's work as poet, literary critic, and folklorist.

"Jay Wright's Poetics: An Appreciation" by Ron Welburn (*MELUS* 18,
iii: 51–70) is a well-balanced introduction to the poet's complex mixture
of Southwestern Hispanic history, African American vernacular culture,
and West African Dogon cosmology. Comparing the initial response to
T. S. Eliot's *The Waste Land* (1922) and Wright's current reception,
Welburn notes that "the poet whose language, style and treatment of
subject matter show seemingly esoteric, even postmodernist referential
proclivities, is increasingly at the disadvantageous mercies of a dysfunc-
tionally literate audience." Welburn argues that Wright's uniquely personal blending of mythologies does not necessarily make him a "difficult" poet, and this essay gives the interested reader many useful cues for
properly appreciating his work.

C. K. Doreski's erudite "Living Through History: Sam Cornish's

Generations" (*CLAJ* 38: 193–210) notes that "recent efforts of African-American theoreticians (like Henry Louis Gates and Houston Baker) and new historicists encourage a rereading of the structure, language and aesthetic of *Generations*," a long poem composed at the height of the 1960s Black Arts Movement. Doreski accomplishes an intelligent reading of Cornish's "social and literary project" while outlining issues of interpretation among African Americanists that have been simmering into controversy at recent conferences. Shamoon Zamir also does a good job of exploring "the interdependence of tradition and innovation" in "The Artist as Prophet, Priest and Gunslinger: Ishmael Reed's *Cowboy in the Boat of Ra*" (*Callaloo* 17: 1205–35). Zamir shows how Reed's widely anthologized 1968 poem revises William Butler Yeats's "The Second Coming" and "Leda and the Swan" while incorporating Reed's understanding of Marshall McLuhan's communication theories and the aesthetics of jazz improvisation. Zamir offers an informed and multidimensional explication that suggests useful approaches to Reed's fiction as well.

ix Melvin B. Tolson, Amiri Baraka, and Others

John Lowe in "An Interview with Brenda Marie Osbey" (*SoR* 30: 812–23), in addition to important details about the poet's method and her interest in an African American poetic idiom, elicits the comment that Melvin B. Tolson is a recent influence because Osbey understands him as a writer "who sees his poems as a kind of correction of history." Tolson, long neglected, has also been cited by Amiri Baraka as a model (along with William Carlos Williams, Langston Hughes, and Charles Olson) for his own most recent series of poems, *Wise, Why's, Y's: The Griot's Song* (Third World, 1995). The similarities Baraka points to are not matters of poetic diction but of poetic structure.

Offering an attentive and perceptive comparison of Baraka's poems and those of the British poet and musician Roy Fisher, Mary Ellison finds that "neither poet has ever been prepared to live with conventional constructs of themselves any more than they accepted forms or definitions which had become normative." In "Jazz in the Poetry of Amiri Baraka and Roy Fisher" (*YES* 24: 117–45) Ellison posits jazz as "quintessentially subversive" and approves Fisher's idea that a poem is "always capable of being a subversive agent." Baraka's more complex view and the direct relationship of his poetic ideas to political activism gets a thorough investigation. Ellison's apparent respect for the personal and cultural specificity of each poet makes this essay valuable.

Among this year's most important books is Aldon L. Nielsen's *Writing Between the Lines: Race and Intertextuality* (Georgia). Arguing that "our language is the body that carries the virus of racism," Nielsen questions some recent notions about pluralism and cultural diversity. "Rather than segregating our readings of African-American literary creations," he writes, "we must, as the very name African-American literature implies, read black texts in their fulsome implication in all English writing." Such a view—suggested somewhat differently in Toni Morrison's *Playing in the Dark* (1992)—allows Nielsen to provide brilliant discussions of the two-way influence shared by such writers as Baraka, Frank O'Hara, and Ed Dorn. Other chapters discuss Melvin B. Tolson, William Carlos Williams, Charles Olson, and several fiction writers. Nielsen's chapter "Whose Blues?" (pp. 185–213) on the influence of jazz on poetic diction is also one of the best studies of Clark Coolidge's work yet to appear. While Nielsen believes "all writing presents the text of an other to another," his meticulous research makes it clear that he feels secure in the old-fashioned faith that reading really does result in understanding. A good example is found in his chapter "LeRoi Jones as Intertext" (pp. 214–51), which presents a well-informed account of Baraka's literary exchanges with Allen Ginsberg, Olson, and others. Attentive readers will see that Lewis Turco's essay "Amiri Baraka's Black Mountain" (*HC* 31: 1–10), while it is full of unfortunate inaccuracies, actually supplies evidence to support Nielsen's statement that "Baraka was one of the first African-American poets whose works were also enormously and almost immediately influential among white poets." In its clear-sightedness, Nielsen's work makes one wonder if the heated debate about theorizing "multiculturalism" has not, in fact, distracted us from recognizing who we already are.

University of Houston-Downtown

19 Drama

James J. Martine

The paucity of scholarly activity on drama remarked here at the decade's opening is now past. To the contrary, times are so flush that there scarcely seems space merely to enumerate the items published this year. The flood tide is different in character, with interest in matters of race, gender, and sexual preference riding peaks of the waves, but a strong current of traditional literary research and scholarship is evident. Matthew C. Roudané, in the *Annual Report 1993* of the American Literature Section of the MLA, proposes that in an era of thinking anew about questions reshaping the field of literary study, American drama prepares to leave the sidelines. American drama was once relegated to hostility or indifference, and scholars who seldom regard it on the same level as the novel, poem, or short story must recognize, says Roudané, that "since 1945, the U.S. has produced a drama that at least matches the brilliance of our best novelists and poets. So scholars who authorize our literary canon . . . would do well to *in*clude American drama as part of our literary history." The outpouring of fresh scholarship supports that contention.

i Reference Works and Anthologies

Dramatic reference texts continue to proliferate. Of the 49 Southern writers of "the last two or three decades" included in *Contemporary Poets, Dramatists, Essayists, and Novelists of the South: A Bio-Bibliographical Source Book,* ed. Robert Bain and Joseph M. Flora (Greenwood), a half-dozen are dramatists. The format of this volume follows that of an earlier companion, *Contemporary Fiction Writers of the South* (1993). Entries, arranged alphabetically, provide biography, a discussion of major themes, a survey of criticism, and a brief bibliography of dramatic.productions, published plays, and studies of playwrights. Entries appear on Alice

Childress, James Duff, and Lonne Elder III; noteworthy are Hilary Holladay's essay on Beth Henley (pp. 238–48), the section on Marsha Norman by Billy J. Harbin and Jill Stapleton Bergeron (pp. 388–95), and Kimball King's solid piece on Preston Jones (pp. 249–59). Updating Terry Helbing's *The Gay Theatre Alliance Directory of Gay Plays* (1979), which has since gone out of print, Ken Furtado and Nancy Hellner's *Gay and Lesbian American Plays: An Annotated Bibliography* (Scarecrow, 1993) lists nearly 700 plays arranged alphabetically by author. The annotations are intelligent, often helpful, but criteria for inclusion are quirky. Listed "are works containing major characters whose gay or lesbian sexuality is integral to the play's message and plays whose primary themes are gay or lesbian." Yet Lillian Hellman's *The Children's Hour,* D. H. Hwang's *M. Butterfly,* and James Kirkwood's *P. S. Your Cat Is Dead!* are included. Not included are performance pieces; camp, drag or radical theater; works by gay or lesbian authors that do not have gay or lesbian charac-ters; or works given gay or lesbian interpretations though the characters's sexuality is never stated outright. Thus, *Something Cloudy, Something Clear* and *Vieux Carré* are the only entries for Tennessee Williams. There is a useful index of plays by title, but some gratuitous things, too, such as a list of agents and agencies, the names and addresses of 75 playwrights—no, the most famous authors are not included here—and a list of theaters.

Two inexpensive anthologies in Penguin's Mentor imprint continue the recent interest in drama outside what used to be called the main-stream. The first is *Nuestro New York: An Anthology of Puerto Rican Plays,* ed. John V. Antush, an expert in the subject, who provides a brief commentary on the background of *puertorriqueñidad* and its place in the tradition of American drama. While the volume contains works by the first generation of New York playwrights born in Puerto Rico, such as Roberto Rodriguez Suárez's *The Betrothal* and Oscar A. Colón's *Siempre en mi corazón,* the anthology principally focuses on the achievements of a talented new generation: the cross-cultural drama *Julia* by Carmen Rivera; Eduardo Ivan Lopez's *Spanish Eyes,* which dramatizes the clash of Anglo and Hispanic cultures; Reuben González's surrealistic *The Boiler Room;* the earthy and lively farce *I Am a Winner* by Fred Valle; Yolanda Rodriguez's tragic depiction of a world of drug dealers and family, *Rising Sun, Falling Star;* Juan Shamsul Alám's *Zookeeper;* Candido Tirado's "fantastic" comedy *Some People Have All the Luck;* Eva Lopez's drama of ethnic identity among the second generation, *Marlene;* and José Rivera's poetic fantasy *Marisol.* The plays are in English and are authentically American. Ross Wetzsteon of the *Village Voice* and chairman of the Obie awards committee has gathered a collection by far more famous authors in *The Best of Off-Broadway: Eight Contemporary Obie-Winning Plays* (Mentor). Household names grouped here are David Mamet (*Edmond*); Christopher Durang (*The Marriage of Bette and Boo*); Wallace Shawn (*Aunt Dan and Lemon*); Eric Bogosian (the performance piece *Sex, Drugs, Rock & Roll*); and Craig Lucas (*Prelude to a Kiss*). Also included are *Imperceptible Mutabilities in the Third Kingdom* by Suzan-Lori Parks, much lionized by New York critics, and *The Danube,* by Maria Irene Fornes. Rarely produced outside Off-Off Broadway and little anthologized, Fornes's work is now eliciting wider appreciation. Wetzsteon provides a brief, readable introduction, a briefer appendix of Obie-winning plays from 1979 through 1993, and he even tosses Samuel Beckett's four-page *Ohio Impromptu* into this otherwise star-spangled collection. The playwrights gathered reject slice-of-life naturalism, psychological realism, and lyric populism; the eight scripts under one cover constitute a bargain.

Claudia Allen's *She's Always Liked the Girls Best: Lesbian Plays* (Third Side, 1993) gathers Allen's *Roomers, Raincheck, Hannah Free,* and *Movie Queens,* the first three appearing in print for the first time, and the last in a full two-act version of the 1986 one-act New York production; *Roomers* and *Raincheck* have not yet been fully produced. Carol Klimick Cyganowski's brief foreword introduces the Chicago-based playwright whose comic dramas begin to draw attention from a wider national audience. This anthology establishes Allen's importance in lesbian theater.

It is difficult to provide a commentary on a new anthology program without sounding like a commercial for the publisher, but in this case there is no help for it. The Smith and Kraus Contemporary Playwrights Series is a worthy set of volumes. *Women Playwrights: The Best of 1993,* ed. Marisa Smith, is an excellent gathering of Cherylene Lee's moving *Arthur and Leila;* J. e. Franklin's moral pilgrimage of African American life, *Christchild;* Erin Cressida Wilson's haunting *Cross-Dressing in the Depression;* Eve Ensler's tender and funny *Floating Rhoda and the Glue Man;* Cheryl Royce's inspired monologue *My Son Susie;* and Claire Chafee's collage of scenes meant to reflect the "lesbian brain" in form as well as content, *Why We Have a Body.* Liz Diamond provides a brief introduction. Also notable in the Contemporary Playwrights Series are *Terrance McNally: 15 Short Plays* (Smith and Kraus) with a short intro-

duction by John Guare; *Horton Foote: Four New Plays* (1993), including
Night Seasons, which had a New York production in 1994 with Jean
Stapleton and Hallie Foote, the playwright's daughter, in the memorable
role of Laura Lee; *William Mastrosimone: Collected Plays* (1993); *Eric
Overmyer: Collected Plays* (1993); *Romulus Linney: Seventeen Short Plays*
(1992); *Lanford Wilson: 21 Short Plays* (1993); and *Israel Horovitz Collected
Works: Volume I—Sixteen Short Plays.*

ii Theater History

While demands for new reference texts have been limited, interest in
theater history has expanded exponentially. Gerald Bordman's *American
Theatre: A Chronicle of Comedy and Drama, 1869–1914* (Oxford) is the
first of a projected three-volume set on nonmusical theater that proposes
to parallel Oxford's *American Musical Theatre: A Chronicle* (published in
1978 and much updated since then). The volume in hand details the
American theater, season by season, with plot synopses, principal players,
and other significant information. This detailed, yearly chronological
organization straightforwardly presents the story of American drama as it
unfolded. The difficulty for its use in research is that to find information
the reader has to refer to multiple locations. For example, there is a one-
paragraph entry on Joseph Jefferson during the 1870–71 year, but 33
other places in the volume have to be checked for additional data. So it
goes for John Drew (85 index entries), Ethel and John Barrymore (23 and
12 entries), and Edwin Booth (66 separate references). The quality of the
volume is consistent with that of other works provided by Bordman and
Oxford, like *The Oxford Companion to American Theatre* (1992).

Cambridge University Press provides three notable volumes this year.
Marc Robinson's *The Other American Drama* is an exciting book which
describes a loose cluster of affinities rather than a tradition; it posits a way
of looking at American drama more than a way of classifying it. Disen-
chanted by standard anthologies and textbooks, Robinson will be ac-
cused of having given the received 20th-century canon short shrift by
characterizing it as "sluggish, bloated, mechanical." But by setting the
dramas of Gertrude Stein alongside O'Neill in importance, his view is
not merely revisionist but instructive. The writers he discusses reduce the
importance of plots, and Robinson can focus on language, gesture, and
presence. His crucial initial chapter establishing Stein as an alternative to
O'Neill is separated from his final "Afterword: New Directions" on

Wallace Shawn, David Greenspan, Suzan-Lori Parks, and Mac Well-man—a disparate quartet Robinson gathered last year in "Four Writers" (*Theater* 24, i [1993]: 31–42)—by individual chapters on Tennessee Williams, Sam Shepard, Maria Irene Fornes, Adrienne Kennedy, and Richard Foreman. Robinson builds his commentary on Williams around the central characters—all women: Amanda of *The Glass Menagerie,* Blanche of *A Streetcar Named Desire,* and *Cat on a Hot Tin Roof*'s Maggie—and he is interesting on the restless energy and impatience Shepard brings to playwriting. He is especially suggestive on the use of language and movement by Fornes; Kennedy's experiments with stasis and the emotional quality of her incantory, repetitive dialogue—attributable to Stein; and Foreman's movement into inner, psychological realms. Robinson writes clearly, and his book will be a topic of serious discussion.

Samuel A. Hay's *African American Theatre: An Historical and Critical Analysis* (Cambridge) charts the history of African American theater beginning with the tension between the W. E. B. Du Bois school, which was strictly political, and the philosopher Alain Locke, who tried to change the Du Bois school from within, to shift it from protest to art theater. Hay devotes two chapters to the results of exchange and growth arising from this tension, covering everything from Bob Cole's *A Trip to Coontown* (1898) to Suzan-Lori Parks's *The Death of the Last Black Man in the Whole Entire World* (1990), identifying Parks's play as fusing the two schools by melding the central Du Bois theme into a Locke form. Hay's third chapter, which he characterizes as a pep talk to young African Americans, points out splendid examples of individuals whose stories provide illustrations of courage, such as James Hewlett and Ira Aldridge, William Wells Brown, Charles Hicks, and Alice Childress. Chapter 4 turns its attention to the governance of theater organizations, and it is followed by a chapter on development, with observations on marketing and finances. His conclusion and three appendices advance his vision of the future of African American theater. If this book sometimes seems discursive and its prose style less than perfect, it is not without energy, enthusiasm, and its own anecdotal humor. The book takes its subtitle seriously; it is as much critical analysis as history.

Using papers of the Federal Theatre Project discovered during the 1970s in a Baltimore airplane hangar, and now in the archives of the FTP Special Collections at George Mason University, Rena Fraden's *Blueprints for a Black Federal Theatre, 1935–1939* (Cambridge) is shaped thematically rather than chronologically; it takes almost two chapters to get to the FTP's so-called Negro units, the book's real subject. One of those chapters is devoted to the background of liberal politics, and a second details debates in the black community. The study concentrates, however, on the misunderstandings and struggles which occurred within and between races as to who would constitute an audience and what would be considered appropriate material for black actors. To illustrate the difficulties and triumphs, Fraden examines two productions in detail, Hall Johnson's *Run, Little Chillun* and the 1938 *Swing Mikado.* The book is doubly valuable in its argument that groups can be misrepresented, often humiliated, but still remain able to create national cultural treasures, and in its demonstration that American culture consists of always-changing, mixing, overlapping, and appropriating cultures. Fraden illustrates that denial of cultural hybridization is futile and that no "subculture" remains pure for long. Full of dates, data, photos, and specific details, *Blueprints* is a carefully documented look into a worthwhile corner of American theatrical history.

A step from the theater and economics of the '30s to the theater and politics of the '60s brings us to J. W. Fenn's *Levitating the Pentagon: Evolutions in the American Theatre of the Vietnam War Era* (Delaware, 1992), my nominee for the book that does not quite live up to the promise of its prodigious title. The book's principal aim is to examine dramatic scripts and productions inspired by the Vietnam War and to explore how theater responded to the age's political and social upheaval. Fenn, like Claude Rains's character in *Casablanca,* rounds up the usual suspects: there is a nice synopsis of Daniel Berrigan's *The Trial of the Catonsville Nine* (1969); David Rabe's *The Basic Training of Pavlo Hummel, Sticks and Bones,* and *Streamers* get extended coverage; and Fenn is good on the little-written-about Gerome Ragni and James Rado musical *Hair* as a transitional moment in theater. Other works, authors, and experimental theater groups are presented, although one wonders why, though *Vietnam Campesino, Vietnam Discourse,* and Christopher Durang's *The Vietnamization of New Jersey* are included, no mention is made of Maria Irene Fornes's experimental piece *A Vietnamese Wedding,* first presented in February 1967 as part of "Angry Arts Week," a protest against American involvement in Vietnam. Still, Fenn does not claim too much for the works covered, conceding that none are commercially produced today. The opening chapter on the social, economic, political, and spiritual ambiance of the 1960s is an excellent précis of the situation, and three appendices—one each on the chronology of major events of the Vietnam engagement, significant American and world events, and theater groups, plays, and productions—will be a convenient aid for students too young and an affecting nostalgic reminder for the gray-beards among us.

Perhaps the year's best history of theatrical and dramatic activity is Thomas P. Adler's *American Drama: 1940–1960: A Critical History* (Twayne). Adler's initial chapter on the sociocultural milieu and the political and economic backgrounds is, like the rest of the volume, without agenda, free of politically correct cant, unbiased, with no object but to be objective. This is to suggest not that Adler ignores the important matters of race and gender but that he provides intelligent proportion and perspective. With no specific ax to grind, he deals with the realities of racial, ethnic, class, and gender divisions in a way that is liberating rather than self-consciously "liberated." A chapter each is devoted to O'Neill's oeuvre during the years after he won the Nobel Prize and Lillian Hellman, a person Adler rightly presents as the conscience of American culture. Adler also deals with Arthur Miller's great plays from *All My Sons* and *Death of a Salesman* to *The Crucible* and *A View from the Bridge,* leaving consideration of the later plays for the next volume in Twayne's Critical History of American Drama series under general editor Jordan Y. Miller. A central chapter is devoted to William Inge, including the dramatist's "circumscribed" females and vulnerable male characters in *Bus Stop* and *The Dark at the Top of the Stairs* through to his last full-length play *Where's Daddy?* Another chapter is devoted to Robert Anderson, Arthur Laurents, Jerome Lawrence and Robert E. Lee, William Gibson, and Paddy Chayefsky, with a brief digression into Archibald MacLeish's Pulitzer Prize-winning *J.B.* as representative of the '50s. Two chapters are given to Tennessee Williams; a balanced and balancing chapter on Lorraine Hansberry precedes a concluding chapter on Edward Albee. Also here are a brief, informative chronology and a good selected bibliography. This is a fine history, no fads or fancy stuff, of the classic period, the meat and potatoes, of American drama.

Another solid contribution to the study of theater history is Dinnah Pladott's "Nineteenth-Century American Drama: A Romantic Quest," pp. 343–58 in *Romantic Drama,* ed. Gerald Gillespie (Benjamins). This revaluation of that portion of American drama which is habitually considered aesthetically inferior, provincial, and devoid of interest has long been in order; Pladott's scholarly documentation and specific illustrations urge a reconsideration of the prevalent critical denigration of

American dramas written and produced before the '20s. As if on cue, enter, stage right, a Spring 1994 number of *American Drama* (3, ii), largely devoted to pre-1920 national drama. The lead article is Gary A. Richardson's "The Greening of America: The Cultural Business of Dion Boucicault's *The Shaughraun*" (pp. 1–28), a discussion of that popular play which premiered in 1874 and is regularly discussed in histories of American drama. Lucy Rinehart's "A Nation's 'Noble Spectacle': Royall Tyler's *The Contrast* as Metatheatrical Commentary" (pp. 29–52) reconsiders this famous play, the first to be registered under the nation's initial copyright law. The peak of romantic verse tragedy is described by Thomas M. Kitts in "An Argument for Boker's *Francesca da Rimini*" (pp. 53–70). Several essays are of related interest. Richard Butsch's "Bowery B'hoys and Matinee Ladies: The Re-gendering of Nineteenth-Century American Theater Audiences" (*AQ* 46: 374–405) provides a sociologist's description of the process of gender transformation from the 1820s theater as male club, having less to do with respectability than with consumer culture. Kim Marra's feminist approach to "Elsie de Wolfe *Circa* 1901: The Dynamics of Prescriptive Feminine Performance in American Theatre and Society" (*ThS* 35: 100–119) concludes that de Wolfe "simply cleared out the Victoriana and let in the twentieth century." Also using a feminist revisionist approach, Susan McCully in "Oh I Love Mother, I Love Her Power: Shaker Spirit Possession and the Performance of Desire" (*ThS* 35: 88–98) argues that the trance state of Shaker spirit possession is a consciously induced performance. American expatriate Elizabeth Robins is the subject of Joanne E. Gates's *Elizabeth Robins, 1862–1952: Actress, Novelist, Feminist* (Alabama). Better seen against a British background dotted with Bernard Shaw and Henry James, Robins, who traveled the United States with Edwin Booth and toured as the female lead opposite James O'Neill in the now memorialized *The Count of Monte Cristo,* is also given the initial chapter, "Elizabeth Robins, 'What we need is a Battle Cry,'" pp. 9–39 in Sheila Stowell's *A Stage of Their Own: Feminist Playwrights of the Suffrage Era* (Michigan, 1992), a volume devoted to drama of Edwardian Britain.

African American Review provides three noteworthy items of theater history. Will Harris's "Early Black Women Playwrights and the Dual Liberation Motif" (*AAR* 28: 205–21) examines a close group of nine artists and the challenges they faced from 1916 until 1950, explaining both the general focus of these early dramatists on black women trapped in domestic situations and the virtual absence of black male authority figures. Bernth Lindfors in " 'Nothing Extenuate, nor Set Down Aught in Malice': New Biographical Information on Ira Aldridge" (*AAR* 28: 457–72) fills in previously missing details while providing an introduction for those unacquainted with America's earliest important black actor. Rich with statistics and details, Jack Shalom's "The Ira Aldridge Troupe: Early Black Minstrelsy in Philadelphia" (*AAR* 28: 653–58) provides an unrelated but interesting essay on a troupe unique in the annals of minstrelsy that played Franklin Hall in 1863; the players derived their name from the actor who had left his homeland in 1825, never to return. The reader will also find interesting Glenda E. Gill's "The Alabama A&M Thespians, 1944–1963: Triumph of the Human Spirit" (*TDR* 38, iv: 48–70), a story of realized possibilities, survival, success, and affirmation of humanity and self-worth by one who was there. Also of interest is Harley Erdman's "Caught in the 'Eye of the Eternal': Justice, Race, and the Camera, from *The Octoroon* to Rodney King" (*TJ* 45, iii: 333–48), which connects Dion Boucicault's 1859 melodrama with the excessive police force case in Los Angeles in 1991.

Enriching our approaches to American drama if not always to dramatic literature are books and articles by and about producers, critics, and performers such as Florenz Ziegfeld, Joe Papp, Harold Clurman, Burgess Meredith, Eric Bentley, and Frank Rich. The celebrated producers are Ziegfeld and Papp. Like a revue which makes no claim on dramatic literature, Michael Lasser's "The Glorifier: Florenz Ziegfeld and the Creation of the American Showgirl" (*ASch* 63: 441–48) is a readable article on the great impresario. Feminism has correctly provided the necessary cautionary lessons about the public ogling of women, but Lasser recaptures Ziegfeld's gift for theatricality and mastery of illusion to create theater now faded forever from view. On the other hand, Benedict Nightingale said that Joseph Papirofsky was smaller than average and larger than life, a sleek vole with the charisma of the tragic hero, an irresistible force that changed that immovable object, the American theater. Anyone with an interest in American *theater* will want to see Helen Epstein's popular—as distinguished from scholarly—*Joe Papp: An American Life* (Little, Brown). Anyone interested in American *drama* will want to read the book's sections on David Rabe, once Papp's premier playwright; Ntozake Shange; Wallace Shawn; John Guare; and Sam Shepard's acrimonious dispute with Papp over *True West*. Also of passing interest are Epstein's "How a King Did and Did Not Seek a Successor" (*New York Times*, 21 Aug., sec. 2, p. 5), and Richard Hornby's very wicked

"Remembering Joe Papp: 'A Whim of Iron'" (*HudR* 47: 429–36) on the producer as a charlatan and self-promoting radical-chic politician.

Quite another matter, and a significant addition to the history of American drama, is *The Collected Works of Harold Clurman: Six Decades of Commentary on Theatre, Dance, Music, Film, Arts and Letters,* ed. Marjorie Loggia and Glenn Young (Applause), which gathers one-third of Clurman's writings, including nearly 600 of his weekly and monthly essays. Producer and director, he was drama critic for the *New Republic* from 1949 to 1952 and for the *Nation* from 1953 until his death in 1980. Clurman was aware of the small ironies of wearing many hats. His discussion of Miller's *All My Sons,* for example, is suggestive, carefully anticipating any charge of partiality since he was one of the play's producers. Believing social and political content to be vital, Clurman was primarily interested in a playwright's ideas, and if the chronological organization allows repetitive material, that is to be expected in a collection which spans April 1931 until May 1980. Included as well are "A Conversation with Kenneth Tynan"; a lengthy oral history, tape-recorded reminiscences of interviews by Louis Sheaffer; appendices of *Daily Worker* essays, previously unpublished papers, and a concluding 1947 letter to Clifford Odets. A thorough index is a sine qua non for a book of 1,101 pages, suffering from what Terry Teachout calls bibliobesity, and the 42-page index—if still incomplete—is usable. For example, there are 16 references to David Mamet, and *American Buffalo* turns up three times in the index. It is convenient to have so much commentary, a testimony to Clurman's consistency, available in a single volume.

Burgess Meredith's *So Far, So Good: A Memoir* (Little, Brown) is an autobiography of the sort that celebrated people are asked to write, full of discursive anecdotes and rambling reminiscences of other celebrities (here they include Tallulah Bankhead, Katharine Cornell, Lee Strasberg, and Zero Mostel). It is worth mention here for an initial chapter on the 1935 opening night of Maxwell Anderson's *Winterset,* a mildly interesting chapter on Actor's Equity and the Federal Theatre Project 1938, and slim sketches on Meredith's directing Amiri Baraka's *The Toilet* and *Dutchman* and James Baldwin's *Blues for Mr. Charlie,* all in 1964. Words of cautionary wisdom and practical advice appear in Arthur H. Ballet's "After-Dinner Thoughts of America's Oldest Living Dramaturg" (*NTQ* 10, xxxvii: 24–27). Ballet wittily decries excess seriousness, pomposity, anger, and pretentiousness in the theater.

Critics Eric Bentley and Frank Rich form an odd couple. Charles

Marowitz's "From Half-Century to Millennium: the Theatre and the Electric Spectator" (*NTQ* 10, xxxvii: 3–10) is an interview with Bentley, who in his eighties regards himself as primarily a playwright: this allows the person who in some ways redefined the agenda of serious criticism during the postwar years to reflect on the present state of both the active theater and the critical trade. Frank Rich's "Exit the Critic" (*New York Times Magazine,* 13 Feb., pp. 32–39 et seq.) is the breezy reflection of the "Butcher of Broadway" on the omnipotence that strangers attached to his 13 years as that paper's drama critic. Rich settles some old scores and makes some new enemies.

No annual survey of theater history would be complete without a glance at Williamsburg to see what Bruce A. McConachie is up to. Ian Watson's "Realizing a Postpositivist Theatre History" (*NTQ* 10, xxxix: 217–22) presents Watson's interview with the theater historian. Mc-Conachie himself provides "The 'Oriental' Musicals of Rodgers and Hammerstein and the U.S. War in Southeast Asia" (*TJ* 46, iii: 385–98), the most recent demonstration of McConachie's ideal that it is the historian's responsibility to analyze theater in terms of the much larger sociocultural complex. The quickest way for students to begin a crash course in neo-Marxist methodology is to read "Marxism, Melodrama, and Theatre Historiography" (*TDR* 38, i: 31–34), an exchange of letters between McConachie and Daniel Gerould, who does not accept McConachie's presuppositions. Each year with anticipation I seek out Gerald Weales's *Georgia Review* essay. In this year's "American Theater Watch, 1993–1994" (*GaR* 48: 571–82), this highly respected scholar evaluates Albee's *Three Tall Women,* Tony Kushner's *Perestroika,* Arthur Miller's *Broken Glass,* and Robert Schenkkan's *The Kentucky Cycle,* which had already won its Pulitzer when it arrived on Broadway (Weales clarifies the attendant contretemps over the nine-play cycle). There are also succinct comments on plays by David Ives, Neil Simon, Mac Wellman, Jonathan Tolins, Romulus Linney, Joyce Carol Oates, and Terrance McNally's *A Perfect Ganesh.* As always, Weales is a pleasure to read. Speaking of which, joyful bits of theater history may be found in a singular 31 May 1993 issue of the *New Yorker,* which includes "Broadway Jubilee" (pp. 54–168), a special section celebrating Broadway's centennial. John Lahr provides an introduction and John Guare a satiric coda, "Broadway 2003: The New Generation Arrives." In between are cameos, interludes, interviews, reviews, and critics' roundtables reprinting Dorothy Parker, Robert Benchley, Wolcott Gibbs, Kenneth Tynan, Brendan

Gill, Truman Capote, and Lillian Ross, among others. Whoever said
research and scholarship couldn't be fun?

iii Criticism and Theory

Walter A. Davis's *Get the Guests* attempts to initiate a new direction for
psychoanalytic theory, "to show that what theatre offers is not yet
another safe space in which we enact the rituals needed to restore our
guarantees, but the place where the secrets we hide from one another are
made public." Davis constructs his theory of the psyche through psychoanalysis and literary interpretation. His theory is developed by submit-
ting five plays to close interpretation, two by O'Neill, one each by
Williams and Miller, concluding, of course, with Albee's *Who's Afraid of
Virginia Woolf?* As might be expected in a work intended to illustrate the
process Davis labels a hermeneutics of engagement, the dialectical theory
of interpretation he constructed for his *Inwardness and Existence* (Wisconsin, 1989), the intricate prose here is like a rococo maze—appropriate
to its heady subject matter. Some readers will be thrilled and amazed by
the language performance, while the less sophisticated may become lost
in the verbal labyrinth. Readings of the plays and their relation to the
audience will reward the discerning reader. John M. Clum's *Acting Gay:
Male Homosexuality in Modern Drama* (Columbia, 1992) delivers what
its title promises, an interpretation of the central works of gay male
drama. Clum distinguishes two categories, plays written primarily for
gay audiences which speak of the audience members' shared experience,
and those written for the mainstream theater by homosexuals (the latter,
including works by Inge and Williams, Clum terms "closet dramas" and
sees as expressions of the playwrights' negative feelings about their own
homosexuality). The book is divided into three sections: "Bodies and
Taboos" centers on the physical aspects of homosexuality including
AIDS; "Codes and Closets" surveys plays written from 1930 through
1968 which made way for gay characters but dealt with homosexuality in
an elliptical or coded manner; and "Staging 'A Culture That Isn't Just
Sexual'" focuses on the dramas of the past three decades which present
homosexuality directly. Clum is good on Crowley's *The Boys in the Band,*
McNally's *The Lisbon Traviata,* and Fierstein's *Torch Song Trilogy,* all
brilliant plays no matter what one's sexual disposition. If his approach
has a weakness, it is the reduction of plays such as *Death of a Salesman,
The Crucible,* and especially *A View from the Bridge* and their author

Arthur Miller to expressions of "the attitude of a well-meaning liberal of the forties and fifties." New to the 1994 paperback edition of Clum's book is a chapter on the proliferation of gay drama in the '90s, including Tony Kushner's *Angels in America* and Larry Kramer's *The Destiny of Me*.

A culmination of those articles which see theater at a "crossroads" or in crisis, Bradley Boney's "Going, Going, Gone: Theatre and American Culture(s)" (*TDR* 38, i: 98–105) is a penetrating and perplexing essay that challenges theater's future role in relation to mass culture. Using the current theatrical mainstream of Broadway as evidence, Boney says that since the 1960s "queers" (his word), women, and people of color have seized the power of producing their own representations on a large scale. Seen in the best light, the article asks theater *quo vadis?* At worst, it is an apocalyptic vision of Armageddon upon a theater which Boney sees as going, going, gone. On the other hand, Nina Rapi's "Hide and Seek: The Search for a Lesbian Theatre Aesthetic" (*NTQ* 9, xxxiv: 147–58) perceives the dominant theater as remaining specifically white, male, and bourgeois. Focusing on a number of lesbian texts, including her own play *Ithaka*, Rapi explores both the theory and practice of an emerging aesthetic. Continuing *NTQ*'s series on the actuality and ideology of lesbian performance, Stacy Wolf's "All about Eve: Apple Island and the Fictions of Lesbian Community" (*NTQ* 10, xxxvii: 28–32) examines how the women's cultural and art space in Madison, Wisconsin, helps to redefine the meaning of cultural feminism. And a special aspect of autoperformance is the topic of Deborah R. Geis in " 'And this strength is in me still': Embodying Memory in Works by Jewish Women Performance Artists" (*YES* 24: 172–79), which establishes the complexities and contradictions of memory as central to performance art.

iv Eugene O'Neill

Most folks with a moderate interest in American drama will not find news in the fact that O'Neill was an autobiographical author, and many can name the plays which demonstrate that fact. Doris Alexander's *Eugene O'Neill's Creative Struggle: The Decisive Decade, 1924–1933* (Penn. State, 1992) is the work of an experienced O'Neill scholar, and her effort here goes well beyond the obvious. Exactly 30 years after publishing *The Tempering of Eugene O'Neill,* Alexander returns to the topic of how O'Neill transmuted life experience into art and by doing so was able to approach his own problems. Her present book selects the nine plays the dramatist completed from 1924 to 1933—*Desire Under the Elms; Marco Millions; The Great God Brown; Lazarus Laughed; Strange Interlude; Dynamo; Mourning Becomes Electra; Ah, Wilderness!;* and *Days Without End*—and demonstrates the procedure by which O'Neill siphoned off his personal sorrow in creating his plays, a complicated process in a writer as philosophical as O'Neill with an active intellectual existence. O'Neill scholars such as Michael Hinden, Michael Manheim, and Steven F. Bloom have commented favorably on the enormous research and sound approach of this study, each at lengths not possible here, and I am happy to add my voice—that of a simple country schoolteacher—to their paean.

Demonstrating a secure command of O'Neill scholarship from Peter Egri to John Henry Raleigh, Kurt Eisen's *The Inner Strength of Opposites: O'Neill's Novelistic Drama and the Melodramatic Imagination* (Georgia) explores trails blazed by Arthur Gelb, Egil Törnqvist, Louis Sheaffer, and most notably Egri indicating elements of the novel in O'Neill's plays. Acknowledging their earlier observations, Eisen gains more authority to support his theme by carefully illustrating O'Neill's awareness and oft-reiterated intention to exploit the novel's capacities. Not merely experimenting with a novelistic drama, O'Neill turned to the resources of the novel as a means of transforming American stage melodrama into more probing images of character and relationships. While O'Neill never attempted a novel, his novelistic tendencies are inseparable from the elements of traditional melodrama conspicuous in even his most experimental plays. Eisen demonstrates how the playwright undercuts melodramatic action by novelistic elements such as "thought asides." While Eisen is thorough in his examination of O'Neill's canon, the chapter on "The Spare Room: *Long Day's Journey into Night,*" which demonstrates how the novelistic technique of establishing multiple perspectives on the same set of events provides the basis of familial tragedy, is especially memorable. That play is the subject of back-to-back articles in *Literature/Film Quarterly.* Donald P. Costello's "Sidney Lumet's *Long Day's Journey into Night*" (22, ii: 78–92) enumerates cuts and changes made in the 1962 film adaptation necessary to remain faithful to the play. Conceding that neither has the visual power of Lumet's motion picture, Edward T. Jones's "The Tyrones as TV Family: O'Neill's *Long Day's Journey into Night,* Primetime" (22, ii: 93–97) compares Jonathan Miller's 1986 made-for-cable production and Peter Wood's 1971 broadcast adaptation with Laurence Olivier as James Tyrone. The penultimate chapter of Walter A. Davis's *Get the Guests,* "Drug of Choice: *Long Day's Journey into Night*" (pp. 147–208), demonstrates that while naturalism is the means, revealing the structure of a collective psychology is the goal of this great play. The essay concludes that O'Neill made dramatic form an independent way of knowing and literally saw there is nothing but drama; thus, drama becomes a principle of exploration and discovery. Davis's initial chapter, "Souls on Ice: *The Iceman Cometh*" (pp. 13–59), posits that the merit of that play resides in the intricate logic of reversal and recognition which forms its structure.

Although experiencing its longest hiatus yet between issues, *EONR* (17, i and ii) Spring/Fall 1993 has arrived, and the "double issue" is worth the wait. As its title suggests, Frank R. Cunningham's "O'Neill's Beginnings and the Birth of Modernism in American Drama" (pp. 11–20) seeks to establish O'Neill's place among significant modernists in American literature, and following hard upon it, Brenda Murphy's "McTeague's Dream and *The Emperor Jones:* O'Neill's Move from Naturalism to Modernism" (pp. 21–29) uses Frank Norris's novel to demonstrate that it would be hard to find a better example of American modernism than O'Neill's play. Laurin R. Porter provides a rich commentary on the parallels in two Pulitzer Prize winners, "Modern and Postmodern Wastelands: *Long Day's Journey into Night* and Shepard's *Buried Child*" (pp. 106–19). There are an additional baker's dozen essays of uniform quality. Also included is a 1949 letter from O'Neill to Arthur Miller with an introduction by Travis Bogard and Jackson R. Bryer, an assessment by Dan Isaac, and an earlier letter from Miller to O'Neill. Robert Conklin in "The Expression of Character in O'Neill's *The Emperor Jones* and *The Hairy Ape*" (*WVUPP* 39: 101–7), acknowledging the plays as early experiments in Expressionism, argues that Jones and Yank are stock characters resisting Expressionistic form. James R. Keller's "Eugene O'Neill's Stokehole and Spenser's Cave of Mammon" (*ELN* 31, iii: 66–73) seeks to add one more potential influence to the list of possible origins for *The Hairy Ape.* The essay points to "significant contrast," but Keller might have been more convincing about O'Neill's "borrowing" if he could add when and under what circumstances O'Neill read *The Faerie Queene.* Joseph Rice's "The Blinding of Mannon House: O'Neill, Electra, and Oedipus" (*T&P* 13: 45–51) adds a Sophoclean thread to the relation of *Mourning Becomes Electra* to Aeschylus's *Oresteia,* finding a partial explanation in Freudian psychology. Electra becomes blinded Oedipus, and Mannon House serves as the Blind Seer. In another temper, readers interested in the ambiance in which O'Neill developed may want to see Leona Rust Egan's *Provincetown as a Stage: Provincetown, The Provincetown Players, and the Discovery of Eugene O'Neill* (Parnassus).

v Sam Shepard

The boom of the last few years in scholarly activity concerning Shepard continues. A book-length study is David J. DeRose's *Sam Shepard* (Twayne, 1992) which *MD* (37: 542–43) calls "the most comprehensive survey of Shepard's plays to date." DeRose offers analyses of both individual plays and the shape of Shepard's canon. Popular audiences and some previous commentaries have focused on Shepard's Western maverick persona, treating him as a social and show business phenomenon rather than as a playwright. DeRose's study provides close readings of Shepard's plays and production reviews, centering on his stage directions, visual imagery, and physical staging. The real advantage of De-Rose's book is that it makes use of previously unpublished plays and includes discussions of the "lost" plays such as *Cowboys, Dog, The Rocking Chair, Up to Thursday,* and *Blue Bitch,* using minor works to cast light on major efforts like *La Turista, The Tooth of Crime, Action,* and the family plays like *Curse of the Starving Class, Buried Child,* and *True West.* Concluding with a selected bibliography, DeRose's book is a smart and readable addition to Shepard studies as the old experimental plays give way to a "new" Sam Shepard whose dramas elicit comparison to O'Neill, Williams, and Miller. Moreover, Shepard continues to appear in distinguished international company. A volume devoted to Ibsen, Strindberg, Brecht, Pinter, and Beckett, Gay Gibson Cima's *Performing Women: Female Characters, Male Playwrights, and the Modern Stage* (Cornell, 1993), commits an entire chapter to "Shepard and the Improvisational Actor" (pp. 159–83). Cima's book generally identifies interconnections among parts of a theatrical production, hopeful that feminists eager to transform social roles can benefit from an examination of the relationship between "new" playwriting and acting styles. Cima sees a complex intertwining of "hegemonic scripting" and feminist counter movements. Her chapter on Shepard, however, draws from the world of art theory, using artist Robert Rauschenberg's "combines"—constructions merging painting and sculpture—as a metaphor to describe the way in which Shepard "joins" two dramatic actions like found objects. This structural approach, claims Cima, prepares an audience to make sense of the peculiar double actions in plays like *Buried Child*. Cima goes on to comment on *Angel City*, *The Tooth of Crime*, and *A Lie of the Mind*, but the chapter's most complete exegesis is of Shepard's combination of realistic and nonrealistic, contradictory but simultaneous multiple dramatic actions in *Buried Child*.

Tucker Orbison's "Authorization and Subversion of Myth in Shepard's *Buried Child*" (*MD* 37: 509–20) argues that while Shepard authorizes the validity of the vegetation myth of the Corn King, he subverts the legend of the Holy Grail: the natural world is renewed, but the human world is not. Using substantial commentary on O'Neill's, Miller's, and Williams's staging of synchronic time as reference points, Enoch Brater's "American Clocks: Sam Shepard's Time Plays" (*MD* 37: 603–12) focuses on *A Lie of the Mind* and *Fool for Love* to demonstrate that in Shepard's theater the movement of time has been vastly and eccentrically accelerated. "Sam Shepard," pp. 60–88 in Marc Robinson's *The Other American Drama*, explores the unpredictability of Shepard's art, which Robinson likens to the liberating, raunchy irresistibility of rock and roll—from *The Tooth of Crime*, *Angel City*, and *Operation Sidewinder* through to *A Lie of the Mind*, Shepard's longest work. Also worth brief mention are two *New York Times* pieces: Ben Brantley's "Sam Shepard, Storyteller" (13 Nov., sec. 2, pp. 1, 26) and Vincent Canby's "Sam Shepard Goes to the Races and Wins" (20 Nov., sec. 2, pp. 5, 8), on the opening of *Simpatico*, to get a sense of Shepard's present standing with critics. Also see Laurin R. Porter's fine essay on Shepard and O'Neill, mentioned earlier.

vi Tennessee Williams and Arthur Miller

In a year which saw the Roundabout Theater bring an intelligent new production of *The Glass Menagerie* with Julie Harris as Amanda Wingfield to the Criterion Center in New York, interest has ebbed a bit from the flood of scholarship during the previous two years. As we catch our breath, we can catch up with Brenda Murphy's *Tennessee Williams and Elia Kazan: A Collaboration in the Theatre* (Cambridge, 1992), the first book-length study of the active relationship of two of the most important figures of 20th-century American drama. Murphy shows the reader how the playwright's language in a preproduction script is affected by the "director's language" and even the "designer's language"—for Jo Mielziner is a participant too in this creative process. Williams, who wrote every word that appears in his published scripts, may have often been uneasy about cuts and changes, and Murphy charts the growing tensions in this complex and fortunate relation. Readers of her excellent book, however, will never read or see *A Streetcar Named Desire, Camino Real, Cat on a Hot Tin Roof,* or *Sweet Bird of Youth* the same way again. That is high praise for Murphy's thorough examination of the process, evolution, and development wrought by collaboration.

Philip C. Kolin last year added eight or more items to our understanding of Williams, including a special number of *Studies in American Drama, 1945–Present,* ed. Colby H. Kullman and Kolin. This journal is experiencing an interruption in publication, though Kolin assures me that it will return after a brief hiatus. This year, Kolin's " 'Cruelty . . . and Sweaty Intimacy': The Reception of the Spanish Premiere of *A Streetcar Named Desire*" (*ThS* 35, ii: 45–56) details the political, cultural, and economic reasons for the play's delayed Spanish debut in 1961, 14 years after it appeared on Broadway, and the mixed response of Spanish critics. The reader will also want to see "Tennessee Williams," pp. 29–59 in Marc Robinson's *The Other American Drama.* Another item, this of unique interest, is John Lahr's "The Lady and Tennessee" (*NY* 19 Dec., pp. 76–97), describing Williams's association with Lady Maria St. Just, the self-appointed "keeper of the playwright's flame." Lahr's account of the friendship is racy, breezy, gossipy, sad, amusing, and serious about the dark implications of the relationship for Williams's literary estate. He reminds us of the problems a litany of potential biographers have had and the twisted legacy of the co-trustee of the Williams Trust, St. Just, who had no academic training and no understanding of how to sustain Williams's literary reputation—thus scholars were refused the right to quote, letters remained unedited and journals unpublished, and organized plans for Williams's unpublished works had not been made at her death on 15 Feb. 1994. Lahr's summary suggests that such work will occupy a generation of scholars. Except for the fact that the heroine totters between the pathetic and the laughable, it all might have made a Tennessee Williams play. Two items concern *Streetcar:* Linda Costanzo Cahir's "The Artful Rerouting of *A Streetcar Named Desire*" (*LFQ* 22: 72–77) discusses the play's transition to film, and Walter A. Davis devotes a chapter to "The Perfect Couple: *A Streetcar Named Desire,*" pp. 60–102 in *Get the Guests,* which begins by examining the relation of role-playing to identity and proposes that Blanche and Stanley are made for each other. Stressing as always the relation to the audience, Davis argues that the play's purpose is to dissolve the difference between desire and death, libido and destruction.

Davis follows his chapter on Williams with "All in the Family: *Death of a Salesman*" (pp. 103–46). He sees the play as involving efforts at transcendence that fail because the values on which the efforts are based actually function to advance the disorder from which they promise deliverance by blinding characters to what they are doing to one another. Davis claims the humanistic Miller is not a critic of the American Dream but its defender. Willy becomes the scapegoat who bears the punishment for the illusions of which the audience is thereby "cleansed." Miller-bashing, already well-established in several forms, has now become a gay sport. Bradley Boney, a theater scholar and gay man, condemns Miller as "a homophobe and a sexist" (*TDR* 38, iii: 199). If some gays find this playwright who was anathema to the political right suddenly offensive, those who would ban books were out before them. Miller has been often censured in his career for his political and social views; still, it comes as a small surprise to find two essays responding to censorship of his most celebrated works. *Censored Books: Critical Viewpoints*, ed. Nicholas J. Karolides et al. (Scarecrow, 1993), is a collection of essays designed to assist persons confronting censorship situations in libraries and public school curricula. Miller's plays are *the* two dramas most frequently the subject of attempts at censorship in the '80s and '90s. The essays are Joan DelFattore's "Fueling The Fire Of Hell: A Reply to Censors of *The Crucible*" (pp. 201–08) and Harry Harder's "*Death of a Salesman*: An American Classic" (pp. 209–19). The volume also includes Miller's own "On Censorship" (pp. 3–10).

Noncombative scholarship on Miller, meanwhile, continues to flourish. Steve Centola's *Arthur Miller in Conversation* (Northouse and Northouse, 1993) is the work of the brightest and most dedicated of a new generation of Miller scholars. Centola provides a well-written introduction comparing the dramatist's reputation at home and abroad, suggestively proposing why Miller's plays, including his early work, are currently received far better around the world than in the United States. The volume's raisons d'être are a pair of interviews, and here Centola is at his best. Miller is, and always has been, warmly generous with academics, and Centola's inquiry is excellent: he is carefully prepared, asks intelligent questions, then gets out of the way and lets Miller answer. Thus, the focus remains on Miller. Especially valuable is the second conversation on Miller's works in the late 1970s and 1980s. The book is marred by distracting typographical flaws. I am not sure of the intended audience for a "Summary of Arthur Miller's Major Works" (pp. 55–64), a necessarily oversimplified one-paragraph synopsis devoted to each of 23 works (try to imagine, if you can, the one paragraph précis of *Salesman* or *Crucible*). Centola, a scholar of taste and intelligence, concludes with a detailed selected bibliography (pp. 65–80).

The Crucible attracts the attention of two essays. Valerie Lowe's " 'Unsafe Convictions': 'Unhappy' Confessions in *The Crucible*" (*Lang&Lit* 3: 175–95) applies speech act theory as a framework to explain differing perceptions in the play according to who is speaking, particularly Tituba; and Wendy Schissel in "Re(dis)covering the Witches in Arthur Miller's *The Crucible:* A Feminist Reading" (*MD* 37: 461–73) is troubled by the way the play reinforces gender stereotypes in its treatment of Abigail and Elizabeth. Stefan Tai, on the other hand, in "Arthur Miller's 'Last Yankee'—A Male Depressive" (*ContempR* 264: 147–48) is impressed by Miller's skill in depicting how individuals, regardless of gender, struggle with the illness of depression. John S. Shockley's "*Death of a Salesman* and American Leadership: Life Imitates Art" (*JACult* 17, ii: 49–56) argues that the play still resonates powerfully in American life and culture by enumerating a number of important traits Willy Loman shares with Ronald Reagan. Helge Normann Nilsen's "From *Honors at Dawn* to *Death of a Salesman:* Marxism and the Early Plays of Arthur Miller" (*ES* 75: 146–56) is not unique in exploring the influence Marxism may have had on the dramatist, but especially impressive here is Nilsen's scholarship in the use of typescripts of Miller's unpublished earliest plays like *The Great Disobedience,* unpublished versions of other plays, and longhand notebooks at the University of Michigan.

vii Edward Albee and David Mamet

Inspired by the first appearance in New York of two Albee plays from the 1970s, *Counting the Ways* and *Listening,* Richard Hornby in "Albee and Pinter" (*HudR* 47: 109–16), examining the parallel careers of these contemporaries, concludes that while Albee's late plays are imaginative and poignant, they belong in the study, not in the theater. Later, Hornby comments (*HudR* 47, iii: 434–35) that *Three Tall Women,* though beautifully written, suffers from an excessive narrative which Hornby says makes so much of Albee's late work sluggish. John Lahr in "Sons and

Mothers" (*NY* 16 May, pp. 102–05) sees *Three Tall Women* as a wary act of reconciliation from Albee to his late mother, Frances Cotter Albee. Walter A. Davis devotes the final chapter of *Get the Guests* to "The Academic Festival Overture: *Who's Afraid of Virginia Woolf?*" (pp. 209–62). He concludes that the emotions which rhetorical criticism claims as basic to human character are precisely those that Albee exposes as defenses developed to conceal more disruptive feelings, and he insists that the play's greatness is its refusal to restore any illusions. Albee, Davis states, like O'Neill and Williams, practiced the best game in town: get the guests. And those who are "gotten" are not just the characters. For Davis, the play's not the thing; it is the audience. Pointing to Albee's powerful subtlety, Carlos Campo in "The Role of *Beyond the Forest* in Albee's *Who's Afraid of Virginia Woolf?*" (*LFQ* 22: 170–73) indicates similarities in both theme and plot between the play and the film discussed in the play's opening scene. Campo proposes that the film's star Bette Davis serves as a role model for Albee's Martha in the play which Hornby claims still looms like Pikes Peak over the modest range of American drama of the past 35 years.

If the reader is not put off by its subtitle, there are rewards in Ilkka Joki's *Mamet, Bakhtin, and the Dramatic: The Demotic as a Variable of Addressivity* (Åbo Akademi, 1993), the focus of which is the role of American vernacular speech in the work of Mamet. Despite daunting forays into recondite aspects of sociolinguistic poetics, an audience interested in the American playwright will find commentary on Mamet's dramatic dialogue in four media: radio, television, film, and theater. Of interest are the first chapter, "David Mamet, an American Dramatist," a response to views of Mamet as obscene and misogynistic; chapters on Mamet's radio and television scripts, especially his work for *Hill Street Blues;* and the chapter on Mamet's cinematic drama. The most interesting aspect of Joki's survey is the section on *American Buffalo* and *Glengarry Glen Ross.* Another bit of the out-of-the-ordinary is Leslie Kane's "'In Blood, in Blood Thou Shalt Remember': David Mamet's *Marranos*" (*YES* 24: 157–71), a first-rate piece of research which deals with the earliest example of ethnic representation in the Mamet canon, a little-known unpublished two-act play, framed by a prologue and an epilogue, that stages the past and the present as contiguous historical events. Written concurrently with *American Buffalo, Marranos* is seen as arguably a seminal work; Kane points to similarities to Beckett and Pinter before concluding that "*Marranos* illustrates Mamet's personal

quest to rediscover Jewish history and reaffirm its teachings." Quite
another matter is Bronwyn Drainie's "*Oleanna's* Popularity Is Deeply
Disturbing" (*Toronto Globe and Mail*, 17 Nov., p. E-1), an inquiry into
why 12 theaters across Canada put on the same play about the same time.
The principles of feminism guide all the chapters of *Fictions of Masculinity*, and David Radavich's chapter therein, "Man among Men:
David Mamet's Homosocial Order" (pp. 123–36), analyzes the quest by
Mamet's characters for lasting male friendship protected from the threats
of women and masculine vulnerability on the one hand and the pursuit
of power and domination on the other. David Worster in "How to Do
Things with Salesmen: David Mamet's Speech-Act Play" (*MD* 37: 375–
90) uses speech-act theory, carefully restricting his discussion to *Glengarry Glen Ross*.

viii The Wilsons: August and Lanford

Once upon a time and not all that long ago, a mention of the surname
Wilson would have referred to Meredith Willson. Presently, Wilson
might be August, Lanford, or Robert. None of the recent attention
afforded Robert Wilson by C. W. E. Bigsby was apparent this year except
for Dean Wilcox's "Sign and Referent in the Work of Robert Wilson:
Reconstituting the Human Form" (*T&P* 13: 97–103), which deals with
the split between form and function and the role of artistic signification.

The other Wilsons saw a burgeoning of scholarship. Mary L. Bogu-
mil's "'Tomorrow Never Comes': Songs of Cultural Identity in August
Wilson's *Joe Turner's Come and Gone*" (*TJ* 46, iv: 463–76) explores the
use of song, whether the juba or the blues, to explain the attempt to
reconnect a character's identity as an African American living in the
United States. *May All Your Fences Have Gates: Essays on the Drama of
August Wilson*, ed. Alan Nadel (Iowa), prints 13 articles and an "Annotated Bibliography of Works by and about August Wilson" (pp. 230–66)
by Sandra G. Shannon. Nadel has gathered an outstanding group of
essays, demonstrating how Wilson makes visible African American culture's connection with a white culture that too often takes it for granted.
Nadel provides a succinct and thought-provoking introduction (pp. 1–
8), and he captures perfectly the situation of characters in a double
diaspora—first from Africa and then from the South in "Boundaries,
Logistics, and Identity: The Property of Metaphor in *Fences* and *Joe
Turner's Come and Gone*" (pp. 86–104). Nadel chooses also to reprint

Wilson's "I Want a Black Director" (pp. 200–204) occasioned by the sale of film rights for *Fences* to Paramount Pictures; this is followed by an original essay, " 'The Crookeds with the Straights': *Fences,* Race, and the Politics of Adaptation" (pp. 205–29) by Michael Awkward, who plays out the implications of Wilson's argument, calling for the education of white Americans in the ethos of black experience in the same way that black Americans are educated to white experience. Wilson has long believed that blacks know more about white culture than whites know about blacks because blacks "have to know because our survival depends on it." Although Sandra G. Shannon's "The Ground on Which I Stand: August Wilson's Perspective on African American Women" (pp. 150–64) reminds us that Wilson's male-centered plays rarely include more than one adult woman, Missy Dehn Kubitschek's "August Wilson's Gender Lesson" (pp. 183–99) explores Wilson's depiction of gender relationships and, like Harry J. Elam, Jr.'s "August Wilson's Women" (pp. 165–82), examines the politics of gender relations in Wilson's plays. Michael Morales's brief "Ghosts on the Piano: August Wilson and the Representation of Black American History" (pp. 105–15) suggests that the dramatist employs African ritual and its forms to challenge American naturalist tradition, and Mark William Rocha's "American History as 'Loud Talking' in *Two Trains Running*" (pp. 116–32) is convincing in the view that a white theater audience is being given angry lessons in a nonconfrontational manner, a form of "loud talking" common in black culture, speaking intended to be overheard by a third party for whom the instruction is intended. Craig Werner and Sandra Adell approach Wilson through jazz and the blues, and Joan Fishman connects the playwright with painter Romare Bearden through art which captures the energy of African American experience. John Timpane's article and Anne Flèche's opening essay evoke histories, competing histories, and historical narrative in their approaches. The essays throughout the volume are of uniform excellence, and the collection suggests that while whimsy and an innate disposition to integration harness two Wilsons here for organizational convenience, August Wilson may be in the process of creating a canon which might eventually place him comfortably in the company of Miller and O'Neill, to whom Nadel points resemblances. Yet the profound difference is that in Wilson's plays community is both the source of the dramatic tension and its product. This may set this multiple prizewinning playwright apart. His accomplishments evoke great expectations.

Audiences also expect a great deal from Lanford Wilson. Anne M. Dean's *Discovery and Invention: The Urban Plays of Lanford Wilson* (Fairleigh Dickinson) opens with "From Missouri to Manhattan," a brief overview and circumspect biographical introduction. This is followed by "Concerns, Poetry, and Dramatized Experience," which provides a commentary on linguistic patterns and rhythms; Dean identifies recurrent themes in Wilson, but one hardly sees that "his work bestrides the United States, reflections of his experiences echoing throughout . . . " (front flap). "Bestrides" suits Caesar, but will seem excessive even to Wilson's admirers. Dean's principal concentration, however, is on Wilson's major "city" plays, nicely spanning three decades: *Balm in Gilead* (1964), *The Hot l Baltimore* (1973), and *Burn This* (1987). The chapter on the earliest play is informative, especially on Wilson's use of language and visual imagery. The chapter on *Hot l,* Wilson's metaphor for the decline of urban America, is readable, especially on the combination of humorous, often hilarious, aspects with the poignant wistfulness and nostalgia in this wonderful play. The chapter on *Burn This* is an appropriate concluding essay, for it proposes that the play "encompasses and expands upon almost every dramatic idea ever expressed by Wilson." While this is hyperbole, the final chapter is competent in the progression traced from *Balm* to *Burn This,* and the substantial quotations from director Marshall Mason, playwright Wilson, and various performers are the book's best passages. Small oversights, confusions, and omissions have escaped Dean's editors. *Lemon Sky,* for example, is omitted from her half-page bibliography (p. 134), and her list of secondary sources is weak.

One is better off with Martin J. Jacobi's six-page bibliography of primary works (pp. 235–40) and his 17-page record of major criticism in *Lanford Wilson: A Casebook,* ed. Jackson R. Bryer (Garland), one of America's busiest and most respected scholars. This volume contains a dozen items plus a chronology. Of the ten essays written especially for this volume, the first four take long views of Wilson's canon. The opening essay, Thomas P. Adler's "The Artist in the Garden: Theatre Space and Place in Lanford Wilson" (pp. 3–20), explores how settings both real and imagined relate to theme. In "The Playwright Continues: Lanford Wilson and the Counter Culture" (pp. 21–35) Barry B. Witham sees Wilson's earliest work in the context of performance techniques created by groups within counterculture theater and assimilated by him. My own "Charlotte's Daughters: Changing Gender Roles and Family Structures in Lanford Wilson" (pp. 37–63) focuses on the playwright's portrayal of the developing role of American women as captured in plays from *Lemon Sky* to *Burn This,* and Robert Cooperman's "The Talley Plays and the Evolution of the American Family" (pp. 65–84) concentrates on Wilson's trilogy. Two fine essays, one by Richard Wattenberg (pp. 85–101), another by Susan Harris Smith (pp. 103–18), look carefully at *Angels Fall.* The essay by the prolific Felicia Hardison Londré (pp. 119–29) examines Wilson's translation of Chekhov's *Three Sisters* in context with *Burn This.* Three essays, by Martin J. Jacobi (pp. 131–149), Henry I. Schvey (pp. 151–60), and Daniel J. Watermeier (pp. 161–81), pay especially close attention to *Burn This.* The volume concludes with two interviews conducted by Bryer, the first with Wilson (pp. 183–203) and a second with his long-time director and collaborator Marshall Mason (pp. 205–34). It would be neither immodest nor inappropriate to say that Lanford Wilson studies take a step forward with this casebook.

ix Closed Canons

There is a wonderful old shaggy-dog story about theater with the recurrent line "Hark, I hear the cannon's roar!" Many American dramatists have left canons which continue to attract scholarly and popular attention. Shaun Considine has written a well-received popular biography, *Mad as Hell: The Life and Work of Paddy Chayefsky* (Random House). While the bulk of the book, as its title suggests, is devoted to Chayefsky's lionized successes in Hollywood and on television, an audience interested in his stage dramas *The Middle of the Night, The Tenth Man,* and *Gideon* will want to consider Considine's thesis, which places the writer alongside Miller, Inge, and Williams. If the volume does not fully support that thesis or carefully weigh the merit and meaning of Chayefsky's plays, peripheral interest can be found in tales of casting the plays and in theater anecdotes meant to color perceptions of Chayefsky's character and his relations with other writers.

    Paul Green's Celebration of Man, with a Bibliography, ed. Lynn Veach Sadler and Sue Laslie Kimball (Human Technology), publishes the proceedings of the Sixth Annual Southern Writers' Symposium. Green, a writer who was correct before it was politically correct, is remembered here not as a playwright who had to endure put-downs and outright mockery, as one friend recalls, but by comments of his daughter, banquet remarks, and recollections. Nine formal articles are devoted to Green's novels, short stories, and 14 outdoor historical plays. Of interest are three essays: Glenda E. Gill's "Paul Green and the Black Actor" (pp. 30–33), commenting on Green's 1927 Pulitzer Prize-winning *In Abraham's Bosom* and his one-act *Hymn to the Rising Sun;* Dahlys Hamilton's "The Struggle of the Mulatto as Seen by Paul Green" (pp. 34–36), which deals with *In Abraham's Bosom* and *White Dresses;* and Frances Roe Kestler's "Paul Green's Celebration of Man Through His Female Characters" (pp. 37–42), which looks at Green's portrayal of women, from the young and flirtatious through the good wives to bitter and disillusioned females. The volume concludes with a substantial bibliography of primary sources (pp. 73–92) and secondary sources (pp. 92–125).

Lorraine Hansberry, *A Raisin in the Sun: The Unfilmed Original Screenplay* (Signet), edited by the late Robert Nemiroff, restores excisions and revisions made to Hansberry's original screenplay for the 1961 motion picture version of her play. A lengthy foreword by Nemiroff's widow, Jewell Handy Gresham-Nemiroff, traces the provenance of the screenplay and her husband's intimate relationship with Hansberry and her works; Hansberry's biographer Margaret B. Wilkerson provides a perceptive scholarly introduction which points to subtle but telling changes in the screenplay; and filmmaker Spike Lee's brief commentary proposes that the deletion of nearly one-third of the original text essentially softened what otherwise might be perceived as a too defiant black voice. Since at least 40 percent of the text is brand-new, the audience of this important play will want to see this untruncated and unfilmed script.

Modern Drama provides two more intelligent, readable pieces of scholarship. Jennifer Jones's "In Defense of the Woman: Sophie Treadwell's *Machinal* (37: 485–96) is an excellent study of the rediscovered 1928 play and the curious circumstances surrounding this Expressionist drama. Like other essays which inspire interest in women's works of the early decades of this century as a fresh generation of scholars rediscover and resurrect neglected but deserving *corpora*, Mary Maddock's "Alice Gerstenberg's *Overtones:* The Demon in the Doll" (37: 474–84) calls our attention to a 1915 experimental one-act drama which is added to a growing list of feminist documents and indictments of patriarchal society.

x The Quick

In a year rich in collections, two more are worthy of note: *Conversations with Amiri Baraka,* ed. Charlie Reilly (Miss.), is a collection of two-dozen interviews presented in chronological order as originally pub-

lished from 1960 to the 1990s, and is part of the Literary Conversations
Series under the general editorship of Peggy Whitman Prenshaw. The
interviews are largely unedited, and the inevitable degree of repetition
occurs as the volume gathers the writer's observations while it traces the
evolution of the rebel, enraged poet-philosopher, and crusader LeRoi
Jones through Imamu Amiri Baraka to the still angry cultural historian
and teacher Amiri Baraka for whom art and politics remain inseparable.
Included are transcripts of a televised 1969 interview with David Frost
and an illuminating 1993 televised conversation with Maya Angelou
published here for the first time. There are a brace of interviews by
Charlie Reilly, the first in 1976 and another in 1991. Of special interest are
Mike Coleman's 1971 "What Is Black Theater?" (pp. 84–88), Sandra G.
Shannon's 1987 "Amiri Baraka on Directing" (pp. 230–38), and especially
for our purposes a reprint of C. W. E. Bigsby's 1978 *Theatre Quarterly*
interview "The Theatre and the Coming Revolution" (pp. 130–45), in
which Baraka rues the tacked-on ending to *The Toilet*, reveals why the
hero of *The Slave* remains a slave, and provides background material
relating to the composition of *Dutchman*. If the interviews are uneven,
the volume provides a convenient gathering of Baraka's social commentary *cum* art.

Escaping the seine in the transition to last year's *ALS* essay is *Intersect-
ing Boundaries: The Theatre of Adrienne Kennedy*, ed. Paul K. Bryant-
Jackson and Lois More Overbeck (Minnesota, 1992), the first book-
length study of Kennedy's contribution to American theater. Included
are a series of interviews with directors, performers, and dramaturges.
Howard Stein interviews two directors central to Kennedy's early work,
Michael Kahn and Gaby Rodgers; also interviewed are director Gerald
Freedman and performer and director Billie Allen; and director David
Willinger both provides his own recollections and interviews Robbie
McCauley. Of the 19 articles and interviews, note should be taken of
Bryant-Jackson's work in African American dramaturgy and the multi-
cultural origins of Kennedy's drama from the Transcendentalists and
Absurdists to an Afrocentric framework (pp. 45–57); Elin Diamond's
"Mimesis in Syncopated Time: Reading Adrienne Kennedy" (pp. 131–
41); Werner Sollors's discussion of Kennedy's autobiography (pp. 13–20);
Margaret B. Wilkerson's outstanding essay comparing the journalistic
and dialectical drama of Lorraine Hansberry with the imagistic and
poetic work of Kennedy (pp. 58–75); and Robert Scanlan's impressive
structural analysis of Kennedy's antirealistic, phantasmagoric, and sur-

realistic *Funnyhouse of a Negro* (pp. 93–109). Overbeck's introductory
essay on the production history of Kennedy's plays (pp. 21–41) is especially welcome since there is as yet no comprehensive stage history or
consolidated archive of Kennedy's manuscripts. Readers expecting a bit
more on *The Ohio State Murders* are cautioned that that work is too
recent for inclusion here. Other essays of interest and a nice selected
bibliography (pp. 231–35) also are included. Philip C. Kolin, who last
year did comment on *The Ohio State Murders,* this year gives us "Or-
pheus Ascending: Music, Race, and Gender in Adrienne Kennedy's *She
Talks to Beethoven*" (*AAR* 28: 293–304), which he sees marking a new
direction for the playwright in its happy conjugal closure and racial
reconciliation. Marc Robinson's "Adrienne Kennedy," pp. 115–49 in *The
Other American Drama,* comments on the relationship between Kennedy's characters and their environments and her genius at portraying
chambered emotions, which are the most difficult impulses and preoccupations to explain in public language. Kennedy's biography is detailed
as a key to the difficulty and frequent inaccessibility of some of her art,
yet Robinson is especially good on the dramatic focus in *The Ohio State
Murders,* Kennedy's variation on the mystery story. Robinson devotes his
penultimate chapter to "Richard Foreman" (pp. 150–77). Foreman creates "pieces" and "works" that have "wound up in the theatre almost by
accident." Robinson suggests why the parts of Foreman's text, intelligible
as they are, refuse to add up to accepted ideas of a completed work. If the
arrangements of narrative elements seem too random, Robinson points
to the pleasures of encounters with the text. Robinson, who teaches at
the Yale School of Drama, argues that Foreman (who attended Yale in
the late 1950s, where, under the guidance of John Gassner, he learned to
turn out mostly unproduced plays) was left "with little choice but to
make a theater of his own."

Robinson's chapter "Maria Irene Fornes" (pp. 89–114) explores the
deep seriousness in even Fornes's most lighthearted plays, which he
examines from *Tango Palace, Promenade,* and *The Danube* to *Abingdon
Square,* with special attention to *Fefu and Her Friends,* her 1977 master-
piece. There is perhaps a fashion to critics' approbation. The cycle of
attention devoted a year ago to Anna Deavere Smith seems this year to be
shared by Smith, Suzan-Lori Parks, and Fornes, whose *The Danube* is
included in Wetzsteon's *The Best of Off-Broadway* (see above). Scarcely
new to New York theater, Fornes, playwright, director, translator, and
teacher for three decades, has won Obies and is well-known Off-

Broadway. What is new is the attention her dramaturgy has begun to draw beyond Manhattan, although feminist scholarship has been tracking her work since the 1980s. Robinson is not alone. For example, William E. Gruber's *Missing Persons: Character and Characterization in Modern Drama* (Georgia) devotes a chapter to "The Characters of Maria Irene Fornes: Public and Private Identities" (pp. 155–81), placing her in the company of Brecht and Beckett. Gruber's question is why Fornes has a profound fascination with the mechanics of theatrical representation—quoting, reciting, reproducing, or impersonating an absent text—and he reiterates that Fornes, like other contemporary women dramatists, collapses distinctions between public and private notions of identity. Gruber is intelligent on the avant-garde *A Vietnamese Wedding* and its use of the four female "presenters" rather than actors who are in character as in conventional—and "masculine"—theater. He is cursory on her best-known work *Fefu and Her Friends,* which portrays the disastrous consequences of men (who never appear onstage) "inscribing their own agenda on women." And he centers his discussion of *Mud* not on matters of form and character but on language, as he does with the use of repetition—the tripled speech—in *The Danube,* to which he devotes the bulk of his essay. Essentially on the same tack as Robinson, Gruber sees Fornes's commedia as "darkened permanently by her sense of ethical crisis."

David Henry Hwang inspired a quartet of articles. As the title indicates, Karen Shimakawa's " 'Who's to Say?' Or, Making Space for Gender and Ethnicity in *M. Butterfly*" (*TJ* 45, iii: 349–61) deals with matters of gender and ethnic identity. Kathryn Remen's "The Theatre of Punishment: David Henry Hwang's *M. Butterfly* and Michel Foucault's *Discipline and Punish*" (*MD* 37: 391–400) applies Foucault's analysis of the prison system, suggesting that observational theater and prison operate in similar fashions, relying on a psychoanalytic privileging of knowledge. In "Engendering the Imperial Subject: The (De)Construction of (Western) Masculinity in David Henry Hwang's *M. Butterfly* and Graham Greene's *The Quiet American*" (this year's nominee for most tortured title), pp. 241–54 in *Fictions of Masculinity,* Suzanne Kehde emphasizes the political implication of gender construction, reminding us that Hwang's play debunks traditional Western ideas of masculinity and femininity. William H. Sun and Faye C. Fei's "Masks or Faces Re-visited: A Study of Four Theatrical Works Concerning Cultural Identity" (*TDR* 38, iv: 120–32) considers cultural misunderstanding in the works of

Hwang, Chinese-born Sherwood Xuehua Hu, Asian American author
Han Ong, and Anna Deavere Smith's one-person documentary perfor-
mances in *Fires in the Mirror,* which has been published by Anchor
Books (1993). I should add that New York critics were abundant in their
celebration of Smith when her extraordinary one-person drama *Twilight:
Los Angeles, 1992* opened at the Public Theater early in 1994.

A play panned by New York critics is the subject of Mary Ellen
Jordan's "Lyle Kessler's *Orphans* and 'The Father's Breasts'" (*AmDram* 3,
ii: 71–88), which Jordan sees precipitating a cultural shift in gender
relations. The same journal prints Daniel Kiefer's "*Angels in America* and
the Failure of Revelation" (*AmDram* 4, i: 21–38), a still early scholarly
estimation of Tony Kushner's seven-hour extravaganza. As yet, only
Richard Hornby's "New Plays in Louisville" (*HudR* 47: 277–83) and two
New York Times pieces, William Harris's "In 'Slavs!' Are the Echoes of
'Angels'" (4 Dec., sec. 2, pp. 5, 36) and Vincent Canby's "In 'Slavs!'
Kushner Creates Tragic Burlesque" (18 Dec., sec. 2, pp. 5, 24), have made
passes worthy of note at Kushner's latest play. Iris Smith's "'Who Speaks
and Who Is Spoken For?': Playwright, Director, and Producer Joan
Lipkin" (*TDR* 38, iii: 96–127) is a lengthy interview with the creator of
politically and socially engaged activist theater. Terrance McNally's *Love!
Valour! Compassion!* is the subject of Vincent Canby's "McNally, True,
but Vaguely Neo-Chekhovian" (*New York Times,* 6 Nov., sec. 2, pp. 5,
32), and Canby has taken singular notice of the new *The American Play*
by Suzan-Lori Parks, who is the subject of Alice Rayner and Harry J.
Elam, Jr.'s "Unfinished Business: Reconfiguring History in Suzan-Lori
Parks's *The Death of the Last Black Man in the Whole Entire World*" (*TJ*
46, iv: 447–61), the play with which Parks burst onto the American stage
in 1990. An American playwright whose work has been staged across the
world but not performed professionally in his own country since 1975 is
the subject of two items by Daniel Larner, "Anywhere But Home: The
Life and Work of Barrie Stavis" (*AmDram* 4, i: 39–61) and "An Interview
with Barrie Stavis" (*AmDram* 4, i: 62–91). Paul C. Castagno in "Varieties
of Monologic Strategy: the Dramaturgy of Len Jenkin and Mac Well-
man" (*NTQ* 9: 134–46) presents an analysis of the present expanded
function of contemporary dramatic monologue with reference to the
works of these two Americans.

St. Bonaventure University

20 Themes, Topics, Criticism

Gary Lee Stonum

This chapter has always been devoted to covering scholarship that straddles the boundaries set for the volume's other chapters, especially if it has broad implications for American literary culture. Once upon a time such work would have stressed themes and topics, as the chapter title still promises. Themes and topics were once prime alternatives to author-centered scholarship, our hardiest critical category, and they opened a door for the contextual and the extrinsic, thereby somewhat countering the textualist biases of the New Criticism. More recently, the third term in the title has assumed greater prominence, first as a result of the theory boom and now in the 1990s out of increasing attention to the role criticism plays in constituting a nation's literary culture. The history of American literary studies is thus now regularly seen as an aspect of the history that it studies.

This inclusion of the discipline within the material it studies is particularly evident in David Shumway's timely *Creating American Civilization: A Genealogy of American Literature as an Academic Discipline* (Minnesota). Shumway stresses a genealogical, that is to say, Foucauldian, perspective on the inclusion, arguing that we need first and foremost to examine how the "disciplinary object" called American civilization gets constructed. The argument is meant to open some distance between Shumway's project and concerns of a standard history of ideas or history of criticism; it is also meant to distinguish his book from what he regards as the established but "internal" history provided by Kermit Vanderbilt's *American Literature and the Academy* (1986).

Shumway does intermittently foreground questions of professionalization and of the disciplinary assumptions behind various material

Thanks to David Rutledge for help with the research on this chapter.

practices. For example, he links the emergence of a new scholarly genre, the anthology of critical essays exemplified by Norton Critical Editions and Prentice Hall's Twentieth-Century Interpretations series, to an understanding of the discipline's work in which debating meaning has replaced the task of establishing facts. Whereas positivist historiography triumphs in the lone scholar's definitive essay or monograph, interpretation flourishes in the give-and-take of divergent readings, the production of which is more or less expected to continue indefinitely. On the other hand, Shumway's focus on disciplinarity supplements rather than displaces familiar historical methods, and this probably is to his book's advantage. It gives *Creating American Civilization* a comprehensiveness that might not have been possible if it had been methodologically fiercer.

Shumway's primary thesis is that in the years around World War II, American literary study went through a fundamental change: redefining its task as criticism rather than history and thereby transforming itself from a positivist to a hermeneutical discipline. By comparison, the heated and highly visible disputes between New Critics and New York Intellectuals that followed this shift were inconsequential squabbles within a single disciplinary paradigm. Both groups inadvertently made common and successful cause against their predecessors in the university, the literary historians who had founded the American Literature Group of the Modern Language Association and had until then dominated institutionalized study of American literature.

This is not quite news. Not only American literature studies but most literary scholarship in the United States has for some time been accustomed to understanding itself as having come to intellectual maturity by driving out the Old History. Except in avoiding triumphalism, Shumway's story does not then differ notably from the Whiggish history that New Critics and their allies in English departments have regularly told about vanquishing Professor Dryasdust. Shumway adds a shrewd twist to the familiar story, however, one which at once helps account for the fact of the victory, usefully highlights the common ground over which the battle raged, and defines the leading role played by American literature. Hermeneutics provided Americanists a way of handling an issue the historians had explicitly regarded as central but were methodologically ill-equipped to address, namely, the distinctiveness of American civilization as an object of study. Americanness appears not in factual circumstances but in the persistent meanings of American texts—themes and topics, in other words—and then also and as a somewhat later consequence in the activity of construing meaning, that is to say, in the territory that literature and literary study are understood to share.

Shumway sees the hermeneutic paradigm as continuing to dominate the field so thoroughly as to cast doubt on the efficacy or importance of subsequent reforms. Indeed, except for an afterword that fixes a surprisingly cold eye on the significance of both transformations in the canon and New Americanist scholarship, Shumway ends his account with the publication in 1964 of Leo Marx's *Machine in the Garden*. Nothing has happened since to dislodge the hermeneutic paradigm, he suggests. Moreover, earlier campaigns to reform or transform it have only contributed to the paradigm's power. For example, against the claims of Gene Wise and other advocates of American Studies, Shumway insists that most work in that putatively interdisciplinary field has been dominated by hermeneutics and thus belongs far more to literary study than to intellectual or social history.

Shumway seems to regard the hermeneutic paradigm as inherently antiprogressive and even as playing out what he regards as a conservative political program built into its origins. In contrast to the tendency of many historians of American criticism to dismiss the influence of the New Humanists, Shumway argues that Norman Foerster was the single figure most responsible for the theoretical and disciplinary underpinnings of American literature studies. One consequence of Foerster's success, he hints darkly, is that even the politically radical critics associated with *Partisan Review* in the 1930's and 1940's have contributed to a fundamentally conservative cause, the celebratory interpretation of American civilization understood as a single, distinctive, and predominantly literary achievement. So also, he implies, have more recent radicals.

i Identities and Genres

Contra Shumway, the antiuniversalist or multiculturalist assumptions of much contemporary scholarship on American literature may define an important difference from earlier pursuits of a singular national identity. However, in spite of much work on this or that matter of local identity and in spite of the continued bandying of slogans from the culture wars, we still have relatively little scholarship that broadly takes account of new perspectives or addresses the implications and consequences of displacing the old myths. The task is a daunting one, and perhaps as a way of circumventing the difficulty much of the scholarship emphasizing cultural diversity this year foregrounds questions of genre and literary type. It thus belongs to a species of criticism that has often happily stressed multiplicity and divergence.

In "Commentary: Nineteenth-Century American Women Writers and the Politics of Recovery" (*AmLH* 6: 600–611) Judith Fetterly worries that critical analysis of rediscovered women writers, particularly novelists, has lagged far behind republication of their writings. No new synthesis has yet emerged from this work of recovery, she further laments, so established, patriarchal versions of literary history remain in place if no longer in the place of honor. Moreover, even such initial attempts at an overview as Richard Brodhead's *Cultures of Letters* (1993) display insufficient enthusiasm for the rediscovered writers. One major obstacle is deciding the artistic and social value of sentimentality, Fetterly rightly notes. She may also make her own position an example of this obstacle in explicitly demanding that the needed scholarship celebrate women's fiction both aesthetically and politically.

In *Engendering Romance* Emily Miller Budick perhaps answers Fetterly's call for a new or in this case renewed synthesis, but the one she offers is probably not what Fetterly has in mind. Indeed, Budick almost explicitly disavows as insufficiently skeptical the moral righteousness that Fetterly regards as essential. Budick proposes an extensive rethinking of the American romance tradition, which she values as a prime narrative instrument of skepticism (in Stanley Cavell's sense) and which she accordingly seeks to reclaim for modern women writers. Budick sees Carson McCullers, Toni Morrison, and Grace Paley as inheriting from the largely male line of 19th-century romancers an admirably distanced but responsive and responsible attitude toward social formations, one which they would not so easily have been able to derive from the women writers of the period.

Budick's concerns resemble Sacvan Bercovitch's attention to the rhetoric of consent, but she gives such concerns a more domestic and epistemological coloring than a political one. Like Cavell in his work on film comedies of remarriage, she sees philosophical skepticism as a family matter, in her case one that centers on knowing who one's kinfolk are and accepting responsibility for them even when one cannot know their identity with absolute certainty. The claiming of doubtful kin exemplifies a more general situation of "aversion," a term that Cavell singles out to describe the Emersonian self's properly cautious but binding acknowledgment of society's claims.

For Budick, the cardinal instances of such aversion in American fiction include Hester Prynne's return to Boston, Isabel Archer's to Osmond, and Sethe's daughter Denver to a life outside 124 Bluestone Road in Toni Morrison's *Beloved.* Each of these events exemplifies compromise and hence leaves room for doubt about the rightness of one's actions and views. Budick links such doubt to what she sees as the inevitable uncertainties that family members (particularly fathers and children) have about their true relations to one another. In American fiction, she argues, such uncertainty has been the special province of the romance, even in the seemingly domesticity-free spaces imagined by Poe and Melville.

Realism, by contrast, and apparently also sentimental fiction, both establish a subversive relation to society, one which Budick understands as demanding epistemological and ideological certainty about the measure to be applied. This may also be what Fetterly demands, but as an exemplary warning of its consequences, Budick cites the suicides of Wharton's and Chopin's key heroines.

Across a broad spectrum of opinion, women's fiction has for some time persistently been seen as arrayed against the melodramas of beset manhood. Budick by contrast understands such melodrama as offering resources for a woman-centered fiction. She likewise goes against the grain of other recent scholarship in celebrating an updated form of liberal humanism, largely the one that underpins Richard Chase's idea of American romance. Budick's speculations about genre and history are often deeper and more persuasive, however, than many of the detailed readings with which she seeks to demonstrate the broad scheme. For example, she asks at one point whether Pearl is not the most "human" character in *The Scarlet Letter,* a rhetorical question that both begs important issues and blithely disregards even the narrator's express doubts.

No other single work this year is so far-reaching as the books by Shumway and Budick. Two essays from the interdisciplinary *Regionalism Reconsidered* seek to redefine American literary regionalism. In "Bioregional Perspectives in American Literature" (pp. 29–46) Michael Kowalewski renames the genre of nature writing as bioregional literature. In "Reading Regionalism: The 'Difference' It Makes" (pp. 47–63) Marjorie Pryse revisits a polemical distinction between local-color writers who

depict a region as an object for others to view and regionalists who write
from the disempowered perspective of its denizens; Pryse argues that the
regionalists embody an admirably progressive "pedagogy." Her claim is
striking for its unblinking assumption that fiction exists to be taught, or
at least to teach, its readers.

Richard Brodhead takes up regionalism more trenchantly in "Regionalism and the Upper Class," pp. 150–74 in *Rethinking Class: Literary
Studies and Social Formations* ed. Wai Chee Dimock and Michael T.
Gilmore (Columbia), emphasizing that the market for such fiction in the
late 19th century was so great that "virtually anyone who could supply
this commodity could get his or her work into print." Careers were thus
open to a larger number of authors from across social classes, but such
writers at the same time were conscripted into writing about local
experience for metropolitan consumption. Moreover, Brodhead argues,
this process also helped bring into place the new elite hungering to read
about such matters. Noting that the same magazines published regional
fiction and new forms of travel writing side by side and that both genres
depicted locale and quaintness as items to be sampled by the cultivated
tourist, Brodhead also proposes that these two seemingly independent
genres functioned as part of a single textual program.

In "Palimpsest of Desire: The Re-Emergence of the American Captivity Narrative as Pulp Romance" (*JPC* 27: 43–56) Kate McCafferty
studies how recent Zebra Books productions shuffle the motifs of an
otherwise moribund genre. Whereas captivity narratives celebrate a
white woman's rescue from captivity and restoration to civilization, the
new pulps represent her as escaping from patriarchy into an idealized
Indian community. McCafferty analyzes such ideological shifts in terms
of Raymond Williams's ideas about emergence.

I confess to being puzzled by Douglas Tallack's *The Nineteenth-
Century American Short Story: Language, Form, and Ideology* (Routledge).
Ostensibly a reconsideration of the genre by means of deconstruction,
the book offers along the way a number of interesting local exegeses but
does so according to a plan I am unable to fathom. Apparently Tallack
wants to challenge Frank O'Connor's influential stress on alienation and
epiphany as the hallmarks of the short story, but his attempts to complicate or contest that view seem as often to wind up reinforcing it.

F. Brett Cox's " 'What Need, Then, for Poetry?': The Genteel Tradition and the Continuity of American Literature" (*NEQ* 67: 212–33)
reconsiders a common understanding: that New Criticism reinforced

the modernist disdain for genteel poetry and genteel poetic values. He notes that Brooks and Warren continued to advocate a version of gentility's central claim: that poetry expresses a different, higher truth than what everyday life makes available. Admittedly sweeping aside nuance and context in making the comparison, Cox concludes that New Criticism owes something of its success and influence to perpetuating such an idealizing and idealistic view.

ii Literary History

With a few notable exceptions, American literary history has been slow to benefit from interest in the history of the book, but this may change now that Ronald J. Zboray's *A Fictive People: Antebellum Economic Development and the American Reading Public* (Oxford) conveniently collects his scattered essays on the material history of American literature. Zboray splendidly demonstrates how much can be gleaned from the archives of early printers, booksellers, and libraries. His primary argument is that the formation of anything like a single and national reading public lingered well behind the economic and technical changes that made it possible: the consolidation of the publishing industry in Boston, New York, and Philadelphia, the growth of railroads as a distribution system for printed matter and for booksellers' correspondence, and the appearance of national advertising and marketing mechanisms. His claim is based in part on studies of publishing industry records which he has gathered and updated, and it is augmented by new studies that focus more directly on readers, including an analysis of the New York Society library's lending records and a detailed examination of one bookstore's merchandise, layout, and sales.

In addition to the empirical findings at the core of his work, Zboray offers a broader, more speculative framework for the changing fate of reading in the republic, suggesting, for example, that by the 1840s fiction played an increasingly important role in constructing a sense of community. The view thus corroborates from the side of readers and of the publishing industry a claim regularly made with respect to the aims and achievements of authors.

David Minter's *A Cultural History of the American Novel* bids fair to become the standard history of prose and its tributaries from 1880 to 1940. Originating as a contribution to the multivolume history in progress from Cambridge University Press, Minter's book resembles its parent in needing to address both specialists and an audience requiring plot summaries and reminders about key cultural and historical events of the time. No new interpretation of the age gets proposed, nor does Minter challenge a long-established periodization. On the other hand, Minter does assemble and integrate much recent work on the era's specific moments, and he does winningly advocate a now widespread understanding that, rather than escaping, transcending, or standing apart from the conditions of American society, the major novelists of the time did important cultural work in their fiction.

Minter's basic itinerary is the familiar story of the American novel as the genre modernizes and as it deals with cultural tensions that scholars have long regarded as formative: individuality versus community, agrarian versus urban, and so on. Several of his side trips are equally familiar: the Jazz Age, the radical '30s, the Southern renaissance. Into this specifically literary history Minter blends many of the concerns of contemporary cultural studies: the importance of popular and nonliterary cultural representations (the Chicago World's Fair, advertising and mass-circulation magazines, documentary photography, the Armory Show and its aftermath), gender issues as they are represented or evaded by both men and women, and tensions between a white hegemony that often gets tacitly assumed and the concerns of American Indians, blacks, and the new immigrants. As might be expected, women writers—especially Cather, Wharton, and Stein—get as much attention as James, Henry Adams, Dreiser, Fitzgerald, Hemingway, and Faulkner continue to do, but Minter pays surprisingly little attention to African American writing.

Minter's more pointed arguments include a claim that Progressive writers and intellectuals from what he calls the "lyric years," 1900–1916, anticipate and shape the '20s and '30s far more than they are given credit for, especially by the writers who owe the most to them. He also revives and bolsters Sartre's case for regarding Dos Passos as one of the major modernists, doing so at the same time that he portrays the left-wing radicalism of the '30s as thinner and shallower than its adherents at the time would have thought or that its current champions would like to believe.

After a brief decline of interest in conceptualizing modernism, postmodernism, and the distinctions between them, the topic has returned to the fore. Whereas Minter largely avoids theorizing about modernism or its origins, Michael North in *The Dialect of Modernism: Race, Lan-*

guage, and Twentieth-Century Literature (Oxford) offers a most original and striking thesis. He sees the whole of Anglo-American modernism as linked to and largely reacting against late Victorian anxieties about the English language's decline. In other words, modernism partly defines itself against upholders of language standards, standards that in many cases have been newly invented for the express purpose of maintaining the privileges of English gentlemen. The politics of this strategy contain some surprises. North argues that modernist writers, even those on the right such as Pound and Eliot, become modern by mimicking dialect, especially the blackface speech of the minstrel shows. As a consequence (and in contrast to such views as Houston Baker's), international modernism is closely linked to the contemporaneous Harlem Renaissance.

North's book belongs with other recent scholarship that has emphasized the interdependence of black and white culture, especially the degree to which the dominant tradition has covertly depended on African American sources. By contrast to its predecessors, however, *The Dialect of Modernism* is thin or even wishful in historical demonstration. On the one hand, North offers an extensive and fascinating portrait of the politics of dialect and of standard English in the years up to World War I, but on the other he recruits Pound and Eliot as blackface modernists not on the basis of their poetry or their criticism but on the strength of the dialect they used mainly in private letters to one another. In other words, he establishes a climate of concern with linguistic propriety more convincingly than he shows white writers significantly using black dialect to flout it.

While downplaying the importance of direct interaction between dominant and minority cultures, including African American writing, in *Framing the Margins: The Social Logic of Postmodern Culture* (Oxford) Philip Brian Harper also sees them as closely linked. He begins with the attractive and important thesis that postmodernism, defined mainly as fragmentation of the self and literarily most visible in American metafiction in the '60s and '70s, is anticipated by much of the otherwise modernist literature produced between the '30s and the '50s by writers from marginalized groups. This earlier fragmentation of the self has more obvious social and historical causes, ones that Harper implies are occulted or ignored by a later generation. At best, the fragmentation earlier writers portray gets confused with modernist alienation, which Harper regards as a distinct phenomenon. Unfortunately, most of Harper's book does little to demonstrate and extend this argument,

402 Themes, Topics, Criticism

either with reference to cultural theory or to the many, aptly chosen novelists and poets he considers. Instead, we get a series of miniessays and exegeses that vary widely in scope, depth, and clarity. Knowing nothing of the specific circumstances, I wonder if Harper's is another promising and even potentially brilliant study that has been rushed prematurely into print.

In *The Trouble with Genius* Bob Perelman asks us to take seriously the characteristically extraordinary claims that some modernists made for themselves and the typically meager success they enjoyed with any public larger than a coterie. "Genius," he notes wryly, is their self-proclaimed job description, and he argues that it departs both from earlier meanings of the term and from a simple allegiance to the avant-garde. Geniuses write masterpieces that fuse social and literary value—indeed, abolish the distinction between them. In seeming contradiction to this achievement, however, they also expect and through the textual obscurity of their work easily secure a position in which they have almost no readers and no influence on society. Perelman establishes no general vantage on the questions he raises about the relation between the artist and society, but his study does perform the important and refreshing work of seeing authorial ambition as an issue requiring both rhetorical and historical analysis. More often we hear either from the disciple who inadvertently begs key questions—why read Zukofsky?—in seeking to answer them through better understanding of the genius's texts or from the theorist who peremptorily folds such issues into the larger operations of history, language, or some other equally large and impersonal agent.

A more familiar ground for discussing modernist and postmodernist writing can be found in the formalist attention to metafiction, which often stresses similarities between 20th-century experimental novels and the novelistic or proto-novelistic texts of the 17th and 18th centuries. In *Textual Bodies: Modernism, Postmodernism, and Print* (Bucknell) Michael Kaufmann slightly extends this claim in noting how several such texts also call attention to themselves as printed artifacts.

By contrast to other studies published this year, all of which largely derive their notions of modernism or postmodernism from literary phenomena, Art Berman's magisterial *Preface to Modernism* (Illinois) takes philosophy as the engine of artistic and cultural change. This is an unusually learned book and also an unusually old-fashioned one, which ranges across all of the arts and sciences and a fair bit of the political history of the modern West. Berman sees all such phenomena as a part of a procession of isms that devolve from Locke's and Hobbes's empiricism, the defining philosophical condition of modernity. Modernism is merely one aesthetic response to this condition, and it is distinguished in careful if relentlessly airy terms from such other responses as romanticism.

Berman intends *Preface to Modernism* to offer not a narrative history of the consequences of empiricism but "a way of thinking about that history," and in one respect, like Hegel lecturing on the philosophy of history, he does just that. Moreover, the book can be recommended as an intensively panoptical synthesis of the sort we have not seen for many years. On the other hand, it is likely to annoy those who doubt its central, unargued thesis about the primacy of philosophical concepts or who expect some explanation of how the ideas of the philosophers have effected the vast influence claimed for them.

iii Critics and Methods

Paul Giles's "Reconstructing American Studies: Transnational Paradoxes, Comparative Perspectives' (*JAmS* 28: 335–58) offers Gene Wise-like reflections on the underpinnings of American Studies in the '90s, refreshingly emphasizing British motives and methods for studying the United States. (Until the Beatles helped redeem the long postwar drabness, for example, America appeared to its British students as wonderfully colorful and alluring, and so British Americanists were happy to join in the celebratory essentialism of the cold war period.) However, beyond a somewhat vague comparativism and a deference to continental theory, it is unclear what Giles advocates or what opportunities he sees for Americans from contemporary British culture.

In *V. L. Parrington: Through the Avenue of Art* (Kent State) H. Lark Hall offers a timely and thorough biography of one of the founders of American Studies. Although she paints an engaging picture of the man, she has more trouble defending *Main Currents in American Thought* against the still influential dismissals by Lionel Trilling and Richard Hofstadter. Against the charge of populist philistinism, she does show that his true Penelope was William Morris, but her account does not dispel the more damning suspicion that his thought lacked real originality or power. Likewise, his early but less than pioneering role in establishing American literature in the academy confirms more than refutes his reputation as a supporting actor rather than a principal.

Two essays consider Trilling's legacy. Before getting weirdly sidetracked by debating the murderousness of Stalin's regime, Russell J. Reising's "Lionel Trilling, *The Liberal Imagination*, and the Emergence of the Cultural Discourse of Anti-Stalinism" (*Boundary II* 20: 94–124) asks if Trilling does not victimize certain opponents—Parrington, Dreiser, and Stalin himself—by means of the same brutal indifference to complexity that he derides as the essence of Stalinism. Emily Miller Budick offers a more positive but also a more elusive view in "Lionel Trilling and the 'Being' of Culture" (*MR* 35: 63–82). She finds in some of Trilling's key essays a subtle dependence on rabbinic Judaism and a tacit acknowledgment of the centrality of the Holocaust to the modern situation, factors she proposes are crucial to a respect for the other's individuality and hence the basis of Trilling's sense of the dialectical relation of self and community. In other words, she depicts a Trilling who advocates the same aversion to society she sees in Cavell's Emerson and the American romance tradition.

Two very different accounts of New Criticism are offered by Murray Krieger's *The Institution of Theory* (Hopkins) and Mark Jancovich's *The Cultural Politics of the New Criticism* (Cambridge). Writing as an avuncular insider and as someone who is simplifying drastically for an originally Taiwanese lecture audience, Krieger once more links the battle between New Criticism and old historicism to the dispute between deconstruction and post-Foucauldian historicisms. He characterizes both as skirmishes in a perennial war over the degree to which concepts, ideologies, social formations, or anything else can prescribe the limits of art. Himself an unreconstructed Coleridgean who obviously still feels blindsided by deconstruction, Krieger rehearses a largely orthodox history, particularly in emphasizing New Criticism's disinterested defense of poetry and the democratizing role it played in postwar American colleges.

Jancovitch, however, stresses how interested Ransom, Tate, and Warren continued to be in politics, even after turning in the '30s from Agrarian social criticism to literary criticism. He accordingly claims that they saw poetry less as an autonomous realm than one to be prized because it was comparatively free from the hated ills of modern industrial capitalism and thus offered a weapon against them. Whereas Krieger writes as a participant, eager on occasion to gossip about his own role in the history of American criticism, Jancovitch knows the material only as a series of texts. This gives a certain freshness to his ideas (Tate as a precursor of Derrida; Brooks, Warren, and Ransom as all anticipating de Man), but the originality usually comes at the expense of contextual savvy. In *Encounters with Kenneth Burke* (Illinois) William H. Rueckert collects two decades' worth of writings on Burke. Often garrulous in the manner of the master, the essays and talks emphasize three things: Burke's kinship with Emerson, Whitman, and William Carlos Williams; the comic ground of all of his work; and the critique of technology that Burke offers in his late, still uncollected writings.

Sandra Adell's somewhat diffuse *Double-Consciousness/Double Bind: Theoretical Issues in Twentieth-Century Black Literature* (Illinois) contains in addition to more narrowly focused essays one argument of major importance to current controversies about the relative importance of European and African perspectives on black literature. She claims that W. E. B. Du Bois's famous notion about the American Negro's double-consciousness derives from his reading of Hegel and that it deliberately recontextualizes Hegel's depiction of the Unhappy Consciousness.

Joseph Alkana's preface to *Cohesion and Dissent in America* (SUNY) offers a helpful summary of Sacvan Bercovitch's ideas in the process of introducing a number of previously published essays by Bercovitch's followers and admirers. Bercovitch's own contribution, "Cohesion, Dissent, and the Aims of Criticism" (pp. 3–30), a reprint of the first chapter of *The Rites of Assent* (1993), narrates the development of his work as the study of ideological mimesis. "Ideology" is defined by Bercovitch as the symbolic practices by which a society characterizes and perpetuates itself; rival versions of that definition seem to deny that ideology can ever be true, that is, adequate to its cultural task.

Heated as the culture wars have been in popular media, it is surprising that no full-scale defense of the old orthodoxies about American writing has come from the right. Peter Shaw's *Recovering American Literature* seems meant to fill that gap, and Shaw predictably has many harsh things to say about how classic American fiction has been interpreted over the last quarter century. (He is also the only critic I have encountered who regularly cites *American Literary Scholarship* for evidence about current opinion!) However, his argument is surprisingly diffuse, for he has considerable difficulty identifying and characterizing the ideologically wrongheaded readings he would have us deplore. By contrast, he is a fine reporter of the older opinions he cherishes, most of them coming not from conservatives or apolitical commentators but from such cold war liberals as Matthiessen, Chase, and Trilling. One is left wondering if his dismay at contemporary criticism does not owe more to generational piety than ideological fervor. Shaw seems mainly concerned with defending any and all of the received truths from his own handsome education, whatever the ideological coloring or even the internal consistency of those truths.

Case Western Reserve University

21 Foreign Scholarship

i French Contributions: Daniel Royot

a. General The long-awaited *Dictionnaire universel des littératures* (PUF, 3 vols.) was a welcome overture early this year, with contributions on individual authors and major themes, covering the spectrum of the United States within the all-inclusive panorama of world literature. Scores of French Americanists wrote entries on subjects ranging from colonial pamphleteers to West Coast writers and postmodern production, under the supervision of Jacqueline Ollier. The second edition of the *Anthologie de la littérature américaine* (PUF) by Daniel Royot, Jean Béranger, Yves Carlet, and Kermit Vanderbilt gives additional space to 20th-century drama and contains an extract from Toni Morrison's *Jazz* in a new chapter entitled "Race, Class, and Gender." Following the 1993 conference of the Société des anglicistes de l'enseignement supérieur (SAES), a volume of abstracts, ed. Paul Carmignani, was published by the Presses universitaires de Perpignan under the title *SAES XXXIIIe Congrès, Monde méditerranéen et culture anglo-saxonne.* Three workshops deserve special mention: "Lectures critiques" chaired by Jean-Jacques Lecercle and André Topia, "Nouvelles" by Claude Maisonnat, and "Etudes américaines" by Patrick Badonnel. *Le Fleuve et ses métamorphoses,* ed. François Piquet (Didier-Erudition), is an interdisciplinary collection of articles on river culture throughout the world. Contents relevant to American literature are reported below, under several headings, except for Daniel Royot's reappraisal of writings on New England streams (pp. 507–10) and "Reading Pacific Northwest Rivers" (pp. 479–82) by Glen Love, an exhilarating presentation of the "legions of watergazers," including Herman Melville, William Stafford, and Ken Kesey. In *Méditerranée, Imaginaires de l'espace* (PUP) Paul Carmignani lays out

Mediterranean lore in American fiction, with examples from Hawthorne, James, Hemingway, Fitzgerald, and Faulkner ("Epiphanies méditerranéennes dans la littérature américaine," pp. 91–112).

As American studies centers crop up all over French academia, the newborn *Annales du monde anglophone* seems to be a promising review funded by the Université de Provence, under the general editorship of Serge Ricard. *L'esthétique de la représentation* (n.s. 19), ed. Nicole Ollier, constitutes the annual issue of the Centre de recherches sur l'Amérique anglophone (CRAA) of the Université Michel Montaigne in Bordeaux. Mostly devoted to multicultural studies, the volume includes articles on Chicano, Native American, and Italian-American literatures. At the same university, the research center in women's studies has published *Le genre et la loi*, vol. 2, ed. Elisabeth Béranger and Ginette Castro, specifically stressing feminine imagination and creativeness over the last two centuries. Also noteworthy is a scholarly venture involving a research team at the University of Valenciennes, which yielded *Le groupe et l'individu dans le monde anglophone*, ed. Bleuette Pion (*Lez* 15 [1993]) and includes several articles on American authors.

This year's volume of *Americana* (11), published by the University of Paris-Sorbonne, is subdivided into three sections (Kate Chopin, John Dos Passos, and Toni Morrison) to meet the needs of a national postgraduate program, with contributions by Roger Asselineau, Colette Gerbaud, Jean Rouberol, Jeanne-Marie Santraud, Michèle Bonnet, Peggy Castex, and Anne-Marie Paquet. Last, the proceedings of the 1993 conference in La Rochelle of the Association française d'études américaines, ed. Christine Raguet-Bouvart, were published under the title *Eclats de voix, crises en représentation dans la littérature nord-américaine* (Rumeur des Ages).

b. 19th-Century Literature With a powerful escort of pundits such as Eliade, Derrida, Todorov, and Lacan, Bernard Terramorsi engages in a provocative reevaluation of the fantastic in the short fiction of Washington Irving and William Austin. His *Le mauvais rêve américain, Les origines du fantastique et le fantastique des origines* (Paris: L'Harmattan) deconstructs the fantasies allegedly born of the American Revolution and results in an assessment of "Rip Van Winkle," "The Legend of Sleepy Hollow," and "Peter Rugg the Missing Man" as "étatsuniennes" etiological tales. The evocation of "*poros* and chaos" as nightmarish substitutes for the dominion of "supernature" is intended to explain the impulse toward "superpower" of uncontrollable, inexpressible forces at work in the American psyche. Challenging and brilliant though such arguments may be, Terramorsi's apocalyptic vision of the young nation regrettably overlooks the function of humor. In the volume of *Les Cahiers de l'Herne* devoted to Thoreau (ed. Michel Granger), a dozen articles, besides translations of significant texts, reflect the complexities of the Walden hermit. In "Gestes spectaculaires, texte vécu" (pp. 21–31) Granger sees Thoreau's autobiographical vision as a token of authenticity, both disclosing personality and setting the boundaries of self-knowledge through demonstrative attitudes. Maurice Gonnaud contrasts Emerson's distance from the substance of language with Thoreau's "linguistic consciousness" and alertness to the constructive power of speech ("Emerson and Thoreau: Où est le maître? Où est le disciple?" pp. 129–36). Revisiting Kant, Daniel Charles is attentive to Thoreau's sense of "natural music" ("De Thoreau à Charles Ives: Musique et transcendantalisme," pp. 137–45). For Sandra Laugier, a continuum exists between the author of *Walden* and Wittgenstein in the use of plain language and the value ascribed to silence ("Du silence à la langue paternelle: Thoreau et la philosophie du langage," pp. 153–64). According to Bertrand Rougé, the writing of *Walden* is comparable to filling the gaps of memory to build a new abode for the sense of being (pp. 165–72). Christian Susini, Pierre Hadot, and Maurice Gonnaud further explore the philosophical implications of Thoreau's discourse. It is then the process of purification and rebirth at Walden Pond that Yves Carlet describes in his analysis of the "dialectics of the margin, the fence and the circle" ("La marge, la clôture et le cercle," pp. 207–19). For Roland Tissot inmost urges are mediated by animal imagery through hyperbolic thrusts which paradoxically pave the way to truth (pp. 223–31). Thoreau's poetry is covered by several articles. Alain Suberchicot sees in the *Collected Poems* a shift to aesthetic preoccupations through utter withdrawal in an age of moralism ("Thoreau Poète," pp. 260–73). Kenneth White inscribes Thoreau's *Journal* in a broader vision which he calls "geopoetic" (pp. 274–80). For Maurice Couturier, the didactic intent subsides into poetic utterances, which no longer fit into any narrative convention, though sometimes close to the *kunstlerroman*, as the echo of the author's voice reaches the reader ("L'encoche et l'écho dans *Walden*," pp. 290–99).

Femmes de conscience, ed. Susan Goodman and Daniel Royot (Presses de la Sorbonne Nouvelle), a book-length study of the women's rights movement in the mid-19th century, allows space for literary studies, with guest contributors such as Cameron Nickels and Timothy H. Scherman, "Elizabeth Oakes Smith: The Puritan as Feminist," pp. 109–26; Mary Suzanne Schriber, "Assuming a Public Voice: The Travel Writing of Margaret Fuller and Harriet Beecher Stowe," pp. 127–48; Deborah Garfield, "Melodrama's Breakdowns: Generic Subversion and Harriet Jacobs," pp. 149–68; Alfred Bendixen, "The Emergence of Realism in Fiction by Women," pp. 189–200; Susan Goodman, "Elizabeth Stuart Phelps and the American Literary Renaissance," pp. 201–16; Katherine Joslin, "Literary Cross-Dressing: Jane Addams Finds Her Voice in Democracy and Social Ethics," pp. 217–36; and Charles Simic, "Chinese Boxes and Puppet Theatres," pp. 239–42.

Late-century realism and naturalism are allotted equal attention. In "Henry James: l'écriture du retournement" (*SAES*: 42) Evelyne Labbé investigates the "technique of reversal," as exemplified by "perverted conversions" and the abhorrence of a "body of difference" with reference to *The Wings of the Dove*. Jamesian intertextuality is scrutinized by Annick Duperray, especially borrowings from French culture ("Henry James et la France: une sympathie récente," *Cahiers Ivan Tourgueniev* 17–18: 153–57). Henry Adams's exotic quest in French Polynesia is the subject of Felix Atem's well-documented study in "Henry Adams, Tahiti et les mémoires d'Ariitaimai" (*Alizés-Trade Winds* 8: 91–102). It thus appears that delving into insular mythology, the so-called Puritan in paradise, was indeed inclined to liken the spirituality of a pagan queen with that of medieval noble women. *QWERTY* 4 hosts six contributions on Stephen Crane's *The Red Badge of Courage:* Paul Carmignani bridges the gap between the novel and "The Veteran" published in *The Little Regiment and Other Episodes of the American Civil War* (1896), in which Henry Fleming settles accounts with his past through self-sacrifice in old age (pp. 219–23); Christine Savinel explores the territory of myth and fable along Fleming's itinerary (" 'La grande parade bleue,' ou la vérité de la fable dans *The Red Badge of Courage,*" pp. 247–54); other contributors are Daniel Baylon ("Henry Fleming, du paraître à l'être," pp. 209–18), Bernard Cosker ("Couleur et métaphore dans *The Red Badge of Courage,*" pp. 225–36), Evelyne Labbé ("Machines of Reflection: *The Red Badge of Courage* et ses doubles," pp. 237–46); and Joseph Urbas ("The Emblematics of Invulnerability in *The Red Badge of Courage,*" pp. 255–64).

c. 20th-Century Fiction to World War II   Compared to the profuse output on postmodern works, a stasis seems to affect French scholarship

on fiction from the first decades through the Great Depression. Significant critiques, however, daringly run counter to the trend. For Peter L.
Hays, Edith Wharton targets American society through Undine Spragg
in *The Custom of the Country* (1913), considered as an onslaught on
modern commercialism ("Undine is US: Wharton's attack on American
Greed," *EA* 47: 22–31). In "Hudson River (Bracketed)" (*Le fleuve et ses
métamorphoses*, pp. 473–76) Susan Goodman contends that for Wharton
the river must bring one home again because home is memory. Ellen
Glasgow is shown by Brigitte Intissar-Zaugg to turn away from dogma
and the man-made myth of sacredness in *Barren Ground* (1925). The
Southern novelist's existential values thereby vindicate feminine resistance, emancipation, and reconstruction in an age of decadent humanism ("Théologie et idéologie sudiste: l'approche d'Ellen Glasgow," *Annales du monde anglophone* 1: 97–104). Bleuette Pion sees Willa Cather's
Southwest as a palimpsest whose pictorial quality depends on the imaginary re-creation of three cultures ("Willa Cather et 'le roman démeublé,'
étude de *La mort vient pour l'archevêque, L'effacement des genres dans les
lettres et les arts*," *Lez* 17: 231–41).

For Paule Lévy, John Dos Passos's Adamic vision in *USA* transcends
the perplexity of the intellectual "peeling the speculative onion of doubt"
in a fragmented universe; disjunctive effects substitute a new dynamic
for discursive logic throughout a magic discourse (" 'We Have Only
Words Against Power Superpower': langage et idéologies dans *The Big
Money* de John Dos Passos," *Annales du monde anglophone* 1: 83–96).
Patricia Bleu surveys Dos Passos's struggle with modernity and nostalgia
for "a lost unity," in "Chambre obscure: le 'Camera Eye' de *USA*"
(*Caliban* 31: 115–22). In "Le Mississippi de l'écriture: *The Wild Palms* de
William Faulkner" (*Le fleuve et ses métamorphoses*, pp. 501–05), Jean
Claude Pichardie sees the narrative and the river as a common medium,
the consciousness of the writer reflecting the complexity of the stream. It
is Henry Miller's indebtedness to romanticism that Charles Holdefer
acknowledges in his view of "The Tailor Shop" ("Henry Miller's 'The
Tailor Shop': The Apprentice as American Romantic," *SAES XXXIIIe
Congrès*, p. 51).

d. Contemporary Literature   Criticism on postmodern experimental
fiction is far from ebbing. Revisiting John Barth's *Tidewater Tales*, Elaine
Safer ascribes the specific vein of humor in the work to the opposition
between traditional expectations for great literary figures and the loss of

meaning for the metamorphosed characters in the "follow-up stories" (*Le Fleuve et ses métamorphoses,* pp. 485–89). Patrick Badonnel applies Lacanian concepts such as "symbolic castration" and "the name of the father" to map out the highly unpredictable and often uncharted Hawkesian territory in "*Second Skin* ou la mue de l'écriture" (*EA* 47: 436–44). In "No Clear Bounded Shape: Forme et Définition dans *Vineland* de Thomas Pynchon" (*SAES XXXIIIe Congrès,* p. 37) Bénédicte Chorier shows how Pynchon's dense networks of "coextensive meanings" erase earlier readings while blurring approved boundaries and suggesting the validity of indigenous perceptions rather than Puritan visions. Patrick Badonnel enlists Lacan to analyze lures, symptoms, and relations in "Le travail du signifiant dans *Cathedral* de Raymond Carver" (*SAES XXXIIIe Congrès,* p. 106). Jean Marie Fournier resorts to Schelling's concept of *Umheimlichkeit* to regard Carver's "Preservation" as coherently reviving repressed memories through textual disclosure (*SAES XXXIIIe Congrès,* p. 55). Claire Maniez reveals Carver's critical attitude toward Hemingway's fiction through the study of "The Aficionados," a short story included in *No Heroics, Please* (*SAES XXXIIIe Congrès,* p. 101). The symbolic values of the volcano are finely circumscribed by Patrick Badonnel in "Le monde méditerranéen dans *Set This House on Fire* de William Styron" (*SAES XXXIIIe Congrès,* pp. 104–05). For Badonnel, the intrusion of the real is indicated by the symptom bearing the stamp of time through those very words: "I realized at last that all this time his face had been a face which, in the space of a day, had aged a dozen years." A productive group of Nabokov scholars has completed new studies, including Danièle Roth-Souton's *Vladimir Nabokov, l'enchantement de l'exil* (Paris: L'Harmattan), in which history and biography are instrumental in disclosing the function of exile and strangeness. Christine Raguet-Bouvart is concerned with the representation of crisis ("Etat de création ou état de crise? Vladimir Nabokov en quête d'une voix américaine," *Eclats de voix,* pp. 49–60). Suzanne Fraysse contends that *Lolita* owes its popularity to a misinterpretation of narrative priorities, the deconstruction of realistic illusion thus prevailing over the breaking of taboos on incest and pedophilia ("Lolita à juste titre," *SAES XXXIIIe Congrès,* p. 38).

Profils américains 6, ed. Jean-Louis Brunel and Michel Gresset, is devoted to William Gaddis, with a wealth of articles, interviews, and bibliographical data exploring the maze of a metafiction given over to masquerading. Brigitte Felix sees laughter as increasingly undermined by

its own ambiguity in *Carpenter's Gothic* and *A Frolic of His Own* (pp. 19–
38). For Brunel, the city stages the aesthetics of dissolution (pp. 39–62).
After translating *The Recognitions,* Jean Lambert has emerged from the
task with the conviction that the writer's baroque style needs the reader's
never-failing connivance to yield its creative power (pp. 63–72). It is
through the same novel that Jean François Chassay follows a fictionalized
image of Hemingway in a "carnival where masks presume themselves as
reality" (pp. 73–84). Three articles deal with *JR:* John Johnston examines
its rich intertextuality, through the figure of Jack Gibbs as a theoretician
of chaos (pp. 97–112); James Massender elaborates on "fields and forces,
influence and electricity" (pp. 113–23); and alluding to Richard Wagner's
Ring tetralogy, Michel Imbert considers that the voices surfacing from
"the damped dump" bring out "a background noise that ruins calcula-
tions" (pp. 127–48). Michel Gresset lists the self-defeating modes of
communication in *Carpenter's Gothic* (mail, telephone, radio, television,
and . . . the doorway) to reveal that verbal messages are equated with
general misunderstanding "while doors are neither open nor closed"
(pp. 149–60). Three articles center on *A Frolic of His Own.* Patrick
O'Donnel analyzes the nature of Gaddis's satire of language in the era of
electronic culture (pp. 161–72). Johan Thielmans explains the function
of *Once at Antietam,* the "lost play recovered," as allowing Gaddis to
substantiate negative views of traditional culture (pp. 173–84). Gregory
Comne concludes with a look at Gaddis's suggestion that aesthetic
improvisation, as expressed in jazz, may help individuals to cope with a
"problematic universe" (pp. 185–98).

A zestful tightrope walker over the quicksands of reiterative critical
values, Marc Chénetier reinterprets Carver, Gass, Hawkes, Theroux,
Elkin, and Barth, together with Toby Olson and William S. Wilson, in
Sgraffites Encres et Sanguines (Paris: Offshore/Presses de l'école normale
supérieure). Chénetier thus responds with spirited virtuosity to the
challenges of contemporary metafiction by resorting to his own palette of
metaphors, applying his choice of red chalk, bister, and India ink to
render the scratches, scorches, and scars pervading "American graffiti,
action writing and all-over" on postmodern literary canvases. Often
thriving on dazzling formulae, Chénetier sometimes lapses into long-
winded, esoteric phraseology, which may turn his guided tour into an
ordeal for the uninitiated.

Women writers are given particular attention by scholars in various
critical modes. Stephanie Adams Genty provides an insightful treatment

of Marilyn French's *The Women's Room* by watching feminine "atavistic corporal alienation" and alternative efforts "to transgress mandatory heterosexuality" ("Marilyn French et l'au-delà du genre ou le malaise féminin: muse, méduse et mort," *Le genre et la loi* 2: 159–68). In the same volume Ginette Castro argues that Joanna Russ deconstructs gender by satirizing the narrative norms of science fiction in *The Female Man* (pp. 205–12).

A specialist of the short story and Southern fiction, Claudine Verley is interested in the architectonics of Eudora Welty's *The Golden Apples,* especially the chiasma which, "setting new boundaries, perturbs a stable pattern." Such effective "decentering," Verley contends, "would seem to be at the core of the characters' fate" ("Décentrement et excentricité: *The Golden Apples* de Eudora Welti," *EA* 47: 32–42). Geneviève Cohen-Cheminet's "Silences et exil de la parole dans *The Cannibal Galaxy* de Cynthia Ozick" approaches Ozick's metaphor of the crack in *The Cannibal Galaxy* and further points to narrative discontinuities, suggesting how the author denounces the illusion of a discursive community of diasporic Jews, in fact lost to themselves, in an illusory American Promised Land (*EA* 47: 43–55). In *L'esthétique de la représentation* Françoise Brousse examines Sarah Schulman's parodic style, namely, the prose merging romantic irony with urban realism to debunk the "sanitized discourse" and protective myth surrounding "vanilla sex" ("Sarah Schulman. Vers une esthétique gaie," pp. 120–28).

RFEA 62 bears on "the return of history" in the fiction of the '80s. In this respect, John Barth's narratives capture Thomas Carmichael's attention as "they transform the imperatives of formalism in the service of contingency, history and possibility" ("Postmodernism Reconsidered: The Return of the Real in John Barth's *Sabbatical* and the *Tidewater Tales,*" pp. 329–38). Geoffrey Green evaluates shifting relationships between fiction and history in " 'I'm sick of this, I might as well just make it all': Gilbert Sorrentino's Fictive Navigations in the 1980s" (pp. 339–48). In "Le yoyo de l'histoire: *Vineland* de Pynchon" (pp. 349–59) Bénédicte Chorier elucidates the interplay between past and present, namely, the way "history is written into the original space of Vineland county," when Pynchon's unstable prose challenges time. William Gass's recent fiction is analyzed by Claire Maniez, whose major interest centers on the reader's identification with the autobiographical narrator ("Innocence and Guilt in William Gass's *The Tunnel,*" pp. 360–70). Thomas Pughe interprets Cormac McCarthy's *Blood Meridian* in the light of Georg Lukács's conception of the historical novel (pp. 371–82), while apropos *White Noise* Maurice Couturier mobilizes Paul Ricoeur's concept of "refiguration" with regard to Don DeLillo's treatment of history in the making (pp. 383–92). The new bend toward the "minorization" of literature is illustrated through Theo d'Haen's views of T. Coraghessan Boyle and Richard Russo with reference to Gilles Deleuze's and Félix Guattari's approaches to Kafka (pp. 393–403). And, to conclude, "Reconciliation dans *Moon Palace* de Paul Auster" by Chantal Coulomb-Buffa justifies the author's "questioning of the infinite power of text" and his attempts to capture "the ontological experience of things" (pp. 404–15).

e. Ethnic Literature   In *Analyses et réflexions sur Césaire* (Paris: Ellipses), a volume of essays on Caribbean writer Aimé Césaire, Anne-Marie Paquet introduces French readers to African American "négritude" in a comparative perspective. Françoise Clary, dedicated scholar in African American studies, observes in "Idéologie de l'authenticité dans l'écriture féminine noire à partir des années soixante" (*Annales du monde anglophone* 1: 105–18) that black women writers often appropriate the voice of the blues singer through sustained metaphors, sometimes ironically borrowing a male vision to disclose prevailing tensions in a patriarchal community intent on defeating woman's longing for independence. In the same vein, Clary also expresses her interest in a new generation that is "no longer enclosed in an island of marginality" or simply voicing the predicaments of "a feminine other to the male self" ("Black Writing as Other: An Island of Feminine Otherness," *Alizés-Trade Winds* 8: 35–50). The concept of the black self as creator of culture is also developed by Clary in "Décider les divergences dans le Roman afro-américain contemporain" (*Eclats de voix,* pp. 29–40). She then turns to Chester Himes's *Lonely Crusade* to define the tension between dream and reality in a context of violence ("Noir ou américain? L'individu et le groupe dans *Lonely Crusade* de Chester Himes," *Le Groupe et l'individu dans le monde anglophone* 15 [1993]: 140–49). Another contribution to this volume is Nicole Terrien's treatment of myth, utopia, and identity in Gloria Naylor's *Mama Day* ("From Staten Island to No-State Island," pp. 51–63). Toni Morrison's temporary residence in Paris may have spurred the interest of Americanists, as evidenced by several articles. For Wendy Harding, the tension between individual election and collective attachment is reconciled in accordance with the wisdom vital to black survival ("Community in Toni Morrison's fiction," *Le groupe et l'individu dans le* *monde anglophone* 15 [1993]: 151–68). Three studies are devoted to *Beloved*. Ellen Pifer brilliantly demonstrates that the current of memory travels down the Mississippi River, deposing the detritus of America's history—with all its cruelty, pain, violence and injustice—on its muddy banks ("Toni Morrison's *Beloved:* Twain's Mississippi Recollected and Rewritten," *Le Fleuve et ses métamorphoses,* pp. 510–14). Michel Bernard links the process toward madness with the motifs of the narrative ("The Mad Trio in Toni Morrison's *Beloved,*" *Alizés-Trade Winds* 7: 43–56). And in the same journal Anne-Marie Paquet clarifies the strategies of survival through the themes of love, death, and desire (pp. 33–40). Also valuable is Paquet's "Patterns of Transition: Rites of Passage in Toni Morrison's *Beloved*" (*Americana* 11: 112–19). Martine Chard-Hutchinson sees the quest for the absent mother and its consequences on character behavior in *Jazz* ("Lady Writes the Blues, *Jazz* de Toni Morrison ou le texte affranch," *Le genre et la loi* 2: 89–96). In the same volume Gayle Wurst analyzes Ann Petry's strategic irony in the evocation of the American Dream as seen by a Harlem black woman in the '40s ("La lettre de la loi et l'héroïne hors-la-loi: l'autobiography de Benjamin Franklin dans *The Street* d'Ann Petry," pp. 169–82). Suzy Durruty treats Marge Piercy's use of language and history when Piercy revisits the national scene through the eyes of a Mexican-American woman at odds with confusing landmarks set by conflicting modes of speech ("*Woman on the Edge of Time,* ou la subversion du genre," pp. 213–20). *L'esthétique de la Représentation* offers a harvest of ethnic studies. Michel Coupal contrasts the poetic nature of Big Bear's discourse with the quasi-documentary rendition of the background narrative in "Voix et construction narrative dans *The Temptations of Big Bear* de Rudy Wiebe" (pp. 25–34). The visual art of the Native American underdog is analyzed by Elyette Benjamin-Labarthe with reference to Luis Valdez's theater in "Le rasquachisme, ou la genèse d'une esthétique chicano" (pp. 51–62). Bernadette Rigal-Cellard's article focuses on the intertextual and "intermythological" themes Louis Owens uses to stage the identity quest of his protagonists in a Californian environment ("Le rouge et le noir selon Louis Owens: l'esthétique hybride d'un polar choctaw, *The Sharpest Sight,*" pp. 69–86). For Christian Lerat, Alejandro Morales strives to comprehend complex ethnic forces and transcend a sense of failure, by promoting a "voice beyond the grave," thus achieving the restoration of communication channels ('Esthétique de la 'Reconstruction' du chaos et de la nostalgie de l'ordre dans *Caras Viejas y Vino Nuevo* d'Alejandro Morales," pp. 87–

104). Marcienne Rocard's views of Sandra Cisneros's short stories point to the process of "mestizage" in the narrative form, which partakes both of the traditional telling mode of the "cuento" and of mainstream storywriting ("L'écriture délibérément métissée de Sandra Cisneros dans *Woman Hollering Creek*," pp. 139–48). It is the little world of Grace Paley that Ginette Castro considers in her essay "*Enormous Changes at the Last Minute* ou le petit monde de Grace Paley," emphasizing especially Paley's rendition of the multilingual speech of New York City neighborhoods, translated through a Jewish-American ear (pp. 127–38). The dual theme of ethnic solidarity and sacredness in Tillie Olsen's *Yonnondio* is analyzed by Suzy Durruty in terms of conflicting issues, voiced by an artist torn between aesthetic urges and proletarian concerns ("*Yonnondio: une esthétique proletarienne*," pp. 157–64). Jean Cazemajou sees Oscar Hijuelos's fiction in the light of the "polyphonic novel" described by Bakhtin. It brings together individual voices functioning dialogically within "aesthetic architectonics" in relation to the modern media ("*The Fourteen Sisters of Emilio Montez O'Brien* d'Oscar Hijuelos: une esthétique de la plénitude," pp. 181–92). Nicole Bensoussan addresses the issue of Tina DeRosa's ambiguous symbolism in *Paper Fish,* especially the creation of a universe beyond the barriers of time and space ("*Paper Fish: une esthétique du temps,*" pp. 149–56). Jean Béranger appraises the Italian touch in experimental fiction with the techniques of fragmentation revealing the protagonist's chaotic destiny in Francis Pollini's *Night* ("L'esthétique de la violence et sa résolution poétique dans *Night* de Francis Pollini," pp. 165–80). *Parcours identitaires* (Presses de la Sorbonne nouvelle), ed. Geneviève Fabre, provides a collection of articles on ethnic issues, some of them in terms of literary expression. For William Boelhower, ethnic fictions "summon up ghosts" to discover a place of secrecy and "refound identity" (pp. 81–96). Ha-Hong-Van Ha-Van's approach to Isamu Noguchi's *A Sculptor's World* brings out the devices of autobiographical writing in the makeup of an aesthetic quest (pp. 69–80). Michel Feith traces the pattern of initiation through the "dislocation of exile" in the works of Carlos Busan, John Okada, and Louis Chu (pp. 97–110). *Borderlands–La Frontera* by Gloria Anzaldúa is seen by Ada Savin to lay the foundation of "a new syncretic self" (pp. 111–20). In Klaus Benesch's eyes "The Education of Mingo" by Charles Johnson shows the master-slave connection as a metaphor of the cross-cultural formation of identity (pp. 335–46). Alice Mills sees syncretic illustrations of both Gilbert Durand's *Structures anthropologiques de l'imaginaire* and the African-inspired studies of Henry Louis Gates, Jr., and De Weever in the plays of August Wilson (pp. 159–70).

f. Poetry   A richly suggestive article by Jacqueline Ollier reveals the poetic potentialities of American landscape paintings, with insights into the works of Bryant, Whitman, and Ginsberg ("La découverte de l'Amerique par ses peintres," *Interspace* 8: 56–60). In "Longfellow and the Meandering Charles River" (*Le Fleuve et ses métamorphoses,* pp. 455–58) Edward Geary notes that throughout his verse the New England poet seeks "a stasis, a Claudian landscape to be kept open forever," thereby reducing Cambridge to a minimalist composition of elemental forms. In "Walt Whitman: les passages autocensurés de 'The Sleepers,'" Thérèse Vichy returns to the "pre-surrealistic lines" deleted from the poem that a critic once called "erotic gibberish" (*Le groupe et l'individu dans le monde anglophone,* pp. 75–80). Alain Suberchicot concentrates on *The Man with a Blue Guitar* by Wallace Stevens to appraise "the aesthetics of self-achievement" through elements of restraint, speculation, and revolt nurtured on the Puritan heritage ("Le sens de la beauté et la beauté du sens chez Wallace Stevens," *Ecriture poétique moderne,* Numéro spécial, "Réflexion théorique et communication esthétique," ed. Marie-Jeanne Ortemann [Nantes: Crini], pp. 215–28). Suberchicot further examines Stevens's austerity and repression of desire in the light of Merleau-Ponty's restrictive views of language; unadorned intellectual beauty, he concludes of Stevens' position, can be attained only by surprise ("Ordre et désordre du sens chez Wallace Stevens," *Ecriture poétique moderne* 3: 283–94). Christine Savinel presents the poet's abstract language in terms of French translations ("Wallace Stevens: un ordre abstrait de la traduction," *Cahiers Charles V* 17: 95–109). Savinel has also authored "Wallace Stevens: la crise à la lettre C" (*Eclats de voix,* pp. 147–56). In "La conscience et ses limites: pour une meta-lecture du *Paterson* de William Carlos Williams" (*Ecriture poétique moderne* 3: 183–89), Michèle Merzoug-Garnier stresses the ontological power of the creative metaphors springing from the unconscious and eluding control in *Paterson,* which he identifies in turn as a "phallic poem."

   Turning to Robert Lowell's confessional poetry, Jacky Martin defines it as dealing "with the web of plausibility one needs to weave to make the split in the modern consciousness bearable" ("Masks of Self in Robert Lowell's Poetry," *Le groupe et l'individu dans le monde anglophone,* pp. 103–18). Jeannine Belgodère studies the sense of space and movement in Sylvia Plath's "Ariel," asserting that words let loose a flux of entropic images, thus expressing "creative fury" in the self as a reflection of its metamorphoses ("L'identité personelle: trouver et perdre le sens du moi dans l'oeuvre poétique de Sylvia Plath," *Ecriture poétique moderne* 3: 75–87). *Eclats de voix* has a special section on "modalités poétiques" with Gayle Wurst (" 'Daddy' revu et corrigé: Sylvia Plath et le legs de l'art extrémiste," pp. 111–24), Evelyne Labbé ("Mort et crise: le travail du négatif dans deux poèmes de Robert Lowell, 'The Flaw' et 'Ice'," pp. 125–36), Marie-Christine Lemardeley-Cunc ("Crises exquises: persistance de la douleur dans la poésie d'Anne Sexton," pp. 137–46).

There is a conjunction of ethnic and poetic studies in several contributions to books and reviews. Taffy Martin sees an imaginary autobiography in the poetry of Lorine Niedecker, who appropriates Jefferson's language among others as an attempt at desecration and transgression through a protean narrative stance ("Par opposition: Lorine Niedecker et la subversion du genre," *Le genre et la loi* 2: 53–64). In "Le fruit mâle et femelle ou la pomme de concorde d'Olga Broumas" (*Le genre et la loi* 2: 41–51), Nicole Ollier focuses on the syncretic reinterpretations of Hellenic mythology by the Greek-American woman poet whose verse "invents a new syntax of love," thus reaching the omega of femininity by luxuriantly expressing a prelapsarian unity, in accordance with the superior laws of nature. Françoise Clary sees Langston Hughes's original quest for identity in the rhetorical overlapping of the lyrical with the discursive in an effort to transcend isolation through outbursts of sensuality ("De l'identité ethnique à l'identité personnelle: trouver et perdre le sens du moi dans l'oeuvre poétique de Langston Hughes," *Ecriture poétique et moderne* 3: 51–65). *La frontière Mexique-Etats-Unis, rejets, osmoses et mutations* (Publications de l'Université de Provence), ed. Maryse Gachie-Pineda and Serge Ricard, constitutes an interdisciplinary approach to borderland literature with articles in French and Spanish. Especially noteworthy is "Bilinguisme poétique chicano" (pp. 199–217), by Elyette Benjamin-Labarthe, who examines the linguistic challenges of such poets as Abelardo Delgado, Ricardo Sanchez, Sergio Elizondo, Bernice Zamora, and Alurista. "Come down my cheek raza roja" by Alurista exemplifies the multicultural dimension of hybridization, diglossic disharmony, and subversion of codes; similarly, Alurista's "Salsa con crackers" illustrates cultural antagonisms. Meanwhile, Spanish words with gnostic overtones assume the value of age-old allegories set off against American norms. Such a spirit of renewal, Benjamin-Labarthe concludes, is reminiscent of Dante's quest, leading away from apocalyptic mutations toward Beatrice's "articulate bliss." In *L'esthétique de la représentation,* the works of Ricardo Sanchez and Gary Soto are shown to exemplify the various ways in which negation inscribes itself in the Chicano poetic text (Yves-Charles Grandjeat, "Surcharge ou ellipse, Sanchez ou Soto: à propos d'esthétique chicano," pp. 105–19).

Sorbonne Nouvelle, Paris

ii German Contributions: Christoph Irmscher

a. Literary Scholarship and the "New American Studies" America as a "multiculture," a society marked by ceaseless struggle rather than ideological uniformity, home of the plight and play of "difference": many of this year's more general contributions in the area of American Studies rehearse a catalog of reasons for challenging and ultimately abandoning a "Eurocentric" point of view. What exactly it needs to be replaced with remains largely, and perhaps productively, unclear. Gone are the days of Siegfried von Turpitz, it seems: that memorable German professor gracing David Lodge's novel *Small World* used to thump the table with his leather-gloved hand whenever he mentioned the one critical category he appreciated—"the reader." Under the impact of the New American Studies, which most critics agree should be seen less as a synthesis of previous work than an opportunity for theoretical proliferation and expansion, German scholarship on American literature now is informed not by one or two or even several overarching paradigms but instead basks in a healthy plethora of models and critical approaches.

In his contribution to a session on "American Studies in the Postmodern Era" held at the 1993 meeting of the German Anglistentag in Eichstätt ("The Status of Literature Within the Changing Self-Definition of American Studies," *Anglistentag 1993: Eichstätt,* ed. Günther Blaicher and Brigitte Glaser [Niemeyer], pp. 340–49), Heinz Ickstadt writes: "I believe that the house of fiction has many windows." With its clever mixing of Jamesian detachment and biblical pathos, Ickstadt's metaphor reminds us that our new awareness of American culture as a multiplicity of discourses and practices still depends, indeed *needs* to depend, on an "assumed frame of coherence without which the context of difference would not make much sense." Alfred Hornung's essay in the same volume (" 'Make It New!': The Concept of Newness in American Studies," pp. 307–19) is an admirable case study of such identity within difference: Hornung locates a tradition of "newness" (a wonderfully oxymoronic phrase) in definitions of American identity ranging from early attempts to rename the "Newfound Land" to Pound's famous modernist injunction to "MAKE IT NEW." The latter, in Hornung's view, already encapsulates the quasi-ritualistic insistence on innovation among the practitioners of the New American Studies. In "Postmodernism and the Proliferation of Aesthetics: The Interrelation of Culture and Aesthetics in American Studies" (pp. 320–39) Gerhard Hoffmann sketches out his theory of the "aesthetic attitude," which he defines as a playful balancing of mutually exclusive viewpoints, delighting in paradox and parody. This, he claims, is the ideal paradigm for the study of American culture, where literature has lost its privileged role in the realm of art and the "interrelations between popular and sophisticated modes of discourse" are more flexible than in Europe.

Some of these reflections are developed in a volume Hoffmann has coedited with Alfred Hornung, *Affirmation and Negation in Contemporary Culture*. In their preface the editors explain how since the 1960s, under the impact of popular culture, the distinctions between high and low art in the United States have been thoroughly eroded to give way to a new, more pragmatic conception of culture. In a long essay on the "uses of pleasure" ("Meaning versus Pleasure: Conflicting Aspects of Twentieth-Century Aesthetics," pp. 1–71) Hoffmann looks at works by Barth, Barthelme, Pynchon, and Sukenick and asks himself what exactly literature has to offer its readers after the triumph of "incoherence" and the death of the subject, at a time when the pleasure principle "turns its back on the over-complex text." At the end of literature's autonomy, Hoffmann muses, the aesthetic is no longer "unassailable": the responsibility for an integration of "pleasure and meaning" lies with the recipients and the choices they make in their reading.

As if responding to Hoffmann's plea for an ethics of communication, Heinz Ickstadt and Günter Lenz, in their jointly written contribution to *Affirmation and Negation* ("After Poststructuralism and Deconstruction: A New American Exceptionalism?" pp. 178–94), have some harsh words for a new "exceptionalism" in American critical thought. Such a one-sided reading of American tradition(s) rejoices not in the play of difference, but invokes a kind of anti-European emphasis on American uniqueness and specificity; remaining deaf to the dialogue of the many cultural voices of the United States, it privileges the educated conversation of the few.

Holistic or narrowly exclusive concepts of American literature also come under scrutiny in a collection of essays by European and American scholars programmatically titled *American Studies in Germany: European Contexts and Intercultural Relations* (Campus/St. Martin's). In their introduction editors Günter Lenz and Klaus Milich argue for a reconception of European-American Studies in the light of recent political developments, notably German unification and European integration. In a thoughtful piece, "The Making of Americans: Mary Rowlandson, Benjamin Franklin, Gertrude Stein, Maxine Hong Kingston" (pp. 96–117), Alfred Hornung compares different enactments of the process of "Americanization" in Rowlandson's *Captivity Narrative*, Franklin's *Autobiography*, Stein's *The Making of Americans*, and Kingston's *The Woman Warrior*, and he concludes that, at least in its more tolerant versions, "the making of Americans" acquires universal significance, inviting "potentially all people" to "become Americans." Europeans have much to gain from this insight and the American dedication to "the advantages of a multicultural practice."

In an essay on "The New Historicism: History as Process and Narratives of Emergence" (pp. 68–76) Ulfried Reichardt suggests that the New Historicist preference for synchronic rather than diachronic treatments of history reflects the conviction that linear narratives usually presuppose a single point of view and therefore best represent the history of the more successful rather than the underprivileged groups of society, the "preterites," in Thomas Pynchon's phrase. Reichardt pleads for a juxtaposition of diachronic and synchronic accounts of history and envisions a fruitful "field of contending narratives," which can be surveyed only from an insider's always changing and shifting point of view. Rüdiger Kunow, in "Beginning/Ending/Rewriting History: Historiographical Scenarios in the Multiculturalism Debate" (pp. 77–95), uses texts by Toni Morrison and Sandra Cisneros to emphasize his point that while white mainstream America is darkly musing about the end of history, hitherto disempowered ethnic minorities are only beginning to establish a history for themselves.

It is a bit disappointing to see that Mario Klarer's otherwise useful little book *Einführung in die englische und amerikanische Literaturwissenschaft* (Darmstadt: Wissenschaftliche Buchgesellschaft) makes no mention of these developments in the area of cultural studies and their influence on literary scholarship (just as it forgets to include "native" German traditions of textual interpretation, such as Gadamer's version of hermeneutics). In a time of increasing commitment to interdisciplinary research Klarer does not discuss the always problematic but sometimes also fruitful relations between literature and the sciences. Even his treatment of New Historicism and feminism—for him obviously the state of the art in theory—foregrounds their status as literary scholarship (New Historicism, he writes, uses the tools of literary criticism to confront historical phenomena) rather than their value as cultural analysis. All this is not to gainsay the value of Klarer's lucidly written and structured chapters on literary genres with their illustrative readings of short passages from novels, poems, or plays, or to deny that his patient, exemplary advice on research techniques will be of considerable help to students in mastering the nitty-gritty of textual interpretation.

b. Literary History *Die Salemer Hexenverfolgungen: Perspektiven, Kontexte, Repräsentationen,* ed. Winfried Herget (Wissenschaftlicher Verlag Trier) is a collection of 11 articles addressing the Salem witchcraft persecutions from a variety of viewpoints. Essays deal with Edward Taylor's medical practice and with the relationship between New England millennialism and Thomas Hobbes's *Leviathan,* but the literary scholar will probably be most interested in the three pieces dealing with the literary aftermath of the trials: Udo Hebel's assessment of the late 17th- and early 18th-century treatments (" 'The Events of That Sad Catastrophe, *Anno 1692:* A Note on Contemporary Representations of the Salem Witchcraft Persecutions," pp. 263–75); Heike Hartrath's reading of John Neal's novel *Rachel Dyer* ("Die Salemer Hexenverfolgung in der amerikanischen Literatur des 19. Jahrhunderts," pp. 209–31); and Hans-Joachim Lang's meditation on how 19th-century American literature missed the chance to adequately confront the historical reality of the Salem trials ("Die Salemer Hexenprozesse als versäumte Chance der amerikanischen Nationalliteratur," pp. 233–62).

A festschrift compiled by Konrad Gross, Kurt Müller, and Meinhard Winkgens in honor of Paul Goetsch's 60th birthday and published under the title *Das Natur/Kultur-Paradigma in der englischsprachigen Erzählliteratur des 19. und 20. Jahrhunderts* (Gunter Narr) is a welcome exception to the rule in that its various contributions actually do have a common theme. The 21 essays assembled deal with the various metaphorical or metonymical guises under which the well-worn opposition of nature and culture has appeared in post-Romantic English, American, and Canadian fiction. Only a few of the many insights proffered by the contributors can be summarized here. Bernd Engler, for example, in "'Grandeur, Sublimity and the Heroic Attitudes of Western Nature': Bret Hartes Kritik an romantischen Naturkonzeptionen" (pp. 237–57), questions Harte's established role as the initiator of the local color movement. Fortified by generous quotations from Harte's journalistic pieces published in the Springfield *Republican,* Engler demonstrates that while Alfred Bierstadt's paintings created heroically stylized images of Western landscape, and Eadweard Muybridge's and Carleton E. Watkins's panoramic photographs successfully commodified Californian nature, Harte rejected the romanticization of nature just as he stubbornly avoided "authentic" description of Western landscape. Manfred Pütz discusses the precarious and somewhat desperate—hence "utopian"—balancing of nature and civilization in Edward Bellamy's *Looking Backward,* a case of "environmental engineering" *avant la lettre* ("Von der Naturhaftigkeit utopischer Zivilisation: Edward Bellamy's *Looking Backward,*" pp. 258–73).

In 20th-century American literature the machine in the garden, for better or worse, has become a familiar sight. Gerd Hurm's essay on Hemingway's stylized treatment of nature ("'I Made It All Up': Die gestaltete Natur in Hemingway's 'Big Two-Hearted River'," pp. 275–303) usefully invokes Theodore Roosevelt as Nick Adams's imaginary guide in the wilderness. Hurm establishes links with contemporary American middle-class celebrations of the "great outdoors" to prove that in Hemingway's story nature appears as a rational construction rather than a mythic refuge or latter-day version of Walden Pond. Helmbrecht Breinig deals with *Incidents of Travel in Central America, Chiapas and Yucatan* by the American diplomat John L. Stephens, who traveled through Central America in 1841 admiring and, at the same time, shuddering at a landscape "which human hands had never attempted to improve" ("'So Beautiful a Country in Such Miserable Hands': Das Natur/Kultur-Paradigma in nordamerikanischen Texten über Lateinamerika," pp. 304–19). Breinig argues that the role of North American entrepreneurs is viewed more critically in 20th-century texts such as Rex Beach's *Jungle Gold* (1935), and he concludes his discussion with a look at Paul Theroux's *The Mosquito Coast,* a bitter anticipation of a world swamped in garbage, where the borders between nature and culture have lost their relevance. Finally, Franz Link believes that B. F. Skinner in *Walden Two* is playing fast and loose with the consequences of a scientific approach to human behavior, the dangers of which Link feels are accurately predicted in Bernard Malamud's *God's Grace,* Kurt Vonnegut's *Galápagos,* and Walker Percy's *The Thanatos Syndrome* ("Evolutionistische Utopien in der neueren englischsprachigen Erzählkunst: Skinner-Burgess-Percy-Malamud-Vonnegut," pp. 320–38).

c. 18th- and 19th-Century Literature One of the most important books to come out this year is Klaus Lubbers's *Born For the Shade: Stereotypes of the Native American in United States Literature and the Visual Arts, 1778–1894* (Rodopi). Refreshingly catholic in its conception of literature, Lubbers's book covers the period from the Declaration of Independence to Frederick Jackson Turner's retrospective evocation of America's mythic frontier. Taking his cue from works such as Louise Barnett's *The Ignoble Savage,* Roy Harvey Pearce's *Savagery and Civilization,* and Robert Berkhofer's *The White Man's Indian,* Lubbers shows how rigidly defined generic boundaries as well as a history of ethnocentric prejudice prevented generations of American writers, artists, and politicians—some rare exceptions notwithstanding—from adopting a stance toward Native Americans that would have allowed them to consider, even for a moment, alternative concepts "of the coexistence of cultures." In 11 chapters, packed with references to well-known, half-forgotten, and totally obscure figures in late 18th- and 19th-century American culture, Lubbers offers his readers a wealth of factual information, textual summary, cultural analysis, and provocative commentary.

In the first part of his study Lubbers demonstrates how Independence Day orators quickly moved from scattered early suspicions that "the native was better than the European" toward ritualistic denunciations of the "savages" as belonging either to the colonial past or to the margins of an imagined glorious Anglo-Saxon future. Despite isolated examples of "transcultural sympathy" (notably in Thoreau's journals), 19th-century essayists, fearing history's censure, believed that natives needed to be "incorporated" or, failing that, had been "destined to disappear" anyway. In the numerous schoolbooks and children's books he has examined, Lubbers finds occasional images of acculturation and pleas for compassion interspersed with more frequent disingenuous justifications of Native American removal.

The second part of his study is devoted to the visual arts, which

Lubbers finds to be in a sorry state. Images on peace medals, for example, helped to convey racial prejudice by relegating Indians to their periphery; and accurate representations of Indian life in Seth Eastman's documentary portfolios soon gave way to the more fanciful images of the Indian as fiend, enemy, or menace in the art of John Vanderlyn, George Caleb Bingham, or Horatio Greenough.

But it is the last part of Lubbers's book which is particularly interesting for literary scholars, because here he succeeds in wiping the dust off a number of exhibits in the museum of literary history. While drama, in which Indians appeared either as tragic or pathetically ridiculous figures, allowed the least thematic latitude, poetry with its many subgenres offered "a wider range of possibilities." Lubbers is particularly impressive on Freneau's cultural relativism, his "overall inconsistency," which placed him in a "cultural void" but did not allow him to see Native American culture as anything but a vaguely defined alternative to the shortcomings he perceived in his own culture. Lubbers points out how Bryant and notably Whitman modified the tradition of the "Indian lament" by imagining the possible future extinction of white civilization. Poems about "historical Indians" mourn their disappearance but celebrate their removal, vacillate between pro-native and pro-pioneer viewpoints, to leave us, as Ernest McGaffrey's "Geronimo" does, with the distorted vision of an Indian whose eagle-like wings are broken and whose brow is disfigured by the "mark of Cain." Lubbers usefully traces the deterioration of the frontier romance into "melodramatic formula fiction," and he shows how novelists such as Emerson Bennett and John Esten Cooke helped to entrench the ideology of savagism even more firmly, perversely imagining either miserable barbarians brandishing their tomahawks or shifty, sallow-complexioned half-breeds. During the second half of the 19th century, interest in Native Americans declined considerably: in the world of Owen Wister's *The Virginian,* Indians have "become so marginal as to be no longer a problem."

Strangely, Lubbers totally omits natural history writers (whose work frequently defied conventional definitions of genre). In his *Notes on the State of Virginia* Jefferson infamously claimed that Indians, like blacks, needed to be treated as "subjects of natural history"; Charles Willson Peale included wax figures of Shawnee chiefs in his Philadelphia museum, and John Godman, in his otherwise groundbreaking *American Natural History* (1826), while conceding the existence of just one species, if different "varieties," of homo sapiens, still felt compelled to deplore the

depravity of the "civilized aboriginal," degenerated to a state lower than
that of the domesticated animal. But perhaps the inclusion of natural
history would have unduly strained the limits of an inquiry whose scope
is encyclopedic enough.

Kate Chopin's oeuvre has caused a lot of ink to be spilt, and Benita
von Heynitz's book *Literarische Kontexte von Kate Chopin's* The Awakening (Gunter Narr) at first seems as narrowly focused as Lubbers's *Born for
the Shade* is wide-ranging. A revised version of von Heynitz's dissertation,
it offers a comparative approach to Chopin's often-analyzed novel. The
study is conceived as a "tour d'horizon," which takes us around some of
the better-known sights and for visits with some of the more familiar
19th-century figures (Maupassant, Flaubert, George Sand), but it also
opens up more startling vistas. Von Heynitz is not looking for influences
but for contexts. She focuses on *The Awakening* as a novel about adultery
(her argument here would have profited from taking note of Peter
von Matt's wonderful study of the "faithless" in literature: *Liebesverrat*
[1989]), and she—convincingly, I think—disputes interpretations which
see Edna as a "new woman," pointing out how Chopin's character shares
a number of important characteristics with the longing, wistful, intro-
spective heroines of English Pre-Raphaelite iconography. Theodor Fontane's well-heeled, well-educated protagonists were fluent in French, to
be sure, but the parallels von Heynitz develops between Fontane's novel
L'Adultera and the Creole world of *The Awakening* rarely seem to point to
anything but the well-known fact that other novels were written about
adultery in the late 19th century. Comparisons with Richard Wagner's
Tristan und Isolde are more instructive. Edna's death is an expurgated
version of Isolde's *liebestod,* but while the Wagnerian heroine's final
ecstasy takes her toward eternal reunion with Tristan, Edna drowns in
her memories of a sweet past. She retreats, as it were, into an "aesthetic
enclave" that reminds von Heynitz of art nouveau and induces her to
read the Undine-like Edna's death as a kind of *Gesamtkunstwerk,* a term
that can, as von Heynitz suggests, easily be applied to the novel as a
whole.

A few essay-length studies are particularly worth mentioning. Roland
Hagenbüchle, in "Emily Dickinson's Poetic Covenant" (*Anglia* 112: 309–
40), notes that Emily Dickinson is a "deeply provincial" yet a truly
"transatlantic, even cosmopolitan author." He offers a detailed "reappraisal" of Dickinson's "There came a Day at Summer's full" (P 322) as a
starting point for a reflection on Dickinson's "testing of semantic bound-

aries," her "pioneering" exploration of the borderline experiences of despair and ecstasy, which, for Hagenbüchle, makes her work the 19th-century equivalent or perhaps even fulfillment of Samuel Danforth's 17th-century vision of an "errand into the wilderness," or, within another frame of reference, the perfect embodiment of the "westering spirit" in poetry. This approach, to be sure, should not lead us to regard Dickinson as a kind of Buffalo Bill of American poetry, but what it does tell us is that she was no nihilist either. Hagenbüchle reassuringly points out that Dickinson kept her faith, not the least because her creativity remained undiminished throughout her life. In a word, she was very much "unlike Melville." Steffi Habermeier, in "On Interpreting Bartleby" (ZAA 42: 352–63), would certainly agree. In her Lacanian reading of Melville's story, the lawyer cannot "fix" the meaning of Bartleby, cannot "write" him (just as we cannot "read" him) because this clerk, the nightmare of office coordinators everywhere, represents the "intrusion of the Real" into the order of the Symbolic: "Bartleby has become an ab-*sens* as a dead letter."

One essay is devoted to the master of literary sleight of hand: in "Repräsentation, Illustration und Simulation bei Henry James" (ZAA 42: 340–51) Mario Klarer claims that the interaction of verbal and visual modes of representation in James's "The Real Thing" powerfully anticipates modernist and postmodernist theories of imitation and mimesis. And, finally, Kurt Albert Mayer, in "Some German Chapters of Henry Adams's *Education:* 'Berlin (1858–1859),' Heine and Goethe" (*ArAA* 19: 1–25), asks us not to take at face value the harsh criticism that *The Education of Henry Adams* heaped on Germany and the Germans and to reconsider the hapless Adams's disparaging references to Berlin and his dismissive treatment of Heine, tinged by barely concealed anti-Semitic prejudice. Meyer wonders if Goethe's *Dichtung und Wahrheit* would not have been a more appropriate model for Adams's narrative than the authors cited by Adams himself, Rousseau and Franklin.

d. 20th-Century Literature Martin Meyer's *Nachkriegsdeutschland im Spiegel amerikanischer Romane der Besatzungzeit* (Gunter Narr) is as much a documentation as it is a study of characteristic images of postwar Germany in American fiction. Its 60-page appendix provides short biographical sketches and lists, and it summarizes 21 novels ranging from Thomas Berger's *Crazy in Berlin* to Leon Uris's *Armaggedon,* all of them set in the landscape of Germany during the decade of occupation after

World War II. Among the books recovered from the dustbin appear to be some real finds, such as Charles Haldeman's novel *The Sun's Attendant* (1964), of which Meyer gives an extended interpretation in the third chapter of his study. One of the conclusions reached by Meyer is that American postwar writers took a livelier interest in Germany than is generally assumed and that American writers with no known traces of a German background have tended to be more sympathetic to the realities of the postwar Germany than have those of German descent.

If Meyer's ambition is to retrieve a body of texts that have, perhaps unjustly, been forgotten almost as soon as they were written, Bernd Graff, in *Das Geheimnis der Oberfläche: Der Raum der Postmoderne und die Bühnenkunst Robert Wilsons* (Niemeyer), looks ahead—at an art form that our more traditional critical concepts, even language itself, cannot adequately describe. Phil Glass once claimed that we should not ask what Robert Wilson's "operas" (to use his own preferred term) "meant" but instead simply realize that "it's meaningful." Wilson's postmodernist refusal to generate "meaning," writes Graff in his theoretically sophisticated, at times somewhat opaquely written, book, creates an "art without works of art." Drawing on the holdings of the Wilson Collection at Columbia University, Graff sketches out Wilson's aesthetic program, which aims not for artistic authenticity, the telling of a coherent "story," but, following the practices established by minimal and performance art, only provides "materials for art," theatrical "ready-mades," or "Real-Lifes," asking spectators to supply their own meaning out of their own different experiences. Graff quotes the New York playbill for Wilson's *The Life & Times of Josef Stalin,* the front and back cover of which encouraged the audience to "please compose—."

Interest in postmodernism has soared again. In this year's edition of *REAL,* devoted to the relations of "Aesthetics and Contemporary Discourse," Gerhard Hoffmann seeks to define what he himself suggests is impossible to define ("The Comic and the Sublime in Postmodern American Fiction: Comedy and Humor in Contemporary Culture," *REAL* 10: 231–91). In a critical tour de force Hoffmann explains that the postmodern is "a series of often quite diverse and contradictory attitudes, practices and styles," a form of "interactions and transitions, of cross-purposes and mixed codes," which brings out the contradictions, contingencies, and exclusions in the discourse of modernism. Hoffmann notes that the last resort of the sublime in contemporary society, namely, the area of technological achievement, has been ironized and "com-

icalized." Hence, the importance of the "free comic viewpoint," which
has a number of good things to offer: it accepts discontinuities and
rejects causality; it is in love with difference and hates sameness; it
opts for multiple viewpoints and flexible structures. In other words, it is
just what we need today as our own homes comes crashing down around
our ears. Shooting rapid glances at texts by Barth, Barthelme, Gass,
Pynchon, and Sukenick and at an impressive range of theoretical contributions on the subject, Hoffmann warns us, however, that outside the
realm of literature the free comic mode lacks the power to teach us
"empathy" or "understanding and hope for the future." Hoffmann
introduces the notion of "humor" as a possible panacea for our present
problems: it "engages in sympathetic understanding" and, in its utopian
dimension, retains at least part of the project of the Enlightenment. Both
"humor" and the "free comic view," however, will enhance, thus Hoffmann hopes, the mind's adaptability to a confusing environment.

A similar concern drives Alfred Hornung in "The Transgression of
Postmodern Fiction: Philip Roth and Cynthia Ozick" (*Affirmation and
Negation,* pp. 229–49). Reading Roth's autobiographical trilogy (*The
Ghost Writer, Zuckerman Unbound,* and *The Prague Orgy*) and Ozick's
novel *The Messiah,* Hornung argues that their shared Jewish background
has predisposed both authors to write "transgressive" texts, fictions
which know about and skillfully exploit the tricks of postmodernist free
play but remain politically "conscious of the effects of language in the
real world."

Such contact with the "real world," perhaps even at the expense of
postmodern "anything-goes," seems to be one of the givens in a fictional
genre addressed by several scholars this year. In an issue of *Amerikastudien* devoted to recent American crime fiction, Evelyne Keitel ("The
Woman's Private Eye View," *Amst* 39: 161–82) considers feminist mysteries by Sue Grafton, Sara Paretsky, and Joan Hess and finds that while
these novels successfully tap into the male tradition of hard-boiled
detective fiction, their first-person narrators usually are strong women
who can "beat any man" with their fists. Thus, they offer utopian
counterimages "to the relative powerlessness of women in patriarchal
societies." According to Michael Porsche ("Journey Into the Past: Tony
Hillerman's *A Thief of Time,*" *Amst* 39: 183–95), Hillerman's mysteries
effectively dramatize the conflict between traditional Navajo culture and
the "encroaching white world." Porsche meticulously traces Navajo po-
liceman Joe Leaphorn's healing process and intellectual coming-of-age in

A Thief of Time, which he sees as illustrating Hillerman's "recipe for Native American consciousness," but he neglects to mention the strong Native criticism which has been leveled against the non-Native writer Hillerman's appropriation of tribal viewpoints and traditions. Thomas Michael Stein, in "The Ethnic Vision in Walter Mosley's Crime Fiction," (*Amst* 39: 197–212) reads African American writer Mosley's Easy Rawlins novels (*Devil in a Blue Dress, A Red Death,* and *White Butterfly*) as attacks on both white and black racism. Stein, it seems to me, somewhat simplifies W. E. B. Du Bois's complex evocation of the two "unreconciled strivings" in black "double-consciousness" to argue that Mosley's fiction transfers a " 'double vision' of black and white Americans into a trans-ethnic concept of American culture."

An entire issue of *Amerikastudien*, guest-edited by Sabine Sielke and me, is devoted to theoretically oriented contributions by younger German Americanists from various disciplines, all of them members of the Post-Graduate Forum in the German Association of American Studies. Among the essays of more immediate relevance for the literary scholar is Carmen Birkle's " 'To Create a Space for Myself': Carolyn Heilbrun aka Amanda Cross and the Detective Novel" (*Amst* 39: 525–35), which continues the exploration of new crime fiction as a medium for literary as well as political self-expression. A noteworthy essay is Georg Schiller's "Organizing Energies: Reference and Experience in the Work of Gertrude Stein" (*Amst* 39: 511–24), which situates Stein's playful deferral of meaning in *Tender Buttons* and *Lifting Belly* in the context of John Dewey's aesthetic theory and Wolfgang Iser's literary anthropology. Andreas Müller-Hartmann suggests a framework of "interracial dynamics" for the exploration of texts by modern African American authors and celebrates the emergence of the "invisible black" from under the woodpile in Arna Bontemps's *Black Thunder* or Zora Neale Hurston's *Their Eyes Were Watching God* (" 'The Nigger in the Woodpile': The Southern Literary Discourse of Race," *Amst* 39: 537–49). Finally, Monika Kaup sets out to redraw the border on the literary map of Mexico and the United States by locating "oppositional" strategies in texts by Chicano writers Estela Portillo Trambley, Aristeo Brito, and Rolando Hinojosa ("Reterritorializing the Border in Chicano/a Fiction," *Amst* 39: 579–95).

Poetry did not have much of a showing this year, but on the shelf of 20th-century materials Barbara Honrath's modestly entitled *Die New York Poets und die bildende Kunst* (Würzburg: Verlag Königshausen und Neumann) deserves special mention. Honrath provides a nuanced and precise mapping of the many points of contact between the poetry of John Ashbery, Barbara Guest, Kenneth Koch, Frank O'Hara, and James Schuyler and the visual arts, but she is ultimately more interested in the textual practices invented by these poets to respond in their work to what Schuyler once called "the floods of paint in whose crashing surf we all scramble." After a biographical and sociohistorical prelude, Honrath first surveys poems which more or less explicitly deal with the arts or the work of individual artists and then probes what she calls "aesthetic affinities" between the New York Poets and contemporary painters. John Ashbery defined the poem as "the history of its own coming into being," and Honrath discovers related notions of the "work-as-process" not only in Ashbery's and Koch's poems, but, for example, in the practice of painters such as Jane Freilicher and Grace Hartigan, who both claimed that they could not "preconceive." In a series of detailed and deft interpretations, Honrath demonstrates that O'Hara wrote a kind of modified "action poetry," and she explains how Ashbery and Koch, but also Schuyler and Guest in their less obviously heterogeneous texts, have succeeded in capturing the "kinetic quality" of experience. For the New York writers, poetry is, Honrath contends, "asymbolical," always open to interpretation, in which, as in Larry Rivers's or Michael Goldberg's art, the meaning is (on) the surface.

Honrath's argument is an effective rejoinder to Rüdiger Kunow's "'You Have It But You Don't Have it': John Ashbery's Guarded Affirmations of Life" (*Affirmation and Negation,* pp. 251–71). Kunow doubts that Ashbery's poetry can be understood by importing "second-order" frames of reference. Critics have read Ashbery's poetry, he says, as a manifestation of his well-known interest in, and commitment to, the visual arts (this is what Honrath has done); they have hailed it as a perfect realization of the fashionable postmodernist ideal of indeterminacy, or they have commented on the influence of Wallace Stevens on his work (*pace* Kunow I do not believe that Stevens, unlike Ashbery, still kept grasping at the "essence of life"; remember that, late modernist or not, he claimed a poem should resist the intelligence "almost successfully"). Kunow considers most of these critical frameworks to be unsatisfactory: Ashbery's poetry, from *Houseboat Days* to *Flow Chart,* functions according to its own intrinsic laws, being engaged as it is in a "constant reproduction of sense." Casually using everyday language, even cliché, Ashbery's poems never "transcend" themselves but remain part and parcel of the world of ordinary experience. This gives me the cue for my own favorite and final quotation this year, which comes not from literary scholarship but from Ashbery's poem "Grand Galop." It begins with the lines (a reviewer's dream, perhaps?): "All things seem mention of themselves,/ And the names which stem from them branch out to other referents."

Universität Bonn

iii Italian Contributions: Algerina Neri

The proceedings of two conferences and an annual seminar of the Italian Association of North American Studies have been published this year. The two thick volumes of proceedings gather the work of most Italian Americanists on two topics, gender and technology; the smaller seminar contribution is dedicated to Walt Whitman. They give the idea of a lively, engaged, expanding literary community. Besides the usual attention to Hawthorne, Melville, James, and Pound, ethnic studies are back in favor. And this year has seen the birth of *Acoma,* a new literary quarterly.

a. General Work, Criticism, Travel Literature *Methodologies of Gender,* ed. Mario Corona and Giuseppe Lombardo (Rome: Herder), at 622 pages, represents the proceedings of the 1991 A.I.S.N.A. Conference at Messina. Cristina Giorcelli's foreword introduces the three main lectures by Sandra Gilbert, Mark C. Carnes, and Rosi Braidotti, and these are followed by eight workshops and a total of 45 papers. The contributions to "Representation of the Body," coordinated by Guido Carboni and Annalisa Goldoni, can be clustered into three groups: explorations of how the body is both revealed and concealed (Lombardo on Oliver Wendell Holmes, Gianfranca Balestra on Edith Wharton); issues of multiplicity and marginality in the use of the "body" as a reference for identity dealing with the range of forms of homosexuality in contemporary fiction (Gordon Poole's "Ungendering versus Unsexing") and in Gwendolyn Brooks's works (Ugo Rubeo); the third cluster deals with reification and erasure of the female body in Poe on the one hand (Paola Gemme) and its exaltation and liberation into poetry on the other (Paola Zaccaria on Emily Dickinson). The papers on "Strategies of Subject Representation," coordinated by Marina Camboni and Biancamaria Tedeschini Lalli, have a common theoretical focus. Born from a national research project on "Language, Gender and Cultures in 20th-Century Women Poets," the contributions deal with subject representation. Marina Camboni supplies a general introduction, while Cinzia Biagiotti speaks of Leslie Marmon Silko, Liana Borghi of Irena Klepfisz, Daniela Ciani of Laura Riding, Bernardette Falzon of Sylvia Plath and Stevie Smith, and Gabriella Morisco of Sylvia Plath's *Juvenilia.* Maria Vittoria D'Amico and Rosella Mamoli Zorzi coordinate another workshop, "Gender and the Canon," analyzing the formation of the canon during the '70s and '80s and its tendency to pragmatism. Giovanna Covi chooses Kathy Acker while Gigliola Nocera chooses Richard Ford as primary examples of anticanonical subversion in the postmodern era. Francesca Orestano and Massimo Bacigalupo investigate John Neal and H.D. as their original choices for an American canon and for their anticanonical stances, both central to an understanding of late modernism. Mario Corona surveys recent editions of literary histories and anthologies; his remarks on the meaningful inclusion of women and ethnic authors generates a lively debate on the teaching of American literature and the question of inclusion and exclusion of major and minor figures in the short span of a literature course. Guido Fink coordinates "Gender and War," dealing with general aspects of the interaction between war, the novel, and woman since the Civil War. Woman's traditional role is explored in depth—woman as a victim of war, as the enemy's representation, as author, character, and spectator, and as a feminine personification. Aldo Celli speaks of Willa Cather, M. Giulia Fabi writes about Thomas Nelson Page's and Frances Harper's post-Reconstruction re-visions of the "true woman" and the Civil War, and Alberta Fabris Gubre explores Edith Wharton's narrative on World War I. Concettina Tramontano Magno explores the antiutopian view of war and gender in William Blake's *America;* Franco Minganti reflects on the confusion of gender roles in the cyberpunk world; Stefano Rosso investigates problematic masculinity in Tim O'Brien's fiction; Gigliola Sacerdoti Mariani shows how Muriel Rukeyser's poetry tries to dissect and interpret wars, searching for values which will outlast violence.

History, literature, and philosophy are involved in Tiziano Bonazzi's workshop, "Gender and Religion." Franca Bacchiega gives a portrait of Bernice Zamora and her religious traditions, and Lina Unali examines projection of gender in spiritual and secular autobiographical writings of the 18th century. In "Mythologies of Gendered Representation in Literary and Historical Narratives," coordinated by Barbara Lanati and Maddalena Tirabassi, the five speakers inquire into different literary genres to see how they are used to express gender differences and how certain genres are connected to gender. Rita Cavigioli explores women's diaries and the problems they pose; I use travel journals and diaries to investigate the self-representation of 19th-century women; Maddalena Tirabassi demonstrates how an Italo-American woman's biography raises questions which can modify current historical stereotypes; Annalucia Accardo speaks of representation and the use of voice in some writings by Appalachian women.

After a foreword by Rosella Mamoli Zorzi, the volume on *Technology and the American Imagination: An Ongoing Challenge,* ed. Mamoli Zorzi and Francesca Bisutti De Riz (Venice: Supernova), presents important lectures by Cecelia Tichi, Miles Orvell, David E. Nye, and Pierre-Yves Petillon. Italian, European, and American speakers contributed to the nine workshops of this conference, making it lively and interesting and the book dramatically thick (636 pages). "Textuality, Intertexuality, Hypertexuality: The more it changes . . . ," coordinated by Guido Carboni, discusses the changes in the notion of textuality that different media have brought at different points in history. Contributions range from analysis of 19th-century textuality (Alessandra Calanchi on Poe) to the contemporary opening from words to images and electronic support (Daniela Daniele on Robert Smithson, Franco Minganti on Rob Swigart). Andrea Carosso offers some theoretical coordinates to move from telegraph to Internet, and Martin Pedersen adds his views on the perspectives of oral texts. "Icons of Technology in the American Visual Arts" is coordinated by Andrea Mariani, who analyzes the significance of technology as a theme and as a means through which reality is described, reproduced, and interpreted. Renzo Crivelli offers a dense parallel analysis of Parmigianino's *Self-Portrait in a Convex Mirror* and Ashbery's verse inspired by that canvas. The shocking invention of the telegraph is investigated in its reverberations on cultural, literary, and filmic discourse in "The Telegraphic Imagination," coordinated by Alide Cagidemetrio. Francesca Orestano presents the internal connections between aesthetic and scientific mental attitudes in the practice of Samuel F. B. Morse; Maurizio Ascari's reading of Henry James's *In the Cage,* centered on the figure of the telegraphist, leads to a discussion of Jamesian poetics and the choice of the telegraph as its technological metaphor. The impact that technological innovation and mass production have had on the modern and contemporary American literary imagination is the subject of a roundtable directed by Biancamaria Pisapia. The 10 members of the group select a single work of one contemporary author in which a machine, an industrial product, or a technological innovation plays a major role, both in terms of its relevance to the narrative plot and as an influence on each author's writing technique. This multifaceted presentation demonstrates the participants' common concern with some of the major aspects of the theoretical debate on postmodernism, while affording a series of detailed, personal, and provocative analyses on Vonnegut, Nathanael West, Asimov, Stephen King, John Barth, William Burroughs, and Coover.

"Technology and Ethnicity," coordinated by Lina Unali, presents a complex system of reactions to the evolution of technology on American soil. Franco Mulas deals with the ambiguous stand of Italo-American characters in the novels of Italo-American authors, showing that in the immigrant's mind the machine was both a blessing and a curse. Maria Anita Stefanelli uses "descent" as defined by Werner Sollors in *Beyond Ethnicity: Consent and Descent in American Culture* (1986) to analyze the production of a popular novel such as Michael Crichton's *Jurassic Park*. Chiara Midolo speaks about the machine and the body in Paule Marshall's novels. Paola Boi associates the image of the steam engine as a powerful reservoir of multilayered meanings to artistic creation. Elena Mortara Di Veroli shows the relationship between Isaac Bashevis Singer and the technological writing instrument; Heather Gardner presents the theatrical world of Elmer Rice; Giorgio Mariani talks about technology and storytelling in Leslie Marmon Silko's *Ceremony*. The essays in the section "Science Fiction and Technology," coordinated by Liana Borghi, range from a reading of Philip Dick's fiction through Heidegger's critique of technology (Umberto Rossi) to a close reading of future cyberpunk elements in a story by James Tiptree, Jr. (Nicoletta Vallorani), to assessments of the catastrophic scenarios in cyberpunk authors William Gibson and Pat Cadigan (Angela Vistarchi and Tiziana Terranova). Giovanna Covi analyzes Jessica Hagedorn's *Dogeaters,* emphasizing devices of social inscription. In his presentation on the "disseminated body," Antonio Caronia discusses the influence of technology on recent changes in the definition of subject. In "Technology and Imagination in Contemporary American Literature" Clara Bartocci traces a sort of continuity between *The Education of Henry Adams* and John Barth's *Giles Goat-Boy.* "The Automobile and the American Imagination" deals with the automobile, a cultural icon which has become an integral part of the American dream and its attendant nightmare. Gianfranca Balestra examines travel books and shows how the car has radically altered the sensibilities of travelers, from Henry James to Edith Wharton. Roberto Cagliero investigates the role of the automobile in terms of fictional form, showing the development from a modernist "literature of exhaust" to a postmodern "literature of exhaustion." Finally, Mario Materassi examines mutilated vehicles, stripped of their function and situated in the American landscape. Literature and new technologies combine as the theme of a dossier by Andrea Carosso, Daniela Daniele, and Filippo La Porta, "Hyper, Cyber e Chimere. Gli scrittori del futuro" (*Linea d'Ombra* 96: 35–50): they comment on new fiction and interview Robert Coover, Joseph McElroy, and Bruce Sterling.

Il Veltro dedicates two numbers (38, iii–iv) to American travelers (in the broadest sense) to Italy. The first volume has a more historical orientation. Alessandra Pinto Surdi points out the cultural reasons which brought Americans to Italy in the 19th century. Pinto Surdi also gives a selective list of American travelers who visited Italy up to 1870. Ellen Ginsburg Migliorino and Luca Codignola dwell on the Italian sojourns of Charles Sumner and Francis Parkman. The second volume has a more literary flavor, with some incursions into art. A Henry James piece written in 1877 on his arrival in Rome, translated by Alessandro Gebbia, evokes literary and artistic atmospheres; as part of her analysis, Gebbia re-creates the Roman scene depicted earlier by the American painter James De Veaux, whose work—like James's—reflects a continuous search for truth, for the absolute, emphasized by the equation art/life. Valerio Massimo De Angelis describes Hawthorne's journey to Rome as an initiation into the knowledge of art and history, but also of pain and sin; on the other hand, Maria Enrica Balestra suggests that Hawthorne exploits the Roman setting in *The Marble Faun* to highlight and criticize the mental outlook of the American middle class. Gaetano Prampolini reviews the circumstances and conditions of the Italian experience of poets Richard Hugo and Charles Wright. Franco Marenco offers a sound contribution on an Italian traveler to the United States, "Luigi Castiglioni and the Rhetoric of American Travel, 1770–1790," pp. 94–108 in *Semeia*. Castiglioni's travel book contrasts with contemporary texts, with his naturalistic observations seen as representative of a scientifically ambitious, if politically timid, perhaps perspectiveless, culture.

Tommaso Pisanti publishes a brief history of American literature, *Storia della letteratura americana* (Rome: Newton Compton), a useful compendium for nonspecialists. *L'Asino d'oro* (4, viii: 3–154) includes four contributions on the New Historicism, with a critical introduction by Barbara Gastaldello, "Il 'nuovo storicismo' negli studi letterari anglo-americani."

b. Colonial and 19th-Century Literature   Paola Gemme's "Representing the World in Discourse: A Socio-stylistic Analysis of Multivocality in *The Journal of Madam Knight*" (*QDLLSM* 6 [1993]: 83–100) is a sound analysis of Sarah Kemble Knight's *Journal*. Gemme aims at mediating between the original discussion of the *Journal* as interesting only because of the events it records and recent, equally distorted analysis of it as a complex but ahistorical verbal artifact, and she reconciles these two modes of reading. She shows that the *Journal*'s significance lies both in the contest of languages waged within it and in the facts it recounts. Michele Bottalico examines Royall Tyler's *The Algerine Captive* in "Il viaggio come materia narrative in *The Algerine Captive* di Royall Tyler" (*Athanor* 5: 120–26). In this novel Tyler made a sort of parody of the travel narrative which is also faithful to reality, but he used it to counterpoint the hostility of his time toward the novel. Bottalico discusses another novel in "The American Frontier and the Initiation Rite to a National Literature: The Example of *Edgar Huntly* by Charles Brockden Brown" (*RSAJ* 4: 3–16). For the novelists of the New Republic, internal migration to the West becomes a national archetype from which many American myths were to spring. In Charles Brockden Brown's *Edgar Huntly* the frontier environment becomes the projection of a condition of the human mind; the American wilderness and its native inhabitants generate horror, and evil takes on an ontological rather than historical dimension. Luisanna Fodde dedicates a book to *Noah Webster: National Language and Cultural History in the United States of America* (Padua: CEDAM). Fodde gives a comprehensive and detailed outline of the man and the author, who contributed to the creation of the American mind not simply as a lexicographer. His life and achievements reflect political and cultural developments during the period of the Declaration of Independence.

Sergio Perosa publishes a remarkable contribution on Poe in "Poetica di Poe," pp. 109–20 in *Semeia*. Perosa shows how Poe builds a fantastic universe where science and imagination are the two engines of a circular movement. This movement is more apparent in *Eureka* where the circle does not enlarge but revolves round itself and builds its indissoluble identity from contrary elements—reality/fancy, science/imagination. In

"La critica speculare: Baudelaire/Poe, Bataille/Sade" (*Il Piccolo Hans* 82: 47–57) Carlo Pasi dwells on Poe's influence on Baudelaire: the American writer becomes a sort of projection through which the French poet seems to trace his poetic destiny. A good choice of Nathaniel Hawthorne's short stories, all his novels (except *The Marble Faun*), excerpts from his *Diary*, and a good number of letters have been collected in an edition by Vito Amoruso in *Opere Scelte* (Milan: Mondadori). Amoruso's remarkable introduction seems to have adopted Hawthorne's narrative technique; it suggests and insinuates more than defines, and it offers a polyhedric analysis of the writer, of his themes and methods. Amoruso also gives a perceptive cultural background to Hawthorne's time and shows how Hawthorne chooses the role of mediator between the cultural elitism of Transcendentalism and the public taste that preferred legends and romantic novels.

Massimo Bacigalupo writes again on one of his favorite authors, Herman Melville. In "Reading the Melville Macrotext," pp. 33–46 in Teresa Ferreira de Almeida and Teresa Cid, eds., *Colòquio Herman Melville* (Lisbon: Colibri) Bacigalupo emphasizes the recurrence of images, ideas, quotations, and references throughout Melville's work. He considers their ever-changing and deeply ambivalent significance, which lends itself to endless interpretation. Bacigalupo translates and introduces the 1853 text of *Bartleby the Scrivener* (Milan: Mondadori), which he publishes in a bilingual version with Melville's less well-known "Jimmy Rose." In his foreword Baciagalupo points out themes, suggests reading methods, and dwells on Melville's language; he compares *Bartleby* to *Moby-Dick* and *Benito Cereno,* and he shows how *Bartleby* proposes the same themes, although the work has an unusual environment. Giuseppe Nori presents a version of Melville's 1851–52 letters to Hawthorne, *Lettere a Hawthorne* (Macerata: liberilibri), adding extracts from Melville's *Diary* and Hawthorne's *Notebooks*. The result is an agile, clear, philologically accurate, adventurous book in its structure and the intense passions that the letters reveal. In his introduction Nori tries to uncover the inscrutable links that united these two authors.

The essays in *Utopia in the Present Tense: Walt Whitman and the Language of the New World* (Rome: Il Calamo), ed. Marina Camboni, were presented at an international conference at the University of Macerata in 1992 to celebrate the centennial of Whitman's deathbed edition of *Leaves of Grass.* The essays center on three major topics: *Leaves of Grass* as Whitman's projection of a language and a culture cut to fit the

American context of present and future times; changes and differences in
the nine editions of Whitman's work; and the European reception of
Leaves of Grass. Biancamaria Tedeschini Lalli highlights the poet's use of
linguistic and rhetorical devices to build a visual and virtual projection of
identity; Marina Camboni concentrates on the first three editions and
on the poet's opening up of the English language to make space for the
American polyethnic society; the male body as the center of Whitman's
religion of love in the 1860 edition is the concern of Mario Corona's
essay; and Andrea Mariani focuses on the "atmospheric" landscapes
created by Whitman's poems and on his chromatic sensitivity. Maria
Anita Stefanelli isolates the words and the rhetorical figures which
connect Whitman's 1860 "chants" to the language of Genesis; Italy and
Whitman's influence on Italian Futurists is the focus of Caterina Ric-
ciardi's discourse; and Viviana Benetazzo evaluates the Italian translations of *Leaves of Grass* through their reception. In "Griffith e Whitman:
le mani sulla culla," pp. 541–53 in *Semeia*, Guido Fink follows the use of
the cradle from Whitman's verse to D. W. Griffith's *Intolerance* (1916).
Fink compares Griffith's use of montage to Whitman's and thinks that
the dream behind *Intolerance* is similar to Whitman's.

Annalisa Goldoni edits and introduces a fine contribution on *La
comunicazione non verbale in "The Pupil" di Henry James* (Rome: Nuova
Arnica Editrice). After the English text the nine essays discuss customs,
postures, and clothes as different means to approach and understand
James's text. The autobiographical element can be seen in the re-creation
of cities (Biancamaria Pisapia's "Il silenzioso discorso della topografia di
Parigi"), in ambiguous and complex family relations (Maria Antonietta
Saracino's "A new and untasted bitterness: la seduzione del legame"), and
in the importance of clothes and appearance (Vanda Perretta's "Paper
Dolls"). Other contributions deal with the Jamesian technique of "seeing
through": Gianfranca Balestra's "Epifanie dello sguardo e del silenzio,"
Francesca Trusso's " 'The delicate subject of his remuneration': alcune
coordinate della transcodificazione," and Valerio Massimo De Angelis's
"L'abbraccio della morte: il contatto fisico." Donatella Izzo's "Tradimenti
e traduzioni: la problematicità della comunicazione verbale" examines
the interplay of the two different means of communication. In "La casa
della critica" (*Il piccolo Hans* 79/80: 118–38) Paola Colaiacomo also
explores the importance of the "sense of place" in James's fiction. In "An
Hermetic Reading of Money in Henry James's *The Coxon Fund*"
Cristina Giorcelli talks about money's role in James's fiction and how it

evolves during his literary career (*LAmer* 50 [1993]: 51–70). In the 1894 novella James concludes that his belief in money as a way to leisure and to a richer social life is wishful thinking. He prepares the way for the works of other American novelists, in which money becomes an end in itself, not the sine qua non of culture. Maurizio Ascari presents James's essays on Matilde Serao in "Henry James: Matilde Serao" (*Paragone* 44: 3–19). Ascari points out how James is both attracted to and scared by Serao's sentimental and realistic novels.

Erina Siciliani presents and translates three short stories from Stephen Crane's *Wounds in the Rain, Racconti cubani* (Milan: Tranchida). In her foreword Siciliani underlines Crane's careful search for the right word; his brief poetic sentences portray the inexorability of death and war. Giorgio Mariani translates and introduces *The Red Badge of Courage, Il segno rosso del coraggio* (Rome: Newton Compton); the translation is based on the original manuscript, not on the Appleton 1895 edition. In his short but sound introduction Mariani discusses the differences between these two versions.

d. 20th-Century Prose The Italian literary world continues to pay homage to Edith Wharton. Tommaso Pisanti's introduction to *Ethan Frome* (Rome: Newton Compton) points out the characteristics and peculiarities of this short novel about which critics differ in their evaluation. *The Valley of Decision* has never been translated into Italian, though it takes place in Italy in the second half of the 18th century. In her fine contribution "Il Settecento italiano di Edith Wharton," pp. 471–87 in *Il passaggiere italiano. Saggi sulle letterature di lingua inglese in onore di Sergio Rossi* (Rome: Bulzoni), ed. Renzo Crivelli and Luigi Sampietro, Gianfranca Balestra does not offer a critical-aesthetic appreciation of this historical novel; rather, she speaks about the research Wharton did in order to write it. The historical reconstruction is accurate and rich in detail, though sometimes encumbered by documentation. A different milieu is represented in Jack London's *The Game, the Mexican and a Piece of Steak (La sfida e altre storie di boxe)* (Rome: Newton Compton). Walter Mauro gives a short but useful introduction to this Italian edition.

Winifred Farrant Bevilacqua publishes *The Great Gatsby* (Genoa: Cideb) with a long introduction, critical extracts, a selective bibliography, and a chronology. A thorough introduction to the English text is followed by some suggested activities for students, which make this book a key to enter Fitzgerald's world and times. Agostino Lombardo has written a brilliant and perceptive essay on "Faulkner e la tradizione americana," pp. 247–58 in *A più voci. Saggi in onore di Dario Puccini* (Milan: Scheiwiller). Faulkner's work is closely linked to the American literary tradition, especially to one of its most important features—faith in the strength of language. Language can tell a story, represent life, but it can also reveal secrets, unveil mysteries, and build worlds that have the substance of reality and are even more lasting than reality itself. Faulkner's faith in language is an affirmation of life which survives the tragedy of life and of death. It is the faith in man for his compassion, self-sacrifice, endurance. Cristina Saffiotti too, in "Faulkner: il silenzio e il libro" (*Paragone* 45: 109–17), says that Faulkner preferred the silence of the written word to music. Saffiotti finds *The Sound and the Fury,* one of Faulkner's sonorous novels, particularly dense with silence. Richard Ford boasts of his affinity with Faulkner, which Sergio Nelli puts under scrutiny in "A proposito di Richard Ford minore e non" (*Il Lettore di Provincia* 91: 87–90). Nelli appreciates *Wildlife* and other short stories from *Rock Strings,* but is highly critical of Ford's recently translated book, *Il Donnaiolo (The Womanizer).* Anaïs Nin's diary, *Incesto* (Milan: Bompiani, 1993), is the starting point for a discussion on the diary as a genre in Idolina Landolfi's "Il miglior maieutico. Appunti su un diario di Anais Nin" (*Il Ponte* 50: 122–25). Clara Bartocci writes on John Barth's first two novels in "Dal teatro galleggiante alla 'Fine della strada': percorsi di vita e di scrittura nei primi due romanzi di John Barth," pp. 517–30 in M. Streiff Moretti et al., eds., *Il Senso del Nonsenso* (Naples: Edizioni Scientifiche Italiane). In his first two works Barth experiments with the main narrative forms of the novel to realize that literature too is at "the end of the road"; from that moment on he will promote and theorize a new postmodern poetics.

This year the Italian public has the opportunity to read a fair number of contemporary American writers in translation. An entire issue of *Panta* is dedicated to 16 young writers; Jay McInerney offers a helpful introduction to their work. Mario Materassi and Stefano Tani translate Henry Roth's *Alla mercé di una brutale corrente. Una stella sulla collina del Parco di Monte Morris* (Milan: Garzanti), which has been widely reviewed. Aldo Rosselli in "Incontro con io" (*Leggere* 63: 40–41) finds Philip Roth's *Operazione Shylock* (Milan: Mondadori) a sort of spy story and the most obsessive and paranoid repertoire of Jewish contradictory codes and allegories. Paolo Bertinetti admires Joyce Carol Oates's capability and intellectual courage to describe the most diverse social milieux in "Ragazzini. I racconti di J. C. Oates" (*Linea d'Ombra* 93: 72–73).

Michele de Mieri finds some similarities between Ian McEwan's *Cani Neri* (Turin: Einaudi) and Antonio Tabucchi's *Sostiene Pereira* (Milan: Feltrinelli) in "Ian McEwan e Antonio Tabucchi: Storie di Storia" (*Il Ponte* 50: 148–52). An extensive dossier on Vladimir Nabokov takes up most of number 56 of the literary magazine *Leggere* (pp. 27–52).

e. Ethnic Literature   This year has seen the birth of a new quarterly of North American studies, *Acoma,* which takes its name from a pueblo north of Mexico where the colonizers believed they would find gold, but where they instead met only a rich cultural tradition, which they proceeded to change with the violence of their guns and with the supposed superiority of their civilization. *Acoma* wants to present American culture through ethnic minorities, as the editors Bruno Cartosio and Sandro Portelli explain, and it will publish essays, interviews, short stories, poems, reviews, and bibliographical information. The first issue is rich and varied. It opens and closes with two pieces by Grace Paley, "It Is the Responsibility" and "Midrash on Happiness." Sandro Portelli discusses the determination of the United States to regard the world as a source of possibilities and danger, imaginative wealth and uncertain identity, democratic vistas and imperialistic threats in "The Sky's a Limit: On the Boundaries and Shape of America" (pp. 8–18). She then examines metaphors of boundaries and borders, which set limits on America's hegemonic dream and are grounds of creation and conflict, in the works of Ralph Ellison, Richard Wright, Toni Morrison, Alice Walker, and Anzaldúa. Portelli publishes another interesting book on a similar subject, *La linea del colore. Saggi sulla cultura afroamericana* (Rome: manifestolibri), which explores the limits between blacks and whites, slaves and masters, orality and written work, sound and sense, folklore and intellectualism, past and present. It is a book about the building of identities that redefine themselves constantly. The color line is the key point, obvious but ever changing, which vanishes as soon as it is looked at from up close, but it is still a base for other artificial and violent borders; thus, this is also a book about the borders and contradictions that tear apart the identities of both blacks and whites. Portelli ranges from the autobiography of Frederick Douglass to Zora Neale Hurston, from Toni Morrison and Richard Wright to the Los Angeles riots of 1992. Giulia Scarpa too writes about Morrison's narrative in *Acoma* (1: 68–77). Scarpa thinks that through her work Morrison re-

writes the heritage of African American culture and history, thus rethinking the multiple codes and signs that make up the entire American
literary tradition. The award of the Nobel Prize to Morrison recognizes a
black female literary tradition, which Elizabetta Porfiri discusses in
"L'Opera al nero e rosa" (*Leggere* 61: 48–50).

Anna Scannavini speaks about code-switching, which she thinks is the
key feature of second-generation Puerto Rican literature in the continental United States; far from being a source of embarrassment, the
hybrid linguistic nature of code-switching provides a wealth of stylistic
and expressive solutions. Scannavini dedicates an entire book to the
subject, *Per una poetica del Bilinguismo* (Bulzoni), which shows how the
Spanglish of Puerto Ricans has moved from everyday language of the
community to literary language, becoming a specific way of expression,
an element of civil identification, of pride and creative potentiality. The
book analyzes some ways through which Spanish and English find a way
to express themselves in writers, voices, and characters. A good introduction to Puerto Rican, Chicano, and Asian American literatures comes
from Mario Maffi's "Scritture dei Latinos e degli Asian Americans"
(*Acoma* 1: 62–67). At the center of this American polyphony Maffi sees
storytelling as an authentic source of energy which can recover the oral
traditions of all these cultures, adapting them to the written page.
Storytelling is also able to combine past and present, origins and becomings. The past, the conquest of Cuzco by the Spaniards, comes back in
Rudolfo Anaya's "Message from the Inca," a short story presented by
Michele Bottalico (*RSAJ* 4 [1993]: 83–96). Bottalico finds Anaya's work
"a blending of fantastic symbolism and imagery, visionary approaches to
reality, magical realism, mythopoeic references, and occasional, overt,
although not always successful hints to socio-political issues." The idea
of the storyteller and mythmaker also has been extremely important for
Anaya, as he confesses in his interview with Mario Materassi (*RSAJ* 4
[1993]: 67–79). Chicano women writers seem vital, exuberant, original,
lively, restless, willing to see their identity recognized, as Franca Bacchiega, a specialist of Chicano literature, affirms in "Fiori di bronzo.
Scrittura femminile nella etnia chicana degli Stati Uniti," pp. 123–37 in
Maschere (Bulzoni), ed. Susanna Regazzoni and Leonardo Buonomo.
Bacchiega also presents the poetry of Angela De Hoyos in "La poesia di
Angela De Hoyos fra critica, ironia e mito" (*Si Scrive* 1: 167–85).

Leslie Marmon Silko's collection of 41 short pieces and 39 black-and-
white photographs, *Sacred Waters,* forms a collective story, where water is

the thread guiding the author through a ritual and a celebration. In "Le *Sacred Waters* di Leslie Marmon Silko" (*RSAJ* 4: 57–66) Laura Coltelli shows how the water stories bond with the innumerable narrations of Indian land which speak of the landscape as a direct manifestation of time's cyclical continuity and cohesion. Silko's autobiography, *Storyteller,* is discussed by Fedora Giordano in "Cosa leggere secondo me sulle autobiografie degli Indiani d'America" (*Indice* 7: 27). Giordano shows how contemporary Indian writers' autobiographies differ from the first autobiographies, which were recorded by editors or ethnographers. Native American theater exploded and flowered in the '70s. For the first time in Italy, Annamaria Pinazzi presents and translates four texts by Hanay Geiogamah, the most famous Native American playwright, in *Teatro* (Rome: Castelvecchi). In her thoughtful afterword Pinazzi explains the problems which Native American theater has to overcome because of lack of financial support and because of Native Americans' way of thinking, which is alien to forms of dramatic art lacking a religious context. Geiogamah blames Native Americans' anachronistic attachment to the past and underlines the role theater must take to awaken and strengthen their ability to recover, change, and look after themselves.

The word "wilderness" has no Italian counterpart, but it has had great relevance in American culture from colonial times to the present. In "Nuovi saggi sulla 'wilderness' americana" (*Indice* 7: 15) Fedora Giordano analyzes which form the wilderness takes in three translated books, Gary Snyder's *Nel mondo selvaggio* (Como: Red, 1992), Gretel Ehrlich's *L'incanto degli spazi aperti* (Milan: La Tartaruga, 1993), and Etel Adnan's *Viaggio al Monte Tamalpais* (Salerno: Multimedia, 1993). In "Uno scrittore in erba" (*Leggere* 64: 43) Mario Maffi finds William Least Heat Moon's *Prateria. Una mappa in profondità* both annoying and fascinating; the 680 pages, so dense of eterogenic subjects, would be boring if the voice of the narrator did not capture the reader's attention. Marisa Caramella interviews Least Heat Moon in "Traversate ed esplorazioni" (*Linea d'Ombra* 96: 51–55). A very interesting contribution about the West comes from Mario Materassi's "I saguari a noleggio: John Ford, Ernest Haycox e la vendita del West," pp. 555–66 in *Semeia*. Materassi recalls his first encounter with the West through film director John Ford's *Stagecoach* (1939), which he compares to Ernest Haycox's short story, "Stage to Lordsburg." Ford has created the myth of the West and sold it throughout the world by playing with and intermingling everyday, well-known, limited subjects with exceptional, unknown, unlimited atmospheres. However, the accessibility to the myth, which is a constant feature of American culture, also contains the painful awareness of its precariousness and condemns it to its death.

f. 20th-Century Poetry and Drama Massimo Bacigalupo has been concerned with H.D.'s Pound memoir *End to Torment* for some years (see *ALS 1990*, p. 455). He goes over the intriguing story of this text in his "H.D. and Ezra Pound in 1958–1959: An Uncanonical Confrontation" (*Quaderni dei Nuovi Annali di Messina* [1993]: 371–79). He notices that the American edition omits several passages of H.D.'s typescript and changes the name of one of the principal characters; he quotes some of these important passages. Furthermore, Bacigalupo points out that Ezra Pound responded to H.D.'s account of their relationship in a series of extraordinary letters, among the last he wrote (1959–61). These were intended for publication by H.D. along with *End to Torment,* but this did not happen. Now Bacigalupo has prepared a painstaking Italian edition of the memoir, *Fine al tormento: ricordo di Ezra Pound* (Milan: Archinto), which translates H.D.'s unexpurgated text and includes 21 unpublished letters from Pound (1958–61). These reveal his continuing devotion to and admiration for H.D., and they paint a moving self-portrait of the embattled poet in the final months of his creative life, as he tried to fight against old age and silence. These letters are the closest prose equivalent we have to Pound's final *Cantos,* which were, in fact, written in the same period. *Fine al tormento* also includes David Rattray's brilliant and controversial essay, "Weekend with Ezra Pound" (1957), and a helpful biographical index. Perhaps this is the first time that what is surely a 20th-century American classic has been first published abroad in its full text. But then there are *Tropic of Cancer* and *Lolita!*

One would think that Ezra Pound's *ABC of Economics* (1934) is a rightly forgotten pamphlet. In Italy, however, there are not one but two concurrent editions of this minor work from Pound's Rapallo years: *L'ABC dell'economia e altri scritti* (Milan: Bollati Boringhieri), which has a preface by Mary de Rachewiltz, an introduction by an economist, Giorgio Lunghini, and a note by the translator, Andrea Colombo; and *ABC dell'economia: lavorare meno lavorare tutti,* ed. Giusee Leuzzi (Florence: Shakespeare and Company). The first translation is more accurate and includes some other writings and broadcasts; the second is technically pirated and omits chapter numbers, but it includes an impassioned biography of Pound by the editor. The publication of two editions of Pound's *ABC* is probably explained by the recent Italian depression, since it was originally written during the American depression of the '30s. Whether it will be of any help to the Italian economy remains to be seen.

Pound's reading of Dante is addressed by Massimo Bacigalupo in his " 'Una bella arrampicata': Pound legge Dante" (*SGym* 46 [1993]: 789–802), the title being a translation of the phrase "and some climbing" (Canto 116), Pound's vernacular comment on Dante's long climb to heaven. Bacigalupo provides an illuminating general perspective on Pound's and Eliot's concern with Dante and some telling close readings of singular passages, especially the one mentioned above. He also recounts an interesting episode involving Pound and Robert Lowell, throwing light on the continuing interest in Dante of major American poets. Bacigalupo also offers an account of the 1993 international conference, which took place in Rapallo, in a witty article, "Pound oggi" (*Verri* iii–iv: 80–95), which amounts to an informative survey of current developments in Pound criticism and makes Pound studies look like fun. In another short piece, "L'onda di Excideuil" (*Poesia* 75: 64–65), Bacigalupo follows Pound's footsteps in Provence, commenting on *A Walking Tour in Southern France* (1992). Bacigalupo agrees with Donald Davie in seeing Pound's poetry as topographical. A friendly overview by a scholar-poet is Tomaso Kemeny's "Ezra Pound: il *formato locho*" in *Scritti in ricordo di Silvano Gerevini*, ed. Tomaso Kemeny and Lia Guerra (Florence: La Nuova Italia). Kemeny remembers a reading by Pound at the University of Milan in 1960. The poet was greeted ironically by students with the Roman salute, until he began reading "With Usura . . . " and the students became sadder and wiser men. The role of Pound as critic and adviser of literary magazines is brilliantly discussed by Gabriella Barfoot in her "Pound e la sua idea di rivista letteraria" (*Il lettore di Provincia* 89: 31–36). Barfoot underlines Pound's authority (Ezthority), his critical and creative intelligence, his superiority over the banality of literary society. Pound's talent to appreciate little-known poets made him translate Saturno Montanari. His translations have been presented by Mario Giosa in "Cinque versioni di Saturno Montanari" (*Testo a Fronte* 10: 6–15). The only contribution dedicated to T. S. Eliot comes from Laura Giovanelli, who tries to locate references to Heraclitus in *Four Quartets*. In her "La presenza di Eraclito nei *Four Quartets* di T. S. Eliot" (*Il Confronto Letterario* 20 [1993]: 185–99) Giovanelli shows that these references do not become the basis for a cosmogony, but they

supply an essential and determinative ontological structure, over which
Eliot is able to build interpretations of the world that combine elements
of Greek and Christian philosophical tradition.

As I predicted in *ALS 1992* (pp. 342–43), the indefatigable Bacigalupo
is back this year with a Wallace Stevens book, and an excellent one at
that. *Harmonium: poesie 1915–55* (Turin: Einaudi), which he edited and
translated, is, with its 700 pages, the largest selection of Stevens poems to
have appeared outside the United States. Bacigalupo has used the title
Harmonium for the whole, taking his cue from Stevens, who wanted to
call his collected poems *The Whole of Harmonium.* It includes nearly all
of the major poems and sequences and is particularly interesting because
it offers new translations of several poems included in Renato Poggioli's
Mattino domenicale e altre poesie, which the same publisher, Einaudi,
brought out in 1954 and which gave great pleasure to Stevens, as it was his
first book in another language. Bacigalupo's volume, appropriately illustrated with Pennsylvania Dutch art, comes just 40 years after that
pioneer work, and pays homage to Poggioli by reprinting his version of
"Peter Quince at the Clavier." But Bacigalupo has retranslated, among
other poems, "Sunday Morning" and "The Man with the Blue Guitar,"
and he has explained some of his rationale in "La musica dell'uomo con
la chitarra blu" (*Poesia* 77: 10–12). From a scholarly point of view,
Harmonium is of great interest because of its introduction and survey of
criticism and because of the ample notes. Bacigalupo's interpretations,
given the obscurity of some of the texts, are refreshingly sane, and on the
whole he offers a largely sympathetic account of the Hartford genius.
The book has been widely reviewed, though there have been some
grumblings about Stevens's obscurity.

In his perceptive essay "James Merrill: A Postmodern Poet? Yes & No
(With a New poem by James Merrill)" (*RSAJ* 4 [1993]: 31–56) Andrea
Mariani analyzes the space/time paradigm in Merrill's trilogy *The Changing Light at Sandover.* He uses this paradigm to show the poet's progress
toward a critical awareness and acceptance of his position within American postmodernism. Mariani then presents and comments on an unpublished Merrill poem, "Volcanic Holiday." Francesco Rognoni publishes an informative and thorough essay on John Ashbery, "Distanza e
Circondamento. Un'introduzione all'opera di John Ashbery" (*Il Confronto Letterario* 20 [1993]: 395–412), which covers his life, comments on
his work, and offers an extensive bibliography. Franco Marenco interviews Ashbery and comments on some passages of "Self-Portrait in a

Convex Mirror" in "La grande insalata. John Ashbery risponde a Franco Marenco" (*L'Indice* 9: 17–19).

In "Mamet and Money: *American Buffalo*" (*LAmer* 50 [1993]: 105–13) Annalisa Goldoni brilliantly points out how money, American identity, and the imagination are connected from the start in David Mamet's *American Buffalo*. Things change through exchange; language too is a means of exchange in the back-and-forth of communication. Irony alone will reverse any message, as Mamet keeps showing us.

University of Pisa

iv Japanese Contributions: Hiroko Sato

Although several interesting papers were published this year, on the whole the fruit of Japanese scholarship in American literature has been disappointing. More than 20 books on the subject were published, but except for one volume on poetry and one each on feminist science fiction and present-day American literature, none seems to be truly outstanding.

Discussions on the canon flourish in Japan. In September the American Studies Foundation sponsored a seminar on pedagogic strategies, and one topic taken up was how to revise approaches to teaching American writers. Discussions reflected the confusion that Japanese university teachers have been facing while the canon in the United States is being revised on the bases of gender, class, and ethnicity. Although the idea of multiculturalism has been accepted by younger scholars, the older generation still resists it, insisting on the value of an aesthetics of absolutes. Two leading scholars of the older group wrote articles for *Eigo Seinen* on this question. Toshio Watanabe's "Revising the Canon of American Literature: Its Aftermath" (139: 494–96, 506) introduces the ideas expressed in such journals as *American Literary History, Partisan Review,* and *American Literature* concerning canon revision following publication of *The Heath Anthology of American Literature* and the awarding of a Nobel Prize to Toni Morrison. In 1991 Watanabe also wrote an article titled "Revising the Revision of the American Canon" (*EigoS*). In it, he warned about the danger of bringing politics into literary criticism. However, his more recent conclusion is ambivalent. He admits to the need for revising the canon, considering upheavals in American society, and, with reservations, he admits the legitimacy of work done by such scholars as Paul Lauter; yet he is still concerned about the "literary value" of specific texts. Quoting Lauter's article, "Revising the *Heath Anthology of American Literature*" (*AL* 65 [1993]: 327–30), Watanabe says that he will wait to see the results of that revision before commenting further.

Taro Shimada has written a short article on the publication of the first volume of *The Cambridge History of American Literature,* ed. Sacvan Bercovitch, "Some Thoughts on the Literary History of the United States: On the Publication of *The Cambridge History of American Litera-ture*" (*EigoS* 140: 238–39). Shimada compares it with such earlier works as *The Cambridge History of American Literature* (ed. William Peterfield Trent et al.), *The Literary History of the United States* (ed. Robert Spiller et al.), and the *Columbia Literary History of the United States* (ed. Emory Elliott et al.), and he points out the lack of any unifying ideas in more recent history—a lack also apparent in *CLHUS.* However, Shimada notices a difference between the Cambridge and Columbia histories. While *CLHUS* was compiled on the basis of multiculturalism and tried to give well-balanced information, which resulted in an impression of fragmentation, the new Cambridge is more subjective and more biased— hence, more interesting to scholars. These discussions of canon and pedagogy will continue for some time, a fair indication of the current scholarly atmosphere.

Before reviewing this year's other achievements, I note that articles surveyed here are restricted to those in the major Japanese periodicals *EigoS, SALit, SELit,* and *American Review.* Unless otherwise indicated, all books have been published in Tokyo.

a. 19th-Century Prose Two articles on Nathaniel Hawthorne ap-peared, both dealing with the periphery of his literary life. Fumio Ano in "Hawthorne and *Narrative of the Expedition of an American Squadron to the China Seas and Japan*" (*EigoS* 140: 464–66) points out that in 1854 Commodore Matthew Perry visited Hawthorne in Liverpool, hoping to persuade him to do the hackwork of writing a book about his expedition to the Orient. After being turned down by Hawthorne, this work finally was done by Francis L. Hawks, an Episcopalian minister in New York. Though a travelogue, which requires an objective point of view and realistic description, seems not to be suited to Hawthorne's literary talent, Ano concludes that if the novelist had accepted the job he might have been saved from the dearth of literary materials from which he suffered in his later years. Since Hawthorne was very interested in the

Orient, he might have found some materials for his work in Perry's narrative. "Fame and Guilt: Hawthorne's Pilgrimage to Uttoxeter" by Takaaki Niwa (*SALit* 31: 41–56) attempts to find the significance of Hawthorne's visit to a city where Samuel Johnson allegedly went to expiate a sin of disloyalty he had committed as a young man. Niwa emphasizes that Hawthorne wrote a biography of the man of letters in 1842 and that Hawthorne himself was disloyal to his benevolent uncle, Robert Manning, his father surrogate, who died the same year, because Hawthorne at that time was striving for literary fame. Hawthorne's visit, therefore, might be interpreted as his secret penance.

Reiko Maeda's Moby-Dick: *Its Hellenism and Christian Doctrine* (Osaka: Osaka Kyoiku Shuppan) should be mentioned. Maeda attempts to reveal the book's obscure meaning. To do so, she uses her rich knowledge of the Bible and mythology, and through minute textual and linguistic analysis, she tries to prove that *Moby-Dick*'s main theme is Paradise Regained. Though a unique look at Melville's novel, and partly convincing when it sticks to its subject, Maeda's work lacks perspective by failing to place *Moby-Dick* among Melville's other works; this shortcoming undermines some points she tries to make.

Takayuki Tatsumi's "The Bad Woman in the Attic: Reading the Autobiography of a Black Slave Woman—Harriet Ann Jacobs" (*EigoS* 139: 540–43, 598–600) is one of this year's most stimulating articles. Jacobs's slave narrative, *Incidents in the Life of a Slave Girl*, was published in 1861 with the editorial help of Lydia Maria Child. Tatsumi emphasizes that Jacobs decided from the start that her readership was to be white middle-class women, which led her to use the technique of the sensational novel, popular among white women of the time. Her intention was not a simplistic desire to form a sisterhood with white women; on the contrary, she was trying to prove she possessed a cultural asset of white people, much as they had possessed her physical body as a slave. Tatsumi points out two things that need careful examination: one is the reason why Jacobs gave birth to a white man's child; the other is Jacobs's relationship with Harriet Beecher Stowe. When Stowe was planning to visit England in 1853, Jacobs offered that her daughter, Louisa, should join her as a companion. Jacobs's intention was that Stowe would be attracted by Louisa, a charming mulatto, and eventually would be interested enough in Jacobs herself to help her in writing her autobiography. Though this strategy failed, it clearly shows Jacobs's intention of exploiting white women's means of expression. Moreover, Tatsumi contends,

Louisa, a mixed-blood child, was conceived not as a love child but a product of a black woman's politics, as a symbol of the period's black nationalism, which asserted that assimilation and racial identity were not contradictory. Tatsumi concludes that Jacobs's autobiography, in trying to assimilate politics and literature, became a miscegenation of discourses. This is the first solid article written in Japan on Jacobs, a writer to whom future attention should be paid.

In *Mark Twain: The Fountainhead of American Literature* (Shin-nihon Shuppan) Hideo Ikegami, using hitherto unnoticed materials, tries to place Twain in the tradition of such "pamphleteers" as Benjamin Franklin and Thomas Paine. Ikegami also says that Twain is a symbol of the American folk spirit, and he asserts that Twain believed it his mission to keenly observe the problems that arose from the conflict between the governing and the governed in American society. He contends that Twain was dedicated to the ideas of the Declaration of Independence and the Emancipation Proclamation.

Two articles on Frank Norris, both using a trendy method of cultural study, are led off by Yoko Tanji's stimulating "Darwinism as an Intertext: Lombroso and Frank Norris" (*EigoS* 139: 482–86). Although Stephen Crane's *Maggie* is generally recognized as the first American novel written under the influence of French naturalism, Tanji insists that the direct descendant of Zola in the United States is Frank Norris and his novel *McTeague*. Zola wrote *The Beast* under the strong influence of Cesare Lombroso's idea of biological determinism. Throughout the second half of the 19th century biology versus environment in determining evil and the criminal nature of human beings was a crucial issue. Although toward the end of the century environment came to seem dominant, it is natural that Norris, an advocate of Zola, was highly interested in Lombroso's notion that human beings cannot wholly discard animalism through evolution. Through his analysis of the characters in *McTeague*, Tanji convincingly indicates how Norris demonstrated his belief in this idea. Though Norris treats this animalism negatively, Tanji points out a completely different treatment by Kate Chopin: the animal in Edna Pontellier in *The Awakening* is closely connected with her emancipation as a woman.

Masashi Orishima's "Invisible San Francisco: City Description in Frank Norris" (*American Review* 28: 21–34) attempts to see how naturalist writers such as Norris, Dreiser, and Crane tried to cope with the expanding cityscape of their time. They invented a classificatory descriptive system, based on the division of cities according to wealth, class, ethnicity, occupation, social status, and business activity. Orishima says that Norris's description of Polk Street in *McTeague* is the best example of this system. However, the complex development and expansion of cities seem to be beyond the system's grasp, and Norris finally had to admit to the misty vagueness of San Francisco.

Masatoshi Miyashita's "The 'Counterfeit' Aspect of 19th-Century American Society" (*EigoS* 139: 586–90), which tells about the lives and deeds of Stephen Burroughs and Jim the Penman, supplies interesting background for such writers as Emerson, Bronson Alcott, Louisa May Alcott, Melville, and Emily Dickinson, all of whom showed an interest in "money," whether solid gold or counterfeit.

b. 19th-Century Poetry   Hiroyuki Koguchi's " 'Existence with a Wall': Emily Dickinson's Prison Imagery" (*SELit* English number: 65–80) is a solid work, based on textual analysis of the prison images in Dickinson's poems. Koguchi thinks that Dickinson "uses a prison as the dark center of her poetic world, revealing her deep and far-reaching understanding of the human mind and the universe." Though Dickinson's own "self-imprisonment" might be considered tragic, Koguchi indicates that in some of her poems the poet transcends her prison's walls and is "liberated into the freedom of eternity." When Dickinson reaches this stage, her poems present a vision similar to Walt Whitman's. Hitoshi Noda's " 'Called Back': A View of Dickinson's Last Years" (*EigoS* 140: 124–26) tries to understand Dickinson's attitude toward death in her final years. Concentrating on her letters to the Norcross sisters, Noda doubts that Dickinson died with a firm Christian belief: instead, Noda believes, she must have died with an agnostic attitude toward life after death. Shinji Watanabe's book-length study *I Hear Singing Voices from the Wilderness: The Essential Quality and Its Transformation of American Poetics* (Chobun-sha) is an appropriate introduction to eight major American poets—Poe, Whitman, Dickinson, Stevens, Pound, Eliot, Ammons, and Ashbery. Although no distinct ideas connect these writers, Watanabe's clear reading reveals the poetic world of each one.

c. 20th-Century Prose   No internationally recognized writers (except Faulkner in one book) were discussed in either books or major periodicals this year. Suguru Hanaoka's *Collected Stories of William Faulkner: On Its Spacial Structure* (Kyoto: Yamaguchi-shoten) examines the collection that Faulkner published in 1950. Using Faulkner's letters to the publisher written while he arranged these stories, Hanaoka shows how the author was sensitive about their positioning, as if putting together a unified novel. Nobuaki Namiki's "Reading Welty's 'Curtain of Green'" (*EigoS* 139: 552–54) attempts to show what a significant role "curtains" play in Eudora Welty's story. Namiki presents various meanings of curtains, but little else that is new to the interpretation of this well-known story. Ralph Ellison's death is mourned in "Departure for Another Territory. On Hearing of the Death of Ralph Ellison" by Takeo Hamamoto (*EigoS* 140: 240–41). Hamamoto aptly reviews Ellison's biography and his only novel, so that this obituary serves as a good introduction to Ellison's achievement and encourages us to look forward to the publication of his posthumous novel, which reportedly was almost completed at his death.

Another novelist remembered primarily for one published book is Henry Roth. After *Call It Sleep* in 1934, Roth ceased publishing and dropped from sight; whether he was alive or not was unknown to many readers until 1958. Hajime Sasaki's "Henry Roth: Awakening after 60 Years" (*EigoS* 140: 234–37) is mostly on Roth's novel *Mercy of a Rude Stream,* published in January 1994. Sasaki's informative survey of Roth's life, his relationship with the Communist Party, his marriages, and more newly excite our interest in this once-forgotten writer.

Katsuaki Watanabe's "Wealth and Gift Exchange in Saul Bellow's *Humboldt's Gift*" (*SALit* 31: 57–73) points out that Bellow's novels are full of references to the exchange of gifts and wealth. Watanabe says that "the symbolic exchange of a 'gift' between the protagonist and his partner plays a crucial role in consolidating their relationship." The ways in which these worldly exchanges come to represent mythical exchanges of life and death in Bellow's novels are convincingly traced.

Minoru Suda's *Ideology and Literature of African American People* (Osaka: Osaka Kyoiku Tosho) is a collection of scholarly essays on literature by African Americans written during the past 20 years. The book is divided into five parts. In the first part, "Slavery and Studies of American Literature," the author insists that it is impossible to study American literature while ignoring the questions of slavery and African Americans. In the second section, assimilation and nationalism, two ideas cherished among black intellectuals of the 19th century, are analyzed from a historical perspective. How white writers such as William Faulkner and William Styron depicted black characters in their novels is examined in the next section. The book's center seems to be its fourth part, in which some works of African American women writers are explicated. Novels by Toni Morrison, Alice Walker, and Sherley Anne Williams are analyzed through a critique of the Japanese translation of *The Color Purple,* a bibliography of Walker studies in Japan, and the first serious study of *Dessa Rose,* among other means. Although sometimes confusing and fragmentary, this work is based on a firm belief in the importance of African American culture in the United States; it greatly helps in furthering Japanese studies of African American literature. Toni Morrison's notable honor is celebrated in Atsuko Furomoto's "Toni Morrison Awarded a Nobel Prize" (*EigoS* 139: 492–93). When the award was announced, a rumor suggested that gender and ethnicity influenced the decision. Through an examination of her literary achievement, this article asserts Morrison's right to the prize. Maxine Hong Kingston's literary development from *The Woman Warrior* to *China Men* is studied in Toshi Ishihara's "A 'Moving' History-Story in Maxine Hong Kingston's *China Men:* In the Steps of Williams and Stein" (*SALit* 31: 23–40). Ishihara asserts that, while *The Woman Warrior* is a novel of an individual's transplanting, *China Men* expands the theme to a universal scale—hence, its similarities to ideas expressed by William Carlos Williams (*In the American Grain*) and Gertrude Stein (*The Making of Americans*).

The August issue of *Eigo Seinen* (140: 216–28) features Thomas Pynchon's *Gravity's Rainbow.* Six essays view the controversial novel. Kenji Kobayashi's "The Position of *Gravity's Rainbow,*" which points out similarities of this novel to Jorge Luis Borges's works, serves as a kind of introduction to the project. Hideaki Hatayama examines Pynchon's techniques and style in the novel. Takayuki Tatsumi points out the possibility of reading the novel in terms of computer technology, pointing to the emergence of a hypertext in the future. Fumiyo Hayashi's "Grotesque/Carnival in *Gravity's Rainbow*" is an analysis using Bakhtin's ideas. In "Rainbow Stocking" Mari Kotani regards the novel as a precursor of the arrival of the Plastic Age. Hiroshi Narasaki views the novel from various aspects in "Is the Interpretation Game Useless?" On the whole, these essays define Pynchon's work as a symbol of the disruption of the modernist conception of the novel; such literary breakdowns will be inevitable in our technological society.

Yoshiaki Koshikawa's *Beyond America: Contemporary American Literature after Pynchon* (Jiyukokumin-sha) should be attractive to those who would like to know literary events in the United States in the '70s and '80s. As one reviewer aptly said, this book plays much the same role as

Tony Tanner's *City of Words* performed for the literature of the '60s. It is a source of information on contemporary American writers, and it tempts the reader to speculate on the future of the novel. Mari Kotani's *Techno-Gynesis: The Political Unconscious of Feminist Science Fiction* (Keiso-shobo) is another radical book. Divided into "Sexuality," "Alien Nation," and "Gynesis", the book traces the conceptual development of techno-gynesis from Freud to Julia Kristeva. Although incomprehensible in some places for old-school readers like me, this first book by a brilliant young critic invites speculation on the development of science fiction in our age of high technology.

d. 20th-Century Poetry   Tomoyuki Iino's *Modern American Poetry: The Lineage of the Rearguard* (Sairyu-sha) is possibly one of the best books written in Japan on modern American poetry. A sympathetic reading of works by such poets as Randall Jarrell and Karl Shapiro in the first chapter leads into the world of American poets who are regarded and criticized as conservative and who are less well-known in Japan. The charm of their verse is revealed through Iino's analysis. Iino's explications of poems by Robert Pinsky, Frank Bidart, and C. K. Williams invite us to the exciting experience of widening the vista of American poetry.

As this review has shown, no major achievements were recorded in the study of American literature this year. However, Eiichiro Otsu's study of Henry James, which began serialization in *Eigo Seinen* in April, continues into 1995: it promises to be an extensive study of the novelist.

Tokyo Woman's Christian University

v   Scandinavian Contributions: Jan Nordby Gretlund, Elisabeth Herion-Sarafidis, and Hans Skei

To an American, the striking fact about the Scandinavian contributions to American literary scholarship this year, as indeed in most years, would be the emphasis on contemporary prose and poetry. Although canonical writers receive their share of attention, notably a monograph on Emerson the moralist and a collection of essays on T. S. Eliot, the body of this year's work by Danish, Norwegian, and Swedish scholars concerns more recent poets and fiction writers. Examples that might be mentioned are a book-length investigation of Sylvia Plath's *Ariel* poems, John Ashbery as the subject of several contributions, and work done on William Carlos

Williams and Robert Bly. Some of the main items when it comes to fiction are a study on Eudora Welty, a book of essays devoted to the work of African American women writers, and a longer work on the Jewish breakthrough in American literature.

a. 19th-Century Prose   In the effort to locate the set of axioms from which not only his aesthetic ideas but his political reasoning derive, Anders Hallengren focuses on Emerson the moralist in *The Code of Concord: Emerson's Search for Universal Laws* (Almqvist and Wiksell), pursuing the concordance of "Ethics and Aesthetics, Poetics and Politics" in Emerson's work. Hallengren finds such a basic structure in the emergence of Emerson's ideas of universal laws that repeat themselves on all levels of reality.

Divided into four main parts, *The Code of Concord* begins with a general introduction in which the "crisis in Emerson's life is seen as representing and foreshadowing the deeper existential crisis of modern man." Part 2 deals with the early development of Emerson's philosophy of nature and the emergence of his moral philosophy, part 3 with politics, and part 4 with aesthetics and poetics. Hallengren contends that Emerson's philosophy might be considered both traditional and antitraditional; while in many respects it appears to be a last attempt "to save a traditional worldview with Christian as well as Classicist tenets," at the same time it belongs in the forefront of the liberalism of the day. As Emerson realized the innate unity between spiritual matters and material facts—organic forms recurring in inorganic forms—he saw similar patterns repeated throughout the universe, "from the microcosm to the macrocosm." These parallels were connected with an idea of laws governing the dynamic process of reality, a collapse of traditional static hierarchies. The essential paradigm of Concord philosophy was the perception of laws that repeat themselves on all levels of reality, including social life and the human mind. The criticism directed at Emerson's failure to present a complete and consistent system is wrongheaded because, actually, the "haze is a quality of the ever-changing reality Emerson saw, the flux of being." Instead of seeking consistency where there is none, then, Hallenberg has "approached some central texts with the questions 'why?' and 'how?' and 'in what sense?'" The result is a learned and, at times, engaging study, clearly the work of longtime involvement with Emerson's philosophical universe. The organization of *The Code of Concord*, however, is marred by countless repetitions, and it seems really to be contradicted by its content. The lack of connections between parts suggests their being essays conceived at different times.

A contemporary of Emerson's who often appears in Scandinavian scholarship is Edgar Allan Poe. This year's contribution is Finn Barlby's "Den braendende talen" [burning speech] (*Plys* 8: 100–108), a discussion of Poe's ideas of horror and terror. On the basis of "The Spectacles," "The Sphinx," and "The Black Cat," Barlby points out that the truly frightening elements of Poe's tales are that they actualize and actually deal with the tale, as tale told, and with the tale-teller and his situation. To be able to see the world behind delusions, disturbing intrusions, and distortions, the storyteller's vision always needs adjustment; and he is willing to do anything to eliminate that which troubles and threatens his vision.

Initially, Erik Kielland-Lund's " 'I Have Heard of Krakens': Melville's Shipwreck in *Pierre*" (*Excursions in Fiction*, pp. 131–41) presents the biographical background material for this novel, discussing its commercial and critical failure. The essay then speculates on the underlying reasons for the artistic failure which *Pierre* represents. Kielland-Lund convincingly outlines the inherent discrepancies between Melville's desire to write a novel for a large audience and his urge to discuss philosophical and existential matters. The attempted parody of genre and not least the use of satire are alien to the rest of the work and to the romantic sensibility of Pierre; ultimately, the book fails in bringing together its many disparate and diverse attitudes and approaches. Kielland-Lund amply demonstrates the impossibility of achieving coherence in *Pierre,* connecting it to Melville's situation, for example, his relation to the market and the literary institution at a certain point in his career. The essay shows that Melville survived this shipwreck and went on to write important short stories and novels over the remainder of his literary career.

Domhnall Mitchell in "Narrative Failure and the Fall in Henry James's 'The Turn of the Screw' " (*AmerSS* 26: 113–25) presents non-apparitionist and apparationist readings of this well-known text, before moving on to her own reading, one which finds competing narratives that seem to converge in the person of the governess. The ambiguity of the novel is not, Mitchell argues, simply a result of its narrating consciousness, but it is rather "conditioned by the premise of post-lapsarian experience." Hence, the essay sets out to investigate the consequences of this premise for the narrative, especially when it comes to the governess and her role as an isolated, inner narrator. Mitchell argues that in "The Turn of the Screw," meaning is constantly deferred, accidental, provisional. Concerned with another aspect of bondage, in "Of Slaves and Masters:" Constructed Identities in Mark Twain's *Pudd'nhead Wilson" (Excursions in Fiction,* pp. 174–90), Vidar Pedersen outlines the main ideas about power structures and discursive formation in Michel Foucault's "The Discourse on Language" before applying Foucault's understanding to Twain's last major novel. Pedersen contends that a "Foucaldian system of power relations" is at work in Twain's novel, that the institution of slavery and its claim of the inferiority of blacks is treated ironically, even sarcastically. The institution of slavery, however, survives all challenges and preserves the status quo.

In "Courageous Souls: Kate Chopin's Women Artists" (*AmerSS* 26: 96–112) it is K. J. Weatherford's contention that Chopin created only one "triumphant woman artist" in her fiction, and that was in her first published story, "Wiser than God." Weatherford considers Paula von Stolz to be Chopin's alter ego, and her fate implies that a woman may become a successful artist without giving up "everything else"—whereas in *The Awakening* Chopin was, supposedly, ambivalent about "the roles available to women artists." It is, however, difficult to see the ambivalence, and the references to Chopin's biography do not really help. Finding it to be an inconsistency of portrayal in the novel that Mademoiselle Reisz is given a grotesque quality, Weatherford is bothered by the fact that the self-absorbed woman is only worthy of imitation in her role as masterful pianist. But should we expect artists to be worth imitating in areas other than the artistic?

Orm Øverland is an expert on Norwegian-American literature or the literature of "Vesterheimen" (The Home in the West) in the period when there was a vital and flowering literature in the Norwegian language in the United States. In "Dorthea Dahl: Fiction from the Margin of the Margin" (*Excursions in Fiction,* pp. 157–72) Øverland presents the Idaho-based woman writer whose desire it was to become a missionary, but who worked as a bookkeeper because of failing health and lived alone after the death of her parents. While she, in fact, lived very much outside the Norwegian cultural and literary life, she nevertheless wrote a considerable number of stories and novels, won prizes, had works serialized, and even moved from writing in Norwegian to English without much hesitation. Outlining and interpreting the larger part of her work in his essay, Øverland finds Dahl to be a minor writer worthy of attention.

b. 20th-Century Poetry The origin of *T. S. Eliot at the Turn of the Century*, a collection of essays by a dozen Eliot scholars from six countries, was a 1993 colloquium held at Lund University. The participants sought, on the one hand, to probe into the contemporary state of Eliot studies—at a time when it begins to seem as if his status as a major poet is far from generally accepted—and, on the other, attempted to investigate possible future research approaches. The contributions in this volume thus cover a wide variety of topics, including analyses of motifs and themes of fundamental importance, in-depth explorations of Eliot's thought, a discussion of his standing as a literary critic, studies into various aspects of his plays, as well as a close reading of an often neglected group of poems. Stephen Medcalf's interestingly argued "T. S. Eliot's Punk Poems: Sweeney and the Quatrains" (pp. 133–45) deals with the quatrain poems that fit awkwardly into the corpus of his verse because they are written in strict meter, and, unlike most of his other poems, carry "their structure on the outside not only in metre but in image and story." Outlining Eliot's concern with the city as poetic material in "Eliot's Cities" (pp. 59–76), Bernard Bergonzi takes as his point of departure the first lines of "The Love Song of J. Alfred Prufrock," and moves on to a thematic inventory of cities of the mind as well as physical ones in the poet's production. The project in "Making a Space in Time: T. S. Eliot, Evolution, and *Four Quartets*" (pp. 77–90) is a very different one; it is Lois A. Cuddy's argument that Eliot, documenting the history of human thought and action through his poetry, translated the principles of evolution in different ways until he finally "summarized—and unified—concepts of scientific, cultural, personal, and cosmic evolution in *Four Quartets.*"

Fredrik Chr. Brøgger's "Design and Disconnection In W. C. Williams' *Spring and All*" (*Excursions in Fiction*, pp. 46–67) contrasts Williams's book with Eliot's *The Waste Land*, published the year before *Spring and All*. The contrasts are worked out to show that they comprise verse as well as poetics, and Brøgger goes on to investigate conflicting formal techniques and the two main directions in which Williams's insistence on imaginative separateness takes him: "A few poems serve as embodiments of an autonomous artistic unity. On the other hand, Williams' volume also features some poems that are predominantly expressions of fragmentation." The opposition between what Brøgger terms "design and disconnection" is used to analyze a few poems in some detail and to show how ambiguous and open-ended *Spring and All* finally is. The volume, writes Brøgger, creates an atmosphere of excitement and merriment, something which links it very much to sentiments of the decade during which it appeared—the '20s.

Aiming to challenge the generally accepted view that Sylvia Plath's early poetry has little value except as a foreshadowing of the later great work, Nancy D. Hargrove's *The Journey Toward* Ariel: *Sylvia Plath's Poems of 1956–1959* (Lund) establishes a more accurate chronology for the composition dates of Plath's *Ariel* poems and corrects errors made by Ted Hughes in *The Collected Poems* (1981), whose chronological order has not been seriously challenged before. Contending that since a "valid assessment of Plath's development as a poet and of the worth of her work as a whole is partially dependent on accurate chronology," Hargrove at some length traces the course of Plath's poetic development from 1956 through 1959 and seeks to demonstrate the complexity, variety, and experimentation evident in content and craft of the poems from this period. *The Journey Toward Ariel* sheds light on the circumstances of the creation of these poems, offers close readings—in some cases new readings—of individual poems, and, finally, corroborates the general view that the early poems and the ones of 1960–63 should not be viewed as two separate and distinctly different types of poetry.

John Ashbery, who seems to be at the very heart of contemporary American poetry, has been interviewed by Bo Green Jensen: "Hokus pokus eller mindre er værre" [Hocus Pocus or Less is Worse] (*Kritik* 112: 40–45). While poetry is often humorous and even comic to Ashbery, it is never privately confessional. He acknowledges the influence of W. H. Auden, Wallace Stevens, and Vaslav Nijinsky (the diary), but points out that self-discipline and a sense of method may also be learned from old movies, modern painting, or even by writing criticism. Ashbery talks of the importance of preserving the possibilities embedded in the uncertainty of our lives. It is a mistake to write only about things the poet knows well, he says, and he compares creative writing programs to the sausage-making industry—the products all look the same. Conceptual poetry is all right as long as the concept is never allowed to dominate. The most important creative writing program in Denmark is the one organized by Poul Borum, a poet who throughout the years has trans-

lated a number of American poets into Danish. In "Po/etik til halvfem-
serne" [Po/ethics for the 90s] (*Kritik* 107: 9–12) Borum considers Ashbery's poetry to be the greatest challenge and best alternative to the
contemporary poetry of experience. Inspired by several new verse anthologies and the collections of critical essays edited by Vernon Shetley
and Mary Kinzie, Borum's essay focuses on ethical (and, at times, reactionary) demands imposed on new American poets.

Robert Bly is the subject of two issues of the Norwegian magazine
Dyade (nos. 3, 4). While Bly's poems and essays are printed in English,
the other contributions are in Norwegian. An article worth mentioning
from the point of view of literary scholarship is Øyvind T. Gulliksen's
"Robert Blys lyrikk" [The Poetry of Robert Bly], in which Gulliksen
describes three different personal encounters with Bly's poetry and with
the poet himself; he then succinctly describes the particular strength of
his poetry. Bly's friend, the late Norwegian poet Olav H. Hauge, and his
translations of numerous Bly poems are used to provide a detailed portrait of the Minnesota poet. Finally, Gulliksen considers Bly's own readings of his poetry in a discussion of the writer as preacher.

c. 20th-Century Prose   When the publishing house Solum in Oslo
brought out the first Norwegian translation of *Absalom, Absalom!* it devoted a special issue of its journal *Ergo* to William Faulkner (25, iv). The
essays are all in Norwegian. Hans H. Skei provides a survey of the
reception and reputation of Faulkner in Norway, from the first translation (the first ever) of *Soldiers' Pay* in 1932 to the publication of selected
short stories and *As I Lay Dying* in 1992 (see *ALS 1992*, pp. 359–60). Skei's
introduction to a book club edition of *The Sound and the Fury* is reprinted here, as is Ole Pramli's afterword to his own translation of *As I
Lay Dying*. Two articles deal with *Absalom, Absalom!* In Jakob Lothe's
"Foreljingas gåte og romanens univers" [The Riddle of the Narrative and
the Universe of the Novel] Lothe outlines the narrative intricacies of this
difficult novel, insisting that everything in it cannot be understood completely, but that Lothe's reading is framed by a modernistic understanding of the complexities of the world and, hence, of the representations of
this world in literature. Sandra Lee Kleppe's "Om å brenne ned hus og å
skrive romaner" [On the Burning of Houses and the Writing of Novels]
also works with the intriguing difficulties of *Absalom, Absalom!* After an
opening discussion of the enigmatic Knut Hamsun, Lee Kleppe focuses
on the relations between social class and environment. While accepting

and defending the novel's brilliance, she ends her article with a reference to Alice Walker's desire to burn the house of Faulkner—one built by slaves. The final essay is Espen Holtestaul's discussion of *The Wild Palms* and the significance of the structural problems presented by this contrapuntal novel.

The opening of Michael Funch's "The Intentional Phallacy: The Art and Life of Ernest Hemingway—A Biographical Angle?" (*AmerSS* 26: 65–78) seems promising as regards the gender perspective and the interplay between fact and fiction. But deteriorating into ordinary gossip, the essay in the end turns out to be simply another tiresome discussion of Hemingway's supposed latent homosexuality. Unfortunately, the worthwhile discussion of the metafictional qualities of Hemingway's writing (in *A Moveable Feast* and *The Garden of Eden*) is cut short and dwarfed by Funch's focusing on the public image of the man rather than on his fiction. For Funch, "the question is whether there is a discrepancy between the man and the artist." But is this a question that we have to ask about Hemingway? Does anybody still believe that "he wanted his art to be as hard as the toughest nail"? Could it still be a surprise to us that Hemingway was a sensitive and emotional man?

Using a simple and straightforward definition of "feminist," in which the political is a central element, Helge Normann Nilsen presents a reading of one of Katherine Anne Porter's stories which is an interesting alternative to previous interpretations, although reductive in its own ways. In "Laura against Sexism: A Feminist Reading of Katherine Anne Porter's 'Flowering Judas'" (*Excursions in Fiction*, pp. 145–56) Nilsen insists that all previous readings of this story have been either misleading or simply wrong because they have failed to understand the text's central character, Laura, and the motives behind her behavior.

Jan Nordby Gretlund's *Eudora Welty's Aesthetics of Place* (Odense) has as its thesis that Welty's works represent the collective Southern experience from the depression until today. Welty's literary achievement is further understood as demonstrating a cultural continuity of Agrarian ideas from their origin in the rural South to their importance in the contemporary South. The South, or, more precisely, Welty's native Mississippi, or even specified local settings, all represent the many "places" that are such vital ingredients in her fictional creations. The book presents close readings of Welty's writings against a background of her own and her native state's history, including most aspects of what today are often called "cultural studies": history, geography, politics, customs, culture, economics. Having stated his purpose and his preferred approach to her fiction, in the four chapters of the first part, "Wedded to Place," Gretlund establishes Welty's career, rooting it firmly in her "sense of place." Reading early short stories and a diversity of facts behind them, he demonstrates both the importance early in her career of family unity and the fact that some of the stories ("Death of a Traveling Salesman," "The Whistle") come close to preaching Agrarian ideas. An opposition between transient people (artists, musicians, circus people, performers) and those who are "wedded to place" may be detected, although not much is made of it here, since a new chapter takes us to the city. The short stories "Flowers for Marjorie" and "Music from Spain" are read against Welty's experiences of New York and San Francisco, respectively, and are used to make a case for Welty's strong Agrarianism. The first part is rounded off with a wide-sweeping and highly informative chapter on Welty's use of humor, and here most of her work is touched on, more or less preparing the ground for the second part of the study, "Part of Our Own Map." This section is really a mapping of Mississippi through fairly close readings of key works in her career. The relationship of fact and fiction and the investigations of Welty's use of place thus inform Gretlund's readings of the novels *Delta Wedding, Losing Battles,* and *The Optimist's Daughter,* of the short story collection *The Golden Apples,* and of the short story "Where Is the Voice Coming From?" That Gretlund also deals with minor works such as *The Ponder Heart* and *The Robber Bridegroom* as well as numerous short stories discussed in the first part of his work makes it clear that *Eudora Welty's Aesthetics of Place* truly attempts to be all-inclusive.

In an interesting penultimate chapter, surprising, and really at odds with the book's overall design, Gretlund brings in Chekhov to discuss similarities in technique and thematic interest between Welty and the Russian writer. This is the most "literary" chapter, offering perceptive comments on Welty's realism and on her short story art. It is a brave and dangerous chapter to have at this point because it suggests that other texts and other authors could have been brought in and could thus have contributed to an intertextual study of Welty's work—and not a study of *influences* in the traditional sense. Gretlund's insistence on Agrarianism makes various of those texts more interesting than the literary ones.

An important contribution to the rapidly growing field of Welty scholarship, *Eudora Welty's Aesthetics of Place* shows that Welty is a writer wedded to place, her place, a writer who makes use of place in her fiction.

Perhaps she does not have an aesthetics of place, or even a theory of aesthetics in general; she is, in any case, a much better writer than thinker. An appendix to the book with two highly interesting interviews with Welty, conducted 15 years apart, adds to the value of Gretlund's work.

Two other Southern writers are the focus of Karl-Heinz Westarp's "Shades of Evil in the Fictions of Flannery O'Connor and Walker Percy" (*P. E. O.* Special Issue [June]: 373–81), an analysis of O'Connor's "The Lame Shall Enter First" and Percy's *Lancelot* that demonstrates how they describe the presence of grace by dramatizing its absence. The mystery of evil, writes Westarp, is destructively present in the work of both writers, where it functions as a means to bring the characters to start their lives anew. Percy is a presence also in "Citified Carolina: Josephine Humphreys's Fiction" (*OASIS* 10: 1–16), in which Jan Nordby Gretlund sees Humphreys as the inheritor of Walker Percy's role as Southern city novelist. Gretlund considers the public, the private, the existential, and the ethical dimensions of Humphreys's cityscape; contrastingly, landscape in her fiction is seen as "a fusion of human and natural order, and the result may offer a window on the whole."

Brita Lindberg-Seyersted's fine and slender volume, *Black and Female: Essays on Writings by Black Women in the Diaspora* (Scandinavian), is a collection of seven essays with at least one central concern in common: "What it means to live and work as a black woman in the New World." Although the writers discussed may be grouped together because they are female and "Diaspora writers with a common ur-home," Lindberg-Seyersted is very much aware of the heterogeneity of their literary texts— produced in different cultures and in different periods. While the authors thus cannot be said to form a unified group, the collection as a whole demonstrates that much is gained by seeing them from a common perspective or by emphasizing their similarities. Nonetheless, the seven essays may also be read as individual studies.

In the first essay, Lindberg-Seyersted offers an analysis of the significance of skin color as social, ethical, and aesthetic sign in writings by black American women. This is a more general study than the second essay, which examines "New World Black Heritage in Paule Marshall's *The Chosen Place, the Timeless People* and *Praisesong for the Widow*" (see *ALS 1992*, p. 362), whereas the third essay deals with Maya Angelou's experiences on returning to Africa and remaining there for some time. Also, "Who Is Nettie? and What Is She Doing in Alice Walker's *The*

Color Purple" is devoted to the African connection, and the focus on Nettie may well be said to enhance and enrich this novel's meaning. The fifth essay returns to a more general theme: the uses of the universal symbol of the tree in works by contemporary black women writers. (On the sixth essay, the image of Europe in writings by African American Women, see *ALS 1993,* pp. 401–02.) The final essay—"Jamaica Kincaid's Postcolonial Monologues"—is a study of the autobiographical fiction of this self-exiled West Indian. *Black and Female* points up the signifi-cance of the African heritage in the writings of many African American women, demonstrating the importance of this kind of perspective for a better understanding of them and their works.

In his "Inventing and Controlling the Vernacular" (*AmerSS* 26: 24–37) Christen Kold Thomsen shows how African American studies, like American studies, is founded on ideas of the vernacular roots of Ameri-can culture. On the basis of Leo Marx's 1958 discussion of the "vernacular tradition," and with references to Houston Baker, Henry Louis Gates, Jr., and Ralph Ellison, Thomsen points out that "the vernacular may suggest consensus about blackness that on closer examination breaks down in different views." As an example, Thomsen mentions that most black intellectuals have responded to rap music with the lack of enthusi-asm that most white intellectuals show for popular culture.

The Jewish breakthrough in American literature is the subject of Claus Secher's impressive study *Den Moralske Don Juan* [The Moral Don Juan] (Borgen). Inspired by Leslie Fiedler's observations on Jewish-American novels of the early decades of this century, Secher sees his material through the idea of Jewish Don Juan figures. He focuses on the achievement of Singer, Bellow, Malamud, and Philip Roth—but he never makes clear why Mailer, Heller, Doctorow, or Auster do not qual-ify for consideration. A good introduction to the religion, history, and culture rooted in the lives of East European Ashkenazi Jews, the main part of the book is a description of how Jewish literature after World War II moved from the periphery of the American literary scene to its center in the 1970s. Secher explains this development through the repre-sentative value of the lives of contemporary American Jews, whose exis-tence is divided between a disciplined observation of traditional (Jewish) ethical ways of life and a modern (American) urge to live individualized lives at the aesthetic stage of existence. The powerful desire for some-thing different is accompanied by a pronounced sense of guilt, a situa-tion that has an obvious parallel in early Puritan thinking. As indicated by the study's title, this division is exemplified by a Kierkegaardian clash between inherited morals (and inherited male identity) and modern dreams of (sexual) emancipation. With Philip Rahv, Secher considers this division the classic one between intellect and body. It is also a clash between a minority and the majority in a democracy. All four writers see "fathers" as figures to be rebelled against, but they also see them as men whose values should be upheld. As Secher's study demonstrates, the writers' problems with a life straddling acceptance and rebellion are characteristic of modern man.

Jacques Caron has retrieved and published "De Jack Kerouac à Ti-Jean Kerouac" (Odense), an interview aired from Montreal by Radio Canada in 1967. It has not been available and has remained unknown to most Kerouac scholars. Fernand Seguin, the interviewer, brings to light Kerouac's French-Canadian background through the author's memories of his parents. Kerouac expresses his views on language, his method of composition, his concepts of "spontaneous prose" and of the Beat Generation, which for him was associated with man's religious dimension.

For some 40 years, with curiosity and sensitivity, Claes-Göran Holmberg has introduced American fiction into Sweden. The recent *Crossroads: Möten med den amerikanska litteraturen* [Crossroads: Encounters with Contemporary American Literature] (Nora: Nya Doxa), a collection of interviews, essays, and short reviews, some of which have been published before, bears witness to what surely is a passionate involvement with contemporary American fiction. Generally, Holmberg is in pursuit of writers who have been labeled either too experimental, too academic or, simply, too "immersed in an untranslatable American reality of political intrigue, drugs, violence, and mass culture" to have attracted a wider audience in Sweden. They are writers like Barth, Pynchon, and DeLillo, but also Richard Ford and Tobias Wolff, whose work has been available in translation from the beginning, but who have, nevertheless, failed to secure a larger readership. *Crossroads* also contains essays on such writers as Bharati Mukherjee and Maxine Hong Kingston, as well as less celebrated writers such as Gilbert Sorrentino and Richard Stern. Holmberg's mix is, to be sure, an eclectic one—he deals almost exclusively with writers who have in some way intrigued him—but the result of the personal angle and his great knowledge of American writers and their work is an inspiring and thought-provoking work.

While the best-selling American author in Scandinavia, Stephen King, is not among Holmberg's chosen writers, he is the focus of Hans

Henrik Møller's "Snoskebolle" [Bungling Bumpkin] (*Plys* 8: 176–87). Møller attempts an evaluation of King's *Misery* as postmodern fiction, arguing that the thriller is the natural literary reaction to the chaos and fragmentation of our contemporary world. King meets our need for suspense, and he does it with a refreshing twist toward metafiction and self-reflection.

d. Drama   *Strindberg in Hollywood,* a play (1993) by Drury Pifer, was successfully staged in Odense in Lise Christiansen's translation. The play addresses the question whether the integrity and idealism of Strindberg are alive anywhere today. Was Strindberg insane, or is Hollywood? Or have we managed to reduce our existence to a level where people accept that their lives are staged by others? In Peter Simonsen's interview with Drury Pifer for *The Workshop* ([Odense] 13, ii: 42–51), the playwright argues that in Hollywood (as in American publishing and television) artists are forced to aim at a broad cross-section of people, which "means it won't be the best." Pifer complains that American culture disregards the power of language. Constant change in the United States causes Americans to become stuck in an eternal present. Instead of words, they have images to connect with the past. In the new play Pifer has Strindberg attempt to bring the word back to Hollywood and the entire Americanized world.

   In a recent production, *American Psycho* was staged in Copenhagen in Bo Green Jensen's translation. The interest in Bret Easton Ellis's controversial novel is manifest also in a collection of essays edited by Kasper Michaelsen, American Psycho: *Ondskab og livsstil* [Evil and Lifestyle] (Copenhagen: Arte and Dansklaererforeningen). One of the contributions, Rikke Schubart's "Bateman: maske, menneske, morder" [Mask, Human Being, Murderer] (pp. 17–20) considers the novel "an ultrarealistic portrait of the American yuppie-society." Ellis's achievement is his locating "evil," ignored by everybody else in the consumer society, at the heart of a social demise. Finally, sadism becomes the sole way of demonstrating one's painful loss of humanity.

e. Theory and Criticism   Inge Birgitte Siegumfeldt has written two essays on the influence of traditional Jewish thought on modern American literary theory: "On the Judaization of Postmodern Theory" (*P.E.O.* 77: 1–8), and "Bloom, Derrida, and the Kabbalah: the Invocation of Ancestral Voices" (*OL* 49: 307–14). Siegumfeldt's main argument is that contemporary text-centered, nonfigural postmodernist criticism is influenced by traditional rabbinic modes of interpretation and Jewish kabbalistic speculation. The Judaization is obvious in Harold Bloom's criticism, but it is also reflected in Derridean theory.

In a perceptive essay on "Reader-response Criticism as Ideological Criticism: Traditions and Innovations" (*P.E.O.* Special Issue [June]: 335–53) Christen Kold Thomsen argues that after the death of the "Ideal Reader without class or gender," the current critical scene in the United States combines apparent diversity with a rigid determinism, whose mainspring is an ideologically defined reader. The effects, Thomsen suggests, are reflected in Paul Lauter's *Heath Anthology*. But the pressure to force us to read in terms of already held prejudices and sentiments is "nowhere more apparent than in feminist literary criticism." As proof Thomsen details Sandra Gilbert's treatment of Wallace Stevens and Jane Tompkins's attempt to recover Margaret Mitchell for the canon of American literature, readings that are viewed as the ultimate triumph of Stanley Fish's idea of the prejudiced interpretive community. Thomsen argues that it is possible to offer arguments that do not depend on specific ideological commitments. In the same volume Lars Ole Sauerberg's "Canon(s) in Twentieth-Century Criticism" (pp. 288–301) takes its point of departure in Leslie Fiedler's, Houston Baker's, and Paul Lauter's calls for expansion and diversification. Seeking to evaluate the effect of American discussions on the British canon debates, Sauerberg claims that although the literary canon is a "somewhat shaky concept," an understanding of it is both "a premise and an objective of any critical activity."

Odense, Uppsala, Oslo Universities

22 General Reference Works

David J. Nordloh

The Cambridge History of American Literature, Volume I: 1590–1820, ed. Sacvan Bercovitch and Cyrus R. K. Patell, launches a project at least as ambitious as its Cambridge University Press predecessor. The 1917 edition, prepared by William Peterfield Trent and colleagues, required four volumes to tell its story; this new one will eventually fill eight. The expansion will accommodate not only the substantial demands of the 20th century but also the articulation of a more complex critical terrain. The 1917 *CHAL* wore its authority easily; the new edition is more self-aware, defining perhaps but not really definitive. The attitude is appropriate to the general mode of skeptical inquiry which takes nothing as true, everything as contingent. Bercovitch asserts in his introduction to this first volume, for example, that "What distinguishes our *History*... is its variety of adversarial approaches and, more strikingly, the presence throughout of revisionary, nonoppositional ways of relating text and context." So thorough is this mode of thinking that even the crucial words do not mean what they did: "the term 'American' is neither a narrative premise in these volumes nor an objective background. Quite the reverse: it is the complex subject of a series of literary-historical inquiries." Nationality is thus "a rhetorical battleground."

And yet the new *Cambridge History* is after all not so thoroughly revisionist as to be unrecognizable: what is being revised is less the content of American literary history than the interpretation of that content. The vocabulary may be too laden with "subjectivizing" and "problematizing," but the persons, texts, and events are still familiar. The five sections of volume I—"The Literature of Colonization" by Myra Jehlen, "New England Puritan Literature" by Emory Elliott, "British-American Belles Lettres" by David S. Shields, "The American Enlightenment, 1750–1820," by Robert A. Ferguson, and "The Literature of the

Revolutionary and Early National Periods" by Michael T. Gilmore—
cover mostly well-established territory, often with very conventional
judgments. Elliott remarks of Anne Bradstreet, for example, that "What
is clear in her poetry . . . is a frequent tension between a passion for
the material world—natural beauty, books, home, and family—and the
countervailing Christian dictim [*sic*] that the world is corrupt and vile
and vastly incomparable to the love of Christ." Gilmore says of Washington Irving's *Knickerbocker's History of New York* that what gives it "its
radically dissident edge is Irving's awareness that all histories are partial
and reflect the viewpoint of the winners." Occasionally the story is
enlarged, not just revised: Jehlen's invocation of multiple European
perspectives of the American continent is striking, as is Shields's survey of
the literature of social pleasure that infused life outside religious and
political controversy. The volume includes a 14-page bibliography, un-
categorized and unannotated, of secondary works the contributors have
found "especially useful or influential," and a parallel chronology of New
World and Old World texts and events.

New editions appeared this year of two comprehensive reference
works directed at general rather than specialist audiences. The third edition of *Reference Guide to American Literature,* ed. Jim Kamp (St. James),
adds 145 new author entries, predominantly African American, Asian
American, Hispanic American, and Native American, plus science fiction writers and women, and 26 new essays on individual works—and
removes 11 essays that had appeared in the previous edition. The interpretative component of the signed critical essays on works and authors is
fairly flat and unsophisticated, but the bibliographical surveys of primary
and secondary materials on authors and the "Reading List" of major
bibliographical handbooks, general studies, and critical works (organized by period) are thorough and up-to-date. The *Reference Guide*
remains a good resource for beginners. Biographical and critical commentary are briefer but bibliographical information more extensive (entries even include price and ISBN numbers) in *The Reader's Adviser,
Volume I: The Best in Reference Works, British Literature, and American
Literature,* ed. David Scott Kastan and Emory Elliott (Bowker), now in
its 14th edition. The difference in emphasis is appropriate to a series
directed to librarians and booksellers rather than readers. With minor
exceptions, the record consists of items currently in print. In its own way
The Reader's Adviser is impressive nonetheless, with its numerous sub-

divisions into historical periods, genres, and recent developments, each with a capsule headnote. *Facts on File Bibliography of American Fiction Through 1865,* ed. Kent P. Ljungquist (Facts on File), joins the two volumes covering 1919–88 (1991) and the one covering 1866–1918 (1993) to complete this series. The listings emphasize accurate bibliographical information in both the primary and selected secondary author bibliographies. I commented on this project when the earlier volumes appeared (see *ALS 1991,* p. 474, and *ALS 1992,* p. 368).

Women writers and regional writing remain the chief areas of reference work in the subdivisions of American literary landscape. *Feminist Criticism of American Women Poets: An Annotated Bibliography 1975–1993,* ed. Liana Sakelliou-Schultz (Garland), is as narrow as its title suggests. More expansive is *Great Women Mystery Writers: Classic to Contemporary,* ed. Kathleen Gregory Klein (Greenwood), featuring signed biographical-critical essays on 117 writers of all nationalities, each essay accompanied by complete listing of the writer's mystery works and a selected critical bibliography. The volume is apparently intended for both mystery writers and readers, since its appendices include inventories of major mystery-fiction awards, conferences, and organizations. None of the indices identify writers by nationality, but it is easy enough to spot such American luminaries as Anna Katherine Green, Annette Meyers, Barbara Paul, Amanda Cross (a pseudonym of Carolyn Heilbrun), Elizabeth Linington—oh, and Margaret Truman. *Jewish American Women Writers: A Bio-Bibliographical and Critical Sourcebook,* ed. Ann R. Shapiro et al. (Greenwood), presents individually authored biographical-critical essays plus primary and secondary bibliographies on 57 writers— the focus of selection is belles lettres—plus an additional essay on "Jewish American Women's Autobiography" by Barbara Shollar. The selection of authors is broadly historical—from Emma Lazarus, Anzia Yezierska, Edna Ferber, and Gertrude Stein to Grace Paley and Emily Mann—and its judiciousness makes this a competent first resource on its topic. I should add that the "production values" (typesetting, paper, binding) are a notch above the typical Greenwood reference title. Rosemary M. Canfield Reisman and Christopher J. Canfield's *Contemporary Southern Women Fiction Writers: An Annotated Bibliography* (Scarecrow), one of the Magill Bibliographies, is a more modest contribution—too bad it is also so relatively expensive. The 28 authors represented here by selective listings of critical books and essays, each accompanied by a paragraph or more of descriptive rather than evaluative annotation, include Toni Morrison, Mary Lee Settle, Alice Walker, Bobbie Ann Mason, and Anne Tyler. Despite an introduction that very carefully defines the terms of the title, the compilers do not make clear why they must apparently limit their coverage to 28 authors, or why these 28 rather than some others.

Also concerned with contemporary Southern writers, but not women writers only, is *Contemporary Poets, Dramatists, Essayists, and Novelists of the South: A Bio-Bibliographical Sourcebook,* ed. Robert Bain and Joseph M. Flora (Greenwood). The volume is a companion to *Contemporary Fiction Writers of the South* (1993) by the same editors (see *ALS 1993,* p. 411), and the two volumes together are successors to Bain and Flora's *Fifty Southern Writers Before 1900* and *Fifty Southern Writers After 1900* (1987; see *ALS 1987,* p. 497). Maya Angelou, Beth Henley, Donald Justice, and Ishmael Reed are among the 49 authors given chapters in this volume, and the term "contemporary" is expansive enough to also gather in LeRoy Leatherman (died 1984), Guy Owen (died 1981), and Preston Jones (died 1979). The current listing does not include any writers also covered in *Fifty Southern Writers After 1900,* but the editors take the opportunity in an appendix to update their earlier primary and secondary bibliographies on A. R. Ammons, James Dickey, and Shelby Foote.

The regional component features too in Robert B. Slocum's *New England in Fiction, 1787–1990: An Annotated Bibliography* (Locust Hill), in two volumes. Slocum's interest is books, not authors, however, and though the 4,975 entries are arranged alphabetically by author, then by title, the annotations feature plot summary (typically derived from a previous published entry, like *Book Review Digest*) instead of biographies or critical essays. The list is not meant to be exhaustive, with only selected titles for the more prolific writers, Hawthorne, Stowe, and Updike among them. Only first publication is recorded, and the definition of fiction excludes children's literature as well as plays and poetry— except for two "narratives in poetic format," James Wallis Washburn's *Yamoyden . . . In Six Cantos* (1820) and Christopher La Farge's *Hoxie Sells His Acres,* a novel in verse (1934).

"Western" signals genre, not region, in Bernard A. Drew's *Western Series and Sequels, Second Edition* (Garland). Drew invokes "a broad definition of Western in selecting entries"—whatever that means, since he does not supply any definition at all—and lists 750 series and sequels, more than double the number of the first edition. Entries appear alphabetically by series title, or by the title of the volume which produced sequels, and supply lists of all associated titles. Drew suggests that organizing by authors' names would have been complicated because of the welter of multiauthor series and pseudonyms. An interesting example of this complication is the "Powder Valley" series begun by Morrow in 1934 and continued into the 1960s by Jefferson House: "Peter Field," the title-page author of all 83 titles in the series, was actually 11 different house authors! Even so, dealing with pseudonyms in some way in the volume would have been helpful: neither the introductory alphabetical list of authors nor the entries distinguish real names from assumed ones. A section with information about 32 additional series not incorporated into the master list confuses matters further, as does Drew's not very coherent shotgun-scattering of history and commentary in his introduction. The intriguing cultural phenomenon addressed by *Western Series and Sequels* deserves better. Another resource dealing with genre is the third edition of *Twentieth-Century Romance and Historical Writers* (St. James), ed. Aruna Vasudevan and Lesley Henderson, which updates the previous edition and adds some 100 new entries. The primary bibliographies for each author record pseudonymous publication in separate lists; entries present biographical profiles and critical essays as distinct items, and some also include contributed comments by authors on themselves and their work. New to this edition is a record of film adaptations.

Broader cultural matters are the focus of several other items. Jeutonne P. Brewer's *The Federal Writers' Project: A Bibliography* (Scarecrow) consists of three sections: works about the FWP—almost 1000 disparate items, from Daniel Aaron's *Writers on the Left* (1961) to state and local inventories of WPA materials; works produced under the auspices of the FWP, divided into state, city, and local guides, regional guides, other publications, and archives; and recordings produced by the FWP. The lists are supplemented by "A List of Federal Writers' Project Writers," cross-indexed to city and state. Tillie Olsen is here, and Claude McKay, and Weldon Kees, among many others. John S. Baky's "Literary Resources of the Vietnam War" (*WL&A* 5, i [1993]: 15–24) describes five major resources, four of them physical collections, the other a microform publication: the Colorado State University Vietnam War Literature Collection; Imaginative Representations of the Vietnam War Collection, La Salle University, Philadelphia; the John M. Echols Collection, Cornell University; the National Archives; and "The History of the Vietnam War on Microfiche," ed. Douglas Pike. Baky's introductory essay mostly compares the Colorado State and La Salle collections. (Incidentally, *WL&A* is a publication of the English department of the U.S. Air Force Academy.) Franklin Brooks and Timothy F. Murphy's "Annotated Bibliography of AIDS Literature, 1982–91," pp. 321–39 in *Writing AIDS: Gay Literature, Language and Analysis,* ed. Murphy and Suzanne Poirier (Columbia, 1993), catalogs items by genre and then author, and supplies brief descriptive annotation. The bibliography accompanies 13 essays on writers and topics.

A new category and additions to three previously established ones continue the relentless expansion of *Dictionary of Literary Biography* (Gale). *American Book-Collectors and Bibliographers, First Series,* ed. Joseph Rosenblum (DLB 140), extends the usual series treatment to 43 leading lights in American bibliography. The selection of figures spans American history—from Thomas Prince and Cotton Mather to Henry Stevens and George Brinley, Jr., to some of the names behind major institutional collections, like J. K. Lilly, Jr., Carl H. Pforzheimer, and A. S. W. Rosenbach—and provides a glimpse not simply into lives and careers but formative influences on the preservation of the literary and historical past. The additions to the series within the series are *American Novelists Since World War II, Third Series,* ed. James R. Giles and Wanda H. Giles (DLB 143), which continues, after a considerable hiatus, *American Novelists Since World War II* (DLB 2 [1978]) and *American Novelists Since World War II, Second Series* (DLB 6 [1980]); *American Magazine Journalists, 1900–1960, Second Series* (DLB 137), ed. Sam G. Riley, which succeeds Riley's first volume devoted to this period (DLB 91 [1990]), as well as his volumes in the same category for the periods 1741– 1850 (DLB 73 [1988]) and 1850–1900 (DLB 79 [1988]); and the DLB *Yearbook: 1993,* ed. James W. Hipp. The current *Yearbook* volume includes the usual annual surveys by genre, among them "The Year in the Novel" by George Garrett and Kristin van Ogtrop and "The Year in Literary Theory" by Barry Faulk and Amy Farmer; installment VII of Garrett and van Ogtrop's "Book Reviewing in America"; an essay focused on Toni Morrison as Nobel Prize winner; a review of the Scarecrow Press Great Bibliographers Series by Dean Keller (to which series Keller's *David Anton Randall, 1905–1975* [1994] is the latest contribution); obituaries of Kay Boyle, Albert Erskine, and Wallace Stegner; a tribute to James Dickey at 70 by Ernest Suarez; a most useful "Guide to the

Archives of Publishers, Journals, and Literary Agents in North American Libraries" by Nan Bowman Albinski; and the annual list of literary awards and honors. And there is more besides; the *Yearbook* is, as ever, a somewhat eccentric treasure trove of critical, historical, and reference information. I wonder how many people will ever find it among the rest of the welter of information publications.

American Biographical Index (Saur), ed. Laureen Baillie, in six volumes, is a print record of all persons represented by biographical entries in the 127 volumes reproduced in the Saur microfiche publication *American Biographical Archive*. The focus of the archive as a whole is American history to 1980. Since the titles selected for the *Archive* range from Elizabeth F. Ellet's *Pioneer Women of the West* (1852) and Charles Sutton's *The New York Tombs* (1874) to the Marquis publication *Who's Who in Filmland*, and since the *Index* provides an introductory table of its biographical sources and annotates entries not only by fiche and frame numbers but page numbers too, the *Index* is useful even without the fiche set. It is indeed a "key," as the publisher's advertisement puts it, "to over three hundred years of American history, as exemplified in the lives of some 280,000 of its citizens."

Readers with an inclination to step out of the reference room briefly to see where the field has been or where it is going might enjoy a look in one direction at a special issue of *PBSA* (86 [June 1992]), featuring eight appreciative and retrospective essays on the now-complete nine-volume *Bibliography of American Literature* (see *ALS 1991*, pp. 473–74), and in the other at Geoffrey D. Smith's "National Bibliography in the Electronic Age" (*AEB* 6, i [1992]: 3–9).

Indiana University

Author Index

Subject Index